THE
OPEN
LEARNING
FOUNDATION

An Active Learning Approach

Quantitative Methods

THE OPEN LEARNING FOUNDATION

An Active Learning Approach

QUANTITATIVE METHODS

Graham Hackett and David Caunt

Business

Copyright © Open Learning Foundation Enterprises Ltd 1994

First published 1994

Blackwell Publishers, the publishing imprint of
Basil Blackwell Ltd
108 Cowley Road
Oxford OX4 1JF
UK

Basil Blackwell Inc.
238 Main Street
Cambridge, Massachusetts 02142
USA

British Library Cataloguing in Publication Data

A CIP catalogue record for this book is available from
the British Library.

Library of Congress Cataloging-in-Publication Data

A catalog record is available from the Library of Congress

ISBN 0-631-19537-8

Typeset in 10 on 12 pt Times New Roman

Printed in Great Britain by T.J. Press Ltd, Cornwall

This book is printed on acid-free paper

CONTENTS

Unit 3 Linear Programming   301

Unit 4 Regression and Correlation   395

Unit 5 Probability   483

Unit 6   Probability Distribution

583

Unit 7   Introduction to Sampling

691

Unit 8   Index Numbers

785

STUDENT GUIDE

1. PURPOSE

Welcome to this student guide which will

- introduce you to the subject of Quantitative Methods (QM)

- explain why you should study this subject

- outline the contents of each of the study units

- give you advice and hints on how to use the study units and any other material to understand this subject

2. WHY YOU SHOULD STUDY QUANTITATIVE METHODS (QM)

All degree courses in business studies include a compulsory element of QM, usually in the first year of the programme. Many degrees also continue the study of QM into the second and final years, sometimes as a compulsory element, but more usually as an option.

This particular course is intended as a first introduction to mathematics for business studies students.

Many business problems cannot be solved without the use of mathematical methods. All businesses collect masses of data during the course of their daily activities. This data must be organised and analysed in such a way that all of the key decision-makers (usually managers) can make sense of it. You will also notice that much of this data is financial, which is why you will need to study a programme of accounting on your course. However, financial or not, the data required by a business must be **collected** in a methodical way. Data collection requires techniques which are often sophisticated. Collected data must then be **analysed**; the business must have some idea of the meaning of their data. The data can be used to **diagnose** the problems faced by the business. When business problems have been diagnosed, then a whole range of techniques (many of them mathematical) can be used to help provide **solutions** to problems. This is why a QM course is inevitably concerned with the techniques used for problem solving. But as you will see from the above, the concern does not just end at the use of the technique, it extends back to the collection of the data required by the technique, and the inevitable questions raised about whether the correct methods are being used.

The importance of the above is to prevent you from making the mistake of thinking that QM will merely consist of a set of techniques. Techniques are important, but the reasons why we use them, and the degree of success we can expect from them are much more important.

3. QUANTITATIVE METHODS CAN HELP WITH BUSINESS PROBLEMS

Quantitative Methods can help in four key areas:

Collection and Analysis of Data

All businesses depend on information. In this course you will see examples of the methods used to collect high quality data (unit 7, *Introduction to Sampling*) and of the techniques used to organise and present data (unit 1, section 2, *Graphs*, and unit 2, *Data Presentation*).

Uncertainty and Risk

Many of the decisions taken by the business are high risk, because the data collected may be ambiguous or misleading. We can never say with certainty whether a particular decision will have a given effect, although we may be able to find the **degree** of risk attached to a decision. You will, for this reason, find that you will be studying the laws of probability in this course (units 5 and 6, *Probability* and *Probability Distribution*).

The Best Way to Use Resources

Resources, such as labour, materials, etc, used by a business are often scarce. Therefore the problem of their most effective use arises. For example, what use of labour, materials, finance and so on will produce the highest possible profit or return? Should we spend our money on buying a piece of equipment, or should we rent it? This combination of scarce resources and competing decisions will give you some idea why you should study techniques such as linear programming (unit 3) and investment appraisal (unit 1).

Predicting the Future

Another major business problem can be caused by the fact that the effects of our decisions are an unknown factor in the future. For instance, we decide to produce a new product on the basis of high anticipated sales in the future. However, no decision maker will proceed with important decisions like this without at least trying to forecast the future. Will the product be a success or failure? This explains why a QM course will include subjects such as forecasting (unit 4, *Regression and Correlation*, and unit 8 *Index Numbers*).

This course is about quantifying many of the every-day concepts of business. Every decision maker needs to have an intuitive 'feel' for the size of things. Think of the number of times you need to use words such as 'large' 'small', 'larger than...', smaller than...', 'growing', 'falling', and so on. These words are vague references to the size of things. However, it is not sufficient for decision makers to make such statements. They must be more precise. Only when we are able to say 'how large', or 'how small', etc, will our words begin to have meaning. That is what a course in QM is about.

4. How Much Maths do I Need to Know?

First of all, you should be in no doubt as to the importance of this subject. Numeracy is as important in educational terms as literacy. However, you might be apprehensive of subjects like QM because of some unpleasant memories of earlier studies, or perhaps a belief that you have a 'numbers block'.

This QM course is **not** a mathematics course. There are no techniques used here which should be beyond your capabilities if you have attained the GCSE (O level) in maths.

You will find no calculus, or rigorous proofs, or any of the things typically found in a standard maths course. This course is wholly directed at achieving results; we are not concerned so much with **why** and **how** a method works, but only that it **does** work. You will, of course, be expected to know something of the circumstances in which these methods can be effective, when to use them and when not to, but this is a long way from having to know full mathematical proofs.

You can acquire the ability to think quantitatively without having to study a full length formal mathematics course.

However, you should not become too complacent about your level of numeracy. Success in QM is as much a matter of practice, or 'drill' as it is of inspiration. If, after reading the units you consider your mathematics a little weak or rusty, you should use the opportunity to revise your skills. This is why we have included a foundation unit (unit 0). This unit covers many of the basic techniques which you may have forgotten or not practised for years. If you find that you are able to work your way through this foundation unit fairly easily, then you should not have any really serious problems with the maths and be ready to tackle the rest of the course.

5. THE STUDY UNITS

The QM course is built around nine study units. You may find that the institution where you are studying does not use all of the units listed in this section. This will entirely depend on how your tutors wish to organise the course and will not affect your studies.

The units have been written in such a way as to facilitate a method of study called 'open learning'. We shall say a little more about open learning and what it means in the next section. Here is a brief description of what you can expect to find in each unit, and the reason it is included. We recommend that you study the units in the order listed, unless there is some reason to do otherwise, or as you may be directed.

UNIT 0: BASIC MATHS

Unit 0 is a foundation unit and should be treated differently from the other units.

Many students coming on to business studies courses have backgrounds very different from the traditional A-level entrant. You may be a 'mature' student (don't be annoyed, 'mature' refers to anyone over 24 years old) whose last formal encounter with mathematics may have occurred several years ago. You may also think that, although fresh from school, you did not acquire the understanding in mathematics that you would like to have. Whatever the reason, this unit is designed to help you to revise the techniques which are often taken for granted as the basic prerequisites for a business studies course. We suggest that you work through, and consult this unit selectively. We do not regard it as a taught part of the course, but intended to address some of the remedial problems which always occur in a maths based course. Topics included are: the numbering system, the language of algebra, including simple and simultaneous equations, order of precedence of numerical operations, scientific notation and basic use of a calculator. In short, these are topics which are regarded as the necessary 'toolkit' of a business studies student.

Do not think that this unit is of too low a level for you. Look through it first, and try some of the problems. Check your answers, and if they are correct, you probably do not need remedial assistance. You will soon find out if you need extra help.

Unit 1: Business Maths

This is the first unit of the taught course. Two basic mathematical techniques are included because of their intrinsic importance in business studies and because they illustrate the technique of mathematical model building. The financial mathematics section introduces the idea of **series** and **progressions**.

The unit then demonstrates how certain kinds of models of growth might be used to model compound interest, the concept of present value and other important areas in the study of finance. In this unit you will learn techniques which help you to decide whether investments are worthwhile, how to work out mortgage payments and how to monitor the progress of loans, investments and sinking funds.

Included also is a section on functions and graphs, which is essential if you wish to understand later work on linear programming, regression and correlation and the behaviour of time series. Later units in the course on these subjects cannot be fully understood unless you have a firm grasp of the contents of this unit.

Unit 2: Data Presentation

This is a long unit. The difficulty with such a unit is not what should be **included** in it, but what should be **left out**.

The overall theme of the unit is how to present statistical information in such a way as to show up any pattern or 'shape' in the data without distorting it. In other words, if we think the numbers have a 'story' to tell, how do we tell it? This unit covers how we measure data, the progress of data from the 'raw', or just collected stage to the 'grouped', or organised stage. Then we deal with specialised methods of representation of grouped data in frequency distributions and graphs and finally the calculation of summary statistics.

The emphasis in the unit is on the understanding of the principles rather than on computational techniques. We have included the basic minimum in this unit: we could easily have doubled its size by including preliminary data analysis and a full coverage of every type of graph or chart. This unit is a basic requirement for any statistics course, and explains why you should study it.

UNIT 3: LINEAR PROGRAMMING

Although linear programming is not always included in a statistics course we have included a unit for several reasons. Firstly, it extends the basic mathematics material of Units 0 and 1. Secondly, it vividly illustrates the importance of mathematical modelling in business problems (a central preoccupation of this course) and thirdly it provides a good introduction to the use of computer software.

Linear programming is concerned with finding a best solution to a business problem (if such a solution exists at all). For example, how should we best use our resources to attain the maximum profit, or the minimum cost?

Although most of the problems in this unit can be solved using the graphical methods discussed in unit 1, there is a final section involving problems where computer software has to be used. It is recognised that in some cases you may not have access to the appropriate computer software. However, even if this is the case, you will find that it is still a valuable experience to read through the last section.

UNIT 4: REGRESSION AND CORRELATION

In many cases a business would like to be able to forecast the behaviour of some important business characteristic, such as sales. Perhaps the business decision-makers think that sales depend upon the general level of peoples incomes. This raises two problems: firstly, are they right? Secondly, if they are right, how do we use this information? For instance, if income rises by 10%, what are the implications for our sales? This unit is concerned with such problems. We deal with the basic relationships between business variables throughout most of the unit, and then a final section which will give you a taste of more complex methods.

The graphics sections of unit 1 (*Business Maths*) and unit 2 (*Data Presentation*) are prerequisites for this unit. The treatment of this subject can also be based on the use of computer software, but if this is not possible, a simple scientific pocket calculator will suffice for all but the very last section of the unit.

UNIT 5: PROBABILITY

This is another long unit. Most business decisions are made under conditions of risk. We may not be able to say whether a given decision will have a definite outcome, but we may be able to calculate the degree of risk which will be incurred. For example, what is the probability that we make a profit of £1 million? What is the probability that we make a loss? And so on. Probability is at the very centre of a course in QM for business, which is why we include it. You will need to know the basic rules for calculating probability.

The mathematical techniques used in probability are very simple, but the logical reasoning processes are complex. You might find some difficulty with this subject. The unit is essential if you are to understand the further material on distributions and sampling.

The unit covers the main rules of probability and also illustrates various techniques for visualising the rules of chance, such as contingency tables, Venn diagrams and trees.

UNIT 6: PROBABILITY DISTRIBUTION

The rationale behind this unit is

to extend the treatment of probability given in unit 5;

to further develop the mathematical modelling bias of this course by providing students with models of the behaviour of probability;

to provide the necessary backing for a unit on sampling.

Statisticians have discovered certain underlying rules which explain the behaviour of probability in certain cases. These rules are often called 'probability distributions'. There are a number of these so-called probability distributions, and we have chosen just two for inclusion in this course. These two distributions – the binomial distribution and the normal distribution have been selected for special study because of their importance to the business world.

UNIT 7: SAMPLING

Much business data is collected by sampling. For example, if you wish to know the percentages of consumers buying different brands of a product, you would not usually be able to contact every consumer but would have to collect data from a sample.

As soon as we use information gathered from a sample, there are problems. How do we know that our sample is representative of the whole population? How can we make allowances for possible errors in our sample data? If our sample data seems to be pointing us in the direction of one decision rather than another, what procedures should we use to minimise the chance of making a costly error?

This unit introduces and demonstrates what could be called 'statistical reasoning'. We must develop rules for analysing the kind of information we get from sample surveys.

UNIT 8: INDEX NUMBERS

Decision makers need to know two things about change in important variables, such as sales, prices, unemployment, imports and exports, etc. They need to be able to measure how these variables have changed in the recent past, and they need to be able to forecast how they might change in the future.

The first part of this unit introduces you to some of the methods for measuring change. An often-used method of measurement is known as the 'index number'. The construction and interpretation of index numbers and the different rationale for their calculation is an important part of this unit. However, the unit is mostly about correct use and interpretation, rather than on the detailed rules of calculation.

In the second section of this unit we will introduce you to some of the methods for dealing with the behaviour of data in the future. What might the sales of our products be next year? This part of the unit can be very time-consuming unless computer spreadsheet software is used.

6. OPEN LEARNING AND 'TRADITIONAL' METHODS

The study units are written in what is called an 'open learning' style. What does this mean? To get a clear idea of this we need to describe traditional methods. These methods are based upon the lecture and tutorial. There is nothing wrong with these methods – in fact, they are very good ways of imparting certain kinds of information. However, the lecture is not always the most suitable way of learning quantitative methods because it assumes that everyone progresses at the same rate. Furthermore, the lecture puts the lecturer at the centre of the learning process, and gives the mistaken impression that they are responsible for your learning. This is not the case; YOU should be at the centre of the learning process, taking responsibility for your own studies.

Open learning means, therefore, organising a course in such a way that you manage your own learning at your own pace, but within the college year.

You will find that a combination of open learning and traditional methods make for a much more stimulating learning experience.

To facilitate this open learning approach, you will find that the study units

are sequenced very carefully, so that there is a clear logical progression from one idea to another;

adopt an approach whereby you are made familiar with one concept before you move on to another;

have a very clear layout with clearly headed short sections;

have many worked examples of problems so that you can see how a technique is used;

have plenty of opportunities to test your own knowledge and then check your answers with worked answers given in the text.

In addition to the study units there is a great deal of extra material provided in the form of a Tutor Guide. This contains extra questions of the same kind that you will find in the units, and also some extra case studies, which are more demanding, and have been provided to give you extra insight into how QM is applied in the business world. Your course tutor will decide how this extra material will be used.

7. HINTS FOR STUDY

When you have access to the study units, you have all you need to start the course, but how should you set about this process?

There is no single answer to this question, but this flexibility is a deliberate part of the method of open learning. If you already have a very solid maths background, then you may find that you can read rapidly through the material. However, remember to check your understanding by answering the problems in the text; never be tempted to skip them, for they are the centre of the units. In most cases you are encouraged to write down your answers in the actual units themselves, so that you have a written record. If you can understand the written material, and find that you are answering the problems correctly, then you need little help from your tutors, apart from perhaps asking them for more challenging problems.

If you are finding the material difficult, then reread and rework it. Then look at some of the worked answers, and then try the activities in the units. If your answers are incorrect, read the solutions in the text, and try to understand why you were wrong. The solutions to the problems will help you to see why you went wrong.

Don't get too despondent about wrong answers. It can be more educationally useful to get wrong answers and subsequently understand the reasons for the error than to get a problem right first time round. This may result in a better understanding of the material.

If you still find that you can make no headway with the problem, it is at this point that you approach your tutor. You are the best person to decide when you need this extra help. But remember, a problem diagnosed early is more easily solved. If you feel that you are not coping with the material then do not delay contacting your tutor.

We re-emphasise the point of open learning; YOU decide the pace of your learning, YOU accept responsibility for your own progress. However, YOU must also decide when you need extra help.

The rest is up to you. Enjoy your course!

UNIT 0

BASIC MATHS

CONTENTS

Unit Objectives

UNIT OBJECTIVES

This unit deals with a number of basic mathematical concepts that will be used during your study of the other units in this module. When you have worked through this unit you will be able to

- understand the number system and relationships between sizes of objects

- appreciate and work with some basic elements in algebra and algebraic manipulation

- solve simple and simultaneous equations and transpose equations

- apply rounding rules to the results of calculations

- calculate binomial coefficients

- use an extended set of calculator functions

Throughout all these units you should also bear in mind the reasons given for studying quantitative techniques that you have read in the student handbook that accompanies these notes.

SECTION 1

NUMBERS

1. OUR NUMBER SYSTEM

Let us start by considering the number system, which forms the basis of all our numerical conversation. We are all familiar with counting, and have accepted that the system we use is based on the number 10. Each number, or digit, in a string represents a group which is related to 10. So 64 is shorthand for 6 groups of 10 and 4 groups of 1.

$$64 = 6 \times 10 + 4 \times 1$$

You may remember when you started 'add-ups' at school that you labelled your columns with 't' for tens and 'u' for units.

So you wrote

```
t      u
2      3 +
4      5
_____
6      8
```

Examples

$$275 = 2 \times 100 + 7 \times 10 + 5 \times 1$$

$$3526 = 3 \times 1000 + 5 \times 100 + 2 \times 10 + 6 \times 1$$

SELF CHECK 1

Expand the numbers in the same way as in the above examples.

1. $526 =$

2. $70132 =$

2. THE NUMBER LINE

Pictures are a valuable tool and often save many sentences of explanation. They can be used to see a problem more clearly. So to represent numbers and their interrelations we use a **number line**. This is just a scaled straight line on which we can indicate the position of a number. On the number line, let us take a portion of the numbers between 0 and 20.

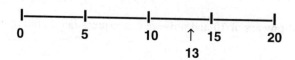

I have drawn an arrow to show the position of the number 13 on the line.

SELF CHECK 2

1.   Show on the number line above, the position of the numbers 7, 16, 19, 2.

2.   In the space below draw your own number line to show the position of the numbers 250, 750, 800, 550.

3. COUNTING NUMBERS

These numbers can also be called the **counting numbers** as we use them for counting objects. If a machine is producing washers then we use these numbers to count how many are produced. The machine will only produce a whole number of washers, each one can be counted as a unit. If these washers are packed in bags, and each bag contained 10 washers, then each bag represents the tens digit. If they are then boxed so that each box contains 10 bags, then each box represents the hundreds digit. If they are then crated so that each crate contains 10 boxes, then each crate represents the thousands digit.

Using the same idea you will be able to see that

$$100 = 10 \times 10 = 10^2 \quad \text{(ie 10 multiplied by itself twice)}$$

$$1000 = 10 \times 10 \times 10 = 10^3 \quad \text{(ie 10 multiplied by itself three times)}$$

which can be extended to

$$10,000 = 10 \times 10 \times 10 \times 10 = 10^4$$

$$10,000,000 = 10^7$$

These are called **powers of 10** and now we can express our counting numbers in these powers.

Example

$$47,652 = 4 \times 10,000 + 7 \times 1000 + 6 \times 100 + 5 \times 10 + 2 \times 1$$

which, in powers of 10 form becomes

$$= 4 \times 10^4 + 7 \times 10^3 + 6 \times 10^2 + 5 \times 10 + 2 \times 1$$

SELF CHECK 3

Write the following numbers in the powers of 10 form.

1. $526 =$

2. $70132 =$

3. $2375100 =$

You will notice that as we proceed to the left, so the power of 10 increases.

4. PARTS OF COUNTING NUMBERS

Let us consider this power of 10 form in relation to our monetary system which is based on the pound (£), with fractions, or parts of a pound called pence. The price £253.67 is a mixture of whole pounds (253) and whole pence (67). The two parts are separated and distinguished by the decimal point, which converts the whole pence and expresses them as a part of a pound.

So, 67 pence represents 6 groups of 10 pence and 7 groups of 1 pence.

However, 10 pence represents 1/10th of a pound and 1 pence represents 1/100th of a pound or

$$\frac{1}{10^2}$$

which we could rewrite as

$$253.67 = 2 \times 10^2 + 5 \times 10 + 3 \times 1 + 6 \times \frac{1}{10} + 7 \times \frac{1}{10^2}$$

SELF CHECK 4

Express these monetary sums in the same form as the example above.

1.   £63.75   =

2.   £1032.23   =

This can be extended beyond the two decimal places that we need in our monetary system, so that

$$7.23469 =$$

$$7 \times 1 + 2 \times \frac{1}{10} + 3 \times \frac{1}{10^2} + 4 \times \frac{1}{10^3} + 6 \times \frac{1}{10^4} + 9 \times \frac{1}{10^5}$$

You will notice that as we proceed to the right the power of 10 in the denominator below the dividing line increases.

SELF CHECK 5

Using the example above, express these numbers in expanded power of 10 form

1.   31.216   =

2.   10.20015   =

3.   123.001   =

5. ROUNDING

Use your calculator to find the value of the multiplication

23.78 × 8.24

Your calculator will most likely give you the answer

195.9472

(if not consult your calculator handbook). If these numbers relate to a monetary sum, it has no money meaning after the 94 pence as we do not deal in parts of pence. But should we call it 94p or 95p?

Such a decision is called **rounding**. When dealing in money terms we would need to round to the nearest penny. With non-monetary numbers we might wish to round to two decimal places (dp), ie two digits after the decimal point.

So what are the rules for rounding?

Look at the digit immediately to the right of the last digit that you wish to retain. Ignore all other digits to the right of that. If the digit you are looking at is 5 or above then the previous digit is uplifted by 1, otherwise it remains unchanged.

So if we wanted to take the answer we had on our calculator, above and round to two decimal places, then we would look at the 7 in the third decimal place, and uplift the 4 to 5 to give

195.95   correct to 2 dp

If we had wished to round to one decimal place then you would look at the 4 in the second decimal place and so leave the previous 9 alone to give

195.9   correct to 1 dp

SELF CHECK 6

1.   Round the following numbers to the accuracy given

(a)   19.276   to 2 dp

(b)   211.349   to 1 dp

(c)   0.4735   to 3 dp

(d)   10.967   to 1 dp

2.   A shopkeeper calculates the selling price of a particular item from the cost price list. As a result of this calculation he obtains a selling price of £1.245. What price should be marked on the item?

6. COMPARISONS OF NUMBERS

If a machine makes 10 washers and 1 is defective in some way, we can express this information in a number of ways;

1 in 10 is defective   or

one tenth of the total is defective   or

0.1 of the total is defective

SELF CHECK 7

1.   Express in three ways the information that, after a quality control inspection, 2 tennis balls out of every batch of 24 are rejected.

    (a)   (b)   (c)

2.   Can you refine this new data by obtaining numerically simpler fractions?

7. PERCENTAGES

Your employer tells you that you will receive an end of year bonus of $4\frac{1}{2}\%$ of your gross annual salary of £12,500. You would need to calculate how much money you would actually receive.

Percentages are used frequently in every-day salary negotiations but how many employees actually understand and can calculate what they mean?

To understand percentages you have to interpret the word. Literally it means 'per hundred'. So a percentage is a fraction with the implied denominator of 100 missed out.

       Thus 10% is the same as 10/100 or 0.1

       and 8% is the same as 8/100 or 0.08

Notice that the easy way of dividing by 100 is to move the decimal point, or implied decimal point, two places to the left of the numerator.

SELF CHECK 8

Express the following as both fractions and decimals

		Fraction	Decimal
1.	15%		
2.	7%		
3.	25%		

Sometimes, as in the example above, we may have more than just a whole number, and in these cases we need to do some conversions first.

Example

$$4\frac{1}{2}\% = 4.5\% = \frac{4.5}{100} = 0.045$$

$$10\frac{1}{8}\% = 10.125\% = \frac{10.125}{100} = 0.10125$$

SELF CHECK 9

Convert these percentages into decimal equivalents

1. $7\frac{1}{4}\%$

2. $15\frac{3}{8}\%$

We can also reverse the process to express fractional and decimal numbers as percentages.

You have seen that to make a percentage into another form we divide by 100. The reverse of this process would be to multiply by 100.

$$\frac{1}{10} \quad becomes \quad \frac{1}{10} \times 100 \quad = \quad 10\%$$

$$0.15 \quad becomes \quad 0.15 \times 100 \quad = \quad 15\%$$

$$0.125 \quad becomes \quad 0.125 \times 100 \quad = \quad 12.5\% \quad = \quad 12\frac{1}{2}\%$$

SELF CHECK 10

Convert these fractions and decimals into percentages

1. $\frac{1}{4}$

2. 0.11

3. $\frac{3}{8}$

4. 0.2125

Now let us return to the question I asked at the beginning of this section about your end of year bonus. The word 'of' in mathematics can be interpreted as 'multiply'. This allows us to write down the question and its solution in this form

$$\text{Bonus} = 4\tfrac{1}{2}\% \text{ of } 12,500$$
$$= 4.5\% \times 12,500$$
$$= 0.045 \times 12,500$$
$$= £562.50$$

which will be the amount of your bonus.

SELF CHECK 11

Calculate the percentages in the following:

1. Calculate 5% of 1200.

2. A pay rise of 4% of a weekly wage of £220.10 is agreed. Calculate, correct to the nearest penny, the amount of the rise.

   Calculate the new weekly wage.

3. The price of a component is to rise by $7\tfrac{1}{2}\%$. Calculate the new list price if it previously cost £3.25.

4. The price of a river boat licence is to rise from £1350 to £1440. Calculate the rise as a percentage of the old price.

   Calculate the rise as a percentage of the new price.

8. SUMMARY

In this section we have

- looked at the number system and in particular the **number line**

- discussed **counting numbers** and **powers of 10**

- established and practised some **rounding rules**

- used our calculator for the first time in this unit

- revised **number comparisons**

- looked at percentage and decimal conversions

If you are unsure of any of these topics, check back **now** to the appropriate sections before you read on.

SECTION 2
ALGEBRA

1. LETTERS FOR NUMBERS

So that flexibility can be maintained we often use letters to represent and replace numbers. For example, if the width of your rectangular office is w metres and the breadth is b metres then the floor area, A, of your office could be given by

$$A = w \times b$$

and the perimeter, or length of wall surrounding your office, P, could be given by

$$P = 2w + 2b$$

Similarly, if one parcel weighs x grams and a second weighs y grams then the total weight of the two parcels is x grams + y grams which we write as

(x + y) grams

using the brackets to show that x + y is to be taken as a single number.

Examine these two sets of questions below and see if you can work out what happens when you use letters to replace numbers.

SELF CHECK 12

1. If a thermometer reads 48° F and the temperature rises by 10° F, what is the new reading?

    If the temperature rises by 7° F, what is the new reading?

    If the temperature rises by 12° F, what is the new reading?

    (Have you noticed how you manipulate the numbers?)

    If the temperature rises by T° F, what is the new reading?

    If the temperature falls by T° F, what is the new reading?

2. The price of a piece of equipment is £p and the price is to rise by x%. Write down the price increase and then the new price.

When you go shopping and buy 3 tins of dog food at 32p each, you will be charged 3 × 32p or 96p at the check-out.

If you buy 4 articles at £x each then you will be charged £4x.

If you also bought 3 articles at £y each then your total bill would be 4x + 3y.

SELF CHECK 13

Using the above example, write down the expressions for

1.   The total cost of buying p cars at £10,000 and q vans at £8,000.

2.   The income received by selling x components at £4 and y components at £7.

Often we find it useful to use a fractional form of the operation of division. In this we replace the instruction

$$24 \div 6 \quad by \quad \frac{24}{6}$$

and in algebraic form

$$15 \div x \quad becomes \quad \frac{15}{x}$$

$$a \div 2 \quad becomes \quad \frac{a}{2}$$

$$p \div q \quad becomes \quad \frac{p}{q}$$

SELF CHECK 14

Write these in the alternative form

1. $y \div 3$

2.   5/a

3. $2b \div a$

4. $c \div 2d$

So we have now introduced the language of algebra. Letters are used to replace numbers to give expressions, or mathematical statements greater generality.

Expressions such as

$$\frac{3p - 8}{5}$$

can also be written in word form. In this example it reads: multiply p by 3, subtract 8 from this and divide the result by 5.

The reverse process is also true. In word form we might say: multiply p by 4, then subtract 3 and the result is equal to 27.

As an expression we would show this as

$$4p - 3 = 27$$

SELF CHECK 15

Rewrite the following in algebraic language

1. Three times p is equal to 12.

2. Take x away from 4; the result is 7.

3. Four times N gives the same answer as adding N to 10.

4. The total cost of buying x units at £5 per unit and y units at £7 per unit.

5. The time taken to make x units of A if each unit takes 2 hours and y units of B if each unit takes 3 hours.

2. INDICES, POWERS AND EXPONENTS

Indices, powrs and exponents are alternative words for exactly the same operation. When we were considering our number system, in section 1 above, we used an **index** or power to simplify the writing down of a product of 10 with itself several times. We wrote

$$10 \times 10 = 10^2$$
$$10 \times 10 \times 10 = 10^3$$

and so on.

This can be immediately extended to algebra with the power being used to indicate the number of times that an object is multiplied by itself.

So for example

q^3 stands for $q \times q \times q$
p^5 stands for $p \times p \times p \times p \times p$

SELF CHECK 16

1.   Write in short (index) form

   (a) $a \times a \times a \times a$.

   (b) $y \times y$.

2.   Write in expanded form

   (a) r^6

   (b) b^7

Just as the square root of 9 can be written as $\sqrt{9}$ so the square root of x is written $\sqrt{x}$. We know that 4x means $4 \times x$ so that

$$4x^2 \text{ means } 4 \times x^2$$

Similarly

$$5y^3 \text{ means } 5 \times y^3$$

$$3x^2y \text{ means } 3 \times x^2 \times y$$

$$(4x)^2 \text{ means } 4x \times 4x$$

Be careful though with the interpretation of an expression containing brackets.

Example

$$3a^4 \text{ means } 3 \times a^4 \text{ but}$$

$$(3a)^4 \text{ means } 3a \times 3a \times 3a \times 3a$$

SELF CHECK 17

Write out these expressions in expanded form, taking care with those with brackets.

(1) $(2a)^3$ (3) $4y^5$

(2) $2a^3$ (4) $(4y)^5$

We have seen that to maintain generality we have used letters to represent numbers, and each algebraic expression will have a value if we are given the values that the letters represent.

You have also found in Self Check 13 that the total cost of buying p cars at £10,000 and q vans at £8,000 could be written as

$$10000p + 8000q$$

and the total cost of buying 9 cars and 8 vans is then

$$(10000 \times 9) + (8000 \times 8) = 154000$$

Notice in our second example that we have not started again but have used the original expression putting in the values p = 9 and q = 8.

Practice this idea of substitution with these questions.

SELF CHECK 18

1. Use the expression 10000p + 8000q to find the total cost of buying 7 cars and 11 vans.

2. If a = 3 and b = 4, find the value of each of the algebraic expressions

    (a) $5ab$

    (b) $2a^3$

    (c) $(2a)^3$

    (d) $\sqrt{9b}$

    (e) $7a^2b$

    (f) $5a + 6b$

    (g) $(4a)/b$

    (h) $12/a - 12/b$

3. BASIC RULES FOR PRODUCTS INVOLVING INDICES

Although there are many rules for manipulating indices you will find as you proceed through the units that only one will be important to you. We now consider this one.

We have seen earlier that an index is the number of times that the object is multiplied by itself. Let us look at

$$10^2 \times 10^3 = (10 \times 10) \times (10 \times 10 \times 10)$$

Now notice that on the right hand side we have 10 multiplied by itself 5 times, or, it is 10^5, ie

$$10^2 \times 10^3 = 10^5$$

Similarly, we can see that

$$p^4 \times p^5 = (p \times p \times p \times p) \times (p \times p \times p \times p \times p) = p^9$$

The general form of these results state that

$$a^m \times a^n = a^{m+n}$$

You will notice two things

1.   **the letter a remains the same throughout**
2.   **the two indices on the left are added to give the single index on the right**

Using this result we can simplify products, therefore

$$2^7 \times 2^5 = 2^{12}$$

$$p^3 \times p^8 = p^{11}$$

$$(2a)^3 \times (2a)^4 = (2a)^7$$

SELF CHECK 19

Write these expressions in simpler form

1. $3^3 \times 3^5$

2. $q^2 \times q^4$

3. 2×2^3

4. $(3x)^2 \times (3x)^3$

---

4. SEQUENCE OF OPERATIONS

When carrying out arithmetic calculations we need to know in which order to apply the operations. At first sight it may appear that $5 + 2 \times 3$ could have the two different values of 21 or 11 depending on whether we multiply before adding, or add before multiplying. There is a convention which puts the operations into priority order. The mnemonic **BEDMAS** summarises this convention.

Brackets first

Exponents (or powers) next

Division and

Multiplication next, then

Addition and

Subtraction.

Hence our original problem now has a unique result as multiplication is carried out before addition.

$$5 + 2 \times 3 = 5 + 6 = 11$$

If it had been required to add 2 to 5 before multiplying then the expression would have to be written as

$$(5 + 2) \times 3$$

Now look carefully at the expression below and see how it is set out for full evaluation.

$$2 \times 3^2 + (2 \times 2^2 - 1)^2 \div 3 = 2 \times 9 + (2 \times 4 - 1)^2 \div 3$$
$$= 18 + (8 - 1)^2 \div 3$$
$$= 18 + 7^2 \div 3$$
$$= 18 + 49 \div 3$$
$$= 18 + 16\frac{1}{3}$$
$$= 34\frac{1}{3}$$

SELF CHECK 20

Evaluate the following, keeping to the BEDMAS convention.

1. $7 - 2 \times 3$

2. $(7 - 2) \times 3$

3. $(4 \div 2)^3 - (9 - 3)$.

4. $(4 \times 3)^2 \div 2^3$

5. $(6 - 2)^3 - 2 \times 5$

1.

2.

3.

4.

5.

Now repeat all the above calculations using your calculator. You should find that your calculator has built into it the convention regarding order of operations.

Check the operating instructions if you are not sure.

5. DIRECTED (OR SIGNED) NUMBERS

A centigrade thermometer represents a number line. It makes no difference whether the thermometer lies horizontally on a table or hangs vertically from a hook, it still represents the same number line. The number line will represent numbers, or temperatures, that are above freezing or below freezing. That is above 0 or below 0.

Temperatures above freezing are represented by positive numbers, for instance +5, +9, +12, or more simply 5, 9, 12. Temperatures below freezing are represented by negative numbers, for instance -7, -10, -14. We see that the sign is giving the number **direction** which in the case of temperature is above or below freezing. You will know from experience that a temperature of -15° is extremely cold while 15° is warm. Directed numbers are often written using brackets to firmly fix the sign to the number.

Using these ideas we can learn how to add and subtract directed numbers.

Using the number scale, as shown below, consisting of positive and negative numbers and moving up for positive numbers and down for negative numbers, consider these values

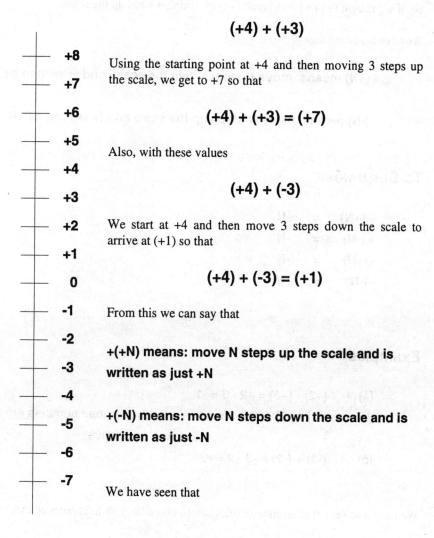

(+4) + (+3)

Using the starting point at +4 and then moving 3 steps up the scale, we get to +7 so that

(+4) + (+3) = (+7)

Also, with these values

(+4) + (-3)

We start at +4 and then move 3 steps down the scale to arrive at (+1) so that

(+4) + (-3) = (+1)

From this we can say that

+(+N) means: move N steps up the scale and is written as just +N

+(-N) means: move N steps down the scale and is written as just -N

We have seen that

(+1) = (-3) + (+4)

and if we subtract (+4) from both sides we obtain

$$(+1) - (+4) = (-3) + (+4) - (+4) \text{ or}$$
$$(+1) - (+4) = (-3).$$

So, if we start at (+1) we can reach (-3) by taking 4 steps down the scale.
If we start again and this time subtract (-3) from both sides we obtain

$$(+1) - (-3) = (-3) + (+4) - (-3) \text{ or}$$
$$(+1) - (-3) = (+4)$$

So, if we start at (+1) we can reach (+4) by taking 3 steps up the scale.

We have thus seen that

- (+N) means: move N steps down the scale, and is written as -N

- (-N) means: move N steps up the scale and is written as +N

To Summarise

$$+ (+N) \quad = \quad +N$$
$$+ (-N) \quad = \quad -N$$
$$- (+N) \quad = \quad -N$$
$$- (-N) \quad = \quad +N$$

Examples

(a) $(+2) - (+3) = +2 - 3 = -1$

(b) $(-2) - (-3) = -2 + 3 = +1$ (= 1, as unsigned numbers are taken as positive)

(c) $(-3) + (-2) = -3 - 2 = -5$

We have also seen that arithmetic rules can be taken through to algebra so that

$$(-2a) - (-8a) = -2a + 8a = 6a$$
$$(+3b) + (+2b) + (-4b) = 3b + 2b - 4b = b$$

SELF CHECK 21

Simplify the following directed (signed) numbers, referring to the number scale as necessary.

1.	$(+3) + (-2)$		7.	$(-2x) - (-x)$
2.	$(-2) - (+3)$		8.	$(-x) - (+3x)$
3.	$(-4) + (-7)$		9.	$0 - (-3a)$
4.	$(+5) - (+2)$		10.	$(+3t) + (-6t) - (-t)$
5.	$(-6) + (-6)$		11.	$(-x) - (-2x) + (-3x)$
6.	$(-3) + (+1)$		12.	$(+a) + (-a)$

Let us suppose that the temperature of water in a boiler is being raised at a steady rate of 5° C per hour throughout the day. If we regard midday as zero hour, then the temperature at n o'clock is $(+5° C) \times n$ above that at midday.

But n is a directed number - at 2pm, $n = (+2)$

- at 9am, $n = (-3)$

and at 2pm the temperature has risen by 10° C so that

$$(+5) \times (+2) = (+10)$$

and at 9am the temperature was 15° C below that at mid- day

$$(+5) \times (-3) = (-15)$$

If we now suppose that the temperature falls by 5° C per hour then we obtain results such as

$$(-5) \times (+2) = (-10)$$
$$(-5) \times (-3) = (+15)$$

This same argument can be applied to any numbers so that in general we have

$$(+a) \times (+b) = (+ab) = \ ab$$
$$(+a) \times (-b) = (-ab) = -ab$$
$$(-a) \times (+b) = (-ab) = -ab$$
$$(-a) \times (-b) = (+ab) = \ ab$$

or with multiplication

like signs produce a +

unlike signs produce a -

If we were to take the above set of results and divide through by a suitable quantity we could obtain

$$(+a) \div (+b) = (+\tfrac{a}{b}) = \tfrac{a}{b}$$
$$(+a) \div (-b) = (-\tfrac{a}{b}) = -\tfrac{a}{b}$$
$$(-a) \div (+b) = (-\tfrac{a}{b}) = -\tfrac{a}{b}$$
$$(-a) \div (-b) = (+\tfrac{a}{b}) = \tfrac{a}{b}$$

or the same concise result as before.

Once again these arithmetic rules can be transferred to algebra.

(*a*) $(-2) \times (-3) = +2 \times 3 = +6 = 6$

(*b*) $(-2) \times (+4) = -2 \times 4 = -8$

(c) $\dfrac{(+8)}{(+4)} = +\dfrac{8}{4} = +2 = 2$

(d) $\dfrac{(+12)}{(-3)} = -\dfrac{12}{3} = -4$

(e) $(-5p) \times (+2p) = -10p^2$

(f) $\dfrac{(+18q)}{(-2q)} = -9$

Try a few more for yourself.

SELF CHECK 22

Simplify the following 12 expressions, again referring to the number scale as necessary.

1. $(-2) \times (+3)$

2. $(-3) \times (-4)$

3. $(+5) \times (-2)$

4. $(+5) \times (+1)$

5. $\dfrac{(-12)}{(-4)}$

6. $\dfrac{(-6)}{(+1)}$

7. $(+2t)(-t)$

8. $(-xy)(-1)$

9. $(-s)(3s)$

10. $\dfrac{(-12xy)}{(-4)}$

11. $\dfrac{(-4x^6)}{(+2x^3)}$

12. $\dfrac{(6ab)}{(-ab)}$

6. MANIPULATING ARITHMETIC FRACTIONS

If you were to cut a whole cake into four equal portions then each portion would represent a quarter of the whole and the four quarters together would represent the whole. Arithmetically we could write this as

$$\frac{1}{4} + \frac{1}{4} + \frac{1}{4} + \frac{1}{4} = 1$$

You will also appreciate that if one portion is now divided into two equal parts then each part is one eighth of the whole, and two of these eighths gives a quarter. Then

$$\frac{1}{8} + \frac{1}{8} = \frac{2}{8} = \frac{1}{4}$$

Similarly

$$\frac{1}{8} + \frac{1}{8} + \frac{1}{8} + \frac{1}{8} = \frac{4}{8} = \frac{1}{2}$$

The final simplification is carried out by dividing the top and bottom of the fraction by the same number. This is true for all fractions:

$$\frac{3}{12} = \frac{1}{4} \quad \textit{dividing by } 3$$

$$\frac{8}{24} = \frac{1}{3} \quad \textit{dividing by } 8$$

This simplification process can also be reversed

$$\frac{1}{2} = \frac{3}{6} = \frac{7}{14} = \frac{9}{18}$$

SELF CHECK 23

1. Simplify the following fractions

(a) $\dfrac{4}{16}$ 　　　　　　　　(c) $\dfrac{14}{35}$

(b) $\dfrac{12}{16}$ 　　　　　　　　(d) $\dfrac{10}{25}$

2. Complete the following

(a) $\dfrac{1}{3} = \dfrac{\ }{6} = \dfrac{7}{\ } = \dfrac{\ }{24}$

(b) $\dfrac{1}{5} = \dfrac{\ }{15} = \dfrac{2}{\ } = \dfrac{\ }{50}$

If we now refer back to our original cake cutting we can draw some more conclusions

$$\frac{1}{4} + \frac{1}{4} + \frac{1}{4} + \frac{1}{4} = \frac{1 + 1 + 1 + 1}{4} = 1$$

So that if all the fractions have the same denominator, then they can be added by simply adding the numerators (above the dividing line).

$$\frac{2}{5} + \frac{1}{5} + \frac{3}{5} = \frac{2 + 1 + 3}{5} = \frac{6}{5} = 1\frac{1}{5}\,(= 1.2)$$

However, if the denominators are not all the same we must start the process by converting them to be the same (ie, reversing the previous simplification).

$$\frac{1}{3} + \frac{2}{9} + \frac{4}{27} = \frac{9}{27} + \frac{6}{27} + \frac{4}{27} = \frac{19}{27}$$

Notice that we have to begin by selecting a suitable common denominator. We have chosen 27 above, as it can be divided by 3, 9 and 27 and is the smallest such number. To select 54 would not be wrong but would add extra work.

SELF CHECK 24

Add the following fractions

1. $\dfrac{2}{5} + \dfrac{3}{10}$

4. $\dfrac{1}{2} + \dfrac{1}{4} + \dfrac{1}{8}$

2. $\dfrac{3}{4} + \dfrac{1}{2}$

5. $\dfrac{1}{2} + \dfrac{2}{3} + \dfrac{3}{4} + \dfrac{7}{8}$

3. $\dfrac{1}{2} + \dfrac{1}{3} + \dfrac{1}{6}$

6. $1 + \dfrac{1}{2} + \dfrac{1}{4} + \dfrac{1}{8}$

We also saw with the slices of cake that half of a quarter is an eighth, or

$$\frac{1}{2} \times \frac{1}{4} = \frac{1}{8}$$

So we can conclude that to multiply fractions we merely multiply numerators to form the numerator and multiply denominators to form the denominator.

$$\frac{2}{3} \times \frac{4}{5} = \frac{2 \times 4}{3 \times 5} = \frac{8}{15}$$

SELF CHECK 25

Simplify by multiplying

1. $\dfrac{1}{4} \times \dfrac{2}{3}$

2. $\dfrac{1}{3} \times \dfrac{4}{5}$

3. $\dfrac{1}{2} \times \dfrac{1}{4} \times \dfrac{1}{8}$

4. $\dfrac{2}{3} \times \dfrac{3}{4} \times \dfrac{4}{5}$

You will have found that to obtain the final answer you will either have simplified after multiplication or used the process of cancelling before multiplication.

So either

$$\frac{2}{3} \times \frac{3}{4} \times \frac{4}{5} = \frac{24}{60} = \frac{2}{5}$$

or

$$\frac{2}{3} \times \frac{3}{4} \times \frac{4}{5} = \frac{2 \times \cancel{3}^{1} \times \cancel{4}^{1}}{\cancel{3}_{1} \times \cancel{4}_{1} \times 5} = \frac{2}{5}$$

Division is closely related to multiplication. Dividing by 2 is the same as multiplying by $\frac{1}{2}$. Dividing by 3 is the same as multiplying by $\frac{1}{3}$ and so on. The relation between the dividing number and the multiplying number is that one is the reciprocal of the other.

Example

the reciprocal of 5 is 1/5

the reciprocal of 7 is 1/7

the reciprocal of a is 1/a

So we now need to decide how to find the reciprocal of a fraction.

We know that there are two halves in a whole

$$Example \quad \frac{1}{\frac{1}{2}} = 2 \quad \left(\frac{2}{1}\right)$$

and there are three thirds in a whole

$$\frac{1}{\frac{1}{3}} = 3 \quad \left(\frac{3}{1}\right)$$

And so we can conclude that the reciprocal of a fraction is obtained by interchanging the numerator and denominator. This means that we can replace the operation of division by a fraction by the operation of multiplication by its reciprocal.

Hence

$$\frac{\frac{2}{3}}{\frac{4}{5}} = \frac{2}{3} \times \frac{5}{4} = \frac{10}{12} = \frac{5}{6}$$

SELF CHECK 26

Simplify the following four divisions.

1. $\dfrac{\frac{2}{1}}{3}$

2. $\dfrac{\frac{1}{7}}{\frac{1}{2}}$

3. $\dfrac{\frac{3}{8}}{\frac{1}{4}}$

4. $\dfrac{\frac{6}{7}}{\frac{2}{7}}$

7. MULTIPLICATION AND DIVISION IN ALGEBRA

There is no new idea involved in multiplication. You know how to multiply numbers together and like objects together and that it is not possible to multiply apples by pears to obtain oranges. Hence

$$
\begin{aligned}
5 \times 2x &= 10x \\
5 \times 2 \times 3x &= 30x \\
3ab \times 8 &= 24ab \\
3y \times 4y &= 12y^2 \\
3a \times 2b &= 6ab
\end{aligned}
$$

For division, exactly as in arithmetic, we can divide both numerator (the top of a fraction) and denominator (the bottom of a fraction) by the same factor.

In arithmetic you know that

$$
\frac{16}{12} = \frac{4}{3} \quad (\textit{divide } 16 \textit{ and } 12 \textit{ by } 4)
$$

so that in algebra

(a) $\quad \dfrac{12a}{3a} = \dfrac{12}{3} \qquad\qquad\qquad$ divide top and bottom by a

$\qquad\qquad\ = 4 \qquad\qquad\qquad\qquad$ divide top and bottom by 3

(b) $\quad \dfrac{10xy}{5y} = \dfrac{10x}{5} = 2x$

(c) $\quad \dfrac{12a^2}{3a} = \dfrac{12 \times a \times a}{3 \times a} = \dfrac{12a}{3} = 4a$

SELF CHECK 27

Simplify each of the following expressions into a single term.

1. $2x \times 3$

8. $14x \div 7$

13. $\dfrac{28p^2q}{7q}$

2. $6a \times 4b$

9. $12q \div q$

14. $\dfrac{6 \times 14a}{7a}$

3. $7 \times 4y$

10. $24xy^2 \div 12y$

15. $\dfrac{(3x)^2}{9x}$

4. $9a \times 2a$

11. $\dfrac{18xy}{9y}$

5. $3a \times 4b \times 2c$

12. $\dfrac{2x \times 3y}{6}$

6. $2P \times R \times 7$

7. $(10p)^2$

8. USE OF BRACKETS

Just as we put several objects in a parcel and tie it up with string, so we use brackets in mathematics to show that the contents are to be taken together. For instance

(x + 3)	means the number obtained by adding **3** to **x**
6(5 + 3)	means **6 × (5 + 3) = 6× 8 = 48**
(x - y)÷4	means that **y** is to be subtracted from **x** and the result divided by **4**.

This last expression could also be written in two other forms

$$(x - y) \div 4 = \tfrac{1}{4}(x - y) = \frac{x - y}{4}$$

It is arithmetically easy to see that

$$6(2 + 3) = 6 \times 2 + 6 \times 3$$

$$6 \times 5 = 12 + 18$$

$$30 = 30$$

Now we obtain the algebraic equivalent of the use and removal of brackets.

The diagram below shows a split rectangle which is $(x + y)$ long and p wide, so its area is $p(x + y)$.

The total area must be equal to the sum of the two small areas so that $p(x + y) = px + py$.

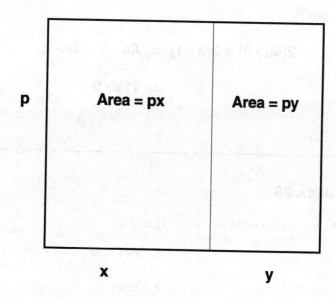

Also, the diagram below shows a rectangle which is p by x, a shaded rectangle which is p by y and a small rectangle which is p by $(x - y)$, and by looking at the relationships between the areas we can see that

$$p(x - y) = px - py$$

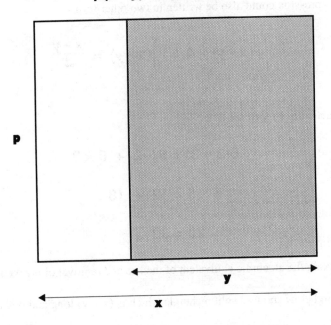

We can draw the conclusion that whenever an expression in a bracket is multiplied by a number, every term in the bracket has to be multiplied by that number.

And to show this

$$2(4a - 3) + 3(a - 1) = 8a - 6 + 3a - 3$$

$$= 11a - 9$$

SELF CHECK 28

Remove the brackets from the following expressions.

1. $2(3x - y)$

2. $7(2a - 3b)$

3. $3x(x - 1)$

6. $5a(2a - 4b)$

7. $2x(a + 3b)$

8. $5(a + 4) + 2$

➡

Self Check 28 continued...

4. $4(x^2 - x + 1)$

9. $a + b(c + d)$

5. $a(2x - t)$

10. $4x(1 - 8x)$

Consider the following arithmetic calculations

(1) $\left.\begin{array}{l} 9 + (5 + 3) = 9 + 8 \\ = 9 + 5 + 3 \end{array}\right\} = 17$

(2) $\left.\begin{array}{l} 9 - (5 + 3) = 9 - 8 \\ = 9 - 5 - 3 \end{array}\right\} = 1$

(3) $\left.\begin{array}{l} 9 + (5 - 3) = 9 + 2 \\ = 9 + 5 - 3 \end{array}\right\} = 11$

(4) $\left.\begin{array}{l} 9 - (5 - 3) = 9 - 2 \\ = 9 - 5 + 3 \end{array}\right\} = 7$

After close inspection of the above we can generate further rules for the removal of brackets:

If a bracket is immediately preceded by a '+' sign then the signs inside the bracket remain unchanged on removal of the brackets (as in (1) and (3) above).

If a bracket is immediately preceded by a '-' sign then all the signs inside the bracket are changed on removal of the brackets (as in (2) and (4) above).

Here are some more examples

(a) $2 - 2x - (x + 1) = 2 - 2x - x - 1$
$$= 1 - 3x$$

(b) $2(5x - 1) - 4(2x - 3) = (10x - 2) - (8x - 12)$
$$= 10x - 2 - 8x + 12$$
$$= 2x + 10$$

(c) $a - (b - c + d) = a - b + c - d$

(d) $2x(4x - 3) - 5(x + 1) = (8x^2 - 6x) - (5x + 5)$
$$= 8x^2 - 6x - 5x - 5$$
$$= 8x^2 - 11x - 5$$

Until you feel confident **you should multiply brackets by the number in front as a first step and then remove brackets as a second step.**

SELF CHECK 29

Remove the brackets from, and hence simplify, the following expressions.

1. $x + (y - z)$

13. $2(4x + 3y) - 3(2x + y)$

2. $y - (x + z)$

14. $5(x - y) - 4(x + y)$

3. $(x - y) - z$

15. $\frac{1}{2}(2x - 6)$

Self Check 29 continued...

4. $(a - b) - (c + d)$

16. $x(x + 2y) - y(x - y)$

5. $1 - (x - 1)$

17. $2x(3x - 5) - 5(x - 4)$

6. $(x + 4) - (x - 1)$

18. $4(3a - 2) - 2(4 - 3a)$

7. $8 - (3 + 2a)$

19. $4(p - 2) - 3(p + 1)$

8. $2p + (3 - p)$

20. $y(2y + x) - x(y - x)$

9. $3(a + 4) + (a - 1)$

21. $3(x + 1) + 2(x - 1)$

10. $5(3c - 2) - (4 + 5c)$

22. $4(y - x) + 3(x - y)$

11. $(2a - b) - (7a - 5b)$

23. $\dfrac{a - (a - b)}{a}$

12. $5 - x^2 - (x^2 + 1)$

9. SUMMARY

In this section we have

- examined the basics of **algebraic functions**

- looked at **written** and **algebraic** forms

- calculated **indices, powers** and **exponents**

- reviewed the **BEDMAS** convention for carrying out arithmetic calculations in the correct order

- used the calculator to confirm the BEDMAS rules

- worked with **directed (signed)** numbers

- revised **multiplication** and **division** in algebra

- practised and revised algebraic expressions involving **brackets**

If you are unsure of any of these topics, check back **now** to the appropriate sections before you read on.

SECTION 3

EQUATIONS AND COEFFICIENTS

1. SIMPLE EQUATIONS

When we started algebra we saw that often we could express a sentence as a mathematical equation. So the total cost of buying x articles at £4 each and y articles at £3 each became

$$C = 4x + 3y$$

Building on this we now need to develop some techniques for solving equations.

So what do we mean by the solution of an equation?

Usually an equation is a **complicated** statement. The solution is a **simple** statement but still an equation. Whereas the original equation may contain the symbol representing the unknown several times and be within other composite terms, the solution will be an extremely simple equation stating the value that the unknown must take. It is this simple equation that we have to obtain.

It is useful to remember that the equals sign in an equation acts very much like the balance of a set of scales. Having obtained the balance point then it will remain in balance if we do the same thing to the contents of each scale pan. So we could add the same to both pans, or we could double or treble the contents of each pan without disturbing the balance. Using this idea of the scales we can add, subtract, multiply and divide examples of equations.

For example

$$p - 17 = 46$$

Adding 17 to each side (ie to each scale pan)

$$p - 17 + 17 = 46 + 17$$

$$p = 63$$

This equation represents the solution as it tells us the value that p must take if the original equation is to be valid.

For example

$$q + 17 = 46$$

Subtracting 17 from each side

$$q + 17 - 17 = 46 - 17$$
$$q = 29$$

Which represents the solution.

For example

$$p/3 = 14$$

Multiplying both sides by 3

$$(p/3) \times 3 = 14 \times 3$$
$$p = 42$$

Which represents the solution.

For example

$$7x = 91$$

Dividing each side by 7

$$(7x)/7 = 91/7$$
$$x = 13$$

Which represents the solution.

SELF CHECK 30

Using the examples above, solve the following equations

1. $n - 3 = 15$

2. $m + 4 = 6$

3. $a/4 = 5$

4. $3b = 27$

So we now have four simple operations which may be applied to equations which will eventually allow us to isolate the unknown, ie solve the equation. In summary these are

Equal numbers may be added to each side.

Equal numbers may be subtracted from each side.

Each side may be divided by the same number.

Each side may be multiplied by the same number.

Often it is necessary to apply a series of these operations to solve an equation.

For example, in order to solve

$$3x - 12 = \frac{2x}{3} + 16$$

remove the fraction, multiply each side by 3

$$3(3x - 12) = 3\left(\frac{2x}{3} + 16\right)$$

$$9x - 36 = 2x + 48$$

subtract 2x from each side

$$9x - 36 - 2x = 2x + 48 - 2x$$

$$7x - 36 = 48$$

add 36 to each side

$$7x - 36 + 36 = 48 + 36$$

$$7x = 84$$

and finally, divide each side by 7

$$\frac{7x}{7} = \frac{84}{7}$$

$$x = 12$$

We can also reinterpret the first two operations to generate two equivalent operations that are more practical to apply.

$$\text{If} \qquad x - a \;=\; b \qquad\qquad \text{then adding a to each side}$$

$$x - a + a \;=\; b + a$$

$$\text{or} \qquad x \;=\; b + a$$

$$\text{If} \qquad x + a \;=\; b \qquad\qquad \text{then subtracting a from each side}$$

$$x + a - a \;=\; b - a$$

$$\text{or} \qquad x \;=\; b - a$$

So it appears we can replace rules 1 and 2 by a single operation; **any term may be removed from one side of an equation to the other if the sign of the term is changed on transfer.**

Finally, we are in a position to do a complete reversal of an equation, ie totally interchange the sides, because if $a = b$ then this implies that $b = a$ as well.

For example, to solve

$$1 - \frac{1}{6}(t + 5) \;=\; \frac{2t + 7}{3} - \frac{t - 10}{4}$$

multiply through by 12 to remove the fractions.

$$12 - 2(t + 5) \;=\; 4(2t + 7) - 3(t - 10)$$

remove the brackets

$$12 - 2t - 10 \;=\; 8t + 28 - 3t + 30$$

$$2 - 2t \;=\; 5t + 58$$

and finally to move the terms about, changing their signs

$$2 - 58 \quad = \quad 5t + 2t$$

$$- 56 \quad = \quad 7t$$

or $$\qquad 7t \quad = \quad -56$$

or $$\qquad t \quad = \quad -\frac{56}{7} = -8$$

SELF CHECK 31

Solve the following equations looking back at the examples as guidance.

1. $2x - 8 = x - 3$

2. $2t + 4 = 19 - t$

3. $3(n - 7) = 12$

4. $7(3m - 1) = 28$

5. $\dfrac{3k - 1}{4} = 5$

6. $5(x - 2) - 3(x - 1) = -1$

7. $p + 1 = 2(p - 3) - 3(p - 1)$

8. $\dfrac{2x - 1}{5} = 3 + \dfrac{1 - 3x}{4}$

2. CHANGING THE SUBJECT OF A FORMULA

When we looked at solving equations we were making the unknown the subject of the equation by a series of modifications of the way that the equation was written down. With equations we are usually dealing with numbers and an unknown. We have seen that in algebra we use letters to represent numbers to give more general expressions. This is often said to generate a formula rather than an equation but essentially they are the same. This means that we can modify formulae using the same basic rules as we used for equations.

So if we are given the formula

$$P = \frac{A(a+b)}{ab}$$

and need to solve for A, ie make A the subject of the formula, then

multiply through by ab: $$Pab = A(a+b)$$

divide through by (a + b): $$\frac{Pab}{(a+b)} = A$$

So that $$A = \frac{Pab}{(a+b)}$$

As another example, suppose we need to make N the subject of the formula

$$s = \frac{2xy}{\sqrt{N}}$$

then we can proceed as follows. (At each stage of the following work you should ensure that you can recognise the operation being used and appreciate why it is being used.)

$$s\sqrt{N} = 2xy$$

$$\sqrt{N} = \frac{2xy}{s}$$

$$N = \left\{\frac{2xy}{s}\right\}^2$$

SELF CHECK 32

For the following expressions, use the basic operations to make the given letter the subject.

1. $2a + b = 3c$, a

2. $3xy = 4y + 1$, x

3. $3xy = 4y + 1$, y

4. $5p = \dfrac{2p - 1}{\sqrt{q}}$, q

5. $P = \dfrac{A[(1 + r)^n - 1]}{r(1 + r)^n}$, A

6. $S = \dfrac{a(1 + r)[(1 + r)^n - 1]}{r}$, a

3. SIMULTANEOUS EQUATIONS

Often equations contain more than unknown and on such occasions so long as we have at least as many equations as unknowns then we may be able to proceed to solve for unknowns. We will only consider two equations in two unknowns. This type of equation is also referred to and used in unit 3, *Linear Programming*.

Consider the equations

$$3x - 2y = 11 \qquad\qquad (1)$$
$$5x + 2y = 29 \qquad\qquad (2)$$

The result of adding the left hand sides will be the removal of y and the retention of x, or a simple equation in x. Hence form the sum of (1) and (2)

$$3x + 5x = 11 + 29$$
$$8x = 40$$
$$= 5$$

We can now put this value for x into either of the original equations to form a simple equation in y.

Put $x = 5$ into (1)

$$15 - 2y = 11$$
$$- 2y = -4$$
$$y = 2$$

giving the simultaneous solution as $x = 5$, $y = 2$. You should now check in (1) and (2) that these values satisfy both of the original equations.

(1) Left hand side $= 3 \times 5 - 2 \times 2 = 15 - 4 = 11 =$ Right hand side

(2) Left hand side $= 5 \times 5 + 2 \times 2 = 25 + 4 = 29 =$ Right hand side

The process of getting rid of y is called **elimination** but is not restricted to y as our next example will show.
Consider

$$2x - 5y = 27 \qquad \textbf{(1)}$$
$$2x + 3y = 3 \qquad \textbf{(2)}$$

Notice that adding will not remove either x or y but subtraction will eliminate x.
Subtract (1) - (2):

$$2x - 2x - 5y - +3y = 27 - 3$$

(take care with the signs).

$$-8y = 24$$
$$y = -3$$

Now we can resubstitute the value for y into (1) or (2).

Suppose we select (2), then

$$2x + 3(-3) = 3$$
$$2x - 9 = 3$$
$$2x = 12$$
$$x = 6$$

giving the simultaneous solution $x = 6$, $y = -3$.

Now check these values in (1) and (2).

Often it is not possible to immediately add or subtract to eliminate one of the unknowns, but we have seen that we can multiply any equation by any number without destroying its validity.

Consider

$$7x - 6y = 20 \qquad (1)$$
$$3x + 4y = 2 \qquad (2)$$

(1) × 2 gives $14x - 12y = 40$ **(3)**

(2) × 3 gives $9x + 12y = 6$ **(4)**

(3) + (4) gives $23x = 46$

$$x = 2$$

Put $x = 2$ into (1)

$$7 \times 2 - 6y = 20$$
$$14 - 6y = 20$$
$$-6y = 6$$
$$y = -1$$

So we have generated the following rules:

1. **Decide which variable you are to eliminate.**

2. **Arrange by choosing suitable multipliers, that this unknown has the same multiplier in each equation.**

3. **Eliminate this unknown by adding or subtracting.**

4.   Solve the resulting simple equation for the remaining unknown.

5.   Substitute this value back into one of the original equations to find the value of the other unknown.

6.   Check your solutions.

7.   It is conventional to number the main equations so that these numbers can be used to explain what you are doing.

Example

Solve the simultaneous equations

$$2r - 7s = 9 \qquad (1)$$
$$3r - 2s = 5 \qquad (2)$$

Let us set out to eliminate s

$(1) \times 2$	$4r - 14s = 18$	(3)
$(2) \times 7$	$21r - 14s = 35$	(4)
$(3) - (4)$	$-17r = -17$	
	$r = 1$	

Substitute $r = 1$ into (2)

$$3 \times 1 - 2s = 5$$
$$-2s = 2$$
$$s = -1$$

Solution is

$$r = 1, s = -1$$

Check

(1)   Left hand side = $2 \times 1 - 7 \times -1 = 2 + 7 = 9$ = Right hand side

(2)   Left hand side = $3 \times 1 - 2 \times -1 = 3 + 2 = 5$ = Right hand side

Try some examples for yourself.

SELF CHECK 33

Solve the following pairs of simultaneous equations.

1. $a + b = 11$
     $a - b = 5$

2. $3p + q = 11$
     $p + q = 7$

3. $r + 3s = 8$
     $r - 2s = 3$

4. $2s - t = 1$
     $5s + t = 20$

5. $6a - 5b = 21$
     $5a + 4b = 17\frac{1}{2}$

---

4. EXPANDING BRACKETS

In section 2 part 8 (use of brackets) we saw that

$$p(x + y) = px + py$$

Now we consider what happens if p itself is a bracketed set of terms. Let us replace p by the expression $(a + b)$ in the above, then we obtain

$$(a + b)(x + y)$$
$$= (a + b)x + (a + b)y$$

$$=x(a + b) + y(a + b)$$
$$= xa + xb + ya + yb$$
$$= ax + bx + ay + by$$
$$= ax + ay + bx + by$$

by interchanging the order of multiplication

By comparison of the two sides of the expression, we can see that the right hand side is obtained by multiplying each of the terms in (a + b) by each of the terms in (x + y) and adding all the separate products, ie

we multiply a by x to give ax

we multiply a by y to give ay

we multiply b by x to give bx

we multiply b by y to give by

and then we add the four resulting terms. It helps if we draw a simple diagram, as below, of this procedure which will represent this method.

Look carefully at it and make sure you understand it.

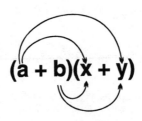

Remember any sign is attached to the following term and care must be taken with sign combinations using the rules on signed or directed numbers.

So in detail

$$(p - q)(r - s) \quad = \qquad pr \qquad \text{first} \times \text{first}$$
$$-ps \qquad \text{first} \times \text{second}$$
$$-qr \qquad \text{second} \times \text{first}$$
$$+qs \qquad \text{second} \times \text{second}$$
$$= \qquad pr - ps - qr + qs$$

and similarly, but with less detail

$$(3x - 2)(4x + 1) = 12x^2 + 3x - 8x - 2$$
$$= 12x^2 - 5x - 2$$

and

$$(2a - 3)(3a - 5) = 6a^2 - 10a - 9a + 15$$
$$= 6a^2 - 19a + 15$$

SELF CHECK 34

Try to expand the following products

1. $(x + 2)(x + 3)$

2. $(a + 5)(a - 2)$

3. $(b - 7)(b + 3)$

4. $(4 + t)(3 - t)$

5. $(2x + 1)(3x + 1)$

6. $(2a + 3)(3a - 4)$

7. $(2x - 1)(3x - 2)$

8. $(3a - 1)(3a + 1)$

Our simple rule can now be extended to brackets containing more terms.

$$(2x^2 - 5x - 3)(3x^2 + 2x - 1)$$

$= 6x^4 + 4x^3 - 2x^2$	first $\times$ second bracket
$- 15x^3 - 10x^2 + 5x$	second $\times$ second bracket
$- 9x^2 - 6x + 3$	third $\times$ second bracket

$$= 6x^4 - 11x^3 - 21x^2 - x + 3$$

SELF CHECK 35

Expand the following brackets in these more complex expressions

1. $(x + 1)(x^2 - 2x + 3)$

2. $(2x^2 - 3x + 2)(4x^2 - 2x - 3)$

We have learnt that an index or power of 2 means that the expression is to be multiplied by itself.

So that

$$(p + q)^2 = (p + q)(p + q)$$
$$= p^2 + pq + qp + q^2$$
$$= p^2 + 2pq + q^2 \quad \text{(as pq = qp)}$$
$$(2x - 3)^2 = (2x - 3)(2x - 3)$$
$$= 4x^2 - 6x - 6x + 9$$
$$= 4x^2 - 12x + 9$$

SELF CHECK 36

Remove the brackets

1. $(p + 2)^2$.

2. $(3a - 4d)^2$.

Now what about higher powers?

$$(p + q)^3 = (p + q)\underbrace{(p + q)(p + q)}$$

$$= (p + q)(p^2 + 2pq + q^2)$$

$$= p^3 + 2p^2q + pq^2 + p^2q + 2pq^2 + q^3$$

$$= p^3 + 3p^2q + 3pq^2 + q^3$$

$$(p + q)^4 = \underbrace{(p + q)(p + q)}\underbrace{(p + q)(p + q)}$$

$$= (p^2 + 2pq + q^2)(p^2 + 2pq + q^2)$$

$$= p^4 + 2p^3q + 4p^2q^2 + 2pq^3 + p^2q^2 + 2pq^3 + q^4$$

$$= p^4 + 4p^3q + 6p^2q^2 + 4pq^3 + q^4$$

(As an alternative we could have multiplied $(p + q)$ by the result of $(p + q)^3$ – you should try it and confirm that the same result is obtained.)

Let us now summarise these results that we have found

$$(p + q)^1 = \qquad p + q$$
$$(p + q)^2 = \qquad p^2 + 2pq + q^2$$
$$(p + q)^3 = \qquad p^3 + 3p^2q + 3pq^2 + q^3$$
$$(p + q)^3 = p^4 + 4p^3q + 6p^2q^2 + 4pq^3 + q^4$$

By inspection we can see a number of things:

1. The resulting number of terms on the right hand side is always 1 greater than the original power.

2. The power on p starts with the original power and descends whereas the power on q ascends finally reaching the original power.

3. The numbers, or coefficients, do not at first sight seem to form any well defined pattern.

Let us now extract just the numbers and consider the pattern

$$
\begin{array}{ccccccccc}
 & & & 1 & & 1 & & & \\
 & & 1 & & 2 & & 1 & & \\
 & 1 & & 3 & & 3 & & 1 & \\
1 & & 4 & & 6 & & 4 & & 1
\end{array}
$$

We can see that each row of numbers starts and ends with a 1. The intervening numbers are generated by adding the two numbers directly above in the previous line.

So the next line in the pattern will be

$$
\begin{array}{cccccc}
1 & 5 & 10 & 10 & 5 & 1
\end{array}
$$

which gives

$$(p + q)^5 = p^5 + 5p^4q + 10p^3q^2 + 10p^2q^3 + 5pq^4 + q^5$$

SELF CHECK 37

Write down the next line in the pattern and so generate the expansion of $(p + q)^6$.

---

5. COEFFICIENTS

It should be clear that as long as the power remains relatively low then this method of generating the coefficients is very simple and easy to apply and remember. The resulting pattern is called **Pascals triangle.**

But, as we will see in a later unit, if the power becomes larger then the effort and arithmetic becomes longer and more tedious.

So far we have generated the coefficients from a triangle but can a method of generating them be obtained without the triangle?

We must first become familiar with the **factorial notation**. This is a shorthand method of writing the product of consecutive whole numbers starting or ending with 1.

We can define

$$n! = 1 \times 2 \times 3 \times \ldots \times (n-1) \times n$$

so that

$$3! = 1 \times 2 \times 3 = 6$$
$$5! = 1 \times 2 \times 3 \times 4 \times 5 = 120$$

SELF CHECK 38

Write down and evaluate the factorials of

1. 4!   3.   2!

2. 6!   4.   1!

You may already have appreciated that as each factorial is a product then simplification of expressions can be obtained by cancelling without a lot of wasteful calculation.

Hence,

$$\frac{12!}{10!} = \frac{1 \times 2 \times 3 \times 4 \times 5 \times 6 \times 7 \times 8 \times 9 \times 10 \times 11 \times 12}{1 \times 2 \times 3 \times 4 \times 5 \times 6 \times 7 \times 8 \times 9 \times 10}$$

$$= 11 \times 12 = 132$$

SELF CHECK 39

Simplify and then evaluate

1. $\dfrac{5!}{4!}$

3. $\dfrac{20!}{19!}$

2. $\dfrac{9!}{6!}$

4. $\dfrac{100!}{99!}$

When you have completed Self Check 39 you should appreciate that the factorial notation is a very efficient method of writing down certain products.

For our purposes we have to define the value of 0! as 1. (This is a definition as it falls outside the definition of the factorial notation.)

Let us now look at five particular arrangements of factorial numbers

$$\frac{4!}{4!\ 0!} = 1$$

$$\frac{4!}{3!\ 1!} = 4$$

$$\frac{4!}{2!\ 2!} = 6$$

$$\frac{4!}{1!\ 3!} = 4$$

$$\frac{4!}{0!\ 4!} = 1$$

You may be able to evaluate these in your head. If not, write in the intermediate steps until you are confident.

SELF CHECK 40

Determine the value of each of the following

$$\frac{5!}{5!\ 0!}$$

$$\frac{5!}{4!\ 1!}$$

$$\frac{5!}{3!\ 2!}$$

$$\frac{5!}{2!\ 3!}$$

$$\frac{5!}{1!\ 4!}$$

$$\frac{5!}{0!\ 5!}$$

You may have realised that these arrangements have generated the fourth and fifth rows of Pascals triangle, or the coefficients that we need to expand $(p + q)^4$ and $(p + q)^5$.

Let us now look again at the expansion of $(p + q)^4$.

$$(p + q)^4 \ = \ p^4 + 4p^3q + 6p^2q^2 + 4pq^3 + q^4$$

$$= \frac{4!}{4!\,0!}p^4 + \frac{4!}{3!\,1!}p^3q + \frac{4!}{2!\,2!}p^2q^2 + \frac{4!}{1!\,3!}pq^3 + \frac{4!}{0!\,4!}q^4$$

SELF CHECK 41

Repeat what we have just done for $(p + q)^4$ for the expression $(p + q)^5$ using the results from Self Check 40.

Let us now look at the relationships between the various powers (or times that it is multiplied by itself) and the arrangements of the factorials. You will see that the numerator is the factorial of the power on the original bracket.

The two terms in the denominator represent the number of times p is multiplied by itself and the number of times q is multiplied by itself in the particular term on the right hand side. So we can now generate coefficients.

The coefficients of the term containing p^5q^3 in the expansion of $(p + q)^8$ will be

$$\frac{8!}{5!\ 3!} = \frac{6 \times 7 \times 8}{1 \times 2 \times 3} = 56$$

SELF CHECK 42

1.   Calculate the coefficient of the term containing p^7q^3 in the expansion of $(p + q)^{10}$.

2.   Find the coefficient of the term containing $p^{10}q^{10}$ in the expansion of $(p + q)^{20}$.

These coefficients, or numbers, are usually called **binomial** coefficients and are further abbreviated. We write

$$\frac{4!}{3!\ 1!} \quad as \quad \binom{4}{1}$$

and

$$\frac{10!}{7!\ 3!} \quad as \quad \binom{10}{3}$$

This is called the binomial form.

Using this notation we can rewrite our expansion of $(p + q)^4$ in the form

$$(p + q)^4 = \binom{4}{0}p^4 + \binom{4}{1}p^3q + \binom{4}{2}p^2q^2 + \binom{4}{3}pq^3 + \binom{4}{4}q^4$$

$$= p^4 + 4p^3q + 6p^2q^2 + 4pq^3 + q^4$$

using our previous evaluations.

Looking at the symmetry of the result here we can immediately conclude that

$$\binom{4}{1} = \binom{4}{3}$$

as each is equal to 4.

SELF CHECK 43

Use the binomial form to rewrite the expansion of $(p + q)^6$.

If you now compare the binomial form for $(p + q)^6$ that you obtained in Self Check 43 with the answer you obtained in Self Check 37 you will once again notice the symmetry. From this we can conclude that

$$\binom{6}{1} = \binom{6}{5} \quad and \quad \binom{6}{2} = \binom{6}{4}$$

Do you now see that the sum of the two lower numbers in each of these two expressions is the upper number?

Having noted this relation we can obtain

$$\binom{10}{3} = \binom{10}{7} \text{ and } \binom{12}{4} = \binom{12}{8}$$

and so on, as a direct result of the symmetry of the expansions.

In general terms we now have that

$$\binom{n}{r} = \frac{n!}{(n-r)!r!}$$

so that

$$\binom{15}{10} = \frac{15!}{5!10!} = \frac{11 \times 12 \times 13 \times 14 \times 15}{1 \times 2 \times 3 \times 4 \times 5} = 3003$$

We also have, as a result of the symmetry of the expansion that

$$\binom{n}{r} = \binom{n}{n-r}$$

SELF CHECK 44

Finally, in this section, use the above general form to calculate

1. $\binom{7}{3}$

Self Check 44 continued...

2. $\begin{pmatrix} 10 \\ 2 \end{pmatrix}$

3. $\begin{pmatrix} 12 \\ 6 \end{pmatrix}$

6. INEQUALITIES

We may wish to express in mathematical form statements that contain comparisons. Such statements could be:

1.   **My salary is bigger than my colleague's.**

2.   **We do not have time to make as many as 10 machines.**

3.   **The bank manager demands that the overdraft stays below £100,000.**

4.   **I must spend less than I earn.**

Each of the above statements is comparing the respective size of two quantities.

We have seen that an equation represents an exact balance. These statements represent an **imbalance**. To express these we introduce two new symbols:

'**a < b**' reads '**a is less than b**'

'**a > b**' reads '**a is greater than b**'

So returning to the original four statements we can write

1. **If my salary is x and that of my colleague is y then x > y.**

2. **If we make m machines then m < 10.**

3. **If the overdraft is P then P < 100,000.**

4. **If I earn e and spend s then e > s.**

Notice how a wordy statement of comparison becomes a concise algebraic inequality.

SELF CHECK 45

Express as an inequality

'the cost of buying x articles at £4 each and y articles at £3 each must be less than £50'.

If we think back again to our number line, in section 1 part 1, then these two inequalities represent the two portions to the left and right of some predetermined position.

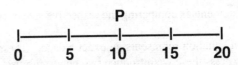

Look at this number line and take the point represented by the number 10.

Any number x to the left of P satisfies

$$x < 10$$

and to the right of P satisfies

$$x > 10$$

The number 10 represents the boundary between the two ranges and is contained within neither.

If the bank manager demanded that the overdraft was to be up to a maximum of £100,000 then the figure of £100,000 would be allowable.

We could restate the demand by saying that the overdraft must be less than or equal to £100,000 or

$$P \leq 100,000 \quad \text{(note the new inequality sign)}$$

With this notation the boundary point is included in the lower range.

The statement 'I must not spend more than I earn' now allows you to spend exactly the sum that you earn so the algebraic inequality becomes

$$e \geq s \qquad \text{or} \qquad s \leq e$$

SELF CHECK 46

Express as an inequality

'the cost of buying a bicycles at £45 each and b scooters at £15 each must not exceed £3,000'.

Using the answer from Self Check 46, your expression should be

$$45a + 15b \leq £\ 3000 \qquad \text{or}$$
$$15(3a + b) \leq £\ 15 \times 200$$

Notice that the common factor of 15 is on both sides of this inequality.

Can we divide through by 15?

Think about the problem from an unbalanced scale point of view.

You will come to the conclusion that we can, and so

$$15(3a + b) \leq £\ 15 \times 200 \qquad \text{and}$$
$$3a + b \leq £\ 200$$

are equivalent statements.

So, we can divide any inequality throughout by any positive number.

SELF CHECK 47

Express, and simplify, the inequality representing the statement

'it will take 20 minutes to make each of x soft bound books and 40 minutes to make each of y hard bound books but must not spend more than 8 hours in total'.

But a note of caution. Using the number line we can say

$$-6 < -2$$

but if we divide this throughout by -2 then it is **not true** that 3 is less than 1.

So unlike equations, inequalities only remain valid when multiplied or divided throughout by a positive number.

7. SUMMARY

In this section we have

- revised **simple equations**

- **changed subjects** in formulae

- worked through **simultaneous equations**

- **expanded brackets**

- looked at **coefficients**

- revised **factorials**

- examined **inequalities**

If you are unsure of any of these topics, check back **now** to the appropriate sections before reading on.

SECTION 4

USING A CALCULATOR

You will own a calculator and the associated instruction manual. The following section should be worked through with your calculator and manual, bearing in mind that the official manual for your machine may override what is written here.

1. BASIC CALCULATIONS

You have already used your calculator with this unit (sections 1 and 2) to perform the arithmetic operations of addition, subtraction, multiplication and division. You may also be aware that your calculator has the correct order of precedence of operations built into it (provided that you do not press the 'equals' button part way through a calculation!)

Earlier we considered the evaluation of

$$5 + 2 \times 3$$

Now try it on your calculator.

You should press the keys in this order

Enter 5 ⊞ enter 2 ⊠ enter 3 ⊟

to give the answer 11.

But if you wanted

$$(5 + 2) \times 3$$

then you would need to press

Enter 5 ⊞ enter 2 ⊟ ⊠ enter 3 ⊟

to give the answer 21.

SELF CHECK 48

Use your calculator to evaluate each of the following, giving each answer correct to one decimal place.

1. $10.27 + 13.51 + 6.73 - 5.92$.

2. $10.1 \times 13.21 - 5.76 \times 7.32$.

3. $\dfrac{14.77 - 3.26}{4.51}$

2. THE SQUARE ROOT FUNCTION

You should find a key on your machine labelled with the square root sign

Use of this key allows you to find the square root of the number held in your calculator and shown on the display window. Let us first check to ensure that you have located the correct key by performing a simple calculation whose result you already know. To find the square root of 4

$$\sqrt{4} = 2$$

Proceed as follows

Enter **4** then $\boxed{\sqrt{}}$ and the result should appear in the display window.

If your answer is anything other than 2, then have a look at your manual, read it and try again.

We can now obtain the square root of any number.

Try these below, and check them with my answers, then go on to Self Check 49.

$$\sqrt{14.76} = 3.842 \quad \textit{to three decimal places}$$

$$\sqrt{7.21 \times 4.56} = 5.734 \quad \textit{to three decimal places}$$

SELF CHECK 49

Evaluate the following expressions to two decimal places.

1. $\sqrt{8.23}$

2. $\sqrt{\dfrac{7.51 - 2.76}{3.25}}$

3. $\sqrt{\dfrac{2ab}{c}}$ where $a = 2.42$, $b = 4.71$, $c = 3.21$

3. THE SQUARE FUNCTION

Find the key on your calculator labelled

Use of this key allows you to find the square of the number held in your calculator and shown in the display window.

Once again, to check that you have located the correct key, try

$$4^2 = 16$$

enter **4** then x^2 and the result should appear on the display window.

Using this key, we can now obtain the square of any number displayed on the display window. Try these and check your results with my answers, then move on to Self Check 50 for more practice.

$$2.52^2 = 6.350 \text{ to three decimal places.}$$

$$(1.21 + 3.67)^2 = 23.81 \text{ to two decimal places.}$$

SELF CHECK 50

Evaluate the following expressions to three decimal places

1. 5.33^2

2. $(1.29 - 0.07)^2$

Self Check 50 continued...

3. $\quad \left\{ \dfrac{15.46 - 12.31}{1.76} \right\}^2$

4. $\quad \left\{ \dfrac{2(p + q)}{3p} \right\}^2$ where $p = 7.29$ $q = 1.34$

4. THE GENERAL POWER FUNCTION

You should find a key on your machine labelled

either $\boxed{X^y}$ or $\boxed{Y^x}$

The use of this key allows you to raise a number to a power where the number is displayed on the screen and the power is to be entered after pressing this key.

Once again, to check that you have located the correct key try

$2^3 = 8$

enter **2** then $\boxed{X^y}$ enter **3** $\boxed{=}$ and the result should appear in the display window.

We can now raise any number to any power using this key. Try it with

$(1.72)^4 = 8.75$ to two decimal places.

$$(1.01 + 0.03)^7 = 1.3159 \text{ to four decimal places.}$$

Note

 use of this key is not confined to whole number powers and it will generate the value for any power.

Try it with

$$(1.56)^{3.5} = 4.742 \text{ to three decimal places}$$

$$(4.37)^{\frac{1}{4}} = 1.4458 \text{ to four decimal places.}$$

Notice here we must first express the power $\frac{1}{4}$ as 0.25.

SELF CHECK 51

Evaluate the following to four decimal places.

1. 1.751^5

2. $(1 + 0.155)^{10}$

3. $7.62^{4.6}$

4. $(1.635)^{\frac{1}{3}}$

---

5. THE FACTORIAL FUNCTION

You should find a key on your calculator labelled

Use of this key allows you to find the value of x factorial which you will remember is important when calculating binomial coefficients.

Once again, to check that you have located the correct key try

3! = 6

Enter **3** then **x!** and the result should appear on the display window.

You can now evaluate the factorial of any number. Try it with

7! = 5040

10! = 3,628,800

and for binomial coefficients

$$\binom{7}{3} = \frac{7!}{4!\ 3!} = 35$$

Check your answers with mine and then move on to Self Check 52.

SELF CHECK 52

Evaluate the following factorial expressions.

1.   9!

2. $\dfrac{13!}{10!}$

3. $\dbinom{6}{2}$

4. $\dbinom{10}{5}$

---

6. THE SCIENTIFIC NOTATION

In section 3 you were only required to find factorials of small numbers although your calculator may be capable of dealing with some larger values.

Try finding 20! Your calculator will give either

$$2.432902008^{18}$$

or signpost an error message. If the error is signposted then consult your manual.

But what do all the numbers in the first option mean? This is an example of the scientific notation which your calculator has built in, as it is unable to give you a display of such a large number on the screen in familiar number form.

It means

$$2.432902008 \times 10^{18}$$

You will remember from section 1 that multiplying by 10 moves the decimal point one place to the right so multiplying by 10 eighteen times requires that movement to take place eighteen times. This will give the extremely large number

$$2\ 432\ 902\ 008\ 000\ 000\ 000$$

Such numbers are so large that they are hard to imagine. However your calculator can handle them efficiently within calculations. Try

$$\binom{20}{15} = \frac{20!}{5!\ 15!} = 15504$$

or

$$\binom{18}{16} = 153$$

7. USE OF THE MEMORY FACILITY

Your calculator will have a memory facility represented by the three keys,

$$\boxed{\text{M+}} \quad \boxed{\text{Min}} \quad \boxed{\text{MR}}$$

If the notation on your calculator differs, refer to your manual.

These three keys allow you to

$\boxed{\text{M+}}$ – add the value shown in the display window to the contents of the memory

| Min | – | clear the memory of any previous contents and transfer the displayed value to the memory |

| MR | – | recall the memory by transferring the contents of the memory to the display window |

The [M+] key is used to accumulate the sum of intermediate calculations rather than have to note them down on a separate piece of paper and then re-enter them and sum them. However, when performing this process you must take great care to ensure the correct order of procedure.

We can show the proper use of the memory function with this example. Given the pairs of values represented by x and y calculate for each pair the product xy and accumulate those products as we proceed.

If we draw this out as a table (with values of x and y as shown) it would look like this

x	y	xy
1	5	5
3	9	27
5	14	70
7	21	147
	Total	249

If we then key the values in for each pair as

enter **x** value [x]

enter **y** value [=] then press [M+]

and then having completed the four calculations press

[MR]

SELF CHECK 58

Complete the following table, accumulating the values of x^2 and then of xy as you calculate each individual value.

Use your calculator and the methods just described.

x	y	x^2	xy
2.1	20.2		
3.4	18.5		
7.5	16.7		
8.3	14.3		
10.5	11.8		
11.7	8.2		
	Totals equal		

---

8. COMBINATIONS OF FUNCTIONS

So far we have considered each function separately. Your calculator will handle a sequence of functions. You should always aim to perform the complete evaluation without taking partial results out of the calculator if they have to be re-entered at a later stage of the calculation.

You should also be careful to ensure that your calculator has completed one calculation before proceeding with the sequence. You can do this by watching the display window.

Follow through this example in order to find $87(1.035)^{18}$

enter **87** press ☒ enter **1.035** and press ☒^{y}

enter **18** press $\boxed{=}$

and you should see displayed 161.60156.

You can reverse the order of the sequence. Try it!

enter **1.035** press $\boxed{\mathbf{x^y}}$ enter **18** $\boxed{=}$

then press $\boxed{\mathbf{x}}$ enter **87** $\boxed{=}$

and again you should see displayed 161.60156.

Now practice with these

$$1000(1.1225)^{20} = 10086.18648 \ \text{ or } 10086.19 \ \text{(two dp)}$$

and

$$100(1.06)^{80} = 10579.59935 \ \text{ or } 10579.60 \ \text{(two dp)}$$

In a more complex example, find

$$\frac{100\{(1.07)^{10} - 1\}}{0.07(1.07)^{10}}$$

You would calculate the value of the denominator and use the memory to hold this value whilst evaluating the numerator before doing the final division. So we can proceed:

evaluate and store denominator:

enter **1.07** press $\boxed{\mathbf{x^y}}$ enter **10** $\boxed{=}$ $\boxed{\mathbf{x}}$

enter **0.07** press ☐= ☐Min

evaluate the numerator:

enter **1.07** press ☐x^y enter **10** ☐= ☐−

enter **1** ☐= ☐× enter **100** ☐=

complete the division:

press ☐÷ ☐MR ☐=

and your display should show

702.358154 or 702.36 (two dp)

Now try

$$\frac{200\{(1.08)^{16} - 1\}}{0.08(1.08)^{16}} = 1770.27 \quad \text{(2 dp)}$$

or

$$\frac{100 \times 0.05 \times (1.05)^{25}}{\{(1.05)^{25} - 1\}} = 7.10 \quad \text{(2 dp)}$$

As you work through other related units in this module you will be introduced to further facilities available on your calculator that will save you time and effort.

9. SUMMARY

In this final section we have covered

- **basic calculations** performed on your calculator

- the **square** and **square root** functions

- the **general power** function

- the **factorial** function

- **scientific notation**

- use of the **memory**

- a look at **combined functions.**

If you are unsure of any of the topics covered in this unit then check back to the appropriate sections.

SECTION 5

ANSWERS TO SELF CHECK QUESTIONS

SECTION 1. NUMBERS

SELF CHECK 1

1.   526   = $5 \times 100 + 2 \times 10 + 6 \times 1.$

2.   70132   = $7 \times 10000 + 0 \times 1000 + 1 \times 100$
             $+ 3 \times 10 + 2 \times 1.$

      = $7 \times 10000 + 1 \times 100 + 3 \times 10 + 2 \times 1$

SELF CHECK 2

1.

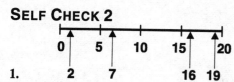

2.   Here we need that portion of the line that includes 250 at the left hand end and 800 at the right hand end. It would not be wrong to use a longer scale, it would be unproductive.

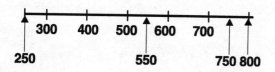

SELF CHECK 3

1.   526 $= 5 \times 10^2 + 2 \times 10 + 6 \times 1.$
2.   70132 $= 7 \times 10^4 + 1 \times 10^2 + 3 \times 10 + 2 \times 1.$
3.   2375100 $= 2 \times 10^6 + 3 \times 10^5 + 7 \times 10^4 +$
            $5 \times 10^3 + 1 \times 10^2.$

SELF CHECK 4

1. $£63.75 = 6{\times}10 + 3{\times}1 + 7{\times}\dfrac{1}{10} + 5{\times}\dfrac{1}{10^2}$

2. $£1032.23 = 1{\times}10^3 + 3{\times}10 + 2{\times}1 + 2{\times}\dfrac{1}{10} + 3{\times}\dfrac{1}{10^2}$

SELF CHECK 5

1. $31.216 = 3{\times}10 + 1{\times}1 + 2{\times}\dfrac{1}{10} + 1{\times}\dfrac{1}{10^2} + 6{\times}\dfrac{1}{10^3}$

2. $10.20015 = 1{\times}10 + 2{\times}\dfrac{1}{10} + 1{\times}\dfrac{1}{10^4} + 5{\times}\dfrac{1}{10^5}$

3. $123.001 = 1{\times}10^2 + 2{\times}10 + 3{\times}1 + 1{\times}\dfrac{1}{10^3}$

SELF CHECK 6

1.   (a) 19.28
       (b) 211.3
       (c) 0.474
       (d) 11.0
2.   £1.25

SELF CHECK 7

1.   (a) 2 in 24 are rejected
       (b) 2/24 are rejected
       (c) 0.0833 are rejected.
2.   The second form may be written as 1/12.

SELF CHECK 8

1.   15/100,   0.15.
2.   7/100,   0.07.
3.   25/100,   0.25.

SELF CHECK 9

1.   0.0725.
2.   0.15375.

SELF CHECK 10

1.   25%
2.   11%
3.   37.5%
4.   21.25%

SELF CHECK 11

1.   60
2.   (a) £8.80,   (b) £228.90
3.   £3.49
4. $6\frac{2}{3}\%$, $6\frac{1}{4}\%$

SECTION 2. ALGEBRA

SELF CHECK 12

1.   (a) 58°F,   (b) 55°F   (c) 60°F   (d) (48 + T)°F
       (e) (48 - t)°F.
2.   (a) Increase = px/100   (b) new price = p + px/100.

SELF CHECK 13

1.   10000p + 8000q
2.   4x + 7y

SELF CHECK 14

1.   y/3
2.   5 _ a
3.   2b/a
4.   c/2d

SELF CHECK 15

1. $3p = 12$
2. $4 - x = 7$
3. $4N = 10 + N$
4. $5x + 7y$
5. $2x + 3y$

SELF CHECK 16

1. (a) a^4 (b) y^2
2. (a) $r \times r \times r \times r \times r \times r$
   (b) $b \times b \times b \times b \times b \times b \times b$

SELF CHECK 17

1. $2a \times 2a \times 2a$
2. $2 \times a \times a \times a$
3. $4 \times y \times y \times y \times y \times y$
4. $4y \times 4y \times 4y \times 4y \times 4y$

SELF CHECK 18

1. £158,000
2. (a) 60   (b) 54   (c) 216
   (d) 6   (e) 252   (f) 39
   (g) 3   (h) 1

SELF CHECK 19

1. 3^8 3. 2^4
2. q^6 4. $(3x)^5$

SELF CHECK 20

1. 1   4. 18
2. 15   5. 54
3. 2

SELF CHECK 21

1. 1   7. $-x$
2. -5   8. $-4x$
3. -11   9. $3a$
4. 3   10. $-2t$
5. -12   11. $-2x$
6. -2   12. 0

SELF CHECK 22

1. -6   7. $-2t^2$
2. 12   8. xy
3. -10   9. $-3s^2$

4.   5
5.   3
6.   -6

10.   3xy
11. $-2x^3$
12.   -6

SELF CHECK 23

1.   (a)   1/4   (b)   3/4   (c)   2/5   (d)   2/5
2.   (a)   1/3 = 2/6 = 7/21 = 8/24
      (b)   1/5 = 3/15 = 2/10 = 10/50

SELF CHECK 24

1.   7/10

2.   5/4 or $1\frac{1}{4}$

3.   1

4.   7/8

5.   67/24 or $2\frac{19}{24}$

6.   15/8 or $1\frac{7}{8}$

SELF CHECK 25

1.   1/6
2.   4/15

3.   1/64
4.   2/5

SELF CHECK 26

1.   6

2.   2/7

3.   3/2 or $1\frac{1}{2}$

4.   3

SELF CHECK 27

1.   6x
2.   24ab
3.   28y
4. $18a^2$
5.   24abc
6.   14PR

7. $100p^2$
8.   2x
9.   12
10.   2xy
11.   2x
12.   xy

13. $4p^2$
14.   12
15.   x

SELF CHECK 28

1.   6x - 2y
2.   14a - 21b
3. $3x^2 - 3x$
4. $4x^2 - 4x + 4$
5.   2ax - at
6. $10a^2 - 20ab$

7.   2ax + 6bx
8.   5a + 22
9.   a + bc + bd
10. $4x - 32x^2$

SELF CHECK 29

1.   x + y - z
2.   y - x - z
3.   x - y - z
4.   a - b - c - d

13.   2x + 3y
14.   x - 9y
15.   x - 3
16. $x^2 + xy + y^2$

5.	2 - x		**17.**	$6x^2 - 15x + 20$
6.	5		**18.**	$18a - 16$
7.	5 - 2a		**19.**	$p - 11$
8.	p + 3		**20.**	$2y^2 + x^2$
9.	4a + 11		**21.**	5x + 1
10.	10c - 14		**22.**	y - x
11.	4b - 5a		**23.**	b/a
12.	$4 - 2x^2$			

SECTION 3. EQUATIONS AND COEFFICIENTS

SELF CHECK 30

1.	n = 18		**3.**	a = 20
2.	m = 2		**4.**	b = 9

SELF CHECK 31

1.	x = 5		**5.**	k = 7
2.	t = 5		**6.**	x = 3
3.	n = 11		**7.**	p = -2
4.	m = 5/3		**8.**	x = 3

SELF CHECK 32

1. $a = \dfrac{3c - b}{2}$

2. $x = \dfrac{4y + 1}{3y}$

3. $y = \dfrac{1}{3x - 4}$

4. $q = \left\{\dfrac{2p - 1}{5p}\right\}2$

5. $A = \dfrac{Pr(1 + r)^n}{[(1 + r)^n - 1]}$

6. $a = \dfrac{Sr}{(1 + r)[(1 + r)^n - 1]}$

SELF CHECK 33

1.	a = 8		b = 3
2.	p = 2		q = 5
3.	r = 5		s = 1
4.	s = 3		t = 5
5.	a = 3.5		b = 0

SELF CHECK 34

1.	$x^2 + 5x + 6$		**5.**	$6x^2 + 5x + 1$
2.	$a^2 + 3a - 10$		**6.**	$6a^2 + a - 12$
3.	$b^2 - 4b - 21$		**7.**	$6x^2 - 7x + 2$
4.	$12 - t - t^2$		**8.**	$9a^2 - 1$

SELF CHECK 35
1. $x^3 - x^2 + x + 3$
2. $8x^4 - 16x^3 + 8x^2 + 5x - 6$

SELF CHECK 36
1. $p^2 + 4p + 4$
2. $9a^2 - 24ad + 16d^2$

SELF CHECK 37

| 1 | 6 | 15 | 20 | 15 | 6 | 1 |

$(p + q)^6 =$
$p^6 + 6p^5q + 15p^4q^2 + 20p^3q^3 + 15p^2q^4 + 6pq^5 + q^6$

SELF CHECK 38
1. 24   3. 2
2. 720   4. 1

SELF CHECK 39
1. 5   3. 20
2. 504   4. 100

SELF CHECK 40

| 1, | 5, | 10, | 10, | 5, | 1 |

SELF CHECK 41
$(p + q)^5 =$
$$\frac{5!}{5!\ 0!}p^5 + \frac{5!}{4!\ 1!}p^4q + \frac{5!}{3!\ 2!}p^3q^2 + \frac{5!}{2!\ 3!}p^2q^3 + \frac{5!}{1!\ 4!}pq^4 + \frac{5!}{0!\ 5!}q^5$$

SELF CHECK 42
1. $\dfrac{10!}{7!\ 3!} = 120$

2. $\dfrac{20!}{10!\ 10!} = 184756$

SELF CHECK 43
$(p + q)^6 =$
$$\binom{6}{0}p^6 + \binom{6}{1}p^5q + \binom{6}{2}p^4q^2 + \binom{6}{3}p^3q^3 + \binom{6}{4}p^2q^4 + \binom{6}{5}pq^5 + \binom{6}{6}q^6$$

SELF CHECK 44
1. 35   2. 45   3. 924

SELF CHECK 45
$4x + 3y < 50$

SELF CHECK 46
$45a + 15b \leq 3000$

SELF CHECK 47
$20x + 40y \leq 8 \times 60$
$x + 2y \leq 24$

SECTION 4. USING A CALCULATOR

SELF CHECK 48
1. 24.6   **2.** 91.3   **3.** 2.6

SELF CHECK 49
1. 2.87   **2.** 1.21   **3.** 2.66

SELF CHECK 50
1. 28.409   **2.** 1.488   **3.** 3.203   **4.** 0.623

SELF CHECK 51
1. 16.4600   **2.** 4.2249   **3.** 11402.3106   **4.** 1.1781

SELF CHECK 52
1. 362880   **2.** 1716   **3.** 15   **4.** 252

SELF CHECK 53

x	y	x^2	xy
2.1	20.2	4.41	42.42
3.4	18.5	11.56	62.90
7.5	16.7	56.25	125.25
8.3	14.3	68.89	118.69
10.5	11.8	110.25	123.90
11.7	8.2	136.89	95.94
		388.25	569.10

UNIT 1

BUSINESS MATHS

CONTENTS

UNIT OBJECTIVES

This unit contains two sections in which we use basic mathematics in two different ways to analyse business problems and situations.

After studying the *Financial Analysis* section you should

- be much more familiar with your calculator and its functions

- be able to analyse financial schemes using basic mathematics

- be able to model financial systems and appreciate the use of diagrams

- appreciate how the value of money changes with time

- be able to make financial comparisons and decisions

After studying the *Graphs* section you should

- be able to quickly and accurately draw a straight line graph

- recognise the equation of a straight line

- understand the idea of a slope and intercept

- be able to draw graphs of equations that give curves rather than straight lines

- understand the interpretation of graphs

- appreciate continuously changing values

- identify maximum and minimum points of a graph and their significance to problem solving

SECTION 1

FINANCIAL ANALYSIS

1. INTEREST RATES

You will have seen in newspapers, banks, building societies and shops, interest rates advertised as percentages per annum (pa). In the introductory unit 0, *Basic Mathematics*, we learned about percentages. Now we are going to apply them to investments. But first let us revise how a percentage can be written as an equivalent decimal.

SELF CHECK 1

Write as equivalent decimals

1.   9%

2. $11\frac{1}{2}\%$

3. $15\frac{1}{4}\%$

4. $4\frac{3}{16}\%$

You will remember that a percentage is a fraction with an implied denominator of 100. This means that R% is equivalent to R/100.

You will also recall that dividing by 100 is easily done by moving the decimal point two places to the left. This gives us the decimal equivalent and is the most useful form for use in your calculator.

When we looked at percentages in unit 0 we used them to calculate bonus payments. We found that to calculate a bonus of $4\frac{1}{2}$% of £12,000 we had to multiply the sum by the decimal equivalent of the percentage. In this case the bonus is

$$12{,}000 \times 0.045 = £540$$

Try these:

SELF CHECK 2

1.　Calculate 2% of £1500.

2.　Calculate $15\frac{1}{4}$ % of £700.

---

2. NUMBER PATTERNS

This subsection considers the effect of time on money. Before looking at this we need to obtain some basic results about numbers that behave in a predetermined pattern. There are two basic patterns that are important.

2.1　PATTERN 1. ARITHMETIC PROGRESSIONS

In the public sector of employment, salary scales are often set at a basic level with a series of increments which are equal sums. As the years pass the employee gains further increments and the salary increases by equal steps. Such a salary progression is called an arithmetic progression. Let us now look at this progression from an abstract point of view.

Suppose that the basic salary, or first term, is u_1 and the increment is d then the second term, u_2, is given by u_2 $\quad=\quad u_1 + d$

the third term, u_3, is given by u_3 $\quad=\quad u_2 + d$

$\qquad\qquad\qquad\qquad\qquad\qquad = \quad u_1 + d + d$

$\qquad\qquad\qquad\qquad\qquad\qquad = \quad u_1 + 2d$

the fourth term, u_4, is given by u_4 $\quad=\quad u_3 + d$

$\qquad\qquad\qquad\qquad\qquad\qquad = \quad u_1 + 2d + d$

$\qquad\qquad\qquad\qquad\qquad\qquad = \quad u_1 + 3d$

Each new term is generated by adding d to the previous term. We call d the common difference as it represents the difference between consecutive terms.

Looking at the results sequence above we can generalise this to obtain

the nth term u_n, is given by $u_n = u_1 + (n-1)d$

SELF CHECK 3

1.   The base salary of a civil servant is £12,000 per year with annual increments of £600. Calculate the annual salary in the seventh year.

2.   An arithmetic progression starts with the number 5 and has a common difference of 3. Calculate

        (a) u_2
        (b) u_3
        (c) u_{10}
        (d) u_{50}

Previously we have looked at examples where the common difference is a positive number. This need not necessarily be so and an arithmetic progression can have a negative difference, such as with straight line depreciation. In this, the book value of a piece of equipment is reduced by a fixed sum at the end of each year. This reduction reflects the fact that as the equipment is used so it is worn out and its resale value is reduced. The number of years over which the value will be reduced from its buying value to zero is often determined in advance. This in turn determines the amount to be written off each year.

SELF CHECK 4

A piece of computer equipment costs £25,500 and has a useful life of 7 years. Calculate, to the nearest pound, the annual write down figure so as to reduce its book value to zero at the end of its useful life.

If the equipment has a trade-in value of £3,000 at the end of its useful life, calculate the write-down figure.

2.2 PATTERN 2. GEOMETRIC PROGRESSIONS

Another way of writing down the book value of equipment is called the diminishing or reducing balance method. In this, a fixed percentage of the previous book value is used to reduce that value to produce the new book value. If the chosen percentage is fixed at 15% then the book value remaining will be 85% of the previous value. To obtain the new value the book value is multiplied by 0.85.

Here we see the new terms (values) being generated by multiplying the last term (value) by a fixed number.

Let us take the first term to be u_1, and the fixed number to be r, called the common ratio, then

the second term u_2 is given by u_2 $\quad = \quad ru_1$

the third term u_3 is given by u_3 $\quad = \quad ru_2$

$\qquad\qquad\qquad\qquad\qquad = \quad r(ru_1)$

$\qquad\qquad\qquad\qquad\qquad = \quad r^2u_1$

the fourth term u_4 is given by u_4 $\quad = \quad ru_3$

$\qquad\qquad\qquad\qquad\qquad = \quad r(r^2u_1)$

$\qquad\qquad\qquad\qquad\qquad = \quad r^3u_1$

SELF CHECK 5

In the same way as above generate the fifth and sixth term in the sequence expressed in terms of u_1 and r.

You may have now noticed a pattern that has emerged allowing us to generalise and write

$$u_n = r^{n-1}u_1$$

If we now return to the diminishing balance depreciation method with which we started, we can take the new value to be £120,000, that is u_1, the value of r will be 0.85 and the book value in the ninth year will be

$$u_9 = (0.85)^8 \times 120,000$$
$$= £32,698.86$$

The actual sum written down at the end of the ninth year will therefore be

$$32,698.86 \times 0.15 = £4904.83$$

SELF CHECK 6

1. Calculate the book value of a piece of equipment in the 12th year if it cost £250,000 and is written down at a rate of 20% per year by the diminishing balance method.

2. A piece of equipment that costs £27,600 has a useful life of 6 years and a trade in value of £2500 at the end of its useful life. Calculate the fixed percentage that must be used in the diminishing balance method.

2.3   SUMMING THE TERMS OF A GEOMETRIC PROGRESSION

You will find that as we work through we will need to sum the terms of a geometric progression. Let us now deal with this problem.

We have seen that the terms are

$$u_1, \ ru_1, \ r^2u_1, \ r^3u_1, \ r^4u_1 \ ..... \ r^{n-1}u_1$$

and if we add these terms together to form the sum of the first n terms, denoted by S_n we write

$$S_n = u_1 + ru_1 + r^2u_1 + r^3u_1 + ... + r^{n-2}u_1 + r^{n-1}u_1$$

Suppose we multiply this expression throughout by r then

$$rS_n = ru_1 + r^2u_1 + r^3u_1 + ... + r^{n-1}u_1 + r^nu_1$$

You will see in the first sum that from the second term the terms reoccur in the second sum with the exception of the last term in the second sum.

If we were now to subtract these two lines these reoccurring terms will cancel out one another leaving only the first term in the first sum and the last term in the second sum. We obtain by subtraction

$$S_n - rS_n = u_1 - r^n u_1$$

which we can now treat as an equation for S_n and solve

$$S_n(1 - r) = u_1(1 - r^n)$$

$$S_n = \frac{u_1(1 - r^n)}{(1 - r)}$$

This formula allows us to calculate the sum of the first n terms of a geometric progression, S_n, provided we know the first term and the common ratio, r.

SELF CHECK 7

1.   Find the sum of the first seven terms of a geometric progression whose first term is 3 and whose common ratio is 4.

2.   Calculate the total amount written off the value of a piece of equipment in 11 years if it cost £250,000 and is written down at a rate of 20% per year.

3. CALCULATION OF INTEREST EARNED

If you invest a sum of money into an account that pays interest annually, at the end of each year you could calculate the interest due to you. So by investing £1000 at 6% pa (per annum, or per year) the interest to be paid to you at the end of the year would be

$$1000 \times 0.06 = £60$$

SELF CHECK 8

1.   Calculate the interest due at the end of the year on an investment of £1000 at 10% pa.

2.   Calculate the interest due at the end of the month on an investment of £100,000 at $1\frac{1}{2}$% per month.

3.   Find the half yearly interest to be paid on a deposit of £1500 at an investment rate of $4\frac{1}{4}$% per half year.

You have now learnt that, as long as the time periods are consistent, the calculation of interest is simply a matter of forming the product of the invested sum and the decimal equivalent of the interest rate.

4. NOTATION

You have already seen how important the decimal equivalent of the interest rate has become to us. We will adopt the notation convention that r will denote this form of the rate.

A sum, P, invested at a rate r per period will attract an interest payment of Pr per period.

5. COMPOUND INTEREST

The usual commercial procedure for dealing with interest earned is to add it to the investment at the end of each interest period. This is how a deposit in a building society is dealt with. This system of adding interest to the investment is called a **compound interest system**.

Let us begin our analysis by considering a sum of £1000 invested at 10% pa over a 5 year period. It is easiest to tabulate the calculation as in figure 1 below.

YEAR	START OF YEAR INVESTMENT	ANNUAL INTEREST EARNED	END OF YEAR INVESTMENT
1	1000.00	1000.00×0.1 $= 100.00$	1000.00 + 100.00
2	1100.00	1100.00×0.1 $= 110.00$	1100.00 + 110.00
3	1210.00	1210.00×0.1 $= 121.00$	1210.00 + 121.00
4	1331.00	1331.00×0.1 $= 133.10$	1331.00 + 133.10
5	1464.10	1464.10×0.1 $= 146.41$	1610.51

FIGURE 1: **Interest on an Investment of £1000**

You will notice from this table a couple of facts about this calculation:

All calculations are exact and there was no need to round the sums to the nearest penny. If we had wanted to go on for year 6 then rounding would have become necessary.

(If we had originally chosen less convenient numbers then rounding would have become necessary earlier in the calculations.)

The amount of interest earned steadily increases as the years go by. This in turn means that the invested sum increases steadily and this increases the interest earned. The system of compound interest has its own built-in momentum in that the invested sum gets bigger and bigger without any action by the investor. The longer that the investment is left in place then the bigger will be the final sum.

SELF CHECK 9

Working to the nearest penny for each calculation complete the following table concerning an investment of £900 at $8\frac{1}{2}$% pa for 4 years.

Year	Start of Year Investment	Annual Interest	End of Year Investment
1			
2			
3			
4			

You will have had to do a lot of calculation to fill up the table. Can you imagine the effort that would be necessary if the investment had been over 40 years rather than 4 years?

We will now have a look at a way to obtain the last figure without having to calculate all the intermediate figures.

6. A MORE GENERAL APPROACH TO INTEREST

Let us consider a sum P invested at a decimal equivalent rate r per period and follow this investment for a number of periods.

Period 1

Invested sum for the period $= P$

Interest earned for the period $= Pr$ (ie sum x interest rate)

Sum invested by end of period 1 $= P + Pr = P(1 + r)$

We have factorised this final sum by taking out a factor of P.

Period 2

Invested sum for the period $= P(1 + r)$ (ie sum at the end period 1)

Interest earned for the period $= P(1 + r)r$ (ie sum times interest rate)

Sum invested by end of period 2 $= P(1 + r) + P(1 + r)r$

$= P(1 + r)(1 + r)$

$= P(1 + r)^2$

We have factorised this final sum by taking out a factor of $P(1 + r)$ and then consolidating the result.

Period 3

Invested sum for the period $= P(1 + r)^2$ (ie sum at the end of period 2)

Interest earned for the period $= P(1 + r)^2 r$ (ie sum times interest rate)

Sum invested by end of period 3 $= P(1 + r)^2 + P(1 + r)^2 r$

$= P(1 + r)^2(1 + r)$

$= P(1 + r)^3$

(Note again the factorisation and consolidation.)

SELF CHECK 10

Working from the above examples calculate the expression for period 4.

As a result of your calculation you should have obtained the sum $P(1 + r)^4$ as the sum invested by the end of period 4. If you didn't, look at the solution pages.

We can now summarise the results so far as

Sum at the end of period 1 = P(1 + r)
Sum at the end of period 2 = P(1 + r)^2
Sum at the end of period 3 = P(1 + r)^3
Sum at the end of period 4 = P(1 + r)^4

SELF CHECK 11

Look at the relationship between the period number and the power that occurs in the result in the summary above, and then write down

sum at the end of period 5 =

sum at the end of period 6 =

If you have had difficulty here then turn to the solution pages and read the comment.

You will have now noticed the relationship and applied it to extend the results without the intermediate considerations. Taking this one stage further we can now write down the general result which will give the sum invested, A, by the end of period n, as

$$A = P(1 + r)^n$$

---

7. APPLYING THE GENERAL RESULT TO PARTICULAR CASES

Let us now return to our original problem of investing £1000 at 10% pa for 5 years. In our general terminology we have here that

P = 1000

r = 0.1

n = 5

and wish to find A. Substituting these numbers into our formula we have

$$A = 1000(1 + 0.1)^5$$
$$= 1000(1.1)^5$$

The calculation can now be completed using your calculator, to give

A = £1610.51

If you have a problem evaluating this with your calculator, then look at the section on calculators in unit 0, *Basic Maths*.

SELF CHECK 12

1.   If £900 is invested for 4 years at $8\frac{1}{2}$% pa calculate the final sum accumulated. Compare this with the previous Self Check where you had to calculate all the intermediate figures.

⟹

Self Check 12 continued...

2.   If £8,500 is invested for 15 years at 5% per half-year, with interest being added every half-year, calculate the value at the end of the 15th year. Take care to work in consistent time periods.

3.   If £30,000 is invested at 1% per month with interest added monthly, calculate the value at the end of the tenth year.

8. COMPARISON OF INTEREST RATES

Suppose we have a sum of £100 invested at a number of apparently equivalent rates for a single year.

(a)   at 12% pa, then the value at the end of the year will be
$100(1 + 0.12) = £112.$

(b)   at 6% per half-year then the value at the end of the year will be
$100(1 + 0.06)^2 = £112.36.$

(c)   at 3% per quarter then the value at the end of the year will be
$100(1 + 0.03)^4 = £112.55.$

(d)   at 1% per month then the value at the end of the year will
$100(1 + 0.01)^{12} = £112.68.$

You will see from the above calculations that the more frequently interest is added to the investment then the larger the final sum will be.

This means that when comparing interest rates to decide on the best investment we must not only compare the rate but also the frequency that interest is applied to the investment.

Alternatively we must ensure that the rates being compared are expressed in comparable terms. Looking at the calculations above you can see that 1% per month is actually 12.68% pa.

SELF CHECK 13

1.   Write down the annual equivalent rate of

   (a)   6% per half year

   (b)   3% per quarter.

2.   Interest is calculated at 1.8% per month. Find the annual equivalent rate.

---

9. PRESENT VALUE OF A FUTURE SUM

Your favourite rich uncle dies and you are summoned to attend the formal reading of his will. You are elated to hear that he has left you a sum of £10,000 but then hear that you are not to receive the money for 15 years. However you would like to have the money now so you arrange to see your bank manager. He is willing to buy your inheritance now, but the problem is what is it worth today.

You and he know that the sum of £10,000 is guaranteed in 15 years time and you assume a fixed interest rate over the 15 years of $7\frac{1}{2}$% pa. The sum that he should give you now is called the present value of the future sum. It is that sum of money, which, if invested for 15 years at $7\frac{1}{2}$% pa would amount to £10,000. In our previous notation we have

A = 10,000

r = 0.075

n = 15

and wish to find P. So using the compound interest formula we have

$$10{,}000 = P(1 + 0.075)^{15}$$

or, on transposing or solving this equation for P

$$P = \frac{10{,}000}{(1.075)^{15}} = £3379.66$$

This means that the present value of £10,000 payable in 15 years with a fixed interest rate of $7\frac{1}{2}\%$ is £3379.66. This is the sum that the bank manager should be offering to you.

In general, the present value of a sum A payable after n periods with a rate r per period is given by

$$P = \frac{A}{(1 + r)^n}$$

We will say that P and A are financially equivalent sums expressed at different times.

SELF CHECK 14

1. Calculate the present value of £100,000 payable in 20 years time with a fixed interest rate of 9%.

2. Find the total present value of my debts which are £300 after 1 year, £500 after 3 years and £800 after 7 years assuming an interest rate of 10.2%. However you come to an arrangement to pay off all your debts with a single payment after 4 years. Find the sum you will have to pay.

⟱

Self Check 14 continued...

3.   You are owed £2000 in 3 years time and £5000 in 7 years time. You agree to receive a single payment in 5 years time. Taking an interest rate of 8.4% pa, calculate the sum that you should receive.

10. FINANCIALLY EQUIVALENT SUMS

We have now reached the position where sums of money can be moved forwards or backwards in time and replaced by **financially equivalent sums**. This is an important idea. Only when sums are expressed at the same time can they be added, subtracted, compared or contrasted.

£100 now and another £200 in 1 years time are not the same as £300 now nor £300 in 1 years time. If the interest rate is 8% pa then the equivalent value **now** will be

$$100 + \frac{200}{1.08} = £285.19$$

and the equivalent value in **1 years time** will be

$$100(1.08) + 200 = £308$$

SELF CHECK 15

1.   You have two offers to consider:

Offer 1: £500 to be paid now
Offer 2: £715 to be paid after 4 years?

Which of the offers is financially best if you assume a rate of 9.3% pa?

⟫

Self Check 15 continued...

2.   Considering the future of your washing machine which you expect to last for
      another 5 years you predict the following repair costs

Minor repairs now	£56
Major overhaul after 18 months	£160
Minor repairs after 36 months	£65
Minor repairs after 50 months	£43

Alternatively you could take out an insurance policy costing £65 now with a
further payment of £65 at the start of years 2, 3, 4 and 5.

Which is the best method, financially, to proceed with taking an interest rate
of 0.8% per month?

11. SUMMARY

Before we proceed further let us just review what we have covered and learned so far.
We have

- looked at **interest rates** and how to calculate them

- discussed **arithmetic** and **geometric** progressions

- calculated **compound interest**

- applied general results to particular cases

- calculated **present values** of future sums

If you are unsure of any of these topics check back over the section before you
move on.

12. REPAYING A LOAN

Although you may not have obtained a loan to buy a car or a television or a washing machine and had to repay it by instalments, I am sure that you have been stranded by a coffee machine without the right amount of change. So you turn to a friend and ask them if they can change 50p for you. In exchange for your 50p piece they give you 20p, 10p, 10p, 5p, 5p pieces. This transaction is an example of a loan and its instantaneous repayment where the sum borrowed and the sum repaid are exactly equal and take place at the same time.

If you repay a loan at the instant when you take out the loan then the repayment sum will be exactly the same as the amount borrowed.

However this is not usual as the whole purpose of obtaining a loan is that you cannot afford to repay it immediately. You want to spread the repayments into the future but have to accept that by so doing you will have to pay interest charges.

Suppose you were considering buying a car and eventually agree a price with the salesman. Some of this cost you want to finance by a loan. After considering your own finances you decide the sum you wish to borrow. The salesman will then be able to tell you what your monthly repayments will be and how many repayments you will have to make. In other words, the periodic regular repayment sum will be fixed and the number of repayments will be fixed at the outset.

Let us now take this example and analyse it.

We have seen that the amount of the loan, P, is fixed, the repayments, a, are fixed, the number of repayments, n, is fixed and so the interest rate, r per period is fixed. We will also assume, as is normal practice, that the first repayment is made at the end of the first period after receipt of the loan.

Diagrammatically we have generated the system shown in figure 2 below.

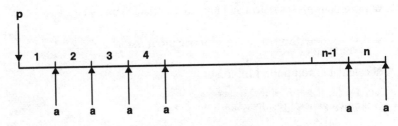

FIGURE 2: **Loan Repayments (1)**

Each of the future repayments has a financial equivalent value, its present value, at the start of the first period. The diagram shows clearly how many periods each repayment has to be moved, brought back, and using our present value formula we can replace each in turn.

This gives the next diagram, figure 3.

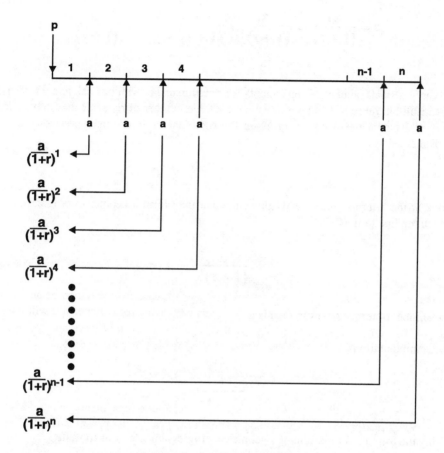

FIGURE 3: **Loan Repayments (2)**

Now we need to remember two things:

we can replace any sum or sums by their financial equivalent(s) at a different time so the row of sums, a, can be replaced by the column of sums on the left of the diagram;

to repay a loan of P at the time of receiving the loan requires a payment P.

Consequently the sum of the present values of our future repayments must be equal to P. Both are expressed at the same time allowing comparisons to be made.

So we can write

$$P = \frac{a}{(1+r)^1} + \frac{a}{(1+r)^2} + \frac{a}{(1+r)^3} + \cdots\cdots + \frac{a}{(1+r)^n}$$

For only a small number of repayments we could manage, with our calculators, to use this result but more often than not we have a large number of repayments. So we need to consider how the string of terms on the right hand side of our expression can be consolidated.

Look at these terms closely and appreciate that they form a geometric progression in which the first term is

$$\frac{a}{(1+r)^1}$$

the number of terms to be summed is n

the common ratio is

$$\frac{1}{(1+r)}$$

Using the formula for the sum of a geometric progression allows us to write

$$P = \frac{\frac{a}{(1+r)}\left\{1 - \left\{\frac{1}{1+r}\right\}^n\right\}}{\left\{1 - \left\{\frac{1}{1+r}\right\}\right\}}$$

$$= \frac{\frac{a}{(1+r)}\left\{1 - \frac{1}{(1+r)^n}\right\}}{\left\{1 - \frac{1}{(1+r)}\right\}} \qquad \textbf{(Step 1)}$$

$$= \frac{\dfrac{a}{(1+r)} \left\{ \dfrac{(1+r)^n - 1}{(1+r)^n} \right\}}{\left\{ \dfrac{(1+r) - 1}{(1+r)} \right\}}$$ **(Step 2)**

$$= \frac{\dfrac{a}{(1+r)} \left\{ \dfrac{(1+r)^n - 1}{(1+r)^n} \right\}}{\dfrac{r}{(1+r)}}$$ **(Step 3)**

$$= \frac{a}{(1+r)} \left\{ \frac{(1+r)^n - 1}{(1+r)^n} \right\} \times \frac{(1+r)}{r}$$ **(Step 4)**

$$P = P = \frac{a[(1+r)^n - 1]}{r(1+r)^n}$$

We have here done some algebraic manipulations which you may be able to follow. If you have trouble then have a look at the solution section where you will find some notes on the various stages that should help you.

12.1 CALCULATING THE AMOUNT OF A LOAN

As a result we now have a formula which will allow us to calculate the amount of a loan, P, when we are given the regular periodic payments, a, the number of repayments, n, and the rate, r, per period. The formula looks complicated but you have already evaluated formulae like this in unit 0. (You may need to go back to that unit just to revise using your calculator on expressions like this.)

Suppose you are told that to repay a loan will require 36 monthly repayments of £198.49 with an interest rate of 1.6% per month. The amount of the loan is then

$$P = \frac{198.49 \, (1.016^{36} - 1)}{0.016 \, (1.016)^{36}}$$

$$= £5400 \text{ (to the nearest pound)}.$$

SELF CHECK 16

1. Calculate the amount of the loan that will be repaid by 24 monthly repayments of £120 with an interest rate of 1% per month.

    With this loan calculate the total sum repaid over the life of the loan and so find the total amount of interest paid.

2. A person agrees to repay a loan by making 10 annual repayments of £1000. The agreed fixed interest rate will be 6% pa. However, the first 4 repayments are not made and the lender then demands that the debt is immediately repaid together with accrued interest. Calculate the sum to be repaid at this time.

12.2 CALCULATING THE REPAYMENTS

Taking the formula that we have just been using we can transpose it to make a the subject. This gives

$$a = \frac{Pr(1 + r)^n}{[(1 + r)^n - 1]}$$

We now have a formula that will allow us to calculate the periodic payments, a, when we are given the amount of the loan, P, the number of repayments required, n, and the fixed rate, r, per period.

Suppose you need a loan of £2,500 to be repaid over 30 months at a fixed interest rate of $1\frac{1}{2}\%$ per month, then

$$a = \frac{2500 \times 0.015 \times (1.015)^{30}}{[(1.015)^{30} - 1]}$$

$$= £104.10$$

ie, you will be required to make 30 monthly repayments of £104.10.

In total, over the life of the loan, you will pay $30 \times £104.10$ or £3123 to the lender which represents repaying the loan sum and the accrued interest.

So over the life of the loan you pay £623 interest in total.

SELF CHECK 17

1.   In order to fit new windows and doors to your home you take out a loan of £7,000 and agree to repay it by ten equal annual repayments with an annual interest rate of $12\frac{1}{4}\%$. Calculate the annual repayment sum.

2.   Your firm has a bank overdraft of £250,000 and after long negotiations with the bankers agree to pay it off by 20 equal annual repayments with a fixed annual interest rate of 14%. Calculate the annual sum to be repaid. What is the total interest paid over the life of the repayments of the overdraft?

12.3   LOAN REPAYMENT SCHEDULES

You have now been able to calculate the total amount of interest paid to the lender over the life of the loan. We now consider how this interest is paid. Clearly it is not uniformly distributed over the repayments as the debt, and so the interest, decreases with time. Each repayment is made up of two parts from the lender's view point; it is only the total that is of concern to the borrower. The first part covers the amount of interest due on the outstanding debt since the last repayment. The second part, which is the residue of the repayment, is used to reduce the outstanding debt.

When you think about this system then you will appreciate that in the early part of the life of a loan, when the debt is high, the interest component will be high and the residual sum for paying off the debt will be low. As time goes on so the debt decreases, and with it the interest component, leaving a larger sum to pay off the debt.

The period by period consideration, containing the breaking down of each repayment into its two parts, is called a **loan repayment schedule**.

Consider a loan of £5,000 at 10% pa over 5 years. The annual repayment can be calculated

$$a = \frac{5000 \times 0.1 \times (1.1)^5}{[(1.1)^5 - 1]}$$

= **£1318.99** (to the nearest penny).

This represents the total of the interest due and the debt repaid in each year.

Now we can construct the year by year schedule (figure 4), calculating the sum in column 4 as the difference between the annual repayment, calculated above, and the interest due in column 3.

YEAR	DEBT AT START OF YEAR	INTEREST DUE ON DEBT	RESIDUAL SUM TO REPAY DEBT	DEBT AT END OF YEAR
1	5000.00	5000.00 × 0.1 = 500.00	1318.99- 500.00 = 818.99	5000.00- 818.9= 4181.01
2	4181.00	4181.01 × 0.1 = 418.10	1318.99- 418.10 = 900.89	4181.01- 900.89= 3280.12
3	3280.12	3280.12 × 0.1 = 328.01	990.98	2289.14
4	2289.14	228.91	1090.08	1199.07
5	1199.07	119.91	1199.08	Overpaid 1p

FIGURE 4: **Loan Repayment Schedule**

You can see from the table that the sum of columns 4 and 5 is always the repayment sum. Every entry in the table has been made correct to the nearest penny. Every figure has been rounded up or rounded down. The result of this rounding is always liable to leave a few pence shown in the last entry as a sum overpaid or underpaid.

You will also see how the interest component has reduced allowing the residual sum to increase over the 5 years.

SELF CHECK 18

1. Construct a loan repayment schedule for a loan of £7,500 at 8% pa to be repaid by seven equal annual repayments.

2. It is agreed that a loan of £3,000 will be repaid by a number of repayments of £700 followed by a single smaller repayment. Taking an interest rate of 7% pa draw up a loan repayment schedule and use it to find

    (a)   the number of payments of £700
    (b)   the final smaller repayment.

12.4 MORTGAGES

A mortgage is a loan. The difference between this and the loans we have previously considered is that a mortgage is usually secured on property and can be very long in terms of time of repayment. To calculate the periodic repayment sum we use the same formula. So the annual repayments on a mortgage of £45,000 over 30 years at 9.6% pa will be

$$a = \frac{45000 \times 0.096 \times (1.096)^{30}}{[(1.096)^{30} - 1]}$$

$$= £4615.02 \text{ pa}$$

When you sell a particular property on which a mortgage is secured then it is necessary to repay the mortgage. If you are selling one property and buying another then usually the mortgage cannot be transferred and you will be required to settle the old mortgage and take out a new mortgage on the new property. So how do we find the outstanding debt on a loan or mortgage at a particular time?

Standing at that time and looking forwards you see a series of equal regular repayments that, if you were not settling the loan, you would eventually have to make. Your debt at the point where you are standing will be the sum of the values of these repayments expressed at that time. However our loan formula does just that for us – replaces each repayment by its financially equivalent sum at present and adds them all up. Returning to the example above then we can find the debt outstanding after 12 years. At this time there will be 18 repayments of £4615.02 left, so

$$P = \frac{4615.02[(1.096)^{18} - 1]}{0.096(1.096)^{18}} = £38840.77$$

will be the outstanding debt.

This calculation could have been completed by using a loan repayment schedule, but that would have involved a great deal more work and effort.

SELF CHECK 19

1.   Calculate the outstanding debt on a loan of £7,500 at 8% pa over 7 years at the end of the fourth year.
     (Compare your result with question 1 of Self Check 18.)

2.   A mortgage of £30,000 at 10% pa over 25 years.

     (a)   Calculate the annual repayments.

⮕

Self Check 19 continued...

(b)   Find the amount of debt paid off in the first year.

(c)   Find the outstanding debt after

i.   5 years

ii.   10 years

iii.   15 years

iv.   20 years

v.   22 years

vi.   24 years

(d)   Use this information to draw a graph of outstanding debt against time. (Use a piece of graph paper.)

12.5 ANNUITIES

An annuity is a loan viewed from the point of view of the lender. From this point of view the lender has invested a lump sum in order to gain a regular periodic fixed sum income. At the end, the lump sum will have been exhausted, having been drawn down as income but having gained interest whilst invested. However, as we are basically looking at a loan then you can use the loan formula that we have previously used.

SELF CHECK 20

1.   Find the capital cost of an annuity that pays £2,500 for 15 years, paid in equal half yearly sums, if interest is paid at 4% per half year.

2.   A civil servant retires at the age of 63 and receives a lump sum retirement payment of £35,000. He raises a loan of £70,000 against his house and has savings of £16,000. He invests all his capital in an annuity which pays an interest rate of 8.7% pa and provides an annual income for the next 20 years
   (a)   calculate the annual income
   (b)   if he dies after receiving the 12th sum, what is the residual value of the annuity?

13. INVESTMENT DECISIONS

We have now used the loan formula for a number of different applications. You will remember that this formula takes a regular income or expenditure stream and calculates the equivalent total sum expressed at present value. Such a calculation can be important when having to decide whether to buy or lease equipment.

A company has to decide whether to buy or lease a new printing press. It would cost £180,000 to buy it now, or £2,500 per month to lease with the first leasing payment at the end of the first month. Assuming money to be worth 1% per month, and that the useful life of the press is 10 years, they will have to compare the today cost of buying with the present value cost of leasing. This present value cost can be calculated as

$$P = \frac{2500[(1.01)^{120} - 1]}{0.01(1.01)^{120}} = £174251.31$$

and so it would appear to be cheaper to lease because £174,251.31 is less than £180,000.

However if they buy the press they will own it and after 10 years may be able to dispose of it and raise a sale income. If they lease it then it never becomes owned by them – ownership remains with the leasing company. Suppose they expect to be able to sell the press after 10 years for £25,000 then this expected resale income will have a present value of

$$\frac{25,000}{(1.01)^{121}} = £7574.87$$

In this case they would have to compare £174,251.31 with £172,425.13 and should choose to buy.

However there may be other considerations to be made which may alter this decision, such as whether the company has the capital sum available to buy the press, and the cash flow of the company.

SELF CHECK 21

This is a very long question – use your own sheet of paper.
You are trying to decide whether to buy or rent a new colour television set. After researching the existing prices you arrive at the following information

1.   A new set will cost £449.95 to buy with a 1 year manufacturer's guarantee covering parts and labour.

2.   If you buy the set it is probable that you will have repair/service costs of £40 in year 2, £60 in year 3 and £75 in years 4 and 5. Assume that these costs occur at mid-year.

3.   As an alternative to repair/service costs you could take out an insurance contract which would cost £50 at the start of the years 2 to 5.

4.   If you rent the same set over a fixed 5 year period you will have to pay a monthly rental of £12.95 in arrears (at the end of each month) together with an initial payment of £20.

Taking an interest rate of 1% per month decide which option is financially best.
Give reasons for your answer.

14. REGULAR SAVINGS SCHEMES

Some years ago the investment institutions introduced schemes for regular savings which gave slightly higher fixed interest rates in return for a commitment to regular savings. These schemes required a fixed sum to be invested at the start of each period. The valuation is calculated at the end of the final period.

Suppose the sum is fixed at D, the interest rate at r (decimal equivalent) per period and the number of periods at n with the final valuation, V, at the end of the nth period. Below we see the diagram of these investments in figure 5.

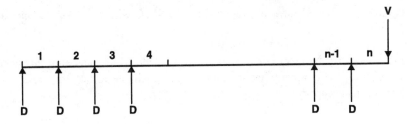

FIGURE 5: **Regular Investments**

Each investment contributes towards the final sum V but each has earned interest by the time of final valuation. This interest also contributes the final sum. You should be able to see that

the investment at the start of period 1 will have been invested for n periods by the time of the valuation, its contribution to V will be $D(1 + r)^n$

the investment at the start of period 2 will have been invested for n-1 periods by the time of the valuation, its contribution to V will be $D(1 + r)^{n-1}$

the investment at the start of period 3 will have been invested for n-2 periods by the time of the valuation, its contribution to V will be $D(1 + r)^{n-2}$

and so we can continue along the row and eventually reach

the investment at the start of period n-1 will have been invested for two periods by the time of the valuation, its contribution to V will be $D(1 + r)^2$

the last investment will have been invested for one period by the time of the valuation, its contribution to V will be $D(1 + r)$.

We have taken each investment forward to its financially equivalent value at the time of valuation. Now as all these are expressed at the same time they can be added. The sum of these will be V, so

$$V = D(1+r)^n + D(1+r)^{n-1} + D(1+r)^{n-2} + ... + D(1+r)^2 + D(1+r)$$

Once again we have on the right hand side a potentially large number of terms. We need to consider how these terms can be added. Look at these terms closely and appreciate that they form a geometric progression in which the first term is

$$D(1+r)^n,$$

the number of terms to be summed is n,

the common ration is

$$\frac{1}{(1 + r)}$$

Using the formula for the sum of a geometric progression allows us to write

$$V = \frac{D(1 + r)^n \left\{1 - \left\{\frac{1}{1 + r}\right\}^n\right\}}{\left\{1 - \frac{1}{(1 + r)}\right\}}$$

$$= \frac{D(1 + r)^n \left\{\frac{(1 + r)^n - 1}{(1 + r)^n}\right\}}{\left\{\frac{(1 + r) - 1}{1 + r}\right\}} \qquad \text{(Step 1)}$$

$$= \frac{D(1 + r)^n [(1 + r)^n - 1]}{(1 + r)^n} \times \frac{1 + r}{r} \qquad \text{(Step 2)}$$

$$V = \frac{D(1 + r) [(1 + r)^n - 1]}{r} \qquad \text{(Step 3)}$$

If you have not understood this algebraic manipulation look at the solution section at the end of the unit for help.

14.1 CALCULATING THE VALUE OF A SCHEME

Suppose you enter into a savings contract in which you agree to save £100 at the start of each month for the next 7 years. The institution agrees to pay 1.2% per month. The valuation of the contract can be calculated as you now know that

$$D = 100, n = 84, r = 0.012$$

and so

$$V = \frac{100(1.012)\,[(1.012)^{84} - 1]}{0.012}$$

$$= \pounds14536.74$$

The total sum that you have invested over the contract period is £8,400 so you have earned £6,136.74 of interest over the contract period.

SELF CHECK 22

A firm predicts that it will need to replace a piece of equipment in 10 years time. Considering the future profitability of the firm it is decided to invest £1,500 at the start of each year starting now. Calculate the accumulated sum at the end of the tenth year if the interest rate is fixed at 8% pa.

14.2   CALCULATING THE SUM TO ACHIEVE A GIVEN VALUATION

On the first birthday of your daughter you begin to plan for her future aware that it is customary for you to pay for her wedding. You make the assumption that she will get married sometime after her 20th birthday and that it is likely to cost you £15,000 then. You decide to start saving immediately and save the same amount on each of her birthdays with the last sum being saved on her 19th birthday. Your local building society will give you a fixed interest rate of $7\frac{1}{2}\%$ pa and you have to calculate the amount of each year's saving.

The problem here is very similar to that which you have just solved, except you now know V and need to find D.

Taking the previous formula we can transpose it to make D the subject and get

$$D = \frac{Vr}{(1 + r)[(1 + r)^n - 1]}$$

Using this formula with

$$V = 15{,}000, \quad r = 0.075, \quad n = 19$$

we obtain

$$D = \frac{15000 \times 0.075}{1.075[(1.075)^{19} - 1]} = £354.57$$

It is interesting here to note that you only pay £6736.84 over the life of the scheme so have gained £8263.16 in interest.

In the industrial and commercial world these savings schemes are often referred to as **sinking funds**. There is no difference between domestic and commercial funds except that the sums are usually larger with the latter.

SELF CHECK 23

1. A company requires to set up a sinking fund to fund an expected expenditure of £10,000 in 10 years time. If interest on the fund is 5% pa, calculate the sum that has to be deposited at the start of each year.

2. A company now has £1000 in a sinking fund that pays interest at 5% pa. What annual deposit is required to cause the fund to amount to £10,000 in 10 years' time?

Finally in this section, let us remember the 4 conditions that we made to generate the savings formula. They were

each investment occurs at the beginning of each period

the valuation is obtained at the end of the last period

the interest rate remains fixed throughout

the invested sums remain fixed throughout.

If any of these 4 conditions are not valid then further thought about how to use our formula will become necessary. However, often the formula can still be used by first interpreting the problem so that it conforms to our conditions, but remembering that the conditions cannot be changed.

SELF CHECK 24

This is a long exercise – use your own sheet of paper.

1. A company pays £10,000 each year into a sinking fund that pays 6% pa interest. At the time of making the sixth deposit the rate of interest on the fund is reduced to 4% pa and the company decides to increase its sixth and future deposits to £12,000. Calculate the amount in the fund at the end of 15 years.

2. Reconsider the above problem if the company had decided to leave its sixth deposit at £10,000 but then to increase its seventh and future deposits to £12,000.

3. Reconsider the above problem if the company does not increase deposits until the tenth deposit when they increase to £14,000.

15. SUMMARY

You have now completed the section on financial analysis. We have

- looked at **loans** and **loan repayment calculations**

- discussed and illustrated **loan repayment schedules**

- reviewed **mortgages and annuities**

- appreciated the problems of comparing payments made at different times

- made **investment decisions**

- shown how to calculate **values of investment schedules** and **investments to achieve a given valuation**

- analysed some complex schemes

If you are not sure about the topics and calculations check back over the section before reading on.

SECTION 2

GRAPHS

A picture saves a thousand words. In mathematics pictures are often replaced by graphs. Graphs can be used to show how relations behave.

1. THE GRID SYSTEM

In unit 0 we saw how a number line can be used to represent the relationships between numbers. This was a one-dimensional system. However, as everyday things such as a sheet of paper are two-dimensional – in that it has width and height – so we need a number line to represent width and a second number line to represent height.

If these number lines are placed at right angles then we have set up a grid system on our paper. Each point on our paper now has a unique two-number reference called its **co-ordinates**, the first number representing the position on the width number line and the second the position on the height number line. The number lines are to be called the axes of our graph and are often referred to as the X-axis (representing width) and the Y-axis (representing height. However, the use of X and Y is not necessary and any two letters or objects can be used.

Look at the axes in figure 6. You can see that the point P is the point where X = 3 and Y = 8, that is, the point P is 3 units across the sheet and 8 units up the sheet. This notation and terminology is very cumbersome and we adopt an abbreviated notation. In this the point referred to will be given by P(3, 8).

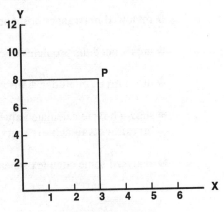

FIGURE 6: **Co-ordinates**

SELF CHECK 25

Redraw the set of axes that we have just been referring to on a separate piece of graph paper and plot the additional points

A(6,2) B(2,10)   C(4,12)   D($4\frac{1}{2}$,5)   E(2,6)

You should notice how important the order of the two numbers is by looking at A and E where the numbers are the same but the order is different.

We adopt the convention that the numbers in our co-ordinates refer to the axes in alphabetical order, so that A(6,2) is the point where X = 6 and Y = 2, whereas the E(2,6) is the point where X = 2 and Y = 6.

SELF CHECK 26

On a separate sheet of graph paper draw two axes representing values of p from 10 to 90 and values of q from 0 to 10 and plot on your axes the points

G(30,5)   H(50,7)   J(90,10) K(70,0)

So we now have a system of identifying points by their co-ordinates and of plotting points using their co-ordinates. This represents the basis of drawing graphs.

With graphs the points are joined by a suitable line or curve. This line or curve is the physical representation of the equation of the line or curve.

Let us start with straight lines and their graphs.

2. STRAIGHT LINE GRAPHS

If we have two non-coincident points then these points will uniquely determine a straight line, ie, there is only one line through two given points.

SELF CHECK 27

Go back to your solution Self Check 26 and on it draw the lines

GH   GJ   GK

You will notice on each occasion you had no choice about which line to draw as there is only one line through the given points.

2.1   STRAIGHT LINE FROM AN EQUATION

The equation is the rule in algebraic form that forces a general point to lie exactly on the line. The general point can be expressed as a particular point by introducing numbers to replace letters. Let us take the equation

$$y = 4 + 3x$$

We will eventually be able to recognise this equation as the equation of a straight line, but for now you should accept that this is so.

When x = 2, say, then y = 4 + 3.2 = 10

When x = 5, say, then y = 4 + 3.5 = 19

In the abbreviated notation we have the two points

A(2,10) and B(5,19)

SELF CHECK 28

Using the equation $y = 4 + 3x$ find the value of y corresponding to

x = 1

x = 3

x = 7

Now we can draw a pair of axes with values of x from 0 to 8 and values of y from 0 to 25.

You should redraw this diagram using a sheet of graph paper which will give you greater accuracy. On these axes you can now plot the points A and B and join them with a straight line (use your ruler!) This line represents the graph of the equation

$$y = 4 + 3x$$

which we add to the graph so that we know what the graph represents at any future date.

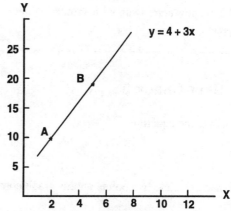

FIGURE 7: **Graph of the Equation Y = 4 + 3x**

SELF CHECK 29

Using your more accurate graph of this straight line plot the three other points whose co-ordinates you calculated in Self Check 28, ie the points

(1,7),   (3,13),   (7,25).

You will notice that each of these points also lies exactly on our original line. Do you think this is coincidence?

SELF CHECK 30

Select another value of x that we have not previously used and calculate the corresponding value of y using

y = 4 + 3x

Plot this new point.

Are you now convinced that it is not coincidence?

Let us now start again with another equation but your original set of axes on your graph paper.

SELF CHECK 31

Take the equation

$$y = 6 + 2x$$

and calculate two points on this graph corresponding to

$$x = 2 \text{ and } x = 8.$$

Plot these points on your graph paper and join them with a straight line. Don't forget to label this line with its equation.

You now have the graphs of two straight lines drawn on the same sheet of graph paper.

We can now compare these lines. Clearly they are different lines but how are they different? In two basic respects – they cross the y axis at two different points and one slopes more than the other.

2.2   SLOPE OF A LINE

Let us look again at the first line that we drew (figure 7) of the equation $y = 4 + 3x$, and consider how the x and y values change as we move from A to B.

At A, $x = 2$ and at B, $x = 5$ so x increases by 3, or the change in x is +3.

At A, $y = 10$ and at B, $y = 19$ so y increases by 9, or the change in y is +9.

We can define the slope of the line as the ratio of the change in y to the change in x, or in our particular case

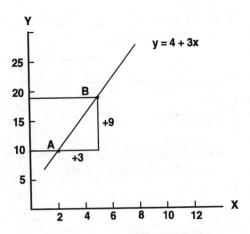

FIGURE 8: **Slope of the Line Y = 4 + 3X**

$$\frac{BC}{AC} = \frac{+9}{+3} = 3$$

We will denote the slope of a line with the letter b, and in this example we have that b = 3.

SELF CHECK 32

Turn to your graph of the line given by y = 6 + 2x and calculate its slope.

Let us now take another equation and repeat this exercise.

Consider y = 10 - 2x.

When x = 1, y = 8,
ie the point A(1,8).

When x = 4, y = 2,
ie the point B(4,2).

These points allow us to draw the graph (figure 9). As we move from A to B so x increases by 3 (+3) and y decreases by 6 (-6).

Hence the slope is

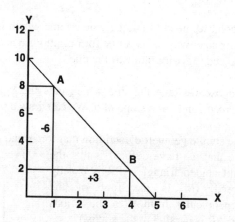

FIGURE 9: **Slope of the Line Y = 10 - 2X**

$$b = \frac{-6}{+3} = -2$$

SELF CHECK 33

Look back to your solution of Self Check 27 and calculate the slope of the lines

GH,   GJ,   GK

2.3   THE EQUATION OF A STRAIGHT LINE

Previously we have started with an equation, used it to calculate and plot two points and so drawn the straight line.

Now we are going to reverse this process – starting with a line and obtaining its equation.

First we need to remember that the equation is the condition that forces every point represented by (x,y) to lie exactly on the line.

Second we need to uniquely determine which line we are going to consider. The most convenient way to fix a line for our purpose is to fix the point where the line cuts the y axis and to fix the slope of the line.

Suppose we take the line which cuts the y axis at the point A(0,a), called the y-intercept, and has a slope of b. We can draw a picture of such a line (figure 10).

The simple geometric condition that forces the general point P(x,y) to lie exactly on the line that we have defined is that the right angled triangle APR is exactly closed. (M is the foot of the perpendicular from P to the x axis and AR is parallel to the x axis.)

Our picture now has a right angled triangle APR sitting on a rectangle OARM.

As A and P lie on the line then the slope of the line, b, is given by

$$\text{Slope of line} = b = \frac{PR}{AR}$$

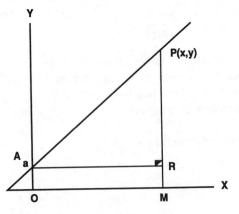

FIGURE 10: **Y - Intercept**

However, because we know the co-ordinates of A and P we can calculate various dimensions in our picture.

As we know that A is the point (0, a) then

OA = a

but OARM is a rectangle so

OA = MR = a

As we know that P is the point (x,y) then

OM = x

but OARM is a rectangle so

OM = AR = x

and

MP = y

This means that we can now calculate the height of the triangle PR by

PR = MP - MR = y - a

We can build these into our slope condition to give

$$b = \frac{y - a}{x}$$

We now tidy up this condition using the basic rules of equation manipulation

bx = y - a

a + bx = y

or our condition, the equation of the line, is

y = a + bx

2.4   DETAILED INSPECTION OF THE EQUATION

We have just obtained the equation of a straight line in the form

$$y = a + bx$$

This is called the **standard form of the equation**. Notice that in this form

y stands alone on the left hand side of the equation

two terms occur on the right hand side

      i. a simple number, a,
      ii. a term containing an x multiplied by a number b.

The numbers a and b have particular meaning – a is the y-intercept, ie the value of y where the line cuts the y axis; b is the slope of the line.

SELF CHECK 34

1. Look back at your graph of y = 4 + 3x and notice the relevance of the numbers 4 and 3 in relation to the y-intercept and slope of the line.

2. Look back at your graph of y = 6 + 2x and notice the relevance of the numbers 6 and 2 in relation to the y-intercept and slope of the line.

3. Draw a set of axes on a piece of graph paper representing p across the page from 0 to 8 and q up the page from 0 to 20 and on these axes draw the graph of q = 20 - 2p

4. Use your graph to identify the value of q where the line cuts the q-axis and to calculate the slope of the line.

2.5   OTHER FORMS OF THE EQUATION

We now understand the significance of the numbers contained within the standard form of the equation but is this the only equation which gives a straight line graph?

Let us start with the equation

$$6x + 3y = 36$$

Using the basic equation manipulations we can proceed as follows

$$3y = 36 - 6x$$
$$y = 12 - 2x$$

which is now in standard form so has a straight line graph. However the equations y = 12 - 2x and 6x + 3y = 36 are the same but in different guises. This means that the graph of 6x + 3y = 36 is a straight line.

SELF CHECK 35

On a separate piece of graph paper and using the equation 6x + 3y = 36 calculate the value of y corresponding to

(a) $x = 0$ (b) $x = 2$
(c) $x = 4$ (d) $x = 6$

Construct a suitable set of axes and plot these four points.

Using a ruler join the points with a straight line.

Read off the y-intercept and calculate the slope and compare these results with the equivalent equation
$$y = 12 - 2x$$

We can now repeat the previous numerical rearrangement of the equation 6x + 3y = 36 but this time starting with the more general equation

$$kx + my + n = 0$$

where k, m, n are numbers. Proceeding as before

$$my = -n - kx$$

$$y = \frac{-n - kx}{m}$$

$$y = \left\{-\frac{n}{m}\right\} + \left\{-\frac{k}{m}\right\}x$$

which is again in our standard form. This represents a straight line having the y-intercept of -n/m and the slope of -k/m.

Hence we can conclude that any equation of the form $kx + my + n = 0$ has a graph that is a straight line. This equation is called the general linear equation.

Any equation that is linear has a graph that is a straight line. This is important because if we know we are going to draw a straight line graph then we know that we need only calculate and plot two points to completely draw the graph.

SELF CHECK 36

Which of the following equations would generate a straight line graph?

(a) $y = 3 + 2x$
(b) $3y = 5 - 4x$
(c) $2y^2 = 3 + 2x$
(d) $5x - 2y - 6 = 0$

(e) $3x - 2y = 7$
(f) $x = 5$
(g) $y = 2$
(h) $3y = 2 - x^2$

SELF CHECK 37

On a separate sheet of graph paper and using a single set of axes representing x from -2 to +3 and y from -6 to 7 draw the graphs of the lines representing the equations

(a) $y = 2x - 2$
(b) $2y - 1 = x$
(c) $x + 2y + 2 = 0$

(d) $y + 2x = 3$
(e) $x = 3$
(f) $y = -2$

2.6   COMPARATIVE SLOPES

By now you will have drawn a lot of lines and you will have realised the significant difference between a line that has a positive slope and a line that has a negative slope. We can draw two sketch graphs showing this difference (figures 11 and 12)

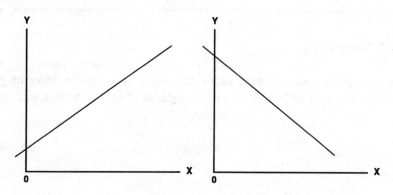

FIGURE 11: **Positive Slope**   FIGURE 12: **Negative Slope**

An uphill line as we read across   A downhill line as we read across
the page from left to right.   the page from left to right.

SELF CHECK 38

Without drawing the graphs decide which of the following represent uphill lines and downhill lines

(a)	$y = 3 - 2x$	(d)	$2x + 3y = 6$
(b)	$y = 5 + 4x$	(e)	$2x - 3y = 6$
(c)	$2y = 5 + 4x$	(f)	$4x + 3y + 7 = 0$

The slope represents the rate at which y changes when compared with the change in x. So for the same change in x, if y takes a bigger change then the slope will be bigger or the line will be steeper uphill (or downhill).

The line represented by

$$y = 3 + 5x$$

will be steeper than the line represented by

$$y = 4 + 2x$$

SELF CHECK 39

Check the above statement by drawing the graphs on a separate piece of graph paper of $y = 3 + 5x$ and $y = 4 + 2x$ on a single set of axes with the x axis from 0 to 4.

2.7   SUMMARY

You will learn more about straight line graphs in unit 3, *Linear Programming*. Here we have laid the foundations and you should now be able to

- recognise the equation that leads to a straight line graph

- minimise the amount of work that you have to do to draw such a graph

- understand the significance of the intercept on the vertical axis in relation to the equation

- understand the significance of the slope of the line in relation to the rate of change

- appreciate that steeper slopes represent greater rates of change

Now try Self Check 40 to bring some of these points together.

SELF CHECK 40

Following, we have a series of graphs, figures 13 - 20 representing cost (C) on the vertical axis plotted against the level of activity (A) on the horizontal axis.

Which of graphs in figures 13 - 20 best depicts the costs described below? In each case add some scales to the axes.

A.   The rental of a machine for which the charges are £50 per hour, subject to a minimum charge of £1000 and a maximum charge of £5000.

B.   The total amount of an electricity bill where there is a basic standing charge of £100 plus an amount based on units consumed according to

1-100 units	–	16p per unit
next 100 units	–	8p per unit
thereafter	–	4p per unit

C.   Supervisor's salaries are £1000 each per month. One supervisor is required for the first 100 units of production. For production between 101 - 300 units 2 supervisors are required and for all levels above 300 units 3 supervisors are required.

D.   The rental of a vehicle for which the charge is 60p per mile travelled with a maximum charge of £300.

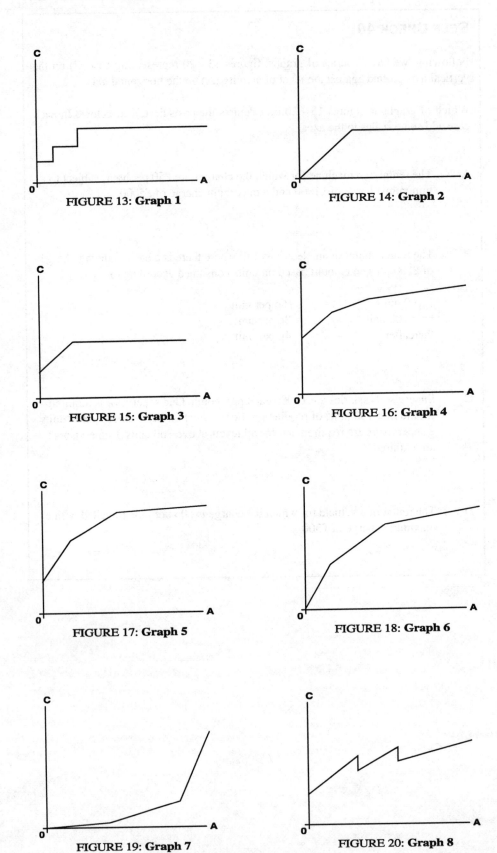

FIGURE 13: **Graph 1**

FIGURE 14: **Graph 2**

FIGURE 15: **Graph 3**

FIGURE 16: **Graph 4**

FIGURE 17: **Graph 5**

FIGURE 18: **Graph 6**

FIGURE 19: **Graph 7**

FIGURE 20: **Graph 8**

3. OTHER GRAPHS

If a linear equation gives rise to a straight line graph then a non-linear equation will give rise to a graph that is a curve.

There are several problems associated with drawing curves

you will no longer be able to us a ruler to draw a good smooth graph

you will need to calculate and plot many more than two points

however good your graph looks, because you have drawn the curve free-hand it will only be a good approximation.

Let us take the firm that produces a commodity. It can produce q batches of this commodity but physical constraints limit their capacity to no more than 9 batches per week. They have a cost function which is given by the equation

$$C = \frac{2}{5}(25 + 10q - q^2)$$

This equation indicates that their fixed costs, such as rent rates, general overheads are 2/5 x 25 = 10 which is the cost of producing no batches of the commodity.

The variable costs are $(2/5)(10q - q^2)$ which represents the direct cost of producing q batches. We will now draw the cost curve for this commodity.

It is a non-linear equation and so the graph will be a curve. This means that we will have to calculate and plot more than two points. It has already been indicated that we are to draw this curve for values of q from q = 0, the smallest production to q = 9, the largest level of production and we now set about calculating the points. Clearly we have to do a lot of arithmetic and we now construct a stage-by-stage table designed so that only one arithmetic operation is done at a time to try to avoid any arithmetic errors.

We first set up the value contained within the bracket and then the value of C.

1	q	0	1	2	3	4	5	6	7	8	9
2	q^2	0	1	4	9	16	25	36	49	64	81
3	$-q^2$	0	-1	-4	-9	-16	-25	-36	-49	-64	-81
4	+10q	0	10	20	30	40	50	60	70	80	90
5	+25	25	25	25	25	25	25	25	25	25	25
6		25	34	41	46	49	50	49	46	41	34
7	C	10.0	13.6	16.4	18.4	19.6	20.0	19.6	18.4	16.4	13.6

FIGURE 21: **Values for C**

In the table above (figure 21) the rows are numbered so that we can now describe the method of obtaining each row.

In row 1 we have the base values of q which are then squared to give row 2. However, our formula, or equation requires $-q^2$ so row 3 is generated from row 2 by changing the sign of row 2. Our equation also requires 10q so in row 4 we have calculated this value for each value of q. Our equation also requires the number 25 and this is entered in row 5. Now to obtain the value of the bracket in row 6 we have to add the entries in rows 3, 4, 5. Finally to find the value of C we have to multiply by 2/5 the entries in row 6.

Now that we have calculated our table of values we see that to draw the graph of this cost function we need a scale of 0 to 9 on the q-axis and 10.0 to 20.0 on the C-axis. So on graph paper we set up these axes. When you do this you should use as much of the graph paper as possible by selecting suitable scales. We want as large a graph as possible so that it can be used accurately.

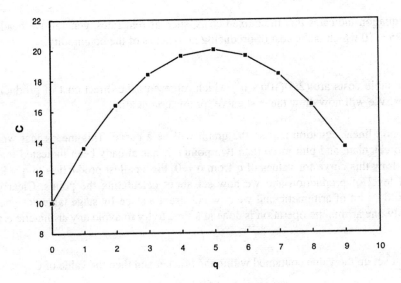

FIGURE 22: **Graph of Values of C**

You will once again have labelled your axes and scaled them, plotted the points and joined them and labelled the graph. The major difference here compared to your previous straight line graphs is that your graph has had to be drawn freehand as it is a smooth curve and not a straight line or series of segments of straight lines.

Inspecting the graph you can now see that costs of production rise to a maximum of 20 when 5 batches are produced and then fall again. Presumably the firm may be interested in keeping its costs down and we can now see that the smallest cost will occur when there is no production but this is unlikely to be of practical interest to any company. However we can also see that the cost of making 1 batch is the same as making 9 batches and this information could be critical in deciding on production levels.

SELF CHECK 41

Another consideration that the firm may take into account when deciding on its best production level could be the average cost of production . This is given by C/q.

For values of q between $q = 1$ and $q = 9$ on a separate sheet of graph paper draw the graph of average cost plotted against q.

Note: you should draw up the table of values, select axes for your graph, plot the points and then join them with a smooth curve.

Keeping costs down will not guarantee profitability, so deciding on production levels on the basis of costs alone will not necessarily be the wisest course of action. So what other considerations could the firm look at?

Let us suppose that the selling price that the firm can obtain from this commodity is governed by the relation

$$p = 30 - 2q$$

then the income, or revenue R, obtained by selling its production will be given by

$$R = pq$$
$$= (30 - 2q)q$$
$$= 30q - 2q^2$$

Once again we can draw the graph of this equation in the range of the production levels available. Setting up the table of values gives figure 23.

q	0	1	2	3	4	5	6	7	8	9
q^2	0	1	4	9	16	25	36	49	64	81
$-2q^2$	0	-2	-8	-18	-32	-50	-72	-98	-128	-162
30q	0	30	60	90	120	150	180	210	240	270
R	0	28	52	72	88	100	108	112	112	108

FIGURE 23: **Revenue Values**

Again you should now take a piece of graph paper, set up your axes, plot your points and draw your graph showing how the revenue varies against quantity produced.

Your graph should look like this

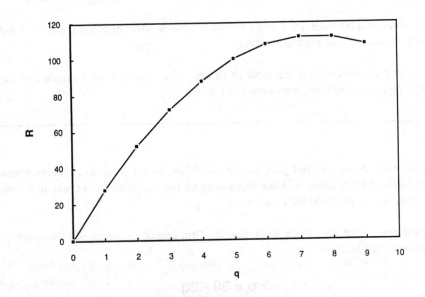

FIGURE 24: **Graph of Revenue**

Looking at this graph you will see how the revenue increases up to a maximum value when $q = 7\frac{1}{2}$ and then starts to decrease again. We can calculate the maximum revenue by putting $q = 7\frac{1}{2}$ into the revenue function to give

$$R = 30 \times 7.5 - 2 \times (7.5)^2$$
$$= 112.5$$

So using revenue as a criterion to determine the best level of production will lead us to producing between 7 and 8 batches per week. However you will remember that at this level of production the costs are not at a minimum so we would appear to have two contradictary views of the problem.

We have now looked at two different views of the same problem but neither guarantees that the company is making its best profit.

Finally let us look at the gross profit function, G, which is a measure of the difference between revenue and cost, ie

$$G = R - C$$

Taking our previous revenue and cost function

$$G = (30q - 2q^2) - \frac{2}{5}(25 + 10q - q^2)$$

$$= 30q - 2q^2 - 10 - 4q + \frac{2}{5}q^2$$

$$= 26q - \frac{8}{5}q^2 - 10$$

$$= \frac{2}{5}(65q - 4q^2 - 25)$$

Again we can draw the graph of this equation in the range of the production levels available. Setting up the table of values (figure 25) gives

q	0	1	2	3	4	5	6	7	8	9
q^2	0	1	4	9	16	25	36	49	64	81
$-4q^2$	0	-4	-16	-36	-64	-100	-144	-196	-256	-324
65q	0	65	130	195	260	325	390	455	520	585
-25	-25	-25	-25	-25	-25	-25	-25	-25	-25	-25
	-25	36	89	134	171	200	221	234	239	236
P	-10.0	14.4	35.6	53.6	68.4	80.0	88.4	93.6	95.6	94.4

FIGURE 25: **Gross Profit Values**

Again you should now take a piece of graph paper, set up your axes, plot your points and draw your graph showing how profit varies against quantity produced.

Your graph should look like this

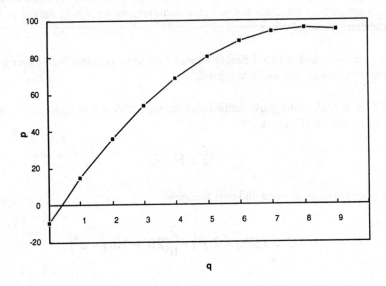

FIGURE 26: **Graph of Gross Profit**

Looking at the graph in figure 26 you will see how the profit increases up to a maximum near to q = 8 and then starts to decrease again.

The graph clearly shows that this maximum profit occurs for a value of q slightly greater than 8 and if greater accuracy is required then either we can redraw the relevant section of the graph (ie, for values of q between 7 and 9) to a bigger scale more accurately or else we can proceed by an arithmetic procedure shown below but still based on the shape of the graph between q = 8 and q = 9.

When q = 8, G = 95.6 (from the table of values).

When q = 8.5, G = 2/5(65 x 8.5 -4(8.5)^2 - 25) = 95.4.

So the maximum profit lies between q = 8 and q = 8.5.

When q = 8.1 G = 95.624

When q = 8.3 G = 95.576

So the maximum profit lies between q = 8.1 and q = 8.3.

When q = 8.1   G = 95.624

When q = 8.15 G = 95.624

So the maximum profit lies between q = 8.1 and q = 8.15.

As the value of G for each of these values of q is the same then the maximum profit will occur at the mid-point between q = 8.1 and q = 8.15.

That is for q = 8.125 when the profit will be 95.625.

Clearly it appears that the increased level of profit generated by producing 8.125 batches per week as against producing 8 batches per week is small. So for production simplicity the firm may decide to produce 8 batches per week but notice that at this level neither the cost is at a minimum nor is the revenue at a maximum.

You have now learnt to draw graphs of non-linear equations. You have seen that you can no longer use a ruler, that you need to calculate and plot a lot more points than for a straight line and your graph will only be an approximation because you have drawn it freehand. With this knowledge now try the final Self Check on graphs.

SELF CHECK 42

Economists talk a lot about supply and demand.

Given the supply equation

$$q = 16 + 4p + p^2$$

and the demand equation

$$q = 48 - 3p^2$$

where q is the quantity at a price p, on a separate piece of graph paper draw on a single set of axes the supply and demand curves for values of p from p = 0 to p = 5. The point at which the two curves intersect is called the point of market equilibrium. It is the point where supply and demand are equal and the market is exactly balanced. From your graph read off the equilibrium price and equilibrium quantity.

Can you use another way of finding this equilibrium point?

4.	SUMMARY

In this final section we have concentrated on

- graphs that are not straight lines

- the extra points that are needed to draw a **smooth curve**

- drawing a **big graph** to obtain accuracy

- being aware that a good curve will only give good **approximate** results

- other ideas that will refine approximate results

If you are not sure of any of the areas of work in this or earlier sections check back now.

SECTION 3

ANSWERS TO SELF CHECK QUESTIONS

SECTION 1: FINANCIAL ANALYSIS

SELF CHECK 1

1. You should have remembered that a percentage is just a way of writing a fraction where the denominator is missed out because it is always 100.

    $$9\% = \frac{9}{100} = 0.09$$

    You have also learnt that division by 100 is simply carried out by moving the decimal point, or implied decimal point, two places to the left.

2. Here we have a fraction that first needs to be converted to a decimal before we can proceed

    $$11\frac{1}{2}\% = 11.5\% = \frac{11.5}{100} = 0.115$$

Now you have remembered these three basic ideas the last two examples should be straightforward.

3. $15\frac{1}{4}\% = 15.25\% = \dfrac{15.25}{100} = 0.1525$

4.   If you have a problem here then it maybe that you do not know the decimal equivalent of the fraction 3/16. Your calculator can assist you here – just divide 3 by 16 to obtain 0.1875 – and then proceed as before

$4\frac{3}{16}\% = 4.1875\% = \dfrac{4.1875}{100} = 0.041875$

SELF CHECK 2

You have learned that the easiest way of calculating these results is to express the percentage in its equivalent decimal form and to multiply this form by the sum given.

1.   2% converts to 0.02 so that

   2% of £1500 $= 0.02 \times 1500 = £30.$

2. $15\frac{1}{4}\%$ converts to 0.1525 so that

   $15\frac{1}{4}\%$ of £700 $= 0.1525 \times 700 = £106.75.$

SELF CHECK 3

1.   Using the formula that we have just obtained then we know that $u_1 = 12000$, d $= 600$ and n $= 7$ so that the salary in the seventh year, u_7, is given by

   $u_7 = 12000 + (7 - 1).600$

   $= 12000 + 3600$

   $= 15600$

2.   In this abstract problem we have been given that $u_1 = 5$, d $= 3$.
   So using the formula we can obtain
   (a) $u_2 = 5 + (2 - 1).3 = 8$
   (b) $u_3 = 5 + (3 - 1).3 = 11$
   (c) $u_{10} = 5 + (10 - 1).3 = 32$
   (d) $u_{50} = 5 + (50 - 1).3 = 152$

Once you have understood what is going on with an arithmetic progression then you may consider the use of the formula as an unnecessary encumbrance.

SELF CHECK 4

With this kind of problem you must be careful to interpret the statements carefully. This computer equipment has been used for the whole of 7 years and its value will have been reduced 7 times to reflect the 7 years of use. So we are being told that the zero value actually occurs in the eighth year.
Using our formula we have that

   $u_1 = 25500, \ u_8 = 0, \ n = 8$

so that

$$0 = 25500 + (8 - 1)d$$

or $\quad 7d = -25500$

$$d = -3642.86$$

$$= -3643 \quad \text{(to the nearest pound)}$$

This means that the annual write down figure has to be £3642 to the nearest pound.
In the second part we now have an eighth year value of £3000 rather than zero. Here we have that

$$u_1 = 25500, u_8 = 3000, n = 8$$

so that

$$3000 = 25500 + (8 - 1)d$$

or $\quad 7d = -22500$

$$d = -3214.29$$

which means that the annual write down figure has to be £3214.29 to the nearest penny. Once again, having appreciated what is going on then these results can be obtained without the use of the formula.

SELF CHECK 5

$$u_5 = \text{common ratio} \times \text{previous term}$$

$$= ru_4$$

$$= r(r^3 u_1)$$

$$= r^4 u_1$$

You should remember that

$$r \times r^3 = r^1 \times r^3 = r^4$$

To multiply when powers, or indices, are involved then we add the powers.
Similarly

$$u_6 = ru_5$$

$$= r(r^4 u_1)$$

$$= r^5 u_1$$

SELF CHECK 6

1. If 20% is written off the value then 80% of the value remains. Here we are being given that $u_1 = 250000$, $r = 0.8$ and we need to find u_{12}, so $n = 12$.

$$u_{12} = (0.8)^{11} \times 250000$$

$$= 21474.84$$

Which means that the book value in the 12th year will be £21474.84 to the nearest penny.
If you had trouble using your calculator to find $(0.8)^{11}$ then go back to unit 0 and rework the section on the use of your calculator.

2.	Here we have a much more difficult problem. If the decimal equivalent of the percentage used to write down the value is p then the value remaining will be 1 - p. This becomes our common ratio. We also know that the initial value, u_1, is £27600 and the seventh year value, u_7, is £2500. Putting this information into our formula leads us to

$2500 = (1 - p)^6 \times 27600$

which gives an equation to be solved for p. Dividing it by 27600 will give

$(1 - p)^6 = 0.09057971$

The problem is how to solve this type of equation where we have a high power on the unknown. If we take the sixth root of both sides of the equation then the power on the left will be reduced to 1 which we know can be omitted as it is always present by implication. But how can we find the 6th root of the number on the right? Once again your calculator comes to your aid but first I need to tell you that the sixth root is the same as the index, or power of 1/6 or 0.1666667. Now you can use the power function in your calculator and obtain

$1 - p = (0.09057971)^{0.1666667}$

$= 0.6701496$

and solving this simple equation gives

$p = 0.3298504$

which means that the percentage write down figure is, as near as makes no difference, 33% p.a.

Now that you have worked your way through this solution have another go at the same problem if the useful life had been 5 years.

(Remember the fifth root is the same as the power 1/5). This time you should obtain the percentage as 38%.

Now do it again with a useful life of 7 years. You should obtain 29% this time.

SELF CHECK 7

1.	This is a straightforward example of the use of the formula that we have just developed with

$u_1 = 3$ **$r = 4$**   **and $n = 7$**

$S_7 = \dfrac{3(1 - 4^7)}{1 - 4}$

$= \dfrac{3 \times -16383}{-3} = 16383$

You will have noticed how careful you must be here with the minus sign.

2.	This is much more difficult to frame in the terms of a geometric progression, although we know at once that n = 11 and the first year write down, u_1, is 0.2×250000 or $u_1 = 50000$. The problem is to find the common ratio, r. Consecutive book values are related, the next being 80% of the previous and as the write down rate is a fixed percentage of these related figures then the common ratio will also be 80% or 0.8.

Thus we have

$u_1 = 50000$ $r = 0.8$ $n = 11$

and

$$S_{11} = \frac{50000(1 - 0.8^{11})}{1 - 0.8}$$

= £228525.16

If this is the total amount written off over 11 complete years then the book value in the 12th year will be 250000 - 228525.16 = £21474.84 which agrees with the answer you obtained in Self Check 6 – which of course it should!

SELF CHECK 8

These three questions are a restatement of the questions, with different numbers, of Self Check 2. The only new concept involved here is that you must ensure that the time periods are consistent.
The answers you should obtain are

1.   £100   (or 0.1×1000)
2.   £1500   (or 0.015×100000)
3.   £63.75 (or 0.0425×1500)

SELF CHECK 9

YEAR	START OF YEAR INVESTMENT	ANNUAL INTEREST	END OF YEAR INVESTMENT
1	900.00	76.50	976.50
2	976.50	83.00	1059.50
3	1059.50	90.06	1149.56
4	1149.56	97.71	1247.27

Hopefully you found no problems here – you calculated the value in the third column by multiplying the value in the second column by 0.085. The value in the final column is the sum of the values in the previous two columns.

Did you use the memory on your calculator to save having to keep re-entering values? If not go back and try the sequence -

   Enter 900 [Min] [×] Enter 0.085 [=]

(note down result in column 3);

   [+] [MR] [=]

(note down result in column 4)

   [Min] and repeat the previous sequence from **[Min]**

SELF CHECK 10

Period 4

Invested sum for the period	$= P(1 + r)^3$
Interest earned for the period	$= P(1 + r)^3 r$
Sum invested by the end of period r	$= P(1 + r)^3(1 + r)$
	$= P(1 + r)^4$

SELF CHECK 11

You should have realised that each result we had in the summary contained P multiplied by $(1 + r)$ raised to a power. The power was the period number. So when the period number is 5 the result will be

$$P(1 + r)^5$$

and when the period number is 6 the result will be

$$P(1 + r)^6$$

SELF CHECK 12

These problems represent a straightforward application of the compound interest formula taking care that you have first organised your data so that your time periods are consistent.

1. $P = 900,\ n = 4,\ r = 0.085$

   $A = 900(1.085)^4 = £1247.27$

2. $P = 8500,\ n = 30$ half years, $r = 0.05$ per half year

   $A = 8500(1.05)^{30} = £36736.51$

3. $P = 30000,\ n = 120$ months, $r = 0.01$ per month

   $A = 30000(1.01)^{120} = £99011.61$

Once again, notice we have calculated correct to the nearest penny.

SELF CHECK 13

1.   Referring back to the text you can pick up the required information.

   (a)   At 6% per half year the end of year value is £112.36. Thus over the year £100 has gained £12.36 interest which expressed as an annual percentage rate is

   $$\frac{12.36}{100} \times 100 = 12.36\%$$

   (Remember to convert a fraction to a percentage we have to multiply the fraction by 100).

   (b)   Exactly as above you obtain 12.55%.

2.   Taking an investment of £100, invested for 12 months at 1.8% per month we can find the end of year value as $100(1.018)^{12} = £123.87$. So the annual equivalent rate is 23.87%

SELF CHECK 14

1.   This is a straightforward application of the present value formula with A = 100000, n = 20 r =0.09 (the time periods are consistent).

$$\frac{100000}{(1.09)^{20}} = £17843.09$$

2.   Here we have a slightly more complex problem, and it will often help to draw a 'picture' of the information. We use a line scale, or set of boxes to represent the years and can analyse our problem with some arrows which represent what we need to do with each sum.

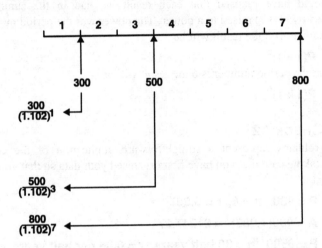

Each future debt has been replaced in the left hand column by its financially equivalent present value. You can now see that total present value =

$$\frac{300}{(1.102)^1} + \frac{500}{(1.102)^3} + \frac{800}{(1.102)^7}$$

= £1051.19

Notice here how we have been able to replace sums at one time by their financially equivalent sums at another time.

Thus the value, or amount to be paid, after 4 years will be £1051.19$(1.102)^4$ = £1550.27

3.   This is very much like the previous question and can be done in the same way of expressing the total at the beginning of the first year and then moving that sum forwards 5 years.

Alternatively, we can move each sum to the time of the single payment. Once again a picture may help.

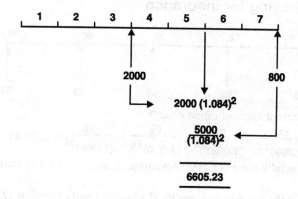

SELF CHECK 15

1.   Remember that you can only add, subtract, compare and contrast sums when they are expressed at the same time. Often we have the option of looking at the equivalent present values or the equivalent future values. Both are equally valid but, on the basis of making your decision now, it would seem more appropriate to look at the present value equivalents.

Offer 1 is already at present value and is £500. The present value equivalent of offer 2 is

$$\frac{715}{(1.093)^4} = £500.99$$

As the present value of offer 2 is 99p more than offer 1 then you should accept offer 2.

2.   Here we have two systems to consider. Look at each separately, drawing a picture to assist your analysis.

System 1 - Paying for repairs

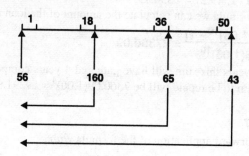

Total present value of repair costs =

$$56 + \frac{160}{(1.008)^{18}} + \frac{65}{(1.008)^{36}} + \frac{43}{(1.008)^{50}} = £272.28$$

System 2 - Paying for insurance

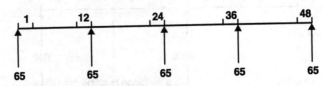

Total present value of repair costs =

$$65 + \frac{65}{(1.008)^{12}} + \frac{65}{(1.008)^{24}} + \frac{65}{(1.008)^{36}} + \frac{65}{(1.008)^{48}} = £270.89$$

So financially there is a clear advantage in taking out the insurance policy.

Further hints on the algebra to simplify the loan formula (Section 12)
(All these algebraic steps you have covered in unit 0.)
Step 1. All we have done here is to write

$$\left\{\frac{1}{1+r}\right\}^n = \frac{1^n}{(1+r)^n} = \frac{1}{(1+r)^n}$$

using the fact that $1 \times 1 \times ... \times 1 = 1$ no matter how many times we multiply 1 by itself.
Step 2. Here we have rewritten each of the square brackets using the relevant common denominator.
Step 3. To obtain this we have realised that in the denominator term we have

$$(1 + r) - 1 = 1 + r - 1 = r$$

SELF CHECK 16

1.   This is a straightforward use of the formula with $a = 120$, $n = 24$, $r = 0.01$
(notice that the time units are consistent).

$$P = \frac{120[(1.01)^{24} - 1]}{0.01(1.01)^{24}} = £2549.21$$

Total amount repaid (ie; 24 payments of £120) = £2880. Amount on interest
paid = 2880 - 2549.21 = £330.79.

2.   Using our formula we can calculate the amount of the loan as

$$P = \frac{1000[(1.06)^{10} - 1]}{0.06(1.06)^{10}} = £7360.09$$

but after 4 years this sum will have gathered 4 years compound interest at 6%
pa so the sum to be repaid will be $7360.09(1.06)^4 = £9291.94$.

SELF CHECK 17

1.   A straightforward application of the formula with

$$P = 7000 \qquad n = 10 \qquad r = 0.1225$$

to give

$$a = \frac{7000 \times 0.1225 \times (1.1225)^{10}}{(1.1225)^{10} - 1} = £1251.59$$

2.   As in the previous question

P = 250000   **n = 20**   **r = 0.14**

to give

$$a = \frac{250000 \times 0.14 \times (1.14)^{20}}{(1.14)^{20} - 1} = £37746.50$$

The total repaid over the 20 years = £754930
so the total interest paid will be £504930.

SELF CHECK 18

1.   First you have to calculate the amount of each repayment using the formula
with

P = 7500   **n = 7**   **r = 0.08**

to give

$$a = \frac{7500 \times 0.08 \times (1.08)^{7}}{(1.08)^{7} - 1} = £1440.54$$

Now remember that this repayment is the sum of the interest due and the debt
repaid.

YEAR	DEBT AT START OF YEAR	INTEREST DUE ON DEBT	RESIDUAL SUM TO REPAY DEBT	DEBT AT END OF YEAR
1	7500.00	600.00	840.54	6659.46
2	6659.46	532.76	907.78	5751.68
3	5751.68	460.13	980.41	4771.27
4	4771.27	381.70	1058.84	3712.43
5	3712.43	296.99	1143.55	2568.88
6	2568.88	205.51	1235.03	1333.85
7	1333.85	106.71	1333.83	2p under

Notice how the interest component has reduced over the 7 years and our
rounding errors have accumulated over the many calculations.

2.   This problem is different in that the repayments are not all the same. However
our loan repayment schedule can still be used but the number of rows is not
determined before we start

Year	Debt at Start of Year	Interest Due On Debt	Residual Sum To Repay Debt	Debt At End of Year
1	3000.00	210.00	490.00	2510.00
2	2510.00	175.70	524.30	1985.70
3	1985.70	139.00	561.00	1424.70
4	1424.70	99.73	600.27	824.43
5	824.43	57.71	642.29	182.14
6	182.14	12.75		

Looking at the schedule you will see that the £700 repayment is made at the end of years 1 to 5, ie; there are 5 repayments of £700.

The final small repayment is made at the end of year 6. It consists of repaying the debt outstanding of £182.14 together with the interest accrued during the sixth year of £12.75. This repayment will be £194.89.

SELF CHECK 19

1. Remember that our formula will total the present values of future regular equal periodic sums. That is how we were able to generate it in the first place.

   In this question we need to consider the last three repayments of £1440.54 so we have

   $a = 1440.54 \qquad n = 3 \qquad r = 0.08$

   to give

   $$P = \frac{1440.54[(1.08)^3 - 1]}{0.08(1.08)^3} = £3712.41$$

   [If you now do the comparison with question 1 of Self Check 18 you will see the 2p caused by rounding has already occurred by the end of year 4.]

2. (a) Use the formula to find $\underline{a}$ given

   $P = 30000 \qquad n = 25 \quad r = 0.1$

   to give

   $$a = \frac{30000 \times 0.1 \times (1.1)^{25}}{(1.1)^{25} - 1} = £3305.04$$

   (b) Interest component in the first year = £3000. Residual sum used to pay off debt in first year = £305.04.

   (c) i. After 5 years, 20 years remain so the debt is

   $$P = \frac{3305.04[(1.1)^{20} - 1]}{0.1 \times (1.1)^{20}} = £28137.67$$

   ii. £25138.40

   iii. £20308.04

   iv. £12528.70

v.   £8219.15

vi.   £3004.58

Looking at these figures you will see that

in the first 5 years the debt is reduced by £1862.33

in the next 5 years by £2999.27 (ie; years 6-10)

in the next 5 years by £4830.36 (ie; years 11-15)

in the next 5 years by £7779.33 (ie; years 16-20)

in the last 5 years by £12528.70 (ie; years 21-25)

which clearly shows how the balance within each repayment of £3305.04 changes as the years go by.

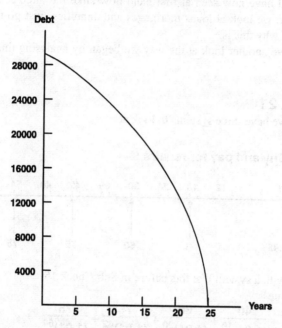

SELF CHECK 20

1.   It is some time since you had to be careful to ensure that time periods are consistent. Here we must generate

a = 1250   n = 30   r = 0.04

then the capital cost is

$$P = \frac{1250[(1.04)^{30} - 1]}{0.04 \times (10.4)^{30}} = £21615.04$$

2.   You should have calculated the capital available as £121000 and you should also have

n = 20   r = 0.087

to give the annual income as

$$P = \frac{121000 \times 0.087 \times (1.087)^{20}}{(1.087)^{20} - 1} = £12972.95$$

After paying out 12 times there are 8 repayments left to be made so the residual value will be

$$P = \frac{12972.95[(1.087)^{8} - 1]}{0.087 \times (1.087)^{8}} = £72610.54$$

You will have now seen at first hand how alike the three sets of calculations are when we look at loans mortgages and annuities. Just go back and remind yourself why this is.

Also have another look at the way we began by analysing the loan repayment system.

SELF CHECK 21

In this problem we have three systems to look at

System 1 - Buy and pay for repairs

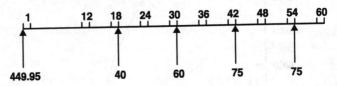

You have dealt with a system like this before in Self Check 15.

Total present value =

$$449.95 + \frac{40}{(1.01)^{18}} + \frac{60}{(1.01)^{30}} + \frac{75}{(1.01)^{42}} + \frac{75}{(1.01)^{54}}$$

$$= £621.11$$

System 2 - Buy and insure

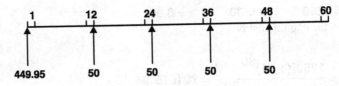

Total present value =

$$449.95 + \frac{50}{(1.01)^{12}} + \frac{50}{(1.01)^{24}} + \frac{50}{(1.01)^{36}} + \frac{50}{(1.01)^{48}}$$

$$= £599.66$$

System 3 - Rent

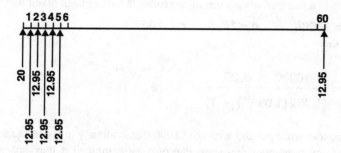

Total present value =

$$20 + \frac{12.95[(1.01)^{60} - 1]}{0.01 \times (1.01)^{60}} = £602.17$$

Comparing the three total present values it would appear marginally better, from a financial view point, to buy and insure the television set.

Further hints on the algebra to simplify the regular savings formula (section 14)
(All these algebraic steps you have covered in unit 0.)
Step 1   Here we have used common denominators in each of the curly brackets.
Step 2   Having simplified the numerator in the denominator we have replaced the division by a fraction by multiplication by its reciprocal.
Step 3   Finally, after cancelling the common terms $(1 + r)^n$, we have rearranged the result remembering that the order of multiplication can be changed.

SELF CHECK 22

This is a straightforward use of our formula having been given that

$$D = 1500 \qquad n = 10 \qquad r = 0.08$$
$$V = \frac{1500(1.08)[(1.08)^{10} - 1]}{0.08}$$
$$= £23468$$

You should note that in this problem the given information conforms exactly to the system that we analysed to obtain the formulation that

investments occurred at the start of each year
valuation occurred at the end of the last year
the investments remained fixed at £1500
the interest rate remained fixed throughout

SELF CHECK 23

1.   This is a straightforward use of our formula having been given that

$$V = 10000 \qquad n = 10 \qquad r = 0.05$$

so that

$$D = \frac{10000 \times 0.05}{(1.05)[(1.05^{10}) - 1]} = 757.19$$

2.   I wonder what you did with the £1000 that is already invested in the fund? Did you remember that sums can only be combined if they are expressed at the same time?

To calculate the contribution that the £1000 makes to the required £10000 we must remember that it remains invested, gaining interest for the whole 10 years. Its contribution will be $1000(1.05)^{10} = £1628.89$ and not just £1000.

The additional sum to be saved will be £8371.11 over 10 years at 5% pa so that

$$D = \frac{8371.11 \times 0.05}{(1.05)[(1.05)^{10} - 1]} = £633.85$$

SELF CHECK 24

In this problem we must clearly work out when we can apply our formula, where the breaks in the application of our formula occur and how we can take our sums through the breaks.

1.   Start by drawing a picture of the information that is given

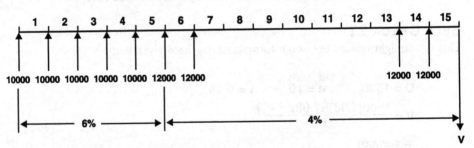

Remember the four conditions that have to apply. Look at the first 5 years. In this period all the conditions apply and our formula will give us the value at the end of the fifth year. It is £59753.19.

We can now use this sum as the financial equivalent of the five investments of £10000. This sum now remains invested in the fund for the next 10 years, gaining interest at the rate of 4% pa. Hence it will contribute $59753.19(1.04)^{10}$ = £88449.32 to the final amount.

Notice how we have replaced financially equivalent sums at one time with financially equivalent sums at different time ending up with the contribution at the required time.

Now look at years 6 to 15. In this period all the conditions apply and our formula will give us the value at the end of the 15th year of £149836.22. This is the contribution made to the amount by the ten investments of £12000.
So we can now add

V = 88449.32 + 149836.22 = £238285.54

2. Draw another picture and look at it carefully. Here we have six investments of £10000, the last being at the time when the interest rate changes. If we use the formula for these six investments it would try to give us the value at the end of year 6 but by this time the rate has changed and we have broken one of the conditions.

Look at it again. See if you can obtain the value of the fund at the end of year 5. It is £69753.19 and this contributes £103251.76 to the final amount. Now look at the remaining nine investments of £12000. They contribute £132073.29 to the final amount. Again we can now add to give the final amount as £235325.05.

Notice that this value is less than the previous one – as you should have expected. If you had not expected this to happen then compare your two pictures.

3. I can show you a summary of the analysis by drawing a picture and adding brackets and arrows to show how we combine sums. But first have you had a try!

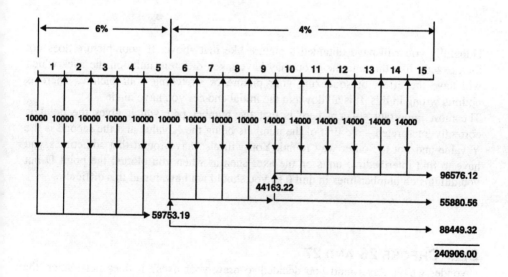

SECTION 2: GRAPHS

SELF CHECK 25

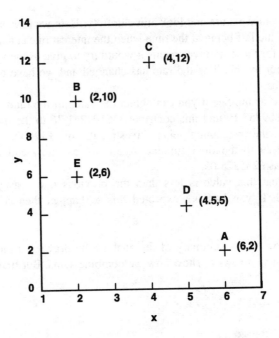

Hopefully you will have obtained a picture like that above. If your picture does not look exactly like this one then you may have taken different units on the axes which will have the effect of squeezing your picture or stretching your picture. There is nothing wrong in this. It is all down to the initial choices you have made.

The most important concept here is that the number pair which gives the point is correctly interpreted – the first of the numbers being the X value and the second is the Y value and not the other way round. You will also have found that sometimes you have to find intermediate units on the axes such as when you plotted the point D but you did this on number lines in unit 0 so you should not have found this difficult.

SELF CHECKS 26 AND 27

I wonder which way round you decided to draw your axes? It does not matter, the choice is yours, but having made that choice it is important that you label the axes to distinguish one from the other.

I have decided to use the cross page axis to represent the p number line and labelled it as such then the up page axis will represent the q number line.

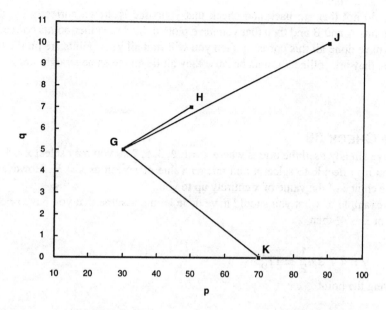

Another point that you should always bear in mind is that you will be drawing graphs to use as tools and so should always try to draw as large a graph as possible.

SELF CHECK 28

Here we have the value of y given as 4 + 3x and we need to calculate this for each given value of x.

> **When x = 1   then y = 4 + 3.1 = 7.**
>
> > **This gives the point (1,7)**
>
> **When x = 3   then y = 4 + 3.3 = 13.**
>
> > **This gives the point (3,13)**
>
> **When x = 7   then y = 4 + 3.7 = 25.**
>
> > **This gives the point (7,25)**

I hope you have remembered the rules regarding the priority of operations in arithmetic that we discussed in unit 0. You should have remembered that multiplication is of higher priority than addition.
This means that

$$4 + 3.3 = 4 + 9 = 13$$

and not 21.

SELF CHECK 29

We have said previously that when you draw a graph you should draw it as big as possible having regard to the size of your graph paper (usually A4). So here your basic graph will be such that it uses the majority of your graph paper.

When you have plotted these three other points you should find that they lie exactly on your original line.

If they do not then go back and check that your line is drawn correctly by checking your points A and B and then that you have plotted the three other points correctly.

If you have done all this correctly then you will find all your points are on the line. We say that they are collinear points because they all lie on the same straight line.

SELF CHECK 30

We have already used the points where x = 1, 2, 3, 5, 7 so you may select x = 4 or x = 6 but you may decide to select a non integer value of x such as x = $3\frac{1}{2}$. However I have left the choice of the value of x entirely up to you.

As an example of what you should have done let me assume that you have selected the value of x as $4\frac{1}{2}$ then

$$y = 4 + 3.4\frac{1}{2} = 17\frac{1}{2}$$

so giving the point

$$(4\frac{1}{2}, 17\frac{1}{2})$$

Now plot this point on your graph paper.

Once again it should lie exactly on your original straight line graph. If not go back and check your arithmetic and the accuracy of your plotting.

SELF CHECK 31

When x = 2 then y = 6 + 2.2 = 10.

This gives the point (2,10), A, say

When x = 8 then y = 6 + 2.8 = 22.

This give the point (8,22), B, say

Looking at these values it would be sufficient to draw your axes for values of x from x = 2 up to x = 8 and for values of y from y = 10 up to y = 22 but on this occasion for reasons that become apparent shortly we will find it better here to use axes for x from 0 to 8 and y from 0 to 22.

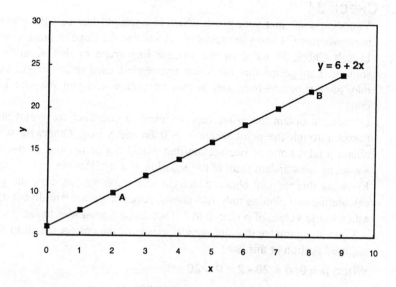

SELF CHECK 32

Having plotted the two points A and B we will use these points. You could choose to use any other pair of points on the line. Try it!

At A, x = 2 and at B, x = 8 so x increases by 6, ie +6.

At A, y = 10 and at B, y = 22 so y increases by 12, ie +12.

$$\textbf{Slope of the line} = \frac{\textbf{change in y}}{\textbf{change in x}}$$

$$= \frac{+12}{+6}$$

$$= 2$$

So here we have found that the straight line given by

y = 6 + 2x has a slope, or value of b, of 2

SELF CHECK 33

For GH we have G(30,5) and H(50,7) so the

change in p = 20

change in q = 2

so that the slope of GH is 2/20 = 1/10 = 0.1.

For GJ the slope is 5/60 = 1/12

For GK the slope is -5/40 = -1/8

You may have noticed the significance of the positive and negative sign on the slope. Reading across the page from left to right the line can be characterised as either sloping uphill as with y = 6 + 2x and GH or downhill as with y = 10 - 2x and GK.

We can conclude that an uphill sloping line has a positive value for its slope while a downhill sloping line has a negative value for its slope.

SELF CHECK 34

1. You should see that your graph which is a straight line cuts the y-axis at the point where y = 4 and you previously calculated the slope of this line to be 3.

2. In Self Check 31 we drew the straight line graph of this equation. In the solution I suggested that for future reasons we used rather longer axes than may have appeared necessary at that time. Now can you see why I suggest that?

    In order to obtain the y-intercept we need to construct the y-axis so that it passes through the point where x = 0 on the x-axis. Otherwise we would obtain a false point of intersection that would not correspond to the way that we set up the standard form of the equation of a straight line.

3. Knowing that we will obtain a straight line graph we can draw the graph by calculating and plotting only two points. Any two points will do but as we are asked to use values of p from 0 to 8 it would be a good idea to use p = 0 and p = 8 and so guarantee that the vertical axis is of the correct length to show the required portion of this line.

    When p = 0, q = 20 - 2 × 0 = 20

    > **This gives the point (0,20), M, say**

    When p = 8, q = 20 - 2 × 8 = 4

    > **This gives the point (8,4), N, say**

    Now we can draw the graph.

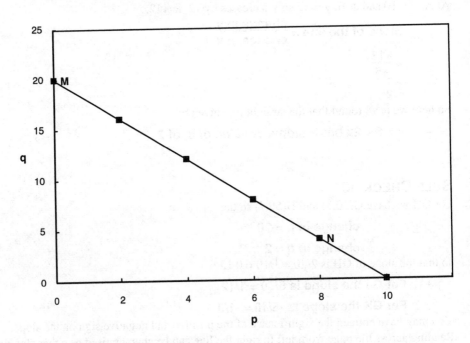

You can immediately read off the q-intercept as we have ensured that q-axis passes through the point where p = 0. It is 20. (As expected from the equation). Using the points M and N we can calculate the slope as -16/8 = -2 (as expected from the equation).

You are now in a position that you know the relevance of the numbers a and b in the standard equation of a straight line.

Given the demand function q = 300 - 10p you can see at once that the q-intercept is 300 and the slope is -10. Alternatively we can say that as the price rises so the demand decreases.

Given the supply function q = 10 + 5p then we have a line with a positive slope so that as the price rises so the supply increases.

SELF CHECK 35

I wonder whether you solved this equation for y first and then used the values of x or whether you substituted the value of x and then solved for y on each of the four occasions. Either way should produce the points

$$(0, 12) \qquad (2, 8) \qquad (4, 4) \qquad (6, 0)$$

Looking at these values indicates that you will need to draw an x-axis from 0 to 6 and a y-axis from 0 to 12 to accommodate these four points.

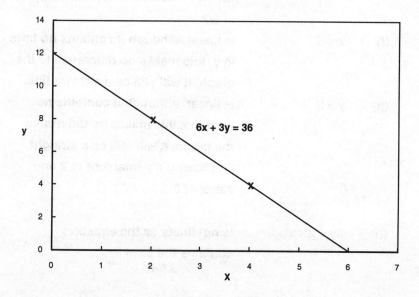

You can now see that the y-intercept is 12 and you can calculate the slope as, for instance, -4/2 = -2.

SELF CHECK 36

Remember that any linear equation will give a straight line graph. But what do we mean by linear when applied to an equation? It means that the equation can contain terms in x but not any other powers of x such as x^2, x^3, x^{-1}, and so on. It can contain terms in y but not any other powers of y and it can contain numbers. Notice that I have used the word 'can' and not 'must' as these terms may not be present without affecting whether the equation is linear or not.

Now look back at the list of equations given

(a) $y = 3 + 2x$ **is linear having a straight line graph with a y-intercept of 3 and a slope of +2.**

(b) $3y = 5 - 4x$ **is linear having a straight line graph with a y-intercept of 5/3 and slope of -4/3.**

(c) $2y^2 = 3 + 2x$ **is not linear as the equation contains the term y^2.**

(d) $5x - 2y - 6 = 0$ **is linear having a straight line graph with a y-intercept of -3 and slope of 5/2.**

(e) $3x - 2y = 7$ **is linear having a straight line graph with a y-intercept of -7/2 and slope of 3/2.**

(f) $x = 5$ **is linear although it contains no term in y, this makes no difference to the graph, it will still be a straight line.**

(g) $y = 2$ **is linear, although it contains no term in x this makes no difference the graph, it will still be a straight line having a y-intercept of 2 and slope of 0.**

(h) $3y = 2 - x^2$ **is not linear as the equation contains the term in x^2.**

SELF CHECK 37

You will first notice that every equation is linear so we are faced with drawing six straight lines. To draw the graph of a straight line you will remember that we only need to calculate and plot two points for each line. Which two points, or values of x you choose is entirely up to you. I have selected the values x = -2 and x = 3 in what follows. Taking each equation in turn

(a) $y = 2x - 2$
When x = -2 then y = 2 x (-2) - 2 = -6 → (-2, 6)
When x = 3 then y = 2 x 3 - 2 = 4 → (3, 4)

(b) $2y - 1 = x$ or $y = \frac{1}{2}(x + 1)$

When $x = -2$ then $y = \frac{1}{2}(-2 + 1) = -\frac{1}{2} \rightarrow (-2, -\frac{1}{2})$

When $x = 3$ then $y = \frac{1}{2}(3 + 1) = 2 \rightarrow (3, 2)$

(c) $x + 2y + 2 = 0$ or $y = \frac{1}{2}(-x - 2)$

When $x = -2$ then $y = \frac{1}{2}(2 - 2) = 0 \rightarrow (-2, 0)$

When $x = 3$ then $y = \frac{1}{2}(-3 - 2) = -5/2 \rightarrow (-3, -5/2)$

(d) $y + 2x = 3$ or $y = 3 - 2x$

When $x = -2$ then $y = 3 - 2 \times (-2) = 7 \rightarrow (-2, 7)$

When $x = 3$ then $y = 3 - 2 \times 3 = -3 \rightarrow (3, -3)$

(e) $x = 3$

This equation, although linear, is more difficult conceptually as it contains no term in y so cannot be solved for y. However, the equation says x = 3 always, other values of x are not allowed and x will be equal to 3 no matter what value y takes.

Or x = 3 for every value of y so we can select any two values of y, say, y = -1 and y = 4, to give the points that lie on this line as (3, -1) and (3, 4). But notice the line that these points generate.

(f) $y = -2$

This is similar to (e) except that the value of y is always -2. We can select the points (1, -2) and (3, 2).

Now you can draw the graph.

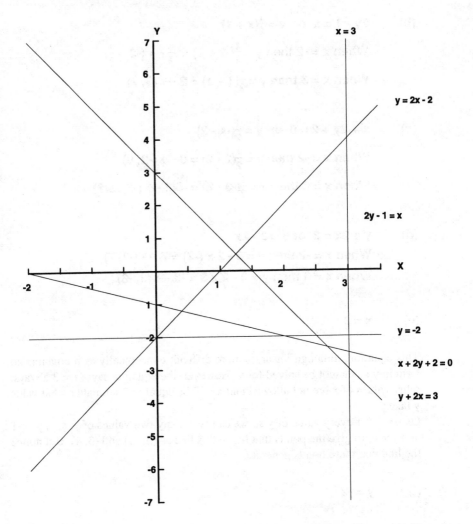

Now have another look at the lines x = 3 and y = -2. In future, now that you have appreciated what these lines look like they will be easy lines to draw without having to plot any points.

SELF CHECK 38

Remember uphill lines have positive value for the slope while downhill lines have negative value for the slope. The slope of a line can be obtained from the equation by recasting the equation into the standard form when the number that multiplies the x term represents the slope of the line.

(a)   **y = 3 - 2x, already in standard form.**

Slope is -2 so line is downhill.

(b)   **y = 5 + 4x, already in standard form.**

Slope is +4 so line is uphill.

(c)   **2y = 5 + 4x has standard form y = 5/2 + 2x.**
       Slope is +2 so line is uphill.

(d)   **2x + 3y = 6 has standard form y = 2 - (2/3)x.**
       Slope is -2/3 so line is downhill.

(e)   **2x - 3y = 6 has standard form y = -2 + (2/3)x.**
       Slope is +2/3 so line is uphill.

(f)   **4x + 3y + 7 has standard form y = -7/3 -(4/3)x.**
       Slope is -4/3 so line is downhill.

SELF CHECK 39

By now you should be having no difficulty in drawing graphs of straight lines. Your graph here should look like the graph below.

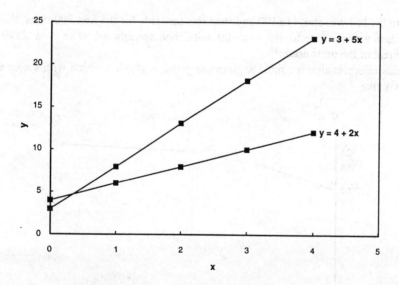

You can see from your graph that the point that lies on both lines is the point $(\frac{1}{3}, 4\frac{2}{3})$. As it lies on both lines then these values satisfy both equations simultaneously. Try it!

SELF CHECK 40

A. Here we are looking for a graph which shows a rental cost of £1000 for the first 20 hours then rises steadily to a rental cost of £5000 after 100 hours and then remains constant thereafter. This is a graph that is parallel to the activity axis for values of A greater than A = 100. In between it is a single straight line.

With this interpretation the only applicable graph is graph 5 which with scales added will look like

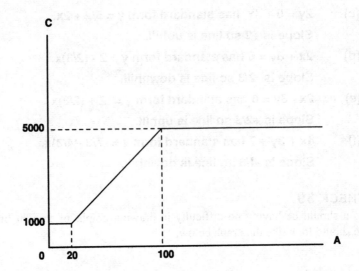

B. Here the bill will start at £100 and then rise upwards for the first 100 units, then rise upwards at a slower rate for the next 100 units, then rise upwards at an even slower rate for the rest of the units used.

With this interpretation the most appropriate graph is graph 4 which with scales added will look like

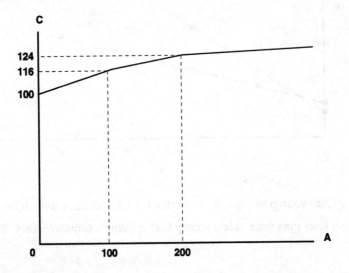

C. Here you will appreciate that we are looking for a graph that jumps upwards as each new supervisor is employed. We can only employ one, two or three supervisors so the salary costs will be

£1000 for 100 units of production

£2000 for 101 - 300 units of production

£3000 thereafter

These costs are represented graphically by segments of lines that are parallel to the activity axis. The only applicable graph is graph 1 which with scales added will look like

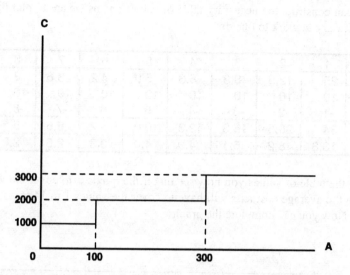

D. You will appreciate very quickly when you consider this situation that the rental rises steadily from zero at zero miles to up to £300 at at 500 miles and then remains fixed. So the graph slopes upwards to start with from the origin and then becomes parallel to the activity axis after 500 miles. This time we need to select graph 2 which with scales added will look like

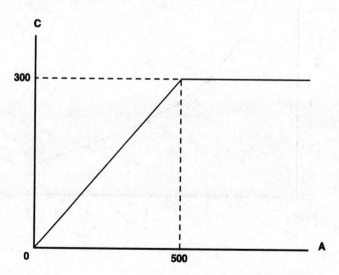

SELF CHECK 41

You can first construct the average cost function dividing the cost function throughout by q

$$AC = \frac{C}{q} = \frac{\frac{2}{5}(25 + 10q - q^3)}{q} = \frac{2}{5}\left(\frac{25}{q} + 10 - q\right)$$

Now you can construct the necessary table of values and as we are to plot the points it is only necessary to work to one dp.

q	1	2	3	4	5	6	7	8	9
25/q	25	12.5	8.3	6.3	5.0	4.2	3.6	3.1	2.8
10	10	10	10	10	10	10	10	10	10
-q	-1	-2	-3	-4	-5	-6	-7	-8	-9
	34	20.5	15.3	12.3	10.0	8.2	6.6	5.1	3.8
AC	13.6	8.2	6.1	4.9	4.0	3.3	2.6	2.0	1.5

Inspecting the table of values you now see that if the q-axis is to cover the values from 1 to 9 then the average cost axis will have to cover the values 1 to 14 to accommodate the graph. Now you can complete the graph.

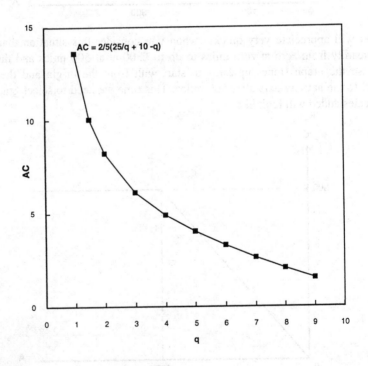

AC = 2/5(25/q + 10 -q)

SELF CHECK 42

You first need to set up two tables of values

1.   For $q = 16 + 4p + p^2$

p	0	1	2	3	4	5
p^2	0	1	4	9	16	25
4p	0	4	8	12	16	20
16	16	16	16	16	16	16
q	16	28	28	37	48	61

2.   for $q = 48 - 3p^2$

p	0	1	2	3	4	5
p^2	0	1	4	9	16	25
$-3p^2$	0	-3	-12	-27	-48	-75
48	48	48	48	48	48	48
q	48	45	36	21	0	-27

Looking at these tables you will see that you will need a q-axis to cover the range from -27 up to 61.

Now you can draw the graphs. I hope you have not forgotten to label your graphs.

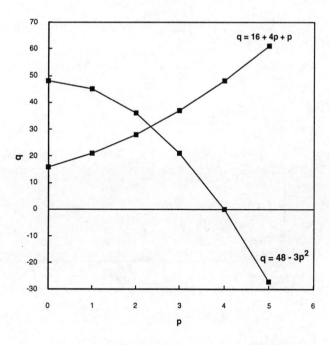

The equilibrium price and quantity is represented by the point of intersection of the two graphs which you can read off as p = 2.4 and q = 31.0.

Another way of finding this equilibrium point is to solve the two equations simultaneously.

If

$$q = 16 + 4p + p^2 \quad \text{and} \quad q = 48 - 3p^2$$

then

$$16 + 4p + p^2 = 48 - 3p^2$$

or $\qquad 4p^2 + 4p - 32 = 0$

or $\qquad p^2 + p - 8 = 0$

and solving using the formula gives

$$p = \frac{-1 \pm \sqrt{1^2 - 4 \times 1 \times (-8)}}{2}$$

$= 2.37 \text{ or } -3.37$

Clearly in this context the negative result has no significance as p is a price so we can only have p = 2.37 and then

$$q = 16 + 4 \times 2.37 + (2.37)^2 = 31.1$$

or $\qquad q = 48 - 3(2.37)^2 = 31.1$

UNIT 2

DATA PRESENTATION

CONTENTS

Unit Objectives

UNIT OBJECTIVES

This unit deals with concepts which are basic to the study of statistics. When you have finished working through you will be able to

- define the terms – variable, data, descriptive statistics, inferential statistics, population and sample

- select suitable measuring scales for different types of data

- construct and use ordinary and cumulative frequency distributions

- calculate or estimate various measures of central tendency (averages) such as means, medians and modes for various kinds of data

- calculate various measures of variation such as range, mean deviation, variance, standard deviation and coefficient of variation

- correctly use, and interpret, measures of central tendency and variation

SECTION 1

DATA, VARIABLES AND MEASUREMENT

1. WHAT IS STATISTICS?

The word 'statistics' is used in two ways:

> a collection of numerical facts gathered and organised so as to **describe** a given situation

> a systematic way of making **inferences** and generalisations about a set of people or things from a subset of numerical facts relating to that set

DESCRIPTIVE STATISTICS

The first of the two definitions is often referred to as **descriptive statistics**. This is normally intended as a reference to the organisation and presentation of information. An essential part of statistical work is to display the important features and patterns inherent in a large collection of numerical facts. From this point of view, statistics has a purely **descriptive** role in that it gives a picture, a 'snapshot', of a situation at a given point in time. Such summaries of data may be either tabular or graphical.

STATISTICAL INFERENCE

The second of the above two definitions is often referred to as **'statistical inference'**. In order to understand the nature of statistical inference you should be familiar with the following terms, which are used frequently in statistics.

> A **population** is the collection of all elements which are of interest to an analyst.

> A **sample** is a subset, or part of the total population

Here is the first Activity.

ACTIVITY 1

Consider the case of an electronics company which wishes to test a new light bulb to see how long it will last.

The only possible way of testing light bulbs is by using them to the point of exhaustion, and then recording the number of hours it took before this happened.

Which of the following do you think is best for testing the light bulbs in this way?

(a)   testing all the light bulbs

(b)   testing a 10% sample of the light bulbs

(c)   testing all the light bulbs produced on Tuesdays

(d)   testing a 1% sample of the light bulbs.

In many cases, such as with the light bulbs and the electronics company in Activity 1, much information is gathered from a sample. The population in this case would be the sum total of **all** products produced by the firm. Clearly, the company cannot test all the bulbs since the testing procedure destroys the product. It will therefore have to make do with a sample.

Testing all the bulbs produced on a Tuesday raises the question as to whether Tuesday is a normal enough day to be considered representative of all the company's production.

To be of any real value, a sample **must** be representative of the population.

A 10% sample of the company's production would be a good test of its product, but could the firm afford to sacrifice 10% of its production?

A 1% sample would certainly test the company's product, and would obviously be less expensive than a 10% sample.

The cost of taking a sample is just as important to a business as the representativeness of the sample.

ACTIVITY 2

As you have seen from the light bulb example, a sample is one way of gathering information. Another way is to take a **census**. A census is a **full enumeration** of the population. Instead of relying on a sample of observations to gather facts, a census would insist on using the whole population.

Can you think of at least two situations where the gathering of information by census might be very difficult?

I think that the example of the electronics company testing lightbulbs is a good example of a situation where a census (meaning the testing of every product) would be extremely difficult or impossible. Sometimes the testing of products involves using or destroying them. In such cases, a sample of products is the only way of obtaining information about product quality.

There will also be situations where it may be possible to take a census, but where the cost and time involved would make it impractical. For example, a television company might need to know viewership figures for its programmes.

It would, in theory, be possible to gather such information by census, ie contacting every single person in the population of viewers. In practice, this would take too long and be too costly. The company normally uses a sample of viewers.

Statistical inference aims to use information in more than just a purely descriptive manner. This branch of statistics is often concerned with collecting a sample from a population. Results are obtained from the sample statistics and inferences are made concerning the whole population. Statistical inference is therefore concerned with the rules which we must use whenever we wish to make generalisations from samples and apply them to the whole population.

Suppose that after all the above considerations, the electronics company decides to take a sample of 100 bulbs, and test them for quality. They could find that the average lifetime for the sample is 75 hours. How can this sample result be generalised to the whole population of light bulbs?

As we shall see later in the unit, the question is not a trivial one as the matter of accuracy (and cost) of the sample has to be considered.

2. MEASUREMENT

Statistical analysis always involves attempts to measure something, such as the lifetime of a company's product. It is worth thinking about the assumptions we make whenever we take statistical measurements.

Since there are different kinds of characteristics in which we may be interested, we must first select a suitable 'yardstick' with which to measure them.

When considering the characteristics of the entity we are measuring there are four possibilities.

NOMINAL MEASURING SCALES

Respondents in a survey about the voting intentions of British electors might be classed as 'Labour', 'Conservative', 'Other', etc. In other words, the statistical entities are classified by **name**, rather than **number**. The scale used for measuring such characteristics as voting intention is said to be **nominal**, not **numerical**. We measure a person's voting intention by attaching labels to them and not by measuring them against some numerical scale.

We must not let the use of numbers in statistical analysis mislead us. In statistics, such categories as voting behaviour are often **coded**, which means giving them a numerical value.

Thus 0 (zero) might represent 'Conservative', 1 'Labour', 2 'other parties', and so on. These numerical values are only given as an aid to computer analysis. Otherwise, such characteristics are not numerical at all, as voting intention can not be measured on a numerical scale. The only kind of statistical analysis possible with nominally scaled information is to count up the number of elements falling into each nominal category. It is impossible to use more sophisticated arithmetical processes with such information as we shall see later.

How about some other examples of nominally scaled information?

Try Activity 3.

ACTIVITY 3

A survey of 1000 people is conducted and all are asked questions relating to the following characteristics:

(a)   their **marital status** (are they single/married/divorced, etc)

(b)   **salary**; how much they earn

(c)   their **occupation**; (are they an engineer, accountant, etc)

(d)   how many **hours of television** do they watch each week

(e)   if they are currently undertaking a course of higher education, **which course of study** (maths, science, etc) are they following

Which of the above can be measured on a nominal scale and which cannot?

How did you get on with this activity? Compare your answers to mine.

Marital status, occupation and study subjects are clearly **labels** we give to certain characteristics. They are purely nominal in nature.

Salary, and number of hours spent watching television are capable of being measured on a numerical scale. They are not nominal in nature.

ORDINAL MEASURING SCALES

Suppose you are conducting a consumer research survey. One of your objectives might be to find how consumers rate five brands of ice cream. One possibility would be to ask a sample of consumers to rank the products on a scale of 1 to 5, where 1 means 'most preferred' and 5 means 'least preferred'.

Such a scale of measurement, which uses numbers, (or sometimes letters) to rank elements is an **ordinal scale**. However, if someone ranks a brand of ice-cream as number 1, then this only tells us that they thought more of this brand than one they rated as number 5.

It certainly does not tell us how **much more** highly they rated it.

Ordinal scales may be numeric or non-numeric; the key characteristic of an ordinal scale is that the numbers (or letters) are used to place objects in ranked order.

For example, an ordinal scale may make statements such as

'A is higher (greater/more than, etc) than **B'**

but not statements such as;

'A is 50% higher (greater/more than, etc) than **B'**

The degree to which it is possible to carry out arithmetic operations on information which is measured ordinally is a matter of fierce debate among researchers. It is probably safer not to try to carry out sophisticated arithmetic analysis on such statistics.

INTERVAL DATA

Think again about the above example, where we asked consumers to rank-order five different brands of ice-cream. The brand ranked by a customer as number 1 is better than the one ranked as number 2, which in turn is better than the one ranked as number 3, etc. However, from this data we are unable to say, for instance, that brand number 1 is rated twice as highly as number 2, or make other similar comparisons.

However, consider a characteristic such as **temperature**. Suppose the temperature yesterday was 15° C, and today it is 20°. It is reasonable to say therefore, that it is 33% warmer than yesterday. In other words, with a characteristic such as temperature, we cannot only make statements such as

'it is warmer today than it was yesterday'

but we can also say

'it is 33% warmer than it was yesterday'

This means that it is not only possible to measure temperature on a numerical scale, but also possible to say that, for example, a change from 10 to 20 is as great a change from 20 to 30. However, the presence of zero in an interval scale is not to be interpreted as a complete absence of the property being measured.

0° does **not** mean a complete absence of heat.

Zero is not the starting point of the scale.

This lack of an absolute zero sometimes causes difficulties with the interpretation of interval-scale data.

RATIO SCALES

It is likely that many of the characteristics you will come across in accounts and business studies will be measurable on a **'ratio scale'**. A ratio scale is identical to the interval scale, with the additional characteristic of starting from zero. 0 means a **complete absence** of the characteristic being measured.

For example, if you are measuring the number of children in a family, then all of the characteristics of interval scales are there. (A family with 5 children is 25% more than a family with 4 children.) It is also the case that a family of 0 children means a complete absence of children!

Both interval and ratio scales use numbers to put objects in order (like the ordinal scale) and also to measure the distance between objects (unlike the ordinal scale).

Interval and ratio scales are always numeric and it is possible to use a full range of arithmetic operations although you should exercise great care if you are analysing interval data.

In statistics, the analysis you can carry out depends on the type of scale used to measure the characteristics which interest you. So an attempt to use analytical methods appropriate to ratio scales on nominal data will produce illogical results.

Now let's take a look at another Activity

ACTIVITY 4

Consider the following two statistical exercises

A sample of lightbulbs from the daily production of an electronics company is collected in order to assess product quality

A sample of people are contacted to find out the numbers who are in various occupational groups.

(a)   what type of measuring scale would need to be used in each of the above cases?

(b)   you are probably familiar with the idea of an 'average' (we shall be discussing it in detail later).

(i) does it make sense to calculate the 'average' lifetime for a sample of lightbulbs?

(ii) does it make sense to calculate the 'average' occupational group of a sample of people?

I hope you will agree that lifetimes of lightbulbs would be measured against a ratio scale. Clearly, it is possible to make numerical comparisons, For example, a bulb lasting 100 hours not only lasts longer than one which lasts 50 hours, but also lasts **twice** as long. In addition, the zero is the starting point of the scale, in that a lifetime of zero hours means a total absence of the quality (lifetime), which is being measured. Since lifetime is a purely numerical characteristic, it is perfectly sensible to speak of 'average lifetime'.

However, if you categorise people according to occupational group, then you are clearly grouping people by label – engineer, teacher and so on. A nominal scale of measurement is being used. It makes no sense to try to calculate 'average occupation' as nominal scales will not allow such an arithmetic computation.

Note

Always try to determine the type of data (nominal, ordinal, interval or ratio-scale) being analysed before making any calculations from it.

3. ELEMENTS, VARIABLES AND DATA

Take a look at the following table:

PRODUCTS MARKETED BY PARANOIA INTERNATIONAL PLC			
BRAND	**TYPE**	**RANK***	**£PROFIT (1990)**
GLEAMO	Detergent	5	1.4m
SHINO	Polish	2	1.9m
RINZIT	Detergent	1	3.4m
WAFT	Deodorant	7	0.8m
PRESTO	Dishwash	3	1.1m
etc...			

* order of brand share of market

FIGURE 1: **Market Brand Shares**

Figure 1 is a (partial) list of the products marketed by a company. We shall now define some important terms using this data as an example.

Elements

Elements are the entities about which information is collected.

In Figure 1 above, an element is an individual product. There are five elements listed in the table.

Variables

Variables are characteristics of the elements which are of special interest to the analyst.

Figure 1 lists product name, product type, rank and profit as characteristics of interest.

There may be many other characteristics of the elements, but they have not been selected as of being of interest by the compiler of this particular table.

You should also notice that product name and type would be measured on a nominal scale, market share rank would be measured on an ordinal scale while profit would be measured on a ratio scale.

Variables are sometimes called nominal, ordinal, interval or ratio-scale variables depending on the scale used to measure them. It is also common to hear variables being described as either 'quantitative' or 'qualitative', depending on whether the characteristic being measured is numeric or non-numeric.

A qualitative variable is always the result of a nominal scale. Interval and ratio-scales always produce quantitative data.

The ordinal scale may produce either quantitative or qualitative data.

Data

Data results from the activity of taking a measurement of each variable for each element in the study. The analyst selects which elements to study such as consumers or households.

Some characteristics of that element are specified, such as consumer preference or size of households.

A measuring scale of an appropriate type is used to obtain values of these characteristics or variables, and the end result is referred to as data.

Suppose the analyst were interested in gathering some facts about domestic water consumption in a certain region. In this case, households would be the elements studied, water usage would be the characteristic (variable) selected, and a ratio-scale employed to obtain the data about quantity of water used.

Try this more detailed Activity.

ACTIVITY 5

The personnel manager of a business is studying employee morale and uses a questionnaire to collect data. The following example is typical of the questions on the questionnaire:

Please read the following statement

'I feel that I am performing a valuable service for society when I do my job well'

Strongly Agree	Agree	Undecided	Disagree	Strongly Disagree
A	B	C	D	E

Circle the letter which most closely represents your agreement/disagreement with this statement.

(a)   For the data generated by this question, state

    i.   the elements to be observed

    ii.   the characteristics about which the question asks

    iii.   the variable being measured, and

    iv.   the measuring scale which should be used to record the variable.

(b)   Are the data quantitative or qualitative?

The **elements** being observed in Activity 5, are employees. Each employee is one element in the study. The **characteristic** being measured is morale. As morale cannot be directly measured, you might reasonably argue that it is the level of agreement with this particular statement which is the subject of measurement. It is being measured on an **ordinal** scale. People in the sample are being asked to rank themselves in order of intensity of agreement or disagreement. Since each person will circle a letter, this makes the resulting data **qualitative**. However, this is an arguable point. What really distinguishes numerical from non-numerical data is whether or not arithmetic operations can be carried out on the data. It is doubtful whether any real arithmetic operations can be carried out on this data beyond the simple act of counting how many people fall into each agreement-disagreement category.

ACTIVITY 6

Every week a clerk in a hypermarket records the number of transactions that occurred in that week at each of the check-out tills

(a)   what is the population of elements being observed?

(b)   define the variable.

(c)   which type of measuring scale is being used?

The **population** under study in Activity 6 is the total number of check-out tills in the store. For each check-out till in this population the **variable** being recorded is the number of transactions. The **scale** used to record it would be the ratio scale. For example, ten transactions are twice as many as five transactions (interval comparison) and zero means a total absence of transactions. All ratio scales have an absolute zero as starting point.

Try another activity so that you are sure you understand what each of these important terms means.

ACTIVITY 7

Once an hour a random sample of 100 battery chargers is selected from an assembly line. The number of battery chargers in each sample that are found to be faulty is divided by 100.

(a)   What elements are being observed?

(b)   What characteristic is being observed?

(c)   What type of measuring scale is being used?

(d)   What is the variable?

I hope you will agree that the **elements** in Activity 7 are battery chargers. The **characteristic** being observed is the number of defectives. This number will be recorded on a **ratio scale**, and the resulting variable, after division by 100, will be the **proportion** of battery chargers which are defective.

Now look at the following activity which should help you distinguish between qualitative and quantitative variables.

ACTIVITY 8

Say whether each of the following variables is qualitative or quantitative and indicate the measurement scale that is appropriate for each.

(a)   age of respondent to a consumer survey

(b)   sex of respondent to a consumer survey

(c)   class rank of pupils taking an exam

(d)   make of motor car owned by a sample of 50 drivers

(e)   percentage of people in favour of Federal European Union in each of the member states of Europe

You should have answered Activity 8 something like this:

(a)   age of respondents is quantitative and measured on a ratio scale

(b)   sex of respondents is qualitative and measured on a nominal scale

(c)   the class rank order of pupils in an exam will be quantitative data and measured on an ordinal scale. However, remember that the type of arithmetic operations which can be carried out on ordinal data is limited. Even if a student's rank in a test (first, second, third, etc) is a number, we are not really justified in treating it numerically, when so few arithmetic operations can be carried out on the data The answer to this particular question is – as we saw in in an earlier example – open to argument.

(d)   the make of motor car is a qualitative variable and only measurable on a nominal scale

(e)   the percentage of people in favour of Federal European Union is a quantitative variable and capable of being measured on a ratio scale. Take careful note however, that if the variable of interest had been **whether or not** a person is in favour, then this would have been nominal, only taking on the values 'Yes', 'No' or 'Don't know'.

ACTIVITY 9

Look carefully at the following data set regarding ten of the 'FORTUNE' 500 largest US corporations.

COMPANY	SALES*	RANK	PROFIT*	ASSETS*	TYPE CODE
Raytheon	8192	53	489.6	4740	7
Texas Ins	6295	75	366.3	4428	7
Clark Equ	1278	283	46.1	951	11
Aristech	1065	321	188.2	676	5
Cons Prs	897	355	149.9	935	9
Dexter	827	369	35.5	626	5
Cooper	748	391	41.1	443	21
Shaklee	628	432	27.2	435	19
Grow Grp	507	495	0.0	223	5
Chemed	501	500	24.1	322.7	5

Source: *Fortune* magazine Apr 24 1989

* in $ millions   Type code = industrial sector.

Activity 9 continued...

(a)   How many elements are there in this data set?

(b)   What is the population from which the sample is drawn?

(c)   How many variables are there in the data set?

(d)   Which of the variables are quantitative and which are qualitative?

(e)   What type of measurement scale is being used for each of the variables?

Your response to Activity 9 should be similar to mine:

(a)   since there are ten companies listed, there are therefore ten elements

(b)   the population from which this sample of ten is drawn is the 500 largest US corporations

(c)
there are 6 variables in the data set

(d) (e)   the qualitative variables are – company name, type code, and are measured on a nominal scale. (Type code is the category of industry to which the business belongs. 7 is, for example the code for electronics.) All of the other variables are quantitative, and are measured on ratio scales, except for rank, which is an ordinal variable. However, you should be aware of the debate on whether ordinal variables are really quantitative in the true sense of the word.

---

4. SUMMARY

In this first section we have

- discussed the **descriptive** and **inferential** use of statistics

- met the terms **sample** and **census** for the first time

- learned how to classify data as either **nominal, ordinal, interval** or **ratio-scale**

- discussed, with examples, **elements, variables** and **data**

If you are unsure of any of the topics encountered in section 1, check back **now** before you read on.

SECTION 2

THE FREQUENCY DISTRIBUTION

1. DATA, FREQUENCIES, CLASSES AND DISTRIBUTIONS

Suppose that you are a work study analyst carrying out timing operations on a group of staff. You have already carried out the timings for a particular clerical operation and have acquired some data.

This data is shown in figure 2 below

```
55 62 71 58 63 50 50 51 54 52 55 48 58 49 59 55 43 51
60 52 54 48 40 59 47 49 43 50 55 62 58 55 49 58 53 62
65 71 59 58 46 59 40 38 71 68 52 47 72 58 54 48 67 50
56 44 61 49 58 49 41 58 52 42 50 68 48 52 48 47 68 50
63 52 44 50 50 64 58 40 48 50 40 49
```

The above times were obtained from observations of 84 clerks carrying out the same simple clerical task.

All times are in seconds.

FIGURE 2: **Times Taken to Complete a Simple Clerical Task**

Figure 2 represents an extract from a much larger set of data taken from 84 clerks working for an electronics firm. Each clerk normally carries out a range of tasks. This particular study consists of timing each of the 84 clerks carrying out ten different operations.

In this data set, an element is equivalent to a **clerk**, and the timings recorded represent just one of the ten operations.

Therefore the work study analyst's complete data file consists of $84 \times 10 = 840$ pieces of data.

You may think that the work study data tells us very little unless we present it in some form which will make sense to us. One of the principal tasks in statistics is to **present** and **group** data in a way which will show up any major features, trends and patterns.

How can the analyst do this?

By using a simple counting process the previously unintelligible mass of 84 figures can be reduced to something more meaningful. The results of this counting process are shown in figure 3 below.

TIME TAKEN TO COMPLETE A SIMPLE CLERICAL TASK				
TIME (Seconds)	FREQUENCY		CUMULATIVE	
	NO.	%	NO.	%
30 and under 35	0	0.00	0	0.00
35 and under 40	1	1.19	1	1.19
40 and under 45	10	11.90	11	13.10
45 and under 50	16	19.05	27	32.14
50 and under 55	21	25.00	48	57.14
55 and under 60	19	22.62	67	79.76
60 and under 65	8	9.52	75	89.29
65 and under 70	5	5.95	80	95.24
70 and under 75	4	4.76	84	100.00
TOTAL NO. OF CLERKS	84			

FIGURE 3: **Frequency Table of Work-Study Data**

The 84 clerks have been counted into nine groups, each bounded by a 'class limit'. For example, the group '60 and under 65' shows that eight clerks belong to this group (9.52% of the total).

Such a form of presentation is often called a **frequency distribution**; '60 and under 65' is a **class interval** of the distribution, the two numbers, 60 and 65, are the **class limits** and 8 (the number of clerks), is the **frequency** for that class.

In the frequency distribution shown in figure 3, you should notice that the data has been shown in both numerical and percentage form. The data has also been arranged cumulatively. Take a closer look at the cumulative column which shows (for example) that 67 clerks (79.76% of the total) took less than 60 seconds. Check out other table entries to make sure you are familiar with this kind of data presentation. The table in figure 3 is both an ordinary and a cumulative frequency distribution.

The frequency distribution is a data presentation method with which you must become familiar. It is a basic building block of statistical method, and is a simple, though powerful method of displaying data. If there is any pattern present in any given data, then the frequency distribution will help to highlight it.

We can summarise our quick look at frequency distributions with short definitions of the following terms:

Frequency is the number of observations which fall into a particular class, or grouping

Cumulative frequency is the number of observations which are below a certain value

Relative frequency is the proportion of observations which fall into a given class. In figure 3 this is shown as a percentage although it could just as well have been a decimal fraction

ACTIVITY 10

Look again at the data in figure 3. What is

(a)   the number of clerks who took more than 40 but less than 45 seconds?

(b)   the frequency for the interval 40 < 60?

(c)   the number of clerks who took less than 55 seconds?

(d)   the relative frequency for the class interval 60 < 65?

Here is how I think you should have responded to Activity 10

(a)   Ten clerks took from 40 to 45 seconds to complete the task

(b)   You will obtain this by adding together several frequencies

         Solution – 10 + 16 + 21 + 19 = 66

         clerks took from 40 to 60 seconds

(c)   48 clerks took less than 55 seconds

(d)   9.52% (0.0952 in decimal terms) have a time between 60 and 65.

---

2. FREQUENCY DISTRIBUTIONS AND VARIABILITY

As you have seen, the understanding of the concept of distributions and their laws is fundamental to statistics.

Why is this so?

Variation always occurs in activities and processes.

Many naturally occurring phenomena clearly show this variability. For instance, adult male heights are commonly between 5ft 7in and 5ft 11in but heights outside this range are by no means rare.

Although it is not so obvious, the creations of the human world are by no means exempt from this kind of variability.

To give you an idea of what this means, look through these:

● a manufacturer of metal washers will find that some washers will have a greater thickness than others, even though they are produced to the same design specification;

● even though electrical filaments may be made at the same time their resistances will not be exactly alike;

● running costs of a department in a business will not be exactly the same each week, even though there appears to be no reason for the difference;

● tensile strength of a steel bar varies at different points along its length;

- the time taken by clerical workers to complete the same office task varies from person to person and from time to time;

- differences will be found in the diameters of components being produced by the same lathe.

Perhaps you can think of other examples.

In manufacturing the aim is to try to make things as alike as possible, or, at least to ensure that the amount of variability is controlled by the specification and the processes, so that variation between certain limits is permitted and acceptable. You should note that even with the greatest precision of manufacture, variability will still exist providing, of course, the measuring equipment used is accurate enough to record it.

ACTIVITY 11

If you have access to a kitchen scales or something similar, try this experiment and see if you can answer the question.

Take a bag of sugar (flour, or any other packaged dry goods) and take a note of the weight printed on the pack.

Now weigh the pack. More likely than not, you will find the weight shown on your scales is not identical to the weight stated on the pack.

Can you account for this variation?

In the case of the variability of package weights described in Activity 11 there are two explanations for this variation. Weighing scales manufactured to the same standards will often give different values when used to weigh the same object. Also, many goods are packaged automatically. Even if the machine is set to measure out, for example, 1 kg of flour, the actual amount delivered will vary from fill to fill because of imperfections in machine performance.

Therefore variation is present in all processes, to a greater or lesser extent, and the use of distributions is necessary to analyse such situations.

3. HOW TO CONSTRUCT A FREQUENCY DISTRIBUTION

We can best explain the general concept behind the construction of frequency distributions by considering the data in figure 4 below. This consists of the weights of a sample of 95 packages that pass through a sorting office.

7.9 7.8 8.0 8.6 8.1 7.9 8.2 8.1 7.3 8.0 8.2 7.8 8.0 7.5 7.4
8.0 8.0 7.7 7.8 7.5 7.8 8.3 7.9 7.8 7.5 7.9 8.2 8.5 7.9 7.5
8.2 8.2 7.9 8.7 7.7 7.8 8.0 8.1 8.5 8.0 8.1 7.8 8.1 7.6 7.8
7.9 7.9 8.3 7.9 8.1 7.6 7.9 8.3 7.4 8.4 7.6 8.0 8.0 8.2 8.2
7.9 8.1 7.7 7.9 7.7 7.9 7.8 7.8 7.7 7.5 8.1 8.1 8.0 8.1 7.7
8.0 8.0 8.0 8.2 7.6 7.9 8.2 8.4 7.9 7.8 8.7 7.6 8.1 7.7 8.1
7.8 7.4 8.1 7.3 7.1

Each of the above figures represents the weight of a package passing through a sorting office.

FIGURE 4: **Package Weights (in kg)**

As with the clerical task timings (figure 3 above), little information about the variable can be deduced. Perhaps the only thing which can be inferred is that the weight of any package passing through this office is likely to be between the lowest and highest values so far recorded, in other words between 7.1 and 8.7 kg.

However, in statistics, data should be looked upon as a whole and not just as a collection of individual readings. It is always surprising to non-statisticians how often regularities appear in these statistical counts.

The process of grouping data into a distribution is done in two stages:

The distance between the smallest and largest value recorded (7.1 to 8.7) is divided into a convenient number of **classes**

Then the **observations** are **counted** into these **classes**

The weight data varies between the two extremes of 7.1 and 8.7 kg, a range extent of 1.6 kg. We must now divide this range into a convenient number of class intervals. In the case of this data, 0.2 has been chosen as a convenient size for the class interval (although it is not the only possibility) which would mean dividing the range up as follows

7.1 and under 7.3
7.3 and under 7.5
.
.

etc
.
8.7 and under 8.9

The exact choice of a class interval depends very much upon the need to make the distribution neat and readable. It would not do to have a distribution which was long and difficult to read, nor would it be useful to have a distribution which only consisted of one or two classes.

After some practice and experience, you will soon gain an understanding of what makes for good presentation.

The next stage is to process the data and count how many observations fall into each class.

This has been done for you and is shown in the table (figure 5 below).

WEIGHT	FREQUENCY		CUMULATIVE FREQUENCY	
	Number	Relative	Number	Relative
7.1 < 7.3	1	0.01 (1%)	1	0.01 (1%)
7.3 < 7.5	5	0.05 (5%)	6	0.06 (6%)
7.5 < 7.7	10	0.11 (11%)	16	0.17 (17%)
7.7 < 7.9	19	0.20 (20%)	35	0.37 (37%)
7.9 < 8.1	27	0.28 (28%)	62	0.65 (65%)
8.1 < 8.3	22	0.23 (23%)	84	0.88 (88%)
8.3 < 8.5	6	0.06 (6%)	90	0.95 (95%)
8.5 < 8.7	3	0.03 (3%)	93	0.98 (98%)
8.7 < 8.9	2	0.02 (2%)	95	1.00 (100%)

FIGURE 6: **Package Weights. Numeric and
Relative Frequencies in Ordinary and Cumulative Form**

Decimals have been rounded to two places, so that the columns may not exactly total 1.00.

Try another activity to make sure you are happy with the calculations and understand how to compile data in this way.

ACTIVITY 13

A study was recently carried out to determine the amount of time that non-secretarial office staff spend using computer terminals. The study involved 50 staff, and the times, in hours per week, spent using the machines were as follows:

0.5	1.2	4.8	10.3	7.0	13.1	16.0	12.7	11.6
5.1	2.2	8.2	0.7	9.0	7.8	2.2	1.8	12.8
12.5	14.1	15.5	13.6	12.2	12.5	12.8	13.5	1.3
5.5	5.0	10.8	2.5	3.9	6.5	4.2	8.8	2.8
2.5	14.4	16.0	12.4	2.8	9.5	1.5	10.5	2.2
7.5	10.5	14.1	14.9	0.3				

Summarise this data in the form of a table and show

(a)   a frequency distribution
(b)   a relative frequency distribution
(c)   a cumulative frequency distribution

How did you manage with this problem? The minimum value in the data is 0.3 hours, and the maximum is 16 hours. My solution starts from 0, and covers the full range of times in intervals of 3 hours. There is no single correct answer to this question, as the distribution you obtain will depend upon the particular class intervals you have chosen. However, you should find that the resulting general 'shape' of the distribution is similar to the one given below in figure 7.

HOURS	NO. OF USERS			
	Frequency		Cumulative Frequency	
	no	%	no	%
Under 3	14	28.00	14	28.00
3 < 6	6	12.00	20	40.00
6 < 9	6	12.00	26	52.00
9 < 12	7	14.00	33	66.00
12 < 15	14	28.00	47	94.00
15 < 18	3	6.00	50	10.00
TOTAL	50			

FIGURE 7: **Distribution of Computer Usage**

Notice how the distribution has two distinct 'peaks'; at the classes 'under 3' and '12 < 15'. Later in the unit, when you read about types of distribution, you will see that this is an example of something we call a 'bi-modal' distribution.

4. FREQUENCY DISTRIBUTIONS AND DIAGRAMS

Tabulating data in the form of a frequency distribution increases our ability to detect pattern and meaning. The use of diagrams can be even more revealing. The package weight data of figure 5 is shown in this way in figure 8 below.

This type of representation is known as a **bar chart**. Sometimes, when the bar chart is used to display a frequency distribution, as is the case here, it is called a **histogram**.

Figure 8 is a histogram displaying the frequencies of package weights. If the class intervals used to construct the frequency distribution are all the same width, as they are in the package weight example, then the height of the bar is proportionate to the number of observations.

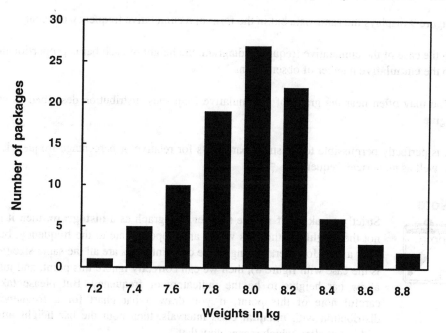

FIGURE 8: **Bar Chart of Package Weight Distribution**

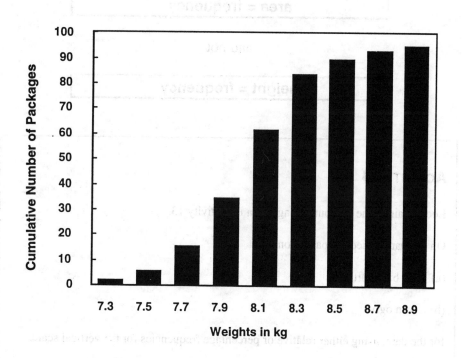

FIGURE 9: **Bar Chart of Cumulative Pack Weight Distribution**

Figure 9 displays the same data but in the form of a cumulative frequency bar chart.

In the case of the cumulative frequency diagram, the height of each bar is proportionate to the **cumulative** number of observations.

You may often hear the graph of a cumulative frequency distribution described as an **ogive**.

It is perfectly permissible to construct bar charts for relative or percentage frequencies as well as numerical frequencies.

Note

Strictly speaking, if we are to refer to a graph as a **histogram**, then it is not the **heights** of the bars which are proportionate to the frequency, but their **area**. However, so long as the class intervals are all the same size (as is the case with figure 8), then we can correctly ignore this point, and just allow bar heights to be the indicators of frequency. But please take careful note of this point; if you draw a bar chart for a frequency distribution with **unequal** class intervals, then both the bar height **and** width will alter, which means now that

| area = frequency |

and not

| height = frequency |

ACTIVITY 14

Look again at the computer usage data in Activity 13.

On a separate piece of paper construct

(a)   a bar chart

(b)   an ogive

for the data, using either relative or percentage frequencies for the vertical scale.

Here are specimen answers to Activity 14 (figures 10 and 11). Your graphs may not be quite the same due to different scales, class intervals, etc.

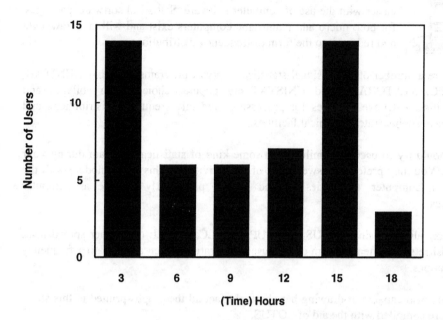

FIGURE 10: **Histogram of Computer Usage Distribution**

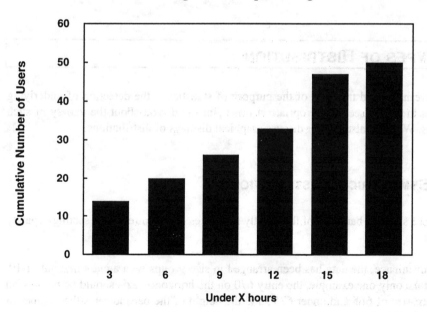

FIGURE 11: **Ogive of Computer Usage**

5. NOTE FOR COMPUTER USERS

 The organising of data into frequency distributions is made a great deal easier with the use of computer software. Statistical software 'packages' for both micro and mainframe computers exist and will take 'raw' data and reduce it to the form of frequency distributions.

There are a number of professional statistical analysis programs available. MINITAB, SPSS-PC, STATGRAPH and UNISTAT are popular choices with colleges and universities. All have facilities for processing data into frequency distributions and some have sophisticated graphical facilities.

You should try to become familiar with some kind of statistical program during your course. You may prefer to answer some of the activities in this study module with the aid of a computer. (Activities 12 and 13 are particularly suitable as computer exercises.)

You may also be using LOTUS 123, SUPERCALC, EXCEL or another spreadsheet. Spreadsheets can often perform certain useful operations, such as tabulating frequency distributions.

Most are also capable of drawing bar charts. In fact all the graphs printed in this study unit were compiled with the aid of LOTUS.

6. TYPES OF DISTRIBUTION

Since we have said that part of the purpose of statistics is the detection of underlying patterns in data it seems appropriate at this point to tell you about the variety of such patterns. We shall also further discuss graphical displays of distributions.

THE SYMMETRICAL DISTRIBUTION

Figure 12 shows a bar chart of the nightly audiences at a theatre with a seating capacity of 800.

For convenience, the data has been arranged in size groups with a class interval of 10. So, to take only one example, the entry 670 on the horizontal axis should be read as 'an audience size of 665 and under 675', and the height of the bar indicates the number of occasions when there was an audience of that size.

Notice the shape of this distribution. We shall be discussing later distributions with this shape.

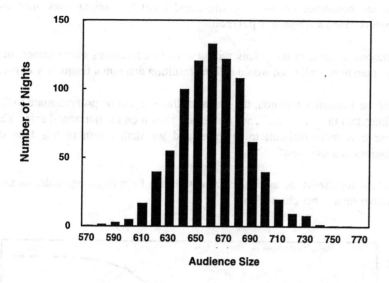

FIGURE 12: **Audience Size Distribution**

The histogram is not the only way of displaying a frequency distribution. Figure 13 below shows the audience size data as a **continuous** line graph. Again, look very carefully at the shape of the distribution, as shown in figure 13.

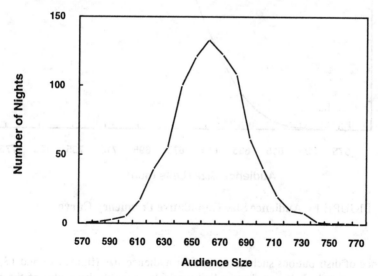

FIGURE 13: **Audience Sizes Frequency Polygon**

To construct the line graph in figure 13, points are drawn on the graph with appropriate co-ordinates, and then these are connected by lines.

If the points are connected (as they are illustrated here) by straight lines, then the resulting graph is called a **frequency polygon.**

If we had chosen to connect the points with a smooth continuous curve rather than straight lines, then technically, we would call the resulting diagram a **frequency curve.**

In the case of the frequency polygon, the height of the line will be proportionate to the number of times that there is an audience of the size shown on the horizontal axis. The frequency curve is more difficult to interpret and we shall return to this type of statistical diagram in a later unit.

Figure 14 below, represents the audience size data in the form of an ogive drawn as a line graph, rather than in bar chart form.

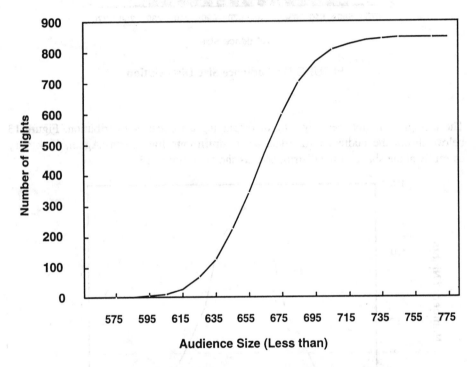

FIGURE 14: **Audience Size Cumulative Frequency Curve**

The importance of distributions such as the one for audience size (figures 12 and 13) is that they are **symmetrical.** If you draw a line vertically through the centre of the bar chart (or curve) you will easily see that the left side of the graph is a 'mirror image' of the right side – or very nearly. Data which are distributed symmetrically are very easy to analyse.

With frequency curves and polygons, care must be taken when reading the graph between data points. This difficulty will be illustrated in the following Activity.

ACTIVITY 15

Try these:

(a)   study the distribution of audience sizes shown in figures 12 and 13. On approximately how many nights did the theatre have audiences of between 715 and 725 people?

(b)   using the ogive in figure 14, estimate the number of nights when the theatre had audiences of less than 685 people

(c)   from the frequency polygon of figure 13, estimate the number of nights the theatre had an audience equal to 699 people

Does it make sense to make such an estimate from this diagram?

Give reasons for your answer.

Your response to Activity 15 might have been along the following lines.

(a)   Look at figure 12. The bar with '720' at the base shows all occasions when there was an audience of from 715 to 725 people. This bar has a height (shown on the vertical scale) of 10. Therefore there were approximately 10 occasions when this theatre had an audience in this range.

(b)   An ogive is always the best way to deal with this type of question. Looking at figure 14 we find the vertical height of the ogive where the horizontal axis is equal to 685. The ogive shows (very approximately), 650 on the vertical scale at this point.

Therefore, on 650 nights there was an audience of **less than** 685 people.

(c)   How would you deal with this type of question? We know the number 699 is in the range 695 - 705. The number of times there was an audience in this size group is shown by the height of the bar chart (or frequency polygon) at 700. (A frequency of approximately 40). We do not know on how many of these occasions the audience was **exactly equal** to 699. We do not have the information to allow us to read between points on the horizontal scale.

Take Care!

You cannot read off values just anywhere on the horizontal scale merely because the points on a graph are connected with a continuous line.

The practice of joining graph co-ordinates with a line is very often to aid the eye to spot trends, or patterns in data. It is not necessarily done to enable you to 'fill in' the gaps between graph co-ordinates.

ASYMMETRICAL DISTRIBUTIONS

A great deal of data cannot be grouped into regular symmetrical distributions. Examine the bar chart in figure 15, below. This displays a sample of people according to the distribution of their incomes.

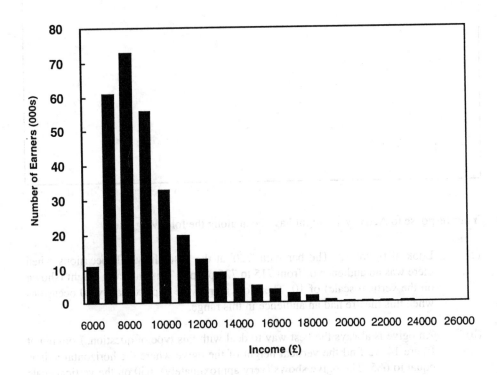

FIGURE 15: **Histogram Showing Income Distribution**

The graph was drawn from data which had been grouped into class intervals of £1000. So, for example, the bar displayed as £10,000, is to be interpreted as showing all people with incomes from £9,500 up to £10,500. The height of the bars shows the number of people who have an income in the class interval shown on the horizontal axis.

Notice carefully the shape of this distribution.

In many countries, most people have incomes in the lower ranges, or at least in the lower to middle ranges. For a histogram representing income distribution, you will find that the bars at the lower end of the age scale will be generally taller than those at the upper end of the income scale.

This distribution has a decidedly lop-sided or asymmetrical look.

Asymmetrical distributions are also often referred to as skew distributions. The words 'skew' and 'asymmetrical' mean much the same. In the case of the income data, we can additionally say that it is positively skew (sometimes just written as ' + skew '). A positively skew distribution will have most of the observations recorded at the lower end of the scale.

There are also negatively skew distributions (written as '- skew'), where most of the observations fall into the upper end of the scale. It is left to you (Activity 16) to find a case of negative skewness.

Try Activity 16 and see if you can.

ACTIVITY 16

(a)   Take another look at the package weight data back in figure 5 section 1.

It is almost, but not quite symmetrical. Would you describe this distribution as positively or negatively skew?

(b)   Try to think of at least two examples of data you think might be negatively skewed.

You would be correct in thinking that it is not easy to detect the direction of asymmetry, or skewness, in the case of the package weight data.

The best way of tackling the question is to study the frequency distribution of weights in figure 5, or the bar chart in figure 8. If we ignore the class 7.9 < 8.1 for the moment, you can easily count that 35 recorded packages are below 7.9, and 33 are above 8.1. The evidence, (in so far as we are able to assess it at this time) seems to suggest that the data is moderately +skew. However, it must be admitted that the tendency is slight.

Concerning the matter of negative skewness, we may quote **mortality rates** as an excellent example. The distribution of age at death (excluding accidents) would be negatively skewed, since we expect most people to live until their 60s or 70s. In any society which has reasonable health care, few deaths would occur in the lower age groups, but this would slowly rise to a peak towards the upper end of the age scale.

To take another example, a distribution of the number of breakdowns in industrial machinery by age of equipment, is quite likely to be negatively skewed. There will be a greater number of breakdowns for older machinery.

As we shall see later, the lack of symmetry in a distribution will mean taking extra care in the analysis of the data. The drawing of a bar chart or other kind of frequency graph is a sound first step in data analysis, because such diagrams will display the underlying shape of the distribution.

THE RECTANGULAR (UNIFORM) DISTRIBUTION

Figure 16 below, is a histogram showing the frequency of occurrence of the digits 0 to 9 in a sample of telephone numbers taken from a directory. It seems fairly reasonable to assume that all of the digits occur with roughly equal likelihood. This means that the bars in the graph will be of roughly the same height.

Such a distribution is known as a **rectangular** or **uniform** distribution. Such distributions occur quite often.

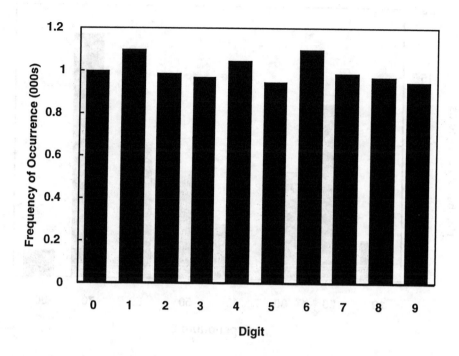

FIGURE 16: **Frequency of Occurrence of Digits 0–9
in the London Telephone Directory**

THE BI-MODAL DISTRIBUTION

Figure 17 below is a histogram of the amount spent on a household product per month by a sample of households. You will see that the bar chart has two distinct separate peaks, or 'modes'.

Such distributions are called **bi-modal distributions**. There may even be cases of data where the distribution has more than two peaks. They are then known as **multi-modal**.

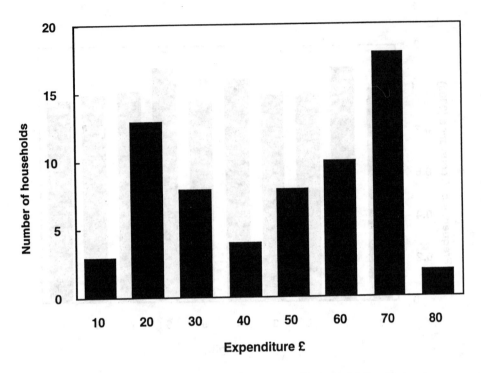

FIGURE 17: **Expenditure Per Month on Household Products**

Distributions with such irregular shapes are very difficult to analyse.

We can conclude this section on distributions by remarking that the underlying shape of the distribution determines the degree of ease or difficulty we shall meet in analysing data, or interpreting results. Regularity (for example, symmetry), makes data easier to interpret.

Constructing frequency tables and drawing bar charts and frequency polygons/curves is a useful first step in the process.

7. SUMMARY

In this second section of this unit we have

● described the type of data presentation known as a **frequency distribution**

● seen how we can present data in **cumulative** and **relative frequency** form

● discussed **variability**, with examples

● practiced the construction of **frequency distributions** by using appropriate **class intervals** and **class limits**

● constructed **histograms**, **ogives** and **frequency polygons** for distribution data

● appreciated the use of **frequency distributions** and **histograms** in showing the pattern, shape and regularity of data

● studied the special cases of **symmetrical, asymmetrical, rectangular** and **bi-modal** distributions, and **positive** and **negative skewness**

If you are unsure of any of these topics, then check back **now** to the appropriate section before starting section 3.

SECTION 3
MEASURES OF CENTRAL TENDENCY

1. INTRODUCTION: SUMMARY STATISTICS

What do you understand by statements like the following?

In 1990, the average weekly wage of boilermen was £150.

The average weight of packages passing through a sorting office is 7.9 kg.

In this town the average age of people is 44.

Section 1 discussed the way in which masses of raw data could be presented in a form in which they could be more easily understood, such as frequency distributions and charts.

It is possible to carry the process of summarising and presenting data even further. Just a few figures (like the ones mentioned above) can tell us a great deal about the data. Hundreds, maybe thousands, of observations may be summarised by these few figures.

These convenient numbers are called '**summary statistics**' and they fall into several groups.

2. WHAT ARE MEASURES OF CENTRAL TENDENCY?

One type of summary statistic is commonly known as an 'average'. This is rather an imprecise term, for as we shall see, there are a number of different statistics meriting this name.

It is worthwhile considering for a moment what is popularly understand by this term.

Numbers known in common language as 'averages' are more precisely described by the statistical analyst as **measures of central tendency**, or **measures of location.**

We often think of data as being centred or located around a fixed point. Therefore if we are told that boilermen have an average weekly wage of £150, then while accepting that individual wages may vary, we have some kind of notion of boilermen's wages being grouped around this amount. Many people interpret an average wage as meaning a typical wage.

To consider another example. If we know that in a particular town the average age of the people is 44, then we think that most people's ages must be grouped or centred around 44. It is regarded as a typical age.

We all seem to have some kind of intuitive idea of the average. We are also likely to know that there can be observations above or below the average and that this does not conflict with the belief that the average is the centre of the data. How justified are these intuitive ideas?

Like all concepts which appear to be basically very simple, you will find that interpreting measures of central tendency is a very elusive task.

The term average is ambiguous because there are several different ways of measuring 'averageness'.

Activity 17 will show you some of the misconceptions many people have concerning the 'average'.

ACTIVITY 17

Now try out your intuitive understanding of the average.

A group of 20 people earn an 'average' weekly salary of £200. Say whether the following statements about these 20 people are **always true, sometimes true**, or **never true**:

(a)   ten of these people earn above the average, and ten of them earn below the average

(b)   more than half of these people earn above the average

(c)   more than half of these people earn below the average

(d)   the total weekly earnings of the 20 people is equal to £4000

It may perhaps surprise you to learn that the answer, for all the statements in Activity 17, is 'sometimes true'.

The major bar to giving a more precise answer to the question is the term average. If we knew which method is being used to arrive at the average of £200, we would be able to answer differently.

Do not worry if you did not do to well with this Activity. It was deliberately worded so as to stress some of the ambiguities in this area. We will return to it later in this section.

If we wish to calculate the average for any set of data, how would we do it?

There are several possibilities; the most popular methods are known as the **arithmetic mean**, the **median** and the **mode**. We will deal with these in turn.

3. THE ARITHMETIC MEAN

When most people speak of the average they are referring to one particular kind of average properly called **the arithmetic mean**. It is a familiar concept.

For example, suppose that by week, a car dealer sold 5, 10, 12, 7 and 3 Rolls-Royces in his first 5 weeks of trading. The arithmetic mean of the number sold would be

$$\frac{5 + 10 + 12 + 7 + 3}{5} = \frac{37}{5} = 7.4$$

The arithmetic mean is the sum of all the values in a collection of observations divided by the number of observations.

Where there is no danger of ambiguity we can drop the term arithmetic and just refer to the measure as the mean.

You should have no trouble with calculating the mean, for the method is widely known.

Expressed mathematically it is computed by the following formula

Formula 1

The Arithmetic Mean

$$\mu = \frac{X_1 + X_2 + X_3 + \ldots + X_N}{N}$$

Where X_1 X_2 X_3 etc, are observations of X.

This can be abbreviated to

$$\mu = \frac{1}{N} \Sigma X$$

If you have not used mathematical notation before, then the Σ symbol in formula 1 is the Greek capital letter sigma, and is used as an abbreviation for add. The letter X is just used as a symbol to identify the variable being averaged (it might be a series of wages, package weights, people's ages or number of Rolls-Royces sold). The Greek symbol μ (pronounced mu), is generally used as an abbreviation for the mean.

Formula 1 is mathematical 'shorthand' for:

> add all the observations (values of X) together, and then divide by the
> number of observations (denoted by the letter N)

Note.

When we wish to make a distinction between the mean of the **whole population** and the mean of just **a sample** of values, we use different symbols. The Greek letter μ is normally used when we refer to the mean of the whole population.

The symbol $\overline{X}$ (pronounced 'X bar') is used when we talk about the mean of a sample.

In the interests of simplicity, we will not make this distinction in this unit but you should be aware of it. We shall return to the difference between sample and population means when we discuss the practice of sampling in a later unit.

ACTIVITY 18

The following figures are the number of Japanese cars imported into the USA for each of the 12 months of 1988:

145	135	100	220	170	145	190	155	210
200	205	180						

(All figures are in 000s)

Calculate the mean number of cars imported per month into the USA from Japan.

Activity 18 should have been answered as follows.

$$\mu = \frac{1}{N}\Sigma X = \textit{(using formula 1)}$$

$$\frac{(145+135+100+220+170+145+190+155+210+200+205+180)}{12}$$

$$= \frac{2055}{12} = 171.25$$

The data is in 000 units, which means an average of 171,250 Japanese cars were imported into the USA each month in 1988.

Let's take this a step further.

Formula 1 is the appropriate method for dealing with raw, ie ungrouped, data.

What if the data is in the form of a **frequency distribution**? How is the mean calculated in such a case?

4. THE MEAN OF A GROUPED FREQUENCY DISTRIBUTION

For a frequency distribution, the method for calculating the mean is summarised below in formula 2.

Formula 2

Arithmetic Mean of a Distribution

$$m = \frac{f_1 X_1 + f_2 X_2 + f_3 X_3 + \ldots + f_N X_N}{N}$$

Where X_1 X_2 X_3 *etc, are observations of X*
and f_1, f_2, f_3, *etc*
are the frequencies with which the values of X occur

This can be abbreviated to

$$\mu = \frac{1}{N} \Sigma fX$$

Please note that for a frequency distribution, N, the total number of data values = Σf.

You should take special notice that for distributions, the observations are often counted into **intervals** rather than as specific observations. If this is the case then, the X_i values in the above formula will be chosen as the mid points of the respective class intervals.

You will understand the use of formula 2 rather better if you can see an example of it in use. Look at the following example.

Example

A publishing company is examining the performance of a typesetting firm. A sample of 100 pages produced by the typesetters shows the following distribution of mistakes:

NUMBER OF ERRORS PER PAGE	NUMBER OF PAGES
0	42
1	33
2	12
3	6
4	3
5	2
6	1
7	0
8	1

For example, 42 pages had no mistakes, 33 pages contained just one mistake, etc.

We shall now calculate μ, the mean number of errors on a page.

In this case, the variable is the number of errors per page. We will symbolise this variable by the letter X. Each value of X (number of errors) may occur more than once, so we need to know the **total number of errors**, and then divide this by the number of pages. Notice that although this is a frequency distribution, the data has been counted into specific values rather than class intervals.

So the total number of errors = ΣfX =

$(0\times42) + (1\times33) + (2\times12) + (3\times6) + (4\times3) + (5\times2) + (6\times1) + (7\times0) + (8\times1)=111$

Notice that to calculate this quantity we have used formula 2, where X represents the number of errors on a page (0, 1, 2, etc), and f represents the number of pages containing those numbers of errors.

So $\Sigma fX = 111$.

Also, N (the total number of pages) = $\Sigma f = 100$

Therefore μ (the mean errors per page) = $111/100 = 1.11$

On average, a page produced by this particular typesetting firm contains 1.11 errors. The next Activity will give you a chance to try out your understanding of this method.

ACTIVITY 19

Using formula 2, calculate the mean weight of the packages from the distribution first shown in figure 6 in section 2.

The distribution of package weights is repeated below for your convenience.

TAKE CARE! These data have been grouped into class intervals, so use formula 2 carefully.

WEIGHT (in kg)	FREQUENCY Number
7.1 < 7.3	1
7.3 < 7.5	5
7.5 < 7.7	10
7.7 < 7.9	19
7.9 < 8.1	27
8.1 < 8.3	22
8.3 < 8.5	6
8.5 < 8.7	3
8.7 < 8.9	2

The package weight data have been grouped into class intervals, so the 'x' value we use in the expression 'ΣfX' will be the mid point of the class. For example, for calculation purposes we assume that all the ten packages in the class 7.5 < 7.7 weigh 7.6 kg.

The working for the mean is shown below.

WEIGHT	NO. OF PACKS (f)	MID POINT OF CLASS (x)	fx
7.1 < 7.3	1	7.2	7.2
7.3 < 7.5	5	7.4	37.0
7.5 < 7.7	10	7.6	76.0
7.7 < 7.9	19	7.8	148.2
7.9 < 8.1	27	8.0	216.0
8.1 < 8.3	22	8.2	180.4
8.3 < 8.5	6	8.4	50.4
8.5 < 8.7	3	8.6	25.8
8.7 < 8.9	2	8.8	17.6
N = Σf = 95			758.6

Using formula 2 you should obtain

$$\mu = (\Sigma fx)/N = 758.6/95 = 7.99 \text{ (to two dp)}$$

Therefore the mean pack weight is 7.99 kg.

Statistical computer programs make tasks such as the above a relatively simple operation. You will find also that software packages such as LOTUS 1-2-3 have facilities for computing the mean. Additionally, if you have a scientific pocket calculator you will find that it will compute some statistical functions, such as the mean. Many calculator models can deal with calculations for frequency distributions. Since there is a great deal of variation between different models of calculator, no general rules can be given. You should try to discover the statistical capabilities of your pocket calculator by referring to the manual which came with it.

5. THE MEDIAN

Although the arithmetic mean is thought by most people to be synonymous with the term average, there are other measures which can be used. One of these is the **median**, defined as follows:

For an odd number of data items, the median is the value of the middle data item, when all items are ranked in ascending order.

If there is an even number of data items, the median is the average of the two middle items.

Whenever the median is used 50% of all our data have values **greater** than the median and 50% have values **smaller** than the median.

The median is very easy to calculate, since all that is required is that you arrange the data in rank order.

Activity 20 illustrates this.

ACTIVITY 20

Over a 7 day period, the number of customers (per day) purchasing at James Leather Goods Shop was as follows

4   100   5   10   51   12   50

Over an 8 day period, the following numbers of purchasing customers were observed at Lees Woollens Shop

21   5   11   7   12   15   20   5

Arrange the two sets of data in ascending rank order and find the median of each data set.

As stressed before, the key to the process of calculating the median lies in the ranking process.

In Activity 20, the James Leather Goods data are rank ordered as follows:

4   5   10   12   50   51   100

↑

**the middle
value**

In the above case there is an odd number (7) of data values and the middle value is clearly the fourth. The fourth data value is 12, so the median is 12.

With the Lees Woollens data, the same procedure is followed, with the results as:

5   5   7   11   12   15   20   21

↑

**the middle
value**

Here we have an even number (8) of data values, so we must take the average of the middle two

$$\text{Median} = (11 + 12)/2 = 11.5$$

Remember to **rank** the data before you select the middle value.

Therefore, assuming that the sample of days used is representative, we have calculated that the average number of purchasing customers coming into the two shops is 12 and 11.5 respectively.

So we now have two ways to calculate an average; the mean and median.

6. CALCULATING THE MEDIAN FOR GROUPED DATA

If there is a great deal of data, the process of ranking may become onerous. In such cases it is often easier to group the data into a cumulative frequency distribution first and then use the ogive to make an estimate of the median.

Look back at figure 6, which contains a distribution of the weights of packages passing through a check-point. Figure 18 below shows the ogive for these data, drawn as a smooth curve. (Remember that the ogive is a graph of cumulative number.)

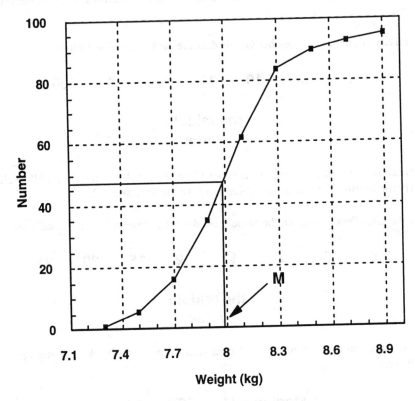

FIGURE 18: **Cumulative Distribution of Package Weights**

How can we use this graph to estimate the median?

Recall that by definition, the median is the middle value of a ranked series. It is the number which divides the data into equal halves. In the package weight example, there are 95 packages. Whatever value the median takes, it must be the case that half of these packages ($95/2 = 47.5$) will weigh more, and half will weigh less than the median.

On the ogive for the data, we look along the vertical, or cumulative scale, until we locate the number 47.5. We then read the corresponding x co-ordinate from the curve. This has been done in figure 18. The required co-ordinate has been marked with the letter M.

You can read from the x scale that this value is approximately 8.

Thus we estimate that the median package weight is 8 kg.

Now you can try this technique in the next Activity.

ACTIVITY 21

Look back at the data of figure 7 in section 2. It consists of the distribution of office personnel by the amount of time spent on the computer.

(a)   On a separate sheet of paper graph the ogive for these data. (Remember to use a smooth curve rather than a bar chart.)

(b)   Use this ogive to estimate the median amount of time spent on the computer.

Figure 19 below shows the ogive for the data of Activity 21.

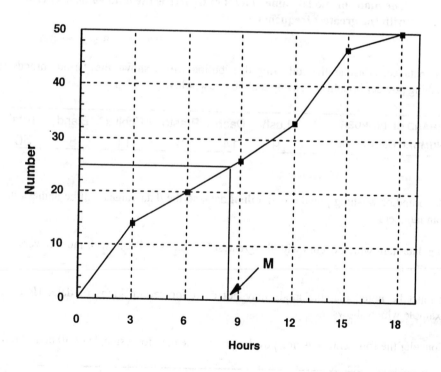

FIGURE 19: **Cumulative Distribution of Computer Use Time**

In this case there are 50 office workers. Thus half of these workers, 50/2 = 25 will spend less than the median time on the computer, and the other half will spend more.

Locate the number 25 on the cumulative vertical scale of the ogive, and check the corresponding x co-ordinate. This has been marked with the letter M on the graph. Very approximately this is 8.1.

Therefore the median time spent on the computer by these staff is 8.1 hours.

Do not worry if your answer does not happen to coincide exactly with the above. Like all estimates based on graphs, we must allow ourselves a little margin of error.

7. THE MODE

There is third measure of central tendency called the mode. It can be defined as

The mode or modal value of a set of figures is the data value occurring with the greatest frequency.

For instance, consider the following distribution which shows the various brands of washing powder bought by a sample of 50 households:

BRAND OF POWDER	Lush	Dash	Presto	Ecolux	Bland	Total
NUMBER OF BUYERS	9	14	8	11	8	50

The brand of washing powder is **nominal** data, so the data values will be names rather than numbers.

The data item which occurs with the greatest frequency is Dash, with more buyers than any others.

It must be noted that the mode may not exist for certain kinds of data. Here's an example which shows this.

Consider the following washing powder preference data for a sample of 50 households

BRAND OF POWDER	Lush	Dash	Presto	Ecolux	Bland	Total
NUMBER OF BUYERS	10	10	10	10	10	50

In this case, each washing powder is bought by exactly ten customers so there is no single modal value.

It is also quite possible that there may be exactly two values of equal (highest) frequency, in which case we would have two possible choices for a mode. Such distributions are called **bimodal** distributions. Remember these from section 2?

In cases where a bimodal or multi-modal distribution is thought to exist the mode is not normally used as a means of measuring the average.

ACTIVITY 22

Business writers report that because of the increasing use of fax machines and home computers, many trained people are working from a home office. The following data give the ages of a sample of 20 people working from home.

22	58	24	50	29	52	57	31	30	49
41	44	40	46	29	31	37	32	44	29

(a)   calculate the mean and modal ages of the group

(b)   suppose that the population of ALL adult workers from which this sample is drawn has a median age of 40.5. Calculate the median age for the sample of 20 home workers, and comment upon whether the at-home group is younger than the population generally.

To tackle this activity we first consider the mean age of these 20 home workers.

The arithmetic mean is given by

$$\mu = \frac{1}{N}\Sigma X$$

now N = 20 (the number of home workers) and $\Sigma X = 775$ the sum of all workers ages.

So

$$\mu = \frac{1}{20} \times 775$$

$$= 38.75$$

As for the mode, the value 29 occurs more often than any other value, so the modal age of this sample of home workers is 29.

For the median age of home workers, we rank order the data as follows:

22 24 29 29 29 30 31 31 32 37 40 41 44 44 46 49 50 52 57 58

We have an even number, 20 in the sample, so the median is the average of the two middle values, these being the 10th and the 11th. Since the 10th and 11th data values are 37 and 40 respectively, then

Median = (37 + 40)/2 = 38.5

Therefore 50% of ALL adult workers are below the age of 40.5, while 50% of our sample are below 38.5. On this basis, the home-based workers are marginally younger, assuming, of course, that our sample can be regarded as representative.

You should note that for these data the mode is very much lower than either the mean or the median. Can you think why?

Section 4 deals with the problem of differences in the three averages so we will discuss this later.

Finally, this is a good time to look back at Activity 17. Can you answer this Activity any better now?

If the average referred to in Activity 17 is the median, then statement (a) is always correct, and statements (b) and (c) always false. The median is, by definition, the middle value of a ranked group of numbers. It **must** be true that half of the people earn less than the average (median) salary and half earn more.

If the average being used is the arithmetic mean then statements (a), (b) and (c) may, or may not be true. This is also dealt with in more detail in the section 4.

Statement (d) is true so long as the average being used is the mean. It **must** be the case that the total wage bill for the 20 is equal to £4,000 **if** the mean wage is £200, as it is a consequence of how the mean is calculated. On the other hand, we have no way of knowing what the total wage bill is, if the only information we have is the median wage.

8. SUMMARY

In section 3 we have

- discussed the role of **summary statistics** in general

- defined what is meant by a **measure of central tendency**

- defined and calculated the **arithmetic mean**

- calculated the **median** by rank-ordering of data

- seen how to **estimate** the mode

If you are unsure of any of these topics, or the calculations, then check back **now** to the appropriate sections now before you read on.

SECTION 4

UNDERSTANDING AVERAGES

The discussion of averages in section 3 has shown that the idea of an average is not a simple one. We have seen that there are several different numbers we could choose, each having a right to be called the average. Even more confusingly, although the mean median and mode are supposed to measure the same thing, they do not often give identical results. How then, do we know which measure of central tendency to use in any given circumstance? Although in the end this will be a matter of judgement and experience, there are various factors which you could consider.

1. WITH WHAT KIND OF VARIABLE ARE WE DEALING?

It may be technically possible to calculate means, medians or modes for all kinds of data but this does not mean that the results will always be sensible.

It is very important to consider the nature of the variable we are analysing. Is it nominal, ordinal etc? Does it, for example, make sense to use the mean for **all** kinds of data regardless of type of variable?

Activity 23 will illustrate this problem. Work through it very carefully.

ACTIVITY 23

In a survey of detergent brand loyalty in the UK, consumers were asked the following question:

'Which brand of automatic washing powder do you **normally** use?

Tick one of the following:

LUSH   DASH   PRESTO   BLAND   OTHER'

In the computer analysis following this survey, the following coding was used for each brand name

0 = LUSH   1 = DASH   2 = PRESTO   3 = BLAND   4 = OTHER

300 households responded to the survey as follows:

Activity 23 continued...

BRAND	NUMBER BUYING
0	100
1	120
2	50
3	15
4	15

Using this coded data

(a)   calculate the mean, median and mode for the variable 'BRAND'

(b)   say what type of measuring scale is being used to measure choice of brand of detergent.

(c)   state which, if any, of the measures of central tendency you have calculated make any sense in this case.

Firstly, we will consider the calculation of the averages required by Activity 23. Secondly, we will decide whether they give us useful information.

To calculate the median we first rank the data.

Remember that the coded brand purchase data is represented in the form of a frequency distribution so that there are 300 values to rank.

$$0\ 0\ 0 \dots 1\ 1\ 1 \dots 2\ 2\ 2 \dots 3\ 3\ 3 \dots 4\ 4\ 4$$

↑	↑	↑	↑	↑
100	**120**	**50**	**15**	**15**
zeros	**ones**	**twos**	**threes**	**fours**

There are an even number (300) of values to be ranked so the two middle values are the 150th and the 151st. Both of these have values of 1. So the median is 1.

The modal value is 1, since this occurred 120 times – more than any other value.

The data is in the form of a frequency distribution, so to calculate the mean, we use formula 2.

We therefore have

$$\mu = (\Sigma fX)/N$$
$$= \{(0 \times 100) + (1 \times 120) + (2 \times 50) + (3 \times 15) + (4 \times 15)\}/300$$
$$= (0 + 120 + 100 + 45 + 60)/300$$
$$\approx 1.08$$

So to summarise

Mean	= 1.08
Median	= 1
Mode	= 1

Remember that the numbers we have calculated are coded values of a nominal variable, and we must bear this point in mind when we decide the problem of whether it is sensible to use these averages for this data. Since detergent brand choice is a nominal variable, it makes no sense to make statements such as

'the mean brand of washing powder is 1.08', or

'the median brand of washing powder is 1'.

Nominal, non-quantitative variables variables are not suitable for sophisticated numerical analysis.

The numerical values assigned to the various brands are codes given purely to make counting and analysis easier for computers.

You therefore cannot validly carry out any arithmetic operations on this data, apart from simple counting.

It **would**, however, make sense to say that the modal brand is 1, (ie 'DAZ'), because the mode **only** involves counting; no arithmetic manipulation is used. The mode is the only measure of central tendency which can be used with nominal data.

Important note

The lesson to be learned from this exercise, is that you **may** be able to go through the **process** of calculating means and medians for any data, but it does not follow that the results will always have a sensible interpretation.

Statistical theory supplies the **methods** for the calculation of descriptive measures; **it is you** who must supply the intelligence to ensure that they are correctly used and interpreted.

The key conclusion which you should draw from Activity 23, is that it does not make sense to compute the mean or median for data measured on nominal scales. The only kind of average you can use with such data is the mode. On ordinal data, you may use either median or mode, although it would be fair to say that there is much argument in the scientific community about the amount of quantitative analysis which may validly be used on ordinal data. With interval and ratio-scale data you can sensibly use either the mean, median or mode.

2. HOW 'REPRESENTATIVE' IS THE MEASURE OF CENTRAL TENDENCY?

The next factor affecting interpretation of the average is not an easy concept to explain. You may remember that an average is supposed to be typical or representative of the data from which it came. Each time you allow a single statistic, such as a mean, to represent a large measure of data items, you lose accuracy and detail.

Activity 24 will illustrate this important point.

ACTIVITY 24

(a)   Calculate the mean weekly income for each of the following two groups of earners:

    i. £100 £120 £122 £130
    ii. £100 £150 £150 £850

(b)   How confident would you be in quoting the arithmetic means calculated in (a) as representative of the earnings of the two groups?

(c)   Calculate the median for the two sets of data in (a).

(d)   How confident are you that the median is representative of the earnings of each group?

Firstly we calculate the mean for both data sets in Activity 24. For data set (i) it is as follows:

$$\mu = \frac{1}{N}\Sigma X = \frac{100 + 120 + 122 + 130}{4} = 118.00$$

And for data set (ii) it is:

$$\mu = \frac{1}{N}\Sigma X = \frac{100 + 150 + 150 + 850}{4} = 312.50$$

The salary data for each group is already in rank order.

The median for the first set of data is £121 (average of the second and third data values; £120 and £122 respectively). The median for the second set of data is £150 (being the average of the second and third data values £150 and £150).

Now what can we say about how representative these averages are? We can consider the means first. £118 seems to be reasonably representative of the first set of data. If you were one of the four earners involved, you would have no difficulty in believing that £118 was a typical earnings figure. However, £312.50 does not seem very representative of the second set of data. None of the four people in the group earn amounts even remotely like this. One person earns a great deal more than the mean, and the other three earn a great deal less.

The point to be made here is that a measure of central tendency (such as the mean) may not, in some cases, be very representative of the data. Never use a statistic (like μ) without knowing something of the data from which it is calculated. In the case of the second set of data, the presence of the very large £850 wage has meant that the mean becomes almost useless as a guide to what these four people are typically earning.

The median is a much more representative earnings figure than the mean for the second set of data.

Remember we asked you why the mean of the second group was so radically different from the mean of the first?

The second group of data had an extreme value of £850 in it. Because of the way in which the mean is calculated unusual extreme values tend to shift it away from the generality of data.

For instance, the mean of the first data set is £118, and this seems quite representative of the set.

However, the mean of the second data set is £312.50 and this is nowhere near any of the wages in the set. The £850 wage has had this affect. Notice however, that the medians for the two sets of figures are £121 and £150 respectively.

The £850 has had little affect on the median. Even if this wage were £10,000 rather than £850, the median would still be £150.

ACTIVITY 25

Now try out for yourself these properties of the mean and median. Write out TWO different series of numbers which have the same median but different means.

There is, of course, a large range of possible answers to Activity 25.
The following is my answer for this activity. The two sets of data following have the same median (100), but different means – (100 and 225 respectively).

i.   99   100   101
ii.   1   99   101   699

The conclusion which we can draw from these considerations is that we should be careful when using and interpreting means, medians and modes. People expect (quite reasonably), that if you make a statement such as

'the average wage is £170 per week'

then you are implicitly stating that £170 is a wage typical of what most people are earning.

Are we really justified in such a belief?

Should we, therefore, ever choose a measure of central tendency which is affected by extreme values? The answer lies in the use we may wish to make of the measure.

ACTIVITY 26

(a)   You are told that a business employs 200 workers at a mean weekly wage of £170. Can you say what the firm's weekly wage bill is?

(b)   If you knew that the median weekly wage of these 200 workers was £160, could you say what the weekly wage bill is?

Activity 26 illustrates an important quality of the mean which the median does not have.

We know that the mean is calculated by taking the sum of the values divided by the number of values:

$$\frac{1}{N}\Sigma X$$

It follows therefore, that if we know the mean and the number of values, we can calculate the sum by using the following expression

$$\Sigma X = N\mu$$

If the mean wage of 200 people is £170, it must follow that the total weekly wage bill is $200 \times £170 = £34,000$.

It is not possible to do this for the median. The median is not calculated by taking the sum, so we cannot say what the total wage bill is.

The mean holds more information about the data set than does the median. The mean might be more useful to a business than the median, because of the characteristic demonstrated in this Activity.

So we have seen one reason why the mean might be preferred over the median, even though it is more prone to be affected by extreme values. We will mention another reason later.

Before we move on to discuss the next factor affecting selection of a measure of central tendency, you should note that the mode is unaffected by extreme values. The mode is very uncomplicated and unlikely to be misinterpreted. However, it should again be pointed out that for same data, we may not be able to use the mode, either because it does not exist, or because there may be more than one (multi-modal distributions).

3. HOW ARE THE DATA DISTRIBUTED?

The form (or shape) of the distribution of our data could strongly affect the magnitude of the different measures of central tendency. Is the data distributed symmetrically or asymmetrically?

It is always important to know something of the underlying 'shape' of our data before we use a particular measure of centrality.

ACTIVITY 27

(a)   Earlier in the unit you encountered a bar chart of the size of nightly audiences at a theatre, (figure 12 section 2). Without making any calculations, try to 'guesstimate' the mean, median and mode of audience size. Do you think there would be much difference between these statistics? Think of reasons for your answer.

(b)   Now do the same for the data in figure 15 section 2. This graph shows a bar chart for a sample of people distributed by income. (You may find the process of making good guesses in this case more difficult than for the audience data, but do your best.)

When using a frequency graph to make estimates, you will find that if the distribution is symmetrical, as is the case with the audience size data, the process is greatly simplified. The mode is easiest to determine. It will be at the point of the highest bar (670). The median height will have 50% of audience sizes below and 50% above. Because of the symmetry of the distribution, it is fairly easy to see that (approximately) half of the distribution is above, and the other half below the centre bar (670). The mean is the more difficult value to estimate from a bar graph, but if you think of it as being the 'centre of gravity' of a distribution, then this will give you a clue. In the case of the median, there will always be half of all data above, and half below this statistic. However, with the mean, the situation is different. There will be half of ΣX above, and half of ΣX below μ. From the symmetry of the bar chart, it can be seen that the centre of gravity is at the point 670.

It seems that with a symmetrical distribution, there is little (or no) difference between mean median and mode. Even if you found it difficult to 'guesstimate' the approximate value of the statistics, you should make a point of remembering this fact.

With the income distribution the situation is different. As always, the mode is the tallest bar (£8000). By definition, half of all people would earn less than the median income. This would seem to be about £9000. The 'centre of gravity' of the distribution is shifted to the right, so that the mean should be between £9000 and £10000.

(Calculations made from the original income data reveals that it is, in fact, £9,700.)

To summarise, for a symmetrical distribution the three measures of central tendency give similar results. However, it appears that with a skew distribution, we cannot expect mean, median and mode to be the same. In fact, if the distribution is +skew then the mean will be greater than the median which will be greater than the mode. If the distribution is -skew, then this order is reversed. If at all possible, it is a good idea to have some knowledge of the underlying distribution before you use a measure of central tendency.

4. A Quick Estimate or a Thorough One?

Some measures of centrality are quicker to calculate than others. This may seem a trivial consideration, but it is a practical one. For instance, in certain kinds of quality control in industry samples are taken at frequent intervals by unskilled staff.

Emphasis here is placed on the swift analysis of data, and in such situations, the user of the statistics might be perfectly prepared to use the mode which is easier to calculate than the mean.

5. Do we Plan to Carry Out Further Analysis?

If we plan to carry out further statistical analysis, (over and above the calculation of an average), then the mean is the correct choice. The exact nature of this further statistical analysis is made clearer in one of the later study units dealing with sampling. The median and mode have little further application beyond their use as descriptive statistics.

To conclude our thoughts concerning choice of a measure of central tendency you should be aware that

> we may not be able to satisfy all of the desirable criteria for selection simultaneously; we may have to make compromises;

> the rules for selecting an appropriate measure of centrality are rules of thumb only. There will always be cases where we use a measure which gives unexpectedly misleading results.

Here is another example for you to try.

ACTIVITY 28

The following shows the advertising expenditure of a car dealer. Each figure represents daily expenditure in £s for 20 days trading.

38	60	20	130	55	150	47	35	86	95
31	46	112	130	55	42	130	35	60	130

Calculate the mean, median and mode of daily expenditure.
Which measure of centrality do you think is most appropriate in this case? Why?

The data of Activity 28 are ranked below.

20 31 35 35 38 42 46 47 55 55 60 60 86 95 112 130 130 130 130 150.

*Since **N** = 20 **and** ΣX = 1487, we have*

$$\mu = \frac{1}{20} \times 1487 = 74.35$$

Median = £57.50
(average of the 10th and 11th data values, 55 and 60).

Mode = £130.00

If we use the mode, then we would be claiming that the average expenditure is £130, although 15 out of the 20 observations are actually less than this. It does not seem that the mode is at all useful in this case. The mean is a little distorted by the presence of the small, but influential number of values above £100.

If you wanted to quote a typical day's expenditure, the median would probably be the most appropriate measure. However, remember that knowledge of the mean daily expenditure would allow us to calculate **total expenditure** over the 20 days trading. This you cannot do this with the median.

ACTIVITY 29

The following table shows the leading Third World debtor nations (1988):

COUNTRY	DEBT $ billions
Brazil	107.8
Mexico	102.0
Argentina	53.0
Indonesia	43.9
Venezuela	34.1
Philippines	28.1
Nigeria	22.1
Chile	21.2
Peru	14.7
Colombia	14.7
Ecuador	9.1

World Almanac and Book of Facts 1988.

(a)   Calculate the mean and median of the debt for these 11 countries.

(b)   Omit Brazil's debt and recalculate the mean and median of the remaining ten countries. Which value, the mean or median, is most affected by the omission of Brazil's debt?

The calculations of the mean and median for the data of Activity 29 are as follows

Since **N = 11 and ΣX = 450.7 (billions) then**

$$\mu = \frac{1}{11} \times 450.7 \approx 41$$

Median = $28.1

If these calculations are repeated without Brazil

*Now **N = 10 and ΣX = 342.9 (billions)** so*

$$\mu = \frac{1}{10} \times 342.9 \approx 34.3$$

Median = $25.1

The mean has been the most affected. This is because of the way the it is calculated. Brazil represents $107.80 extra to ΣX; the sheer size of this figure affects the mean.

However, for the purpose of estimating the median, Brazil is merely just one other country among 11. It is immaterial whether Brazil's debt is $1 billion, $10 billion or $1000 billion; the median will not be affected.

---

6. SUMMARY

In this section we have

- further practiced the calculation of mean, median and mode

- investigated the **affect of type of variable** (nominal, ordinal, interval and ratio-scale) on the choice of an average

- considered the need to make the average **representative of the data** from which it is calculated

- seen how the **shape of the distribution** of the data affects the various averages

Check back over this section **now** if you are unsure of any of the topics covered before you continue.

SECTION 5
MEASURES OF DISPERSION OR VARIATION

1. WHY MEASURE VARIABILITY?

The following Activity is a preparation for the material contained in this section.

ACTIVITY 30

Two companies, company A and company B make industrial cable. A buyer in another business wishes to buy cable from one of these companies and quite naturally, would like to buy from the one making the better product. The products quality is measured by the tensile strength, or breaking strain of the cable. The buyer decides to take a sample of 10 pieces of cable from the production line of each of company A and B, and test them to breaking point. The following are the resulting breaking strengths of each piece of cable (in kg per cm^2).

COMPANY A 9 16 14 10 13 17 9 12 11 9
COMPANY B 10 11 13 12 11 14 13 12 11 13

(a)   Calculate the mean strength of each company's product.

(b)   Is there a difference between the quality of each product as indicated by the mean breaking strength? If there is no difference between the means for the two companies, does this necessarily mean they make products of equal worth?

Think of a reason for your answer.

The following table summarises the calculations for Activity 30

	COMPANY A	COMPANY B
ΣX	120	120
N	10	10
μ	12	12

The fact that the **mean** breaking strengths are the same, might lead us into the belief that the products are of equal quality.

However, notice that the 10 samples of A's cable show more variability than do B's. Surely this variability of performance is an important aspect of quality? The buyer would certainly want a product with high **average** quality, but they would also want a product which performs **consistently**.

A measure of central tendency, such as the mean, is insufficient by itself to summarise data. We can easily get an incorrect impression of our data if we rely on one statistic alone.

Another example will further illustrate the point.

A group of 53 applicants for managerial training take two tests; one in verbal skills and one in numeracy. The following distributions show attainment (on a scale 0 - 100) in the two tests.

TEST SCORE	NO. OF PEOPLE (Verbal Skills)	NO. OF PEOPLE (Numeracy)
20 and under 30	0	2
30 and under 40	3	5
40 and under 50	4	8
50 and under 60	20	12
60 and under 70	18	11
70 and under 80	5	8
80 and under 90	2	5
90 and under 100	1	2
NUMBER TESTED	53	53

Figures 20 and 21 below, show the distribution of test scores in histogram form. In each skill, the mean score obtained is approximately 60%. Check these figures if you need practice in calculating means. (You will need to use formula 2.)

Does the equality of average scores in verbal and numerical skills imply that these 53 managerial trainees show equal ability in these areas?

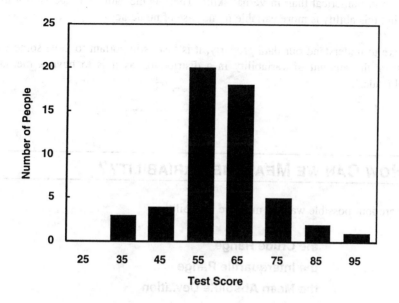

FIGURE 20: **Distribution of Test Scores in Verbal Ability**

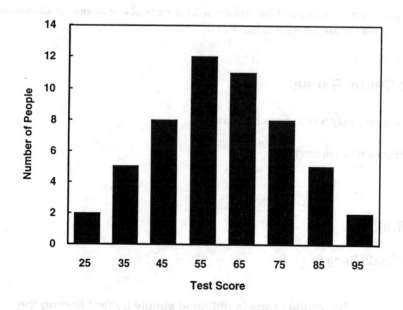

FIGURE 21: **Distribution of Test Scores in Numerical Ability**

It most certainly **does not**. Look at the two bar charts and you will see a greater 'spread' of scores in numerical than in verbal skills. There is the same average ability in both areas, but this ability is more variable in the case of numeracy.

If we are to understand our data properly, it is just as important to have some way of measuring the amount of variability in a distribution as it is to have a measure of central tendency.

2. HOW CAN WE MEASURE VARIABILITY?

There are four possible ways to measure variability:

the Crude Range

the Interquartile Range

the Mean Absolute Deviation

the Variance

Two other statistics commonly met with in the measurement of variability are the standard deviation and the coefficient of variation, which we shall deal with later in this section.

It is important to stress that the selection of a particular measure of dispersion will depend upon the use we wish to make of it.

THE CRUDE RANGE

This is a very easy way to measure variability.

We begin with its definition.

Definition

The Crude Range

The crude range is obtained simply by first finding the maximum and minimum values in the data set.

Crude range = maximum - minimum

The greater the crude range, then we may say (with care), that the more variable will be the data.

Activity 31, below reveals serious problems in the ability of the crude range to measure variability.

ACTIVITY 31

Consider the cable strength data from Activity 30.

(a)   State the crude range of breaking strengths for the cables of each company and say which company produces the most variable product.

(b)   A third cable producing company is also sampled, and the breaking strengths of the 10 cables tested is as follows:

   2 12 12 12 12 12 12 12 12 22

   Calculate the crude range for this company's product and compare it with companies A and B. Comment on the use of the crude range for measuring variability, in the light of this third set of data.

The following table summarises the results for companies A and B.

Company B's product has a smaller crude range so we would (tentatively) argue that it produces the less variable (more consistent) product.

	COMPANY A	COMPANY B
MAXIMUM	9	10
MINIMUM	17	14
CRUDE RANGE	17 - 9 = 8	14 - 10 = 4

However, the crude range for company C is 22-2 = 20. This would be a worse result than either company A or B. However, the large crude range is totally due to the extreme values, or **outliers**; the cables which have breaking strengths of 2 and 22 respectively. Apart from these, all other cables have unvarying breaking strengths. The crude range may be measuring the distance between two freak values. Therefore the measure needs care in its use and interpretation.

THE INTERQUARTILE RANGE

We have seen that the problem with the crude range is that it may be measuring the difference between two highly untypical extreme values. It would be like saying that the difference between the heights of the circus midget and giant is illustrative of the general range of heights.

The **interquartile range** is an attempt to use a measure of variability which does not suffer from this defect.

First, we must define the lower and upper quartiles.

Definition

The Quartiles

> The Lower Quartile is a value, (denoted by Q_1) such that 25% of data values are below Q_1 and 75% of data values are greater than Q_1.
>
> The Upper Quartile denoted by Q_3 is a value such that 75% of data values are below Q_3 and 25% of data values are above Q_3.
>
> The lower and upper quartiles are sometimes referred to as the first and third quartiles respectively.

To find Q_1 and Q_3

> rewrite the data in ascending order,
> calculate N/4 and 3N/4

(where N is the number of values in the data set)

> if N/4 and 3N/4 are not whole numbers, then round up. Q_1 and Q_3 occupy the positions denoted by these numbers
>
> if N/4 and 3N/4 are whole numbers, then Q_1 and Q_3 are found by taking the midpoint of the data values in this position and the one above.

The process is illustrated with the following data showing the monthly take-home salaries of 12 accountants.

EMPLOYEE NUMBER	SALARY (£)	EMPLOYEE NUMBER	SALARY (£)
1	1650	7	1690
2	1750	8	1930
3	1850	9	1740
4	1680	10	2125
5	1555	11	1720
6	1510	12	1680

MONTHLY SALARIES OF 12 ACCOUNTANTS

Firstly, rank the data in ascending order.

1510 1555 1650 1680 1680 1690
1720 1740 1750 1850 1930 2125

Secondly, calculate N/4 and 3N/4. (N = 12 in this case)

$$N/4 = 12/4 = 3 \quad \text{and} \quad 3N/4 = 3 \times 12/4 = 9$$

These are whole numbers, so Q_1 will be the midpoint between the third and fourth data values, and Q_3 will be midway between the ninth and tenth data values.

1510 1555 <u>1650 1680</u> 1680 1690
1720 1740 <u>1750 1850</u> 1930 2125

As shown above, the third and fourth data values are 1650 and 1680, and since the midpoint between these values is 1665, then we take this to be the lower quartile. By a similar argument, the upper quartile is the average of the ninth and tenth data values. The midpoint between 1750 and 1850 is 1800.

Thus: $Q_1 = 1665$ and $Q_3 = 1800$

So if these 12 salaries are representative, 25% of accountants earn £1800 or more per month, while 25% earn less than £1665 per month. By implication, 50% earn between £1665 and £1800.

Quite apart from their use in measuring variability, the quartiles are useful statistics, because they show how a distribution is divided up.

We are now ready to define the interquartile range.

Definition

The Interquartile Range

The interquartile range is the difference between the upper and lower quartiles.

$$Q_3 - Q_1$$

This gives the range for the middle 50% of data.

The interquartile range is an improvement on the crude range, since we are excluding the top and bottom quarters of the data, which might contain unrepresentative extreme values. We are looking only at the range of the middle 50%.

For the accountant's salary data, the interquartile range would be

$$Q_3 - Q_1 = 1800 - 1665 = 135$$

Now we return to the cable strength problem.

ACTIVITY 32

(a) Now calculate the quartiles for the cable strength data in Activity 30, and hence find the interquartile range for each company.

Which company makes the most variable cable, as shown by the interquartile range?

(b) In our calculations, we have mentioned the first and third quartiles. The second quartile, Q_2 is better known by another name. What is it?

In order to calculate the interquartile range for this data we firstly rank the data. The positions of the quartiles are pointed out for each set of data.

Company A

$$9\ 9\ 9\ 10\ 11\ 12\ 13\ 14\ 16\ 17$$
$$\uparrow \qquad\qquad\qquad\qquad \uparrow$$
$$Q_1 \qquad\qquad\qquad\qquad Q_3$$

Company B

$$10\ 11\ 11\ 11\ 12\ 12\ 13\ 13\ 13\ 14$$
$$\uparrow \qquad\qquad\qquad\qquad \uparrow$$
$$Q_1 \qquad\qquad\qquad\qquad Q_3$$

N = 10 in both cases, so that

$$\textbf{N/4 = 10/4 = 2.5 and 3N/4 = (3} \times \textbf{10)/4 = 7.5}$$

As these are not whole numbers, we round up, to 3 and 8 respectively.

Therefore the third data value will be Q_1, and the eighth data value will be Q_3.

The results are summarised below.

	COMPANY A	COMPANY B
Q_1	9	11
Q_3	14	13
Q_3 - Q_1	5	2

Company A has an interquartile range of 5, compared to 2 for company B. So we may assert that company B has the least variable product.

You may perhaps have wandered what has become of the second quartile. There **is** such a statistic but we usually call it by its more well known name of the **median**.

THE MEAN ABSOLUTE DEVIATION (MAD)

None of the methods so far used have attempted to measure variability around a fixed point. It is quite a useful idea to take a fixed value – usually the mean – and measure how much the data differs from this fixed point.

One such approach is known as the mean absolute deviation, or MAD for short.

To calculate MAD take the following steps:

calculate the mean of the data

subtract the mean from each data value hereby obtaining a series of deviations from the mean

disregard the negative signs

add these deviations together

divide by N (the number of data values).

A more formal definition of MAD is given below:

Formula 3

The Mean Absolute Deviation (MAD)

$$MAD = \frac{1}{N} \Sigma |X - \mu| \quad where$$

N = the number of data values and |X| is the absolute value of X.

The **absolute value** of a number is its **magnitude** (ignore negative signs).

So for example, the absolute value of $-6 = |-6| = 6$.

Example of MAD calculation

What is the MAD for the numbers 1 2 3 4 5?

The workings are laid out below in tabular form:

X	X - μ	IX - μI
1	-2	2
2	-1	1
3	0	0
4	1	1
5	2	2
μ = 3		ΣIX - μI = 6

The mean of the values is 3. In the second column, 3 has been subtracted from each data value. We thus obtain a series of deviations from the mean. The third column gives the 'absolute' values of these deviations from the mean. This is an essential stage, because if we did not disregard the negative signs, the sum of the deviations would always be zero. Finally, we divide the sum of the (absolute) deviations by 5 (since $N = 5$ in this case).

Therefore

$$MAD = \frac{1}{N}\Sigma|X - \mu| = \frac{1}{5} \times 6 = 1.2$$

MAD tells us how much, on average, the data values differs from the mean. If the data values showed no variation (meaning that they were all the same), then MAD would be zero. Generally speaking, the higher the MAD, the more variable is the data.

ACTIVITY 33

Calculate the MAD for each of the cable supply companies of Activity 30, and state which company produces the more variable product.

Use a separate piece of paper for your answer.

The calculations for Activity 33 are set out below.

COMPANY A			COMPANY B		
X	X - μ	IX- μI	X	X - μ	IX- μI
9	-3	3	10	-2	2
16	+4	4	11	-1	1
14	+2	2	13	+1	1
10	-2	2	12	0	0
13	+1	1	11	-1	1
17	+5	5	14	+2	2
9	-3	3	13	+1	1
12	0	0	12	0	0
11	-1	1	11	-1	1
9	-3	3	13	+1	1
sum = 120		sum = 24	sum = 120		sum = 10
μ = 12			μ = 12		

Company A MAD =

$$\frac{1}{N}\Sigma \ IX - \mu I = \frac{1}{10} \times 24$$

$$= 2.4$$

Company B MAD =

$$\frac{1}{N}\Sigma \ IX - \mu I = \frac{1}{10} \times 10$$

$$= 1$$

According to the MAD, company B produces the least variable cables.

THE VARIANCE AND STANDARD DEVIATION

MAD is a useful descriptive measure of dispersion but in dealing with absolute deviations from the mean we have resorted to the mathematical trick of ignoring the negative values. Although you need not worry about the details of this process, you should be aware that using absolute deviations restricts the usefulness of MAD. There is a measure called the **variance**, which does not suffer from the defects of the MAD. The variance measures dispersion by dealing with squared deviations from the mean rather than absolute deviations.

To calculate the variance we

> **calculate the mean of the data**
> **subtract the mean from each data value**
> **square the deviations so obtained**
> **calculate the mean of these deviations**

As a formula the variance is defined as:

Formula 4

The Variance

$$\sigma^2 = \frac{1}{N}\Sigma(X - \mu)^2$$

The symbol 'σ^2', is the accepted abbreviation for the variance of the population. (σ is the Greek lower-case letter 'sigma'). If we are dealing with a sample, the symbol s^2 would denote the variance.

The square root of the variance, σ, is known as the **standard deviation**. (The sample standard deviation is denoted by s.)

As with the mean, we shall temporarily ignore the distinction between sample and standard deviation and use σ^2 and σ.

In order to give a simple demonstration of the calculations required for the variance and the standard deviation we may use the following numbers:

1 2 3 4 5

The working is laid out in the table below.

X	(X - μ)	(X - μ)²
1	-2	4
2	-1	1
3	0	0
4	1	1
5	2	4
μ = 3		Σ(X - μ)² = 10

$$\therefore \sigma^2 = \frac{1}{N}\Sigma(X - \mu)^2$$

$$\sigma^2 = \frac{1}{5} \times 10 = 2$$

$$\sigma = \sqrt{2} = 1.414 \text{ ... for the above data.}$$

An alternative method for calculating the variance is available.

Formula 5

The Variance (alternative method)

$$\sigma^2 = \{\frac{1}{N}\Sigma X^2\} - \mu^2$$

This will give precisely the same result as formula 4 and some people prefer to use it because it does not involve the calculation of deviations from the mean. Using formula 5, the workings for calculating the variance and standard deviation of the numbers

$$1 \ 2 \ 3 \ 4 \ 5$$

would be as follows:

X	X²
1	1
2	4
3	9
4	16
5	25
$\mu = 3$	$\Sigma X^2 = 55$

So

$$\therefore \; \sigma^2 = \{\frac{1}{N}\Sigma X^2\} - \mu^2 \qquad (formula\ 5)$$

$$\sigma^2 = \{\frac{1}{5}\times 55\} - 3^2$$

$$\sigma^2 = 11 - 9 = 2$$

as before.

In general (although we shall have more to say about this matter later in this section), the larger the variance (and standard deviation), the more variable is the data from which it is calculated.

ACTIVITY 34

Use either formula 4 or 5, to calculate the variances and standard deviations for the cable strength data of Activity 30.

Use a separate piece of paper for your answer.

The working for Activity 34 is set out below.

Formula 4 has been used in this case.

COMPANY A			COMPANY B		
X	**X - μ**	**(X-μ)²**	**X**	**X - μ**	**(X-μ)²**
9	-3	9	10	-2	4
16	+4	16	11	-1	1
14	+2	4	13	+1	1
10	-2	4	12	0	0
13	+1	1	11	-1	1
17	+5	25	14	+2	4
9	-3	9	13	+1	1
12	0	0	12	0	0
11	-1	1	11	-1	1
9	-3	9	13	+1	1
sum = 120		**sum = 78**	**sum = 120**		**sum = 14**
μ = 12			**μ = 12**		

For company A:

$$\sigma^2 = \frac{1}{N}\Sigma(X - \mu)^2$$

$$= \frac{1}{10} \times 78 = 7.8$$

$$\therefore \sigma = \sqrt{7.8} \approx 2.79$$

For company B:

$$\sigma^2 = \frac{1}{N}\Sigma(X - \mu)^2$$

$$= \frac{1}{10} \times 14 = 1.4$$

$$\therefore \sigma = \sqrt{1.4} \approx 1.18$$

ACTIVITY 35

Two simple clerical tasks are carried out in the post room of a large firm. A work study analyst wishes to investigate how long each task takes. The following are the times for 5 staff members, carrying out each task (times in minutes);

Staff member	1	2	3	4	5
Task 1	0.92	0.98	1.04	0.90	0.99
Task 2	4.52	4.35	4.60	4.70	4.50

The work study analyst thought (after seeing these results) that the times for task 1 were the most consistent (less variable). Calculate the variance and standard deviation of times for each task, and comment upon the analyst's belief.

The working for Activity 35 is set out below.

X	X²	X	X²
0.92	0.8464	4.52	20.4304
0.98	0.9604	4.35	18.9225
1.04	1.0816	4.60	21.1600
0.90	0.8100	4.70	22.0900
0.99	0.9801	4.50	20.2500
ΣX =	ΣX² =	ΣX =	ΣX² =
4.8300	4.6785	22.6700	102.8529
μ = 0.9660		μ = 4.5340	

Variances have been calculated using formula 5, which is easier to use for this data than formula 4.

For task 1

$$\sigma^2 = \{\frac{1}{n}\Sigma X^2\} - \mu^2$$

$$= \{\frac{1}{5} \times 4.6785\} - 0.966^2 \approx 0.0025$$

For task 2

$$= \{\frac{1}{5} \times 102.8529\} - 4.5340^2 \approx 0.0134$$

Thus for task 1

$$\sigma = \sqrt{0.0025} = 0.0500$$

and for task 2

$$\sigma = \sqrt{0.0134} = 0.1158$$

Since σ and σ^2 are larger for task 2, a simplistic interpretation of the results would lead us to conclude that the analyst's belief appears to be correct. (However, see Activity 38 in the next section before coming to firm conclusions on this matter.)

3. CALCULATING σ^2 AND σ FOR FREQUENCY DISTRIBUTION DATA

What if the data have been grouped into a frequeny distribution? How would we set about calculating the variance and standard deviation in such a case?
For data which have been grouped in this way, you may use formula 6.

Formula 6

The Variance

$$\sigma^2 = \frac{1}{N}\{\Sigma fX^2\} - \mu^2$$

In this formula, the symbol 'f' stands for 'frequency'. Thus as we proceed with our calculation we need to multiply each value by its associated frequency. Notice that since the data will probably have been grouped into classes, each X value might represent the mid point of the class.

An example of the calculation of the variance for a grouped frequency distribution is shown below, on the computer usage data (see figure 7 in section 2). The data are set out below, together with necessary workings in column form.

HOURS	NO OF USERS	MID POINT OF CLASS	fX	(X^2)	$f(X^2)$
	(f)	(X)	fX	(X^2)	$f(X^2)$
Under 3	14	1.5	21.0	2.25	31.50
3 < 6	6	4.5	27.0	20.25	121.50
6 < 9	6	7.5	45.0	56.25	337.50
9 < 12	7	10.5	73.5	110.25	771.50
12 < 15	14	13.5	189.0	182.25	2551.50
15 < 18	3	16.5	49.5	272.25	816.75
TOTAL N	$\Sigma fX = 50$		$\Sigma fX = 405.0$		$\Sigma fX^2 = 4630.50$

You will see from formula 6, that we need to calculate the mean first.

So by formula 2, the mean

$$\mu = \frac{1}{N}\Sigma fX = \frac{1}{50} \times 405 = 8.1 \; hours$$

Mean computer usage time is 8.1 hours (exactly).

We can now proceed to calculation of the variance.

By formula 6

$$\sigma^2 = \frac{1}{N}\{\Sigma fX^2\} - \mu^2$$

$$\sigma^2 = \frac{1}{50}\{4630.5\} - 8.1^2 = 92.61 - 65.61 = 27.00$$

So

$$\sigma^2 = 27.00 \; \text{hours}^2$$

and

$$\sigma = \sqrt{(27.00)} = 5.20 \; \text{hours} \; \text{(to two decimal places)}.$$

Now you should try using this method yourself in the following activity.

ACTIVITY 36

Look back at the data contained in figure 6, section 2. It is a distribution of the weight of packages passing through a check point. The table is reproduced below.

WEIGHT	FREQUENCY No of Packs
7.1 < 7.3	1
7.3 < 7.5	5
7.5 < 7.7	10
7.7 < 7.9	19
7.9 < 8.1	27
8.1 < 8.3	22
8.3 < 8.5	6
8.5 < 8.7	3
8.7 < 8.9	2

Calculate the variance and standard deviation of pack weights.

The calculations for Activity 36 are set out below.

WEIGHT	FREQUENCY (f)	MID POINT (X)	f(X)	f(X²)
7.1 < 7.3	1	7.2	7.2	51.84
7.3 < 7.5	5	7.4	37.0	273.80
7.5 < 7.7	10	7.6	76.0	577.60
7.7 < 7.9	19	7.8	148.0	1155.96
7.9 < 8.1	27	8.0	216.0	1728.00
8.1 < 8.3	22	8.2	180.4	1479.28
8.3 < 8.5	6	8.4	50.4	423.36
8.5 < 8.7	3	8.6	25.8	221.88
8.7 < 8.9	2	8.8	17.6	154.88
N = Σf = 95			ΣfX = 758.6	ΣfX² = 6066.6

Note

During calculation of the variance, the mean should be computed to as many decimal places as can be conveniently carried by your calculator. It is always a good rule to round an answer only at **the final stage of**, not (if you can avoid it) **during** a calculation.

So the mean is

$$\mu = \frac{1}{N}\Sigma fX = \frac{1}{95} \times 758.6 = 7.9852632$$

The variance can now be calculated as follows

$$\sigma^2 = \frac{1}{N}\{\Sigma fX^2\} - \mu^2$$

$$\sigma^2 = \frac{1}{95}\{6066.6\} - 7.9852632^2$$

$$= 63.858947 - 63.764428$$

$$= 0.094519$$

Thus

$$\sigma^2 = 0.094519 \text{ kg}^2 \text{ (0.09 to two decimal places).}$$

and

$$\sigma = \sqrt{(0.094519)} = 0.31 \text{ kg (to two decimal places).}$$

 After a little practice using this method you will not find it difficult. However, you will probably agree that it involves a great many tedious calculations, and it is strongly suggested that you use a computer if you have access to one. A good scientific calculator which has some additional statistical functions will make light work of these calculations.

4. SUMMARY

In this section we have

- discussed the importance of measuring the **variability** of data

- defined the **crude range** of a set of data and discussed its efficiency as a **measure of variability**

- used the **lower** and **upper quartiles** to obtain the **interquartile range** and use it as a **measure of variability**

- defined and used the **mean absolute deviation**

- learned how to calculate the **variance** and **standard deviation**

If you are not sure of any of the topics covered in this section, you should check back **now** before reading on.

SECTION 6

INTERPRETING THE VARIANCE AND STANDARD DEVIATION

The variance and standard deviation are the most frequently used measures of variability. This final section covers further analysis of their use.

1. WHY DO WE NEED THE STANDARD DEVIATION?

If we already have a variance, why is this not enough? What is to be gained from taking its square root and obtaining this further measure, the standard deviation?

You should remember that in obtaining the variance we **square** the deviations from the mean. This will mean that the units of measure are **square units**. Therefore, for example, the variances you calculated in Activity 35 are measured in 'square minutes'.

Similarly, if you calculated the variance of earnings of a group of people, the result would be in square £s. Now since it is difficult to deal with such square units, the common practice is to unsquare the variance – take the square root. The result will be a measure which is in ordinary units. So the standard deviation of clerical task times in Activity 35 will be in minutes. The standard deviation is always measured in the same units as the original data from which it was calculated.

This is one reason for using the standard deviation in preference to the variance.

2. COMPARING TWO OR MORE SETS OF DATA

Activity 37 illustrates why we should exercise care when interpreting variances and standard deviations

ACTIVITY 37

Compare the following two sets of data

i.	1	3	5	7	9
ii.	101	103	105	107	109

(a)   Without making any calculations, say which set, (i) or (ii), you think is the most variable. Explain your answer.

(b)   Now calculate the variance and standard deviation for each set. What do these statistics tell you about the variability of the data sets?

   If the answers to (a) and (b) point to different conclusions about the data, can you reconcile this difference?

You may find part (a) of Activity 37 difficult. Notice that the numbers change by the same **absolute** amounts (+2 for each data set). It might therefore seem reasonable to state that they are equally variable. However, a variation of 2 is a large amount when it occurs in numbers of the order of magnitude of 1, 3, 5 etc, but it is a small amount for numbers such as 101, 103, 105 etc. For this reason we could legitimately argue that data set (i) is more variable than data set (ii).

Now let us see what the standard deviations of the two data sets look like. Formula 4 has been used.

X	$(X - \mu)^2$	X	$(X - \mu)^2$
1	16	101	16
3	4	103	4
5	0	105	0
7	4	107	4
9	16	109	16
$\mu = 5$	$\Sigma(X-\mu)^2 = 40$	$\mu = 105$	$\Sigma(X-\mu)^2 = 40$

For both data set (i) and (ii)

$$\sigma^2 = 40/5 = 8 \quad \text{and} \quad \sigma = \sqrt{8} = 2.828$$

Since the values of σ^2 and σ are the same for both data sets, we might argue that they are equally variable. However, bear in mind that 8 is a large variance for numbers such as 1, 3, 5 etc, but not for 101, 103, 105 etc. Size is always relative.

Activity 37 shows that comparing the standard deviations of two completely different sets of data, or distributions, is not a simple matter.

Firstly, a standard deviation may be large just because the numbers it was computed from are of a high magnitude. Similarly, the standard deviation will be small if the numbers giving rise to it are small.

This is now a good time for you to review the work study data of Activity 35.

If you look back at this Activity, you will see that the times for task 1 are generally of the order of magnitude of 1 minute (give or take a few seconds) while the task 2 data is generally over four times greater.

This fact alone will cause the standard deviation for task 2 to be greater than that for task 1.

This does not mean necessarily, that the data with the higher value for σ are more variable than the other data.

Secondly, the standard deviation is measured in the units of the original data.

Therefore for example; suppose we have data on people's weight and height and we have calculated that the standard deviation of weight is 10 kg and the standard deviation of height is 12 cm. How can we possibly use these figures to say whether height or weight is the more variable, when one is measured in centimetres, and the other is measured in kilogrammes?

The solution to our problem lies in a simple calculation called the **coefficient of variation.**

This is defined below as another formula:

Formula 7

The Coefficient of Variation

$$CoVar = \frac{\sigma}{\mu} \times 100$$

Since the coefficient of variation is a percentage, this solves the problem created by different units of measurement. Of two or more distributions, the one with the highest coefficient is the more variable.

ACTIVITY 38

(a)   Calculate the coefficient of variation for the work study data of Activity 35. Do you need to change your opinion of the analysts belief as a result of this calculation?

⟱

Activity 38 continued...

(b)   Calculate the coefficient of variation for the data of Activity 37 and comment on the result obtained.

In order to deal with Activity 38, the work study data are summarised below.

	TASK 1	TASK 2
μ	0.9660	4.5340
σ	0.0500	0.1158
CoVar = $\dfrac{\sigma}{\mu} \times 100$	$\dfrac{0.0500}{0.9660} \times 100$ $\approx 5.2\%$	$\dfrac{0.1158}{4.5340} \times 100$ $\approx 2.6\%$

Even though task 1 shows a larger standard deviation than task 2, the times are less variable comparatively speaking. The task 1 standard deviation is a lower percentage of the mean.

To answer the second part of this activity, the data of Activity 37 are summarised below, together with the calculation of the coefficient of variation.

	DATA SET i.	DATA SET ii.
μ	5	105
σ	2.828	2.828
Covar =	$\dfrac{2.828}{5} \times 100$	$\dfrac{2.828}{105} \times 100$
$\dfrac{\sigma}{\mu} \times 100$	= 56.6%	= 2.7%

Even though s is the same for both sets of data, data set (i) is comparatively more variable than set (ii), because the standard deviation is a larger percentage of the mean.

So whenever a comparison between sets of data, or distributions is required, the coefficient of variation is used.

3. CHEBYSHEV'S THEOREM

This theorem allows us to make useful observations concerning the percentage of a distribution which falls within specified values. The results of the theorem allows us to say, for instance:

at least 75% of the data must be within 2 standard deviations of the mean;

at least 89% of the data must be within 3 standard deviations of the mean;

at least 94% of the data must be within 4 standard deviations of the mean.

As an example of the application of this rule, suppose that the average expenditure on proprietary cold cures is £50 per household per year with a standard deviation of £5.

Then by Chebyshev's theorem 75% of all households expenditure must be within 2 standard deviations of the mean, ie; in the range

$$\mu - 2\sigma \quad \text{to} \quad \mu + 2\sigma$$

Which is;

$$£50 - (2 \times £5) \quad \text{to} \quad £50 + (2 \times £5) \quad \text{or}$$

$$£40 \text{ to } £60$$

By a similar argument, 89% of households spend between £35 and £65.

You may wish to supply the limits for 4 standard deviations yourself, to make sure you understand the value of the theorem.

You may use the Chebyshev theorem on any data; you do not need to know the shape of the distribution from which it came.

4. SYMMETRICAL OR BELL-SHAPED DISTRIBUTIONS

Many distributions are bell shaped and symmetrical (or roughly symmetrical). If you need to refresh your memory on what such a distribution looks like, study the histogram of theatre audience size shown in figure 12.

You will be able to see from the histogram why the description 'bell shaped', is used to describe such distributions.

Now if we know that our data are distributed in such a manner, then we can make even more precise statements than the Chebyshev theorem will allow.

For example, we can say approximately that:

68% of the data lies within one standard deviation of the mean, and the remaining 32%, lies outside these limits

95% of the data lies within two standard deviations of the mean, with the remaining 5% outside these limits

almost all of the data lies within three standard deviations of the mean.

The above results will be roughly true for any data which do not show too much skewness.

The following table (figure 22) summarises the above rules in detail. Please remember that all figures are approximate.

RANGE, OR INTERVAL	PROPORTION OF DISTRIBUTION IN THIS INTERVAL
Below μ-3σ	0.0%
Between μ-3σ and μ-2σ	2.5%
Between μ-2σ and μ-1σ	13.5%
Between μ-1σ and μ	34.0%
Between μ and μ+1σ	34.0%
Between μ+1σ and μ+2σ	13.5%
Between μ+2σ and μ+3σ	2.5%
Above μ+3σ	0.0%

FIGURE 22: **Symmetrical Distributions**

It is very important to remember that the results shown in figure 22 will only hold good if the data does not have a skewed distribution.

ACTIVITY 39

Consider the cable strength data of Activity 30.

(a)   On the supposition that we know nothing about the distribution of cable strengths, use Chebyshev's theorem to compare the variability of strength of the firm's cables.

(b)   Suppose that you have it on good authority that the distribution of cable strengths is bell-shaped, or symmetrical. Use this information to compare the variability of strength of the firm's cables.

The following table lists the appropriate calculations for Activity 39, assuming that we have no knowledge of the underlying distribution of cable strengths. In such a case, we need to use Chebyshev's theorem.

	COMPANY A	COMPANY B
μ	12.00	12.00
σ	2.79	1.18
$\mu-2\sigma$ to $\mu+2\sigma$	6.42 to 17.58	9.64 to 14.36
$\mu-3\sigma$ to $\mu+3\sigma$	3.63 to 20.37	8.46 to 15.54
$\mu-4\sigma$ to $\mu+4\sigma$	0.84 to 23.16	7.28 to 16.72

These figures clearly show that company A's product is more variable. We know that 94% of company B's cables will have breaking strengths between 7.28 and 16.72 kg per sq cm, and 94% of company A's cables will vary from as low as 0.84 to as high as 23.16 kg per sq cm, which is a very high degree of variability.

The following table lists the appropriate calculations if we are convinced that the underlying shape of the distribution is symmetrical.

	COMPANY A	COMPANY B
μ	12.00	12.00
σ	2.79	1.18
$\mu-1\sigma$ to $\mu+1\sigma$	9.21 to 14.79	10.82 to 13.18
$\mu-2\sigma$ to $\mu+2\sigma$	6.42 to 17.58	9.64 to 14.36
$\mu-3\sigma$ to $\mu+3\sigma$	3.63 to 20.37	8.46 to 15.54

If symmetry exists, then we can improve on Chebyshev about the limits within which various percentages of cable strengths will fall. For instance nearly all of company B's cables have a strength between 8.46 and 15.54. This is much less of an interval than company A (3.63 - 20.37).

ACTIVITY 40

(a)   The mean outstanding debt of the 1000 customers of a business is £70 and the the standard deviation of the debt is £5. Use Chebyshev to calculate the number of customers who owe the company between

    i. £60 and £80   ii. £50 and £90

(b)   For the same debtor information, suppose we know that the distribution is bell shaped. How many customers owe between

    i. £65 and £75   ii. £60 and £80

    iii. £55 and £85

A debt of £60 is two standard deviations below the mean, while a debt of £80 is two standard deviations above the mean. By the Chebyshev theorem, 75% of all data must fall in the interval $\mu - 2\sigma$ to $\mu + 2\sigma$. Therefore 750 customers will owe an amount in the range £60 to £80.

By the same theorem, at least 94% of data falls in the range $\mu - 4\sigma$ to $\mu + 4\sigma$. Now since £50 and £60 are 4 standard deviations above and below the mean respectively, then at least 940 customers must have debts in this range.

If we know that the distribution of debt follows a bell shaped distribution then we are able to say the following:

approximately 680 customers owe between £65 and £75 (because 68% of a bell-shaped distribution is in the range $\mu - \sigma$ to $\mu + \sigma$)

approximately 950 customers owe between £60 and £80 (95% of a bell-shaped distribution is in the range $\mu - 2\sigma$ to $\mu + 2\sigma$.)

almost all customers owe between £55 and £85 (virtually all of a bell-shaped distribution is in the range $\mu - 3\sigma$ to $\mu + 3\sigma$).

ACTIVITY 41

A recent report stated that IQ (Intelligence Quotient) for the population had a mean of 100 and a standard deviation 0f 15. The distribution of IQ is known to be bell-shaped.

(a)   What percentage of the population would have an IQ in the range 85 to 115?

(b)   What percentage of the population would have an IQ between 70 and 130?

(c)   What percentage of the population would have an IQ outside the range 70 to 130?

(d)   A person with an IQ of 145 is considered a genius. What proportion of the population would be considered geniuses?

The answers to Activity 41 depend upon using the relationship between the mean and the standard deviation in a symmetrical bell-shaped distribution.

85 and 115 are (respectively) one standard deviation below, and one standard deviation above the average. Therefore, 68% of people must have IQs in this range.

70 and 130 are two standard deviations below and above μ.

Therefore, 95% of people must have IQs between 70 and 130.

It follows from the above, that if 95% of people have IQs in the range 70-130, then the remainder, 5%, must have IQs either above 130 or below 70.

145 is three standard deviations above the mean. Almost all the distribution is in the range $\mu - 3\sigma$ to $\mu + 3\sigma$. Therefore, hardly anybody has an IQ outside this range, and without being able to say exactly what the proportion of geniuses in the population happens to be, we can confidently expect it to be tiny.

5. Z-Scores (Standard Scores)

One further use we can make of the standard deviation (and the mean) is to calculate Z-scores. To explain the concept of Z-scores, consider the following case.

Suppose you are a member of a large business studies course which has recently been tested. The average mark in the test was 50%, with a standard deviation of 10%. Now suppose that your own test score was 60%.

Your Z-score would be +1, because you obtained a mark which was 1 standard deviation greater than the mean.

If another person scored 35%, then the Z-score for this test result would be -1.5, because the result was 1.5 standard deviations below the mean.

The Z-score of a value (sometimes called the 'standard' score), is the number of standard deviations the value is above, or below the mean.

Calculation of the Z-score, is shown by the following formula

Formula 8

Z-Scores

The Z-score of a variable X, coming from a distribution with mean μ and standard deviation σ, is calculated as follows;

$$Z = \frac{X - \mu}{\sigma}$$

Z-scores are useful because they adjust values

for differences in means, standard deviations and measuring units. For example, if we know that someone's Z value in a height distribution is +1, and in a weight distribution it is -0.5, then we know that they are taller and thinner than average.

Example

Suppose we purchase two items produced by ABZ Electronics; one is a torch battery and the other is a light bulb. We compare the lifetimes of our purchases with the overall average lifetimes for these products. The resulting data is as follows:

	TORCH BATTERY	LIGHT BULB
Average life	50	60
Standard deviation of life	5	9
Life of sample purchase	60	69

(lifetimes in hours)

The Z-scores for your battery and light bulb would be calculated as

$$Z = \frac{X - \mu}{\sigma} \qquad \textit{by formula 7}$$

$$Z = \frac{60 - 50}{5} = 2 \qquad \textit{(for the battery)}$$

$$Z = \frac{69 - 60}{9} = 1 \qquad \textit{(for the light bulb)}$$

Although the lifetime of the light bulb is higher than the battery, the battery is actually the better performer. This is because its lifetime is two standard deviations better than the mean, whereas the light bulb is only one standard deviation better than the mean. Also, if the distribution of lifetime is bell-shaped, then we may add that a lifetime of 60 hours for a torch battery ($Z = 2$), would put it in the longest lasting 2.5% of this firm's batteries. This is because only 2.5% of the distribution would be in excess of $\mu + 2\sigma$, or 60. A light bulb lasting 69 hours would be merely in the top 16% of all light bulbs (see figure 22).

ACTIVITY 42

(a)   500 people apply for civil service jobs. Job application requires each applicant to take tests in verbal and mathematical reasoning. Verbal score tests have a mean of 100 and a standard deviation of 10. Maths test scores have a mean of 32, and a standard deviation of 6. One applicant receives marks of 115 in the verbal test and 30 in the maths test. Compare the applicants' performance in the two tests.

(b)   Fill in the blank columns in the following table (assuming that test scores in both verbal and mathematical ability have a bell-shaped distribution). Approximately how many of the 500 applicants will have marks in the following ranges?

VERBAL SCORE	NO. OF PEOPLE	MATHS SCORE	NO. OF PEOPLE
< 70		< 14	
70 < 80		14 < 20	
80 < 90		20 < 26	
90 < 100		26 < 32	
100 < 110		32 < 38	
110 < 120		38 < 44	
120 < 130		44 < 50	
> 130		> 50	

The answer to the first part of Activity 42 is shown in the following table.

	VERBAL TEST	MATHS TEST
μ	100	32
σ	10	6
score	115	30
z score	$\dfrac{115-100}{10} = 1.5$	$\dfrac{30-32}{6} \approx -0.33$

Z-scores have been used in the above. The verbal test score is the best, with an above average score. In fact, since it is more than one standard deviation above the mean, the person scoring 115, will be in the top 16%. (Remember that 68% of a bell shaped distribution is within one standard deviation of the mean. The remaining 32% is outside this range; 16% above, and 16% below.)

The maths score of 30 is below the average, although at -0.33 standard deviations below, you could argue that this is only slightly below the average.

To fill in the table for part (b) of the Activity, we use the relationship between the mean and standard deviation developed earlier (see figure 22).

The following is a summary of the relationships for the verbal and maths test data.

		VERBAL TEST	MATHS TEST
$\mu-\sigma$ to $\mu+\sigma$	is	90 to 110	26 to 38
$\mu-2\sigma$ to $\mu+2\sigma$	is	80 to 120	20 to 44
$\mu-3\sigma$ to $\mu+3\sigma$	is	70 to 130	14 to 50

The table can be filled in as

VERBAL SCORE	NO. OF PEOPLE	MATHS SCORE	NO. OF PEOPLE
< 70	–	< 14	–
70 < 80	2.5% (12)	14 < 20	2.5% (12)
80 < 90	13.5% (68)	20 < 26	13.5% (68)
90 < 100	34.0% (170)	26 < 32	34.0% (170)
100 < 110	34.0% (170)	32 < 38	34.0% (170)
110 < 120	13.5% (68)	38 < 44	13.5% (68)
120 < 130	2.5% (12)	44 < 50	2.5% (12)
> 130	–	> 50	–

We know that virtually all maths scores will be between 70 and 130. (Because this interval is $\mu\pm3\sigma$.)

Thus 250 scores will be in the range 70 < 100, and the other 250 in the range 100 <130.

Also, we know that 95% (475) of maths scores will be in the range 80 < 12, of which 237.5 (238 approximately) will be in the range 80 < 100, and the other 238 in the range 100 < 120.

Since 250 scores are in the range 70 < 100, and 238 in 80 < 100 then 250-238 = 12 scores must be in the range 70 < 80.

Working in this manner the whole table may be completed.

---

6. SUMMARY

In this final section we have

- further practised the technique of calculating **variance** and **standard deviation**

- discussed the affect of the **unit of measurement** on the **variance** and **standard deviation**

- seen how to use the **coefficient of variation** to compare variability between two or more sets of data

- used **Chebyshev's theorem** to make useful observations about the distribution of data

- learned how to use the **symmetry** of a distribution to make observations about the distribution of data

- compared levels of different variables by calculating and using their **Z- Scores**

- made some observations on the conventions used in the **notation** for mean and standard deviations in both **sample** and **census**

If you are unsure of any of the topics covered in this unit, check back **now** to the appropriate section.

REFERENCES

Students who wish to do so may follow up this subject by reading the following texts.

MORRIS. C. *Quantitative Approaches to Business Studies*. Third Edition. Pitman Publishing.
CURWEN & SLATER. *Quantitative Methods for Business Decisions*. Third Edition. Chapman & Hall.

GLOSSARY

The following is an alphabetical listing of the technical terms most often encountered in this unit.

Arithmetic mean The sum of all data values divided by the number of such values. A measure of central tendency.

Asymmetry A condition where data is not evenly distributed about its mean. Another term for skewness.

Asymmetrical distribution A frequency distribution which displays asymmetry.

Average A general term meaning any measure of central tendency.

Bar chart Any statistical diagram where the magnitude of data values is shown by the heights of bars.

Bell-shaped distribution A symmetrical distribution which peaks at the mean and tails away rapidly to left and right. There is a precise relationship between mean and standard deviation in such distributions.

Bimodal distributions A distribution with two distinct peak values.

Central tendency The tendency of data to group around a central point.

Chebyshev theorem A useful theorem which establishes a relationship between mean and standard deviation for data, regardless of the shape of the distribution.

Class frequency The class frequencies are the numbers of data values which fall into each class interval.

Class interval Class intervals are the subdivisions of the variable range used to count data into frequency distributions.

Class limits Class limits are the upper and lower bounds to the class interval.

Coded value A numerical value given to nominal data in order to make computer analysis easier.

Coefficient of variation A measure expressing the standard deviation as a percentage of the mean. A means of comparing variability between data sets.

Crude range The difference between the maximum and minimum values of a set of data, and therefore a measure of dispersion.

Cumulative frequency The recorded frequency of a variable equal to, or less than some specified value.

Data When a variable has been defined, data are the result of taking counts or measurements of the value of this variable.

Dispersion The tendency of data in a distribution to be scattered over a range of values.

Element An element is a basic unit of statistical analysis, such as a household or person. Study of an element may produce several variables.

Frequency curve A smooth line graph which shows the shape of a frequency distribution.

Frequency distribution A general term referring to the tendency of data to have shape or pattern.

Frequency polygon Similar to the frequency curve, but the line graph consists of a series of straight lines drawn between data points rather than a smooth curve.

Histogram A histogram is a special case of the bar chart, where it is used to graphically display a frequency distribution.

Interquartile range The difference between the upper (Q_3) and lower (Q_1) quartiles. A measure of dispersion.

Interval scale A scale of measurement where intervals can be proportionately compared and where zero is not the starting point of the scale.

Interval variable A variable which is capable of being measured on an interval scale.

Mean absolute deviation (MAD) The average of the absolute devations of a data set from the mean. A measure of dispersion.

Median The middle value of a data set when the set has been rank-ordered. A measure of central tendency.

Mode The most frequently occurring value of a data set. A measure of central tendency.

Multimodal distribution A distribution where there are two or more distinct peaks, or modes.

Nominal scale A scale of measurement where the measuring categories are labels rather than numbers.

Nominal variable A variable which is measured using a nominal scale.

Ogive A graph which displays cumulative frequencies.

Ordinal Scale A scale of measurement which places a variable in rank order.

Ordinal variable A variable which must be measured on an ordinal scale.

Population The full collection of entities being studied by the researcher.

Quartiles Measures which divide a data set into quarters. They consist of the lower quartile (Q_1) and the upper quartile (Q_3).

Ratio scale A scale of measurement similar to the interval scale with the additional feature that zero forms the starting point of the scale.

Rectangular distribution A distribution where individual values of the variable tend to occur with equal frequency.

Relative frequency Numerical frequency of a class divided by the total frequency.

Sample A proportion of entities selected from the total population.

Skewness The tendency in a distribution to deviate from symmetry. Can be positive or negative.

Standard deviation The square root of the variance. A measure of dispersion.

Standard score The number of standard deviations between a data value and the mean constitutes the values standard score.

Summary statistics A group of statistics which purport to represent, or sum-up a data set. Measures of variation and central tendency are examples.

Symmetrical distribution A distribution where the shape below the central point is identical to the shape above this point (but inverted).

Uniform distribution Another name for the rectangular distribution.

Variance The average of the squared deviations of a data set from the mean. A measure of dispersion.

Z-score Another name for standard score.

UNIT 3

LINEAR PROGRAMMING

CONTENTS

UNIT OBJECTIVES

When you have finished working through this unit you will be able to

- formulate linear programming problems involving two or more decision variables

- solve linear programming problems involving two decision variables using the graphical method

- use the output from an appropriate software package to solve linear programming problems involving two or more decision variables

- perform a sensitivity analysis on the solution, using computer software output

- determine when it would not be appropriate to use linear programming methods

SECTION 1

A CASE STUDY

1. INTRODUCTION: A LINEAR PROGRAMMING PROBLEM

Suppose that A.R. Jarvis & Partners is a small building firm specialising in the construction of doors to be sold to the DIY market as ready made. The firm make two kinds of door, sold under the brand names 'CHEZ NOUS' and 'MON REPOS'. Jarvis find that they can sell all the doors they make, but are unable to make an unlimited number of them because of limitations on the amount of glass and wood they can obtain, and because an agreement with the trade union restricts availability of labour.

In fact, the firm can obtain 600 m^2 of wood per week at a cost of £4 per m^2, and 300 m^2 of glass per week at a cost of £16 per m^2. They have 8 operators working a 40 hour week at an hourly rate of £6.

Inclu
ding all necessary allowances for wastage, a CHEZ NOUS uses 2 m^2 of wood and 0.5 m^2 of glass, while each MON REPOS requires 1.5 m^2 of wood and 1 m^2 of glass. It takes 1 hour of labour time to cut and assemble each door.

Currently, a CHEZ NOUS sells for £30 and a MON REPOS for £40.

Raj Singh, the accountant who performs occasional tax work for Jarvis has told them that they could increase their profit by changing the number of each type of doors they make. That is to say, the present mix of CHEZ NOUS and MON REPOS is not **optimal**.

Mr Singh says it is possible to alter this mix and therefore improve contribution.

Assuming that what Raj says is true, how can the builders firm find out what would be the best (ie the most profitable, or optimal) mix of the two products? What would this optimum profit be?

2. WHAT DOES LINEAR PROGRAMMING DO?

The case of Jarvis and the doors is a classic example of a problem which would benefit from linear programming. Linear programming (or LP, as we shall often call it in this unit), is an operational research technique concerned with finding **optimum** solutions to a particular class of problems. Optimum is an old Latin word meaning the best and in practice, searching for an optimum means looking for the **maximum or minimum** of something. LP will mean maximising or minimising a given **function** such as cost, revenue, contribution, profit, distance travelled, subject to a number of **constraints** – capacity and supplies available for example. The problem is to determine the values of some **variables**, for example the rate of production of certain items, the number of vehicles to be scheduled for a given task, that optimise this function, without violating any of the constraints.

ACTIVITY 1

Consider the case of Jarvis & Partners for a moment.

(a)   What do you think is the optimum goal for Jarvis?

(b)   What kind of actions should be taken to achieve this optimum?

(c)   List the constraints which are of concern to Jarvis in achieving this optimum.

Any business will have a number of goals or objectives that they need to meet. In the brief statement of the Jarvis case, it is quite clear that optimum means maximum profit or maximum contribution to profit from the manufacture of the two doors.

It appears that obtaining this maximum will involve changing the proportions in which the doors are produced.

Whatever Jarvis do, they are constrained by the limits on the available supplies of labour, glass and wood.

3. Applications of Linear Programming

Linear programming is used to investigate problems such as:

Maximising contribution
In a multi-product environment a common problem is to determine whatever mix of products will maximise contribution

Investment appraisal
Investment managers often need to find the optimum investment in situations where there are various investment options available but finance to invest in them is limited. This is referred to as a capital budgeting problem.

Blending problems
Determining the mixture of raw materials to be input into a process that will satisfy the product requirements and minimise the cost of the raw materials.

Transportation and supply
Many different types of commodity have to be conveyed to destinations by a variety of different types of transport. Constraints are imposed upon the capacities and numbers of vehicles, ships, etc that can be used. Intermediate staging posts may be available for temporary stockpiling of commodities in transport. The objective is to accomplish the supply operation in an optimum way and one which minimises stockpiles and transportation costs.

4. JARVIS & PARTNERS: DEVELOPING A MODEL

SUMMARISING THE DATA

Before taking a more detailed look at LP, it will be useful to us if we probe deeper into the Jarvis doors problem.

The known information regarding the business is summarised below.

Figure 1 shows how much of each resource Jarvis has available each week.

RESOURCE	AVAILABILITY (WEEKLY)	UNIT COST
Wood	600 m²	£4 m²
Glass	300 m²	£16 m²
Labour	320 hours	£6 hour

FIGURE 1: **Resource Data**

Figure 2 shows how much of each resource is required to produce each product.

TO PRODUCE	YOU WILL NEED THIS MUCH			PRODUCT PRICE
	wood	glass	labour	
Chez Nous	2.0 m²	0.5 m²	1 hour	£30
Mon Repos	1.5 m²	1.0 m²	1 hour	£40

FIGURE 2: **Production Data**

THE OBJECTIVE FUNCTION

The objective of the Jarvis firm is to maximise profit. Because we only have material and labour cost, we are concentrating in this example on maximising contribution. We would need to know fixed costs in order to calculate profit.

Contribution per unit produced is equal to selling price minus the variable costs of production.

Using this definition of contribution, try Activity 2.

ACTIVITY 2

Work out the unit contribution for the CHEZ NOUS and the MON REPOS products.

How did you do? You should start with the basic data:

A CHEZ NOUS uses 2 m^2 of wood at £4 per m^2, 0.5 m^2 of glass at £16 per m^2, and 1 hour of labour costing £6. We must now calculate its contribution.

Since it sells at £30, its unit contribution is

$$30 - (2 \times 4) + (0.5 \times 16) + (1 \times 6) = 8$$

The MON REPOS uses 1.5 m^2 of wood, 1 m^2 of glass and 1 hour of labour.

It sells at £40, so its unit contribution is

$$40 - (1.5 \times 4) + (1 \times 16) + (1 \times 6) = 12$$

Now what contribution will Jarvis make if they combine the two products in the optimum manner?

There is not enough information just yet to enable you to do this, but you should be able to deal with the much simpler problem of Activity 3.

ACTIVITY 3

Assume that Jarvis decide to produce X CHEZ NOUS and Y MON REPOS. X and Y may be any number.

Write down a mathematical expression involving X and Y which is equal to the total contribution obtained from this 'mix' of products.

Jarvis earn £8 contribution for each CHEZ NOUS produced. Consequently, if they produce X of these doors the contribution will be £8X.

By the same reasoning, each MON REPOS earns £12, so that a production of Y doors will earn £12Y.

Total contribution therefore, from making X CHEZ NOUS and Y MON REPOS will be 8X + 12Y.

If we allow the letter Z to symbolise total contribution, then the expression becomes

$$Z = 8X + 12Y$$

Jarvis' objective is to find the **maximum** value of Z (contribution) that it is possible to attain by manipulating the values of X and Y which represent the respective quantities of CHEZ NOUS and MON REPOS produced.

The function $Z = 8X + 12Y$ is often called the **objective function** because it is the mathematical representation of the objectives that Jarvis have set for themselves. They wish to find what mix of production will achieve the objective of maximising contribution.

In this instance the objective function has to be maximised. In the case of many other problems, we may be required to **minimise**. The objective differs from situation to situation.

ACTIVITY 4

Consider the objective function for the data of the Jarvis problem. What contribution would Jarvis make if

(a) $X = 10$ and $Y = 15$

(b) $X = 15$ and $Y = 25$

(c) $X = 20$ and $Y = 25$

What generalisation can you make about Z as X and Y increase?

Does the objective function tell us what the optimum mix of doors should be so as to maximise contribution?

The objective function is $Z = 8X + 12Y$, where X and Y represent the quantities of each kind of door produced.

If Jarvis produce 10 CHEZ NOUS and 15 MON REPOS, then the contribution will be

$$Z = 8X + 12Y = (8 \times 10) + (12 \times 15) = 260$$

If they produce 15 and 20 respectively of each type of door then the contribution will be

$$Z = 8X + 12Y = (8 \times 15) + (12 \times 20) = 360$$

Finally, if Jarvis produce 20 and 25 of each door, then the contribution will be

$$Z = 8X + 12Y = (8 \times 20) + (12 \times 25) = 460$$

As you can see, as X and Y increase, the value of Z also increases without limit. If we wish to maximise Z (contribution), the objective function tells us nothing in itself about what X and Y (the number of each type of door) should be in order to achieve this object. You can continually obtain increases in Z by just expanding X and Y.

Fortunately, our knowledge of the problem is not restricted to details regarding contribution. We also have some information about the availability of materials.

Resource Constraints

Activity 4 above, tells us that contribution will increase without limit if more and more doors are produced. But has Jarvis sufficient resources to produce an unlimited number of doors?

ACTIVITY 5

Use figures 1 and 2, which list the resource requirements for the manufacture of the doors to decide whether the following target production figures are possible for the two products;

(a)   100 CHEZ NOUS and 100 MON REPOS.

(b)   200 CHEZ NOUS and 200 MON REPOS.

A CHEZ NOUS uses 2 m^2 and a MON REPOS 1.5 m^2 of wood.

If Jarvis decide to manufacture 100 of each type of door, then it is quite easy to calculate that they will require a total 350 m^2 of wood. Since they have 600 m^2 available per week, they will not be hampered by a scarcity of this material. Likewise, it can easily be calculated that with a glass requirement of 0.5 m^2 and 1 m^2 for a CHEZ NOUS and a MON REPOS respectively, the total glass usage will be 150 m^2. This is well within their weekly glass supply of 300 m^2. In the same way, they will require 200 labour hours to produce 100 of each type of door, and since they can call on 320 hours if necessary, that requirement is easily met.

So the production target of 100 of each type of door is viable. However, if Jarvis decide to manufacture 200 of each type of door, then this is quite another matter. They will require a total of 700 m^2 of wood to achieve this target, and the 600 m^2 available per week, will effectively make it impossible. The glass requirement for this level of production will be 300 m^2 which can be met by their current supply (exactly equal to 300 m^2). They will require 400 labour hours to produce 200 of each type of door, and since only 320 hours are available, they will not be able to meet this target.

Activity 5 has proved that Jarvis cannot just set themselves any production target they care to. They are using resources which are scarce. In Activity 5 you saw that a production target of 100 of each type of door was viable, whereas a target of 200 of each was not.

In linear programming we call these limitations **resource constraints**. Therefore, when we seek to find the maximum value of the contribution function, we must do it subject to the limitations forced on us by these constraints.

These constraints can be expressed in mathematical form.

ACTIVITY 6

Consider the usage of wood. Suppose, as we have previously done, that Jarvis decide to produce X CHEZ NOUS and Y MON REPOS, where X and Y are any whole numbers.

Write down a mathematical expression involving X and Y which states the amount of wood which is used.

From figure 2 we know that the CHEZ NOUS and MON REPOS require 2 m^2 and 1.5 m^2 of wood respectively. So the X MON REPOS units will use 2X m^2 while the Y CHEZ NOUS will use 1.5Y m^2.

Total wood usage from this level of production is therefore

$$2X + 1.5Y \ \ m^2$$

ACTIVITY 7

Assuming production targets of X and Y for the two door types, write down expressions in X and Y which state the usage of glass and labour.

Activity 7 requires that we apply the process used in the solution to Activity 6 to the resources of glass and labour.

The CHEZ NOUS and MON REPOS use 0.5 m^2 and 1 m^2 of glass respectively. A production of X units of the former and Y units of the latter will therefore mean a total glass usage of

$$0.5X + Y \ \ m^2$$

The third and final resource is labour. We need 1 hour to produce a unit of each type of door. Total utilisation of labour is therefore

X + Y hours

As well as knowing how a particular production plan will utilise wood glass and labour, we also know how much **in total** we have of each resource.

The next three Activities will demonstrate how we can put our knowledge of resource **utilisation** and resource **limitation** to good use.

ACTIVITY 8

Consider the builder's wood resources. Jarvis can make X CHEZ NOUS and Y NON REPOS, where X and Y can be ANY number provided they are chosen so that only ONE of the following expressions is ALWAYS true. Which of the following is the correct expression?

(a) $2X + 1.5Y < 600$

(b) $2X + 1.5Y > 600$

(c) $2X + 1.5Y = 600$

(d) $2X + 1.5Y \leq 600$

(e) $2X + 1.5Y \geq 600$

All of the expressions used in Activity 8 (except for (c)) are known as **inequalities** which you will have come across in the foundation unit of this course. Let's look at each of the expressions in turn.

Is expression (a) the correct one?

The expression $2X + 1.5Y < 600$ states that we can choose any value of X and Y so long as $(2X + 1.5Y)$ is less than 600. However, this leaves out the possibility that we may choose a mix of X and Y values where $2X + 1.5Y$ is **exactly equal** to 600. Thus the inequality in option (a) does not include all legitimate possibilities.

Option (b) seems to be suggesting that we may choose any mix of X and Y such that $2X + 1.5Y$ is greater than 600. This cannot possibly be the case; we cannot adopt a production plan which uses more than 600 m^2 of wood.

Option (c) says that we may have any values of X and Y where $2X + 1.5Y$ is exactly equal to 600.

This is certainly true, but it does not allow for the possibility that we may legitimately have a production plan where we use **less** than 600 m^2 of wood.

Expression (d) says that we may choose any value of X and Y where $2X + 1.5Y$ is **less than or equal to** 600. Now this is the only statement which is true in all circumstances and allows for every possible combination of X and Y.

Option (e) would allow us to choose any values of X and Y such that $2X + 1.5Y$ is **equal to** or **greater than** 600. This statement can only be true in the special case where we pick values of X and Y which make it exactly equal to 600; we may NOT use more than 600 m^2 of wood.

We may therefore adopt any production plan (ie choose values of X and Y) that allows the statement

$$2X + 1.5Y \leq 600$$

to be true.

Now work through Activities 9 and 10 making similar decisions on glass and labour.

ACTIVITY 9

Now consider the glass resources available.

Write out an inequality similar to the one for wood, which correctly describes limits on X an Y imposed by the availability of glass.

ACTIVITY 10

Finally, consider the labour available to the business.

Write out an inequality similar to the ones for wood and glass, describing the limits on X an Y imposed by the availability of labour.

We may consider the answers to Activities 9 and 10 together.

We know that the utilisation of glass resulting from a particular production plan is given by the expression

$$0.5X + Y$$

We are also aware that the firm has 300 m^2 of glass. Any production plan is feasible provided that it uses no more than this quantity. Consequently, the correct inequality expression for glass is

$$0.5X + Y \leq 300$$

By a similar process of reasoning, the inequality stating the usage of labour is

$$X + Y \leq 320$$

Check back over these last three Activities to make sure you are happy with the methods and logical reasoning used to obtain these mathematical expressions.

5. SUMMARY

In this section we have used a case study to

- define **linear programming**

- introduce you to the concepts of **linear programming**

- describe typical linear programming **applications**

An understanding of these basics has allowed us to make considerable progress towards solving the problems of Jarvis & Partners as we seek to discover the optimum numbers (producer mix) of CHEZ NOUS and MON REPOS doors they need to produce.

To do this we set out to maximise the objective function value of Z (where $Z = 8X + 12Y$) within certain resource constraints, for wood, glass and labour.

With X and Y explicitly stated as non-negative this is the way we define any linear programming problem:

'an objective function to be optimised within the limits of linear constraints'

If you are unsure of any of the points made in this section, check back **now** before you read on.

SECTION 2

DEVELOPING A LINEAR PROGRAMMING MODEL

1. INTRODUCTION

This second section will do two things. Firstly, we will introduce you to linear equations and linear inequalities both of which are at the heart of the technique of linear programming (LP), and secondly you will gain some practice in setting up a range of LP problems, similar to the Jarvis & Partners case that we worked through in section 1.

2. LINEAR EQUATIONS AND LINEAR INEQUALITIES

What is the reason for the use of the word 'linear' in the expression 'linear programming'? In any linear programming problem the functions stating the objective to be achieved, and the resource constraints all take a **linear** form. Therefore it will be of advantage to you if you spend part of this study session studying the notion of a **linear equation**. If you have worked through unit 1 (*Business Maths*) in this series, then you will already have a good idea about the meaning of linearity.

For two variables, X and Y the general form of a linear equation is

$$Y = a + bX$$

where a and b are constants.

In the above case, only two variables are involved but we can extend the definition to an equation involving n+1 variables

Definition

General Linear Function

A linear function in n+1 variables is written as

$$Y = a_0 + a_1X_1 + a_2X_2 + ... + a_nX_n$$

Where $Y, X_1, X_2 ... X_n$ are the variables

and $a_0, a_1, a_2 ... a_n$ are the constants

If the above expression looks very complex then a few examples, giving specific values to the constants a_0, a_1, ... etc, may help.

$Y = 2X - 10$

$Y - 2X = -10$

$25 = 5X - 2.5Y$

$Y = 6 + 3X_1 - 7X_2 + 0.5X_3$

All of the above are linear functions. The first three are, in fact, the **same** function written in different ways. The last function in the list is an expression involving four variables, whereas the first three are expressions involving only two variables.

ACTIVITY 11

Which of the following are linear equations:

(a) $Y = 3X$

(b) $Y = 2 + 3X + 4X^2$

(c) $Y = 3/X$

(d) $2Y - 3X_1 = X_2 - 4X_3$

(e) $Y = 10$

$Y = 3X$ is a linear equation since it is of the form
$Y = a + bX$, with $b = 3$ and $a = 0$.

$Y = 2 + 3X + 4X^2$ is not a linear equation because of the presence of the term $4X^2$.

$Y = 3/X$. You may remember from the mathematics foundation unit that an expression of this type can be rewritten as $Y = 3X^{-1}$, which is certainly non-linear.

$2Y - 3X_1 = X_2 - 4X_3$ involves four different variables. It can be rewritten as
$Y = (3/2)X_1 + (1/2)X_2 - (4/2)X_3$
which is certainly a equation of the type defined as linear on the previous page.

$Y = 10$ is a linear equation of the type
$Y = a + bX$
where $b = 0$ and $a = 10$.

When a linear equation includes ONLY two variables then it can be represented by a graph.

An expression of the form

$$Y + 2X \leq 12$$

(where £ is read as 'less than or equal to') is termed an **inequality**. To be more precise it is a **linear inequality**. The inequality can be broken down into:

$$\text{the linear equation} \quad Y + 2X = 12$$
$$\text{the strict inequality} \quad Y + 2X < 12$$

As you may have surmised from the Jarvis & Partners case in section 1, the construction of an LP model of a problem depends upon representing an **objective function** by a linear function, and a number of **resource constraints** by appropriate linear inequalities.

Section 3 will show you how to represent linear functions and inequalities consisting of only two variables in graphical form. Graphical representation will help us to find solutions to LP problems. However, it is important right now for you to gain some experience in the **construction** of LP models. We will devote the remainder of this section to developing this important skill. We shall return to the problem of solution later on.

3. MORE CASE STUDIES

PROBLEM 1: SUPERB AUDIO PLC

Suppose that Superb Audio plc produce two types of speaker mechanisms for inclusion in telephone handsets, the 'ECONOMY' and the 'SPECIAL'. Most of their sales are to telecommunications organisations such as British Telecom. Manufacture of each product involves two processes, which we may refer to as assembly and testing. Currently the number of hours required for each production process is as given by the table below:

	Per ECONOMY (Hours)	Per SPECIAL (Hours)
Assembly	2	4
Testing	1	3

The firm considers that it has available no more per week than

2,000   manufacturing hours for assembly

and

1,200   manufacturing hours for testing.

Past experience suggests that sales of the ECONOMY are unlikely to exceed 900 per week.

Finally, each ECONOMY sold earns a contribution of £4 and each SPECIAL a contribution of £9.

The firm would appreciate some advice as to what it should do to maximise its profits.

We start by determining the decision variables; the variables which we must adjust until we arrive at some objective. The decision variables are the quantities of ECONOMY and SPECIAL speakers to be produced each week.

> **Let X** = the number of **ECONOMYs** produced per week
>
> **Let Y** = the number of **SPECIALs** produced per week

What are the resource constraints?

It is fairly clear from this problem that the amount of assembly and testing time available are two important constraints.

ACTIVITY 12

Write out two linear inequalities which state the restrictions imposed by the availability of manufacturing hours for assembly and testing.

From the original table of Superb Audio data, we know that to produce the products requires

2 hours of assembly for each **ECONOMY**

4 hours of assembly for each **SPECIAL**

Consequently, if Superb Audio produce X ECONOMY and Y SPECIAL models then it will require

2X + 4Y hours of assembly time

Since we only have 2,000 hours per week of assembly time available, it must follow that whatever mix of the two speakers we adopt, we cannot exceed this value. Consequently, the resource constraint for assembly time can be expressed by the linear inequality

2X + 4Y ≤ 2,000

By a similar argument Superb Audio will require

X + 3Y hours of testing time

Since we have 1,200 hours available per week, then we may express the limitations placed on production by testing hours by the linear inequality

X + 3Y ≤ 1,200

We refer to these as resource constraints.

ACTIVITY 13

There is also a sales constraint on the weekly production levels of one of the speakers.

Express this constraint in the form of a linear inequality.

The sales constraint is only a restriction on the production of the ECONOMY model. Superb Audio cannot sell more than 900 of this model per week. Therefore

$$X \le 900$$

We do not need to mention Y in this inequality, because the SPECIALs are not subject to a sales limitation.

We cannot leave the discussion of constraints for this problem without mentioning that since we cannot produce a negative amount of each of the speakers, we have;

$$X \ge 0$$

and

$$Y \ge 0$$

Now that we have formally expressed the constraints affecting this problem, we turn to the question of the **objectives** of the business. What do you think Superb Audio plc plan to do?

ACTIVITY 14

What do you think should be the objective of Superb Audio?

Can you express this objective in the form of a linear function?

We have some information regarding the size of contribution obtained from the sale of each of the two loudspeaker models. It seems therefore reasonable to assume that the business would wish to choose the production plan which maximises contribution.

Now each ECONOMY model will contribute £4, and each SPECIAL will contribute £9. Therefore, if the company decides to produce X ECONOMY and Y SPECIAL models, the resulting total contribution will be

$$Z = 4X + 9Y$$

The linear programming model for the Superb Audio problem has now been formulated and can be summarised as

● find the production plan which maximises $Z = 4X + 9Y$

● subject to the following constraints

$$2X + 4Y \leq 2{,}000 \text{ (assembly)}$$
$$X + 3Y \leq 1{,}200 \qquad \text{(testing)}$$
$$X \qquad \leq 900 \qquad \text{(sales)}$$
$$X \qquad \geq 0 \qquad \text{(X non-negative)}$$
$$Y \qquad \geq 0 \qquad \text{(Y non-negative)}$$

We still have a further step to take before we obtain the ultimate solution to this problem. But nevertheless, as was the case with the Jarvis problem in section 1, we have made considerable advances in setting it out in formal mathematical terms.

PROBLEM 2: THE SMALL MINE

Now would be a good time for you to see whether you can take a LP problem from the following initial statement all the way through to formal mathematical model.

A small mine works two coal seams and produces three grades of coal. It costs £100 an hour to work the upper seam, obtaining in that time 1 tonne of anthracite, 5 tonnes of best quality coal and 2 tonnes of ordinary coal. The lower seam is more expensive to work, at a cost of £150 per hour, but it yields in that time 4 tonnes of anthracite, 6 tonnes of best coal and 1 tonne of ordinary coal.

Faced with a requirement for at least 8 tonnes of anthracite, 30 tonnes of best coal and 8 tonnes of ordinary coal each day, how many hours a day should each seam be worked so as to fill this order as cheaply as possible?

ACTIVITY 15

Formulate the small mine problem (problem 2, above) as a linear programming problem.

(In other words, write out the objective function and constraints as linear equations or inequalities.)

There is a useful procedure you can follow when formulating any linear programming problem. This consists of acting out the role of the decision maker at the centre of the problem, and asking various key questions.

What is the Objective?

Is it to maximise or to minimise some variable? Here the objective is clearly to minimise the cost of meeting an order for coal.

What are the variables we must make decisions about?

Another way of putting this same question is as follows

'what are the variables actually under my control?'

Here there might seem to be several options for decision variables: there is reference to two coal seams, rates (per hour) of production for three types of coal, an order for a specified amount of this coal and finally, costs (per hour) of mining each seam.

The factor which is under the mine owner's immediate control is the number of hours spent working each seam. This has an immediate impact on how much of each of the three types of coal is mined and at what cost. Since there are two seams then there must be two decision variables.

Therefore we must decide how many hours are to be spent mining each of the two seams so as to supply an order for coal at minimum cost.

Let X = the number of hours spent on the upper seam

and Y = the number of hours spent on the lower seam

Now since the upper seam costs £100 per hour to work, then mining it for X hours will mean that we incur costs of 100X.

Likewise, we incur costs of 150Y if we work the lower seam for Y hours.

So the total cost of mining both seams must be

$$100X + 150Y$$

and the LP objective function is to minimise Z, where

$$Z = 100X + 150Y$$

What will constrain the decision variables?

How many constraints are there? Here there are constraints due to the quotas which must be met for three types of coal.

There are three constraints in total, which need to be specified algebraically.

(a)   **Anthracite.** The upper seam can produce 1 tonne every hour while the lower seam can produce 4 tonnes in the same time. If we work the upper and lower seams for X and Y hours respectively, then the total production of anthracite must be

$$X + 4Y$$

Now there is a clearly stated quota of at least 8 tonnes of anthracite. Whatever the number of hours spent working the seams they must meet this target. The linear inequality expressing this constraint should be written as

$$X + 4Y \geq 8$$

meaning equal to, or greater than, 8 tonnes.

(b)   **Best Coal.** The upper seam produces 5 tonnes per hour while the lower seam produces 6. Working upper and lower seams X and Y hours respectively, the total production of best must be

$$5X + 6Y$$

At least 30 tonnes of best coal must be produced. The linear inequality expressing this constraint is therefore;

$$5X + 6Y \geq 30$$

(c)   **Ordinary Coal.** Finally, using an argument similar to that used for anthracite and best coal, the linear inequality expressing the constraint for ordinary grade coal is

$$2X + Y \geq 8$$

We are now in a position to formulate the problem.

We must choose a value of X and Y such that the value of Z in the expression

$$Z = 100X + 150Y \text{ (objective function)}$$

is minimised, subject to:

$$
\begin{array}{rll}
X + 4Y \geq & 8 & \text{(Anthracite order)} \\
5X + 6Y \geq & 30 & \text{(Best order)} \\
2X + Y \geq & 8 & \text{(Ordinary order)} \\
X \geq & 0 & \\
Y \geq & 0 &
\end{array}
$$

Notice, as in previous problems, the last two constraints which formally express the non-negativity of X and Y.

PROBLEM 3: REST EASY LOUNGE SUITES

Rest Easy plc manufacture lounge suites solely for the export market. They have two; the 'AMBASSADOR' with leather upholstery and the 'DIPLOMAT' with dralon covering. The firm is organised into three departments: joinery, upholstery and packaging. Both suites can be handled within the joinery and packaging departments, but upholstery is divided into two separate sections. Given the capacity available in the joinery department a maximum of **either** 300 AMBASSADORs **or** 450 DIPLOMATs (or a 'pro rata' production of both types) can be constructed per week. The packaging department can handle a maximum of **either** 400 AMBASSADORs **or** 400 DIPLOMATs (or pro rata) per week. In the upholstery department, the leather section can handle up to 150 AMBASSADORs per week and the dralon section can handle up to 375 DIPLOMATs per week.

Contribution is £110 per AMBASSADOR and £90 per DIPLOMAT.

You are to act as a consultant to the firm.

ACTIVITY 16

Write out (in words) the objective you think Rest Easy should adopt in order to optimise their production plans.

What are the decision variables which affect this production plan?

Write out an objective function which expresses the company's optimum production plan.

You would probably advise Rest Easy to adopt the production plan which obtained the maximum possible contribution.

The variables which are under the control of the decision maker are the number of lounge suites of each type to be made. Consequently, if the firm made X AMBASSADORs and Y DIPLOMATs, then the total contribution earned would be

$$110X + 90Y$$

We therefore have an objective function; Rest Easy would need to maximise Z, where

$$Z = 110X + 90Y$$

ACTIVITY 17

In trying to achieve the objective of maximising contribution, how many constraints are Rest Easy bound by?

In words, describe what these constraints are.

Apart from non-negativity, there appear to be four constraints.

The capacity of the joinery department
The capacity of the packaging department
The capacity of the leather sub-department
The capacity of the Dralon sub-department

We must now express these constraints as linear inequalities.

The constraints relating to the Dralon and leather covering subsections of the upholstery department are straightforward, so we will deal with these first.

ACTIVITY 18

Write down linear inequalities which express the Dralon and leather constraints.

Leather covering capacity only affects the AMBASSADOR. A maximum of 150 can be covered in a week, so that if we make X AMBASSADORs per week, then it must be the case that

$$X \leq 150$$

Likewise, Dralon covering only affects the DIPLOMAT.

A maximum of 375 can be covered in a week. So if Y DIPLOMATs are made per week, then it must be the case that

$$Y \leq 375$$

Now we need to deal with the constraints imposed by capacity in the joinery and packaging departments.

You will find these constraints rather more difficult to deal with.

ACTIVITY 19

Consider the constraint placed on production by the capacity of the joinery department. Reread the part of the Rest Easy problem which describes this constraint, and then try to formulate a linear inequality which expresses it.

Do not spend too long on this problem; if you find it too difficult, try to gain some hints from the solution immediately following.

The key fact about the capacity of the joinery department is that contained in the expression 'pro rata'. If it were to produce AMBASSADORs alone, it could handle 300 of them. At the other extreme, if it were to concentrate solely on DIPLOMATS, it could deal with 450. However, in reality it can handle any pro rata combination of them both together.

How do we formulate a linear inequality for such a situation?

Think back to the definition of a linear function of two variables, which takes the form

$$Y = a + bX$$

Now we know that when the joinery department produces no AMBASSADORs ($X = 0$) it can produce 450 DIPLOMATs ($Y = 450$). If we insert these values into the general two-variable linear function, we have

$$450 = a + (b \times 0)$$

Consequently

$$a = 450$$

Likewise, if the joinery department produces no DIPLOMATs ($Y = 0$), it can produce 300 AMBASSADORs ($X = 300$). Inserting these values (and $a = 450$) into the linear function, we have

$$0 = 450 + (b \times 300)$$

and

$$b = -(450/300) = -(3/2)$$

Since we now know a and b, we have

$$Y = a + bX$$

and since

$$b = -(3/2) \text{ and } a = 450$$

we have

$$Y = -(3/2)X + 450$$

which is better rewritten in the form

$$(3/2)X + Y = 450$$

Multiply through by 2 to remove the fraction

$$3X + 2Y = 900$$

Since we know that production is **less than or equal to** 300 AMBASSADORs or 450 DIPLOMATs, then the linear inequality

$$3X + 2Y \leq 900$$

will correctly describe the joinery constraint.

ACTIVITY 20

Now that you have seen how the linear inequality for the joinery department constraint has been derived, see if you can use a similar process to obtain an inequality for the packaging department constraint.

We are told that packaging can handle a pro-rata mix of suites ranging from the extreme of 400 AMBASSADORs and no DIPLOMATs to 400 DIPLOMATs and no AMBASSADORs. This means that when X =0, Y = 400, and when Y = 0, X = 400. Therefore

$$Y = a + bX$$

$$400 = (b \times 0) + a$$

and

$$a = 400$$

Also

$$0 = 400 + (b \times 400)$$

(Since a = 400)

$$\text{So } b = -1$$

The linear function becomes

$\quad$ **Y = -X + 400** or

$\quad$ **X + Y = 400** and the inequality is

$\quad$ **X + Y ≤ 400**

To summarise the Rest Easy problem we must choose a value of X and Y such that the value of Z in the expression

$$Z = 110X + 90Y \text{ (objective function)}$$

is maximised, subject to

3X +	2Y	≤	900	(joinery department)
X +	Y	≤	400	(packaging department)
X		≤	150	(leather section)
	Y	≤	375	(Dralon section)
X,	Y	≥	0	(non-negativity)

PROBLEM 4: THE DOLLS' WORKSHOP

A training agency sponsored workshop manufactures two types of doll.

The 'Cindy Lou' Doll

Selling price   - £20

Variable costs - £8

The 'Sue-Ellen' (moving mouth) Doll

Selling price   - £32

Variable costs - £12

The joint fixed costs are £400 per day. The workshop has the capacity to produce 2,000 dolls of the 'Cindy Lou' type (alone) per day. The 'Sue Ellen' takes twice as long to produce as the 'Cindy Lou'. The supply of plastic is just sufficient to produce 1,500 dolls ('Cindy Lou' and 'Sue Ellen' combined) each day. The 'Sue Ellen' requires a special mechanism to make its mouth move, and there are only 600 of these available per day.

ACTIVITY 21

Advise the workshop what it should do to maximise daily profit.

Would your advice change if the workshop prefers to maximise **sales revenue** instead?

Since fixed costs must be paid whatever the output of the two dolls, we can treat this as a problem involving the maximisation of daily contribution.

For the decision variables

let

$\qquad$ **X** = the output of **'Cindy Lou' dolls,** and

$\qquad$ **Y** = the output of **'Sue Ellen' dolls**

We can work out contribution for the 'Cindy Lou' as (£20 - £8) = £12, and for the 'Sue Ellen' as (£32 - £12) = £20. The objective function is, therefore

$$Z = 12X + 20Y$$

As constraints there are

$\qquad$ **workshop capacity**

$\qquad$ **supply of plastic**

$\qquad$ **supply of mouth mechanisms**

The last two constraints are fairly straightforward. The supply of mouth mechanisms only affects the 'Sue Ellen', so for that constraint

$$Y \le 600$$

We know that there is sufficient plastic to produce a **sum total** of 1500 dolls, so

$$X + Y \le 1500$$

Workshop capacity is a little more involved.

A 'Sue Ellen' will take up twice as much workshop time as a 'Cindy Lou'. Consequently, the workshop can **either** produce 2,000 'Cindy Lou' dolls (and no 'Sue Ellens') **or** 1000 'Sue Ellen' (and no 'Cindy Lou').

Now because of these facts, we know that when X = 0

Y = 1000, and when Y = 0, X = 2000, which is sufficient information to determine the linear expression required for the workshop constraint. Using a similar process to that used for the joinery and packaging constraints in the Rest Easy problem, we find that this will lead us to the linear inequality

$$X + 2Y \le 2000$$

We are now in a position to summarise the Dolls' Workshop problem.

We must choose a value of X and Y such that the value of Z in the expression

$$Z = 12X + 20Y \text{ (objective function)}$$

is maximised, subject to

X	+	Y	$\leq$	1,500	(plastic supply)
X	+	2Y	$\leq$	2,000	(workshop capacity)
		Y	$\leq$	600	(mouth mechanisms)
X,		Y	$\geq$	0	(non-negativity)

If asked to maximise revenue, rather than contribution, how would the problem change?

We have not altered any of the constraints, so they remain as they are. We have however, altered the **objective** to be attained. The revenue function is

$$20X + 32Y \text{ (price times quantity)}$$

Therefore we maximise

$$Z = 20X + 32Y$$

instead of

$$Z = 12X + 20Y$$

---

4. SUMMARY

In this section we have taken the subject a stage further as we develop the linear programming model.

You should now be developing a fair understanding of the types of problems where linear programming may be of help, and gaining some useful experience in expressing problems as formal mathematical models.

We have discussed with examples from four new case studies

- **linear equations** and **linear inequalities**

- **variables** and **constraints**

- shown how these can be brought together to **define the problem** and help us **find a solution**

Look back through all the examples and calculations in this section and be sure you understand them before you move on to the next section.

SECTION 3

SOLVING LINEAR PROGRAMMING PROBLEMS USING GRAPHICAL METHODS

1. INTRODUCTION

So far in this unit you have learned how to set up certain kinds of problem as LP models using linear functions and inequalities. Although expressing problems in this form is a major step forward, we still have to carry out a further stage before we obtain answers to the all-important question

'what values of the decision variables will maximise or minimise the objective function, yet stay within certain constraints'.

If a problem has only two decision variables – as have all the problems you have encountered so far – then it is possible to use graphical methods. We will now return to the Jarvis & Partners case study from section 1. Reread this problem and have some graph paper handy.

2. JARVIS & PARTNERS REVISITED

You may remember that the Jarvis problem was expressed as

Find the values of X and Y which maximise

$$Z = 8X + 12Y$$

subject to the following resource constraints

2X	+	1.5Y	≤	600	(wood)
0.5X	+	Y	≤	300	(glass)
X	+	Y	≤	320	(labour)
X			≥	0	
Y			≥	0	

The graphical method proceeds by drawing lines to represent the above expressions and then shading in the areas on the graph which correspond to allowable, or feasible values of X and Y.

The Wood Constraint
The linear inequality representing the wood resource is

$$2X + 1.5Y \leq 600$$

How do we draw the graph of such an expression?

The simple answer to this question is that it is not possible to graph an inequality.

We can, for the moment, treat the expression as a strict **equality**. That is, proceed as though it were the linear function

$$2X + 1.5Y = 600$$

Now sketching the graph of a linear function is a fairly straightforward matter.

Such a function by definition, has a straight line graph, so all we need to draw its graph are just two co-ordinates of X and Y, that is to say, two pairs of XY values. We then simply draw a straight line between these points.

In many cases, it is convenient to choose the points where the line cuts through the X and Y axes. At the point where the line cuts through the Y axis, X will be equal to 0. In the case of the wood constraint, when X = 0, Y = 400.

One possible co-ordinate on the graph of this line is

$$X = 0, Y = 400$$

ACTIVITY 22

What are the co-ordinates of the line 2X + 1.5Y = 600, at the point where it passes through the X axis? (ie where Y = 0)

ACTIVITY 23

Draw axes on appropriately scaled graph paper, mark two XY co-ordinates.

Hence graph the function 2X + 1.5Y = 600.

Now if Y = 0, then the expression 2X + 1.5Y = 600 becomes

$$2X + (1.5 \times 0) = 600$$

and X is therefore equal to 300.

We now have two XY co-ordinates: (X=0, Y=400), and (X=300, Y=0).

Constructing suitably scaled axes and then connecting these two co-ordinates, we have a graph as shown in figure 3.

Any co-ordinate XY which lies on this line will satisfy the strict **equality**, $2X + 1.5Y = 600$.

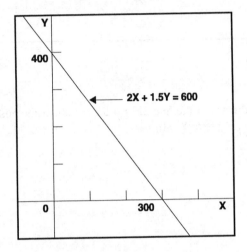

FIGURE 3: **Jarvis & Partners: Wood**

For example; the co-ordinate (X=150, Y=200) happens to lie on this line. However, we are particularly interested in the set of points for which the **inequality** $2X + 1.5Y \pounds 600$ is true.

How do we show these on our graph?

It is a useful exercise to examine a few XY co-ordinates and make a note of their position relative to the graph line drawn in figure 3. For example, we have already seen that the co-ordinate (X=150, Y=200) lies **exactly** on the line. What about the co-ordinate (X=300, Y=100)?

For this co-ordinate

$$2X + 1.5Y = (2 \times 300) + (1.5 \times 100) \geq 600$$

If you mark the co-ordinate on your graph, you will find that it lies to the right of the line $Y = 2X + 1.5Y$.

What about the co-ordinate (X=100, Y=100)?

For this co-ordinate

$$2X + 1.5Y = (2 \times 100) + (1.5 \times 100) \leq 600$$

and if you mark it on your graph, you will find that it lies to the **left** of the line in $Y = 2X + 1.5Y$.

It should be possible to draw some conclusions from this which will help us with our linear programming problem.

ACTIVITY 24

It is possible to shade in an area on your graph corresponding to the set of ALL points XY which satisfy the inequality $2X + 1.5Y \leq 600$.

Try and do this.

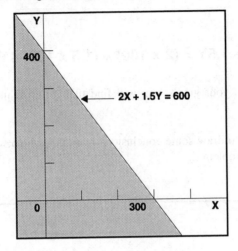

FIGURE 4: **Wood Constraint**

Figure 4 shows the graph of $2X + 1.5Y = 600$, as before.

The shaded area corresponds to the set of all XY values where

$$2X + 1.5Y \leq 600$$

Now since we know that this inequality represents the wood constraint for Jarvis & Partners, then it **must** be the case that any solution to the problem of maximising contribution must be restricted to this shaded area. We cannot choose a solution where X or Y lies outside it.

ACTIVITY 25

You may remember that the glass constraint for Jarvis & Partners could be represented by the linear inequality

$0.5X + Y \leq 300$

Sketch a graph of the equality $0.5X + Y = 300$, and shade in the area you think corresponds to the glass constraint.

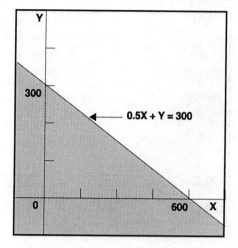

FIGURE 5: **Glass Constraint**

Figure 5 shows a graph of $0.5X + Y = 300$. The region below and to the left of this line has been shaded in, and the resulting area corresponds to the set of all XY values which satisfy the inequality $0.5X + Y \leq 300$. It would be a useful exercise for you to choose a few XY co-ordinates (some where $0.5X + Y < 300$, some where $0.5X + Y > 300$). Marking these co-ordinates on your graph should convince you that the shaded area correctly corresponds with the glass constraint. Any value of X and Y which solves the Jarvis problem will be resricted to this shaded area.

ACTIVITY 26

The last resource constraint inequality is the supply of labour represented by the inequality

$X + Y \leq 320$

Draw a graph of $X + Y = 320$ and shade in the region which you think represents the inequality.

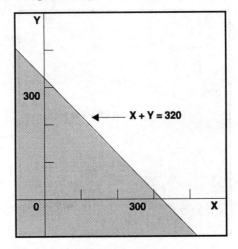

FIGURE 6: **Labour Constraint**

Figure 6 shows a graph of X + Y = 320. The shaded area represents the inequality X + Y ≤ 320. As before, you might find it useful to choose a few XY co-ordinates, (some where X + Y < 320, and some where X +Y > 320). Use these co-ordinates to check that the shaded area correctly corresponds with the labour constraint. Values of X and Y which solve the problem of maximum contribution will be resricted to this shaded area.

ACTIVITY 27

On the same set of graph scales draw the graphs representing the three functions

$$
\begin{array}{rcl}
2X + 1.5Y &=& 600 \\
0.5X + Y &=& 300 \\
X + Y &=& 320
\end{array}
$$

Shade in the area which you think satisfies ALL three resource constraints at the same time.

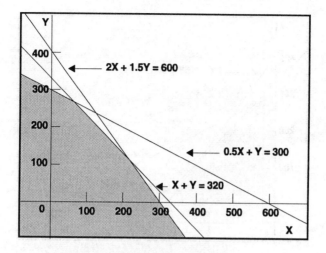

FIGURE 7: **All Constraints**

The shaded area in figure 7 contains ALL of the co-ordinates of X and Y which are solutions to the Jarvis problem AND which satisfy all of the three resource constraints **simultaneously.**

However, although we have represented all of the **resource** constraints on the graph in figure 7, we are still not completely through with this process.

There are still two other constraints to show. These are the 'non-negativity' conditions represented by the expressions

$$X \geq 0$$

and

$$Y \geq 0$$

We cannot produce a negative number of doors. When the graph has been altered to rule out all non-negative values of X and Y, we have the shaded region shown in figure 8.

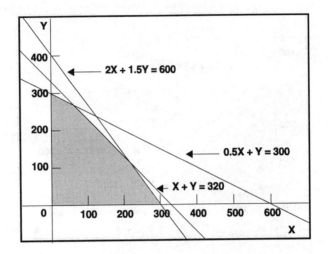

FIGURE 8: **Feasible Region**

The effect of this process has been to shade in an area of the graph paper, bounded by the three functions and the X and Y axes. This area we call the **feasible region**.

Why do you think we call it this?

Any solution (ie, an XY co-ordinate) we select to solve the Jarvis problem must lie within this area. A value of XY chosen from outside this area will not be 'feasible', because it will breach one of the constraints.

Therefore, to summarise our findings so far

we must select an XY co-ordinate from within the feasible region such that contribution is maximised.

How do we do this?

We can proceed to answer this question by examining the objective function. If you remember, for the Jarvis data this is

$$Z = 8X + 12Y$$

The process of solving the maximisation problem will involve drawing the graph of this objective function and then comparing this graph with the feasible region obtained earlier.

However, we cannot draw a graph with three variables; we must give Z a value.

Suppose that we assume that Z takes, for example, the value 1920. The objective function then becomes

$$1920 = 8X + 12Y$$

This is a linear function of two variables, so we can certainly draw its graph.

ACTIVITY 28

On a new sheet of graph paper sketch the graph of the function

$1920 = 8x + 12y$

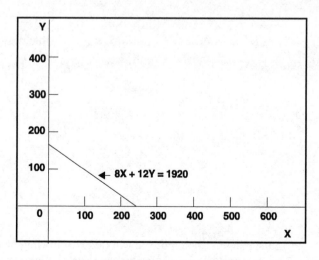

FIGURE 9: **Objective Function**

The graph of this function is shown in figure 9 opposite. Any co-ordinate of XY which is on this line satisfies the equation

$$1920 = 8X + 12Y$$

What would happen to the objective function if we chose Z to be a value other than 1920?

ACTIVITY 29

On the same piece of graph paper you used for Activity 28 draw the graphs of the objective function where

(a)   Z = 3840

(b)   Z = 4800

What do you notice about the behaviour of the objective function as Z increases in size?

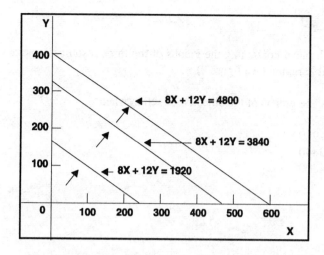

FIGURE 10: **Behaviour of the Objective Function**

The graphs of the function $Z = 8X + 12Y$ for $Z = 1920$, 3840 and 4800 are shown in figure 10. As the value of Z increases, you will see that the graph of the objective function moves further and further away from the origin. You should also take careful note that all three lines are parallel to each other. We can therefore summarise this finding as:

> the graph of the objective function will depend upon the particular value we choose to give Z

> if we **increase** the value of Z, then the graph of the objective function will move further away from the origin

> if we **decrease** the value of Z, then the graph of the objective function will move closer to the origin

> whatever value we give to Z, the graphs of the objective function will always be parallel.

We can now draw together all the information we have on the Jarvis problem. We know what the feasible region is and we know that any solution must lie within this region. We also know what the objective function is and what the graph of it looks like.

ACTIVITY 30

On the graph paper containing the graphs of the three resource constraints, and the shaded feasible region (see figure 8)

(a)   Draw the graphs of the objective function when

$Z = 1920$
$Z = 3840$
$Z = 4800$

(b)   Could the optimum number of doors be equal to some XY co-ordinate on the line

$8X + 12Y = 1920$?

or on the line

$8X + 12Y = 3840$?

or on the line

$8X + 12Y = 4800$?

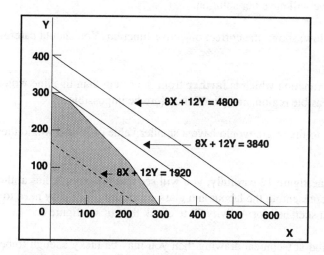

FIGURE 11: **Objective Function and Feasible Region**

The graph needed to answer this question is shown in figure 11 above.

Could the solution to Jarvis's problem be some XY co-ordinate on the line $1920 = 8X + 12Y$?

The answer is that it could not. Why is this?

Recall that the graph line of $Z = 8X + 12Y$ represents the objective function (in this case contribution). We wish to maximise this. Z becomes larger as the graph line representing the objective function moves further away from the origin. We are certainly able to move the line further out, because we are still inside the feasible region.

Could the solution then be an XY co-ordinate on the line $4800 = 8X + 12Y$?

The answer is NO again.

Look at the graph line $4800 = 8X + 12Y$, and then look at the feasible region. They do not coincide at any point. Any value of XY which is a solution to this problem must lie within the feasible region.

What about the line $3840 = 8X + 12Y$?

This line lies **only just** outside the feasible region. It does not contain the solution, but you should now be able to see that as you move the objective function back towards the feasible region, the first point it will make contact with is the point labelled A in figure 11.

Therefore, if we draw a line parallel with the objective function lines, but just touching the point A, we will have our solution.

Figure 12, below, shows the correct objective function. You should carefully study this graph.

An objective function which is **farther** from the origin than this line would lie entirely outside the feasible region, and would therefore be impossible.

A line **closer** to the origin would have a smaller value of Z, and would therefore not be optimal.

If you examine figure 12 carefully, you will see that the point A lies at the intersection of the lines representing the labour and glass constraints. You may need to refer back to the graph you sketched for Activity 27 to check this, or see figure 8.

If you are good at technical drawing then you may be lucky enough to be able to read the co-ordinates of this point from your graph. If not, then you can use simultaneous equations to obtain an answer.

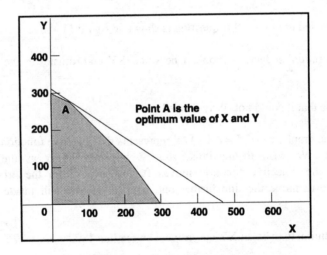

FIGURE 12: **The Correct Objective Function**

You can obtain a solution by simultaneous equations as follows.

We need to obtain values of X and Y such that

0.5X	+	Y	=	300	(1)
X	+	Y	=	320	(2) subtract 1 from 2

0.5X		=	20
X		=	40
Y		=	280

which means that

Now since we originally allowed X to represent the number of CHEZ NOUS and Y the number of MON REPOS type doors, it follows that Jarvis should make 40 of the former and 280 of the latter.

This will be an optimal solution.

What about the amount of contribution from this production plan?

We know that contribution is given by the expression $Z = 8X + 12Y$. If X (the number of CHEZ NOUS) and Y (the number of MON REPOS) are 40 and 280 respectively, then contribution is

$$(8 \times 40) + (12 \times 280) = £3680$$

3. SUMMARY

In this section we have looked back at the Jarvis & Partners problem and reproduced the data in graphical form, concluding that, subject to all constraints, the firm should produce 40 CHEZ NOUS and 280 MON REPOS, yielding £3680 contribution. This solution is optimal, as no other combination of X and Y will achieve a greater contribution.

Here is a summary of the graphical linear programming method

- set up **objective function** and constraints as formal mathematical functions and inequalities

- graph these functions and shade in the '**feasible region**'

- draw the graph of the objective function with a suitably chosen value of Z

- move the objective function slowly out of the feasible region, and note the last XY co-ordinate that it has in common with the region before it finally leaves it

- this XY co-ordinate is the **optimum solution**

Don't leave this section until you are sure of these steps and the graph construction method. When you are ready, move on to section 4 where you will be able to practice this graphical method.

SECTION 4

PRACTISING THE GRAPHICAL SOLUTION TECHNIQUE

1. INTRODUCTION

No new material will be introduced in this section. After having seen the graphical LP method at work in the solution to the problem of Jarvis & Partners, it will be of benefit to you if you practice this technique further.

You will need several sheets of graph paper and also to check back to the formal mathematical statements of the problems from section 2, namely:

Superb Audio plc

The Small Mine

Rest Easy Lounge Suites

The Dolls' Workshop

2. SUPERB AUDIO PLC: A GRAPHICAL SOLUTION

First of all, remind yourself of the nature of Superb Audio's problem by reading the appropriate part of section 2.

The formal statement, in LP terms, of this problem was

find the production plan which maximises $Z = 4X + 9Y$
subject to the following constraints

2X	+	4Y	≤	2,000	(assembly)
X	+	3Y	≤	1,200	(testing)
X			≤	900	(sales)
X			≥	0	(X non-negative)
Y			≥	0	(Y non-negative)

ACTIVITY 31

On the same axes, draw the graphs of the functions representing the constraints on Superb Audio plc's production plan.

Shade in the area of the graph which you think represents the feasible region.

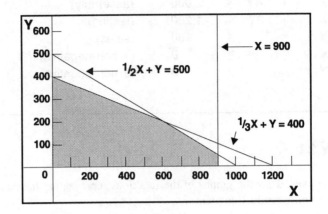

FIGURE 13: **Superb Audio**

Figure 13 shows the graphs of all of the constraints.

Since all of the resource constraints are of the '≤' type, the feasible area is located below and to the left of each graph line. This part of the graph has been shaded, and represents the 'feasible region'. Any solution to the Superb Audio problem must be a point **within** this region.

Notice that the sales constraint only affects manufacture of the ECONOMY model; $X \le 900$; this will be represented by a vertical straight line parallel to the Y axis at the point $X = 900$.

ACTIVITY 32

Now draw the graph of the objective function $Z = 4X + 9Y$ on the same paper you used to show the feasible region.

Before you can do this, you will have to put Z equal to some convenient value. Experiment with a few numbers and you will soon get a 'feel' for the method.

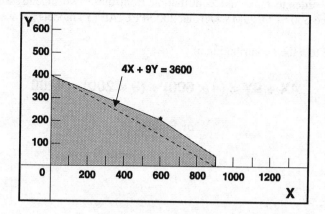

FIGURE 14: **Superb Audio**

Figure 14 shows the feasible region as before, although the graph has been simplified to make matters clearer. In addition, the graph of the function $4X + 9Y = 3,600$ has been drawn. In other words, this is the graph of the objective function where $Z = 3,600$. 3,600 is a convenient choice for this data because it is an exact multiple of 4 and 9 – the contribution figures for ECONOMY and SPECIAL models. This makes it relatively simple to find the XY co-ordinates to draw the graph. It is also important that you select a value of Z which places the graph of the objective function near to the edge of the feasible region. Choose too small a value, and the graph of the objective function may end up being too close to the origin; choose too large a value and it may be right off your graph! A little experimentation with different values for Z will soon develop your skill in deciding what is a convenient choice.

It is fairly clear from figure 14, that as the objective function (currently within the feasible region) moves outwards from the origin, the last point of the shaded area it will be in contact with before it enters the non-feasible area, will be the point marked with a '*'.

If you check this point with your graph, you will see that it is at the intersection of the assembly and testing constraint functions. We need, therefore, to find the XY co-ordinate at this point. If your graph is accurate, it is possible to use it to 'read off' this co-ordinate. Otherwise, it is better to treat the two intersecting graph lines as simultaneous equations, and solve for X and Y. This is done below.

2X	+	4Y	=	2000	**(1)** Assembly
X	+	3Y	=	1200	**(2)** Testing
					Multiply **(1)** by 0.5
X	+	2Y	=	1000	**(3)**
X	+	3Y	=	1200	**(4)** Subtract **(3)** from **(2)**
Y			=	200	therefore X = 600

Therefore, in order to maximise contribution from these two models, Superb Audio should produce 600 ECONOMY (X) and 200 SPECIAL (Y) models per week.

This will lead to a total contribution of

$$4X + 9Y = (4 \times 600) + (9 \times 200) = 4200$$

or £4200

3. THE SMALL MINE: A GRAPHICAL SOLUTION

We now return to Problem 2 discussed in Section 2. Please reread the account of this problem if you need to. It is formally summarised below.

Minimise Z in the objective function expression $Z = 100X + 150Y$ subject to

X	+	4Y	≥	8	(Anthracite order)
5X	+	6Y	≥	30	('Best' order)
2X	+	Y	≥	8	('Ordinary' order)
X			≥	0	
		Y	≥	0	

ACTIVITY 33

On an appropriately scaled sheet of graph paper sketch graphs showing the mining problem constraints.

Shade in the region you think corresponds to the feasible region.

Take care! The constraints are of the '≥' type in this problem.

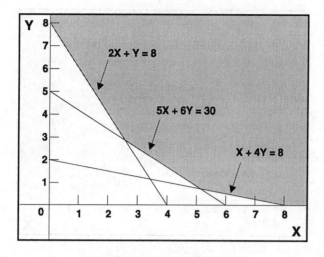

FIGURE 15: **The Small Mine**

Figure 15 shows graphs of functions representing the coal order constraints. The feasible region has been shaded in. Notice that, in this case, the region above and to the right of each graph line, is shaded. This is because the constraints are all of the '≥' type (greater than or equal to) in this problem, rather than the '≤' type.

ACTIVITY 34

On your graph of the feasible region, sketch a line representing the objective function

Z = 100X + 150Y

As before, you will have to select a sutable value for Z before you can do this.

Also, remember that this time, instead of **maximising** profit/contribution, you are **minimising** cost.

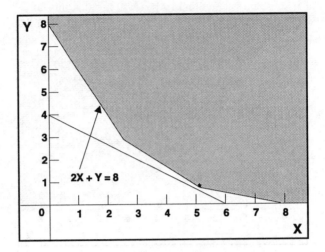

FIGURE 16: **The Small Mine**

The graph of the Small Mine problem is shown in figure 16 with the cost objective function. In this case, Z is equal to 600, so that the objective function shown is that of

$$100X + 150Y = 600$$

As in the problem of Superb Audio, this value of 600 has been chosen because it is a convenient multiple of the factors 100 and 150, and because it has the effect of placing the objective function close to the feasible region, where we can easily see what the likely solution will be.

It is very important to remember that this is a **minimising** problem. Do you remember the discussion of the objective function in section 3?

We noted there that, as the graph of the objective function moved further away from the origin, Z grew larger. Therefore, a maximisation problem consisted in seeing how far we could move the function away from the origin and still have some point in common with the feasible region.

In the minimisation case, Z becomes **smaller** as the objective function moves **closer** to the origin. Therefore, a minimisation problem consists in seeing how far we can move towards the origin and yet still share some point in common with the feasible region.

In the graph of figure 16, the objective function lies just outside the feasible region.

The last point of contact the function had with the region before it moved into the non-feasible zone is marked '*'.

If you check your own graph (or figure 15), you will see that this co-ordinate is at the intersection of the graph lines representing the orders for 'best' coal and anthracite. We therefore either read this point directly from the graph, or solve the simultaneous equations.

X	+	4Y	=	8	**(1)** Anthracite
5X	+	6Y	=	30	**(2)** 'Best'
					Multiply **(1)** by 5
5X	+	20Y	=	40	**(3)**
5X	+	6Y	=	30	Subtract **(2)** from **(3)**
		14Y	=	10	
		Y	=	5/7th	
		X	=	36/7	or $5\frac{1}{7}$

The objective function at this point will be

$$100X + 150Y \quad = (100 \times 36/7) + (150 \times 5/7)$$
$$= (4350)/7 \; ≗ \; 621.42$$

Thus the mine owner should work the upper seam for $5\frac{1}{7}$ th hours and the lower seam for 5/7th of an hour. This will meet the order at the (minimum) cost of £621.42.

---

4. REST EASY LOUNGE SUITES: A GRAPHICAL SOLUTION

You should reread the details of this case study if you need to refresh your memory concerning the details. It is formally summarised here;

Choose a value of X and Y such that $Z = 110X + 90Y$ (objective function) is maximised, subject to

3X	+	2Y	≤	900	(joinery department)
X	+	Y	≤	400	(packaging department)
X			≤	150	(leather section)
Y			≤	375	(dralon section)
X,		Y	≥	0	(non-negativity)

ACTIVITY 35

As with the previous two problems draw a graph representing the resource constraints of this problem.
Shade in the feasible region.

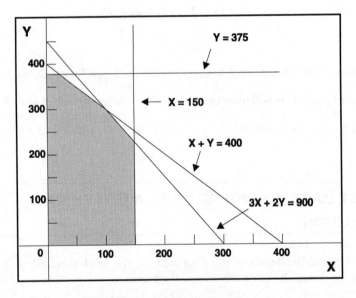

FIGURE 17: **Rest Easy Suites**

The graphs and feasible region for this problem are shown in figure 17.

In this problem there are two constraints which affect only one variable at a time. Such constraints always show up as horizontal lines (if they affect the vertical axis variable – usually Y) or vertical lines if they affect the horizontal axis variable – usually X).

The other two constraints in the problem affect both variables.

ACTIVITY 36

On your graph of the feasible region sketch the objective function for Rest Easy lounge suites,

$$Z = 110X + 90Y$$

Find the optimum production plan for Rest Easy, and the total contribution earned by this plan.

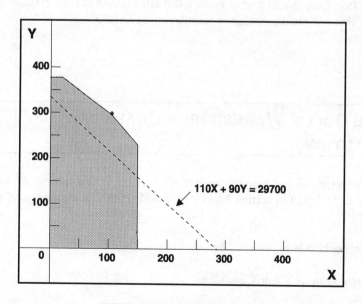

FIGURE 18: **Rest Easy Suites**

Figure 18 shows the feasible region together with the graph of the objective function for Z = 29,700. As with the other problems, this value of Z was chosen to yield an objective function with a graph conveniently near the boundary of the feasible region.

As the objective function moves outward from the origin, it touches the point marked '*' before finally leaving the feasible zone.

If you inspect your own graph (or figure 17), then you will see that this is at the intersection of the joinery and packaging constraints. As before, we either read this co-ordinate directly from the graph, or solve the appropriate equations.

$$
\begin{array}{rcll}
3X + 2Y & = & 900 & \text{(1) Joinery} \\
X + Y & = & 400 & \text{(2) Packaging} \\
& & & \text{Multiply (2) by 3} \\
\hline
3X + 2Y & = & 900 & \text{(3)} \\
3X + 3Y & = & 1200 & \text{(4)} \\
& & & \text{Subtract (3) from (4)} \\
\hline
Y & = & 300 & \\
X & = & 100 &
\end{array}
$$

The objective function at this point will be

$$110X + 90Y = (110 \times 100) + (90 \times 300) = 38,000$$

Therefore Rest Easy should plan to make 100 AMBASSADORs and 300 DIPLOMATs per week. This will yield a maximum contribution of £38,000.

5. THE DOLLS' WORKSHOP: A GRAPHICAL SOLUTION

We now come to the last problem we will try to solve in this section. As earlier, the details are to be found in section 2 and you should refresh your memory by rereading these.

The formal position is summarised below.

We require a value of X and Y such that

$$Z = 12X + 20Y \text{ (objective function)}$$

is maximised, subject to

X	+	Y	≤	1,500	(plastic supply)
X	+	2Y	≤	2,000	(workshop capacity)
		Y	≤	600	(mouth mechanisms)
X,		Y	≥	0	(non-negativity)

ACTIVITY 37

By drawing the graphs of the resource constraints and the objective function for the Dolls' Workshop find the optimum production plan and the profit associated with that plan.

Graphs illustrating the solution to Activity 37 are shown in figures 19 and 20.

Figure 19 illustrates the feasible region for the Dolls' Work Shop problem. The point marked '*' in figure 20 is the last point the objective function has in common with the feasible region as it moves away from the origin.

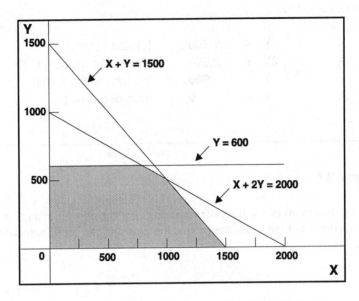

FIGURE 19: **The Dolls' Workshop. The Feasible Region**

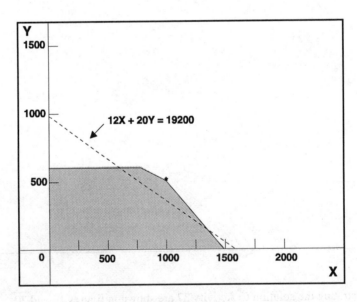

FIGURE 20: **Dolls' Workshop. Feasible Region and Objective Function**

This point is at the intersection of the workshop capacity and plastic supply constraints.

$$
\begin{array}{llll}
X & + & 2Y & = & 2000 \\
X & + & Y & = & 1500 \\
\hline
& & Y & = & 500 \\
& & X & = & 1000
\end{array}
$$

(1) Plastic supply
(2) Workshop capacity
subtract (2) from (1)

The objective function at this point will be

$$12X + 20Y = (12 \times 1000) + (20 \times 500) = 22000$$

Therefore the Dolls' Workshop should produce 1000 'Cindy Lou' and 500 of the 'Sue Ellen' dolls, yielding a contribution of £22000.

We also know that the workshop has fixed costs of £400. Thus optimum profit is £22,000 - £400 = £21,600.

6. SUMMARY

In this section you have had the opportunity through four new case studies, to develop your knowledge of linear programming by

- setting up linear programming problems in a **formal mathematical way**

- using graphical methods to obtain solutions to problems where there are only two **decision variables**

- identifying **feasible solution areas** to help in the decision making process

If you are not sure of any of these areas look back and check **now**, reworking any examples if necessary before you move to the next section.

SECTION 5

SHADOW PRICES AND SENSITIVITY ANALYSIS

1. INTRODUCTION

There are two important aspects of LP problems which we still need to explore, shadow prices and sensitivity analysis.

SHADOW PRICES

Although we may have obtained an optimal solution to a problem this does not mean that all of the resources we are using are employed to the full. For example, in the Jarvis Builders case study, perhaps we are not using all of the available wood, glass and labour when producing at the optimum point. Some resources may therefore be surplus to the decision-makers requirements. Other resources may be scarce in the sense that we are currently using all we have of them. If we had an extra unit of these scarce resources we might be able to achieve a more favourable maximum or minimum. Such resources are therefore valuable and we would be prepared to pay for more of them. The price we are prepared to pay for an extra unit of a scarce resource is known as its **shadow price.**

Definition

Shadow Price

> **The shadow price of a scarce resource is the amount of increase or decrease shown by the objective function as a result of a unit increase or decrease in the amount of the resource available.**

SENSITIVITY ANALYSIS

In practice, whenever we use linear programming to solve problems, one difficulty is that the data we are using may not be known with accuracy or may be subject to error. An important question then becomes

how sensitive is the solution to a change in any of the conditions upon which it is based?

This is explored using a technique called **sensitivity analysis.**

2. SCARCE RESOURCES AND SHADOW PRICES

We can use the Jarvis & Partners problem to illustrate the difference between scarce resources and those where there is some 'slack'.

You may remember that in this case we had to maximise

$$Z = 8X + 12Y$$

subject to keeping within the following resource constraints

2X	+ 1.5Y	≤	600	(wood)
0.5X	+ Y	≤	300	(glass)
X	+ Y	≤	320	(labour)
	X	≥	0	(non-negativity)
	Y	≥	0	

X represents the number of CHEZ NOUS doors and Y the number of MON REPOS doors.

ACTIVITY 38

The optimal solution to the Jarvis problem was to produce 40 CHEZ NOUS and 280 MON REPOS doors making a total contribution of £3680.

Calculate how much of each of the three resources (glass wood and labour) is being used at this optimal production plan.

Which resources, if any, are scarce?

⟾

Activity 38 continued...

Firstly, we may examine the usage of wood.

The linear inequality describing this resource is

$$2X + 1.5Y \leq 600$$

Now at the optimum production plan Jarvis would make 40 CHEZ NOUS ($X = 40$) and 280 MON REPOS ($Y = 280$).

This means that we use

$$(2 \times 40) + (1.5 \times 280) = 500 \text{ square metres of wood}$$

Clearly, since Jarvis have 600 m^2 of wood this is not a scarce resource. Jarvis do not want any more wood; they already have more then they need. Consequently, since extra wood does not improve their optimum position, they would not be willing to pay for more of this resource. It has no **shadow price**.

The situation for glass and labour is different.

The glass constraint is described by the function

$$0.5X + Y \leq 300$$

At the optimum production plan, Jarvis would use

$$(0.5 \times 40) + (1 \times 280) = 300 \text{ square metres of glass}$$

Now Jarvis only have 300 m^2 of glass available, so the production plan will use all of it. Glass is therefore a scarce resource, or to express it using the language of linear programming, the glass constraint is said to be **binding**.

Therefore the scarcity of glass makes it valuable. If Jarvis had more glass, they could earn a higher contribution. Glass is said to have a shadow price.

Labour is also scarce. The function used to describe the labour constraint is

$$X + Y \leq 320.$$

At the optimum production plan, Jarvis would use

$$(1 \times 40) + (1 \times 280) = 320 \text{ hours of labour}$$

Since only 320 labour hours are available, the resource is binding. Labour will thus command a shadow price.

ACTIVITY 39

Now let us reconsider the Superb Audio problem from section 2.

A summary of that problem is maximise

$$Z = 4X + 9Y$$

subject to

2X	+	4Y	$\leq$	2000	(assembly)
X	+	3Y	$\leq$	1200	(testing)
X			$\leq$	900	(sales)
X,		Y	$\geq$	0	(non-negativity)

X, Y are the numbers of ECONOMY and SPECIAL models produced per week.

⟶

Activity 39 continued...

The optimum production plan was for SUPERB to produce 600 of the ECONOMY models and 200 of the SPECIALs.

By making suitable calculations, say which of the three constraints have shadow prices and which have not.

Firstly, we examine the assembly constraint. Superb Audio only have 2,000 hours currently available. At a level of production where X = 600 and Y = 200 their usage of the resource would be

$$2X + 4Y = (2 \times 600) + (4 \times 200) = 2000 \text{ hours per week}$$

The resource is scarce, or binding.

Usage of testing hours at the optimum production level would be

$$X + 3Y = (1 \times 600) + (3 \times 200) = 1200 \text{ hours per week}$$

Therefore, the amount of testing time available is also a binding constraint.

The sales constraint is different. Superb Audio would not find it worthwhile to produce more than 900 because they would not sell more than this amount. Is this a binding constraint on the problem? Would the company be in a better position if this sales constraint were higher?

The answer is NO, because

$$X \leq 900$$

and X = 600 at the optimum production plan. We are not producing anywhere near the market restriction of 900. Therefore the constraint is not binding.

3. CALCULATING SHADOW PRICES

We have seen from an analysis of the constraints for Jarvis Builders that while **wood** is not a scarce resource, **glass** and **labour** certainly are. If Jarvis had more of these resources they would be placed in a more favourable position in the sense that they could produce more doors and thus earn a higher total contribution. Conversely, if the quantity of glass and labour available to them were reduced, they would be in a less favourable position, ie they would earn less total contribution.

How much would they be prepared to pay for one **extra hour** of labour, or an extra one square metre of glass? Clearly, they would be prepared to pay, because they earn extra contribution from the extra resources. The maximum amount that they would pay is clearly limited by the extra amount of contribution gained.

We can approach this problem graphically.

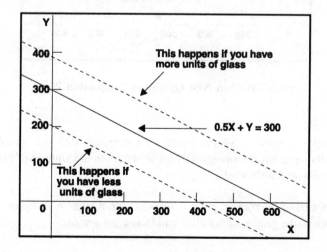

FIGURE 21: **More or Less Glass?**

Figure 21 shows the current availability of glass as a continuous line, the graph of the function $0.5X + Y = 300$. If we **increase** glass availability from its current level of 300, then the graph of the constraint will move outward from the origin. If we **reduce** the amount of glass available, then the graph will move towards the origin. These movements are shown by the dotted lines in figure 21.

We will begin by assuming that we have an extra one square metre of glass. That is, we have 301 instead of 300 m^2. The glass constraint would then become

$$0.5X + Y \leq 301$$

Next, we find out how this alteration to the constraint affects the production plan.

Finally, we substitute the new solution values for X and Y in the objective function and observe how this affects the value of Z.

Now examine the graph in figure 22 below.

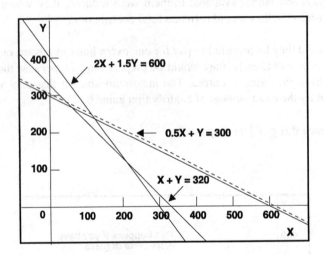

FIGURE 22: **A New Optimum Production Plan**

Figure 22 shows graphs of all the functions connected with this problem. It is a complicated diagram, but the situation which arises when the amount of glass increases can be deduced with a little work.

The current optimum production point is marked with a letter A in figure 22, and is at the intersection of the graphs of the glass and labour constraints.

Now if we increase the amount of glass by one unit, we cause the graph line for the constraint to move further away from the origin.

The optimal solution will still, however, be at the intersection of the glass and labour constraints.

So we proceed to find the new optimum by finding the XY co-ordinate at the point where the graphs of

$$0.5X + Y = 301$$

and

$$X + Y = 320$$

intersect.

ACTIVITY 40

Solve the equations

$$0.5X + Y = 301$$
$$X + Y = 320$$

for X and Y.

Calculate the value of Z for these new values of X and Y. What is the shadow price for glass?

The equations are solved as follows:

$$0.5X + Y = 301 \quad \textbf{(1)}$$
$$X + Y = 320 \quad \textbf{(2)}$$

Subtract **(1)** from **(2)**.

$$0.5X = 19$$
$$X = 38$$
$$Y = 282$$

Thus instead of producing 40 CHEZ NOUS and 280 MON REPOS, Jarvis will **now** be in an optimal position if they change this to 38 and 282.

How does this affect contribution?

The objective function is

$$Z = 8X + 12Y$$

and Z currently takes the value £3,680.

If we let X = 38 and Y = 282, as per the new production plan, we get

$$Z = (8 \times 38) + (12 \times 282) = 3688$$

Thus the increase in contribution is

$$£3688 - £3680 = £8$$

So having more glass will cause total contribution to rise by £8 for each extra square metre added.

The business would be willing to pay up to £8 for each extra unit of glass and so the shadow price for the resource is £8.

It is also the case that if the amount of glass available is reduced, then contribution falls by £8 for every square metre lost.

ACTIVITY 41

You already know from Activity 38 that labour is a binding constraint. What is its shadow price?

We know that the solution to the Jarvis problem is to be found at the intersection of the linear functions for glass and labour. Increasing the amount of labour available by one hour, from 320 to 321 will not alter this fact. Therefore, as in the case for the glass constraint, we need to solve a pair of simultaneous equations for X and Y.

$$
\begin{array}{llll}
0.5X & + & Y = & 300 \quad \text{(1)} \\
X & + & Y = & 321 \quad \text{(2)}
\end{array}
$$

Subtract (1) from (2).

$$
\begin{array}{lll}
0.5X & = & 21 \\
X & = & 42 \\
Y & = & 279
\end{array}
$$

So increasing the amount of labour by one hour will cause the optimum production plan to change from X = 40, Y = 280, to

$$X = 42, Y = 279$$

The new contribution from this production will be

$$8X + 12Y = (8 \times 42) + (12 \times 279) = 3684$$

The increase in total contribution as a result of having one extra hour of labour is

$$£3684 - £3680 = £4$$

Thus the shadow price for labour is £4 per hour.

ACTIVITY 42

What are the shadow prices for the constraints in the Superb Audio problem?

We already know that the sales constraint, $X \leq 900$ is not binding, so that the shadow price is zero in this case (see Activity 39). However, assembly and testing hours **are** scarce, so we will need to calculate their shadow prices.

Figure 23 below, is a graph of the constraints related to this problem.

The solution to Superb Audio's current problem is to produce 60 ECONOMY and 200 SPECIAL models, giving a total contribution of £4,200. This optimum point is shown in figure 23, marked with the letter A. Note that it lies on the intersection of the assembly and testing constraints.

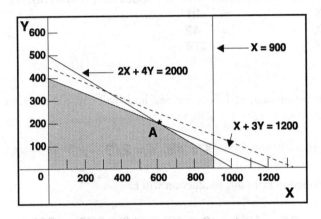

FIGURE 23: **Assembly Hours**

If we increase the amount of assembly time by one hour, the constraint

$$2X + 4Y \leq 2000$$

becomes

$$2X + 4Y \leq 2001$$

We can now consider this new version of the assembly constraint and the testing constraint as a pair of simultaneous equations and solve them for X and Y.

2X	+	4Y	=	2001	(1)
X	+	3Y	=	1200	(2) multiply by 2

2X	+	6Y	=	2400	(3)
2X	+	4Y	=	2001	(1)
					subtract (1) from (3)

		2Y	=	399
		Y	=	199.5
		X	=	601.5

Thus the new optimum will be at X = 601.5 and Y = 199.5.

Checking the effect of this on the objective function we have

$$Z = 4X + 9Y = (4 \times 601.5) + (9 \times 199.5)$$
$$= 4201.5$$

The increase in contribution is

$$£4,201.50 - £4,200 = £1.50$$

So the shadow price for assembly time is therefore £1.50 per hour.

We now turn our attention to testing time. Assume that Superb Audio has 1201 hours of time available instead of 1200. We then need to solve

2X	+	4Y	=	2000	(1)
X	+	3Y	=	1201	(2) multiply by 2
2X	+	6Y	=	2402	(3)
2X	+	4Y	=	2000	subtract (1) from (3)
		2Y	=	402	
		Y	=	201	
		X	=	598	

So having one more hour of testing time will cause the production plan to change from 600, 200 to 598, 201.

The contribution will now be

$$Z = 4X + 9Y = (4 \times 598) + (9 \times 201)$$
$$= 4201$$

The increase in contribution is

$$£4,201 - £4,200 = £1$$

Thus the shadow price for assembly time is £1 per hour.

4. SHADOW PRICES AND SENSITIVITY

We have seen that the optimum solution to a LP problem is sensitive to changes in the amounts of scarce resources available. We can analyse the value of these resources to the decision maker by examining these shadow prices.

One question we might ask is; within what limits are these shadow prices effective?

For example, we are already aware that the shadow price for glass in the Jarvis & Partners problem is £8 per square metre, meaning that we increase/decrease total contribution by £8 every time we add to/reduce the glass supply by this amount. Will this **always** be true? Will glass always be scarce?

The answer to these questions is NO.

Eventually, as the amount of glass increases, it ceases to be scarce and will therefore have no shadow price. Also, if the amount of glass is reduced below a certain point, it will still remain scarce but its shadow price will change.

Although it is possible to calculate these limits for a two-variable problem, you are not required to do this. You should, however, be aware that within certain limits shadow prices will not change and that sensitivity analysis will detect what these limits are.

In section 6 you will look at a typical sample of output from LP computer software. These computer programs usually perform sensitivity analysis for a problem.
Another aspect of sensitivity analysis is concerned with analysing the coefficients of the decision variables in the objective function. How far can they change without upsetting the optimum solution?

For instance, the objective function for the Jarvis & Partners problem is

$$Z = 8X + 12Y$$

The coefficients of X and Y are 8 and 12 respectively.

It is the case that these numbers can be changed (within limits) without upsetting the optimum production plan. This is valuable information to have, because if costs should change, thus upsetting the coefficients of X and Y, Jarvis & Partners will know if the change alters its production plans.

5. SUMMARY

In this section we have examined two further important aspects of linear programming

- shadow prices

- sensitivity analysis

and shown how we need to take account of these as we develop feasible solutions.

As we move to the last section concerning linear programming with three or more variables and the role of computer software check back through this section to be sure that you have fully understood these new concepts.

SECTION 6

THE ROLE OF COMPUTER SOFTWARE

1. INTRODUCTION

In this final section we extend the technique of linear programming to models where there are more than two decision variables. It is not possible to apply graphical solutions to such problems so we therefore need to use computer software. A sample of output from LP software will be studied. Finally, we briefly examine some of the problems arising from the use of LP.

2. THE SIMPLEX ALGORITHM

As we have already made clear, graphical linear programming becomes impossible when there are more than two decision variables. Fortunately, there is a very powerful algorithm (ie computational procedure) called **SIMPLEX** that can be resorted to in such situations. Essentially, simplex is an **iterative procedure**. That is, it works by repeating, or iterating a fixed sequence of steps until the optimal solution is found.

It is possible to carry out the Simplex procedure without using a computer, but in practice, it is a cumbersome process, and is not recommended. You do not need to have any understanding of how the Simplex algorithm works in order to use the computer. It is far more important to know how to formulate a problem prior to using the computer and how to interpret the solution that the computer outputs.

 A suite of computer programs is supplied with a well known text-book (see *References*) and one of them is a version of the simplex algorithm. Because its output is very typical of much LP software, we will use it as an example.

In order to understand the output of the program we use data from the Jarvis problem.

3. SIMPLEX LINEAR PROGRAMMING: SAMPLE OUTPUT

PROBLEM: JARVIS & PARTNERS

MAX 8X1 + 12X2

Subject to

$$2X1 \quad + \quad 1.5X2 \quad <= \quad 600$$
$$0.5X1 \quad + \quad 1X2 \quad <= \quad 300$$
$$1X1 \quad + \quad 1X2 \quad <= \quad 320$$

After 2 iterations, this solution is optimal

VARIABLE	QUANTITY
X1	40
X2	280
S1	100

OPTIMAL Z = 3680

VARIABLE	DUAL OR SHADOW PRICE	CONSTRAINT
X1	0	
X2	0	
S1	0	(1)
S2	8	(2)
S3	4	(3)

SENSITIVITY ANALYSIS OF OBJECTIVE FUNCTION COEFFICIENTS

VARIABLE NAME	LOWER LIMIT	ORIGINAL VALUE	UPPER LIMIT
X1	6	8	12
X2	8	12	16

SENSITIVITY ANALYSIS OF RIGHT HAND SIDE RANGES

CONSTRAINT	LOWER LIMIT	ORIGINAL VALUE	UPPER LIMIT
1	500	600	no limit
2	200	300	320
3	300	320	360

A number of points need to be made about the above output.

Firstly, like most LP software, the decision variables are labelled X1, X2, X3, X4 etc. As the Jarvis problem is a two variable problem we have just X1 (CHEZ NOUS) and X2 (MON REPOS).

Secondly, the software automatically assumes that $X \geq 0$ and $Y \geq 0$.

Thirdly, the simplex algorithm proceeds by converting all of the inequalities into equations. It does this by creating 'slack' variables which are required to be non-negative. As the name implies, these variables measure any 'slack' (ie any unused amount of the resource represented by an inequality). They are labelled as S1, S2, S3, S4 etc, and there will be one created for every constraint. S1 will be the slack variable associated with constraint 1, S2 is the slack variable for constraint 2 etc.

ACTIVITY 43

In the computer output for the Jarvis problem, wood is constraint 1, glass is constraint 2, and labour is constraint 3.

The following information appears in the computer solution;

AFTER 2 ITERATIONS,
THIS SOLUTION IS OPTIMAL

VARIABLE	QUANTITY
X1	40
X2	280
S1	100

There are three constraints but only one slack variable is mentioned. What do you think is the reason for this?

In order to answer Activity 43 you need to recall some of the details of the Jarvis problem. Wood is not a binding constraint for Jarvis, in fact there is $100 \ m^2$ surplus to requirements. Notice that S1 = 100. S1 is the slack variable associated with constraint 1, which is wood. S2 (glass) and S3 (labour) do not appear in this section of the output because they are scarce resources. The amount of slack would be zero. Most software does not usually bother to output zeros.

The next part of the output states the shadow prices for each constraint. Notice that S1 = 0, S2 = 8 and S3 = 4. This is merely reporting that constraint 1 (wood) has no shadow price, while constraint 2 (glass) has a shadow price of £8, and constraint 3 (labour) a shadow price of £4.

The part of the output labelled

'SENSITIVITY ANALYSIS OF OBJECTIVE FUNCTION COEFFICIENTS'

states how much the coefficients of the decision variables can change without altering the optimum production plan. For the Jarvis problem, the coefficients of X1 and X2 are the contributions for each of the two types of door. Other things being unchanged, the contribution for a CHEZ NOUS, currently at £8, could fall as low as £6, or go as high as £12, and the production plan of 40 CHEZ NOUS and 280 MON REPOS would still be optimal even though the amount of total contribution, Z, would alter.

The next section of computer output is labelled

'SENSITIVITY ANALYSIS OF RIGHT HAND SIDE RANGES'

The phrase 'right hand side ranges' refers to the number appearing on the right hand side of each inequality. These numbers are therefore references to the amount of a resource which is available. This particular section of output tells us within what ranges the shadow prices are operative.

For example, constraint 3 (labour) has a current availability of 320 hours. It has a shadow price of £4 per hour, which will be the case for any amount of labour between 300 and 360 hours.

ACTIVITY 44

What is the analysis of right hand side ranges telling us about the wood constraint?

Wood is constraint 1. The current availability of wood is 600 m^2. We know that wood is not a scarce resource. This means that it has no shadow price, and the output appears to be telling us that it will continue to have no shadow price between 500 m^2 and 'no upper limit'. If it is not scarce when we have 600 m^2, it will certainly not be scarce for any larger amount. This is the reason for there being no upper limit for the zero shadow price of wood. Also, if the amount of wood falls to 500 m^2, it will start to become scarce, and thus will have a shadow price.

4. MORE THAN TWO DECISION VARIABLES

Consider the following problem.

A farmer has just bought an unstocked farm of 1045 acres, all in pasture. She has £10,400 available to spend on stocking the farm, and can buy breeding ewes, heifers or beef cattle. The current market price per animal, her estimate of annual profit per animal and the number of acres required per animal are as follows:

ANIMAL	MARKET PRICE PER ANIMAL	ACRES PER ANIMAL	ANNUAL PROFIT PER ANIMAL
EWES	£5	1.0	£12
HEIFERS	£10	0.5	£8
CATTLE	£100	2.0	£40

ACTIVITY 45

Set up the farm data as a formal linear programming problem, assuming that the farmer wishes to maximise profit.

There are three decision variables in this problem symbolising the number of ewes, heifers and cattle to be stocked. Let

X1 be the number of ewes stocked
X2 be the number of heifers stocked
X3 be the number of cattle stocked

Then the objective function will be

$$Z = 12X1 + 8X2 + 40X3$$

Apart from non-negativity, there are only two constraints:

5X1 +10X2+100X2	≤	10,400	(cash limit)
X1 +0.5X2+2X2	≤	1,045	(land limits)
X1, X2, X3	≥	0	

Unless you have access to a computer and software you will not be able to take the problem any further.

The following is the computer output relating to the problem:

$$MAX\ 12X1 + 8X2 + 40X3$$

Subject to

$$5X1 + 10X2 + 100X3 <= 10400$$
$$1X1 + 0.5X2 + 2X3 <= 1045$$

After 3 iterations, this solution is optimal

VARIABLE	QUANTITY
X1	700
X2	690

OPTIMAL Z = 13920

VARIABLE	DUAL OR SHADOW PRICE	CONSTRAINT
X1	0	
X2	0	
X3	8	
S1	0.267	(1)
S2	10.667	(2)

SENSITIVITY ANALYSIS OF OBJECTIVE FUNCTION COEFFICIENTS

VARIABLE NAME	LOWER LIMIT	ORIGINAL VALUE	UPPER LIMIT
X1	4	12	14
X2	7.333	8	24
X3	no limit	40	48

SENSITIVITY ANALYSIS OF RIGHT HAND SIDE RANGES

CONSTRAINT	LOWER LIMIT	ORIGINAL VALUE	UPPER LIMIT
1	5225	10400	20900
2	520	1045	2080

The cash available is constraint 1, and the land available is constraint 2.

ACTIVITY 46

(a)   Using the computer printout for the farm problem, what is the optimum solution? What profit will be made at this optimum point?

(b)   For any type of animal not appearing in the optimum solution mentioned in (a), at what profit would they become attractive?

(c)   The farmer has the opportunity of either purchasing additional land or investing available capital in additional animals. If £c represent the cost of purchasing one additional acre of land, determine the value of c for which
the   two options are equally attractive.

The optimum solution can be simply read from the computer printout; 700 ewes and 690 heifers should be purchased, giving a total profit of £13,920.

Notice that the absence of X3 (cattle) in this part of the output implies that none would be purchased; cattle do not feature in the optimum plan.

At what point would it be an attractive proposition to start stocking cattle?

To answer this question, look at the analysis of objective function coefficients.

Looking at the cattle variable, we see that the coefficient can vary from NO LIMIT to £48 without altering the optimum stock plan. When the profit for cattle exceeds £48 the optimum will change; cattle will then feature in the optimum plan.

The solution to part (c) of Activity 46 will require more thought. How much would an acre of land have to cost before the aquisition of one more unit of land and expenditure on stock became equally attractive?

Let the cost of an acre of land = £c.

Now the shadow price of an acre of land is £10.667 (from the computer solution). The farm profit would benefit by this amount for each extra acre of land bought.

Also for each £ spent on stock, the farms profits benefit by £0.267 (see computer solution). If the farmer has exactly the price of an acre of land – £c available for spending on stock, then the total addition to profit will be £0.267c.

For the two options to be equally attractive, we require that

Benefit from one extra acre of land = benefit from one extra unit of stock

$$10.667 = 0.267c$$

and so

$$c = £40$$

Therefore, if an acre of land cost £40, the benefits to be gained from spending that £40 on either stock or land would be equal.

5. LIMITATIONS OF LINEAR PROGRAMMING

Although linear programming is a powerful tool for the solution on many kinds of managerial problems, it does have a number of limitations. However, before examing these limitations, it is necessary to stress that many of them can be allowed for by using more mathematically sophisticated forms of programming (of which linear programming is only a small part).

These more sophisticated techniques are outside the scope of a first level course.

The limitations of linear programming concern divisibility, linearity and the presumption of a single objective.

Divisibility

Decision variables are assumed to be divisible; to be **continuous** variables. In many problems this is a perfectly reasonable thing to assume. In other problems, the variables are not continuous. For example, in the Jarvis problem the number of doors of each type is a discrete variable; we cannot produce, say, 35.6 doors. In some cases where we encounter a discrete variable and the optimum solution is not a whole number, we may be able to get by with the nearest 'whole number' solution. At other times, if there are a large number of variables, this may be impossible. There is another kind of mathematical programming, called **integer programming** which has been specially devised for problems involving many discrete decision variables.

Linearity

A crucial assumption made in linear programming is that both the objective function and the linear constraints can be expressed in linear form. To deal properly with situations where linearity cannot be assumed, we need to have recourse to non-linear programming, which is a very substantial body of techniques.

Existence of a Single Objective

Linear programming rests on the crucial assumption that in any problem there is only a single objective; a single quantity to be maximised or minimised. Decision makers are often assumed to either want to maximise contribution or minimise costs.

The assumption of a single objective can be very restrictive.

A firm might, for example, have the following objectives:

securing an adequate return for shareholders

achieving an adequate rate of growth

demonstrating a concern for the environment

Since such objectives might well be conflicting, then they cannot be dealt with in the framework of linear programming. There is yet another branch of mathematical programming called game programming which can be employed to illuminate such problems, but it is not a suitable first-level course.

6. SUMMARY

In this final section we have demonstrated and illustrated

- the **Simplex Algorithm**

- **Simplex Linear Programming**

- how to work with **more than two decision variables**

- sample **computer output**

- the **limitations** of the linear programming technique

You should now feel more comfortable with the concepts, applications and methods of linear programming and should take every opportunity to build on the experience you have gained from this unit.

Before you leave the unit, check back **now** to any section or topic you are unsure about.

REFERENCES

Students may follow up this subject by reading the following texts:

1 MORRIS, C. *Quantitative Approaches to Business Studies*. Third edition. Pitman Publishing. Chapter 17.
2 CURWEN & SLATER. *Quantitative Methods for Business Decisions*. Third edition. Chapman & Hall. Chapter 21.
3. RENDER & STAIR. *Quantitative Analysis For Management*. Allyn & Bacon. Chapters 10 - 13.

Thorough coverage for those interested in taking the subject further. A disk with supporting computer software is available with this book.

4. DENNIS & DENNIS. *Micro Computer Models for Management Decision Making.* West Publishing.

This book will be of little help with the theory of linear programming. Its main strength is the packaged computer sofware which comes with it. The software has been used in section 6 of this unit.

GLOSSARY

The following is an alphabetical listing of the technical terms most often encountered in this unit.

Binding A constraint is said to be binding in a linear programming problem if there is no surplus left unused.

Decision variable Decision variables are at the centre of linear programming. A decision must be made respecting respecting the value of these variables necessary to obtain the best solution.

Feasible region The feasible region is the set of all values of the decision variables which could constitute a possible solution to a linear programming variable. Values which do not belong to this set cannot possibly solve the problem. On a graphical solution to a two-variable problem, the feasible region would be represented by a shaded area.

Inequality An inequality is a mathematical statement which puts some unknown value in a relationship where it is less than, less than or equal to, more than or more than or equal to some number. The following are all inequalities:

$X < 200$ (X is less than 200)
$X \leq 200$ (X is less than or equal to 200)
$X > 200$ (X is greater than 200)
$X \geq 200$ (X is greater than, or equal to 200)

Linear constraint If a physical constraint in a LP problen can be formulated in the form of a linear equation, then it is described as a linear constraint.

Linear equation A linear equation takes the form of a linear function.

$Y = a_0 + a_0X_0 + a_1X_1 + ... + a_nX_n$

Objective functions and constraints in LP must be in linear form.

Linear inequality Constraints which affect the solution to a LP problem must be formulated as linear functions and expressed as inequality relationships. They are referred to as linear constraints. The terms 'linear constraint' and 'linear inequality' are often used interchangeably.

Maximise A possible aim of the decision maker may be to maximise some quantity, such as profit, sales or contribution.

Minimise The decision maker may often seek to minimise some quantity, such as costs.

Objective function This is the mathematical expression of the decision makers objective – assumed to be either the maximisation or minimisation of some quantity.

Optimum The optimum means the 'best possible'. The decision maker is usually assumed to be intent on finding the optimum – either the maximum or minimum of some variable.

Sensitivity analysis The process of examining the degree to which the solution to a LP problem is affected by changing the right hand sides of the linear constraints or the coefficients of the objective function.

Shadow price The addition to, or reduction of the optimum solution caused by having one more, or one less unit of a resource which is scarce.

Slack The amount of a constraint which is not totally utilised when the optimum solution is reached.

Simplex algorithm A set of rules which will gradually arive at a solution to a LP problem. The rules can be represented by a computer program, making the implementation of the algorithm a straightforward matter.

UNIT 4

REGRESSION AND CORRELATION

CONTENTS

UNIT OBJECTIVES

On completion of this study unit you will be able to

- describe different kinds of relationship between variables

- build up a model of a simple linear relationship

- be able to calculate the co-efficient of correlation for the simple bivariate linear model

- construct a regression equation for simple bivariate linear data

- interpret the meaning of linear regression and correlation using the output of computer software as an aid

SECTION 1

RELATIONSHIPS BETWEEN VARIABLES

1. WHAT IS CORRELATION AND REGRESSION?

Suppose we are interested in the relationships between certain specified variables. The simplest case would involve just two variables. For example, the two variables of interest to us might be daily production volume for a large factory, and the total cost of producing this volume. Every time we record such data, we take two pieces of information; a daily production volume and its associated total cost. Each piece of data consists of a pair of values. Statisticians refer to the analysis carried out on such data as **bivariate** analysis.

Example

A mail order warehouse employs casual labour on a day-to-day basis to deal with orders recieved. Each morning, the manager needs to be able to forecast very quickly the number of orders there are in the incoming mail, so that the correct number of staff are taken on. The manager considers that the weight of the mail gives a good indication of the number of orders, and has recorded the following data over ten days.

Two kinds of question might arise concerning the analysis of bivariate data such as the mail order firm data in figure 1:

(1)   Is there any evidence that the variables are related in some way? Do the number of orders taken by the firm depend in some way upon the weight of the incoming mail? The mail order manager obviously believes the two variables are connected, and that it is a sufficiently close relationship for him to be able to forecast the number of orders. If we think there is a link between two variables, how might this be measured, and how should we interpret the results so obtained? Variables which are related in this way are often said to be **correlated** and questions relating to the strength and nature of the association are explored using **correlation analysis.**

Day	Weight Kg	Orders 00s
1	23	58
2	17	50
3	24	54
4	35	64
5	10	40
6	16	43
7	15	42
8	24	50
9	18	53
10	30	62

FIGURE 1: **Mail Order Firm Data**

ACTIVITY 1

Think for a moment about the nature of this relationship we call 'correlation'.

Can you think of **three** different situations in the business area where

(a)   variables might be correlated;

(b)   where a knowledge of this correlation might be useful to the decision
          maker?

Your suggestions may be very different from mine, but equally valid. We have already come across one example where the case of total cost and production volume was mentioned. Also of interest would be

● advertising expenditure and sales;

● product price and consumer demand.

In all of these cases it would be of considerable interest to decision makers if they knew the strength and nature of the correlation between these variables.

(2)   The second question which may be posed about bivariate data follows from the first question. If we believe that there is a relationship between two variables, then how do we set about establishing what precise form it takes?

The manager of the mail order business mentioned earlier would be very concerned to have this question answered. Knowing the **form** of the relationship between weight of mail and number of orders will help him/her make such forecasts. Questions of this second type are explored using a technique called **regression analysis.**

ACTIVITY 2

Have another look at the mail order firm data in figure 1, and as far as is possible, say what happens to the number of orders as the weight of the mail goes up and down.

You need no great ability in statistics to deduce that the number of orders received tend to go up as the mail becomes heavier. What little data we have in figure 1 tend to support this. We need, however, to advance beyond crude assertions of this type. Not only do we need to say whether or not a relationship exists, but we must be prepared to measure how strong this relationship is.

2. RELATIONSHIPS BETWEEN VARIABLES

Before we begin exploring possible solutions to the two questions just posed, it would be best if we examined the kind of relationships we shall be dealing with.

Note

Some of this material will be revision of matters dealt with in the units on *Business Maths* and *Linear Programming*. Just 'skim-read' the rest of this section if you feel that you are already familiar with the material it covers.

FUNCTIONAL AND STATISTICAL RELATIONSHIPS

Variables can be related functionally or statistically. An algebraic equation is a good example of a **functional** relationship between variables. Such relationships are **exact**. (Sometimes, the word **deterministic** is used to describe relationships of this type.)

To give a simple example; suppose a rectangle has a base of 5 cm, and a height represented by the variable h. Then area A can be expressed by the following functional relationship;

$$A = 5h$$

Figure 2 is a graph illustrating this relationship.

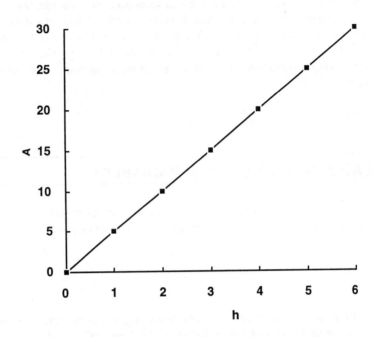

FIGURE 2: **Example of Functional Relationship**

Let height (h) be 4 cm. Area (A) will then be 20 cm². All the data points h and A lie on a straight line.

The relationship between h and A is **deterministic**, or exact. Once the height is known then you can exactly determine the area.

You should not expect to come across exact functional relationships in the study of socio-economic, or business data. You are much more likely to encounter situations where, although relationships may exist, they are anything but exact.

To illustrate this fact, you need only reconsider the relationship between the weight of incoming mail and the number of orders received by a mail order firm (see figure 1). We may well convince ourselves that there is some form of relationship between the two. A heavier postbag will, in all probability, contain more orders than a lighter one. We cannot express this relationship in an exact functional equation; there will always be days when mail is heavy but contains few orders, just as there will be days when a light postbag unaccountably yields considerable orders. The relationship holds for most of the time, but there are exceptions. Such relationships are often referred to as **statistical** relationships.

SCATTERPLOTS

As a first step towards analysing bivariate data, it can be examined visually by plotting it on a special graph called a scatterplot (sometimes called a scattergraph, or scattergram). A scatterplot is the name given to a method of representing data of the type in the mail order example.

The scatterplot consists of a horizontal axis to represent one of the two variables, and a vertical axis to represent the other. Each pair of measurements is represented by a single point on the diagram. See figure 3, for an example of a scatterplot representing some specimen data.

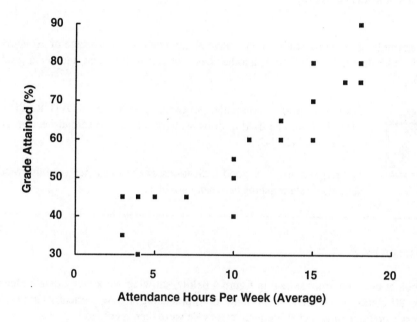

FIGURE 3: **Attendance and Grade of a Group of Students**

In this case the data is from the records of a group of 19 students. For each student two pieces of data were collected; assignment grade and average attendance per week. On the graph shown in figure 3 the horizontal axis represents 'attendance hours per week' – the X variable, and the vertical axis represents 'grade attained' – the Y variable.

One student for example, attended for an average of 7 hours per week and attained a final mark of 45%. This student would be represented on a scatterplot by a single point at the co-ordinates

$$X = 7 \text{ and } Y = 45$$

When drawing a scatterplot, proceed as though you were drawing an ordinary graph – but do not connect the points with a continuous line.

The important feature of such a graph is the pattern shown up by the scatter of points.

As you can see from figure 3, the points show a definite direction; they generally show an upward slope.

There is clearly a relationship between grade and attendance; the more time spent at college, the higher the grade. The points do not exactly lie on a straight upwardly sloping line, but it could be argued that they show an approximate 'linear' relationship. However, the relationship is statistical, not exact, since there is no single unique grade for each attendance figure.

For example, there are 3 students who have all attended for an average of 10 hours per week. One has a grade of 40%, another has a grade of 50% and another a grade of 55%.

Some statistical computer software, such as STATGRAPH and MINITAB can be used to draw scatterplots, as can spreadsheet programs such as LOTUS 1-2-3.

Scatterplots are very good indications of the existence (or otherwise) of statistical relationships between variables.

ACTIVITY 3

Look at the scatterplot shown in figure 4 below, showing work study data collected for 20 clerks. Each clerk spent some time practising a new clerical routine. The clerk's practice time and subsequent error rate were then recorded.

What do you think the scatterplot shows about the relationship between time spent practising and percentage error rate?

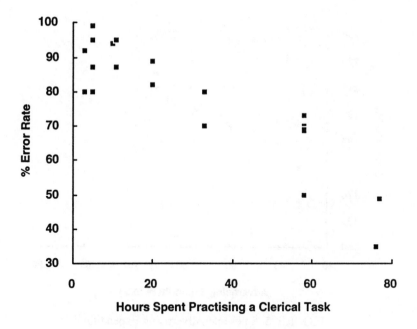

FIGURE 4: **Clerical performance**

You would expect to find a relationship between the two variables shown in figure 4, since, in general, the more a task is practised, the lower the error rate. However, it cannot be an exact relationship, since it will always be the case that some people aquire the 'knack' of carrying out a clerical task more quickly than others. In this case the scatterplot shows a definite downward direction. More practice time seems to mean a lower error rate. The relationship between the two is not so clearly linear as the student grade example (see figure 3). However, if you drew a straight line from the top left to the bottom right corners, the points would lie fairly close around it.

ACTIVITY 4

Figure 5 shows a scatterplot for some sales and advertising data. For each month over a given period, a company recorded its advertising expenditure and resulting sales.

What does the scatterplot show about the relationship between these variables?

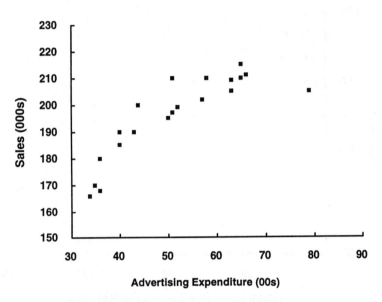

FIGURE 5: Sales and Advertising Expenditure

As you would expect, there is some kind of relationship between the variables shown in figure 5, in the sense that a higher advertising expenditure will encourage a higher sales return. However, such a relationship cannot continue indefinitely; at some point, further advertising expenditure will achieve no discernable return. Notice that the scatter of points does show this pattern. Sales and advertising are related; but it is not a straight line (linear) relationship.

In any case, no advertising manager is able to accurately predict the outcome of a given promotional expenditure.

ACTIVITY 5

Look at the scatterplot, figure 6 below. It shows the amount of labour used by a business and the unit cost incurred at that level of activity.

What do you think is the nature of the relationship (if any) between these variables?

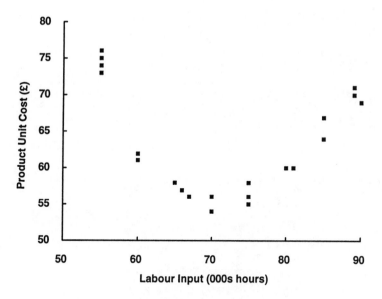

FIGURE 6: **Labour Input and Unit Cost**

Figure 6 shows the influence of increasing and diminishing returns; unit variable cost first falls as more labour is used, but after optimum efficiency is attained, more labour results in higher unit cost. If you are familiar with any economic theory, you may be aware of this relationship. It is not like the exact functional relationship often shown in many economics textbooks, but the general pattern is clear. Whatever the connection between cost and labour, it is certainly not linear.

ACTIVITY 6

Now return to the data for the mail order business (figure 1).

Draw a scatterplot for this data in the space below, and say what you think the scatterplot shows for this data.

Activity 6 continued...

Here is my solution to Activity 6 (see figure 7 below).

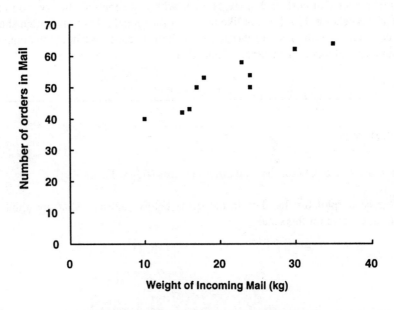

FIGURE 7: **Mail Weight and Mail Orders**

The graph shows the scatterplot of the mail order data.

As you can see, the scatter of points indicates an upward direction; the heavier the mail, the more orders will be received. As far as we are able to see, the data appear to be approximately linear. You could draw a straight upwardly-sloping line right through the scatterplot and the points would lie fairly close to this line.

LINEARITY OF RELATIONSHIPS

As you may know from the units *Business Maths* and *Linear Programming*, any linear function involving two variables can be expressed in the form

$$Y = a + bX$$

Y and X are the two variables in question. What you may not be aware of is that Y is often called the **dependent variable** simply because it 'depends' upon whatever value X happens to take. X is called the **independent variable**. The value of b determines the rate of change of the function; its 'gradient' or slope.

The value of a – usually called the **intercept**, or **Y-intercept** determines the point at which the graph of the function cuts through the Y axis.

So a function such as

$$Y = 100 + 6X$$

is a linear function. Its slope (b) is 6, meaning that each one unit increase in X produces a six units increase in Y. Also, its intercept (a) is 100, which is just another way of saying that if you drew the graph of the function it would pass through the co-ordinate $X = 0, Y = 100$.

Note

Since linearity dependence and independence are crucial matters in this study unit, the next two questions revise your knowledge of them. If you do not need any revision, then skip to the next section.

ACTIVITY 7

(a)   Which of the following functions are linear, and which are not?

i. $Y = 3 - 4X$.

ii. $Y = 4X + 5$.

iii. $Z = e^{-2X}$ (where e = 2.7182818....).

iv. $Q = X^2 - 4X - 2$.

v. $S = 4.5T$.

vi. $F = \dfrac{1}{V}$.

(b)   For each of the linear functions identified in question (a), write down the values of the slope and intercept, and state the symbols representing the dependent variable and independent variables.

In answering this question, remember that the choice of 'X' and 'Y' to represent independent and dependent variables are merely conveniences; any symbol could be used.

If you are unclear about the linearity or otherwise of the functions in Activity 7, you could try sketching rough graphs of them. Alternatively, examine the independent variables; if they are raised to a power other than 1, the function cannot be linear.

(a) i. **Y = 3 - 4X**

This is a linear function. The dependent variable is Y and the independent variable is X. The Y intercept is 3, and the slope is -4. The negative value for the slope means that the line is downward sloping, and in this case, if X increases by 1 unit, Y will decrease by 4 units.

ii. **Y = 4X + 5**

This is also a linear function with dependent/independent variables as in the last example. In this case, the Y intercept is 5 and the slope is 4.

iii. **Z = e^{-2x}**

This is not a linear function.

iv. **Q = X^2 - 4X - 2**

This is not a linear function.

v. **S = 4.5T**

This is a linear function with dependent variable S
and independent variable T.
The slope of the function is 4.5 and its Y intercept is 0.

vi. **F = $\dfrac{1}{V}$**

This is not a linear function.

ACTIVITY 8

It is useful to be able to estimate the mathematical form of a linear relationship merely by studying its graph.

Study the graphs in figures 8, 9 and 10. They all describe linear relationships.

Write down the mathematical form of the linear function shown in each graph.

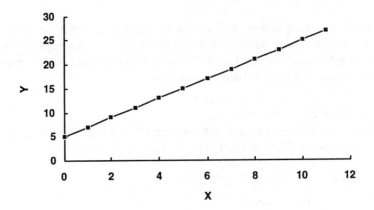

Figure 8

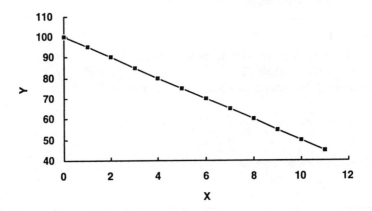

Figure 9

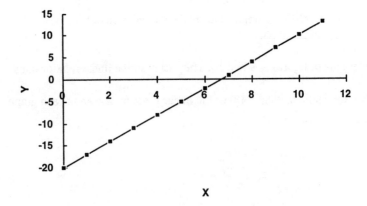

Figure 10

To answer Activity 8, you should keep clearly in mind that all linear functions are expressible in the form

$$Y = A + BX$$

Consequently, for each of the functions illustrated in figures 8, 9 and 10, you will need to make an estimate of the 'a' and 'b' values.

Examine the point at which the line cuts through the Y axis; this will be the a-value.

Also, take any convenient increase in X (say from X_1 to X_2), find the corresponding increase/decrease in Y, (Y_1 to Y_2) and calculate

$$\frac{Y_2 - Y_1}{X_2 - X_1}$$

The resulting value will be the slope, b.

Figure 8

The line cuts through the Y axis at the point Y = 5. When X increases from 0 to 2, Y increases from 5 to 9. This is a slope of

$$\textbf{(change in Y)/(change in X)} = 4/2 = 2$$

Consequently, the linear function is

$$Y = 5 + 2X$$

Figure 9

In this case the line cuts the Y axis at the point Y = 100. The line slopes downwards, so we will have a negative slope. For example, if X changes upwards from 0 to 2, then Y changes downwards from 100 to 90. This is a slope of -10/2 = -5. Thus the linear function is

$$Y = 100 - 5X$$

Figure 10

In this case the line cuts the Y axis below zero; at the point Y = -20. Also, when X changes from 0 to 2, Y changes from -20 to -14. This is a slope of 6/2 = 3. Consequently, the linear function is Y = -20 + 3X, which can be read as Y = 3X - 20.

You now know something about different types of relationships between variables. For example:

that some variables are in a functional, and some are in a statistical relationship

that some variables may also be linearly related, others not

that some variables are 'dependent', others 'independent'

that the decisive factors in a two variable linear function are 'intercept' and 'slope'.

With this knowledge of the nature of functional and statistical relationships, and revision of linearity, we can proceed to examine the techniques used in correlation and regression analysis. In the next study session we shall explore the way in which we may measure the **strength** (correlation) between two linearly related variables.

3. SUMMARY

In this first section we have

● defined **correlation** and **regression**

● examined how **variables** are **related** to each other

● constructed and analysed **scatterplots**

and

● revised **linear relationships**

If you are unsure of any of the topics in section 1, check back **now** before you read on.

SECTION 2

THE COEFFICIENT OF CORRELATION

1. CORRELATION BETWEEN VARIABLES

You will remember the scatterplots drawn in section 1.

In particular, take another look at Activity 6, which required you to draw a scatterplot for the mail order data and figure 7 which shows the answer to this activity. The mail order manager clearly believes that the heavier the weight of the mail, the higher tends to be the number of orders.

This is not an unreasonable view, and there is clearly some evidence supporting this view in the scatterplot.

We have already called the association between variables **correlation**. If two (or more) variables show signs of being associated, we say that they are **correlated**. Furthermore, we may say that variables are **strongly** or **weakly** correlated according to the degree of association between them. Quite clearly, weight of mail and number of orders are strongly correlated – witness the fact that the points on the scatterplot show a definite pattern. In addition, we can also make observations on the direction of the correlation. In the mail order data, it can be clearly seen that as one variable (mail weight) increases, the other variable (orders) also tends to increase.

When both variables change in the same direction, we describe this as **positive correlation**. Some variables also exhibit an **inverse** relationship. For example, consider the two variables 'price of product', and 'amount of product sold'. Now, (other things being equal as economists are fond of saying), you would expect that higher prices tend to be associated with lower sales, and vice versa. In other words, they are related inversely. In such a case the variables are said to be **negatively correlated**. Be very careful about the use of the word 'negative'. Unfortunately, in ordinary language, 'negative' sometimes means 'no'. Thus many students often fall into the trap of interpreting the term 'negative correlation as meaning no correlation at all. This is incorrect. In this context, the term negative refers to the **direction** of the correlation. Thus if variables are correlated we need to know

● how **strong** is the correlation

● whether the correlation is **positive** or **negative**.

ACTIVITY 9

(a)   Describe how you would use a scatterplot to determine whether correlation is strong or weak.

(b)   If there is **no correlation at all** between two variables, what would you expect the scatterplot to look like?

(c)   How would you use a scatterplot to determine if correlation is positive or negative?

To answer the kind of questions posed here, firstly make an attempt to draw a straight line through the scatter of points.

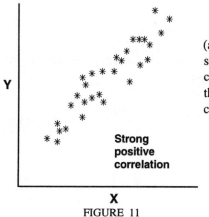

(a) If the XY co-ordinates on a scattergraph are seen to lie close to this straight line, then correlation is **strong**. The more pronounced is the linear tendency, the stronger is the correlation (see figure 11).

FIGURE 11

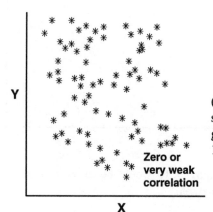

(b) On the other hand, if the co-ordinates are scattered randomly over the graph, then this is good evidence for weak correlation (see figure 12).

FIGURE 12

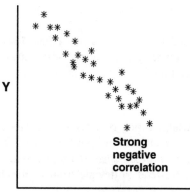

(c) If the overall direction of the points is upward sloping to the right, as in figure 11, then this suggests positive correlation. If the overall direction is downward (see figure 13), then this suggests negative correlation.

FIGURE 13

ACTIVITY 10

Examine the scatterplots in figures 3, 4, 5 and 6. What remarks can you make about the nature of the correlation (if any) in each case?

A simple way to deal with this problem of Activity 10 would be to try to draw a straight line through the scatter of points in each graph.

Figure 3

In figure 3 there is a definite tendency for the XY co-ordinates to slope upwards from left to right, suggesting positive correlation. Also, the co-ordinates lie fairly close to a line drawn through them, suggesting strong correlation.

Figure 4

The XY co-ordinates have a definite direction, and lie fairly close to a line drawn through them, suggesting strong correlation. However, the direction is downward sloping from left to right, suggesting negative correlation.

Figure 5

Here there is also evidence for a positive relationship, which is fairly strong. Notice though, that the relationship is more complex than the examples in figures 3 and 4. The co-ordinates rise from left to right, reach a peak, after which sales fail to respond to further advertising expenditure. The XY co-ordinates tend to deviate from a straight line more and more as X increases.

Figure 6

In figure 6 there is still a definite relationship between X and Y. The relationship appears to be strong but it is too complex to categorise it in terms of negative or positive relationships. It is not possible to draw a straight line through the co-ordinates.

To Summarise Activity 10

the scatter of points on a scatterplot indicates negative correlation if they show a tendency to slope downwards from left to right, and a positive correlation if they slope upward from left to right;

the closer the points on a scatterplot approximate to a straight line (whether upward or downward sloping), the stronger is the linear correlation.

Therefore a scatterplot is a good first indicator of the degree and direction of correlation. It is, however, a very crude instrument. It would be more useful to have a numerical measure. The next section will discuss this matter.

2. THE COEFFICIENT OF CORRELATION

We must now develop a numerical method of measuring correlation called the **product moment coefficient of correlation**. It is an easy enough measure to calculate, although its interpretation is subject to difficulties.

Note

If you find the theory in this section a little hard going at times, do not be worried. Perhaps you could reread it after you have finished the unit. Many people find it easier to understand theory once they have seen a little of the practice.

One way of thinking about correlation is that it indicates the degree to which values of one variable (X) which are bigger than average are associated with values of the other variable (Y) which are also bigger than average, and vice versa.

To see this, we insert on to the mail order problem scatter diagram, horizontal and vertical lines to represent the arithmetic mean values of the two variables. This is shown in figure 14, below.

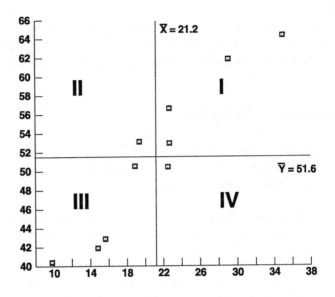

FIGURE 14: **The Mail Order Variables and Their Means**

We can calculate that

$\overline{X}$, (the mean weight of incoming mail) is 21.2 kg, and

$\overline{Y}$, (the mean number of orders received = 51.6 (00).

Using this information, the scattergram in figure 14 has been divided into 4 quadrants labelled I, II, III and IV.

Consider quadrant I. For any point (X,Y) in this quadrant it is the case that

$$(X - \overline{X}).(Y - \overline{Y}) \text{ is positive}$$

For example, on day 1 the mail order company had an incoming mail of 23 kg and 5800 orders. The co-ordinate (23, 58) lies in quadrant 1 and

$$(23 - 21.2).(58 - 51.6) = 11.52 > 0$$

(Remember that '>' means 'greater than').

In quadrant III the same result holds, since we will always be multiplying two minus values together, which produce a plus.

For example, on day 5 the company had a mail weighing 10 kg with 4000 orders. This co-ordinate (10, 40) lies in quadrant lll and;

$$(10 - 21.2).(40 - 51.6) = 129.92 > 0$$

Therefore, for any XY co-ordinates in quadrants l and lll it will be the case that

$$(X - \bar{X}) \text{ multiplied by } (Y - \bar{Y}) \text{ will be positive}$$

ACTIVITY 11

What happens in quadrants ll and IV?

By picking suitable mail weight – number of orders co-ordinates state a general rule for the quantity

$$(X - \bar{X}).(Y - \bar{Y})$$

In quadrants II and IV it is the case that:

$$(X - \bar{X}).(Y - \bar{Y}) \text{ is negative.}$$

For example, on day 9, the mail order company mail weighed 18 kg and there were 5300 orders. Now the co-ordinate (18, 53) is in quadrant IV and

$$(18 - 21.2).(53 - 51.6) = -4.48 < 0$$

('<' means 'less than').

We can put the the foregoing results in another way.

When the mail weighs above average, the company tend to get an above average number of orders, and vice versa. Now if the two variables are **positively related**, then we would expect that **most** of the data pairs would be in quadrants I and III (ie if an observation is above average for X, then it is also above average for Y, and vice versa). In which case

$$\Sigma\ (X - \bar{X}).(Y - \bar{Y}) \text{ would be} > 0$$

NB. The expression 'Σ' means that we would sum the values of $(X - \bar{X}).(Y - \bar{Y})$ over all data points, or observations. In the mail order case, we would need to sum over 10 XY observations.

On the other hand, if the two variables are **negatively** related then we would expect most of the data pairs to be in quadrants II and IV. (If an observation is **above** average for X, it will usually be **below** average for Y, and vice versa.) In which case

$$\Sigma\ (X - \bar{X}).(Y - \bar{Y}) \text{ would be} < 0$$

If there is no association between the two variables, then data points would occur randomly over all four quadrants, in which case

$$\Sigma\ (X - \bar{X}).(Y - \bar{Y}) \text{ would be} \approx 0$$

('≈' means 'approximately equal to')

Now this sounds promising in view of our wish to find a numerical measure of correlation. It seems that an appropriate measure of the degree and direction of correlation between two variables might be

$$\Sigma\ (X - \bar{X}).(Y - \bar{Y})$$

It seems to have all the desirable properties; the measure is negative if negative correlation exists and is positive if positive correlation exists.

If **no** correlation exists, the measure will be very close to zero.

ACTIVITY 12

The measure $\Sigma(X - \bar{X}).(Y - \bar{Y})$ seems to be quite good at telling us the **direction** (ie whether positive or negative) of correlation. Can you think of any disadvantages that it would have in establishing the **degree** of correlation (ie whether strong or weak) between two variables?

Hint
what would happen if we had collected data for 20 days instead of 10?

Suppose we had a sample of 20 days of data rather than 10. This increase in sample size would be sufficient to increase the size of

$$\Sigma (X - \bar{X}).(Y - \bar{Y})$$

without necessarily implying that correlation is correspondingly stronger.

Activity 12 has shown you that the measure may indicate the **direction** of the correlation, but it is useless as an indication of its **strength** of correlation.

However surely there must be some way out of this dilemma? If the number of data observations makes the interpretation of the measure difficult, perhaps we can adjust for this factor by using

$$\frac{1}{N} \Sigma (X - \bar{X}).(Y - \bar{Y})$$

In plain words, divide by N, where N = the number of data pairs. (In the mail order case, N = 10).

In fact, this last measure is known as the **sample covariance of X and Y**. However, there still remains a problem. The sample covariance as defined above is **not independent** of the units in which X and Y are measured.

For example, consider the data pair (23, 58) in quadrant I. We have already seen that (23 - 21.2).(58 - 51.6) is equal to 11.52. Now suppose that X is measured in **grams**, rather than kilograms. There are 1000 grams in a kilogram.
Thus for the same data point we would have

$$(X - \bar{X}).(Y - \bar{Y}) = 1000.(23 - 21.2).(58 - 51.6)$$

$$= 11520$$

Thus if X was measured in grams, rather than kilograms, for all of the data points, then we would obtain a quite different (and larger) figure for

$$\frac{1}{N} \Sigma (X - \bar{X}).(Y - \bar{Y})$$

How can we make our measure of the degree of association between X and Y independent of the units in which the variables are measured?

This is a problem which can easily be solved.

If a quantity is divided by something else measured in the same units, then the result is a pure number.

In the case of our sample covariance, we can divide by the product of the standard deviations of the two variables. The resulting ratio (usually denoted by the symbol 'r') is termed the

Pearson Product Moment Coefficient of Correlation

and is defined in formula 1, below.

Formula 1

The product moment coefficient of correlation is defined as

$$r = \frac{\text{sample covariance of } (X,Y)}{\text{standard deviation } (X) \times \text{standard deviation } (Y)}$$

However, formula 1 is not always convenient to use in computations of the correlation coefficient.

The following (see formula 2) is derived from formula 1 and is normally used in all practical situations.

Formula 2

The Coefficient of Correlation

$$r = \frac{\sum XY - \frac{(\sum X)(\sum Y)}{N}}{\sqrt{\{\sum X^2 - \frac{(\sum X)^2}{N}\} \cdot \{\sum Y^2 - \frac{(\sum Y)^2}{N}\}}}$$

You may find a large formula like the above rather awesome. We shall therefore demonstrate how r is calculated by using some simple data.

Suppose that we have five observations of a pair of variables as follows

X	1	2	3	4	5
Y	2	2	4	6	7

A calculation for r is set out below, using formula 2. Follow the example carefully, making sure that you know what is happening at each stage.

Before we can use the formula, we need to make some preliminary calculations, as shown in the following table.

X	Y	X²	Y²	XY
1	2	1	4	2
2	2	4	4	4
3	4	9	16	12
4	6	16	36	24
5	7	25	49	35
$\sum X = 15$	$\sum Y = 21$	$\sum X^2 = 55$	$\sum Y^2 = 109$	$\sum XY = 77$

In addition, $(\Sigma X)^2 = 15^2 = 225.$ $(\Sigma Y)^2 = 21^2 = 441.$ $N = 5.$

When making calculations for r be very attentive to the following points

ΣX^2 is not the same as $(\Sigma X)^2$
likewise, ΣY^2 is not the same as $(\Sigma Y)^2$
ΣXY is not the same as $(\Sigma X).(\Sigma Y)$

$$r = \frac{\sum XY - \frac{(\sum X)(\sum Y)}{N}}{\sqrt{\{\sum X^2 - \frac{(\sum X)^2}{N}\}.\{\sum Y^2 - \frac{(\sum Y)^2}{N}\}}}$$

$$r = \frac{77 - \frac{(15)(21)}{5}}{\sqrt{\{55 - \frac{15^2}{5}\}.\{109 - \frac{21^2}{5}\}}}$$

$$\frac{14}{\sqrt{208}} = 0.9707$$

Before we offer comments and interpretations of the meaning of this calculation you should try Activity 13.

ACTIVITY 13

Calculate the coefficient of correlation for the mail order data first encountered in Figure 1.

Note

You will probably find the computations involved in Activity 13 tedious rather than difficult. If you have a pocket calculator with some statistical functions, you will find that this lightens the labour somewhat. Also, if you have access to statistical computer programs such as STATGRAPH and MINITAB then the calculations involved in correlation analysis will be much easier. Some spreadsheets, such as LOTUS 1-2-3, will also produce regression/correlation output. Even if the spreadsheet you use does not have such functions, you will still find it a great help in speeding up calculations.

From the mail order data of figure 1 it is possible to compute the following sums

$$\Sigma X = 212 \quad \Sigma Y = 516 \quad \Sigma X^2 = 5000 \quad \Sigma Y = 27242$$

$$\Sigma XY = 11452 \quad (\Sigma X)^2 = 212^2 = 44944$$

$$(\Sigma Y)^2 = 516^2 = 266256 \quad N = 10$$

Then using formula 2 we have

$$r = \frac{11452 - \dfrac{212 \times 516}{10}}{\sqrt{\left\{5000 - \dfrac{44944}{10}\right\} \times \left\{27242 - \dfrac{266256}{10}\right\}}}$$

$$r = \frac{512.8}{\sqrt{505.6 \times 616.4}}$$

$$r \approx 0.919$$

Whatever method you have used to compute the value of r, whether it be a pocket calculator or a computer, more important questions are – what exactly does it mean?

How do we interpret the value of r we have just calculated?

3. INTERPRETATION OF THE COEFFICIENT OF CORRELATION

Considerable care must be taken in the interpretation of r as there are serious pitfalls waiting for the unwary!

When talking of the extent to which variables are correlated, we have in mind some idealised pattern for the scatterplot. This idealised pattern is that the variables exhibit **perfect correlation** if all the data points lie along a straight line.

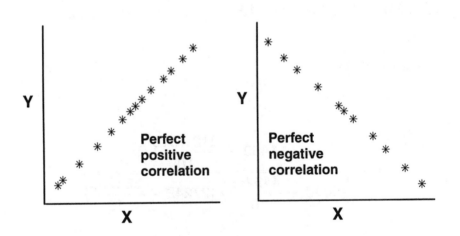

FIGURE 15: **Perfect Positive and Negative Correlation**

The correlation coefficient is a pure number, and it can be shown that

$$-1 \leq r \leq +1$$

('≤' means 'less than or equal to').

If you get a value of r > 0, then this indicates a positive association between the variables. In the extreme case, if r = +1, then all data points lie on a straight upwardly sloping line (see figure 15 above).

If you get a value of r < 0, then this indicates a negative association between the variables.

In the extreme case, if r = -1, then all data points lie along a straight downwardly sloping line.

We may thus summarise as follows:

If the results of a correlation analysis show a value of r close to either -1 or +1, we may argue that the 2 variables are closely related.

If the value of r is close to 0, then we may argue that there is no evidence of any relation between the variables.

Further, if the value of r is negative, we may argue that an upward change in one of the variables is associated with a downward change in the other variable, and vice versa.

If the value of r is positive, then we may argue that an upward change in one variable is associated with an upward change in the other, and vice versa.

ACTIVITY 14

The results of Activity 13 show that the value of r for the mail order data is 0.919.

Comment upon this value of r.

Does it indicate that the manager of the mail order firm is justified in basing his forecasts of orders on the weight of the mail?

The value of r for the mail order data is very high and close to +1. This is high positive correlation. Number of orders is closely connected with weight of mail, and the manager would be justified in using it as a forecasting device.

We shall be dealing with this matter of forecasting in more detail in the next section.

---

4. SUMMARY

In this section we have

- developed a method for measuring the **degree of association** between **two variables**

- calculated the **coefficient of correlation**

- seen how to **interpret** the coefficient of correlation

If you are unsure of any of the topics covered in this section then check back **now** before you read on.

SECTION 3

INTERPRETING THE CORRELATION COEFFICIENT

In this section we will explore a number of issues which arise whenever the need for the interpretation of a particular value of r occurs. What potential problems should we be on the look out for?

1. LINEARITY

ACTIVITY 15

Consider the following data relating to unit cost and number of units of labour used in a manufacturing organisation.

LABOUR (units)	2	3	4	6	8	9	10
UNIT COSTS (£)	9	5	3	1	3	5	9

Draw the scatterplot of the data and calculate r.

What does the calculation of r say about correlation between the variables?

What does the scatterplot say about the correlation between the data?

What do **you** think about the closeness of correlation between the variables?

In calculating r, we make use of the following amounts;
(where X = labour, Y = unit cost).

$\Sigma X = 42$ $\Sigma Y = 35$ $\Sigma X^2 = 310$ $\Sigma Y^2 = 231$
$\Sigma XY = 210$ $(\Sigma X)^2 = 42^2 = 1764$
$(\Sigma Y)^2 = 35^2 = 1225$ $N = 7$

Using formula 2 from section 2

$$r = \frac{210 - \dfrac{42 \times 35}{7}}{\sqrt{\{310 - \dfrac{1764}{7}\} \times \{231 - \dfrac{1225}{7}\}}}$$

$$r = \frac{0}{\sqrt{58 \times 56}}$$

$$r = 0$$

Thus a calculation of r seems to be suggesting a complete lack of linear relationship between labour input and unit cost (r = 0 means no correlation at all).

What does the scatterplot for this data reveal?

A chart showing this data is to be found in figure 16 below.

This scatterplot seems to suggest that there is a very strong (but non-linear) relationship between the two variables.

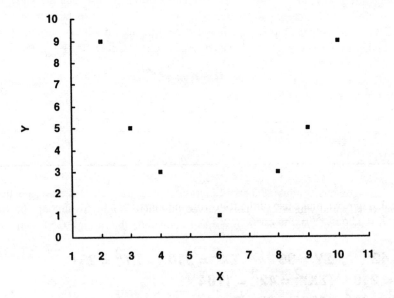

Figure 16: **Labour and Unit Cost**

The scatterplot and the calculation of r seem to be at odds.

What is the cause of this apparent disagreement between our numerical measure and the graph?

The correlation coefficient measures the degree of **linear** association between variables. If we find a value of r close to zero, we cannot rule out the possibility that the variables are associated in some way; all we have done is to establish that there is no **linear** relationship between them.

The important lesson to be learned is that

> absence of correlation should not be confused with a situation where there IS a relationship between the variables, but it does not happen to be linear (as is the case with the labour/unit cost data).

The way to establish whether or not a non-linear relationship might be present is always to construct a scatterplot. There is no point in calculating r unless there are reasonable grounds for supposing that there is **not only** a relationship between X and Y, **but also** that it is linear.

---

2. CAUSALITY

One serious problem connected with the interpretation of r, is that of causality. The coefficient of correlation measures the statistical relationship between the variables. A value of r close to +1 merely tells us that when one of the variables went up (or down), the other variable happened to change in the same direction. It tells us nothing, in itself, about whether or not one of the variables depends upon the other.

High correlation (whether + or -) does NOT equal cause and effect; it does not imply that either X depends upon Y or Y depends upon X.

ACTIVITY 16

Your colleague has conducted a study involving measurement of the gross national product (GNP) and wages. She has observed that there is a high value of r between these two variables over time, and wishes to conclude that a high GNP will cause high wages.

What words of caution might you say to her respecting this claim?

It may well be the case that gross national product and wages both go up at (roughly) the same time. However, you might advise your colleague to be cautious, on the grounds that a third factor, **price inflation** is affecting both variables. It may be this factor which is really the cause of high wages, rather than GNP.

An apparent high correlation between X and Y might be quite spurious. The 'true' situation might be:

- X is positively related to some variable Z, and a rise in Z leads to a rise in X;

- Y is also positively related to the variable Z, and a rise in Z leads to a rise in Y.

Hence we observe (but the inference is quite spurious) that X is positively related to Y. The statistical relationship may be present, but it is devoid of meaning.

Only if we have some model, or theory which asserts such a relationship, and perhaps expounds the nature of the causative mechanism, can we interpret a high value for r as providing evidence for the accuracy (for the time being) of that model or theory.

On the other hand, apart from the problem of non linearity, a low value for r might be thought a convincing demonstration of the lack of association between X and Y.

If the foregoing explanation seems difficult to understand, then do not worry too much; it amounts to stating that we should never jump to rash conclusions if we encounter particularly high (or low) correlations. High correlation is only a first step to establishing a causal connection between X and Y; it should never be taken as final and positive **proof** that Y depends upon X.

3. TRENDS

One of the problems of calculating r for two variables, is that both X and Y might show signs of a trend over time. There are otherwise no grounds for suspecting association; a high r value may show up because the trend for the variables is in the same direction.

For example, let X be monthly sales of video cassette recorders (VCRs), and let Y be monthly figures for the crime of housebreaking. At the time these notes were written, it was the case (in the UK), that the trend in VCR sales was up.
Also, the number of reported instances of housebreaking showed an upward trend. This common trend factor in itself would lead to the appearance of a high r value for variables you would not otherwise assume to be connected.

Take care that the presence of linear trends in the variables does not distort the value of r.

ACTIVITY 17

Over the last two decades, the correlation coefficient between company directors fees and the consumption of wine proves to be +0.94.

What do you conclude from this?

The variables mentioned in this activity have a high value of r. Consequently, we might argue that they are highly positively correlated. However, they are may be both subject to the same upward trend. The presence of the same trend in these variables may be the only thing they have in common. Otherwise they could be completely unrelated.

4. SAMPLE SIZE AND ACCURACY

As with most statistical calculations, the value of r is nearly always obtained from a sample. You therefore need to be aware of the usual factors affecting interpretation; was the sample size large enough to ensure sufficient accuracy?

How do we know that the value of r we have obtained is significantly different from zero (no correlation)? Regrettably, we cannot pursue the question of sample size and confidence in the results of statistical calculations any further in this unit. The topic is beyond the scope of a level one course. Nevertheless, you must be aware that greater confidence in research data tends to come with greater sample size.

5. NON-RATIO SCALE DATA

As is the case with many statistical techniques, the product moment coefficient of correlation can only be used on ratio scale or interval data.

If you are analysing nominal or ordinal variables, then you must use different techniques to measure association.

Now that you are aware of the problems to be borne in mind when interpreting the meaning of r, try applying them to the final problem (Activity 18) in this section.

ACTIVITY 18

Do families with higher incomes tend to buy bigger houses? The following data is extracted from the records of an estate agent, and shows for each of 10 families, total income and the square footage of their homes (in 00s square feet).

FAMILY	1	2	3	4	5	6	7	8	9	10
INCOME (£000s)	22	26	45	37	28	50	56	34	60	40
Sq ft (00s)	16	17	26	24	22	21	32	18	30	20

Draw a scatterplot, calculate r, and comment on the theory that richer families buy larger homes. What words of caution would you advise on interpreting the results?

See the scatterplot for this data (figure 17).

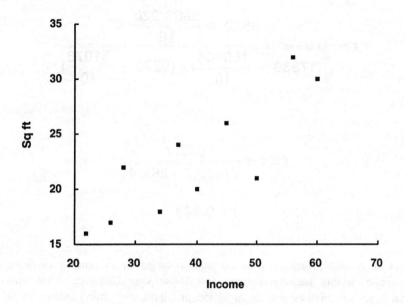

FIGURE 17: **Income – House Size**

There is some inconclusive evidence in the scatterplot for linearity. If you said that you required some more data before you expressed an opinion, then you would be acting well within the tradition of scientific scepticism

However, we shall proceed with the calculation. The data is ratio-scale, which means that it is suitable for this purpose.

Let family income = X and square feet = Y

Then

$\Sigma X = 398$ $\Sigma Y = 226$ $\Sigma XY = 9522$

$\Sigma X^2 = 17330$ $\Sigma Y^2 = 5370$ $N = 10$

$(\Sigma X)^2 = 158404$ $(\Sigma Y)^2 = 51076$

Using formula 2

$$r = \cfrac{9522 - \cfrac{398 \times 226}{10}}{\sqrt{\left\{17330 - \cfrac{158404}{10}\right\} \times \left\{5370 - \cfrac{51076}{10}\right\}}}$$

$$r = r = \cfrac{592.7}{\sqrt{1489.6 \times 262.4}}$$

$$r \approx 0.843$$

This is a fairly high positive correlation, and, as far as the evidence goes, is strongly suggestive of a link between income and house size. However, when analysing correlation results, always bear in mind the problems concerning interpretation of r given in this section.

In this instance, we would would have to recall the inconclusive evidence for linearity shown by the scatterplot.

Also, it would be wise to bear in mind the possibility of a other variables – for example, size of family - of which the above calculation of r has taken no account. Maybe it is true that income and size of house are associated. But perhaps it is the case that size of house is associated even **more** strongly with size of family?

6. SUMMARY

The coefficient of correlation, r, is a valuable measure of the association between two variables. The degree of correlation is a very useful property to be aware of. For example, in the realm of forecasting, we often need to use one variable to forecast another.

If we know that the volume of cash in circulation is correlated with the amount of change in the level of inflation, then we might be able to use the former variable as a forecaster of the latter. It would, of course be pointless to use uncorrelated variables for forecasting purposes.

However, it is not always easy to interpret the result of a calculation of r. Is the relationship linear? Is there any possibility of a spurious result? Such factors make caution necessary when interpreting r.

In section 3 we have

- explored **linearity**

- discussed and demonstrated **causality**

- looked at **trends, sample size and accuracy**

- considered the effects of **non-ratio scale data**

If you are unsure of any of these topics, check back **now** before you read on.

SECTION 4

REGRESSION ANALYSIS

1. WHAT IS REGRESSION ANALYSIS?

In the previous sections we were concerned with the question of correlation; whether there is a linear relationship between two variables, and (if there is), how strong it is, and whether it is positive or negative. Thus we found that there was a strong positive relationship between weight of mail and number of orders placed with a mail order firm. No doubt this finding would gratify the manager of the mail department, who would now be reassured (as far as the evidence goes) as to the correctness of using one variable as a means to forecasting the other. However, the manager would now need to find out what precise form this relationship takes.

Consideration of examples other than the mail order example should serve to underline the kind of activity we are to undertake in this section:

> All accountants know that there is a relationship between total cost and production volume. Would it be possible to calculate a function which describes this relationship?

Economists often discuss the relationship between total UK disposable income and total UK consumer expenditure. (You may, if you have studied any economics, have heard this relationship described as the propensity to consume.) Would it be possible to find out what the functional form of this relationship is?

For examples such as the above, and the mail order data, there is a technique called **regression analysis**. It will be of great assistance in helping us to express the relationship between two variables in a mathematical functional form.

2. THE PURPOSE OF REGRESSION

If it is known that a relationship exists between variables, then it is sometimes useful to develop a 'predictive' function expressing this relationship. In the total cost and production volume example mentioned above, it would be very convenient if we had a 'cost function' which allowed us to forecast what the total cost might be for a given planned production volume. The manager of a mail order department would find a function forecasting number of orders of very great utility.

We have seen how useful it is to have techniques which allow us to relate variables in this way. If we let Y stand for the variable 'total costs' and X stand for the variable 'volume produced' (in units), then regression would allow us to state the cost function in a form such as

$$Y = 400 + 20X$$

Of course, this is only an illustrative example. We would need to do a little more numerical work before we could get to this stage. However, in brief, regression analysis can be described as the process of describing statistical relationships in a functional form, like the above cost equation.

Note: Scope of the Course

Regression is a vast topic, and could easily constitute a course of studies on its own. As with correlation analysis, we restrict ourselves to cases involving two variables only, which are related linearly. Note however, that regression methods can be extended to include non-linear relationships and more than two variables.

3. FINDING THE FORM OF THE REGRESSION EQUATION

Earlier, in Activity 8, you were asked to establish the functional form of several relationships which were displayed in graphical form. When the graphs are exact straight lines it is not difficult to do this. However, look again at the mail order data first shown in figure 1, and as a scatterplot in figure 7. Since the XY data points do not lie on a straight line it is not possible to estimate a linear function by the methods of Activity 8. None the less, the scatterplot of these data strongly suggests that a linear relationship exists between weight of mail and number of orders.

We also have some grounds for thinking (because r = 0.919) that the relationship is strong. It can be shown that it is possible to find a linear equation which is an approximate 'fit' to the data.

Consider figure 18 below. It is a copy of the scatterplot of the mail order data encountered earlier, but with the addition of a straight line drawn through the scatter of points. The line has been drawn 'freehand', and represents an attempt to fit a linear function to the data.

You may not think that the line drawn on this scatterplot is a particularly good fit, and that you could do better. Perhaps you could.

However, let us examine some of the problems involved in attempting to define a functional relationship in this way.

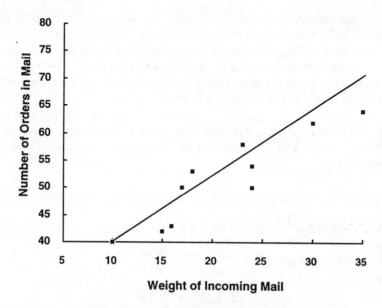

FIGURE 18: **Mail Order Scatterplot**

ACTIVITY 19

(a)   Study the straight line drawn through the scatterplot in figure 18. Make an estimate of the linear function (expressed in the form Y = a + bX) which describes this line.

(Warning – be careful with the X and Y axes)

(b)   Use the linear function obtained in (a) to estimate the number of orders which might be forthcoming from a mailbag weighing 40 g.

To obtain the estimate required for Activity 19, you can use roughly the same techniques used in Activity 8. The answer will be very 'rough and ready' because of the size of scale used on the graph. One complicating factor is that the 'true' origin is not shown on the chart; the horizontal axis does not start at 0, but at 5, and the vertical axis begins at 40. (The graph was drawn using LOTUS 1-2-3, which sometimes adjusts the scales to begin from some origin other than zero.)

Making allowances for this, the line cuts through the (real) Y axis at (very) approximately where Y = 25. Therefore the intercept for the linear function is 25. Therefore a = 25.

Also, when X changes from 10 to 15, Y changes from (very approximately) 40 to 47.

This gives a slope of (47 - 40)/(15 - 10) = 7/5 = 1.4. Therefore b = 1.4

and the linear function would be

$$Y = 25 + 1.4X$$

Remember that the above is a rough estimate only, so if you obtained a result close to this then you can consider it correct.

What would be the forecast for orders from a mail bag of 40 kg?

This would mean that X = 40, giving the result

$$Y = 25 + (1.4).(40) = 81 \ (00s)$$

ie the equation obtained in this solution would predict that a mailbag weighing 40 kg would yield 8100 orders.

In working through Activity 19, you might have formed the conclusion that the line drawn through the points in figure 18 is not a very good 'fit'. You would be right, and I make no special claims for its accuracy.

Perhaps you could draw a line which fits the data better. It is left to you as an exercise.

Problems With the 'Freehand' Method

In answering Activity 19, a drawback to fitting a freehand line to a scatterplot might have occurred to you. If you ask (say) 30 different people to draw a line through a scatterplot, which they believe to be a good estimate of a function describing the relationship, you may well get 30 different answers. Is there a line which can be drawn through the scatterplot which in some sense is the 'best fit' to the data? The answer to this question is 'yes', and we do not have to use crude graphical techniques to find it. Such a line is known sometimes as the 'line of best fit' and sometimes as the 'least squares line', for reasons which will be made clear in the next section.

4. BEST FIT – THE LEAST SQUARES LINE

Graphical methods are therefore not reliable enough for our purpose. There is a method called 'the least squares method' which produces a line of **best fit**. The following is a rough explanation of this expression, 'best fit'. But before describing how to find this so-called best fit line, look again at the mail order data. The scatterplot for the data is reproduced in figure 19, and the line drawn through the points is the **least squares line**. Vertical lines have been drawn connecting the least squares line with the scatterplot points in order to illustrate how good a fit the line is.

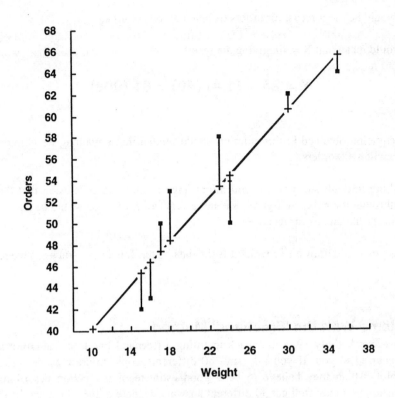

FIGURE 19: **Mail Order Scatterplot (With 'Best Fit' Line)**

The equation of this line is

$$Y = 30.10 + 1.014X$$

But how was this line obtained? Have patience for just a little longer, as you will eventually be introduced to this technique. Before you do however, it is a good idea to understand what 'best fit' means.

The scattered points in figure 19 illustrate the **actual** statistical data, while the least squares line is an **estimate** of Y for a given value of X. Notice the distance between the scattered points and the line; this will give you some idea how good a fit the line is.

For example, the original data shows one day when the mail weighed 15 kg and contained 4200 orders. But what happens if we set X = 15 in the least squares regression line?

ACTIVITY 20

Use the least squares regression line from figure 19 to forecast the number of orders which would result from a postbag weighing 15 kg. Compare this estimate with the **actual** orders recieved on that day.

To answer Activity 20, we will need the least-squares regression line

$$Y = 30.10 + 1.014X$$

where X = weight (kg) and Y = orders (00s).

Now if the postbag weighs 15 kg (X = 15), then the regression line would estimate

$$Y = 30.10 + (1.014).(15) = 45.31 \text{ (in 00s)}$$

We know from the original data that on day 7, the mail actually weighed 15 kg (see figure 1), and there were 4200 orders on that day (Y = 42).

Thus the least squares line would predict 4531 orders compared to the actual 4200. This is an error of 331 orders, or just 7.9% of actual orders.

From your answer to the last question, you will notice that the least squares line gives an estimate for orders which has an error (albeit small). In figure 19, the vertical distances between the actual Y values (scatterplot points) and the estimates of Y (the least squares line) are drawn in, and indicate how large is the error in the regression estimates.

Let Y represent the actual values of sales, and Y_{est} represent the estimates, or predictions of sales obtained from the regression line $(Y = 30.10 + 1.014X)$.

ACTIVITY 21

On day 1 in the table for the mail order firms data, the mail bag is recorded as weighing 23 kg. (See Figure 1).

Use the line of best fit and calculate Y_{est} for $X = 23$. How does this regression estimate compare with the **actual** orders recieved?

On day 10, the incoming mail weighed 30 kg, and there were 6200 orders on that day. Compare this with the forecast value provided by the line of best fit when $X = 30$.

For each value of X, we first calculate the estimate Y_{est}. Then calculate $Y - Y_{est}$. (The difference between the actual orders and the estimated.)

Expressing $Y - Y_{est}$ as a percentage of Y will give some idea of the kind of errors the so-called line of best fit makes.

When   **X = 23**
          Y = 30.10 + (1.014).(23) = 53.422
          = (5342 orders)

Actual orders on day 1 happened to be 5800, so we have an error of 5800 - 5342 = 458, which is 7.9% of actual orders.

When   **X = 30**
              Y = 30.10 + (1.014).(30) = 60.52
              = (6052 orders)

Actual orders on day 10 happened to be 6200, so there is an error of only 6200 - 6052 = 148, or 2.4% of actual orders.

The mail order data have observations for 10 days. Thus there would be 10 possible forecast, or prediction errors (differences between Y and Y_{est}). These are shown in figure 20.

The column headed 'Error is equal to Orders (Y) - Y_{est}.

The final column '% Error is the error as a percentage of actual orders (Y). This last column gives some idea of the degree of error in the regression estimate.

DAY	WEIGHT (X) kg	ORDERS (Y) 00s	Y_{est}	ERROR	ERROR (%)
1	23	58	53.42	4.58	7.9
2	17	50	47.34	2.66	5.3
3	24	54	54.44	-0.44	0.8
4	35	64	65.59	-1.59	2.5
5	10	40	40.24	-0.24	0.6
6	16	43	46.32	-3.32	7.7
7	15	42	45.31	-3.31	7.9
8	24	50	54.44	-4.44	8.9
9	18	53	48.35	4.65	8.8
10	30	62	60.52	1.48	2.4

FIGURE 20: **Actual Orders Obtained Over 10 Days Together With Forecasts Obtained From Using The Least Squares Regression Line Y = 30.10 + 1.014X**

If you examine the last column of percentage forecast errors, you will see that apart from a few cases, the regression line gives fairly accurate estimates (most percentage errors are small).

We have already mentioned that a method of obtaining a best fit line is known as the 'method of least squares'. The reasoning behind it can be stated as follows;

Find the differences between Y and Y_{est} ie $(Y - Y_{est})$.

The least squares method searches for the line which minimises the sum of the squares of these differences, ie $\Sigma(Y - Y_{est})^2$ should be the minimum possible.

The general equation of a straight line is $Y = a + bX$. Therefore $Y_{est} = a + bX$ for suitably chosen values of a and b.

Points 2 and 3 above, imply that we must try and find values of a and b such that $\Sigma(Y - a - bX)^2$ is at a minimum. A line which achieves this is known as a 'best fit' line.

After applying a little calculus (we can skip the details here), we establish the following equations.

Formula 3

The Regression Coefficients
For the general linear equation Y = a + bX

$$b = \frac{\Sigma\ XY\ -\ \bar{X}.\Sigma\ Y}{\Sigma\ X^2\ -\ \bar{X}.\Sigma\ X}$$

$$a = \bar{Y} - b.\bar{X}$$

X is the independent variable (weight of mail in the present example), and Y (number of orders) is the dependent variable. Solving the equations shown in formula 3 will tell us the values of a and b which should be inserted in the standard linear equation $(Y = a + bX)$.

The resulting function will be the least squares line.

ACTIVITY 22

Use formula 3 to make the appropriate calculations, and hence confirm that the least squares regression line for the mail order data is

$$Y = 30.10 + 1.014X$$

Note

If using a pocket calculator to calculate a regression line, it is good practice to carry as many decimal places as possible during the computation, and only round off when finished.

We need to supply the values a and b in the standard linear equation $Y = a + bX$.

From the working for Activity 13, where you were asked to compute the coefficient of correlation for this data we have the following results:

$\Sigma X = 212 \quad \Sigma Y = 516 \quad \Sigma X^2 = 5000 \quad \Sigma Y^2 = 27242$

$\Sigma XY = 11452 \quad (\Sigma X)^2 = 212^2 = 44944$

$(\Sigma Y)^2 = 516^2 = 266256 \quad N = 10$

Using formula(s) 3 we have:

$$b = \frac{\sum XY - \bar{X}.\sum Y}{\sum X^2 - \bar{X}.\sum X}$$

$$b = \frac{11452 - 21.2 \times 516}{5000 - 21.2 \times 212}$$

$$b = 1.0142405$$

and

$$a = \bar{Y} - b\bar{X}$$

$$a = 51.6 - 1.0142405 \times 21.2$$

$$a = 30.098101$$

Rounding these values a little, and inserting them into the standard linear function, we have

$$Y = 30.10 + 1.014X$$

as required.

5. STATISTICAL AND SPREADSHEET PACKAGES

Most statistical packages (STATGRAPHICS, MINITAB, SPSS-PC, etc will calculate a least squares regression line and calculate r, as well as provide scatterplots. Remember that we have restricted ouselves to simple regression in this study module, so that you should be careful to choose the correct model (linear, two variables) from the options the software provides. Many statistical packages will also offer options for multiple and non-linear regression, which are beyond the scope of this course. You should also take note that the output of any statistical software is much more complex, and provides much more detail than needed at this stage. You only need to know r, and the values of a and b; ignore everything else.

LOTUS 1-2-3 will also perform regression analysis on data you you have already entered in a worksheet. Choose the option /Data, Regression from the main menu. It is possible to process every problem in this study unit with LOTUS 1-2-3. LOTUS will also allow you to draw scatterplots of data, but you **must** select the XY type of graph when you choose the type of chart (/Graph, Type, XY). Also, you will need to turn off the connecting lines between points (/Graph, Options, Format, Symbols). Most of the scatterplots shown in this book were drawn with the aid of LOTUS.

There are some examples of LOTUS regression output in the next section.

6. DEPENDENT AND INDEPENDENT VARIABLES

The function $Y = a + bX$, which we have referred to as the regression line, is more correctly known as the regression line of Y on X. The extra wording is important, because it tells us that Y is the dependent variable.

In Activity 22 you calculated the regression line of number of orders on mail weight, which is another way of saying that number of orders is the dependent variable.

You must be careful to correctly identify the dependent variable (it is called Y in the regression formulae). If you nominate the wrong variable as the Y variable, you will end up with the regression line of X on Y, which IS NOT the same as the regression line of Y on X.

In many cases it will be clear which of the variables is dependent and which is independent. You will presumably have some quite good intuitive ideas as to what variable 'depends' on what. In some cases you may have to do a little thinking before you apportion the X and Y labels.

And now, since you will require some practice in this technique, we conclude this section with two problems.

ACTIVITY 23

The following data describe consumer expenditure and personal disposable income in a small economy over the years 1981-1990. Assume that there is a roughly linear relationship between these variables.

YEAR	TOTAL CONSUMER EXPENDITURE (£M)	TOTAL PERSONAL DISPOSABLE INCOME (£M)
1981	22.9	25.0
1982	24.2	26.6
1983	25.4	27.8
1984	27.4	29.7
1985	29.0	31.6
1986	31.5	34.6
1987	35.1	38.5
1988	39.6	44.1
1989	45.1	50.9
1990	51.3	59.0

(a) Find the regression line of consumer expenditure on personal disposable income.

(b) What would consumer expenditure be if personal disposable income were £65 million?

(c) Interpret the meaning of the regression coefficient b. What is its significance?

(d) Interpret the meaning of the regression coefficient a. Does it tell us anything useful about the data? Explain your answer.

In Activity 23 you are required to find the regression line of consumer expenditure on personal disposable income. This tells us that expenditure is the dependent, or Y variable, while income is the independent, or X variable. Remember, you must always carefully identify the X and Y variables before proceeding with regression analysis.

Now for this data you can check that

$\Sigma X = 367.8$ $\Sigma Y = 331.5$ $\Sigma XY = 13162.42$

$\Sigma X^2 = 14682.08$ $\Sigma Y^2 = 11805.09$ $N = 10$

$\bar{X} = 36.78$ $\bar{Y} = 33.15.$

So that

$$b = \frac{\sum XY - \bar{X}.\sum Y}{\sum X^2 - \bar{X}.\sum X}$$

$$b = \frac{13162.42 - 36.78 \times 331.5}{14682.08 - 36.78 \times 367.8}$$

$$b = 0.84013631$$

and

$$a = \bar{Y} - b.\bar{X}$$

$$a = 33.15 - 0.84013631 \times 36.78$$

$$a = 2.24978652$$

Therefore the least squares line for these data is

$$Y = 2.2498 + 0.8401X \quad \text{(to four dp)}$$

If disposable income were £65 million ($X = 65$), then

$$Y = 2.2498 + (0.8401).(65) = 56.8563$$

The estimated consumer expenditure would be £56.8563 million.

The value 'b' is the slope of the function. In this case 'slope' would mean the rate at which consumer expenditure is changing per unit increase in personal disposable income. In this case b is (approximately) 0.84, meaning that for a £1 increase in income, there will be a £0.84 increase in expenditure. This is quite a useful piece of information for economists.

The 'a' is the Y intercept; it is the value of Y when the regression line crosses the vertical axis (when X = 0). For the income-expenditure data a = 2.2498. This implies that when income is zero (X = 0), expenditure is £2.2498 millions. It does not seem likely that the country would be spending this amount when there is no disposable income (unless everyone is spending on credit or using up their savings). Therefore, the 'a' value does not tell us anything useful about the data.

ACTIVITY 24

Costs are to be estimated for the the forthcoming budget. A scatterplot indicates mixed costs and machine usage behaving in the form Y = a + bX.

Over the last 9 months, costs were as follows

MONTH	MACHINE HOURS (000s)	TOTAL MIXED COSTS (£000s)
JAN	22	23
FEB	23	25
MAR	19	20
APR	12	20
MAY	12	20
JUN	9	15
JUL	7	14
AUG	11	14
SEP	14	16

(a)   What would be appropriate choices for dependent and independent variables for this data?

(b)   Use the least squares method to find the cost function for this operation.

⫸

Activity 24 continued...

(c)   Interpret the values of a and b. What do you think is their significance in
      terms of the classification of costs?

A cost function would only make sense if total cost depended on machine usage. This
means that we need to make cost the Y variable and machine usage the X variable. In
other words, we require the regression line of total cost on machine usage (in hours).
For this data

$\Sigma X = 129 \quad \Sigma Y = 167 \quad \Sigma XY = 2552 \quad N = 9$

$\Sigma X^2 = 2109 \quad \Sigma Y^2 = 3227$

$\bar{X} = 14.333...$ $\bar{Y} = 18.555...$ (recurring decimals)

So that

$$b = \frac{\sum XY - \overline{X}.\sum Y}{\sum X^2 - \overline{X}.\sum X}$$

$$b = \frac{2552 - 14.3333...\times167}{2109 - 14.3333...\times129}$$

$$b = 0.60897436$$

and

$$a = \overline{Y} - b\overline{X}$$

$$a = 18.5555... - 0.60897436 \times 14.3333...$$

$$a = 9.82692306$$

Therefore the regression line is

$$Y = 9.8269 + 0.6090X \text{ (to four dp)}$$

The 'b' value tells us the slope of the line: the rate at which total cost is changing for a unit increase in machine usage. Therefore b can be identified with the variable costs of machine usage. For each unit increase in machine hours, total cost will increase by 0.6090 (£000s).

The 'a' value is the Y intercept, or the point where the straight line cuts the Y axis. When X (machine usage) = 0, then total cost is 9.8269 (£000s).

In other words, even if machines are not used there will still be a cost of 9.8269. Thus a is equivalent to a fixed cost which the business will bear irrespective of the amount of activity.

7. SUMMARY

In this section we have developed a method for fitting a straight line; the 'line of best fit'; to variables which are known to be statistically related. The method is of very great value to analysts wishing to develop a model which they can use for forecasting purposes. What we need to do now is find a way of assessing the effectiveness of our model. How good is it at making forecasts? How many mistakes does it make? How big are these mistakes? These are questions which we shall be looking at in the next study session.

In section 4 we have

- defined **regression analysis**

- examined the **purpose of** regression analysis

- seen how to find the **form of** the regression equation

- discussed the **least squares method**

- given some advice on the use of **computer packages** for regression analysis

- discussed **dependent** and **independent** variables

If you are still unsure of any of the topics in this section, check back **now** before you read on.

SECTION 5

HOW EFFECTIVE IS REGRESSION ANALYSIS?

1. WHAT WE HAVE ACCOMPLISHED SO FAR

It is useful at this stage, to stop and consider the aims of correlation and regression analysis. What are we now able to do with these techniques?

We have been able to say whether a linear relationship exists between variables.

We are able to measure the strength of this relationship

We can use the relationship between the variables to make forecasts, estimates, predictions.

But how good is our regression line at the task of estimating? We can continue to use the mail order data as an example. Look at the table in figure 20 in the last section. This is a table consisting of the **actual** orders recieved on each of 10 days, together with the **estimates** of orders we would have got had we used the regression line.

In order to assess the accuracy of our regression line, it would seem a useful idea to start with the differences between actual orders and forecasts. By a lengthy, complicated, argument which we omit here for the sake of brevity, the analysis of error terms yields a measure called the **coefficient of determination**. Now it just so happens that the coefficient of determination is equal to r^2, ie the coefficient of correlation **squared**.

We have already established earlier, that $r = 0.919$ for this data.

Therefore $r^2 = 0.84$ (to two dp).

What, however, does r^2, the coefficient of determination tell us about the data?

2. INTERPRETATION OF THE COEFFICIENT OF DETERMINATION

The dependent variable, Y varies for a number of reasons. Variation in Y can be classified as

- 'explained' variation, because it is due to changes in the dependent variable, X

- 'unexplained' variation, because it is due to factors other than X.

For example, for our mail order data, some of the changes in the number of orders can be 'explained' by references to changes in the weight of the mail. However, some of the variation in orders must be due to other factors. The size of r^2 will give an indication of how much of the variation in Y is due to the independent variable.

In the mail order case, r^2 is 0.84.

Thus we can argue that 0.84, or 84% of variation in orders (Y) is 'explained' by changes in weight of mail (X), implying that the remainder

$$1 - R^2 = 1 - 0.84 = 0.16, \text{ or } 16\%$$

is unexplained variation.

16% of the changes in number of orders cannot be attributed to variation in the weight of the mail recieved. For a regression model to be at all useful, the coefficient of determination must be close to 1.

A regression model with r^2 close to 1 is said to have higher 'explanatory' power than one where r^2 is not close to 1.

ACTIVITY 25

Find the coefficients of determination for the two regression models of Activities 23 and 24. What do the calculations tell you about the effectiveness of the models?

Activity 23 concerned expenditure and income. We have

$$r = \frac{13162.42 - \dfrac{367.8 \times 331.5}{10}}{\sqrt{\{14682.08 - \dfrac{135276.84}{10}\} \times \{11805.09 - \dfrac{109892.25}{10}\}}}$$

$$r = \frac{969.85}{\sqrt{1154.396 \times 815.865}}$$

$$r = \approx 0.999 \quad \therefore r^2 \approx 0.998$$

This is a very high level of r^2 and suggests that the regression line is a very good estimator.

Almost all of the variation in consumer expenditure can be 'explained' by reference to changes in personal disposable income. Our model would have high explanatory power.

For the Activity 24 data (costs – machine usage), we have

$$r = \frac{2552 - \dfrac{129 \times 167}{9}}{\sqrt{\{2109 - \dfrac{16641}{9}\} \times \{3227 - \dfrac{27889}{9}\}}}$$

$$r = \frac{158.3333...}{\sqrt{260 \times 128.2222...}}$$

$$r = \approx 0.867 \quad \therefore r^2 \approx 0.752$$

This is not such a high level of r^2 as in the previous example, but nevertheless, it still implies that 75% of the variation in cost can be explained by variation in machine hours. The evidence, so far as it goes, suggests that the least squares line is a fairly accurate predictor of cost.

ACTIVITY 26

A life insurance company needs to make quick estimates of the net monthly direct costs of servicing a policy per £ of premium paid. The company analyst believes that the age of a policy is a very good indicator of these costs. To test this opinion, the analyst samples 16 policies and records the age of the policy in months (X), and the net cost per £ premium paid (Y).

The following data resulted.

POLICY NUMBER	X	Y
1	8	1.26
2	29	1.15
3	47	0.81
4	24	1.14
5	57	0.61
6	45	0.88
7	39	0.99
8	14	1.11
9	70	0.58
10	40	0.74
11	66	0.67
12	55	0.70
13	68	0.62
14	36	0.91
15	21	1.10
16	38	0.78

Find the regression line for the data. Do you think the model will give good predictive results?

The analyst wishes to estimate policy cost by using age of policy. To make such estimates, we must first find the regression line of policy cost on policy age.

The data can be summarised as follows

$\Sigma X = 657$ $\Sigma Y = 14.05$ $\Sigma XY = 517.96$

$\Sigma X^2 = 32367$ $SY^2 = 13.0783$ $N = 16$

$\bar{X} = 41.0625$ $\bar{Y} = 0.878125$

$$b = \frac{\sum XY - \bar{X}.\sum Y}{\sum X^2 - \bar{X}.\sum X}$$

$$b = \frac{517.96 - 41.0625 \times 14.05}{32367 - 41.0625 \times 657}$$

$$b = -0.01094244$$

and

$$a = \bar{Y} - b.\bar{X}$$

$$a = 0.878125 - (-0.01094244) \times 41.0625$$

$$a = 1.32744894$$

The regression line of policy cost on policy age is

$$Y = 1.3274 - 0.0109X$$

Notice that b is negative, indicating a downward slope to the function; policy cost (per £) falls as the policy ages.

In order to comment on the effectiveness of the regression equation as a predictor, we need to calculate r^2.

$$r = \frac{517.96 \ - \ \dfrac{657 \times 14.05}{16}}{\sqrt{\left\{32367 \ - \ \dfrac{431649}{16}\right\} \times \left\{13.0783 \ - \ \dfrac{197.4025}{16}\right\}}}$$

$$r = \frac{-58.968125}{\sqrt{5388.9375 \times 0.74064375}}$$

$$r = \approx -0.933 \quad \therefore \quad r^2 \approx 0.87$$

Approximately 87% of variation in policy cost can be explained by variation policy age. Thus the equation will be a good predictor of cost.

3. SUMMARY

In this section we have

- looked at the question of **forecasting the behaviour of variables**, given a model of how one variable depends upon another

- discussed the meaning of **explained** and **unexplained variation**

- defined what we mean by the **explanatory power** of a regression model

- shown how the **coefficient of determination** is a measure of the degree of explained variation, and therefore of the explanatory power of regression.

If you are unsure of any of the topics covered in this section, then check back **now** before reading on.

SECTION 6

WHAT NEXT?

1. WHERE DO WE GO FROM HERE?

Most of what you need to know about the subjects of regression and correlation (at this level) has already been dealt with in the previous sections of this unit. You now have a technique for measuring the degree of association between variables (**correlation**), and you are also able to construct a model of the relationship between variables (**regression**).

You may perhaps return to a deeper study of regression techniques at a higher level of your course. This part of the unit exists purely to provide you with a taste of what such further studies may involve. Also, you will find the material here of great value in providing you with a critical insight into the use of the techniques you have already learned.

2. CORRELATION, REGRESSION AND NON-RATIO SCALE DATA

The techniques of regression and correlation discussed in this unit will only work if the data is measured on a ratio scale, or an interval scale.

Note

See the opening section of Unit 2, *Data Presentation* if you have forgotten the meaning of these terms.

Regression analysis is not really applicable to nominal or ordinal variables at all. However, you should be aware that there are techniques for measuring the degree of correlation between such variables.

Example

Suppose that a group of recruits to the government service are given an intelligence test in communication skills and general knowledge. They are then ranked according to whether they came first, second, third, etc in the tests. The resulting data are **ordinal**. It is possible to measure the correlation between general knowledge and communication skills (via rank achieved by each recruit). However, because the data are not ratio-scale or interval, we would not be able to use the methods used in this text. Special methods are available which are outside the scope of this course.

Remember that **at all times** you should examine the type of data you are dealing with before using a technique.

3. DEALING WITH A TIME SERIES

Certain kinds of data are referred to as **time series**. What is meant by this?

If one of the variables you are dealing with is the time period when the data were recorded, then you have a time series.

Consider the following example.

YEAR YEAR C	YEAR CODE	PASSENGERS (000)
1983	1	79
1984	2	85
1985	3	95
1986	4	118
1987	5	140
1988	6	202
1989	7	251
1990	8	334
1991	9	421
1992	10	537

The table shows the annual number of passengers, in 000s using a regional airport.

The airport authority may wish to forecast the number of passengers using the airport in 1994, which will involve it in trying to develop a model of the behaviour of customers over time. In this case, it is treating 'Year' as one of the variables; the independent variable in fact. The other variable 'Passengers' will be the dependent variable.

It is possible to calculate the regression line of passengers on year and use the result for forecasting purposes. Usually, for ease of calculation, the year is numerically 'coded', 1, 2, 3, 4, etc. This has already been done in the above table. The coded value is treated as the X variable.

ACTIVITY 27

For the airport data calculate the line of best fit of passengers on year.

Use the line to forecast the expected number of passengers in 1994.

Take care – remember the year coding!

Treating year code as X and number of passengers as Y the data can be summarised as follows;

$\Sigma X = 55$ $\qquad$ $\Sigma Y = 2262$ $\qquad$ $N = 10$

$\Sigma X^2 = 385$ $\qquad$ $\Sigma Y^2 = 736986$

$\Sigma XY = 16506$ $\qquad$ $\bar{X} = 5.5$ $\qquad$ $\bar{Y} = 226.2$

Thus

$$b = \frac{\sum XY - \bar{X}.\sum Y}{\sum X^2 - \bar{X}.\sum X}$$

$$b = \frac{16506 \ - \ 5.5 \times 2262}{385 \ - \ 5.5 \times 55}$$

$$b \approx 49.2727$$

and

$$a = \bar{Y} - b.\bar{X}$$

$$a = 226.2 - 49.27272727 \times 5.5$$

$$a \approx -44.8$$

So the regression line is

$$Y = -44.8 + 49.2727X$$

The forecast for 1994 would be

$$Y = -44.8 + (49.2727).(12)$$
$$= 546.4724 \ \ (546{,}472 \text{ passengers})$$

Remember the coding! 1994 would mean putting $X = 12$.

We shall not make any further use of regression analysis and time series here.

Note

The subject will appear again in Unit 8, *Index Numbers and Time Series*.

However, from this brief introduction, you should be able to see that the use of the technique offers planners potential (and very powerful) methods for forecasting sales, customers, or other strategically important variables.

4. WHAT CAN WE DO ABOUT NON-LINEARITY?

You are probably only too aware of the number of times the word 'linear' has been used in this text. Because this is a first level course, we have had to restrict the subject by making the assumption that the variables are linearly related.

While this may be true of many variables, it certainly is not universally applicable.

For example, consider the airport data used as the basis of the calculations in Activity 27. We calculated the regression line of passengers on year on the implicit assumption that the relationship was that of a straight line. How true is this?

ACTIVITY 28

Draw a scatterplot of the data for the regional airport usage.

Does it show any evidence to support the assumption of linearity?

If not, what do you conclude about it?

The scatterplot for the airport data is shown in figure 21. It does not support the assumption of linearity. In fact, it appears that the number of passengers using the airport has been growing, not by a **constant** amount, but by an **increasing** amount over the years 1983 - 1992. It seems that we have constructed a linear regression line on a false premise. What effect will this have on the forecast we made for 1994?

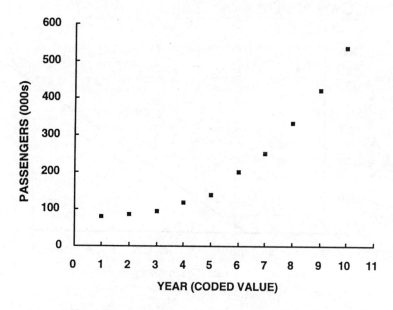

FIGURE 21: **Annual Number of Passengers (000s)**

ACTIVITY 29

On the same diagram used to draw the scatterplot of the airport data draw the line of (linear) best fit Y = -44.8 + 49.2727X.

What observations can you make about the forecast made in Activity 27 of 546,472 passengers for 1994?

The scatterplot for the airport data is repeated in figure 22. The straight line of best fit is shown on the same scale. By year 10 (1992), the regression line has diverged quite considerably from the actual data. This will certainly mean that the forecast for 1994 (year 12) will probably prove wildly inaccurate.

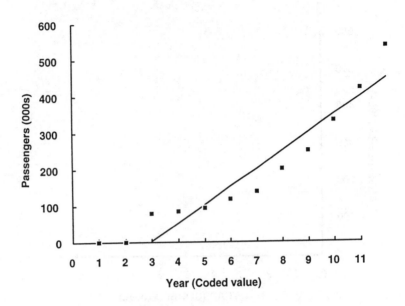

FIGURE 22: **Annual Number of Passengers (000s)**

What can we do if the data is not linear?

Very often, it is possible to carry out mathematical transformations of non-linear data which make it still possible to use linear regression methods. A very large class of functional relationships can be dealt with in this way. If it is not possible to do this, then there are some non-linear regression methods which can be used. In any case, the methods to be used on non-linear data are beyond the scope of this course, although you should be aware of their existence.

5. MUST WE ALWAYS BE LIMITED TO TWO VARIABLES?

In all cases in this study unit, we have restricted ourselves to what is called **bivariate** data. That is to say, where there are two variables only. One of these is a dependent variable, (Y), the other an independent variable, (X).

While many models have high explanatory power with just one independent variable, it is possible to have more. If we have more than one independent variable then we are involved in **multivariate** statistics. There are multivariate regression methods available for such data.

In unit 3, *Linear Programming*, there is a brief introduction to the general linear function in n+1 variables. This function is

$$Y = A_0 + A_1X_1 + A_2X_2 + A_3X_3 + \text{.......} + A_NX_N$$

One of the variables in this expression, (Y), is the dependent variable, and the X_1, X_2, X_3, ... etc ...... X_n are the n independent variables.

a_0 is the **constant**, the multivariate equivalent of the Y intercept, while the values a_1, a_2, a_3, etc are the regression coefficients.

In the simple linear case all of the a values after a_1 would not exist, as there is only one X variable.

For example $Y = a_0 + a_1X_1$

is the two variable version of the above.

Let us have a look at some multivariate data.

Ace Manufacturing PLC

MANUFACTURING HOURS	ORDER SIZE	NUMBER OF OPERATIONS
153	100	6
192	35	11
162	127	7
240	64	12
339	600	5
185	14	16
235	96	11
506	257	13
260	21	9
161	39	8
835	426	14
586	843	6
444	391	8
240	84	13
303	235	9
775	520	12
136	76	8
271	139	11
385	165	14
451	304	10

In Ace Manufacturing PLC, the amount of time (manufacturing hours) it takes to prepare an order for a client depends upon two variables:

● how large the order is (number of pieces);

● how many manufacturing operations are involved in each order.

The above table shows the behaviour of these variables for the last 20 orders. The works manager would like an efficient system for forecasting the length of time it will take to prepare an order.

The next three activities try to give a flavour of multiple regression. If you have access to a statistical software package, or a spreadsheet with regression functions you should attempt them. You can, of course, perform many of the computations required with a pocket calculator, although this will involve much tedious detail. If you do not have the software, or are short of time, then just read the solutions to the activities.

ACTIVITY 30

The works manager initially believes that it will be sufficient just to use order size as a predictor for manufacturing hours.

Calculate the regression line of best fit of manufacturing hours on order size.

Do you think this regression line would give you accurate forecasts? Why? (Or why not?)

In the solution to this activity, the output from a LOTUS 1-2-3 worksheet has been used.

The X data (order size) and the Y data (manufacturing hours) are typed in as separate columns. In version 2.2 of LOTUS, /Data, Regression is entered, and you are then asked to name the ranges for dependent and independent variables.

If you use any other version of LOTUS the procedure may be slightly different.

LOTUS produces the following output:

Regression Line of Hours on Order Size

Regression Output

Constant	192.3894
Std Err of Y Est	140.0244
R Squared	0.545848
No. of Observations	20
Degrees of Freedom	18

X Coefficient(s) 0.663847
Std Err of Coef. 0.142723

For our purposes, there is much in this table which can be ignored. The important values are the 'constant', 'X coefficient' and 'R Squared'.

The 'constant' in the above table corresponds to the Y intercept; the 'a' value in the straight line of best fit, $Y = a + bX$. The 'X coefficient' is the slope, or 'b' value.

Thus the straight line of best fit of manufacturing hours on order size is

$$Y = 192.3894 + 0.663847X$$

But how good would this line be as a forecasting model?

Note that the R Squared value in the above table is approximately 0.55. Remember what we have said about this statistic. It means that the model explains only 55% of the changes in manufacturing hours. Our model would not have very good explanatory power.

Another method of judging whether the line would be a good fit is to examine the scatterplot of the data.

The scatterplot for the two variables 'manufacturing hours' and 'order size' is shown in figure 23 below. It gives ample evidence that there is little relationship between these variables. Any attempt to forecast how long it takes to prepare an order just by reference to the order size seems doomed to failure.

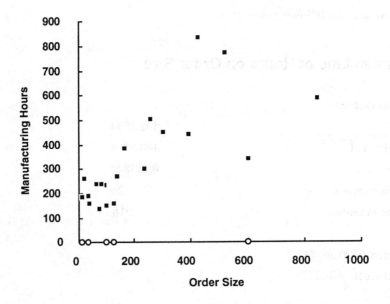

FIGURE 23: **Manufacturing Time and Order Size**

ACTIVITY 31

If the relationship between manufacturing hours and order size is a poor model for making forecasts, perhaps we shall do better if we use number of operations as the independent variable.

Calculate the regression line of manufacturing hours on number of operations.

Do you think this will provide us with good forecasts of manufacturing time?

Activity 31 continued

The following table shows the regression output from using LOTUS 1-2-3.

Hours on operations

Regression Output

Constant	185.1291
Std Err of Y Est	201.9929
R Squared	0.054926
No. of Observations	20
Degrees of Freedom	18

X Coefficient(s) 15.54885
Std Err of Coef. 15.20205

The b value (X coefficient) = 15.54885 and the a value (constant) = 185.1291

Thus the regression line of best fit of manufacturing hours on number of operations is

$$Y = 185.1291 + 15.54885X$$

But what sort of forecasts would this regression equation give us?

Look at the coefficient of determination r^2 in the LOTUS output table. This is only a little over 0.05. The regression model would have hardly any explanatory power at all!

Clearly, forecasts obtained from using this model would be even worse than the ones obtained from the model using order size as independent variable.

To support the answer to Activity 31, the scatterplot of the data is shown in figure 24.

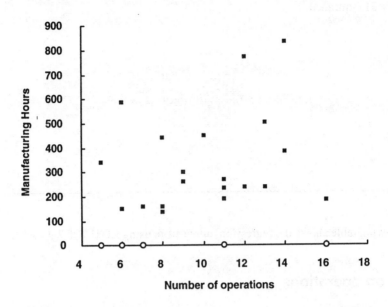

FIGURE 24: **Manufacturing Time – Number of Operations**

This diagram confirms our belief that this particular regression model would give appallingly inaccurate forecasts.

However, instead of considering a forecasting model using only one independent variable, why not use a model which has both variables; order size **and** number of operations as independent variables?

ACTIVITY 32

You are already aware that the simple linear regression model with one independent variable is

$$Y = a + bX$$

Write down an expression for a linear regression model with **two** independent variables.

From the general linear equation we can establish that the model involving two independent variables would be

$$Y = a_0 + a_1X_1 + a_2X_2$$

Suppose we agree to let the X_1 variable represent order size, and the X_2 variable represent number of operations. Y will be manufacturing hours.

What will the LOTUS output for this model look like?

Look at the following table:

Regression Output

Constant	-196.599
Std Err of Y Est	96.96845
R Squared	0.794301
No. of Observations	20
Degrees of Freedom	17

X Coefficient(s) 0.815965 34.92498
Std Err of Coef. 0.104383 7.707335

Notice that there are **two** values shown opposite the heading 'X coefficients'. This is because LOTUS was given two columns of data as the required input for the independent variables; 0.815965 is the coefficient for the X_1 variable (manufacturing hours) and 34.92498 is the coefficient for the X_2 variable (number of operations).

The constant is -196.599. Thus the forecasting model for manufacturing hours would be

$$Y = -196.599 + 0.815965X_1 + 34.92498X_2$$

ACTIVITY 33

Using the multivariate model just developed, forecast how long (how many manufacturing hours) it would take to fulfil an order of size 500 pieces involving seven different operations.

In this case we are letting $X_1 = 500$ and $X_2 = 7$.

We would thus have

$$Y = -196.599 + (0.815965)(500) + (34.924982)(7)$$
$$= 455.858374$$

It would take approximately 456 hours to prepare such an order. It seems therefore that we can sometimes get better results by using more than one independent variable in a regression model.

How good would the forecasts made by such a model be?

Look at the value of r^2 in the LOTUS output from this model. It is approximately 0.79. This means that our multivariate model will explain 79% of the variation in manufacturing hours. This is a very great improvement on the two simple models developed earlier.

The methods of multiple regression constitute a major study in their own right, and we must therefore restrict our comments to the foregoing brief indication of the possibilities.

---

6. SUMMARY

The technique of regression is very powerful, and can be of valuable assistance to people wishing to make business or economic forecasts.

Note

You will be meeting regression analysis later in the course, when you study the unit *Index Numbers*.

In this last section we have

- looked beyond **simple linear models**

- examined time **series** and **non-linearity**

- analysed more **scatterplots**

- discussed the use of **multiple independent variables**

and

- examined some simple **computer output** for regression

If you are unsure of any of the topics covered in this unit, check back **now** to the appropriate section.

REFERENCES

Students may follow up this subject by reading the following texts:

1. CURWIN & SLATER. *Quantitative Methods for Business Decisions*. Third edition. Chapman & Hall.
   Chapters 18 and 19 cover this subject well. In addition, chapter 19 provides a valuable insight into multiple regression.
2. MORRIS. C. *Quantitative Approaches in Business Studies*. Third edition. Pitman Publishing.
   This book is written in a 'user friendly' manner, and covers the same ground as this study unit.

Additionally, if you wish to read a rather more rigorous account of correlation and regression, you might turn to

3. ANDERSON, SWEENEY & WILLIAMS. *Statistics For Business & Economics*. Fifth edition. West Publishing.
   This is an American textbook, and chapters 14, 15 and 16 provide a very good account of the subject. Students are warned however that the coverage goes far beyond the introduction provided in this unit. It might be useful for students who are intending to pursue quantitative analysis in later studies.

GLOSSARY

The following is an alphabetical listing of the technical terms most often encountered in this unit.

Bivariate analysis Any analysis carried out on two data series. Usually the data are paired. Bivariate analysis is a special case of multivariate analysis.

Causal relationship A relationship between variables where movements in one variable are held to cause changes in the other.

Coefficient of determination (r^2) A measure of the explanatory power of a regression model.

Correlation The extent to which variables are associated with each other, and the direction of this association.

Dependent variable In a model of the relationships between variables, the 'dependent' variable is the one which is thought to be determined, or influenced by the others.

Deterministic relationship This is another expression for functional relationship. (Which see).

Direct relationship In bivariate analysis, a direct relationship exists where both variables tend to change in the same direction. Another name for positive correlation.

Explanatory variable In correlation and regression analysis, the explanatory variables are those which are held to determine the behaviour of the dependent variable. Another term for independent variable.

Functional relationship If the relationship between variables is sufficiently precise to be expressed in terms of a mathematical formula, it is said to be 'functional'. It means the same as 'deterministic relationship'.

Independent variable In a regression model, the independent variables are the ones which are held to determine the behaviour of the dependent variable.

Inverse relationship This is a relationship between variables where changes tend to be in opposing directions. It is another term for negative correlation.

Line of best fit This is the functional relationship thought to be the best approximation to bivariate data.

Linear function A relationship between variables which is expressible in the form $Y = a + a_1X_1 + a_2X_2 + ... + a_nX_n$.

Method of least squares A method of obtaining a line of best fit for statistically related data.

Multivariate analysis Any analysis of data which consist of two or more variables. Bivariate analysis is a special case (two variables).

Negative relationship Another term for inverse relationship.

Perfect correlation This is where the relationship between variables is deterministic, or functional; $r = +1$.

Positive relationship Another term for direct relationship.

Product moment coefficient of correlation A method of measuring the degree and direction of the linear relationship between two variables.

Regression A collection of methods directed at expressing the relationship between variables in functional terms. The method of least squares is a major technique in regression analysis.

Regression coefficients These are the values which are associated with the independent variables in a regression model. For example, in the general linear model $Y = a + a_1X_1 + a_2X_2 + ... + a_nX_n$, the values a_1, a_2, ... a_n are the regression coefficients.

Scatterplot A graphical method used to roughly estimate the degree, direction and form of the relationship between two variables.

Statistical relationship This is where a relationship between variables exists, but it cannot be exactly expressed as a mathematical function.

UNIT 5

PROBABILITY

CONTENTS

Unit Objectives

References

Glossary

UNIT OBJECTIVES

After completion of this unit you will be able to

- understand the meaning of basic terms used in probability theory

- make correct use of the rules for calculating probabilities

- use probability trees and contingency tables as a means of presenting probability information

- use the special counting rules involving permutations and combinations

SECTION 1

THE PROBLEM OF MEASUREMENT

1. INTRODUCTION

This part of the course deals with a very important part of statistics – probability. An appreciation of this topic is essential because, without some of understanding of the laws of chance, it is just not possible to gain anything other than a very superficial understanding of statistics and the techniques used in operational research.

2. WHAT IS PROBABILITY?

Most people have some kind of idea or intuition about probability. We all have a notion as to what it means when we say that the probability, or chance of something happening is low, or high.

Likewise, we understand what is meant when people say that the odds are against (or for) some event occurring.

For example, consider the following questions.

What is the probability that

> **a die will score six when it is thrown?**
> **that you will live until your 50th birthday?**
> **that a particular investment plan will make a profit?**

It is plain that when we ask questions like this that we have already gone beyond what our limited intuitive knowledge can tell us. We need to be able to devise some way of measuring probability.

In the course of discussing the measurement of chance events we shall be describing a mathematical technique which is at the heart of business, economic and social statistics.

THE SCALE OF PROBABILITY

If something is **bound** to happen, it is conventional to say that it has a probability equal to 1 (one). If something is impossible, then we say that it has a probability equal to 0 (zero). Any event must have a probability which is somewhere on the scale of zero to one. (See figure 1).

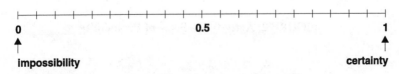

FIGURE 1: **Probability is Measured on a Scale From Zero to One**

The above statements concerning the probabilities of certain and impossible events may seem obvious. However, if we ask for estimates of the probabilities of events which are neither impossible nor certain, we are faced with a problem of quite a different kind. How would we set about calculating the probabilities of such events?

Before outlining some common approaches to this problem, try your hand at the first activity.

ACTIVITY 1

The following line is the scale of probability

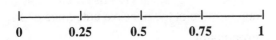

Let A represent the event that you will be struck by lightning (twice) on leaving your home, B represent the event that you will live until your 50th birthday and let C represent the event that a coin will come down heads after being tossed. Mark the letters A, B and C at the points on the above scale which you think correspond to their (approximate) probability.

It is hardly likely (though not impossible) that you will be struck by lightning twice if you step outside your home. Consequently, you would place 'A' close to zero.

Most people (in countries with developed health care) live until their 50th birthday (see the life expectancy figures if you do not believe this). 'B' would therefore be placed close to 1 on the probability scale. Also, it seems only common sense to assume that there is a 50-50 chance that a coin will come down as 'heads', so you would place 'C' in the middle of the scale. The resulting scale of probability might look as in figure 2.

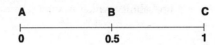

FIGURE 2: **Activity 1 – Scale of Probability**

Perhaps you thought that Activity 1 was common sense.

However, since common sense can often be unreliable when we are faced with unfamiliar problems, we must examine some different and more accurate approaches to the problem of measuring chance events.

THE 'CLASSICAL' WAY OF MEASURING CHANCE

Before we go further look at the following definitions:

Experiment	an activity which has an uncertain outcome
Event	one or more of the possible outcomes of an experiment
Sample Space	the set of all outcomes associated with an experiment
Probability	if we represent a particular event by a letter, such as E, then we write the 'probability of event E' as Pr(E).

The word experiment might conjure up visions of test tubes and Bunsen burners. However, in statistics it refers to something different – something which has a number of possible outcomes. The experiment could be complex or it could be simple. For the moment we shall restrict ourselves to simple experiments, such as the throwing of coins and dice.

Experiment 1

Two coins are thrown.

Let the event 'heads' be represented by this symbol

and the event 'tails' be represented by this symbol

The **sample space** for the experiment of throwing two coins will be a list of pairs of outcomes – the first coin and the second coin.

For instance, this outcome means 'heads on the first coin and tails on the second coin'.

So the sample space for this experiment consists of 4 distinct outcomes, or **events**.

They are listed in figure 3. Notice that the event 'tails on coin 1 and heads on coin 2' is a different outcome from 'heads on coin 1 and tails on coin 2'.

Experiment 2

Throwing a single fair six-sided die

The sample space for this experiment is the set of scores

1   2   3   4   5   6

There are six outcomes, corresponding to the six possible scores on the die.

Thus the sample space for the experiment of a single throw of a fair die consists of six distinct events.

FIGURE 3:
**Event Outcomes –
Two Coin Toss**

ACTIVITY 2

Consider an experiment of throwing three coins.

Describe the sample space which would result.

For example, you could let (H H H) represent the outcome 'three heads'.

Each of the outcomes of a throw of three coins could be represented as the combination of three events

outcome of first coin

outcome of second coin

outcome of third coin

This would give us the result shown in figure 4.

Notice that the outcome 'tails, heads, heads' is different to the outcome 'heads, tails, heads', even though the result is one tail and two heads in both cases. The event 'heads' and 'tails' happen to different coins.

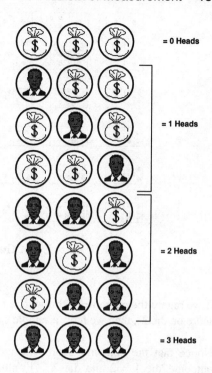

FIGURE 4: **Event Outcomes – Three Coin Toss**

ACTIVITY 3

Consider the experiment of throwing a pair of fair six-sided dice. Write down all of the events in the resulting sample space. Write down each event as a pair of numbers. For example (1 5) would mean a score of 1 on the first die and 5 on the second die.

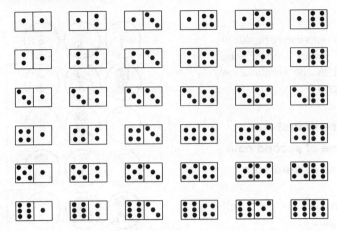

FIGURE 5: **Event Outcomes – Two Dice Throw**

If we regard the outcome of throwing a pair of dice as two numbers, (score on die 1 and score on die 2), then we have a sample space as shown in figure 5.

Notice that the outcome 'score = 1 on die 1 and 2 on die 2' is different from the outcome 'die 1 = 2 and die 2 = 1'; although the scores are the same, they occur on different dice.

Now that you are used to the idea of sample spaces, events and experiments, we can move on to the classical definition of probability. However, before we do this, try to solve the problem in Activity 4. You may not know anything about the formal rules for calculating probabilities at the moment, but you should be able to answer the Activity by using a little intuition.

ACTIVITY 4

A single die is thrown. What is the chance of obtaining an odd number?

Perhaps you thought that the answer to Activity 4 was obvious. In some ways it is, but nevertheless, the reasoning which produced the answer illustrates an important principle of probability. You may well have reasoned

> there are six possible outcomes from throwing a die, and, as half of them are odd numbers, the probability of obtaining an odd number from such an experiment must be 1/2.

So in the die-throwing experiment there are six outcomes in the sample space and if we are interested in the event 'an odd number', then three of the outcomes in this sample space are odd. Therefore we have

$$\textbf{Pr}(odd\,no) \;=\; \frac{3}{6} \;=\; \frac{1}{2}$$

which would be the correct answer for Activity 4.

It should be carefully noted that outcomes in the sample space are assumed to be equally likely.

The rule for using the classical approach to probability is summarised below.

THE CLASSICAL DEFINITION OF PROBABILITY

Let S be a sample space, and E be an event within this sample space. Let n(S) be the number of distinct points in the sample space, n(E) of which belong to the event E. Then

$$Pr(E) = \frac{n(E)}{n(S)}$$

In simpler terms the definition means that we count up the number of possible ways the event E can occur and divide by the total number of **all** possible distinct events in the sample space S.

The terminology used in this definition is very typical of probability notation. A letter, say E, represents a particular event while n(E) represents the number of ways in which the event E can occur.

Similarly, the letter S represents the **whole sample space** for the experiment, and n(S) represents all of the possible equally-likely events in the sample space.

Now try the following questions in Activity 5.

ACTIVITY 5

(a)   In a throw of a pair of dice what is the probability of obtaining a score of seven?

(b)   Three coins are thrown. What is the probability of obtaining

i) exactly 2 heads;   ii) at least 1 head?

(c)   A card is drawn from a well shuffled deck of cards (of the 4 suit, 52 card variety). What is the probability that the card is an ace or a 10?

You can use the sample spaces you drew up for Activities 2 and 3 to help with Activity 5.

In answer to question (a) first let E be the event 'score 7'.

In the two-dice sample space there are a total of 36 outcomes. So n(S) = 36. Of these, six result in a combined score of 7.

These are the number pairs:

1 6, 6 1, 2 5, 5 2, 3 4, 4 3

So n(E) = 6. We have

$$Pr(E) = \frac{n(E)}{n(S)} = \frac{6}{36} = \frac{1}{6}$$

For question (b) examine the sample space for the three coin experiment of Activity 2. There are eight outcomes altogether, so n(S) = 8. Let E be the event 'two heads'. Three of the sample space outcomes result in this event. (H H T, T H H, H T H). So n(E) = 3. We have

$$Pr(E) = \frac{n(E)}{n(S)} = \frac{3}{8}$$

The event 'at least one head' means **one or two or three** heads. Out of the eight total outcomes in the three coin experiment, seven result in either one or two or three heads. So we have

$$Pr(E) = \frac{n(E)}{n(S)} = \frac{7}{8}$$

where E is the event 'at least one head'.

And finally, for question (c), in drawing a card from a deck, there are 52 different possible outcomes, corresponding to all of the different face values of the cards. There are eight cards which are either an ace or a 10.

Consequently

$$Pr(E) = \frac{n(E)}{n(S)} = \frac{8}{52} = \frac{2}{13}$$

where E is the event 'either an ace or a 10.'

Therefore you would conclude that the classical method of determining probability depends upon dividing a sample space up into a number of equally-likely outcomes, and counting the number of those outcomes falling into a particular category.

Sometimes this is not possible, and we cannot use this approach. We then have to look for different ways of measuring chance.

RELATIVE FREQUENCY AND PROBABILITY

Many events involve circumstances which can be repeated again and again. For instance, we can throw a die or a coin as many times as we like. We could then estimate the probability of a score of 6 (say) by observing the frequency of 6s relative to the total number of throws of the die.

This is known as the **relative frequency** method of measuring probability, and is defined below.

The Relative Frequency Definition of Probability

If an experiment is repeated m times, and the event E occurs n times, then

$$Pr(E) = \frac{n}{m}$$

ACTIVITY 6

Records were kept by the maintenance department of a large factory concerning the lifetime, in days, of a particular drill bit.

LIFETIME OF BIT	NUMBER OF DRILL BITS
under 5 days	6
5 and less than 10 days	12
10 and less than 20 days	34
over 20 days	4

Assume that the above sample of drill bits is representative of the departments entire stock.

What is the probability that a drill bit issued at random will last

(a) less than 10 days

(b) 5 or more days?

Let E represent the event 'bit lasts less than 10 days'. The table in Activity 6 lists 56 drill bits in total. Therefore total frequency, m = 56. Of these 56 bits, 18 lasted less than 10 days, so n = 18. Thus the relative frequency in this case is

$$\frac{n}{m} = \frac{18}{56} = \frac{9}{28}$$

Therefore

$$Pr(E) = \frac{9}{28}$$

Now let E be the event 'a drill bit lasts 5 or more days'. Then

$$Pr(E) = \frac{n}{m} = \frac{50}{56} = \frac{25}{28}$$

Note the importance of the assumption that this sample of 56 drill bits is representative of **all** drill bits.

The relative frequency approach to chance is what is called an **empirical** (that is, experimental) approach. We must observe an event many times to establish probabilities in this way. Insurance companies use this method to calculate the risks of certain kinds of event, such as death, sickness, accident and the like. You will be unable to obtain insurance against any risk which cannot be quantified.

For example, where it is possible to observe how many people out of many thousands suffer a certain kind of accident, the insurer can calculate the likelihood of such an accident occurring to the insured, and come to some decision concerning the amount of the premium to be charged.

THE SUBJECTIVE APPROACH

It may be completely impossible to determine some probabilities by either the classical or the relative frequency approach.

For instance

What is the probability that there will be a serious explosion at a nuclear power plant?

What is the probability that global temperature will rise by 2 degrees by 2000 AD?

What is the probability that a particular investment in a new waste processing plant will earn in excess of £2,000,000?

We have no objective basis for determining these probabilities. Given the fairness of a die and the fact that it is six-sided, the probability of a score of (say) 4 is 1/6. We can come to this conclusion because we have an objective basis for determining this probability. We have no objective basis for determining the probability of an explosion at a nuclear power plant. We certainly cannot use relative frequencies, for there have not been enough accidents at nuclear plants to form a basis for empirical judgement. Our assessment of such probabilities can only be subjective.

Some probabilities may be determined by using good judgement but we must accept that peoples judgement will vary. You may think that global temperature has a very high chance of rising two degrees by 2000; some one else may judge that the probability of this happening is small.

3. PERCENTAGES AND ODDS

Probabilities can also be expressed as percentages. So the statement

'the probability of obtaining a six on a throw of a single die is 1/6'

is equivalent to saying

'16.67% (approximately) of all throws of a die should result in a six'.

In effect, in using percentages as probabilities we are really establishing a link between the relative frequency approach and other methods of determining chance.

You may also hear probabilities being expressed as **odds**, either for, or against an event. What is the difference between a probability and an odds statement?

Probabilities are expressed as the ratio of chances **for** an event to **total** chances. Odds are expressed as the ratio of chances **for** an event to chances **against** an event.

For example, we already know that if we toss a fair die, then the probability of scoring a six is written as

$$Pr(\text{Score} = 6) = 1/6$$

However, the odds **in favour** of scoring a six on a fair die is written as the ratio 1:5, (one chance in favour compared with five chances against).

ACTIVITY 7

Express the following odds statements as probability statements

(a)   The odds **for** a heads on a toss of a coin are 50:50

(b)   The odds **for** rain today are 1:4

(c)   The odds **against** a new product design being commercially successful are 199:1.

The first statement 'odds in favour are 50:50' means that there are 50 chances in favour of heads compared with 50 chances against. It would be equally correct to say that the odds for heads are 1:1. So out of 2 chances, 1 is in favour of heads. Therefore

$$Pr(Heads) = \frac{1}{2}$$

The second statement implies that there is 1 chance for rain compared with 4 chances against. Out of 5 chances, 1 is in favour of rain.

Therefore

$$Pr(Rain) = \frac{1}{5}$$

The last statement implies that there are 200 chances, 199 of which are against the success of the new product design.

Therefore

$$Pr(Product \ will \ not \ be \ successful) = \frac{199}{200}$$

4. SUMMARY

In this first section you have

- read about the concept of probability and the scale on which it is measured

- discovered that there are three different approaches to estimating probabilities; the **classical, relative frequency and subjective** approaches

- defined the terms **experiment, sample space** and **event**

- understood that probabilities can be written as decimal or vulgar fractions, or as percentages

- learned about the difference between using **probability** and **odds** statements

If you are unsure about any of these topics check back before you continue with this unit.

SECTION 2

EVENTS, CONTINGENCY TABLES AND VENN DIAGRAMS

1. SIMPLE AND COMPLEX EVENTS

To understand what is said in the following pages you will need to keep in mind the difference between **complex** and **simple** events.

We often need to determine the probabilities of events which are **complex**. By complex we mean events which consist of combinations of other events. For example, the event 'score 12' on a roll of a pair of fair dice is a complex event because it consists of two other (simple) events; score 6 on die 1 and score 6 on die 2.

DATA: AGE AND SEX OF SARDIS LTD STAFF

In this section we will be referring frequently to staff data obtained from a fictitious company called Sardis Ltd, a small firm with 200 employees. Sardis staff includes 120 males, 60 of whom are aged 30 or less, 20 who are aged between 31 and 40 and the rest are aged over 40. Of the female staff, 40 are aged 30 or less, 30 are aged between 31 and 40, and the remainder are over 40. These data are summarised in figure 6 below.

Such tables are known as contingency tables or cross-tabulation diagrams, and are popular ways of summarizing data by dividing it into two categories.

	AGE			
	Up to 30	31 to 40	Over 40	Total
Male	60	20	40	120
Female	40	30	10	80
Total	100	50	50	200

FIGURE 6: **Age–Sex Profile of Employees of Sardis Ltd**

In the contingency table of figure 6 the two categories of age and sex have been used to classify all Sardis employees.

We can now begin discussing different types of probability using the above example.

MARGINAL PROBABILITIES

The probability of an event which is computed over the whole of the sample space of an experiment is known as a **marginal probability**.

For example, refer to the table of Sardis Ltd staff in figure 6, and suppose we select an employee's name at random. What is the probability that the employee is female?.

The contingency table tells us that there are 200 employees, of whom 80 are female. Therefore

$$\textbf{\textit{Pr}}(\textit{Employee is Female}) = \frac{80}{200} = \textbf{0.4}$$

The figure obtained is the probability of selecting a female quite irrespective of her age. To put it another way, the probability was calculated across the whole sample space.

If the outcomes of an experiment are shown in the type of table in figure 6, then marginal probabilities are the probabilities which can be read as relative frequencies from the 'Totals' columns and rows. Therefore

$$\textbf{\textit{Pr}}(\textit{Employee is Male}) = \frac{120}{200} = \textbf{0.6}$$

$$\textbf{\textit{Pr}}(\textit{Employee £30}) = \frac{100}{200} = \textbf{0.5}$$

$$\textbf{\textit{Pr}}(\textit{Employee is aged } 31\text{-}40) = \frac{50}{200} = \textbf{0.25}$$

$$\textbf{\textit{Pr}}(\textit{Employee is more than } 40) = \frac{50}{200} = \textbf{0.25}$$

All of the above are **marginal** probabilities, and have been calculated by referring to the column and row totals relative to the total frequency (200).

JOINT PROBABILITIES

Look at figure 6 again. What is the probability that a randomly selected employee is a male over 40?

This is known as a **joint probability**, since the event 'male and over 40' arises from counting the number of people jointly satisfying two criteria; 'over 40' and' male'. From the Sardis data it can easily be seen that there are 40 people who satisfy both criteria.

Then

$$\textbf{\textit{Pr}}(\textit{Employee is a male and} > 40) = \frac{40}{200} = \textbf{0.2}$$

EITHER-OR PROBABILITIES

Sometimes we need to determine probabilities for the event that either A **or** B will occur. For instance, what is the probability that a randomly selected Sardis employee will be **either** male **or** over 40?

Notice very carefully the difference between this type of event and the joint probability. From figure 6, we can count that there are 130 people who are either over 40 or male. You will notice that this figure results from adding together the 40 people who are **both** over 40 years old **and** male, the 80 who are over 40 and not male and the 10 who are male but not over 40.

Therefore

$$\textbf{\textit{Pr}}(\textit{Employee is} > 40 \textit{ or male}) = \frac{130}{200} = \textbf{0.65}$$

CONDITIONAL PROBABILITIES

Sometimes we are required to determine the probability that a certain event will occur, given that we know some other event has occurred.

Let a Sardis employee be selected at random. We are told that this person is female. What is the probability that she is over 40?

This is known as a conditional probability, and can be written as

$$Pr(\text{Employee is} > 40 \text{ /employee is female})$$

In probability language, the diagonal slash "/" is used as the **conditional** sign, so that an expression such as

$$Pr(A / B)$$

means 'the probability of event A happening, given that event B has happened'.

In the case of the probability of selecting a person over 40, if the person is known to be female, then

$$Pr(\text{Employee} > 40 \text{ /employee is female}) = \frac{10}{80} = 0.125$$

The effect of the prior condition, that is, knowing the employee is female restricts the sample space – in this case it is restricted to the 80 females. We know from figure 6 that 10 of them are over 40.

COMPLEMENTARY EVENTS

The complement of an event 'A', is the event 'A does not occur'. It is usually written as $\bar{A}$. (A with a horizontal bar, which is read 'not A').

Therefore the complementary event to the event 'a male Sardis employee is selected' is the event 'a non-male (ie female), employee is selected'.

You will sometimes find that it is easier to obtain the probability of an event by calculating the probability of its complement, rather than the event itself. This is because

$$Pr(A) + Pr(\bar{A}) = 1 \quad \text{so that}$$

$$Pr(A) = 1 - Pr(\bar{A})$$

Example

Three coins are thrown. What is

Pr(At least one head) ?

The complement of 'at least one head' is 'no heads', so

Pr(At least one head) = 1 - Pr(0 heads)

= 1 - 0.125 = 0.875

You should be able to check the correctness of this answer from your responses to Activities 2 and 5(b).

Activity 8 will give you some practice in these calculations.

ACTIVITY 8

An investment portfolio consists of 100 securities classed as either government stock or equities. Of the 60 government stocks 45 had recently increased in price while 15 of the equities had increased in price. A stock is selected at random from the portfolio.

(a) Draw up a contingency table to illustrate the above data.

Use the contingency table to determine the following probabilities, stating whether they are for marginal, joint, either-or or complementary events

(b) The stock has had an increase in price.

(c) The stock has not increased in price.

(d) The stock is a government stock.

(e) The stock is not a government stock

➠

Activity 8 continued...

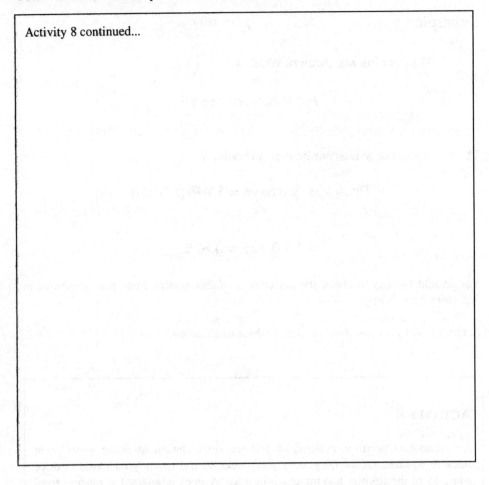

Your contingency table from Activity 8 should look like this

	PRICE INCREASE	NO PRICE INCREASE	TOTAL
Gov't stock	45	15	60
Equities	15	25	40
Total	60	40	100

In calculating

Pr(stock has increased in price)

we are actually calculating a marginal probability. We are not concerned whether the stock is equity or government stock. We only wish to know whether it has had a price increase. Now 60 stocks (out of 100) have had price increases. Therefore

$$Pr(\textit{Price Increase}) = \frac{60}{100} = 0.6$$

Pr(stock has not increased in price)
is also a marginal probability; we are not interested in whether it is an equity or government stock. Forty stocks (of 100) have had no price increases, therefore

$$Pr(\textit{No Price Increase}) = \frac{40}{100}$$

Also, note that the event 'not increased in price' is the complement of the event 'increased in price', which you were asked to calculate in part (b) of this Activity.

So we could also have obtained the required probability as follows

$$Pr(\textit{No Price Increase}) = 1 - Pr(\textit{Price Increase})$$

$$= 1 - 0.6 = 0.4$$

Pr(stock is government issue)
is yet another marginal probability. We wish to know the probability that the stock is government issue, irrespective of whether it has risen in price or not. Sixty (of 100) stocks are government issue. So

$$Pr(\textit{Government issue}) = \frac{60}{100} = 0.6$$

Finally,

Pr(stock is not government issue)
is yet again a marginal probability. There are 40 non-government stocks (ie equities). So

$$Pr(\textit{Non-government stock}) = \frac{40}{100} = 0.4$$

The event is also the complement of the one we looked at in part (d) of Activity 8.

ACTIVITY 9

Using the data from Activity 8, what is the probability that the randomly selected stock is an equity which has increased in price recently?

The event 'the stock is an equity which has increased in price', is a joint event. The stock must satisfy two criteria jointly; it must be an equity and it must have increased in price. From the contingency table, there are 15 (of 100) stocks which satisfy these two criteria.

We therefore have

$$\textbf{\textit{Pr}}(\textit{Stock is an Equity AND has increased in price})$$

$$= \frac{15}{100} = 0.15$$

ACTIVITY 10

Using the data from Activity 8, what is the probability that a randomly selected stock which is known to have increased in price is government stock?

Did you spot that this is a **conditional probability**?

We know that the stock has increased in price. What is the probability that such a stock is government stock?

Using the conditional notation introduced earlier, this can be written as

$$Pr(\text{Stock is Government Issue} \,/\, \text{Price Increase})$$

Out of the 60 stocks which have increased in price, 45 of them are government issue. Therefore the required probability is

$$\frac{45}{60} = \frac{3}{4} = 0.75$$

ACTIVITY 11

Four-hundred randomly selected car owners (250 of whom were female) were asked whether they had selected their latest car on mainly style considerations or mainly performance considerations; 180 people said that they had chosen for reasons of style and 95 of them were male.

Express these data in the form of a contingency or cross tabulation diagram.

What is the probability that

(a) a car owner buys a car mainly because of its style

(b) a car owner is male who has bought mainly because of style

(c) a female car owner purchases a car mainly because of its style?

The contingency table below illustrates the data of Activity 11.

	PURCHASED FOR REASONS OF		TOTAL
	Style	Performance	
Male	95	55	150
Female	85	165	250
Total	180	220	400

It is often useful in probability analysis, to use capital letters to abbreviate the main events.

So

Let A represent the event 'owner is male'

Let B represent the event 'owner is female'

Let C represent the event 'car is purchased for style reasons'

Let D represent the event 'car is purchased for performance reasons'

For part (a) of this Activity we want

$$Pr(C) = \frac{180}{400} = \frac{9}{20} = 0.45$$

Notice that this is a marginal probability.

The event 'a male car owner who buys for style' is a joint event. We have two criteria; the owner is male AND he has bought mainly because of style. This can be expressed as

$$Pr(A \text{ and } C) = \frac{95}{400} = \frac{19}{80} = 0.2375$$

Part (c) requires you to calculate a conditional probability. IF the customer is female THEN what is the chance that they have bought mainly for style reasons?

$$Pr(C/B) = \frac{85}{250} = \frac{17}{50} = 0.34$$

ACTIVITY 12

You are now able to make use of some of the language of probability. However, it is sometimes quite useful to be able to translate probability statements into ordinary language. For example, let a sample space S consist of all sales managers. A sales manager is selected at random. Let A represent the event that the manager is female and let B represent the event that the manager is a graduate. The probability expression Pr(A) can be translated as 'the percentage of sales managers who are female'.

Interpret the following probabilities as percentages.

(a)   Pr(A and B)   (b)   Pr(A/B)

(c)   Pr(B/A)   (d)   Pr(B/$\bar{A}$)

Activity 12 is a reminder of something you learned earlier; that probabilities can be expressed as percentages.

Thus Pr(A and B) means 'the probability that a randomly selected manager is a female graduate'. However, we can also translate it as 'the percentage of all sales managers who are female graduates'.

Likewise, Pr(A/B) could be translated as 'the percentage of graduate managers who are female'.

Pr(B/A) would be the percentage of female managers who are graduates.

Pr(B/$\bar{\text{A}}$) would be the percentage of male managers (complement of female) who are graduates.

2. PROBABILITY NOTATION AND VENN DIAGRAMS

In section 3 we will be examining the formal mathematical rules for calculating probabilities. Before we do this however, you must learn some further technical terms and symbols used in probability analysis.

We have dealt with the relationships between events. Now that you know something about such relationships we can look at them more formally.

THE UNION OF TWO OR MORE EVENTS

Earlier in this section, you looked at something called either-or probabilities. For example, we may need to determine the probability that a randomly selected employee of Sardis Ltd (the company we introduced you to earlier) will be either male or over 40 years of age.

In order to determine this probability we would have to count the number of employees who were

   (a) male

   (b) over 40

   (c) male and over 40

Formally, such 'either-or' events, are known as the **union** of two (or more) simple events. They would be written as

(either A or B) = (A union B)

and the probabilities of such events written as

$$Pr(A \cup B)$$

A and B represent simple events, and the symbol '∪' means 'either A or B (or both)' happen.

We can easily generalise this to more than two events.

THE INTERSECTION OF TWO OR MORE EVENTS

Earlier, you read about joint events. More formally, we call these the **intersection** of two or more events. Therefore, the probability that a randomly selected Sardis employee (see figure 6) is both male and over 40 would involve the enumeration of only those customers who fell into both categories.

Such events would be written

$$(A \text{ and } B) = (A \cap B)$$

and the probability of such events written as

$$Pr(A \cap B)$$

A and B are events, and the symbol '∩' means 'both A and B' happen.

We can generalise this to more than two events.

MUTUALLY EXCLUSIVE EVENTS

There will be many cases where such events as (A and B) cannot occur. For instance, when two dice are thrown, let the outcome be defined as 'a score of 6 and 7'. Put more formally, this would be

$$Pr(Score = 6 \cap Score = 7)$$

which is plainly impossible. You cannot score both a six and a seven on one throw of a pair of dice. Such events are described as **mutually exclusive**. They cannot happen together. It must therefore follow that for such events

$$Pr(A \cap B) = 0$$

On the other hand the events, 'score = 6' and 'score is a double' are not mutually exclusive. A double 3 would mean that both events had occurred.

There are graphical devices called 'Venn diagrams' which can be used to illustrate union and intersection. If you have never encountered a Venn diagram then figure 7 shows an example.

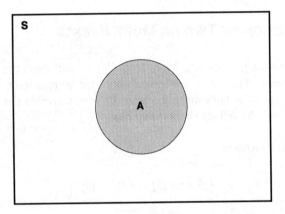

FIGURE 7: **Venn Diagram**

The rectangle 'S' represents the whole sample space for an experiment and the circle A represents any event that can happen in the sample space.

If the experiment involved throwing a pair of dice and the letter A represented the event 'score of 7', then S would consist of 36 outcomes, and A would enclose 6 of those outcomes within its circumference (there are 6 ways of scoring a 7).

In terms of areas, S would have an area of 1, and A would have an area of 6/36.

The **union** of two events would be represented as in figure 8 below.

In figure 8 the experiment is a throw of two dice. Let A be the event 'score 6' and B be the event 'a double'.

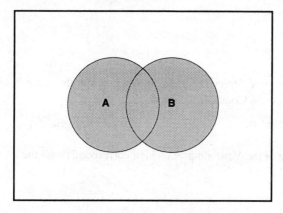

FIGURE 8: **Union Of Two Events**

Event A would consist of five possible outcomes (all the different ways of scoring a six) B would consist of six possible outcomes (all the different ways of scoring a double).

The shaded area shows the event (A ∪ B). You should be able to see that in this case, the overlapping area of the two circles would contain one outcome (a double 3).

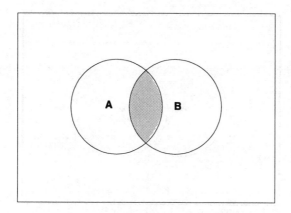

FIGURE 9: **Intersection of Events**

To illustrate the Venn diagram for the **intersection** of events, refer to figure 9. Two dice are thrown. The events A and B are defined as before. The shaded area illustrates the event (A « B). Both events have occurred (though there is only one outcome; the double 3). Notice that if A and B were mutually exclusive, then the circles representing A and B would have no point of intersection.

ACTIVITY 13

Figure 10 below, is a Venn diagram showing a sample space S, in which two events, A and B occur. Consider the event

$\bar{A}$ the complement of A.

Shade in the area of the Venn diagram which corresponds with the complement of A.

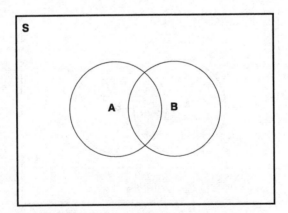

FIGURE 10: **Venn Diagram – Activity 13**

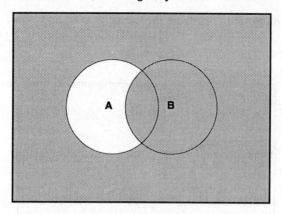

FIGURE 11: **Activity 13 – Solution**

Figure 11 above is the same as figure 10, except for the fact that all of the Venn diagram apart from the circle A has been shaded. The shaded area represents the event $\bar{A}$); everything else EXCEPT A occurs.

ACTIVITY 14

Consider the event $\overline{(A \cap B)}$, which is the complement of $(A \cap B)$. Shade in the area on the Venn diagram in figure 12 below, which corresponds with this complementary event.

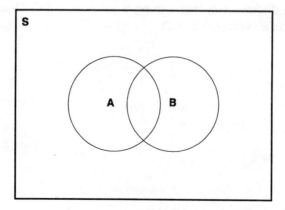

FIGURE 12: **Venn Diagram – Activity 14**

Here is the Venn diagram to illustrate the event

$\overline{(A \cap B)}$

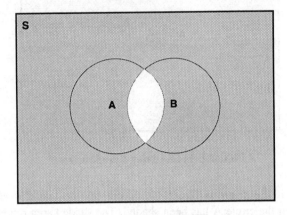

FIGURE 13: **Activity 14 – Solution**

in figure 13. This expression is another way of saying 'the event (A and B) does not happen'. So we should shade in everything on the Venn diagram except for the area representing $A \cap B$.

ACTIVITY 15

Consider a sample space S, and any three events A, B and C which can occur within it.

Suppose that there is some probability that the event $(A \cap B \cap C)$ can occur. Draw your own Venn diagram with circles to represent A, B and C. Shade in the area corresponding to the event $(A \cap B \cap C)$.

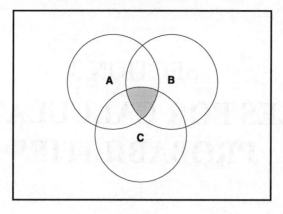

FIGURE 14: **Activity 15 – Solution**

$(A \cap B \cap C)$ means that the three events A, B and C ALL occur together. If this is possible, then the three circles representing them must all have a mutual point of overlap. The Venn diagram in figure 14 represents the event $(A \cap B \cap C)$ as the shaded area of overlap of the circles.

3. SUMMARY

In section 2 you have

- learned how to use **contingency tables** to classify **events** and assist with the estimation of probabilities

- learned the meaning of various **complex events**, such as **unions** and **intersections**

- illustrated **unions** and **intersections** using **Venn diagrams**

You may have come to the conclusion that we will not be able to use contingency tables and Venn diagrams in all situations, as we need some mathematical rules of probability for more complex circumstances.

We shall be looking at these rules in section 3.

If you are unsure of any of the topics covered in this section, check back before you move on to section 3.

SECTION 3
RULES FOR CALCULATING PROBABILITIES

1. INTRODUCTION

In the section 2 we used Venn diagrams to **visualise** the sample space of an experiment and contingency tables to **enumerate** the events within the sample space. It will not always be possible to use a contingency table, a Venn diagram or any other way of listing the outcomes of an experiment.

What techniques can we use in such circumstances?

There are some mathematical rules of probability which will be of help to us, and which we will be discussing in this section. However, the following points cannot be overstressed

  ● the rules for calculating probabilities are simple and the arithmetic involved is never onerous, **but**

  ● it is not always easy to see which rule(s) should be used in order to obtain the desired result

You will need to take care; **using** the rules of probability is easy, the logical problem of deciding **which** rules to use in any given situation is not.

With this warning in mind we can now examine the formal mathematical rules for calculating probabilities.

2. CONDITIONAL PROBABILITIES

For any two events A and B the probability that A will happen given that B has occurred is written

$$Pr(A/B)$$

and can be calculated as follows

Formula 1

$$Pr(A/B) = \frac{Pr(A \cap B)}{Pr(B)}$$

In plan words, we must first calculate the probability of the **intersection** of A and B, and then divide this by the **marginal** probability of B.

EXAMPLE OF A CONDITIONAL PROBABILITY CALCULATION

Sardis Ltd sales representatives have a 70% chance of making a prior appointment to see a potential buyer, and therefore a 30% chance of failing to make such an appointment. However, irrespective of whether or not they have made an appointment, they always try to call on all buyers. The chance that they will succeed in making a prior appointment **and** making a sale is 0.28, while the chance that they will not succeed in making an appointment but still sell the product is 0.018.

What is the probability that a representative will make a sale **if they have made a prior appointment**?

Using formula 1

Let the event A be 'representative makes a sale' and the event B be 'the representative makes a prior appointment'.

Now the event (A ∩ B) means 'the representative makes an appointment and makes a sale'.

Therefore

$$Pr(\text{Sale /appointment made}) = Pr(A/B)$$

$$= \frac{Pr(A \cap B)}{Pr(B)} = \frac{0.28}{0.70} = 0.4$$

What is the probability that a representative will make a sale **if no prior appointment is made**?

In terms of formula 1, event A means 'the representative makes a sale', while event B would be 'no prior appointment is made'.

Thus event (A∩B) is 'a sale is made but no prior appointment is made'.

$$Pr(\textit{Sale /No appointment made}) = \textbf{Pr(A/B)}$$

$$= \frac{Pr(A \cap B)}{Pr(B)} = \frac{0.018}{0.300} = 0.06$$

If we interpret these figures as percentages, they imply that a sale is made on 40% of all visits made with a prior appointment but only on 6% of visits made without appointment.

Clearly, it is worthwhile for the sales representative to make a prearranged appointment!

Here is an example of the use of formula 1 for you to try.

ACTIVITY 16

A pair of fair dice are rolled. What is the probability that a double was the result, given that the score was at least 8?

Use formula 1 and then use the sample space for a two-dice experiment (see the solution to Activity 3, section 1), to check your answer.

To answer Activity 16 we define the following events

A = A double is thrown

B = the score is ≥ 8

then

$$Pr(A \cap B) = \frac{3}{36} \quad (\text{because there are 3 doubles} \geq 8)$$

$$Pr(B) = \frac{15}{36} \quad (\text{because there are 15 scores} \geq 8)$$

$$\therefore \ Pr(A/B) = \frac{Pr(A \cap B)}{Pr(B)} = \frac{\frac{3}{36}}{\frac{15}{36}} = \frac{3}{15}$$

You could have answered this by counting that there are 15 cases in the sample space for the experiment where the score is 8 or more. Of these 15 cases, three are doubles.

However, you will be able to use the formula for calculating conditional probabilities even when it is not possible to list the whole sample space.

CONDITIONAL PROBABILITIES AND INDEPENDENCE

Whenever we discuss conditional probabilities, the subject of **independence** arises. Suppose you toss a fair coin 100 times, and the coin comes down 'heads' on all 100 throws. You throw the coin again.

Let A be the event 'heads on the 101st throw' and B be the event 'heads on the first 100 throws'.

Now what is the probability

$$Pr(A/B) \ ?$$

that is, what is the probability of getting heads on the 101st throw of the coin if the first 100 throws were heads?

The answer to this question is 0.5. It does not matter what the first 100 throws were, there is still an 0.5 probability of getting heads on the next throw.

In this case

$$Pr(A) = 0.5$$

$$Pr(A/B) = 0.5$$

so

$$Pr(A) = Pr(A/B)$$

The condition has made no difference.

Now any two events, A and B, for which the following holds true

$$Pr(A) = Pr(A/B)$$

are said to be **independent**.

In the above example, throws of the coin are independent of each other.

ACTIVITY 17

Study again the data relating to car owners in Activity 11. Calculate the following probabilities for a car owner selected at random.

(a) Style is main reason for buying

(b) Style is the main reason for buying for an owner who is female.

Do the factors sex of buyer, and reason for purchase appear to be independent of each other?

Give reasons for your answer.

Activity 17 continued...

To answer Activity 17 we define the following events

A = Style is main reason for buying
B = Owner is a female

From the table accompanying Activity 11 we have

$$Pr(A) = \frac{180}{400} = 0.45$$

$$Pr(A/B) = \frac{85}{250} = 0.34$$

So Pr(A) ≠ Pr(A/B), meaning that 'sex of buyer' and 'reason for purchase' are NOT independent.

ACTIVITY 18

For any two events A and B, let

$Pr(A) = 0.4$ $Pr(B) = 0.3$ and $Pr(A \cap B) = 0.12$

(a)   What is the probability that A will occur given that B has occurred?

(b)   Are A and B independent events?

   Explain your answer.

We can use formula 1 to answer part (a) of this activity.

Doing this we would have

$$Pr(A/B) = \frac{Pr(A \cap B)}{Pr(B)} = \frac{0.12}{0.30} = 0.4$$

For part (b) we would have

$$Pr(A) = 0.4$$

These two facts mean that since $Pr(A) = Pr(A/B)$ then A and B are independent events.

In many cases it is fairly obvious that two events are independent, without having to prove the fact.

Consider the following two events

A = the event 'Universal Detergents plc will go bankrupt next year'

B = the event 'Hyde Park will be closed this year'.

It seems unlikely that the closure of Hyde Park will have any effect on Universal Detergents, so that

$$Pr(A) = Pr(A/B)$$

The two events are clearly independent. However, suppose that we now let B be re-defined as 'detergents are banned'.

It seems likely that event B **would** have an effect on a company such as Universal Detergents, so that

$$Pr(A) \neq Pr(A/B)$$

3. THE INTERSECTION OF EVENTS

You may remember that the intersection of (say) two events A and B is represented as $(A \cap B)$, and that it can be described as 'the events A and B both occur'.

Suppose we throw a pair of dice. What is the probability that we obtain double-six (score = 12)?

You should have no problems in solving this, since you have listed the sample space for the experiment in section 1.

In fact, the answer is 1/36.

This experiment was quite simple, but what about the following problem?

Six dice are thrown. What is the probability that they will all be sixes?

The difficulty here is that while it was possible to list the sample space for a **two-dice** experiment, it is very time consuming to do the same for a **six-dice** experiment.

We need a mathematical rule which will calculate such probabilities, and hence avoid the tedium of counting points in a sample space. To illustrate how such a rule might work let us return to the two-dice experiment.

The event 'score = 12' is really the intersection of two events;

score 6 on die 1 **and** score 6 on die 2

therefore

$$Pr(Score = 12) = Pr(Die\ 1 = 6 \cap die\ 2 = 6)$$

In other words, the event 'score 12' is really composed of two other events. We know that:

Pr(Score 6 on die 1) = 1/6 and
Pr(Score 6 on die 2) = 1/6

Is there a way we can combine these two probabilities in order to obtain the probability of scoring a 12?

The answer to this question is 'yes' and the rule is stated in formula 2 below.

Let A and B be any two events. Then

Formula 2

$$Pr(A \cap B) = Pr(A) \times Pr(B/A)$$

If the events A and B are independent then this simplifies to

$$Pr(A \cap B) = Pr(A) \times Pr(B)$$

In other words, formula 2 suggests that we can obtain the probability of an intersection by multiplying the probabilities of the separate events making up that intersection.

Now since dice throws are independent, we have

$$Pr(Score = 12) = Pr(Die\ 1 = 6) \times Pr(Die\ 2 = 6)$$
$$= \frac{1}{6} \times \frac{1}{6} = \frac{1}{36}$$

The rule stated in formula 2 is often called the **multiplication rule of probabilities**.

ACTIVITY 19

The rule in formula 2 was stated in a form applicable to two events. It can, however be extended to more than two events. Try doing this with the following problem.

What is the probability of obtaining 4 sixes in 4 throws of a die?

Throws of dice are independent of each other, so we can reason as follows

Pr(**4 sixes**) =

Pr(**die 1 = 6** and **die 2 = 6** and **die 3 = 6** and **die 4 = 6**)

By an extension of Formula 2 this means

Pr(**die 1 = 6**) $\times$ Pr(**die 2 = 6**) $\times$ Pr(**die 3 = 6**) $\times$ Pr(**die 4 = 6**)

$$= \frac{1}{6} \times \frac{1}{6} \times \frac{1}{6} \times \frac{1}{6} = \frac{1}{1296}$$

ACTIVITY 20

A lottery is to be held by a group of 100 people. The prize draw is organised by a 5 person management committee, selected from the group of 100. Five prizes are available, and the winners are to be selected by placing the names of the 100 into a hat. After drawing a name from the hat, that person is announced as a prizewinner, and the name is replaced prior to the next draw. What is the probability that members of the prize draw committee will win all of the prizes?

Activity 20 explicitly states that names are replaced in the hat after a draw. This means that the same person could win more than one prize. On each draw there are 100 possible names which could be drawn, and five of those names could be those of committee members.

Therefore, for each draw, the chance of a committee member winning is 5 in 100, or 0.05.

So the chance of the committee winning all of the prizes is

$$(0.05)^5 = 3.125 \times 10^{-7}$$

ACTIVITY 21

Re-calculate the probability of Activity 20 if names are **not replaced** in the hat after they are drawn.

In Activity 21 names are NOT replaced in the hat. So the committee's chance of winning are not independent for each draw. On the first draw, there is a 5 in 100 chance that a committee member will win a prize. However, given that a committee member won the first prize, there is now a 4 in 99 chance that a committee member will win a prize on the second draw. (This is because there are now only 99 names in the hat, 4 of which are committee members.) On the third draw, there is a 3 in 98 chance of a committee member winning, and so on. The probability of the committee winning all prizes is

$$\frac{5}{100} \times \frac{4}{99} \times \frac{3}{98} \times \frac{2}{97} \times \frac{1}{96}$$

Activity 21 shows the desirability of checking whether or not events are independent before using the multiplication rule of probabilities.

ACTIVITY 22

A chairman and vice-chairman are to be chosen at random from a committee of five men and seven women. What is the probability that they are both female?

The committee described in Activity 22 consists of 5 + 7 = 12 members. Therefore, on selection of the first committee member, there is a 7 in 12 chance of a female being selected. On selection of the second committee member, there is now a 6 in 11 chance of a female being selected.

Therefore, the chance that both selections are female is

$$\frac{7}{12} \times \frac{6}{11} = \frac{42}{132}$$

You will have seen from the answers to Activities 20, 21 and 22 that the main consideration to be taken into account when using the multiplication rule is whether or not the events are independent.

4. THE UNION OF EVENTS

The union of two (or more) events has already been described. However, it is worthwhile restating that if A and B are two events, then (A ∪ B) symbolises the union of these events and means 'either A or B (or both) happen'.

Just as there is a rule for determining the probability of the intersection of events (multiplication rule), there is also a rule for determining the probabilities of unions of events. As always, it is best if we illustrate the rule with a simple example.

Two dice are thrown, and the scores on each die are added together. What is the probability of obtaining a score of **either** 2 or 12?

In terms of unions of events, we require

$$Pr(Score = 2 \cup score = 12)$$

From the sample space of the two dice experiment developed in section 1 you should be able to see that there are only two ways of obtaining a score of 2 or 12, so that the required probability must be 2/36.

Note that

$$Pr(Score = 2) = \frac{1}{36} \quad and$$

$$Pr(Score = 12) = \frac{1}{36}$$

and

$$Pr(Score = 2) + Pr(Score = 12) = \frac{1}{36} + \frac{1}{36} = \frac{2}{36}$$

This is the correct result for the union of these events. Perhaps the above result might lead us to make the following conclusion

for two events A and B

$$Pr(A \cup B) = Pr(A) + Pr(B)$$

In other words, if we want to find the probability of a **union** of events, can we simply **add** the separate event probabilities?

Activity 23 may lead us to the answer.

ACTIVITY 23

Let an experiment consist of a single spin of a roulette wheel. In order to simplify the arithmetic we will assume that the zero does not exist. There are therefore only 36 outcomes, consisting of the numbers 1-36 inclusive.
The roulette wheel is spun once.

(a)   What is the probability that one of the numbers in the range 19-36 (inclusive) comes up?

(b)   What is the probability that an odd number turns up?

(c)   What is the probability that either an odd number, or a number in the range 19-36 turns up?

(d)   Does the sum of the probabilities calculated in (a) and (b) give the correct answer for (c)? If not, why not?

▯▯▮➡

Activity 23 continued...

In the roulette wheel problem, we can calculate

$$Pr(\textit{Number is in range } \mathbf{19\text{-}36}) \quad = \frac{1}{2}$$

$$Pr(\textit{Number is odd}) \quad\quad\quad = \frac{1}{2}$$

Earlier, we asked whether it we could calculate $Pr(A \gg B)$ by adding $Pr(A)$ to $Pr(B)$. We can test out this theorem now.

Let A be the event 'an odd number turns up' Let B be the event 'a number in the range 19-36 turns up.

Then

$$Pr(A) = \frac{1}{2} \quad and \quad Pr(B) = \frac{1}{2}$$

$$Pr(A) + Pr(B) = 1$$

but

$$Pr(A \cup B) \neq 1$$

In fact, of the 36 numbers which could turn up, 27 of them are either odd or in the range 19-36. So

$$Pr(A \cup B) = \frac{27}{36} = \frac{3}{4}$$

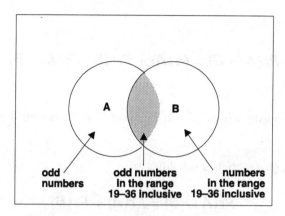

FIGURE 15: **Roulette Wheel Problem**

Obviously, it is not enough just to add Pr(A) and Pr(B) and assume that this will give the correct answer for Pr(A ∪ B). Why not?

Figure 15 above, may help to show why.

There are 18 outcomes in the event 'odd number'. There are 18 outcomes in the event 'a number in the range 19-36'. There are 36 outcomes in the whole sample space. There are, however, 9 outcomes which are both odd and in the range 19-36. If we add the two probabilities, we will mistakenly count the outcomes in this intersection area twice.

The problem has arisen because **the two events are not mutually exclusive**.

If we add the two probabilities, then we must compensate for this 'double counting' as follows;

$$Pr(\textit{Either number is odd or in the range } \textbf{19-36})$$

$$= \frac{18}{36} + \frac{18}{36} - \frac{9}{36} = \frac{27}{36} = \frac{3}{4}$$

The 9/36 which is subtracted in the above calculation is equal to probability of the intersection of these two events.

The full rule for determining the probability of the union of events is given in formula 3 below.

Let A and B be two events. Then

Formula 3

$$Pr(A \cup B) = Pr(A) + Pr(B) - Pr(A \cap B)$$

If A and B are mutually exclusive then the event $(A \cap B)$ **cannot** happen (it has zero probability).

If this is the case, then formula 3 simplifies to

$$Pr(A \cup B) = Pr(A) + Pr(B)$$

This rule is often known as the **addition rule of probabilities**. The main consideration to be taken into account when using this rule is whether or not the events are mutually exclusive.

ACTIVITY 24

In 1990, a special government loan scheme was started to help students finance their higher education. In a study of 100 students who had taken special-purpose loans under the provisions of a this policy, it was found that 40 had also taken part-time jobs. Of the 100 students, 25 were reported as poor attenders, and 15 had taken part-time jobs AND were poor attenders.

(a)   Draw a Venn diagram to illustrate the above situation.

➠

Activity 24 continued...

(b)   What is the probability that a randomly selected loan-aided student has a part-time job?

(c)   What is the probability that a randomly selected loan-aided student is a poor attender?

(d)   What is the probability that a randomly selected loan-aided student is both a poor attender and has a part-time job?

(e)   Use the addition rule to find the probability that a student either has a part-time job or is a poor attender.

A Venn diagram illustrating this sample space is shown below in figure 16.

The sample space consists of all students who are loan-aided.

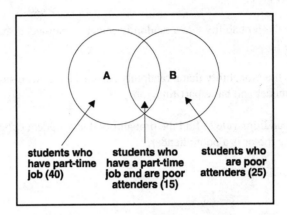

FIGURE 16: **Venn Diagram – Loan Scheme**

We can begin to calculate the probabilities required by Activity 24 by defining the events A and B as follows

A = Students with part-time jobs

B = Students who are poor attenders.

The probability that a student has a part-time job is

40/100 = 0.4

The probability that a student is a poor attender is

25/100 = 0.25

The probability that a student has a part-time job *and* is a poor attender is

15/100 = 0.15

The probability that a randomly selected student is a poor attender or has a part-time job is

$$Pr(A \cup B) = Pr(A) + Pr(B) - Pr(A \cap B)$$

$$= \frac{40}{100} + \frac{25}{100} - \frac{15}{100} = 0.5$$

ACTIVITY 25

The following events are defined

A = a person takes regular exercise
B = a person dies of heart disease
C = a person dies of cancer

Also, Pr(A) = 0.01, Pr(B) = 0.25, Pr(C) = 0.20

(a)   Do you think A and B are mutually exclusive? If not, is it possible to find
       $Pr(A \cap B)$ from the above data? If not, why not?

(b)   Are B and C mutually exclusive? Calculate $Pr(B \cup C)$.

It is unlikely that A and B are mutually exclusive. It is possible to be a regular
exerciser, and still die of heart disease. You cannot use the multiplication rule to find
$Pr(A \cap B)$ in this case, because we do not know $Pr(B/A)$. We cannot assume the events
are independent. In fact, it is likely that they are not independent, because a person who
takes regular exercise (probably) has a lower chance of suffering a heart attack then a
person who does not. So

$$Pr(B/A) < Pr(B/\bar{A})$$

However, B and C are mutually exclusive, in the sense that a person either dies from a heart attack or from cancer (not both). So in this case

$$Pr(B \cup C) = Pr(B) + Pr(C)$$

$$= 0.25 + 0.20 = 0.45$$

ACTIVITY 26

Suppose that a person is randomly selected from the population. The following events are defined

A = the person normally uses a car to get to work

B = the person normally uses a bus to get to work.

Also $Pr(A) = 0.45$ and $Pr(B) = 0.35$.

(a) Are A and B mutually exclusive?

(b) What is $Pr(A \cup B)$?

A and B are mutually exclusive, the word 'normally' implies this. Therefore

$$Pr(A \cup B) = Pr(A) + Pr(B)$$

$$0.45 + 0.35 = 0.80$$

It is possible to generalise the addition rule to more than two events. If the events are mutually exclusive (take note of this important condition), then

$$Pr(A \cup B \cup C \cup D \cup .... etc)$$

$$= Pr(A) + Pr(B) + Pr(C) + Pr(D) + ... etc$$

5. COMPLEMENTARY EVENTS

We begin by stating the law of complements formally. Let A be an event.

Then the event $\bar{A}$ is defined as the complement of A, and

Formula 4

$$Pr(A) = 1 - Pr(\bar{A})$$

In other words, the probability that an event happens can be calculated by subtracting the probability of the event **not** happening from 1.

ACTIVITY 27

Using the data of Activity 25, find the probability that a person dies from causes other than cancer.

By Formula 4

$$Pr(A) = 1 - Pr(\overline{A})$$

From Activity 25, C is the event 'cause of death was cancer'. Therefore 'not-C' is the event 'cause of death was for reasons other than cancer'. So

$$Pr(\overline{C}) = 1 - 0.20 = 0.80$$

ACTIVITY 28

Using the data of Activity 26, find the probability that a person normally uses something other than a car to get to work.

If A is the event 'a person normally uses a car' then $\overline{A}$ is the event 'a person normally uses means other than a car'. So

$$Pr(\overline{A}) = 1 - 0.45 = 0.55$$

6. SUMMARY

In this section you have

- learned about the **addition, multiplication** and **complementary rules** of probability

- calculated **probabilities** in situations where it is not possible to use **contingency tables** or **Venn diagrams**

- constructed and analysed Venn diagrams

Remember, as we remarked at the beginning of the session, even though the actual **arithmetic** required in using the rules is simple, the process of deciding **which rules** to use in any given situation is sometimes difficult.

If you are uncertain about any part of section 3, check back now before starting work on the next section, where we shall be putting these rules of probability to work in more-or-less complex situations.

SECTION 4
PUTTING THE RULES OF PROBABILITY TO WORK

1. INTRODUCTION

In section 3 we said that although the rules of probability are simple, it is not always easy to decide which rules to apply under which circumstances.

In many cases we must restate a problem in terms of the language of probability. Are we being asked to calculate the probability for an **intersection** of events or for a **union**? When do we use the rule for complementary events? How do we know when events are **independent** or **mutually exclusive**?

It is useful to use some examples as an illustration of these difficulties.

BOXES AND BATTERIES

Suppose that two boxes contain batteries of the type used in personal stereo units and other similar devices. The first box contains seven batteries of which four are known to be of the 'long life' variety, while the remaining batteries are ordinary. The second box contains six batteries, of which two are long life, and the rest are ordinary. The batteries are otherwise indistinguishable from each other.

A battery is taken from one of the boxes at random. What is the probability that it is a long life battery?

You should note in this problem that selecting a box comes before selecting a battery. In other words, selecting a box is part of the experiment.

We call these boxes 'box 1' and 'box 2' for reference.

It will be helpful if we define some events as follows. Let

> **A = the event 'select box 1'**
> **B = the event 'select box 2'**
> **C = the event 'select long life battery'**

We can also assume that $Pr(A) = Pr(B) = 1/2$, as there is no reason to suppose that one box has a greater chance of being selected than the other.

Additionally we know that

$$Pr(C/A) = \frac{4}{7}$$

$$Pr(C/B) = \frac{2}{6}$$

These are the conditional probabilities of selecting a long life battery given that box 1 or 2 was chosen.

There are four possible results of the selection experiment

1. We pick box 1 and get a long life battery

2. We pick box 1 and get an ordinary battery

3. We pick box 2 and get a long life battery

4. We pick box 2 and get an ordinary battery

Of these outcomes 1 and 3 result in event C – a long life battery. Therefore the full symbolic statement of the required probability is

$$Pr(C) = Pr[(A \cap C/A) \cup (B \cap C/B)]$$

Which means **either** you pick box 1 **and** get a long life battery, **or** you pick box 2 **and** get a long life battery.

Notice that in this problem, the event C involves both intersections and unions of events.

We will therefore need to use addition and multiplication rules. Using the addition rule we get

$$Pr(C) = Pr(A \cap C/A) + Pr(B \cap C/B)$$

Notice also how the arithmetic sign '+' has replaced the symbol '$\cup$' ($\cup$ = 'or') in this probability statement. Also we note that the events inside each bracket are mutually exclusive.

Next, we apply the multiplication rule

$$Pr(C) = Pr(A) \times Pr(C/A) + Pr(B) \times Pr(C/B)$$

Notice that the arithmetic sign $\times$ has replaced the probability symbol '$\cap$' ($\cap$ = 'and').

Next we substitute numbers

$$Pr(C) = \frac{1}{2} \times \frac{4}{7} + \frac{1}{2} \times \frac{2}{6}$$

$$Pr(C) = \frac{2}{7} + \frac{1}{6}$$

$$= \frac{19}{42}$$

ACTIVITY 29

The probabilities that three customers will buy a product after listening to a sales pitch are 1/3, 1/4 and 1/5 respectively. These events are independent of each other.

What is the probability that

(a) no customer purchases the product

(b) at least one customer purchases the product

(c) exactly two customers fail to purchase.

In order to answer Activity 29 we identify the following events by letters

A = first customer purchases
B = second customer purchases
C = third customer purchases

therefore

$$\bar{A} \quad \bar{B} \quad and \quad \bar{C}$$

will represent the events that each of the customers **do not purchase**. (Complementary events).

Then the probability that **no customer** purchases can be expressed as 'the first and the second and the third customers do not purchase'. Notice the occurrence of the word 'and', which signifies intersections of events, and therefore the use of the multiplication rule.

Also the events are independent, so that we can write

$$Pr(\bar{A} \cap \bar{B} \cap \bar{C}) = Pr(\bar{A}) \times Pr(\bar{B}) \times Pr(\bar{C})$$

$$= \frac{2}{3} \times \frac{3}{4} \times \frac{4}{5} = \frac{2}{5} = 0.4$$

The probability required in part (b) of Activity 29 can be calculated directly, but it is tedious to do this, since the event 'at least one customer purchases' means '**either** one **or** two **or** all customers purchase'. This involves a lengthy calculation.

However, there is an easier method which involves using the complement rule, which is

Pr(At least one customer purchases)
= 1 - *Pr*(No customer purchases)
= 1 - 0.4 = 0.6

Make certain that you understand the use of the complement rule in this question as it can often save a lot of tedious calculation.

To answer part (c) of Activity 29 we must realise that ANY TWO of the three customers may fail to purchase. Therefore, the probability to be calculated is that

EITHER the first AND the second (but not the third)

OR the first AND the third (but not the second)

OR the second AND third (but not the first)

do not purchase. Expressed formally this is

$$Pr[(\bar{A} \cap \bar{B} \cap C) \cup (\bar{A} \cap B \cap \bar{C}) \cup (A \cap \bar{B} \cap \bar{C})]$$

Notice that this involves using multiplication addition and complement rules together.

Now

$$Pr(\bar{A} \cap \bar{B} \cap C) = \frac{2}{3} \times \frac{3}{4} \times \frac{1}{5} = \frac{6}{60}$$

$$Pr(\bar{A} \cap B \cap \bar{C}) = \frac{2}{3} \times \frac{1}{4} \times \frac{4}{5} = \frac{8}{60}$$

$$Pr(A \cap \bar{B} \cap \bar{C}) = \frac{1}{3} \times \frac{3}{4} \times \frac{4}{5} = \frac{12}{60}$$

So the overall probability of two customers not purchasing is

$$\frac{6}{60} + \frac{8}{60} + \frac{12}{60} = \frac{26}{60}$$

ACTIVITY 30

70% of a group of people are male, of whom 60% smoke.

40% of the females are smokers.

A person is selected at random from the group.

What is the probability that

(a)   the person selected is a male smoker?

Activity 30 continued...

(b)   the person selected is a female smoker?

(c)   the person selected is a smoker?

(d)   if the person selected is known to be a smoker, they are female?

From the data of Activity 30 we define the following events

A = the person is male
B = the person is female
C = the person is a smoker

Pr(Person is a male smoker) = $Pr(A \cap C)$
= $Pr(A) \times Pr(C \, / \, A)$
= $0.7 \times 0.6 = 0.42$

Pr(Person is a female smoker) = $Pr(B \cap C)$
= $Pr(B) \times Pr(C \, / \, B)$
= $0.3 \times 0.4 = 0.12$

Part (c) asks for the probability that the selected person is a smoker. This probability does not specify the sex of the smoker, so the selection might be a male or a female smoker. Using the addition rule on the answers to part (a) and (b) above

Pr(Person is a smoker) = Pr(Person is either male smoker or female smoker)

= 0.42 + 0.12 = 0.54

Part (d) of Activity 30 asks for a conditional probability, which can be written as

$$Pr(B \,/\, C) = \frac{\textbf{Pr(B} \cap \textbf{C)}}{\textbf{Pr(C)}}$$

$$\frac{0.3 \times 0.4}{0.54} \; ≜ \; \textbf{0.22}$$

Note the use of the rule for calculating conditional probabilities.

THE COMPUTER SYSTEM

A single-user office data processing system consists of three separate devices, a hard disk drive, a computer and a printer linked together.

The computer reads data from the disk drive, transfers it to the computer and then transfers any computer output to the printer. All three devices must be working in order for the system to be successful. The system can be illustrated as follows:

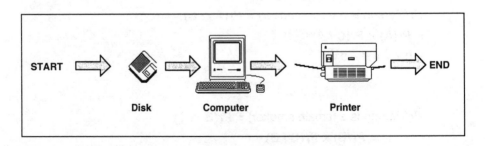

FIGURE 17: **Simple Computer System**

At any one time, the probability that the disk drive will be in working order is 4/5. The probability that the computer will be in working order is 5/6, and the probability that the printer will be in working order is 6/7. To put this a slightly different way, the disk drive, computer and printer are in working order for 4/5, 5/6 and 6/7 of the time respectively.

ACTIVITY 31

What percentage of the time will the data processing system be in working order?

The probability that the data-processing system works is equal to the probability that all of the components are working. We can use the multiplication rule to determine this

Pr(The process works) =

Pr(Drive works ∩ Computer works ∩ Printer works) =

Pr(Drive works) × **Pr**(Computer works) × **Pr**(Printer works)

$$= \frac{4}{5} \times \frac{5}{6} \times \frac{6}{7} = \frac{4}{7}$$

As a percentage, 4/7 = 57%

The answer to Activity 31 reveals that this system is highly inefficient. For a considerable portion of time – 43% – the system will be unworkable because one, or more of the components are inoperable. What can be done to increase its chances of success?

One method often used is a duplicate system, so that if one system fails, then the process can be switched to the alternative system. For instance, most aircraft are all equipped with duplicate circuits operating such key functions as undercarriage or wing flaps. The duplication is provided to increase the probability of trouble-free flight.

Suppose the firm operating the data-processing system mentioned earlier decide to install a duplicate network. In all respects, the duplicate consists of a network of three components, operating completely independently of the original.

If the first system fails, then the second comes into operation. The duplicated process may be illustrated as in figure 18 below.

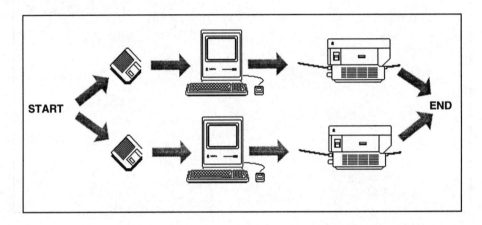

FIGURE 18: **Duplicated Computer System**

ACTIVITY 32

For what percentage of the time will the data processing set-up illustrated in figure 18 be in working order?

As long as at least one of the duplicate systems is in working order the business will have a successful data processing facility.

Therefore, we need to calculate the probability that **either** the original system, **or** the duplicate, or both, will be in working order.

Alternatively, we could approach the problem by using the law of complements.

$$Pr\text{(Duplicate System works)} = 1 - Pr\text{(Duplicate System fails)}$$

The duplicate system will only fail if both the original network and the duplicate fail. Since each network has a probability of working of 4/7, then each must have a probability of 3/7 of failing.

So we have

$$Pr\text{(System works)} = 1 - Pr\text{(Both networks fail)}$$

$$= 1 - \left(\frac{3}{7} \times \frac{3}{7}\right) \approx 0.82$$

So we can see that a considerable gain in efficiency (from 57% to 82%) has been achieved by simply setting up a duplicate network. The management would have to decide whether this gain in efficiency is worth the additional cost of the duplicate system.

The duplicate system shown in figure 18 has an increased chance of working properly. However, it could be improved even further. Suppose that the disk drive in the original network and the computer in the duplicate break down.

Because the two networks operate independently of each other the process cannot continue.

There are still fully-functional versions of each machine working, but the process shown in figure 18 cannot use the disk drive in the duplicate network and then switch back to use the computer in the original. This seems wasteful. What if it were possible to link together every component in the two networks?

The result may resemble figure 19.

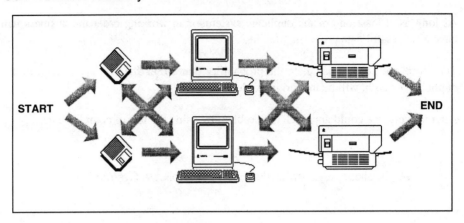

FIGURE 19: **Modified Duplicated Computer System**

The data processing system can now switch between the two networks at any point, if it encounters a broken component. As long as there is **at least one working version of each type of component the whole system will work**.

ACTIVITY 33

What percentage of the time will the modified duplicate system shown in figure 19 be working?

Activity 33 is quite a difficult problem to solve. A clue is given in the last paragraph before the Activity

       ....'as long as there is at least one of each type of component the process will work'.

Therefore we must calculate the probability that there will be at least one disk drive, one computer and one printer in working order.

Now

Pr(*At least one disk drive working*)

= **1** - **Pr**(*No disk drive working*)

$$= 1 - \frac{1}{5} \times \frac{1}{5} = \frac{24}{25}$$

Pr(*At least one computer working*)

= **1** - **Pr**(*No computer working*)

$$= 1 - \frac{1}{6} \times \frac{1}{6} = \frac{35}{36}$$

Pr(*At least one printer working*)

= **1** - **Pr**(*No printer working*)

$$= 1 - \frac{1}{7} \times \frac{1}{7} = \frac{48}{49}$$

So the probability that there will be at least one of each component working can be obtained by using the multiplication rule on the above probabilities.

$$\textbf{Pr}(\textit{The system works}) = \frac{24}{25} \times \frac{35}{36} \times \frac{48}{49} \approx 0.91$$

2. SUMMARY

Although no new material has been introduced in this section, you have seen the rules of probability being used on several complex situations. In general, the difficulty to resolve in any computations of complex probabilities is to detect when to use the multiplication and/or the addition rules.

Look back through the examples used in this section and be sure that you understand the logic used in the solutions before you read further.

SECTION 5

PROBABILITY TREES

1. INTRODUCTION

You have already seen in previous sections the use of such methods as Venn diagrams and contingency tables as aids for visualising sample spaces and events. **Probability trees** are another useful way of showing the mutually exclusive outcomes of a sample space; they may also be of assistance to you in solving problems.

2. PROBABILITY TREES IN USE

A COIN-TOSSING PROBLEM

We begin, as always, by using a deliberately simple example:

Toss three coins. What is the probability that the result will be at least two heads?

Since you have already drawn up a sample space for such an experiment in section 1, you will have an instant check on the results obtained in the probability tree.

Figure 20 shows you a completed probability tree for the three coin toss experiment. The reason for calling it a probability tree should be quite clear from the diagram. It has a root and branches (although unlike ordinary trees, it grows sideways rather than upwards).

Starting with the left-hand side of the diagram, there are two branches representing what happens when the first coin is thrown. We either have a heads or tails, each with a probability of 1/2.

We now pass on to the second set of branches.

For instance, if the first coin came down 'heads' then the second coin could either come down heads or tails, with probability 1/2 in each case.

This will also be true if the first coin came down 'tails'. We therefore have a second set of branches to represent what happens to the second coin.

In a similar manner, for each of the branches representing the outcome on the second coin there is a third set of branches which show the result of tossing the third coin.

By the time the tree is finished, there are eight branches at the right hand side, each branch representing one of the outcomes in the sample space.

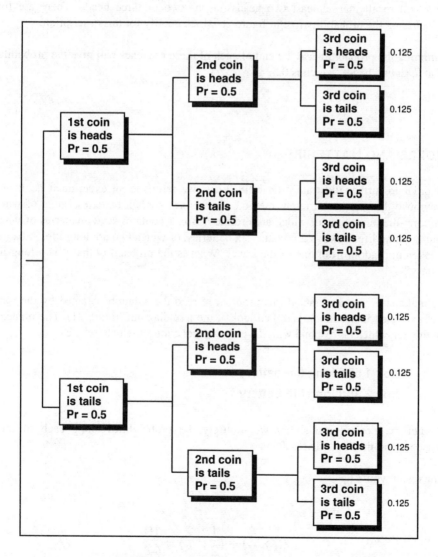

FIGURE 20: **A Throw of Three Coins**

The probabilities of any of the outcomes resulting from a throw of three coins can be obtained by multiplying the individual probabilities shown on each of the branches along a given path. In this case, all of the probabilities will be

$$\frac{1}{2} \times \frac{1}{2} \times \frac{1}{2} = \frac{1}{8} = 0.125$$

We now return to the original problem; what is the probability of obtaining at least two heads?

You will recall that 'at least two heads' means two or three heads. There are four branches on the probability tree in figure 20 which qualify for this description.

Summing the probabilities at the end of each of these branches will give the probability of at least two heads, which is 0.5.

BOXES AND BATTERIES

In order to further illustrate probability trees, we return to an experiment dealt with previously by a rather different method. Two boxes contain batteries, some of which are long-life, and some of which are ordinary. Box 1 contains seven batteries of which four are long life, and box 2 contains six batteries, of which two are long life. A battery is taken at random from one of the boxes. What is the probability that it is a long-life battery?

To make sure you understand this problem re-read the solution obtained by the other methods used in section 4, and then look at the tree diagram (figure 21). The branches on the tree which correspond with the event 'select a long-life battery' are

box 1 and long life battery
box 2 and long life battery

To get the desired probability we multiply the probabilities along each of these branches and then add the results.

The result would be

$$(\frac{1}{2} \times \frac{4}{7}) + (\frac{1}{2} \times \frac{2}{6}) = \frac{19}{42}$$

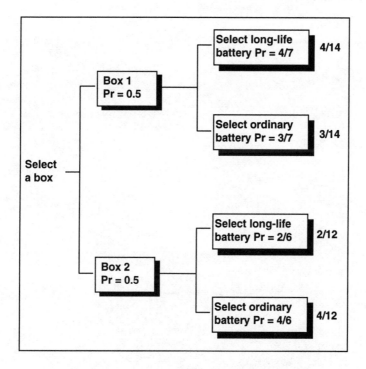

FIGURE 21: **Selecting a Battery From a Box**

ACTIVITY 34

A sales representative believes there is a probability of 0.6 of making a sale on the first call to a prospective customer, and that each following call on a prospect who has not yet purchased sees the probability of making a sale fall by 0.1. The representative is willing to make up to three calls on a prospect.

(a)   Draw probability tree to illustrate this situation.

(b)   Use the tree to determine the probability that the representative will sell to any one customer.

⫸

Activity 34 continued...

A probability tree to illustrate the sample space for the experiment of Activity 34 is shown in figure 22.

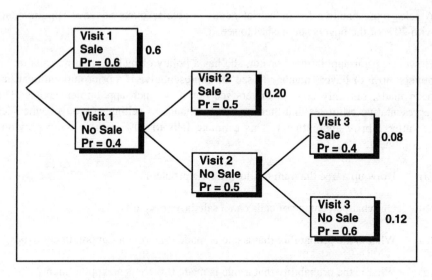

FIGURE 22: **Probability Tree to Illustrate Activity 34**

Now if a sale is made to a customer **at all**, then it will be made **either** on the first, second **or** third visit. Therefore we need to calculate the probability that a sale will be made either on visit 1, or on visit 2, or on visit 3. It is easier to proceed with the complementary event, since

$$Pr(Sale) = 1 - Pr(No\ sale)$$

If you examine the tree carefully, you will see that there is only one branch corresponding to a 'no sale' position on all visits. Multiplying the probabilities along this branch we have

$$Pr(No\ sale) = 0.4 \times 0.5 \times 0.6 = 0.12$$

so

$$Pr(Sale) = 1 - 0.12 = 0.88$$

ACTIVITY 35

A sales representative for industrial goods is able to make advance appointments with 70% of the buyers she wishes to see.

However, prior appointment or not, she has a policy of making routine calls on all buyers. 80% of buyers manage to see the representative if a prior appointment has been made, but only 60% of buyers see her if no such appointment exists. The representative estimates that there is a 50% chance of selling to a buyer who sees her after a prior appointment. This estimate falls to 10% if there is no previous appointment.

(a)   Draw up a tree diagram to illustrate the problem.

(b)   On what percentage of calls can a sale be expected?

(c)   What is the probability that a sale is made if a previous appointment exists?

(d)   What is the probability that a sale is made if there is no appointment?

(e)   Is it worthwhile to call on buyers without an appointment?

The probability tree (figure 23) to illustrate the solution to Activity 35 will be found below.

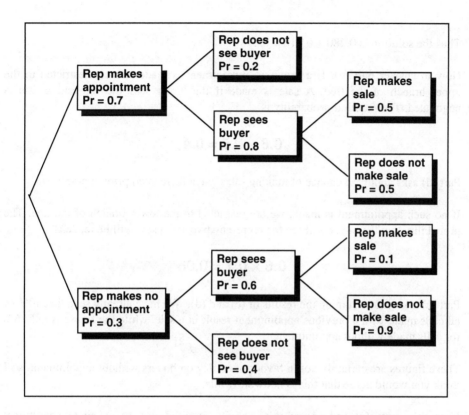

FIGURE 23: **Probability Tree Illustrating Activity 35**

For part (b) of this Activity we need to calculate the probability that a sale will be made. There are two ways in which this can occur, shown by two branches on the tree:

The representative makes an appointment, the buyer sees her and a sale is made.

The rep calls without appointment, but the buyer still sees her, and a sale is made.

Multiplying the probabilities along these branches gives

Branch 1 $0.7 \times 0.8 \times 0.5 = 0.280$

Branch 2 $0.3 \times 0.6 \times 0.1 = 0.018$

Thus the solution is $0.280 + 0.018 = 0.298$

Now to answer part (c). If a previous appointment is made, we are restricted to the upper branch of the tree. A sale is made if the buyer sees the rep and a sale is negotiated. The required probability is

$$0.8 \times 0.5 = 0.4$$

Part (d) asks about the chance of making sales when there is no prior appointment.

If no such appointment is made, we are restricted to the lower branch of the tree. The probability that the buyer will see the representative and a sale will be made is

$$0.6 \times 0.1 = 0.06$$

Part (e) asks you to sum up the results of (c) and (d). We have already seen that 40% of all calls made with a previous appointment result in a sale, while the figure is only 6% for calls made without appointment.

These figures are certainly not in favour of calling on buyers without appointment, so I think you would agree that this is not worthwhile.

Note that parts (c) and (d) of this Activity required you to calculate conditional probabilities.

ACTIVITY 36

This last Activity on probability trees will require considerably more thought.

A quality control inspector checks two processes (A and B) regularly. Process B follows on from process A. 11% of the production units going through the processes are rejected after the completion of process B. Process A rejects 10% of units, but 80% of these units are corrected during process B, and are then finished.

Use a tree diagram to determine the rejection rate for process B for those production units which are acceptable after process A.

⠀⠀ IIII➡

Activity 36 continued...

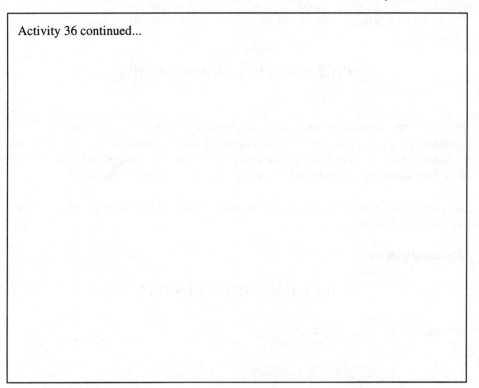

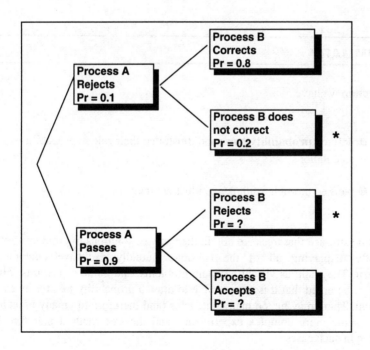

FIGURE 24: **Probability Tree to Illustrate Activity 36**

If you think carefully, you should be able to see that we must find the following probability

Pr(B *rejects unit /* **A** *accepts unit*)

meaning   'the probability of process B rejecting a unit given that process A has accepted it'. This probability can be calculated as 0.1, because the end-of-branch probabilities on the branches marked with a '*' (see the tree diagram), MUST total to 0.11. (We know that 11% of units are rejected after process B is completed.)

In order for this total of 0.11 to occur, the lower branch must have a probability of 0.1 for the event 'B rejects'.

We would then have

$$0.1 \times 0.2 + 0.9 \times 0.1 = 0.11$$

as required.

---

3. SUMMARY

In this section we have

- defined **probability trees** and illustrated their role in probability calculations

- worked through examples to illustrate their use

It should be stressed that trees are not, in themselves, solutions to problems but ways of graphically displaying all of the possible mutually exclusive outcomes of an experiment. They help us visualise certain problems, and guide us towards solutions. It should also be noted that it is not possible to draw a probability tree for every possible experiment. There may be too many outcomes (and therefore too many branches to the tree), for some more complex experiments, and the tree method therefore becomes impossible in such cases.

If you are unsure of this topic recheck through the section before moving on.

SECTION 6
COUNTING TECHNIQUES

1. INTRODUCTION

The title of this final study session may look rather odd. You no doubt consider yourself already able to count, so why do you need to study what is in this session? Sometimes it is not possible to list all of the likely outcomes in a sample space. Even if it is possible, it is usually inconvenient to do so. However, in order to estimate probabilities, it is necessary to have some method for counting outcomes from an experiment. There are three very popular counting rules which can greatly simplify this task.

2. THE 'MN' RULE

This rule says that if there are M ways in which event A can happen, and N ways in which event B can happen, then there are M times N = MN ways in which **both** can happen.

Putting this a different way – if we can fill one 'slot' in M different ways and another 'slot' in N different ways, then there are M times N = MN ways of filling both slots. The rule can be generalised to more than two slots.

Suppose you order a new car and find that you may choose any one of eight external colours, four different interior colours and ten seat colours. How many possible colour schemes are there?

This problem contains three slots:

- external colour (eight types)
- interior colours (four types)
- seat colours (ten types)

To find the total number of colour schemes, just multiply the number of ways of filling each slot.

So there are

$$8 \times 4 \times 10 = 320 \quad \text{different schemes}$$

A more formal statement of this rule follows below.

Formula 5

The MN rule

Let

N_1 = the number of ways of filling the first 'slot'

N_2 = the number of ways of filling the second 'slot'

N_3 = the number of ways of filling the third 'slot'

.

.

.

N_k = the number of ways of filling the kth 'slot'.

Then the number of different ways of filling all the k slots is

$$N_1 \times N_2 \times N_3 \times \ldots \times N_k$$

Here is another example of the MN rule.

Suppose a computer password is to be made up consisting of four characters. Only alpha-numeric characters are allowed. (Chosen from the Western European set of character symbols).

How many different computer passwords can be devised if

repetitions of characters are allowed?

repetitions are not allowed?

In this case there are four slots to be filled - a slot for each number in the password. There are 26 + 10 = 36 alpha-numeric characters, so that if repetitions are allowed, each slot may be filled in any of 36 different ways. Thus there are

$$36 \times 36 \times 36 \times 36 = 1{,}679{,}616$$

different computer passwords.

However, if repetitions **are not allowed** then there are

36 ways of filling the first slot

35 ways of filling the second slot

34 ways of filling the third slot

33 ways of filling the fourth slot

There are thus

$$36 \times 35 \times 34 \times 33 = 1,413,720$$

different computer passwords.

Now try using the MN rule for yourself in the next activity.

ACTIVITY 37

A lottery is to be held by a hospital management board. The lottery will consist of issuing tickets with five boxes covered with foil. After purchase, the gambler rubs off the foil to reveal the boxes. If the contents of the boxes are in the right order, a prize is won.

Each box on the ticket can consist of one of five fruits; an apple, pear, orange, cherry or banana. There is only one winning ticket.

If all possible fruit arrangements are printed and sold, what is the probability that any ticket selected at random will be the winning ticket?

Lottery tickets of this kind are very popular at the moment and you are probably familiar with the way in which they work. Each 'box' on the ticket can consist of any one of five different fruits.

We thus have a situation where we can use the MN rule with five 'slots', each filled in five possible ways. So the number of different possible tickets is

$$5^5 = 3125$$

Which means that the probability of any randomly selected ticket being the prizewinner is

$$\frac{1}{3125}$$

3. THE PERMUTATIONS RULE

Permutations are a way of grouping objects, and represent a special case of the MN rule.

As an example suppose that we need to select a group of 4 people from a larger group of 20. They are to fill the roles of chairman, vice-chairman, secretary and treasurer in a committee. How many possible ways are there of filling these roles from the group of 20?

Consider the following possible selection:

Chan for chair

Theodora for vice-chair

Pandora for secretary

Edward for treasurer

which is not the same selection as

Edward for chair

Pandora for vice-chair

Theodora for secretary

Chan for treasurer.

Even though the same people are involved they are selected in a different order and therefore fill different posts.

Selections of a set of objects from a larger set of objects are known as **permutations** when the **order** in which the objects are selected is a material consideration. In fact, in the case of the committee problem there are 116,280 different ways of filling the four positions from the group of 20 people.

How was this result obtained?

Before this question is answered directly, it will be easier if we tackle a much simpler case first.

Consider a group of three objects. For convenience sake we shall call them A B and C. How many possible permutations are there, taking these objects two at a time? In other words, if we select any two from the three, how many possible selections are there, if order of selection is important?

The possible selections are as follows:

$$\textbf{AB\ \ BA\ \ AC\ \ CA\ \ BC\ \ CB}$$

There are thus six possible different permutations of two objects selected from three. Be careful! Because order is important, the selection 'AB' is not the same as 'BA'.

The following formula (formula 6) gives a general rule for calculating the number of possible permutations of objects taken X at a time from a total of N objects.

Formula 6

X objects are taken from a group of N objects, the order in which they are selected being noted. The number of such selections, or permutations is

$$_NP_X = \frac{N!}{(N-X)!}$$

where N! is defined as

$$N \times (N-1) \times (N-2) \times (N-3) \times .....\times 2 \times 1$$

The expression $_NP_X$ is the customary abbreviated way of writing 'permutations of X from N'.

Firstly, you should remind yourself of the meaning of the expression 'N!' in the above formula. You may recall studying its use in the very first unit in this series. It is read as **N factorial**, and is a shorthand way of writing the product of the whole numbers from N downwards.

So, for example

$$5! = 5 \times 4 \times 3 \times 2 \times 1 = 120$$
$$100! = 100 \times 99 \times 98 \times..........\times 2 \times 1$$

100! is a very large number indeed, and no attempt will be made to calculate it. You may possibly have a pocket calculator which can calculate factorials. The pocket calculator used to make some of the computations during the preparation of this study unit could cope with factorials up to 70! but not beyond.

> **IMPORTANT!**
> It should be carefully noted that 0! = 1.

Using formula 6 the number of permutations of two objects from three is

$$_3P_2 = \frac{3!}{(3-2)!} = \frac{3 \times 2 \times 1}{1} = 6$$

Now we may return to the committee problem discussed earlier.

How many ways are there of filling four posts from a group of 20 people? (How many different permutations of four objects from 20 are there?)

The answer to this is as follows

$$_{20}P_4 = \frac{20!}{(20-4)!} = \frac{20!}{16!}$$

$$= 20 \times 19 \times 18 \times 17 = 116,280$$

Now try the following two activities which require the use of the permutations counting rule.

ACTIVITY 38

Three cards are drawn from a well-shuffled deck of 52 playing cards.

How many different 3-card arrangements are possible if the order in which the cards are drawn is important?

Use your answer to determine the probability that the 3 cards drawn are an ace, a king and a queen (in that order).

To answer Activity 38, you should firstly consider the number of ways there are of drawing any 3 cards from 52.

Thus

$$_{52}P_3 = \frac{52!}{(52 - 3)!} = \frac{52!}{49!} = 52 \times 51 \times 50 = 132,600$$

Now consider how many ways there are of drawing an ace, followed by a king followed by a queen. By the MN rule, there are 3 'slots' to fill (first, second and third card). There are 4 ways of drawing an ace, 4 ways of drawing a king, and 4 ways of drawing a queen. So there are

$$4 \times 4 \times 4 = 4^3 = 64$$

different ways of drawing these particular cards.

So the probability required by Activity 38 is

$$Pr(\text{Ace, King, Queen}) = \frac{64}{132600} \approx 0.00048$$

ACTIVITY 39

An executive must meet with 5 departmental managers during the day. He will see the managers as and when he happens to chance upon them, so the order of meeting is quite random. Two of the managers work in sales, and it would be particularly convenient if he could see them before the others.

What is the probability that this ordering will come about by chance?

To answer Activity 39 first count the number of possible ways there are of coming across the 5 managers.

This is equivalent to counting the number of ways of permutating 5 from 5.

$$_5P_5 = \frac{5!}{(5 - 5)!} = \frac{5!}{0!} = 5! = 120$$

Now how many of these 120 ways involve seeing the 2 particular managers first? The MN rule tells us that there are

2 ways of meeting the first manager

1 way of meeting the second

3 ways of meeting the third

2 ways of meeting the fourth and finally

1 way of meeting the fifth.

There are thus

$$2 \times 1 \times 3 \times 2 \times 1 = 12$$

ways of this ordering coming about. (Remember that we wish to meet 2 particular managers before any of the 3 others.)

So the probability sought for is

$$\frac{12}{120}$$

4. THE COMBINATIONS RULE

What will be the consequences if we are not interested in the order in which the objects are selected?

In order to illustrate such a situation we can reconsider the committee problem which was used as an example in the section on permutations. In that case, 4 people were to be selected from a group of 20 in order to fill 4 designated posts.

Suppose that we now only have to select 4 people to sit on a committee. There are no specific posts to fill. In this case, we are not interested in the order in which we select the 4.

For instance, the selection

Chan

Theodora

Pandora

Edward

is the same as

Edward

Pandora

Theodora

Chan.

The change of order does not matter; they are the same committee.

Selections of objects from a larger set of objects are known as combinations when the order in which the objects are selected is of no consequence.

In the above committee problem, there happen to be 4845 different committees of 4 which can be made up from a group of 20.

Before explaining how this result was obtained, it will be useful to clarify what is meant by combinations by referring to a simple example.

Consider a group of three objects, A, B and C.

How many ways are there of selecting 2 objects from this group, if order of selection is not important?

The possible selections are

AB AC BC

There are 3 different combinations of 2 objects taken from 3.

We do not list BA, CA and CB because they are already listed, that is AB is the same **combination** as BA, although AB and BA are different **permutations**.

With only one exception there are always fewer combinations than there are permutations.

Formula 7 below, states a rule for calculating combinations.

Formula 7

X objects are selected from a group of N objects, the order of selection being unimportant. The number of such selections, or combinations is calculated as follows:

$$\binom{N}{X} = \frac{N!}{X!(N-X)!}$$

The expression

$$\binom{N}{X}$$

is an abbreviated way of writing; 'the number of combinations of X objects from N'.

You may find that some mathematicians prefer to use the expression 'NCx' as the abbreviation for combinations. Either is acceptable.

So the number of combinations of 2 objects from 3 is calculated as follows

$$\binom{3}{2} = \frac{3!}{2! \times (3-2)!} = \frac{3 \times 2 \times 1}{2 \times 1 \times 1} = 3$$

We can now return to the committee problem.

How many possible committees of 4 can be selected from a group of 20 people? (Remember, we are not filling specified posts, so that the order in which we select people is unimportant.)

$$\binom{20}{4} = \frac{20!}{4! \times (20-4)!} = \frac{20 \times 19 \times 18 \times 17}{4 \times 3 \times 2 \times 1} = 4845$$

ACTIVITY 40

Twelve customer accounts from the records of Capital Enterprises Plc were initially selected for special analysis by an auditor.

However, since the auditor is now short of time, only 5 of these accounts can be scrutinised in detail. The 5 accounts are to be selected at random from the 12. Among the original 12 accounts selected there were 3 firms named

Jones Bros   Lever and Co   King and Hurd Ltd .

What is the probability that all 3 will be included in the auditors short list of 5?

Firstly, you must calculate the number of ways there are of picking **any 5** accounts from a group of 12? (The order in which you select the accountants is unimportant.)

$$\binom{12}{5} = \frac{12!}{5!(12 - 5)!} = \frac{12!}{5! \times 7!} = 792$$

Now the required selection MUST include the 3 named firms. The other 2 firms may be any of the remaining 9. There is only one way in which we can select the 3 firms, combined with

$$\binom{9}{2} = \frac{9!}{2! \times 7!} = 36$$

different ways of selecting the remaining 2.

In all, there are therefore 36 x 1 = 36 different ways of choosing 5 firms where the 3 firms are always included.

Thus there is a 36 in 792 chance that the selection of the 5 accounts will consist of the aforementioned names.

5. SUMMARY

In this final section we have discussed and illustrated three important counting rules:

● the **MN** rule

● the **permutations** rule

● the **combinations rule**

If you have worked through the exercises in the unit, you should have a reasonable knowledge of the language of probability. It is a subject of central importance in statistics, and you will certainly encounter it again if you continue your course in business studies. However, you should always keep in mind that the actual **selection** of a problem-solving technique is much more difficult than the **application** of that technique.

The rules of probability are few and relatively simple. Deciding when and how they should be used is a skill requiring a highly developed sense of logic. The following hints may be of use to you when tackling problems:

● define events using letters, A, B, C, etc

● try to translate the words of a problem into probabilities; does a particular statement tell you anything about $Pr(A)$, $Pr(B)$, $Pr(A \mid B)$, $Pr(A \cup B)$, etc

● see if it is possible to draw a Venn diagram in order to visualise the nature of the event under investigation

● ask yourself if it is possible to clarify the sample space using a tree or a contingency table

● if you cannot list all the mutually exclusive outcomes of an experiment using a tree or a contingency table can you count them by using permutations or combinations?

Finally, do not become too downhearted if you find you cannot yet solve many problems in probability. Remember that this is only a first course in the subject. It will take some considerable experience of using the laws of chance before you develop a facility in their use.

You should take a look back now at any of the sections in this unit where you found difficulty, or were uncertain, and rework the examples and Activities.

REFERENCES

Students may follow up this subject by reading the following texts:

1. MORRIS. C. *Quantitative Approaches in Business Studies*. Pitman Publishing. Chapter 8.
2. CURWEN and SLATER. *Quantitative Methods for Business Decisions*. Chapman & Hall. Chapter 10.

The above books give a clear, concise guide to the subject, written in a manner appropriate for a first year course in business statistics. If you wish to see a more formal approach to the subject you should try

3. MOSTWELLER. *Probability With Statistical Applications*. Addison-Wesley.

However, please remember that this book is of an order of magnitude more challenging than the material covered in this unit.

GLOSSARY

The following is an alphabetical listing of the technical terms most often encountered in this unit.

Addition rule of probability This rule applies to the union of events, and states that, for two events A and B
Pr(A ∪ B) = Pr(A) + Pr(B) - Pr(A ∩ B)
The rule can be extended to more than two events.

Classical definition of probability This is based on the ratio of the number of points in a sample space favourable to an event to the total number of points.

Combinations Combinations are groups of things selected from a larger set, where the order of their selection is of no importance.

Complement The complement of an event is the negation of that event.

Complex event A complex event is the union or intersection of two or more other events.

Conditional probability The probability of an event whose calculation is based on the knowledge that some other event has occurred.

Contingency table This is a tabular method of showing a sample space classified according to two variables. Hence the alternative title – two way table. A method of simplifying probability calculations.

Either-or probability The probability of the union of two or more events – that either A or B (or both) have occurred.

Empirical approach to probability Another term for the relative frequency approach.

Event One or more of the possible outcomes of a random experiment.

Experiment A random activity which may result in one of a number of possible events.

Independence Two events, A and B, are formally independent if
Pr(A) = Pr(A / B)

Intersection Events are said to intersect if they all occur simultaneously.

Joint probability This is the probability of intersecting events. Two or more events occur jointly.

Marginal probability An event probability calculated across the whole sample space of an experiment, not dependent on the occurrence of any other event.

MN rule This is a rule for counting the number of combined events resulting from two or more other events, where one event may occur M ways, another may occur N ways, etc.

Multiplication rule of probabilities   Used for calculating the probability of joint (intersecting) events.

$Pr(A \cap B) = Pr(A) \times Pr(B \, / \, A)$.

Mutually exclusive   Events are said to be mutually exclusive if they cannot occur jointly.

Odds   The odds for something happening are calculated from the ratio of chances **in favour** of the event to chances against the event. A method of measuring probability.

Permutation   A permutation is a set of objects drawn from a larger group where the order in which the objects are selected is important.

Probability tree   A method of graphically displaying the sample space of an experiment, where events are compared to the branches of a tree.

Relative frequency definition of probability   In a repeated experiment, the relative frequency measure of probability is the ratio of times an event occurred to the total number of experiments carried out.

Sample space   The set of all possible events likely to happen as the result of an experiment.

Union of events   Sometimes called 'either-or' events. $Pr(A \cup B)$ is the union of A and B, and means 'either A or B or both occur'.

Venn diagram   A graphical method of showing a sample space. A valuable method for visualising intersections and unions of events.

UNIT 6

PROBABILITY DISTRIBUTION

CONTENTS

Unit Objectives

UNIT OBJECTIVES

After completing this study unit you should be able to

- define what is meant by a random variable

- distinguish between continuous and discrete random variables

- use functions tables and graphs to describe the behaviour of probability distributions

- know when to use the binomial distribution to calculate probabilities for appropriate discrete variables

- use the normal distribution to model the behaviour of probability for certain types of continuous variable

SECTION 1
RANDOM VARIABLES

1. INTRODUCTION

Think about the following situations

you throw a pair of dice. What is the resulting total score?

how many readers are there for each copy of a newspaper sold?

what is the breaking strength of a sample of industrial cable?

In each of these cases, there is an experiment, namely

a throw of 2 dice
a count of the readership per paper
a test of a cable.

For each experiment there is a **measurement**, resulting in a **variable**. In the dice throw example, the resulting variable is the combined score (a value between 2 and 12). A count of readership per paper sold will produce a variable with a value from 1 upwards. The test of a cable will result in the breaking strength for that particular cable.

In each of the above examples, the exact value the variable takes is unpredictable, and is therefore known as a **random variable**.

In general, whether it be the outcomes from launching a new product or service, the resulting number of defective products arising from a quality control check or the number of claims that an insurance company will have to pay out in a year, many business situations can be considered as **random experiments**, the outcome of which is a **random variable**. In these examples, as in others, it would be a great advantage if the decision maker had some knowledge of the behaviour of the random variables in question. In this unit we will be studying the notion of a **probability distribution**. A probability distribution explains how certain kinds of variables behave. We shall see that the apparent random nature of some of the events in the business world will not prevent us from acquiring a useful knowledge of their behaviour.

We will start with a definition.

Definition

A Random Variable

A variable whose value is determined by the outcome of an experiment is known as a random variable. A random variable assigns a number to every possible outcome in an experiment, and represents the variable by a letter such as X.

Some Examples of Random Variables

Throw 3 coins and let X = the number of heads obtained. X can be any of the values 0, 1, 2, or 3, but we cannot know which one until the coins are thrown. A block of flats is to be constructed. Let X be the random variable 'percentage of building completed after 4 months'. Anything from none to all of the building may be finished.

Therefore $0 \leq X \leq 100$; we have no idea what X will be until after 4 months.

ACTIVITY 1

(a)   100 products are to be inspected, and the number of defectives noted. Define the random variable which results (ie what kind of numerical value results, what type of measuring scale is used, etc).

�III➡

Activity 1 continued...

(b) A light bulb is to be tested and the lifetime (up to 80,000 minutes) is to be recorded. Define the random variable which results.

The number of defectives is a random variable which can be any whole number (integer) between 0 and 100 inclusive. The variable is numerical, measured on a ratio scale.

Bulb lifetime is a random variable taking any real value between 0 and 80,000. The value observed need not be an integer; it could be, for example, 10,009.00897 hours. Lifetime is measured on a ratio scale.

2. DISCRETE AND CONTINUOUS VARIABLES

Random variables can be **discrete** or **continuous**.

Discrete random variables can only be certain fixed values. For example; the variable 'size of family' can only assume values such as 1, 2, 3 etc. Non-integer values such as 0.37 cannot occur with this variable.

Continuous variables can be any value. A person's weight is a continuous variable, because, within a given range, weight can be measured to any desired accuracy, or number of decimal places (although there may be practical limits on the degree of accuracy we can achieve).

Discrete variables are often said to be **countable**, and continuous variables **measurable**. We make the distinction because techniques suited to discrete variables may not work on continuous variables.

ACTIVITY 2

Here is a list of experiments and the random variables which arise from them.

EXPERIMENT	RESULTING VARIABLE
Analyse rainfall	Number of days that rain fell last month
Analyse rainfall	Amount of rain, in inches, falling last month
Make 200 sales calls	Number of sales achieved
Check progress on building project	Percentage of project completed to date
Audit business in a cafeteria	Number of customers passing through per day
Conduct traffic census	Number of cars passing census checkpoint
Keep record of all parcels passing through a postal department	Weight in grams of a a postal package

Say whether each of the above variables is **continuous** or **discrete**.

We can go through the list of experiments in Activity 2 in turn. The crucial question to ask is 'do we count or do we measure'?

The number of days that rain fell, sales calls achieved, cafeteria customers per day and cars passing a census checkpoint are all **discrete** variables.

The percentage of a project completed, the amount of rain falling and the weight of a parcel, are **continuous** variables.

3. PROBABILITY AND RANDOM VARIABLES

Discrete and continuous variables require different treatment in relation to the measurement of probability. To illustrate this consider the following two problems.

(1)   A manufacturer produces goods 2% of which are defective, and boxes them in sets of 5. If a box contains 1 or more defectives the firm pays the customer a refund. On a consignment of 100 boxes what is the probability that the firm will not have to offer a refund to customers?

(2)   An electric battery may last for up to 30 hours of continuous use and could fail at any time during this lifetime. What is the probability that it will fail during the first 6 hours of use?

What method would you use to solve these probabilities?

If you used the relative frequency method for calculating probabilities then you might have argued that

$$Pr(E) = \frac{n(E)}{n(S)}$$

where E is an event, n(E) is the number of (countable) points in the sample space which satisfy the event and n(S) is the total number of points in the sample space.

This approach will work quite well for the defective products problem (1), you could find the solution by counting up the number of boxes of products in a consignment of 100 which contain at least one defective.

We will not pursue the solution to this problem at this point, since it involves methods which we shall be looking at later on.

However, the lesson to be deduced from this discrete data is that it is possible to count both the number of points in the sample space and the number of those points which are favourable to the event.

What do you make of problem (2), concerning the battery lifetimes? Time is a continuous variable. We cannot count up the number of points in 30 hours, nor in the first 6 hours of life. There are an infinite number of such points. So we cannot estimate the probability by the following method

Pr(Battery fails in the first 6 hours) =

$$\frac{\text{number of points in the time period } 0 \text{ to } 6 \text{ hours}}{\text{number of points in the time period } 0 \text{ to } 30 \text{ hours}}$$

Continuous variables are not countable, but they are measurable, so you might have solved problem (2) using the following argument:

'the time period 0-6 hours is one fifth of the period 0-30 hours, so the probability of the battery failing in the first 6 hours of operation is 1/5 = 0.2.'

Provided that we are sure that the product has equal chances of failing at any time during this period then this is correct reasoning. Try using the same technique on the following Activity.

ACTIVITY 3

You are awaiting the arrival of an aircraft at Heathrow Airport, and are informed that it is late, and could arrive at any time between 14.00 and 16.00 hours. No other information is available. What is the probability that it will arrive between 14.00 and 14.45?

The time between 14.00 and 16.00 hours is of length = 120 minutes. We have 45 minutes between 14.00 and 14.45, so

Pr(Aircraft will arrive between 14.00 and 14.45)
= 45/120 = 3/8 = 0.375.

For the battery life and aircraft problems (Activity 3), it was not possible to estimate probability by simply counting. As we have said, it is not possible to do this with continuous data.

The uncountable nature of continuous data has another consequence.

Consider the battery problem again. What is the probability that a randomly selected battery will last for **exactly** 6 hours?

This is an impossible question to answer. (Try it!). Six hours is one single point out of an infinite number of points in a time period of 30 hours.
We **could** answer a question such as

or

'what is the probability that the battery will last between 5.9 and 6.1 hours'

'what is the probability that the chosen battery will last between 5.999 and 6.001 hours'.

In other words, probabilities regarding continuous variables make sense only for **intervals** (eg 5.9 - 6.1 hours), not for **single values** (eg 6 hours).

4. PROBABILITY DISTRIBUTIONS

The result of a random experiment may be uncertain, but this does not mean that we can say nothing about the outcome. If we throw 3 coins, we cannot say beforehand, whether we will obtain 0, 1, 2 or 3 heads. We can say **how probable** each outcome is.

A specification of the outcomes of a random variable, together with a statement about the probabilities of these outcomes is known as the **probability distribution** of that variable. Since a great deal of statistical analysis is concerned with various kinds of probability distributions, it is necessary to study them in some detail. You may have studied something called a 'frequency distribution' in another unit. Probability distributions are very similar to frequency distributions.

5. WHAT DO PROBABILITY DISTRIBUTIONS LOOK LIKE?

Firstly, we must deal with a practical problem; how can we display probability distributions? We shall examine both tabular and graphical displays of probability distributions in this section.

USING A TABLE OR LIST

An easy way to display some random variables is simply to list them in tabular form. For example, consider a throw of 3 coins with the random variable X equal to the number of 'heads' which result from the experiment. X can only take the values 0, 1, 2 or 3, so is therefore a discrete random variable.

ACTIVITY 4

For the 3-coin experiment mentioned above, fill in the spaces in the following table. X = number of heads, and Pr(X) = the probability of obtaining X heads. The first entry, the probability of obtaining 0 heads – has already been put in for you.

X	Pr(X)
0	0.125
1	
2	
3	

You may be already familiar with the experiment in Activity 4. You will need to use the addition and multiplication rules of probability.

Therefore

Pr(0 Heads)   = Pr(Coins 1, 2 and 3 are all tails)

                    = 0.5 x 0.5 x 0.5 = 0.125.

Pr(1 Head)   = Pr{(Coin 1 = heads and 2 and 3 are tails)

                    or (coin 2 = heads and 1 and 3 are tails)

                    or (coin 3 = heads, 1 and 2 are tails)}

                    = (0.5 x 0.5 x 0.5) + (0.5 x 0.5 x 0.5) +

                    (0.5 x 0.5 x 0.5) = 0.375.

Pr(2 Heads)   = Pr{(Coin 1 and 2 are heads and 3 is tails)

                    or (coins 1 and 3 are heads, 2 is tails)

                    or (coins 2 and 3 are heads, 1 is tails)}

                    = (0.5 x 0.5 x 0.5) + (0.5 x 0.5 x 0.5) +

                    (0.5 x 0.5 x 0.5) = 0.375.

Pr(3 Heads)   = Pr(All 3 coins are heads) = 0.5 x 0.5 x 0.5

                    = 0.125.

The completed distribution is shown in figure 1.

X	PR(X)
0	0.125
1	0.375
2	0.375
3	0.125

FIGURE 1: **Three-Coin Experiment**

Activity 5 describes another probability experiment you will have met before.

ACTIVITY 5

Now consider another simple experiment. Throw a pair of dice, and let X be the random variable of the total score obtained from both dice. Fill in the following table.

X	Pr(X)
2	
3	
4	
5	
6	
7	
8	
9	
10	
11	
12	

The following table, figure 2, shows the distribution for the random variable in Activity 5.

X	Pʀ(X)
2	1/36
3	2/36
4	3/36
5	4/36
6	5/36
7	6/36
8	5/36
9	4/36
10	3/36
11	2/36
12	1/36

FIGURE 2: **Two-Dice Experiment**

Notice the similarity between probability distributions (such as the ones you constructed for Activities 4 and 5) and frequency distributions. Both involve a full statement of all the values the variable can possibly take. Frequency distributions record a physical **count** of how many times a particular value of the variable has been seen to occur. Probability distributions record the **degree of likelihood** with which it will occur.

The solutions to Activities 4 and 5 illustrate examples of discrete variables. Can tables also be used to describe a continuous random variable?

By way of giving you the answer, look at figure 3, below. It shows the result of a quality control check on the lifetimes of 200 electric light bulbs produced by the Ever-Lite Corporation. It is, in fact, a frequency distribution of the kind you have seen before.

The variable shown in figure 3 is continuous, but is not in the form of a probability distribution.

By using the concept of relative frequencies, this can easily be done. The relative frequency definition of probability was covered in an earlier unit in this series.

LIFETIME (in hours)	NO. OF BULBS
280 and less than 300	4
300 " " " 320	6
320 " " " 340	13
340 " " " 360	19
360 " " " 380	26
380 " " " 400	29
400 " " " 420	33
420 " " " 440	27
440 " " " 460	20
460 " " " 480	12
480 " " " 500	6
500 " " " 520	4
520 and above	1
TOTAL NO. TESTED	200

FIGURE 3: **Lifetimes of 200 Ever-Lite bulbs**

Now try Activity 6 and change it from a frequency distribution into a probability distribution.

ACTIVITY 6

(a)   By calculating relative frequencies, convert figure 3 into a probability distribution.

(b)   Now use your table from part (a) to estimate the following probabilities

   (i) a randomly selected light bulb will last between 400 and 500 hours?

   (ii) a randomly selected light bulb will last less than 400 hours?

   (iii) a randomly selected light bulb will last between 370 and 410 hours.

   (iv) a randomly selected light bulb will last exactly 400 hours?

A table of relative frequencies (probabilities) is shown below in figure 4.

LIFETIME (hours)	PROBABILITY	CUMULATIVE PROBABILITY
280 < 300	0.020	0.020
300 < 320	0.030	0.050
320 < 340	0.065	0.115
340 < 360	0.095	0.210
360 < 380	0.130	0.340
380 < 400	0.145	0.485
400 < 420	0.165	0.650
420 < 440	0.135	0.785
440 < 460	0.100	0.885
460 < 480	0.060	0.945
480 < 500	0.030	0.975
500 < 520	0.020	0.995
520 and above	0.005	1.000

FIGURE 4: **Table of Relative Frequencies (Activity 6)**

We can read from the table that the relative frequencies between 400 and 500 hours add up to 0.49.

So $Pr(400 < \text{lifetime} < 500) = 0.49$.

Also, relative frequencies below 400 add up to 0.485.

So $Pr(\text{Lifetime} < 400) = 0.485$.

The relative frequency table is not detailed enough to allow us to determine $Pr(370 < \text{lifetime} < 410)$ with accuracy. Nevertheless, we may make an estimate.

To do this, first note that the relative frequency between 380 and 400 hours is 0.145.

Secondly, since 370 is half-way between 360 and 380, we can tentatively assume that half the relative frequency for this class will be in the range $370 < 380$.

Therefore relative frequency for $370 < 410 =$

0.5 times relative frequency of $360 < 380$ plus
relative frequency of $380 < 400$ plus
0.5 times relative frequency of $400 < 420$

$= 0.065 + 0.145 + 0.0825 = 0.2925.$

It should be borne in mind that this is only an approximate answer since we have had to interpolate from the table.

Activity 6 shows that there is one important difference between tabular presentations of discrete and continuous probability distributions. For the latter, the variable must be stated in the form of class intervals. Put simply, this difference means that statements such as

$$'Pr(X = 400)'$$

are only meaningful in tables where the variable is discrete. Statements such as

$$'Pr(400 < X < 401)'$$

are the only valid way to represent probabilities for continuous variables. This is in line with what has already been said about continuous variables and is the reason why figure 3 shows the data in the form of intervals, for example

280 less than 300

300 less than 320

320 less than 340 etc.

instead of exact values, as in the two discrete cases in Activities 4 and 5.

However, whether discrete or continuous, two conditions must be satisfied by any valid probability distribution.

For every value of X in the case of a discrete random variable, $0 \leq Pr(X) \leq 1$.
For every interval a to b in the case of a continuous random variable, $0 \leq Pr(a < X < b) \leq 1$.

For both types of variable, over the range of X, probabilities must add up to 1.

The first condition restates a fundamental rule of probability. (The measuring scale for probability is in the range 0 to 1 inclusive.)

The second condition says that since the whole range of a variable X is the whole sample space for an experiment, then (by definition) the sum of the probabilities over X must be 1. You can check that the sums of the probabilities for each of the tables of Activities 4, 5 and 6 are equal to 1.

GRAPHICAL DISPLAY OF PROBABILITY DISTRIBUTIONS

Just as frequency distributions may be graphically described, probability distributions can also be illustrated by using a suitable diagram. There are different graphical procedures for discrete and continuous variables.

The Discrete Case

Histograms are a good method for displaying discrete variables. Figures 5 and 6 show the 3-coin and 2-dice experiments of Activities 4 and 5. The horizontal axis shows values taken by X (the random variable), number of heads, dice score, etc. The vertical axis is the scale of probability. Bar heights are proportionate to Pr(X). As with frequency distributions, histograms are excellent for showing shape or pattern in discrete probability distributions.

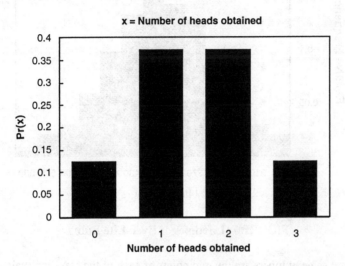

FIGURE 5: **Bar Chart of the Probability Distribution of the Throw of Three Coins**

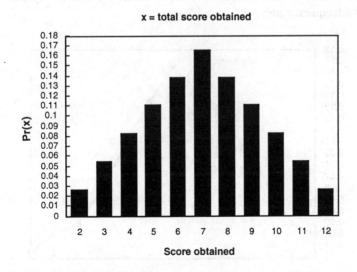

FIGURE 6: **Histogram of the Probability Distribution of the Combined Score Obtained From a Throw of a Pair of Dice**

The Continuous Case

Consider the Ever-Lite light bulb data of figure 3. Figure 7, shows a bar chart of these data.

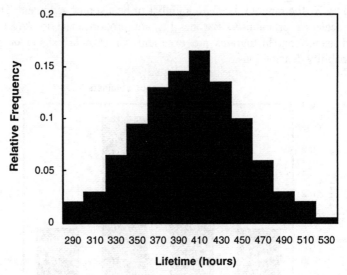

FIGURE 7: **Lifetimes of Ever-Lite Bulbs**

The horizontal scale numbers are the mid points of each of the class intervals.

While it is permissible to use a bar chart, or histogram for continuous data, it is conventional to draw a continuous line, or curve. Figure 8 shows the light bulb data in the form of a **frequency polygon**.

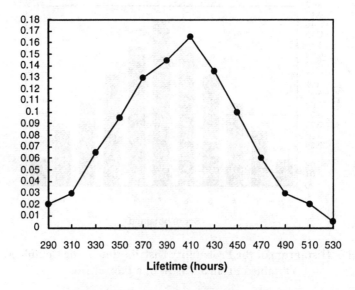

FIGURE 8: **Lifetime of Ever-Lite Bulbs**

This use of different graphical methods reflects the fact that discrete data can only take on a limited number of values, and this is well illustrated by the discontinuous changes from one bar (of the histogram) to another. By comparison, continuous data can take on any value on the horizontal scale of the graph, a fact best illustrated by the smooth continuous line, instead of a series of bars.

There is a further important fact about the graphical interpretation of continuous data. This is illustrated in figure 9, below.

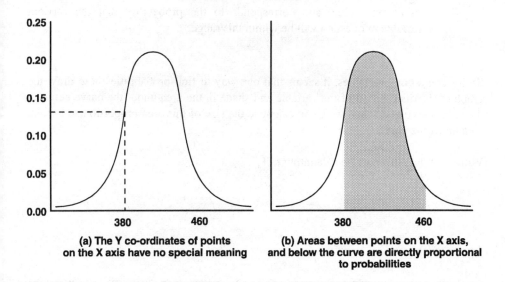

(a) The Y co-ordinates of points on the X axis have no special meaning

(b) Areas between points on the X axis, and below the curve are directly proportional to probabilities

FIGURE 9: **Lifetimes of 200 Ever-Lite Bulbs (Hours)**

The graph (a) of figure 9 shows that the Y co-ordinate of X = 380 is 0.13 (approximately). This number has no significance in the context of continuous probability distributions. Vertical axis co-ordinates on graphs illustrating such data have nothing to do with probabilities. But look at graph (b).

The region between the points X = 380 and X = 460 below the curve is shown as a shaded area.

Now this shaded area happens to be proportionate to the probability that a randomly selected light bulb will last between 380 and 460 hours.

Since (from figure 3) we can count that 109 of 200 bulbs have lifetimes between these values, then the size of the area shown on the second graph of figure 9 must be 109/200 = 0.545, or 54.5% of the total area.

6. CONCLUSION

To summarise on the differences between charts of discrete and continuous probability data, you should note the following points:

- for discrete data, the Y co-ordinate of a value, the height of a bar, corresponds to the probability of that value occurring;

- for continuous data the height of the graph line at a single value has no significance. The area **under the curve** between two values is the significant value, and corresponds to the probability that the random variable in question will be within this range.

So for continuous variables, it seems that one way to find probabilities is to draw the graph of the distribution of the variable and shade in the area under the curve between the values involved. Then we try to calculate the size of this area proportionate to total area under the curve.

With most data this may be a daunting task.

7. SUMMARY

In this first section we have

- defined random variables

- discussed **discrete** and **continuous variables**

- shown the relationship between probability and random variables

- discussed with examples, **probability distributions**

- examined **graphical displays of probability distributions**

If you are unsure of any of these topics check back **now** before you move on to the next section.

SECTION 2

MATHEMATICAL FUNCTIONS OF PROBABILITY DISTRIBUTIONS

1. INTRODUCTION

Tables and lists are convenient when there are a small number of values the variable can take. Histograms and line graphs show pattern and shape, but are mathematically imprecise. The most useful and concise method for depicting a probability distribution is to use functions. As with tables and graphs, there are some important differences between how **functions** are used in the discrete and continuous cases.

2. FUNCTIONS AND DISCRETE DATA

A function is a kind of algebraic formula, and is usually written in the following way

$$Pr(X = \chi) = \text{some algebraic expression containing } \chi$$

When solved, this algebraic expression produces the probability that the random variable X is equal to χ.

Note

take care with this notation. The upper case letter X, is the **general symbol** used in these notes for a random variable, whereas the symbol χ stands for a **particular** value which X can take.

So $Pr(X = 2)$ means

> 'what is the probability that the random variable symbolised by X can take on the value 2?'.

In this case $\chi = 2$.

You may already be familiar with this notation. If not, then be patient a while; you will eventually get used to it. It is impossible to understand statistics without using some mathematical shorthand.

Example of a Function

Single copies of newspapers often have multiple readers. Let the random variable X be the number of readers a single copy may have. Also, suppose that 1/6 of all copies sold are read by 1 reader, 1/3 are read by 2 readers, and 1/2 are read by 3 readers.

Then the probability function for this situation is

$$Pr(X = \chi) = \frac{\chi}{6} \quad \textit{for } \chi = 1, 2 \textit{ or } 3$$

We can check that this is a proper probability   distribution as follows

$$\textit{If } \chi = 1 \quad Pr(X = \chi) = \frac{\chi}{6} = \frac{1}{6}$$

$$\textit{If } \chi = 2 \quad Pr(X = \chi) = \frac{\chi}{6} = \frac{2}{6} = \frac{1}{3}$$

$$\textit{If } \chi = 3 \quad Pr(X = \chi) = \frac{\chi}{6} = \frac{3}{6} = \frac{1}{2}$$

Therefore the function produces the probabilities required. Further, since

$0 \le Pr(X = X) \pounds 1$ for each x and

$\Sigma Pr(X = X) = 1/6 + 1/3 + 1/2 = 1$

then the function is a true probability distribution.

It is important to remember that for a function to be a genuine probability distribution, Pr(c) must always be a value between 0 and 1 for all X, and $\Sigma Pr(\chi)$ must equal 1.

So a reasonable way to check many discrete probability distributions, is to calculate Pr(χ) for all values of X.

Remember these points while you try the next Activity.

ACTIVITY 7

The daily number of customers in a shop who buy size 10 boots is a discrete variable taking the values 1, 2, 3 or 4. Let X represent this variable. The probability function associated with X is

$$Pr(X = \chi) = \frac{\chi}{10} \qquad \text{for } \chi = 1, 2, 3 \text{ or } 4$$

and zero otherwise.

(a) Show that this meets the conditions required for a probability distribution.

(b) What is the probability that on any one day, exactly 2 customers will want size 10 boots?

(c) What is the probability that more than 2 customers will want size 10 boots?

(d) Sketch the histogram for this probability distribution.

We already know the conditions necessary for a valid probability distribution.

We can check the function in Activity 7, and verify that $Pr(X=\chi) \geq 0$ for all χ, and that the sum of the probabilities is 1, or unity.

$$FUNCTION \ \textbf{Pr(X = \chi)} = \frac{\chi}{10}$$

$$If \ \chi = \textbf{1}, \ then \ Pr(X \ = \ \chi) = \frac{1}{10}$$

$$If \ \chi = \textbf{2}, \ then \ Pr(X \ = \ \chi) = \frac{2}{10}$$

$$If \ \chi = \textbf{3}, \ then \ Pr(X \ = \ \chi) = \frac{3}{10}$$

$$If \ \chi = \textbf{4}, \ then \ Pr(X \ = \ \chi) = \frac{4}{10}$$

None of these values is negative, or more than 1. Also their sum is

$$\frac{1}{10} + \frac{2}{10} + \frac{3}{10} + \frac{4}{10} = 1$$

exactly as required, for a valid probability distribution

The probability required in Activity 7(b) is $Pr(X = 2)$ and has already been calculated as $2/10 = 0.2$ in part (a).

The probability required in Activity 7(c) is

$$\textbf{Pr(X > 2) = Pr(X = 3) + Pr(X = 4)} = \frac{7}{10}$$

Finally, figure 10 below shows a bar chart in answer to 7(d).

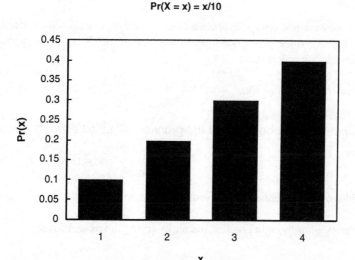

Pr(X = x) = x/10

FIGURE 10: **Bar Chart of Distribution of Purchasers of Boots**

3. FUNCTIONS AND CONTINUOUS DATA

We must take extra care when using probability functions for continuous data. Consider the following continuous probability function.

Example

Time taken to complete an industrial process varies from 0 to 5 hours. The actual time taken is thus a continuous random variable. We further suppose that the probability function can be expressed in the form

$$Y = \frac{2X}{25}$$

where X = number of hours to completion

So   if X=3,   then Y = (2x3)/25 = 6/25 = 0.24   or
    if X=0.5, then Y = (2x0.5)/25 = 1/25 = 0.04 etc.

Can we interpret these figures in the same way as we would the results of discrete probability functions? Can we say, for example, that Pr(Process takes exactly 3 hours) = (2x3)/25 = 6/25?

The answer to this question is **NO**.

Remember, you cannot compute probabilities for single points with continuous data. Therefore the Y value associated with any value of X tells us nothing about probabilities for continuous data.

But we know that questions like

'what is the probability that the process will take between 2 and 3 hours'

are valid.

How would we use the mathematical probability function to answer such a question?

You can clarify your thoughts on this matter by trying the next Activity.

ACTIVITY 8

(a)   On a separate sheet of paper, draw the graph of the function

$$Y = \frac{2X}{25}$$ for values of X between 0 and 5.

(It is a linear function, so you should find this easy.)

(b)   Using your graph, calculate the area beneath the line

$$Y = \frac{2X}{25}$$ between X = 0 and X = 5, and

verify that it is equal to 1. (The area of a triangle is found by calculating 0.5 times length of the triangles base times triangle height.)

(c)   **Why** is the area beneath the graph of the probability function equal to 1?

(d)   Using the graph, show the region between X = 2 and X = 3 under the line as a shaded area. Calculate the size of this area and hence find the probability that the industrial process described by this function will take between 2 and 3 hours to complete.

The graph of the function Y = 2X/25 is shown in figure 11.

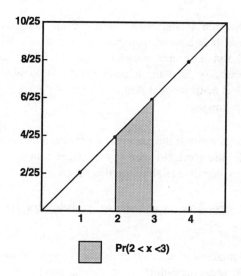

Pr(2 < x <3)

FIGURE 11: **Probability Graph of Y = 2x/25**

It forms a regular triangle with base = 5 - 0 = 5 units and height = (10/25) - 0

= 10/25 units.

The area of this triangle is $0.5 \times$ base $\times$ height =

$0.5 \times 5 \times (10/25) = 1$.

The graph represents the whole sample space for the random variable. (X can be any value between 0 and 5.) The probabilities of every event in the sample space always add up to 1. This is why the **total** area beneath any probability graph of a continuous random variable is equal to 1.

The area under the function between X=2 and X=3 is shown as the darker shaded portion of the graph in figure 11. The best way to calculate this area, is as follows:

area of triangle formed by X = 0 to X = 3,

minus

area of triangle formed by X = 0 to X = 2.

The resulting area is 5/25 = 0.2.

So, Pr(the process takes between 2 - 3 hours) = 0.2.

4. CONCLUSION

The mathematical function is the most useful of all methods used to specify a probability distribution. It is concise, summarising the whole distribution in a single algebraic expression. But it is not always possible to find a mathematical 'law' to describe a known probability distribution, and even if it is possible, it often takes much trial and error, as well as mathematical skill, to find it. In the case of continuous data we can also state the following:

> The whole area beneath the graph of a probability function is equal to 1 and the area under the graph between any 2 numbers on the horizontal axis equals the probability that the variable is in this range.

This leaves us with problems in calculating probabilities for continuous random variables.

Even if we know the mathematical function its graph might be so complicated that it is impossible to calculate areas beneath it.

The graph of the function of Activity 8 was a straight line so calculation of areas was simple.

Few probability functions will be as straight forward as this.

However, we need not worry about finding the mathematical function for a distribution as some of the work has already been done for us.

Statisticians have discovered a number of probability distributions both discrete and continuous which seem to be quite useful in a number of real world situations. We will be dealing with two of these distributions later in this unit, in section 4, the **binomial distribution** and in section 5, the **normal distribution**.

5. SUMMARY

In this second section we have

- introduced the idea of **functions** and **discrete** data

- demonstrated and illustrated **functions** and **continuous** data

- calculated areas under **probability graphs**

If you are unsure of any of these areas, check back **now** before you read on.

SECTION 3

SUMMING UP A PROBABILITY DISTRIBUTION

1. INTRODUCTION

We already know that we can calculate summary statistics for a frequency distribution, such as the mean, the standard deviation, and so on. It is also possible to do the same thing for a probability distribution. This section will deal with the calculation of such quantities, in particular with the expected value and the variance. As before, we will treat the discrete and continuous cases separately.

2. EXPECTED VALUE FOR A DISCRETE VARIABLE

Expected value is very similar to the arithmetic mean of a frequency distribution. It is a measure of central tendency for a random variable, and we calculate it as follows

Formula 1

The expected value E(X) of a discrete random variable X

$$E(X) = \Sigma X.Pr(X)$$

which means multiply each value of the random variable X, by the probability $Pr(X)$, then add the resulting values.

Note that E(X) is here used as an abbreviation for expected value. However, the Greek symbol μ is also used by some writers. In this unit E(X) and μ will be used interchangeably to refer to expected value.

Example

A service engineer handles from 0 to 5 calls on any given day. Figure 12 shows the probability distribution of X, the number of calls for service

NO. OF SERVICE CALLS (X)	0	1	2	3	4	5
PROBABILITY PR(X)	.10	.15	.30	.20	.15	.10

FIGURE 12: **Probability Distribution of Service Calls**

The calculation for finding the expected number of calls per day is set out in figure 13, below.

X	PR(X)	X.PR(X)
0	0.10	0.00
1	0.15	0.15
2	0.30	0.60
3	0.20	0.60
4	0.15	0.60
5	0.10	0.50
		ΣX.Pr(X) = 2.45

FIGURE 13: **Number of Service Calls Per Day; Calculation of Expected Value**

In this case the expected value, E(X) = 2.45, which means that the service engineer can expect 2.45 calls per day.

What does this number tell us?

Do not worry if you cannot yet answer this question. We will return to the question of interpretation when we have dealt with variance of a random variable.

ACTIVITY 9

Look again at the data of Activity 7.
Calculate the expected daily number of customers buying size 10 boots.

The calculations for E(X) are shown in figure 14, below.

X	PR(X)	X.PR(X)
1	0.1	0.1
2	0.2	0.4
3	0.3	0.9
4	0.4	1.6
	ΣX.Pr(X) = 3	

FIGURE 14: **Number of Customers Buying Boots (Activity 9)**

So $E(X) = \Sigma X.\Pr(X) = 3$

3. THE VARIANCE OF A DISCRETE RANDOM VARIABLE

As with the frequency distribution it is possible to calculate the variance and standard deviation of a probability distribution.

Formulae 2 and 3

The variance, σ^2 of a discrete random variable X

$$(2) \quad \sigma^2 = \Sigma(X - \mu)^2.Pr(X) \quad or$$

$$(3) \quad \sigma^2 = \{\Sigma X^2.Pr(X)\} - \mu^2$$

The variance describes the variability of the probability distribution, just as it does with a frequency distribution. Either formula (2 or 3) will calculate the variance. If μ is not an integer, formula 3 is easier to use. The standard deviation is the square root of the variance.

Example

Consider the distribution of number of engineer service calls used to demonstrate the calculation for expected value. Figure 15 demonstrates the calculations needed to determine the variance and standard deviation of a probability distribution.

X	PR(X)	X.PR(X)	X²	PR(X).X²
0	0.10	0.00	0	0.00
1	0.15	0.15	1	0.15
2	0.30	0.60	4	1.20
3	0.20	0.60	9	1.80
4	0.15	0.60	16	2.40
5	0.10	0.50	25	2.50
		ΣX.Pr(X) = 2.45		ΣX².Pr(X) = 8.05

FIGURE 15: **Variance and Standard Deviation of Engineer Service Calls**

$$\sigma^2 = \{\Sigma X^2.Pr(X)\} - \mu^2$$
$$= 8.05 - 2.45^2$$
$$= 2.0475.$$

This particular calculation uses formula 3.

Firstly, the values of X in the above table were squared. The result is shown in column 4. The squares were multiplied by their respective probabilities. The values so obtained (column 5) were summed, and the expected value (m) was squared and subtracted from this sum. Since the standard deviation, s, is the square root of the variance, then

$$\sigma = \sqrt{2.0475}$$
$$= 1.4309$$

Study this example of the calculation of expected value and variance, and make sure you know how they were obtained.

You should compare these calculations with the very similar calculations of mean and variance for a frequency distribution.

ACTIVITY 10

Using the data from Activity 7, calculate the variance of the number of people buying size 10 boots.

The calculations required for Activity 10 are set out below, in figure 16.

X	PR(X)	X.PR(X)	X²	X².PR(X)
1	0.1	0.1	1	0.1
2	0.2	0.4	4	0.8
3	0.3	0.9	9	2.7
4	0.4	1.6	16	6.4
		ΣX.Pr(X) = 3		ΣX.Pr(X)² = 10.0

FIGURE 16: **Variance of Number Buying Boots**

Thus the variance for this distribution is $10.0 - 3^2 = 1$

4. EXPECTED VALUE AND VARIANCE: CONTINUOUS VARIABLES

Formulas 1, 2 and 3 will not calculate the expected value and variance for continuous random variables. In fact, exact calculation of these statistics requires a knowledge of the mathematics of calculus. However, it is possible to obtain approximate estimates of these statistics by using a table of the probability distribution.

Formula 4

The expected value E(X) of a continuous random variable X can be approximately estimated by the following formula

$$E(X) = \Sigma mpc_i.Pr(c_i)$$

Where mpc_i is the mid point of class interval i and $Pr(c_i)$ is the probability that the random variable will be in class interval i.

It is a method very similar to the one used to calculate the mean of a variable in a grouped frequency distribution. You may recall the method if you worked through the earlier unit in this series on data presentation. Figure 17, below, illustrates the use of this formula by using the 'Ever-Lite' data from figure 3 and Activity 6.

CLASS INTERVAL	MID POINT (mpc$_i$)	PR(c$_i$)	mpc$_i$.PR(c$_i$)
280 < 300	290	0.020	5.80
300 < 320	310	0.030	9.30
320 < 340	330	0.065	21.45
340 < 360	350	0.095	33.25
360 < 380	370	0.130	48.10
380 < 400	390	0.145	56.55
400 < 420	410	0.165	67.65
420 < 440	430	0.135	58.05
440 < 460	450	0.100	45.00
460 < 480	470	0.060	28.20
480 < 500	490	0.030	14.70
500 < 520	510	0.020	10.20
520 < 540*	530	0.005	2.65
			Σmpc.Pr(c)= 400.90

FIGURE 17: **Expected Lifetime of Ever-Lite Bulbs**

* In figure 3, this class interval originally read '520 and over'. It has been given an arbitrary upper limit of 540 in order to make calculation possible.

Therefore $E(x) = \Sigma mpc_i.pr(c_i) = 400.90$ which means that the expected lifetime of a light bulb is 400.90 hours.

ACTIVITY 11

A computer will vary from time to time in the speed with which it can carry out tasks. The following is a table illustrating the probability distribution of the time taken to complete a database search by a computer.

TIME (X) (nanosecs)	Pr(X)
30 under 35	0.04
35 under 40	0.07
40 under 45	0.12
45 under 50	0.20
50 under 55	0.21
55 under 60	0.19
60 under 65	0.08
65 under 70	0.05
70 under 75	0.04

Calculate the expected time the computer will take to perform a data base search.

Figure 18, below sets out the calculations necessary to answer Activity 11.

CLASS INTERVAL	MID POINT mpc_i	$Pr(mpc_i)$	$mpc_i.Pr(C_i)$
30 < 35	32.5	0.04	1.300
35 < 40	37.5	0.07	2.625
40 < 45	42.5	0.12	5.100
45 < 50	47.5	0.20	9.500
50 < 55	52.5	0.21	11.025
55 < 60	57.5	0.19	10.925
60 < 65	62.5	0.08	5.000
65 < 70	67.5	0.05	3.375
70 < 75	72.5	0.04	2.900
$\Sigma mpc_i.Pr(c_i) = 51.750$			

FIGURE 18: **Data Bank Search Time (Activity 11)**

The computer therefore takes an expected 51.750 nanosecs search time.

It should again be stressed that this calculation will only give an approximate estimate of the expected value of a continuous random variable. Some scientific pocket calculators have statistical functions which calculate E(X). You may wish to use them.

The following formula shows an approximate method for calculating the variance of a continuous random variable

Formula 5

The variance σ^2 of a continuous random variable X can be approximately estimated by the following formula

$$\sigma^2 = \{\Sigma mpc_i^2 . pr(c_i)\} - \mu^2$$

where mpc_{i2} is the squared mid point of class interval i and $Pr(c_i)$ is the probability that the random variable will be in class interval i.

You may again notice the similarity between this formula and the method used to calculate the variance of a variable from a grouped frequency distribution.

Calculation of the variance is illustrated in figure 19 for the **Ever-Lite** data of figure 3 and Activity 6.

CLASS INTERVAL	MID POINT (mpc_i)	$Pr(c_i)$	$mpc_i^2.Pr(c_i)$
280 < 300	290	0.020	1682.0
300 < 320	310	0.030	2883.0
320 < 340	330	0.065	7078.5
340 < 360	350	0.095	11637.5
360 < 380	370	0.130	17797.0
380 < 400	390	0.145	22054.5
400 < 420	410	0.165	27736.5
420 < 440	430	0.135	24961.5
440 < 460	450	0.100	20250.0
460 < 480	470	0.060	13254.0
480 < 500	490	0.030	7203.0
500 < 520	510	0.020	5202.0
520 < 540	530	0.005	1404.5
			$\Sigma mpc^2.Pr(c)=$ 163,144.

FIGURE 19: **Variance of Lifetime for Ever-Lite Bulbs**

We require

$$\sigma^2 = \{\Sigma mpc_i^2.Pr(c_i)\} - \mu^2$$

We already know that m = 400.90 (figure 17), so

$$\sigma^2 = 163,144 - 400.90^2 = 2423.19 \quad \text{and}$$
$$\sigma = 49.23$$

ACTIVITY 12

Calculate the variance of times taken to perform a data base search by the computer in Activity 11.

⟩

Activity 12 continued...

CLASS INTERVAL	MID POINT mpc_i	$Pr(mpc_i)$	$mpc_i{}^2.Pr(C_i)$
30 < 35	32.5	0.04	42.2500
35 < 40	37.5	0.07	98.4375
40 < 45	42.5	0.12	216.7500
45 < 50	47.5	0.20	451.2500
50 < 55	52.5	0.21	578.8125
55 < 60	57.5	0.19	628.1875
60 < 65	62.5	0.08	312.5000
65 < 70	67.5	0.05	227.8125
70 < 75	72.5	0.04	210.2500
		$\Sigma mpc_i{}^2.Pr(c_i)$ = 2766.25	

FIGURE 20: **Variance of Data Bank Search Times**

We require

$$s^2 = \{Smpc_i{}^2.Pr(c_i)\} - m^2$$

We already know that m = 51.75 nanosecs (Activity 11), so

$\sigma^2 = 2766.25 - 51.75^2 = 88.1875$ **and**

$\sigma = 9.3908$

5. INTERPRETATION OF EXPECTED VALUE AND VARIANCE

We now make good a promise made earlier and explain how the expected value should be interpreted. There are several points to note. We will use the service engineer example first introduced in figure 12 to illustrate.

Firstly, the service engineer never actually makes 2.45 calls.

Sometimes more than 2.45 calls are made, sometimes less. The figure of 2.45 should be regarded as a long run 'average'. Secondly, if (as in the case of this data), we are dealing with a discrete variable, a value such as 2.45 can never occur. Calculation of an expected value for a discrete random variable sometimes results in a fractional figure, in just the same way as the mean of a discrete frequency distribution can be fractional. (You may have heard that a family in the UK will have an average 1.75 children.)

So long as you are aware that the variable is discrete, you can make the necessary mental adjustments when interpreting the value.

This second point does not, of course, apply to continuous data, since the variable can assume any value.

Therefore, if a random variable is the result of carrying out repeated experiments, then the expected value can be thought of as the long run 'average'.

For example, the risk of accidental death among 18-25 year old males is about 100 per 100,000 persons.

So the probability of a fatal accident happening to any particular male in this age group is 0.001. Suppose an insurance company proposes to market a policy against fatal accidents for an annual premium of £30. The policy pays out £20,000 if a fatal accident happens to a policy holder. Therefore, the insurance company experiences one of the following monetary consequences by issuing this policy:

receives a profit of £30 with probability 0.999

suffers a loss of £19970 (£20000 - £30), with probability of 0.001.

ACTIVITY 13

Calculate the expected profit that the insurer makes on a policy, and verify that it is £10.

Does this mean that the insurer will make a profit of £10 **on each and every policy**?

Try and explain your answer in words to this last question.

Firstly we calculate the expected return made by the insurer.

There are two outcomes to this random experiment. The insurer has a 0.999 chance of making £30 (a profit), and a 0.001 chance of making -£19970 (a loss).

Therefore

$$E(X) = \mu = \Sigma X.Pr(X)$$
$$= (30 \times 0.999) + (-19970 \times 0.001) = 10$$

as required.

This does not mean that the insurer **always** makes £10 on each policy. Mostly, the insurer will make a profit of £30 (because most insured people never suffer an accident), but sometimes there will be a loss of £19970 when such an accident occurs. On the average, the long term gain per policy is £10. This is what is meant by the term 'expected value'.

ACTIVITY 14

An investor needs to decide where to place money in any one of three different risk ventures.

Investment A results in either a profit of £60,000, with probability 0.5, or a loss of £40,000 with probability 0.5.

Investment B pays £50,000 with probability 0.2, or loses £150,000 with probability 0.8.

Investment C pays £250,000 with probability 0.2, or loses £50,000 with probability 0.8.

For each investment, calculate the expected value and standard deviation of the return. Interpret the meaning of these figures.

Firstly, we must calculate the expected value and variance for each investment and secondly, interpret the results.

(**Note**: formula 2 has been used to calculate σ^2 in the workings which follow, because it was found to be computationally easier to use in this case than formula 3.)

Investment A

$\mu = (60,000 \times 0.5) + (-40,000 \times 0.5) = 10,000.$

$\sigma^2 = (60,000 - 10,000)^2 \times 0.5 + (-40,000 - 10,000)^2 \times 0.5$

$\therefore \sigma^2 = 2.5 \times 10^9$

$\therefore \sigma = 50,000$

Investment B

$\mu = (50,000 \times 0.2) + (-150,000 \times 0.8) = -110,000.$

$\sigma^2 = (50,000 - (-110,000))^2 \times 0.2 +$

$(-150,000 - (-110,000))^2 \times 0.8$

$\therefore \sigma^2 = 6.4 \times 10^9$

$\therefore \sigma = 80,000$

Investment C

$\mu = (250,000 \times 0.2) + (-50,000 \times 0.8) = 10,000.$

$\sigma^2 = (250,000 - 10,000)^2 \times 0.2 + (-50,000 - 10,000)^2 \times 0.8$

$\therefore \sigma^2 = 1.44 \times 10^{10}$

$\therefore \sigma = 120,000$

We can summarise these results in figure 21

INVESTMENT	EXPECTED RETURN μ	STANDARD DEVIATION OF RETURN σ
A	£10,000	£50,000
B	-£110,000	£80,000
C	£10,000	£120,000

FIGURE 21: **Return on Investments (Activity 14)**

We should firstly remember what the mean (expected value) and the standard deviation measure. μ is a 'long run average', while the standard deviation is a measure of the variability of the return. For example compare investments A and C. They both have the same expected, or mean return. Now this means that if the investments are repeated enough times, the long run return from each of them will average £10,000 per investment.

Notice that while A and C have the same mean returns, the standard deviation for investment C is greater than for A. Since the standard deviation is a measure of variability, this tells us that the return from investment C is more variable than the return from A. In investment analysis, the standard deviation of returns is often used as a measure of the risk. Investments A and C both have the same average return, but investment C is more risky.

ACTIVITY 15

Interpret the following figures as long run averages

(a)   the expected number of customers per evening at the Sizzling Lobster Bistro is 23.7

(b)   the expected number of defective mouldings turned out by a machine shop is 0.7 per 100

(c)   the expected inches of rain per month in a country area is 3.0.

What does it mean to 'expect' 23.7 customers per evening at the Sizzling Lobster? The number of customers will vary from one evening to another; the long run average per evening is 23.7.

Although the variable is discrete, it is perfectly possible to arrive at a fractional value such as '23.7 customers'. This is because of the way m is calculated.

When we have a defective rate of 0.7 mouldings per 100 produced, you would expect to count 0.7 defectives in each batch of 100. This could equally, and perhaps more meaningfully, be expressed as '7 out of every 1000 mouldings are defective'.

You should be careful not to assume that this means a guaranteed 7 defectives for every 1000 mouldings produced. The figure is a long run average.

Lastly in Activity 15, we can see that some days will be dry, other days rainy. The 3.0 inches expected value will refer to an average over a period of time. It would theoretically be possible to have 364 dry days, experience all the rainfall for the year on day 365, and still record an average 3 inches of rain per day. This would, however, be highly unlikely.

6. SUMMARY

In this section we have

- looked at **expected values** for **discrete distributions**

- discussed **the variance** of **discrete distributions** with examples

- shown how to estimate **expected value** and **variance** for **continuous variables**

- interpreted expected values and variances

If you are unsure of any of these topics and examples, check back before you continue with the next section.

SECTION 4

THE BINOMIAL DISTRIBUTION

1. INTRODUCTION: A MATTER OF INSURANCE

Five men, of equal health buy a medical expenses insurance policy which pays out if they are hospitalised before age 65. Actuaries working for the insurance company believe there is an 0.1 chance of any individual male being hospitalised before they are 65.

How would the insurance firm calculate the probability that **none** of the 5 people will be hospitalised before they are 65?

Further, what would be the chance that **only 1** of the 5 will be hospitalised before they are 65?

More generally, how would the actuaries assess the risk that x of the 5 men will be hospitalised before they are 65? (where x is any integer between 0 and 5).

In this section we examine a special discrete probability distribution, known as the **binomial probability distribution**. It has a number of useful applications, especially in the area of quality control. The insurance problem stated above will help to develop our understanding of how it works.

ACTIVITY 16

Think about the insurance example. If each man has the same probability (0.1) of being hospitalised before they are 65, then what is the probability that NONE of them will suffer this fate?

To answer this question you need to refer to the theory developed in unit 5 on probability. The complex event 'no-one is hospitalised' itself consists of 5 component events.

Do you remember how we used the multiplication rule of probabilities to deal with such situations?

It enables us to rewrite

Pr(none hospitalised)

as

Pr(first man and second and third and fourth and fifth are not hospitalised).

Each man has a 0.1 chance of hospitalisation, so they will have a 0.9 chance of **not** being hospitalised. So the required probability is

$$0.9 \times 0.9 \times 0.9 \times 0.9 \times 0.9 = 0.9^5 = 0.59049.$$

The next Activity will require something more than just the multiplication rule.

ACTIVITY 17

Still using the insurance example, what is the probability that ONLY 1 of the 5 men will be hospitalised before they are 65?

(Careful! the event 'only one hospitalised' really means; '1 hospitalised and 4 not hospitalised').

Activity 17 requires thought. What is the probability that only 1 of the 5 men will be hospitalised?

For the moment, assume that it is the **first man** who is hospitalised, while the other 4 **are not**. We use the multiplication rule of probabilities here.

Pr(first man hospitalised and the other 4 not)   =

Pr(first man hospitalised) x Pr(other 4 not)   =

$0.1 \times 0.9 \times 0.9 \times 0.9 \times 0.9 = 0.1 \times 0.9^4$ **= 0.06561**

But this does not end the matter. We have only considered the case where the first man was hospitalised. **Any** of the 5 could be affected in this way.

There are therefore five different ways in which one man could be hospitalised. So to get the correct probability, we must multiply 0.06561 by 5

Pr(**only 1 man is hospitalised) = 5 × 0.06561 = 0.32805.**

Activity 17 may remind you of the law of combinations covered in unit 5. First, we make a calculation to find the probability that any **particular** individual of the 5 ends up hospitalised. But since there are 5 individuals, then there are 5 different ways in which the event could occur. Hence we need to multiply by 5 to obtain the final answer.

ACTIVITY 18

What is the probability that **exactly 2** of the 5 men will be hospitalised before age 65?

To answer Activity 18, first assume that the first and second men are hospitalised and that the other 3 are not.

Pr(Men 1 and 2 hospitalised, 3, 4 and 5 not)   =
Pr(1 and 2 hospitalised) × Pr(3, 4 and 5 not)   =
$0.1^2 \times 0.9^3 = 0.00729$.

But we have only dealt with the specific case where 1 and 2 were hospitalised; we have not yet solved the problem. Any 2 of the 5 could be hospitalised. We need to know how many possible different groups of 2 men could be selected from 5. This is a problem in **combinations** and is equal to

$$\binom{5}{2} = 10$$

We would multiply 0.00729 by this number.
So Pr(2 men will be hospitalised) =

$$\binom{5}{2} \times 0.00729 = 10 \times 0.00729 = 0.0729$$

Activity 18 shows that we must use the law of combinations with such problems. First, you calculated the probability that any particular 2 men out of the 5 would be hospitalised. However, there are

$$\binom{5}{2} = 10$$

ways in which 2 men can be selected from 5 men. Hence the need to multiply by 10. If you found Activities 17 and 18 difficult to answer, then you should reread section 6 on counting techniques from unit 5, *Probability*.

Now we return to the more general problem involving the insurance data, namely

what is the probability that χ of the 5 men will be hospitalised before they are 65?

The symbol χ stands for any whole number between 0 and 5. So we are required to state the **functional form** of this probability distribution.

We must calculate two quantities

what is the probability that any particular set, χ, of the 5 men will be hospitalised

in how many ways can we select χ men from 5.

If we put these two quantities together we will have a calculation like that shown in figure 22

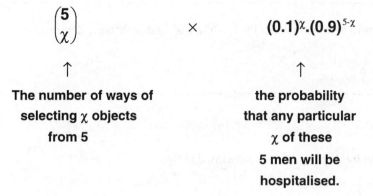

FIGURE 22: **Pr(χ Men are Hospitalised)**

We can express this using the following formula:

Formula 6

The probability that χ men out of 5 will be hospitalised before age 65 is

$$Pr(\chi\,men\ hospitalised) = \binom{5}{\chi}(0.1)^{\chi}(0.9)^{5-\chi}$$

This is a special case of a function known as the binomial distribution (see sub-section 2 below).

ACTIVITY 19

This Activity summarises the insurance problem. Use formula 6 and set χ to the values 0, 1, 2, 3, 4 and 5 respectively to fill in the blank row in the following table,

χ	0	1	2	3	4	5
$Pr(X=\chi)$						

and therefore demonstrate that the formula is a valid probability distribution.

Calculations for Activity 19 are summarised in figure 23.

It can be seen from figure 23 that $Pr(X=\chi) \geq 0$ for all χ (see column 4). Also, the probabilities in column 4 sum to 1. Therefore, the function is a valid probability distribution.

χ	$\binom{5}{\chi}$	$(0.1)^\chi(0.9)^{5-\chi}$	$Pr(X=\chi)$
0	1	0.59049	0.59049
1	5	0.06561	0.32805
2	10	0.00729	0.07290
3	10	0.00081	0.00810
4	5	0.00009	0.00045
5	1	0.00001	0.00001

FIGURE 23: **Valid Probability Distribution (Activity 19)**

The probability distribution developed in Activities 16-19 is a special case of something called the **binomial distribution**. We must now consider binomial distributions in general.

2. THE GENERAL FORM OF THE BINOMIAL DISTRIBUTION

A binomial distribution describes the probability distribution resulting from the outcome of a **binomial experiment**. The experiment involving the health insurance policy was just such an experiment. But what exactly **is** a binomial experiment?

A binomial experiment has four properties:

the experiment must consist of N identical 'trials'

two mutually exclusive outcomes are possible on each trial (technically, one of these outcomes is described as a 'success', and the other as a 'fail')

the probability (which we shall call p) that the trial results in a 'success', remains the same from trial to trial

the trials are **independent** of each other.

Now let us look again at the hospital insurance policy case in the light of these four points.

Consider each man as a separate 'trial'. Then we have N = 5 trials in this case. For each man (or trial), there are 2 possibilities; either he is hospitalised before age 65, which we will call a 'success', or he is not, which we will call a 'fail'. It does not really matter which one we call a success, and which we call a fail so long as we stay consistent.

If we can regard each man as having the same probability of being hospitalised, then the equal probability condition is met. In this case, p, the probability of success = 0.1.

This means that the probability of fail, not being hospitalised

$$= 1 - p = 1 - 0.1 = 0.9.$$

If the men are random selections from the general population, then the independence rule will be met. Refer to unit 5, *Probability*, if you are unsure what independence means.

Random variables resulting from binomial experiments are said to be **binomially distributed**.

It cannot be expected that the necessary conditions for binomial experiments will be met in all cases. Careful examination of all the facts is essential before we can make a judgement.

Now consider each of the experiments described in Activity 20, which will test your ability to distinguish experiments which are binomial from those which are not.

ACTIVITY 20

Consider the following experiments

(a)   throw a coin 10 times and count the number of heads

(b)   a caravan site owner has 10 caravans which are all occupied and also hires out TV sets to any caravan occupant who requires one. It is thought that there is an 0.6 chance that any caravan occupant will want to hire one. The number wanting a TV set is recorded.

(c)   a marksman fires at a target which is either hit or missed. The marksman fires 20 shots and the number of hits is recorded.

Are these binomial experiments? Why? (Or why not?)

Each time a coin is thrown, the outcome can be one of two possibilities, heads or tails. The chance of obtaining heads is the same for each throw of the coin. Furthermore, throws of a coin are independent trials, which means that this experiment is binomial.

In the caravan example, a trial can be thought of as the action taken by a caravan. There are 10 such trials, each resulting in the hire (or otherwise) of a TV set.

It is also reasonable to think of the 10 caravans as independent trials, each of which has a probability, 0.6 of wishing to hire a TV set. Consequently, this experiment could be treated as binomial.

The marksman example presents us with a different situation. It is certainly the case that there are 20 trials, each of which could be classified as 'success' or 'fail'. However, it is unlikely that the trials are independent. The marksman would not have the same probability of hitting the target each time, as there would be a better chance of hitting the target after a little practice. Consequently, this can not be considered as a binomial experiment.

Once we are satisfied that we have a valid binomial experiment with N trials, and that the probability of success is p, then we can define the binomial distribution. This is shown in formula 7.

Formula 7

For a binomial experiment with N trials, with probability of success = p (meaning probability of fail = 1 - p), the probability of χ successes is given as

$$Pr(X = \chi) = \binom{N}{\chi} p^{\chi}.(1-p)^{N-\chi}$$

This formula may look complicated if you are unfamiliar with mathematical notation. However, you have already seen earlier in this section a special case of this binomial distribution formula, where $N = 5$ (the 5 insured men), and $p = 0.1$ (the probability of being hospitalised). Look back to that formula and compare it with formula 7.

The probability of χ successes in N trials is shown in figure 24 as

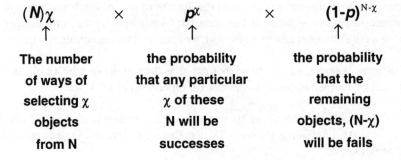

FIGURE 24: **Calculating Binomial Probabilities**

ACTIVITY 21

For each of the binomial experiments mentioned in Activity 20

(a)   state the value of p, 1-p, and N

(b)   write down the formula for the binomial distribution relating to that experiment

(c)   calculate Pr(X = 2) for each binomial distribution.

The first binomial distribution to be checked in Activity 21 is the coin-tossing experiment. We can consider the occurrence of heads as a success. There are 10 throws of the coin, so N = 10. Probability of a success (heads) is 0.5, so p = 0.5, and so the probability of a fail (tails), 1 - p = 0.5.

This coin throwing distribution may be written in functional terms as

$$Pr(X = \chi) = \binom{10}{\chi}(0.5)^{\chi}.(1 - 0.5)^{10-\chi}$$

or more simply

$$\binom{10}{\chi}(0.5)^{10}$$

Consequently

$$Pr(X = 2) = \binom{10}{2}(0.5)^{10} \approx 0.0439$$

We can now deal with the caravan TV hire experiment. There are 10 caravans, so N = 10. If we consider a hire as being a success, then p = 0.6, and consequently a fail, or non-hire is 1 - p = 0.4.

For this experiment the distribution function can be written as

$$Pr(X = \chi) = \binom{10}{\chi}(0.6)^{\chi}.(0.4)^{10-\chi}$$

So for the caravan experiment

$$Pr(X = 2) = \binom{10}{2}(0.6)^{2}.(0.4)^{8} \approx 0.0106$$

The marksman example was not a binomial experiment, so is not considered here.

Now you can try out what you have just learned on some more binomial experiments.

ACTIVITY 22

The manager of a department store considers that 30% of the people who come into the store actually make a purchase.

What is the probability that 2 of the next 4 people coming into the store make a purchase?

In Activity 22 we may consider each customer as a trial, the outcomes being a 'success', (a purchase is made), or a 'fail' (no purchase is made). Since 30% of people entering the store actually buy, we can say that p, the probability of a success is 0.3. This will mean a probability of 0.7 for a fail. In general the probability that c of the next 4 customers will buy is

$$Pr(X = \chi) = \binom{4}{\chi}(0.3)^{\chi}.(0.7)^{4-\chi}$$

therefore, the probability that 2 of the 4 will buy is

$$Pr(X = 2) = \binom{4}{2}(0.3)^2.(0.7)^2 = 0.2646$$

ACTIVITY 23

An auditor inspects a firm's invoices by randomly selecting 5 invoice documents. If 4% of invoices are known to contain errors, what is the probability that the auditor will find

(a)   exactly 1 invoice with an error

(b)   at least 1 invoice with an error?

Each of the 5 invoices of Activity 23 can be considered as a trial. The result of each trial is that we find an error (which we can call a success), or we do not find an error (which we shall call a fail). The probability of a success (error) is 0.04 (because 4% of invoices are known to contain errors). The probability of a fail (no error) will be 0.96.

So the probability of finding χ errors is

$$Pr(X = \chi) = \binom{5}{\chi}(0.04)^{\chi}.(0.96)^{5-\chi}$$

We specifically need to calculate the probability that 1 invoice is in error. This is given by

$$Pr(X = 1) = \binom{5}{1}(0.04)^{1}.(0.96)^{4} \approx 0.1699.$$

The probability of **at least one error** is best tackled using the complement law of probability.

$$Pr(X \geq 1) = 1 - Pr(X = 0) =$$

$$1 - \binom{5}{0}(0.04)^0.(0.96)^5 \approx$$

$$1 - 0.8154 = 0.1846$$

---

3. EXPECTED VALUE AND VARIANCE OF A BINOMIAL DISTRIBUTION

You already know how to calculate the expected value and variance of a probability distribution. We do not need to go through this lengthy calculation of m and s for a binomial variable; there is a 'short cut'. If we know that a random variable has a binomial distribution we can use the following formulae 8 and 9 below. The results are quoted without proof.

Formulae 8 and 9

The expected value of a binomial variable is computed as follows

$\mu = E(X) = Np$

where N is the number of trials and p is the probability of a success.

The variance of a binomial distribution is computed as follows

$\sigma^2 = Np(1 - p)$

Example

The number of heads obtained in a throw of 10 coins is binomially distributed with N = 10 and p = 0.5.

Expected value $\mu = Np = 10 \times 0.5 = 5$.

Variance $\sigma^2 = Np(1 - p) = 10 \times 0.5 \times 0.5 = 2.5$.

As always, the standard deviation σ, is the square root of the variance. So

$$\sigma = \sqrt{Np(1 - p)}.$$

For the coin example above, this will be

$$\sigma = \sqrt{Np(1 - p)} = \sqrt{2.5} = 1.5811.$$

ACTIVITY 24

Normally there is an 0.03 chance that a page of written typescript will contain an error. In documents consisting of 1000 pages, what will be the mean (expected) number of pages with an error? What will be the standard deviation of the number of pages with an error?

We can calculate results for Activity 24 as follows:

Mean number of pages in error = $Np = 1000 \times 0.03 = 30$.

Standard deviation of number of pages in error =
$$\sqrt{Np(1 - p)} = \sqrt{(1000 \times 0.03 \times 0.97)} = \sqrt{29.1} = 5.3944.$$

ACTIVITY 25

Lorries in a firms haulage fleet spend part of their time in overhaul. The number of its lorries which are in overhaul at any one time is binomially distributed with mean = 4 and variance = 3.2.

How many lorries does the firm have in its fleet, and what is the probability that less than 4 will be in overhaul at any one time?

From the statement of Activity 25 we know that

$$\mu \quad = Np = 4 \qquad\qquad \text{and}$$
$$\sigma^2 \quad = Np(1 - p) \quad = 3.2. \qquad \text{therefore}$$

$$\sigma^2 \quad = 4(1 - p) \quad = 3.2$$
$$1 - p \quad = 3.2/4 \quad = 0.8 \qquad \text{so}$$
$$p \quad = 0.2$$

$$\text{If } p \quad = 0.2 \qquad\qquad \text{then}$$

$$Np \quad = 0.2N \quad = 4$$
$$N \quad = 4/0.2 \quad = 20$$

Therefore Pr(less than 4 trucks in overhaul)=
Pr(0 or 1 or 2 or 3 in overhaul) =

$$\binom{20}{0}(0.2)^0.(0.8)^{20} + \binom{20}{1}(0.2)^1(0.8)^{19} +$$

$$\binom{20}{2}(0.2)^2.(0.8)^{18} + \binom{20}{3}(0.2)^3(0.8)^{17}$$

= 0.0115 + 0.0576 + 0.1369 + 0.2053 = 0.4113.

4. SUMMARY

In section 4 we have examined the binomial distribution:

● the **general** form of the distribution

● calculations demonstrating **binomial probabilities**

● **expected value** and **variance** of the **binomial distribution**

If you are unsure of any of these areas, check back **now** before reading on.

SECTION 5

THE NORMAL DISTRIBUTION

1. INTRODUCTION

We now move from discrete probability distributions and turn to one of the more important continuous distributions, the **normal distribution**.

Many measurements in the natural and industrial world, such as height, weight, length, thickness, time and so on, are random variables, and this random variation can be described by the normal distribution.

Take another look at figure 3, and Activity 6. Figure 3 shows a table of lifetimes for 200 Ever-Lite bulbs and, in solving Activity 6 you had to draw up a probability distribution of the data.

In statistics it is important to know the **shape** of the distribution of data. The graphs of the Ever-Lite data (figures 7 and 8) show that the distribution of lifetimes is almost symmetric, around a central or mean life of about 400 hours.

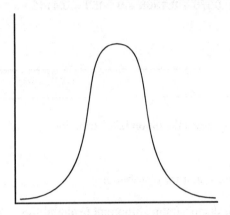

FIGURE 25: **Normal Distribution Curve**

The distribution of Ever-Lite bulb lifetimes can be said to be a **normal distribution**. The main characteristic of such a distribution is that its graph (known as a **normal curve**), has a bell shaped symmetric appearance. The graph peaks at the centre, and flattens out very quickly as it gets further away from the centre (see figure 25).

Actually, Ever-Lite bulb lifetimes are not exactly symmetrically distributed, but they are close enough.

In fact, we have already anticipated many of the characteristics of the normal distribution in the last section of unit 2, *Data Presentation*.

2. CHARACTERISTICS OF THE NORMAL DISTRIBUTION

There are four main characteristics of the normal distribution:

1.   It is bell-shaped, or symmetric, in appearance.

2.   The 'averages' of the distribution, mean, median and mode are identical.

3.   If we know that a distribution is 'normal', then all we need to know are its mean, μ, and standard deviation, σ. In technical jargon, μ and σ are said to be the parameters of the normal distribution, which means that they completely specify it.

4.   The area under the graph of the distribution between any two values of the variable can be easily estimated (see figure 26). It would be possible to find the area under the graph in figure 26 between any two points X_1 and X_2. For example, it is known that   95% of the area under the curve lies between the points μ-1.96σ and μ+1.96σ.

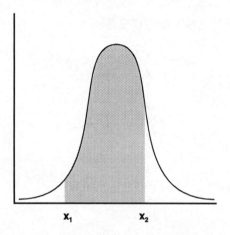

FIGURE 26: **Area Under a Normal Curve**

The last point is particularly important. If, for example, Ever-Lite bulbs have a normally distributed lifetime with mean μ=400 hours and σ=50 hours, then

μ-1.96s $= 400 - 1.96 \times 50$ $= 302$
μ+1.96s $= 400 + 1.96 \times 50$ $= 498$

So the area under the graph of Ever-lite bulbs between 302 and 498 hours is 95% of total area.

To put the matter slightly differently, an Ever-Lite bulb has a 0.95 probability of lasting between 302 and 498 hours.

This characteristic of the normal curve – the ability to estimate areas under the curve – can be generalised, as we will see later. This will prove advantageous because areas under the graph of a continuous probability function correspond to probabilities.

So, **if** we know a variable is normally distributed, and **if** we know its mean and standard deviation, then the task of estimating probabilities is simplified.

However, we need to do a little more work before we are able to take advantage of this particular property of the normal distribution.

Now consider the following Activity.

ACTIVITY 26

The following table shows results from educational tests given to 1000 pupils in a certain school region. The tests examined verbal ability on a scale from 0 to 1000.

SCORE	NO. OF PUPILS
below　225	3
225　<　275	9
275　<　325	28
325　<　375	65
375　<　425	124
425　<　475	172
475　<　525	198
525　<　575	172
575　<　625	124
625　<　675	65
675　<　725	28
725　<　775	9
775 or more	3

(a)　Sketch a frequency curve of the above data.

(b)　The mean test score for these children was 500, with a standard deviation of 100. Calculate the two values $\mu - 1.96\sigma$ and $\mu + 1.96\sigma$. Using the above table, estimate the approximate number of pupils gaining marks between $\mu - 1.96\sigma$ and $\mu + 1.96\sigma$. **Do not** make any assumptions about the normality, or otherwise, of the data when making this estimate.

(c)　Do the results of your answers to (a) and (b) suggest that the test scores are normally distributed?

Use a separate piece of paper for your answer.

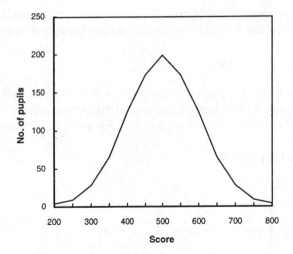

FIGURE 27: **Frequency Curve (Activity 26)**

A frequency curve for the data of Activity 26 is shown in figure 27. If

$\mu = 500$ **and** $\sigma = 100,$
then
$\mu + 1.96\sigma = 500 + 1.96 \times 100 = 696$
and
$\mu - 1.96\sigma = 500 - 1.96 \times 100 = 304.$

If we take these values as approximately 300 and 700, then we can read from the table that an estimated 948 of the 1000 pupils have scores between these numbers. In order to do this you will have to estimate roughly how many pupils score between 300 - 325 and 675 - 700, since the table is not detailed enough to make a direct reading.

If the data is normally distributed, then 95% of all pupils should obtain test scores between 304 and 696. We have seen from the table that approximately 948 pupils have scores from 300 and 700 – almost 95%. Together with the symmetry of the distribution, this is good evidence that test scores are normally distributed.

3. MEAN AND STANDARD DEVIATION OF THE NORMAL DISTRIBUTION

You should already have a good idea of what these statistics measure. Because they define the normal distribution completely, they are often referred to as **parameters** of the distribution. The mean is the value the distribution is **centred** around, while the standard deviation measures the **spread** of the data around this mean. We must know m and s before we can make probability calculations for normally-distributed data.

What happens if μ and σ change?

To understand this we look again at the data for the Ever-Lite bulb problem. Mean lifetime is 400 hours with a standard deviation of 50. If the company is able to improve mean lifetime of its bulbs to 450 hours, how will this affect the distribution?

This is illustrated in figure 28.

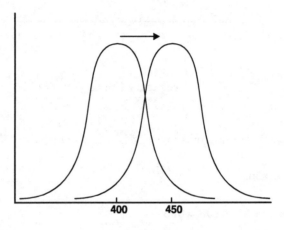

FIGURE 28

The distribution would still be normal, but it would now be centered on 450 instead of 400. The shape would remain the same, but the whole normal curve would shift to the right.

What would happen if the mean of a normal distribution remained the same, but the standard deviation altered?

ACTIVITY 27

Suppose that the standard deviation of lifetimes for Ever-Lite bulbs falls from its existing 50 hours, down to 30 hours.

The existing distribution is shown in the graph box just below this question. Make a rough sketch, on the same axes, showing what would happen after the fall in the value of σ.

⫸

Activity 27 continued...

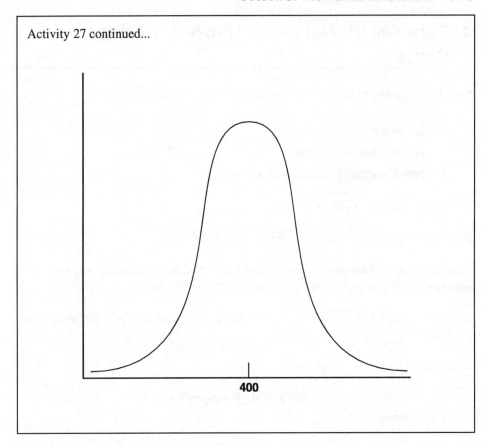

400

Figure 29 shows how the normal curve will react in response to the change described in Activity 27. The curve will remain centred on a mean of 400 hours, but will be more closely grouped around this mean. It will still be normal.

You should be easily able to generalise the result of Activity 27 to what would happen if σ increased rather than decreased.

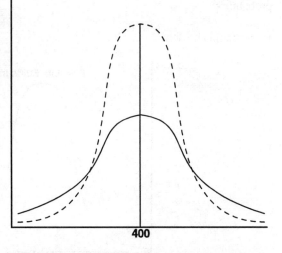

400

FIGURE 29:
Changes in the Normal Curve

—— **Normal curve with standard deviation = 50**
– – – **Normal curve with standard deviation = 30**
Both curves have mean = 400

4. PROBABILITY AND AREAS UNDER THE NORMAL CURVE

It has been established that the distribution of lifetimes of Ever-Lite bulbs

> is normal
>
> has a mean of 400 hours
>
> has a standard deviation of 50 hours.

How can we best use this information?

This question brings us back to the subject of probability.

Since we know that the normal distribution is a continuous distribution, we can answer questions relating to probability by considering areas under the curve.

Suppose we need to know the probability that an Ever-Lite bulb will last longer than 450 hours.

In probability language this is written

$$Pr(X > 450 \text{ hours})$$

where X = lifetime.

The probability $Pr(X > 450)$ can be represented by the shaded area shown in figure 30, below. If we can calculate the size of this area, then we produce the required probability.

How can this be done?

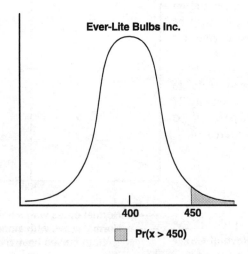

FIGURE 30: **Probability of Bulb Lasting more than 450 Hours**

Unfortunately, we cannot calculate areas under the normal curve by the geometric methods used earlier (see Activity 8). The graph of the normal distribution is not a straight line. Neither can we hope to find much comfort by referring to the mathematical function for the normal distribution. This is

$$Y = \frac{1}{\sqrt{2\pi\sigma}} \exp \ - \ \frac{1}{2} \{ \frac{x \ - \ \mu}{\sigma} \}^2$$

This is a very complex equation, and you will be glad to know that we do not actually have to make direct calculations with it.

It is given here partly for information, partly to illustrate the enormous difficulty we seem to be in. We cannot geometrically calculate areas under the normal curve, and the function is of no immediate use to us. How then, can we calculate probabilities? How can we answer questions such as

> 'what is the probability that a randomly selected Ever-Lite bulb will last longer than 450 hours?'

5. THE STANDARD NORMAL DISTRIBUTION

Statisticians have defined something called the **standard normal distribution**. They have computed areas under this distribution, and published them in table form. The standard normal distribution is

> a **normal** distribution
>
> with a **mean of 0** (zero)
>
> and a **standard deviation of 1**.

You may say that the Ever-Lite bulb lifetime distribution has a mean of 400 (not zero), and a standard deviation of 50 (not 1). So how is a table of areas under this so-called standard normal distribution of any use to us? As it happens, all normal distributions can be expressed in terms of the standard normal which **will** be of help to us. For the moment we will concern ourselves only with the standard normal distribution.

Consider figure 31, which is a small extract from a table of areas under the standard normal curve. You need not worry how these areas were calculated, as the method is beyond the scope of this programme. There is a complete table at the end of this unit.

Z	Area Between Mean and Z	Area Beyond Z
0.00	0.000000	0.500000
0.01	0.003988	0.496011
0.02	0.007977	0.492022
0.03	0.011965	0.488034
0.04	0.015952	0.484047
0.05	0.019938	0.480061
0.06	0.023921	0.476078
0.07	0.027902	0.472097
0.08	0.031880	0.468119
0.09	0.035855	0.464144
0.10	0.039827	0.460172
0.11	0.043794	0.456205

FIGURE 31: **Areas Under the Standard Normal Curve**

The table consists of three separate columns.

Column 1 is labelled '**Z**' in the tables. (Z is the symbol most often used to denote the standard normal variable.) It is the value on the horizontal axis of the graph of the function. In practice it ranges in size from -4 to +4. Look at the complete table of areas at the end of this unit, and you will see it only shows values of Z from 0 to +4. Where are the values of Z from -4 to 0 ? This will be explained shortly.

The second column in the tables is titled **Area between mean and Z.** The numbers in this column give the areas under the curve between the mean (zero) and Z. See figure 32 for an example where z = 1.5.

Area beyond Z heads the third column in the tables, and gives areas under the curve above Z.

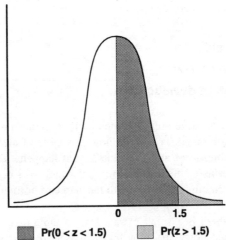

FIGURE 32: **Areas Under Curve Between Mean and Z and beyond Z**

Now suppose that you needed to know the area under the standard normal distribution between the mean and Z = 1.5.

This is equivalent to

$$Pr(0 < Z < 1.5).$$

(Remember that areas under the curve are the same as probabilities.)

Look at the full tables of area under the normal curve at the end of this unit, and you will see that the area between the mean and Z = 1.5 is 0.433192. Figure 33, below, shows an extract from the table with the appropriate line marked with a '*'.

Z	Area Between Mean and Z	Z	Area Beyond Z	Area Between Mean and Z	Area Beyond Z
1.45	0.426470	0.073529	2.00	0.477249	0.022750
1.46	0.427854	0.072145	2.01	0.477784	0.022215
1.47	0.429219	0.070780	2.02	0.478308	0.021691
1.48	0.430563	0.069436	2.03	0.478821	0.021178
1.49	0.431887	0.068112	2.04	0.479324	0.020675
1.50	0.433192*	0.066807**	2.05	0.479817	0.020182
1.51	0.434478	0.065521	2.06	0.480300	0.019699
1.52	0.435744	0.064255	2.07	0.480773	0.019226
1.53	0.436991	0.063008	2.08	0.481237	0.018762
1.54	0.438219	0.061780	2.09	0.481691	0.018308
1.55	0.439429	0.060570	2.10	0.482135	0.017864
1.56	0.440619	0.059380	2.11	0.482570	0.017429
etc	etc	etc	etc	etc	etc

* = area between mean and Z = 1.5
** = area beyond Z = 1.5

FIGURE 33: **Extract from Table of Areas Under the Standard Normal Curve**

Therefore

$$Pr(0 < Z < 1.5) = 0.433192$$

By using the appropriate column of the tables, we can also see that the area under the curve above Z = 1.5 is 0.0668. Therefore

$$Pr(Z > 1.5) = 0.066807 \text{ (see figure 33)}$$

Notice that the 2 areas (for Z > 1.5 and Z between 0 and 1.5) add up to 0.5. This should come as no surprise. As the distribution is symmetrical, you would expect to find 50% (0.5) of the area above the mean, and 50% below the mean. Check for yourself that the two columns described as 'areas between' and 'areas beyond' Z always sum to 0.5.

Now what about areas below $Z = 0$?

For example, suppose you are asked to find the area between $Z = 0$ and $Z = -1.5$. How would you do this? There are no negative values for Z in the tables of area under the normal curve.

This problem can be easily overcome. Recall that the normal distribution is symmetrical. This means that the area between 0 and -1.5 is exactly the same as the area between 0 and $Z = 1.5$. We already know this to be 0.433192.

Similarly, the area beyond $Z = -1.5$ is the same as the area beyond $Z = +1.5$. (ie 0.066807).

In probability terms

$$Pr(0 < Z < +1.5) = Pr(-1.5 < Z < 0) \quad \text{and}$$

$$Pr(Z > +1.5) = Pr(Z < -1.5)$$

This is summed up in figures 34 and 35.

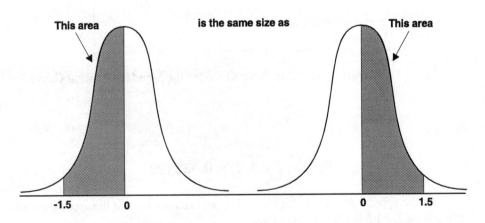

FIGURE 34: **Areas Between 0 and ±1.5**

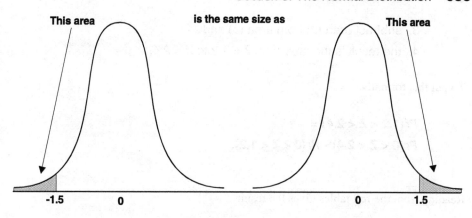

FIGURE 35: **Areas Beyond ±1.5**

Finally, consider the following:

> what is the probability that a randomly selected standard normal
> variable will be in the interval 1.2 to 2.4?

In other words, what is $Pr(1.2 < Z < 2.4)$?

To do this, we must first find the area under the standard normal curve for this interval.

The area is shown in figure 36, below.

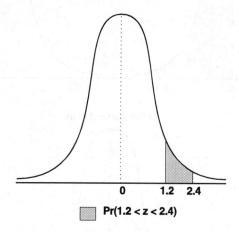

FIGURE 36: **Area Between 1.2 and 2.4**

It is an area neither above the mean, nor between the mean and Z, but is a 'strip' of area to the right of the mean. It can be estimated as follows:

1. Find the area between 0 and $Z = 2.4$ then
2. find the area between 0 and $Z = 1.2$ then

3. subtract area (2) from area (1) and

4. the result is the area from Z = 1.2 to Z = 2.4.

To put this formally

$$Pr(1.2 < Z < 2.4) =$$
$$Pr(0 < Z < 2.4) - Pr(0 < Z < 1.2).$$

Reading from the full tables gives the result

$$Pr(1.2 < Z < 2.4) = 0.491802 - 0.384930 = 0.106872$$

The process is summarised in figure 37.

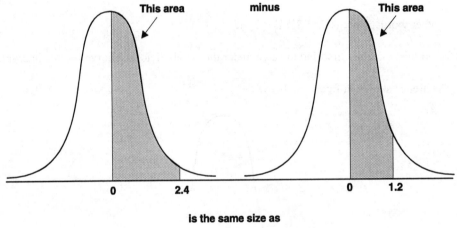

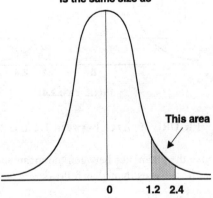

FIGURE 37: **Calculation of Strip Area**

ACTIVITY 28

Now that you know something about estimating areas under the standard normal curve you should be able to solve the following problems. On a separate sheet of paper, make sketches of the normal curve, and shade in the area for the following

(a) $Z < 0$ (b) $Z < 1$

(c) $Z > 1$ (d) $Z < -1$

(e) $0 < Z < 1$ (f) $1 < Z < 1.5$

(g) $-1 < Z < 1$ (h) $-2.5 < Z < -1.5$

Using the tables of areas under the standard normal curve, write down the numerical values of these areas.

Detailed answers are provided for Activity 28, below.

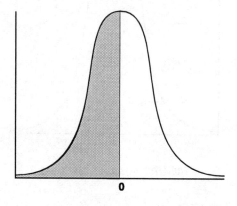

0

FIGURE 38: **Area for Z < 0**

(a) Area for Z < 0 (figure 38)

Since 0 is the mean of the standard normal curve, and the distribution is symmetrical about the mean, it automatically follows that 0.5 (50%) of the distribution is less than this value.

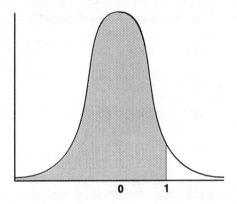

FIGURE 39: **Area for Z < 1**

(b) Area for Z < 1 (figure 39)

This just entails finding the area between the mean and Z = 1. (It is 0.341344). However, since we need the whole of the area below Z = 1, and not just the segment between 0 and 1, we must remember that 0.5 of the normal distribution is below the mean (which is 0 in this case). This makes the total area below 1,

0.341344 + 0.500000 = 0.841344.

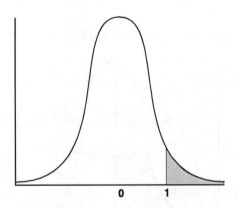

FIGURE 40: **Area for Z > 1**

(c) Area for Z > 1 (figure 40)

This only involves finding the area beyond Z = 1. From tables this is 0.158655.

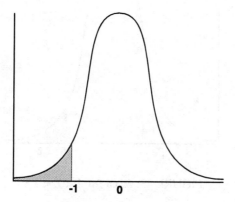

FIGURE 41: **Area for Z < -1**

(d) Area for Z < -1 (figure 41)

The standard normal tables do not give negative values of Z. However, we use the fact that Pr(Z< -1) = Pr(Z > 1). The area beyond Z = 1 we have already established from (c) to be 0.158655.

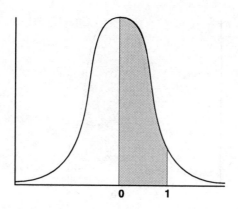

FIGURE 42: **Area for 0 < Z < 1**

(e) Area for 0 < Z < 1 (figure 42)

The area from Z = 0 (the mean) to Z = 1, we already know from (b) to be 0.341344.

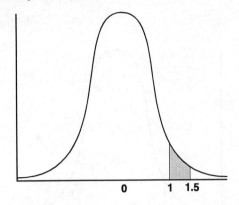

FIGURE 43: **Area for 1 < Z < 1.5**

(f) Area for 1 < Z < 1.5 (figure 43)
This can be obtained by

(area 0 < Z < 1.5) -
(area 0 < Z < 1) =
0.433192 - 0.341344 = 0.091848

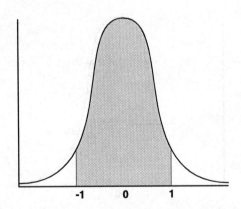

FIGURE 44: **Area -2.5 < Z < -1.5**

(g) Area for -1 < Z < 1 (figure 44)
This is

(area; -1 < Z < 0) +
(area; 0 < Z < 1) =
0.341344 + 0.341344 = 0.682688

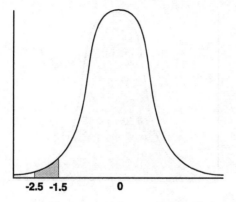

Figure 45: **Area -2.5 < Z < -1.5**

(h) Area for -2.5 < Z < -1.5 (figure 45)

This can be obtained as follows:

> **(area; -2.5 < Z < 0) -**
> **(area; -1.5 < Z < 0) =**
> **0.493790 - 0.433192 = 0.060598**

You can now find an area (probability) given a particular value of Z. Suppose we reverse the situation. If you were given an area, or probability statement relating to an unknown value of Z, could you discover what this value of Z should be?

For example, what value of x would satisfy the following probability statement?

$$Pr(Z < x) = 0.95$$

We are told here that the chance that Z is less than some (unknown) value x, is equal to 0.95. What is this value?

Figure 46 displays this area, together with the approximate position of x on the horizontal axis.

If 0.95 of the area lies below x, then 0.45 of the area must lie between the mean and x, the remaining 0.50 is below the mean.

Now using the normal tables, glance down the column labelled **area between the mean and Z** until you come to the value 0.4500. Figure 47 shows an extract from the appropriate section of the normal curve tables. As you can see, there is no exact value 0.4500 so 0.449497 has been taken as the nearest.

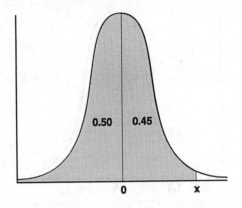

FIGURE 46: **Pr(Z) < X) = 0.95**

Z	Area Between Mean and Z	Area Beyond Z	Z	Area Between Mean and Z	Area Beyond Z
1.10	0.364333	0.135666	1.65	0.450528	0.049471
1.11	0.366500	0.133499	1.66	0.451542	0.048457
1.12	0.368642	0.131357	1.67	0.452540	0.047459
.	.	.	.	.	.
.	.	.	.	.	.
1.59	0.444082	0.055917	2.14	0.483822	0.016177
1.60	0.445200	0.054799	2.15	0.484222	0.015777
1.61	0.446301	0.053698	2.16	0.484613	0.015386
1.62	0.447383	0.052616	2.17	0.484996	0.015003
1.63	0.448449	0.051550	2.18	0.485371	0.014628
1.64	* 0.449497	0.050502	2.19	0.485737	0.014262

FIGURE 47: **Extract from Normal Curve Tables**

This area has been marked with an asterisk in the above table.

The Z value corresponding to this area is Z = 1.64.

Thus the full probability statement is

$$Pr(Z < 1.64) = 0.95$$

The final Activity in this section gives several probability statements. See if you can use the normal curve tables to estimate the unknown values. As previously, it may help to sketch the normal curve, in order to visualise the required area.

ACTIVITY 29

Find the value of x which satisfies the following probability statements

(a) $Pr(Z < x) = 0.10$
(b) $Pr(Z > x) = 0.025$
(c) $Pr(Z > x) = 0.55$
(d) $Pr(-1.8 < Z < x) = 0.6$
(e) $Pr(0 < Z < x) = 0.25$
(f) $Pr(1 < Z < x) = 0.1$
(g) $Pr(-2.8 < Z < x) = 0.05$

Sketches of the normal curve are shown below. The appropriate area, and x, have been included for each probability statement. Some notes on the solutions follow the sketches.

(a) $Pr(Z < x) = 0.1$ (figure 48)

The value, x has an area below it equal to 0.1. This must mean that x is on the left hand, or negative side of the mean (0). The required area 0.1 is below x, so look at the column of 'areas beyond Z' in the tables. The number closest to 0.1 is 0.100272, with a Z value of 1.28. Also, the value of Z sought lies in the **negative** region of the curve, so we add a minus and call it -1.28. Therefore the full probability statement becomes

$Pr(Z < -1.28) \approx 0.1$

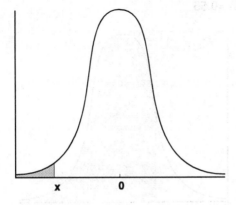

FIGURE 48: $Pr(Z < X) = 0.1$

(b) *Pr(Z > x)* = **0.025** (figure 49)
The value, x has an area above it equal to 0.025.

Since we are looking for an area smaller than 0.5, and it is an area above x, then it follows that x must lie on the positive (right hand side) of the curve. The area sought is above (beyond) Z. The nearest tabulated area is 0.024997, with a Z value of 1.96 and our probability statement becomes

Pr(Z > 1.96) ≈ 0.025

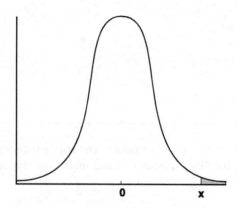

FIGURE 49: $Pr(Z > X) = 0.025$

(c) *Pr(Z > x)* = **0.55** (figure 50)
The unknown x, has an area above it equal to 0.55. As 55% is more than half of the area under the normal curve, x must be to the left of the mean. 50% of the area is above 0, leaving just 5% between 0 and x. Looking at tables, in the column marked 'area between the mean and Z', we find the nearest area to 5%, or 0.05 to be 0.051716, corresponding to a Z of -0.13. (Remember to add the negative, since x is to the left of the mean.) Therefore the probability statement becomes

Pr(Z > -0.13) ≈0.55

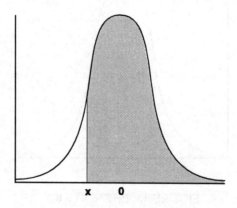

FIGURE 50: $Pr(Z > X) = 0.55$

(d) *Pr(-1.8 < Z < x) = 0.6* (figure 51)

There is an 0.6 probability that Z is above -1.8, but below some unknown x. We know that x is to the right of the mean, because of the size of the area, 0.6. Normal tables tell us that 0.464069 of the total area is between -1.8 and 0, leaving us with 0.6 - 0.464069 = 0.135931 of the required area between 0 and x.

The nearest figure in the 'areas between the mean and Z' to 0.135931 is 0.136830, with a corresponding Z of 0.35. So the probability statement is

  Pr(-1.8 < Z < 0.35) ≈ 0.6

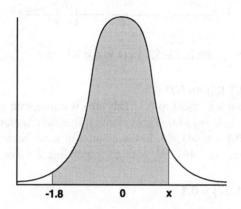

FIGURE 51: **Pr(-1.8 < Z < X) = 0.6**

(e) *Pr(0 < Z < x) = 0.25* (figure 52)

There is a 25% probability of Z being above 0 and less than x.

The required value of x can be found by finding the figure nearest to 0.25 in the 'area between' column. We find 0.248570, with a corresponding Z of 0.67. So the probability statement is

  Pr(0 < Z < 0.67) ≈ 0.25

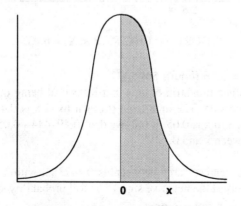

FIGURE 52: **Pr(0 < Z < X) = 0.25**

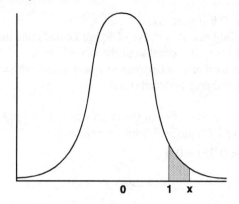

FIGURE 53: **Pr(1 < Z < X) = 0.1**

(f) *Pr*(1 < Z < x) = 0.1 (figure 53)

The area between 1 and x is equal to 0.1. This area is a thin strip to the right of 0. The area between 0 and 1 is 0.341344. (From tables.) Therefore the area between 0 and x must be 0.341344 + 0.1 = 0.441344. In the column of areas between the mean and Z, the nearest to this figure is 0.441792, with corresponding Z value of 1.57. So the full probability statement is

Pr(1 < Z < 1.57) ≈ 0.1

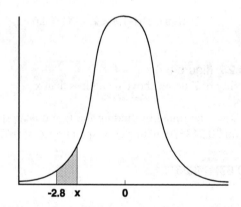

FIGURE 54: **Pr(-2.8 < Z < X) = 0.05**

(g) *Pr*(-2.8 < Z < x) = 0.05 (figure 54)

Like problem (f), this is a thin strip of area, but instead of being on the right of 0, it is on the left, or negative side. The area from 0 down to -2.8 is 0.497444, from tables. Since the area from -2.8 to x is 0.05, it follows that (0.497444 - 0.05) = 0.447444 of the total area must be between x and 0.

Tables tell us that the nearest 'area between' is 0.447383, with a corresponding Z of -1.62. (Remember to insert the negative sign.) The full probability statement is thus

Pr(-2.8 < Z < -1.62) ≈ 0.05

6. SUMMARY

In this section we have concentrated on the normal distribution:

- **characteristics**

- the **mean** and **standard deviation**

- **probability** and **areas under the normal curve**

- the **standard normal distribution**

If you are unsure of any of these topics, check back **now** before you move to the next section.

SECTION 6

USING THE NORMAL DISTRIBUTION

1. NON-STANDARD NORMAL DISTRIBUTIONS

Our introduction to the normal distribution used a rather special example, the distribution of Z, where Z is normally distributed with m = 0 and s = 1. This, as we have seen, is called the **standard normal distribution**. It is easy to deal with because tables of areas are already routinely available.

Although many variables are normally distributed, we would be unlikely to come across one with a mean of zero and a standard deviation of 1.

Consider the familiar example of the Ever-Lite bulb company. Ever-Lite bulb lifetimes are certainly normally distributed, but with mean 400 (not zero) and standard deviation 50 (not 1).

If we select an Ever-Lite bulb at random, what is the probability that it will last longer than 500 hours?

The area we are looking for is shown in figure 55. We cannot use the tables to find this area; the distribution of light bulb lifetimes is not **standard** normal. However, it was mentioned earlier that ANY normal variable could be expressed in terms of the standard normal distribution of Z. How?

We begin by using the following transformation:

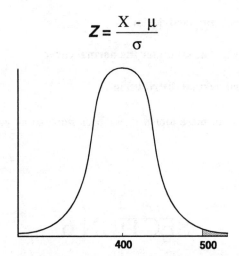

$$Z = \frac{X - \mu}{\sigma}$$

400   500

The shaded area corresponds to the probability that a randomly selected bulb lasts over 500 hours

FIGURE 55: **Probability of Bulb Lifetimes Greater Than 500 Hours**

It is sometimes called the 'Z transformation', since it has the effect of converting any normal variable into a standard normal, or Z value.

X is a non-standard normal variable, such as Ever-Lite bulb lifetimes. μ and σ are its mean and standard deviation, so if we needed to find the probability that an Ever-Lite bulb would last over 500 hours, then X = 500, μ = 400, and σ = 50.

Figure 56 illustrates how the Z-transformation works.

We cannot directly find the area under the curve beyond X in the distribution of bulb lifetimes illustrated by the first graph in figure 56. However, by using the transformation on X, we can convert it to a Z value. The area beyond Z in the second graph of figure 56, (which we can read from tables), is identical to the area beyond X. Thus we can reduce any normal variable to a corresponding Z value in the standard normal distribution.

To determine the probability that a bulb will last for longer than 500 hours, we first transform 500 into its corresponding Z value.

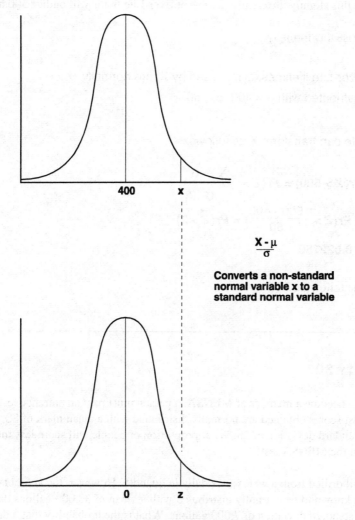

$$\frac{X - \mu}{\sigma}$$

**Converts a non-standard
normal variable x to a
standard normal variable**

FIGURE 56: **Z Transformation**

$$X = 500, \mu = 400, \sigma = 50,$$

so

$$Z = \frac{X - \mu}{\sigma} = \frac{500 - 400}{50} = 2$$

Remember that we wish to find the area greater than 500 in the original distribution, which means finding the area greater than its standard normal equivalent of $Z = 2$. This area is 0.022750, and means that Pr(Bulb last longer than 500 hours) = 0.022750.

Or, putting this slightly differently, 2.28% of Ever-Lite bulbs will outlast 500 hours.

To summarise this formally

> Ever-Lite lifetimes, symbolised by X, are normally distributed with $\mu = 400$, $\sigma = 50$.

> We can transform X as follows:

$$Pr(X > 500) = Pr\left(Z > \frac{X - \mu}{\sigma}\right)$$

$$= Pr\left(Z > \frac{500 - 400}{50}\right) = Pr(Z > 2)$$

$$= 0.022750$$

Now try the following Activity.

ACTIVITY 30

(a)   To become a member of MENSA, a person must pass an entrance test. The test scores obtained are normally distributed with a mean mark of 80, and a standard deviation of 25. What proportion of people will score less than 50 on the MENSA test?

(b)   Oil drilled from a well varies daily in quantity. However, the amount drilled is known to be normally distributed with a mean of 30,000 gallons daily and a standard deviation of 7,000 gallons. What is the probability that a day's production will be

(i)   more than 40,000 gallons?
(ii) within 500 gallons of the mean?

To find the proportion scoring less than the MENSA level of 50 we calculate the area below x = 50 on a normal distribution which has μ = 80 and σ = 25.

We begin, as always by using the Z transformation.

$$Pr(X < 50) = Pr(Z < \frac{X - \mu}{\sigma}) =$$

$$Pr(Z < \frac{50 - 80}{25}) =$$

$$Pr(Z < -1.2) = 0.115069$$

Therefore the area below x = 50 on the **non-standard** MENSA normal distribution, is the same as the area below Z = -1.2 on the **standard** normal distribution. So 11.51% of people score below 50 on the MENSA test.

Part (b) i of Activity 30 is calculated as

$$Pr(X > 40,000 \text{ gallons}) = Pr(Z > \frac{X - \mu}{\sigma}) =$$

$$Pr(Z > \frac{40,000 - 30,000}{7,000}) =$$

$$Pr(Z > 1.43) = 0.076358$$

and part (b) ii

$$Pr(29,500 < X < 30,500) = Pr(\frac{X - \mu}{\sigma} < Z < \frac{X - \mu}{\sigma}) =$$

$$Pr(\frac{29,500 - 30,000}{7,000} < Z < \frac{30,500 - 30,000}{7,000}) =$$

$$Pr(-0.07 < Z < 0.07) = 0.055804$$

If you find difficulty with problems like Activity 30 it may help to visualise the problem by sketching the normal curve and shading the appropriate region.

Activity 30 involved finding areas (probabilities) given known values of the normal variable. The next Activity reverses the procedure. Given statements about probabilities, or areas, you are required to find the appropriate values of the normal variable.

ACTIVITY 31

Look back to Activity 30 part (a). MENSA accept the top 20% of performers in the entrance test. What mark would you need to achieve in order to be admitted to membership?

Activity 31 requires you to find the mark which separates the top 20% of performers from the rest, which means that we need to solve $Pr(Mark > x) = 0.2$ for an unknown x.

$$Pr(Mark > x) = Pr(Z > \frac{X - \mu}{\sigma}) =$$

$$Pr(Z > \frac{x - 80}{25}) = 0.2$$

In this equation, x is the unknown mark.

Now since 20% (approximately) of the normal distribution lies above Z = 0.84, then we have

$$\frac{x - 80}{25} = 0.84$$

So
$$x = 0.84 \times 25 + 80 = 101.$$

So a candidate would need to achieve a mark in excess of 101 in order to be admitted to MENSA.

Activity 32 introduces yet another twist. Given statements about probabilities (areas) and other information, you are required to find the unknown mean of a normal distribution. You may well find this problem rather more demanding than those you have previously dealt with.

ACTIVITY 32

Machinery packs goods into packages advertised as being nominally 9 kg in weight. In fact, because of slight variability in machine performance, the actual pack weight may be above or below 9 kg. However, it is known that the machine produces packs whose weight is normally distributed, with a standard deviation of 0.06 kg. (The mean weight is manually set by the machine operator.) Because of regulations governing short weight, the firm producing the packages must ensure that no more than 1% of packs fall below the advertised 9 kg weight.

(a)   What mean weight should the machine be set at, in order to guarantee the firm meets this regulation?

Activity 32 continued...

(b)   The firm could use an alternative packing machine which operates to a
standard deviation of 0.03 kg. They produce 2,500,000 of these packs each
month. The cost C, in pence, of producing a pack weighing g kilograms
is given by the expression;

$C = 6.5 + 0.5g.$

Determine the monthly savings which could be achieved by changing to the
alternative machine.

The first part of this Activity requires you to calculate a value for m. First, we construct
a probability statement using the data in the question.

We are told that only 1% of packs (at the very most) should be less than 9 kg in weight.

So;

$$\textbf{\textit{Pr}(weight < 9 kg) = 0.01.}$$

$$\textbf{\textit{Pr}(Z < \frac{9 - \mu}{0.06}) = 0.01}$$

Since we are dealing with the 1% of packs with the **lowest** weight we are in the negative left hand side of the distribution. The nearest area beyond Z to 1% (0.01) is 0.009903, with a corresponding Z of -2.33. (Remember always to add the negative sign if needed.) Therefore

$$\frac{9 - \mu}{0.06} = \textbf{-2.33} \quad \therefore \quad \mu = 9 + 0.06 \times 2.33 = 9.1398$$

The mean weight should be set at 9.1398 kg.

If the firm use the alternative machine with a standard deviation of 0.03 kg, how does this affect the mean setting?

All we need do to solve this is to repeat the above calculation, substituting $\sigma = 0.03$ instead of 0.06.

This will give a value for the mean setting of $\mu = 9.0699$ kg.

The existing machine must be set at $\mu = 9.1398$ to comply with the law, while the alternative could be set at $\mu = 9.0699$.

The cost of producing a pack weighing g kilos is

$$\textbf{C = 6.5 + 0.5g}$$

So for a pack weighing (on average) 9.1398 kg we have

$$\textbf{C = 6.5 + 0.5} \times \textbf{9.1398 = 11.0699 pence}$$

For a pack weighing (on average) 9.0699 kg we have

C = 6.5 + 0.5 × 9.0699 = 11.03495 pence

Therefore it costs an average of 11.06990 pence to produce a pack on the existing equipment and 11.03495 pence on the alternative equipment. The alternative machine offers us a saving of 11.06990 - 11.03495 = 0.03495 pence for each pack produced. This is not much of a saving as such, but over a month, and 2,500,000 packs, it would amount to £873.75.

---

2. THE NORMAL CURVE AND BINOMIAL PROBABILITIES

Try to provide answers to the two problems in Activity 33 by using the binomial distribution.

Warning: you may not get very far with problem (2), but try it anyway, just to convince yourself of its difficulty. What is the reason for its difficulty?

ACTIVITY 33

(1)   What is the probability that a sample of 10 products contains 2 or more defectives, if the batch from which the sample came is known to be 5% defective?

(2)   70% of the computer programmers who are hired to work for a major
        computer company have had previous work experience in programming. In
a   sample of 35 of the firm's programmers, what is the probability that less
        than 20 had previous experience in programming?

You should have few difficulties with the first problem of Activity 33, but the second is quite a different matter.

Problem 1

The distribution of the number of defectives in a sample of 10 goods is binomial, with $N = 10$ and $p = 0.05$.

$$Pr(X \text{ defectives}) = \binom{10}{X}(0.05)^X(0.95)^{10-X}$$

So

$$Pr(2 \text{ or more defects}) = 1 - Pr(0 \text{ or } 1 \text{ defects})$$
$$= 1 - [(0.95^{10}) + (10 \times 0.05 \times 0.95^9)] \approx 0.0861.$$

Problem 2

The number of programmers in a sample of 35 who have had previous work experience is a binomial variable with $N = 35$ and $p = 0.70$.

$$Pr(X \text{ employees with experience}) = \binom{35}{X}(0.70)^X(0.30)^{35-X}$$

Therefore

$$Pr(\text{less than 20 have had experience})$$
$$= Pr(0 \text{ or } 1 \text{ or } 2 \text{ or } ..... \text{ or } 19 \text{ have experience}).$$

As this is an awkward calculation we will not proceed with the solution at this point, but we will look at an easier way of solving such problems.

The difficulty lies in the fact that $N = 35$, and it is difficult to calculate binomial probabilities when N reaches any appreciable size.

Fortunately, there is a short cut method for calculating binomial probabilities for large values of N.

As the number of trials, N, in a binomial experiment increases, the 'shape' of the binomial distribution begins to look more and more like the normal curve. For all practical purposes, we can regard the distribution of X, the number of successes, as normal (if N is large).

In order to illustrate, see figure 57, which contains a bar chart for the this problem of Activity 33.

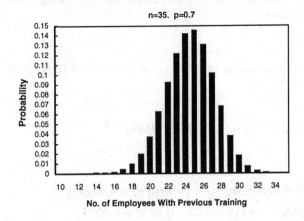

FIGURE 57: **Binomial Distribution (Activity 33)**

Since there is a 70% chance that a programmer has had previous experience before joining the computer firm, we need a binomial distribution with N = 35 and p = 0.7. Figure 57 shows such a bar chart. The heights of the bars show the probabilities of 0, 1, 2, 3 ..... 35 employees having had previous work experience. Notice that the bar chart is very symmetrical.

Recall that the mean of a binomial distribution is Np.

For the distribution in question, the mean number of employees in a sample of 35 who will have had previous relevant work experience is

$$Np = 35 \times 0.7 = 24.5$$

Similarly, the standard deviation for the data is

$$\sigma =$$
$$\sqrt{Np(1 - p)} =$$
$$\sqrt{(35 \times 0.7 \times 0.3)} \approx 2.711$$

Figure 58 shows a normal curve with a mean of 24.5, and a standard deviation of 2.711. Notice the similarity between the binomial bar chart and the normal curve.

This similarity between the two graphs enables us to treat the distribution of the number of programmers with prior experience as though it were a normal distribution, in this case with $\mu = 24.5$ and $\sigma = 2.712$.

Therefore, in order to calculate the probability that less than 20 will have had prior experience, we merely find the area under the normal curve less than X = 20.

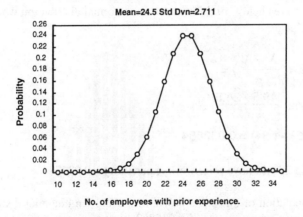

FIGURE 58: **Normal Distribution**

This area is shown in figure 59.

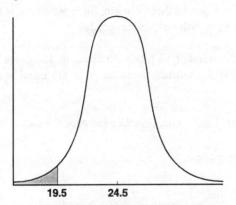

The shaded area corresponds to the
probability that fewer than 20 programmers
will have had previous job experience

FIGURE 59: **Area Showing Previous Experience**

Important Note

One thing you should notice from figure 59 is that the actual area shaded in is the area less than 19.5, **not** 20. Why is this?

It is because the binomial distribution is **discrete**, while the normal distribution is **continuous**. We have to make a correction of 0.5 to the figure we are working with to allow for the difference in nature between the two distributions. What this means in practice is that to calculate the probability of less than 20, we must correct the value to 19.5 before we can use the normal distribution to calculate binomial probabilities. This is known as the **correction for continuity**, and you must use it whenever you use this method to calculate binomial probabilities. You will read more about this so-called correction for continuity later.

Calculating the area below 19.5 for an assumed normal distribution where $\mu = 24.5$ and $\sigma = 2.711$ we have

$$Pr(Z < \frac{X - \mu}{\sigma}) =$$

$$Pr(Z < \frac{19.5 - 24.5}{2.711}) =$$

$$Pr(Z < -1.84) = 0.032884$$

So Pr(less than 20 will have prior work experience) = 0.032884.

A lengthy calculation of this same probability using the binomial distribution formula would have given us an answer of 0.035882, so we can see that comparing these two numbers, the normal approximation gives us an answer accurate to two decimal places. This is close enough for many purposes.

Finally, we consider just one further example. Suppose a coin is tossed 12 times. What is the probability that there will be 4 or less heads?

The distribution of the number of heads obtained in 12 tosses of a coin is certainly binomial. We could, if we wished, calculate it in the usual way using the binomial formula.

But if we use the normal approximation then we need the mean, which is

$$Np = 12 \times 0.5 = 6$$

and the standard deviation

$$\sqrt{Np(1 - p)} = \sqrt{(12 \times 0.5 \times 0.5)} = \sqrt{3}$$

We wish to calculate Pr(No. of heads ≤ 4).

Making the correction for continuity, this would mean finding the area under the assumed normal curve below 4.5. Why? Because the probability statement says '≤ 4'; less than or equal to 4.

To include 4, we would need to correct to 4.5. Had the probability statement been '< 4' we would have had to correct to 3.5, (in order to exclude the 4).

$$Pr(Z < \frac{X - \mu}{\sigma}) =$$

$$Pr(Z < \frac{4.5 - 6}{\sqrt{3}}) =$$

$$Pr(Z < -0.87) = 0.192150$$

Working out this probability the traditional binomial way, we would obtain 0.194. Therefore we conclude that the normal approximation to the binomial distribution gives fairly accurate results. However, does the method always give good approximations?

Earlier, we stated that the binomial distribution resembles the normal distribution only for large values of N. This implies that we cannot use the method for small values of N. How large is large? A reasonable rule of thumb suggests that you use the normal approximation only if Np and N(1-p) are both greater than 5.

ACTIVITY 34

In a throw of 12 coins, what is the probability of obtaining more than 5 heads?

The number of heads obtained in a throw of 12 coins is binomial with N = 12 and p = 0.5.

Also,

$$m = Np = 12 \times 0.5 = 6.$$
$$s = \sqrt{Np(1-p)} = \sqrt{12 \times 0.5 \times 0.5} = \sqrt{3}$$

Notice that Np = 6 is greater than 5, but Np(1 - p) = 3, which is less than 5. Thus we would not strictly have the correct conditions for using this method.

Nevertheless, using the normal approximation we have

$$Pr(Heads{>}5) = Pr(x > 5.5) = Pr(Z > \frac{x - \mu}{\sigma})$$
$$Pr(Z > \frac{5.5 - 6}{\sqrt{3}}) = Pr(Z > -0.29) = 0.614091$$

(Note the correction for continuity).

A calculation using the full binomial distribution gives this probability as 0.613, and the normal approximation gives quite accurate results in this case, even though Np(1 - p) < 5.

ACTIVITY 35

On an exam paper containing 50 questions that ask for a true or false answer, a student scored 35 correct answers. How likely is it that the student was guessing the answers to the question?

If the student is merely guessing whether to answer true or false, then he/she has an 0.5 chance of getting any single question right or wrong. The number of correct questions in a paper of 50 will follow a binomial distribution with N = 50 and p = 0.5. In order to see just how likely it is that a student could correctly guess the answers to 35 questions, we can start by calculating the probability of getting 35 or more correct answers.

$$N = 50 \text{ and } p = 0.5. \ \mu = Np = 50 \times 0.5 = 25$$

$$s = \sqrt{Np(1-p)} = \sqrt{50 \times 0.5 \times 0.5} = \sqrt{12.5}$$

$$Pr(\text{Number of correct answers} \geq 35) = Pr(x > 34.5)$$

$$Pr\left(Z > \frac{x - \mu}{\sigma}\right) = Pr\left(Z > \frac{34.5 - 25}{\sqrt{12.5}}\right) = Pr(Z > 2.69)$$

You will see from tables that for Z = 2.69, there is an area of 0.003572 beyond Z. We can conclude therefore that

$$Pr(\text{Student guesses 35 or more answers}) = 0.003572$$

Since this is a very low probability we can say that a student who gets 35 (or more) correct answers is unlikely to be guessing.

ACTIVITY 36

A customer bought 100 hyacinth bulbs from a nursery which advertised them as 87.5% sure to produce plants if the planting instructions were followed. The customer follows the planting instructions, and finds that only 83 plants are produced. As a result, he considers the nurseries' advertising claim to be false.

Calculate the probability that a sample of 100 hyacinth bulbs would have 17 or more failures if the nursery claim is correct. Use your answer to comment on the customer's belief that the claim is false.

The number of successful germinations from 100 hyacinth bulbs is a binomial variable with $N = 100$ and $p = 0.875$. Also $m = Np = 100 \times 0.875 = 87.5$.

$$s = \sqrt{Np(1-p)} = \sqrt{100 \times 0.875 \times 0.125} = \sqrt{10.9375}$$

In order to test whether the claim is false we can begin by calculating the probability of getting 83 (or fewer) successful germinations.

$$Pr(\text{number of germinations} \leq 83) = Pr(x < 83.5) =$$

$$Pr(Z < \frac{x - \mu}{\sigma}) = Pr(Z < \frac{83.5 - 87.5}{\sqrt{10.9375}}) = Pr(Z < -1.21)$$

The area beyond $Z = -1.21$ is 0.113139. Therefore

$$Pr(\text{There are 83 or fewer germinations}) = 0.113139$$

This means that there is just over an 11% chance that a batch of 100 hyacinth bulbs would have 83 or less successful plants, or 17 unsuccessful plants. Now as 11% is not a low probability, the nurseryman could argue that the customer's result could easily have happened by chance and therefore does not invalidate the advertising claim.

3. SUMMARY

In this final section we have extended the discussion of the normal distribution to cover

- **non-standard** normal distributions

- **normal curves** and **binomial probabilities**

supported by using worked examples.

4. UNIT SUMMARY AND CONCLUSIONS

This unit has been concerned with probability distributions. We have seen that probability statements for continuous variables relate to intervals, while for discrete variables they may also relate to discrete data points. Both types of variables can be described using tables graphs or functions, although we need to be aware of the differences between using these methods for each variable.

The calculation of probabilities for continuous data involves finding the size of an area under the graph of a continuous probability distribution. This presupposes that we know the shape of the graph of a distribution and/or its exact mathematical function. In many cases this knowledge is missing.

Several probability distributions have been discovered which can be used to model real world situations.

In this unit you have read about two of these, the binomial distribution which models discrete variables, and the normal distribution which relates to continuous data. We have seen that resolving probability questions with the normal distribution reduces to dealing with the standard normal curve. Lastly, we saw how, with corrections for continuity, the normal distribution could be used to solve cumbersome calculations for some binomial variables.

If you are uncertain about any part of this unit take the time to look back and, if necessary, reread and rework the explanations and examples.

REFERENCES

Students may follow up this subject by reading the following texts:

1. CURWIN & SLATER. *Quantitative Methods for Business Decisions*. Chapman & Hall.
   Chapters 11 and 12 give a good account of probability distributions. You should note that chapter 11 deals with the Poisson distribution, which has not been covered in this unit.
2. MORRIS. C. *Quantitative Approaches in Business Studies*. Pitman Publishing.
   Chapter 9 gives an overview of the Binomial and Normal distributions.
3. MOSTELLER. *Probability With Statistical Applications*. Addison-Wesley.
   This book offers a very good complete account of probability, including distribution theory. You will find this book fairly challenging, and you should only use it if you have found the material in this unit straightforward and would like some further work.

GLOSSARY

The following is an alphabetical listing of the technical terms most often encountered in this unit.

Binomial variable   A variable which can assume any one of two values, usually described as 'success' and 'fail' is known as a binomial variable. The chance of a success or a fail remains constant for repeated observations of the variable.

Binomial distribution   A binomial distribution describes the probability of obtaining X successes in N observations of a binomial variable.

Continuous probability distribution   Any probability distribution where the variable is continuous.

Continuous variable   A variable which can take any value within a given range is said to be a continuous variable. Continuous variables are measured rather than counted.

Correction for continuity   This is used when attempting to make approximate estimates of binomial probabilities using the normal distribution. The normal distribution is continuous, while the binomial distribution is discrete. Hence the need to make a correction.

Discrete probability distribution   Any probability distribution where the variable is discrete.

Discrete variable   A variable which can only take a limited number of values (for example, integers) within a given range is said to be a discrete variable. Discrete variables are counted rather than measured.

Expected value of a random variable   A measure of central tendency for a random variable. A concept very similar to the arithmetic mean of a frequency distribution.

Failure   One of the two outcomes of a binomial experiment is classified as a failure, or fail. Usually, this term is reserved for the outcome which is not being counted by the analyst.

Normal distribution   A continuous probability distribution which is symmetrical and bell-shaped, and is exactly specified by just its mean and variance.

Normally-distributed variable   Any variable which has a normal distribution is said to be a normal variable, or normally distributed.

Normal approximation to the binomial distribution   In cases where N, the number of trials, is large, the normal distribution can be used to give approximate estimates for binomial probabilities. The method offers a considerable simplification of the calculation process.

Probability distribution   A statement of all of the possible outcomes of a random experiment, together with the probabilities of these outcomes.

Probability function   A mathematical expression which describes a probability distribution.

Standard normal variable   A variable which is normally distributed with mean = 0 and standard deviation = 1 is called a standard normal variable.

Success   The outcome of a binomial trial which is of interest to the analyst is often referred to as a success.

Variance of a random variable   A measure of variability for a random variable. Similar to the variance of a frequency distribution.

Z transformation   This is a mathematical process which transforms non-standard normal variables into standard form, thus allowing the use of special statistical tables.

TABLES OF AREAS UNDER THE STANDARD NORMAL CURVE

TABLE VALUES CALCULATED USING HASTINGS BEST APPROXIMATION

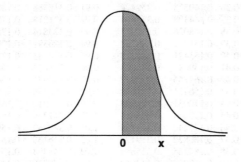

Z	Area Between Mean and Z	Area Beyond Z	Z	Area Between Mean and Z	Area Beyond Z
0.00	0.000000	0.500000	0.55	0.208840	0.291159
0.01	0.003988	0.496011	0.56	0.212259	0.287740
0.02	0.007977	0.492022	0.57	0.215660	0.284339
0.03	0.011965	0.488034	0.58	0.219042	0.280957
0.04	0.015952	0.484047	0.59	0.222404	0.277595
0.05	0.019938	0.480061	0.60	0.225746	0.274253
0.06	0.023921	0.476078	0.61	0.229068	0.270931
0.07	0.027902	0.472097	0.62	0.232370	0.267629
0.08	0.031880	0.468119	0.63	0.235652	0.264347
0.09	0.035855	0.464144	0.64	0.238913	0.261086
0.10	0.039827	0.460172	0.65	0.242153	0.257846
0.11	0.043794	0.456205	0.66	0.245372	0.254627
0.12	0.047757	0.452242	0.67	0.248570	0.251429
0.13	0.051716	0.448283	0.68	0.251747	0.248252
0.14	0.055669	0.444330	0.69	0.254902	0.245097
0.15	0.059617	0.440382	0.70	0.258036	0.241963
0.16	0.063558	0.436441	0.71	0.261147	0.238852
0.17	0.067494	0.432505	0.72	0.264237	0.235762
0.18	0.071423	0.428576	0.73	0.267304	0.232695
0.19	0.075344	0.424655	0.74	0.270349	0.229650
0.20	0.079259	0.420740	0.75	0.273372	0.226627
0.21	0.083165	0.416834	0.76	0.276372	0.223627
0.22	0.087063	0.412936	0.77	0.279349	0.220650
0.23	0.090953	0.409046	0.78	0.282304	0.217695
0.24	0.094834	0.405165	0.79	0.285235	0.214764
0.25	0.098705	0.401294	0.80	0.288144	0.211855
0.26	0.102567	0.397432	0.81	0.291029	0.208970
0.27	0.106419	0.393580	0.82	0.293891	0.206108
0.28	0.110260	0.389739	0.83	0.296730	0.203269
0.29	0.114091	0.385908	0.84	0.299545	0.200454
0.30	0.117910	0.382089	0.85	0.302337	0.197662
0.31	0.121719	0.378280	0.86	0.305105	0.194894
0.32	0.125515	0.374484	0.87	0.307849	0.192150
0.33	0.129299	0.370700	0.88	0.310570	0.189429
0.34	0.133071	0.366928	0.89	0.313266	0.186733
0.35	0.136830	0.363169	0.90	0.315939	0.184060
0.36	0.140575	0.359424	0.91	0.318588	0.181411
0.37	0.144308	0.355691	0.92	0.321213	0.178786
0.38	0.148026	0.351973	0.93	0.323814	0.176185
0.39	0.151731	0.348268	0.94	0.326391	0.173608
0.40	0.155421	0.344578	0.95	0.328943	0.171056
0.41	0.159096	0.340903	0.96	0.331472	0.168527
0.42	0.162756	0.337243	0.97	0.333976	0.166023
0.43	0.166401	0.333598	0.98	0.336456	0.163543
0.44	0.170031	0.329968	0.99	0.338912	0.161087
0.45	0.173644	0.326355	1.00	0.341344	0.158655
0.46	0.177241	0.322758	1.01	0.343752	0.156247
0.47	0.180822	0.319177	1.02	0.346135	0.153864
0.48	0.184385	0.315614	1.03	0.348494	0.151505
0.49	0.187932	0.312067	1.04	0.350829	0.149170
0.50	0.191462	0.308537	1.05	0.353140	0.146859
0.51	0.194973	0.305026	1.06	0.355427	0.144572
0.52	0.198467	0.301532	1.07	0.357690	0.142309
0.53	0.201943	0.298056	1.08	0.359928	0.140071
0.54	0.205401	0.294598	1.09	0.362143	0.137856

Z	Area Between Mean and Z	Area Beyond Z	Z	Area Between Mean and Z	Area Beyond Z
1.10	0.364333	0.135666	1.65	0.450528	0.049471
1.11	0.366500	0.133499	1.66	0.451542	0.048457
1.12	0.368642	0.131357	1.67	0.452540	0.047459
1.13	0.370761	0.129238	1.68	0.453521	0.046478
1.14	0.372856	0.127143	1.69	0.454486	0.045513
1.15	0.374927	0.125072	1.70	0.455434	0.044565
1.16	0.376975	0.123024	1.71	0.456367	0.043632
1.17	0.378999	0.121000	1.72	0.457283	0.042716
1.18	0.380999	0.119000	1.73	0.458184	0.041815
1.19	0.382976	0.117023	1.74	0.459070	0.040929
1.20	0.384930	0.115069	1.75	0.459940	0.040059
1.21	0.386860	0.113139	1.76	0.460796	0.039203
1.22	0.388767	0.111232	1.77	0.461636	0.038363
1.23	0.390651	0.109348	1.78	0.462462	0.037537
1.24	0.392512	0.107487	1.79	0.463273	0.036726
1.25	0.394350	0.105649	1.80	0.464069	0.035930
1.26	0.396165	0.103834	1.81	0.464852	0.035147
1.27	0.397957	0.102042	1.82	0.465620	0.034379
1.28	0.399727	0.100272	1.83	0.466375	0.033624
1.29	0.401474	0.098525	1.84	0.467115	0.032884
1.30	0.403199	0.096800	1.85	0.467843	0.032156
1.31	0.404901	0.095098	1.86	0.468557	0.031442
1.32	0.406582	0.093417	1.87	0.469258	0.030741
1.33	0.408240	0.091759	1.88	0.469945	0.030054
1.34	0.409877	0.090122	1.89	0.470621	0.029378
1.35	0.411491	0.088508	1.90	0.471283	0.028716
1.36	0.413084	0.086915	1.91	0.471933	0.028066
1.37	0.414656	0.085343	1.92	0.472571	0.027428
1.38	0.416206	0.083793	1.93	0.473196	0.026803
1.39	0.417735	0.082264	1.94	0.473810	0.026189
1.40	0.419243	0.080756	1.95	0.474411	0.025588
1.41	0.420730	0.079269	1.96	0.475002	0.024997
1.42	0.422196	0.077803	1.97	0.475580	0.024419
1.43	0.423641	0.076358	1.98	0.476148	0.023851
1.44	0.425066	0.074933	1.99	0.476704	0.023295
1.45	0.426470	0.073529	2.00	0.477249	0.022750
1.46	0.427854	0.072145	2.01	0.477784	0.022215
1.47	0.429219	0.070780	2.02	0.478308	0.021691
1.48	0.430563	0.069436	2.03	0.478821	0.021178
1.49	0.431887	0.068112	2.04	0.479324	0.020675
1.50	0.433192	0.066807	2.05	0.479817	0.020182
1.51	0.434478	0.065521	2.06	0.480300	0.019699
1.52	0.435744	0.064255	2.07	0.480773	0.019226
1.53	0.436991	0.063008	2.08	0.481237	0.018762
1.54	0.438219	0.061780	2.09	0.481691	0.018308
1.55	0.439429	0.060570	2.10	0.482135	0.017864
1.56	0.440619	0.059380	2.11	0.482570	0.017429
1.57	0.441792	0.058207	2.12	0.482997	0.017002
1.58	0.442946	0.057053	2.13	0.483414	0.016585
1.59	0.444082	0.055917	2.14	0.483822	0.016177
1.60	0.445200	0.054799	2.15	0.484222	0.015777
1.61	0.446301	0.053698	2.16	0.484613	0.015386
1.62	0.447383	0.052616	2.17	0.484996	0.015003
1.63	0.448449	0.051550	2.18	0.485371	0.014628
1.64	0.449497	0.050502	2.19	0.485737	0.014262
			2.20	0.486096	0.013903
			2.21	0.486400	0.013600

Z	Area Between Mean and Z	Area Beyond Z	Z	Area Between Mean and Z	Area Beyond Z
2.22	0.486790	0.013209	2.79	0.497364	0.002635
2.23	0.487126	0.012873	2.80	0.497444	0.002555
2.24	0.487454	0.012545	2.81	0.497522	0.002477
2.25	0.487775	0.012224	2.82	0.497598	0.002401
2.26	0.488089	0.011910	2.83	0.497672	0.002327
2.27	0.488396	0.011603	2.84	0.497744	0.002255
2.28	0.488696	0.011303	2.85	0.497813	0.002186
2.29	0.488989	0.011010	2.86	0.497881	0.002118
2.30	0.489275	0.010724	2.87	0.497947	0.002052
2.31	0.489555	0.010444	2.88	0.498011	0.001988
2.32	0.489829	0.010170	2.89	0.498073	0.001926
2.33	0.490096	0.009903	2.90	0.498134	0.001865
2.34	0.490358	0.009641	2.91	0.498192	0.001807
2.35	0.490613	0.009386	2.92	0.498249	0.001750
2.36	0.490862	0.009137	2.93	0.498305	0.001694
2.37	0.491105	0.008894	2.94	0.498358	0.001641
2.38	0.491343	0.008656	2.95	0.498411	0.001588
2.39	0.491575	0.008424	2.96	0.498461	0.001538
2.40	0.491802	0.008197	2.97	0.498510	0.001489
2.41	0.492023	0.007976	2.98	0.498558	0.001441
2.42	0.492239	0.007760	2.99	0.498605	0.001394
2.43	0.492450	0.007549	3.00	0.498650	0.001349
2.44	0.492656	0.007343	3.01	0.498693	0.001306
2.45	0.492857	0.007142	3.02	0.498736	0.001263
2.46	0.493053	0.006946	3.03	0.498777	0.001222
2.47	0.493244	0.006755	3.04	0.498817	0.001182
2.48	0.493430	0.006569	3.05	0.498855	0.001144
2.49	0.493612	0.006387	3.06	0.498893	0.001106
2.50	0.493790	0.006209	3.07	0.498929	0.001070
2.51	0.493963	0.006036	3.08	0.498964	0.001035
2.52	0.494132	0.005867	3.09	0.498999	0.001000
2.53	0.494296	0.005703	3.10	0.499032	0.000967
2.54	0.494457	0.005542	3.11	0.499064	0.000935
2.55	0.494613	0.005386	3.12	0.499095	0.000904
2.56	0.494766	0.005233	3.13	0.499125	0.000874
2.57	0.494915	0.005084	3.14	0.499155	0.000844
2.58	0.495059	0.004940	3.15	0.499183	0.000816
2.59	0.495201	0.004798	3.16	0.499211	0.000788
2.60	0.495338	0.004661	3.17	0.499237	0.000762
2.61	0.495472	0.004527	3.18	0.499263	0.000736
2.62	0.495603	0.004396	3.19	0.499288	0.000711
2.63	0.495730	0.004269	3.20	0.499312	0.000687
2.64	0.495854	0.004145	3.21	0.499336	0.000663
2.65	0.495975	0.004024	3.22	0.499358	0.000641
2.66	0.496092	0.003907	3.23	0.499380	0.000619
2.67	0.496207	0.003792	3.24	0.499402	0.000597
2.68	0.496318	0.003681	3.25	0.499422	0.000577
2.69	0.496427	0.003572	3.30	0.499516	0.000483
2.70	0.496532	0.003467	3.35	0.499595	0.000404
2.71	0.496635	0.003364	3.40	0.499663	0.000336
2.72	0.496735	0.003264	3.45	0.499719	0.000280
2.73	0.496833	0.003166	3.50	0.499767	0.000232
2.74	0.496927	0.003072	3.60	0.499840	0.000159
2.75	0.497020	0.002979	3.70	0.499892	0.000107
2.76	0.497109	0.002890	3.80	0.499927	0.000072
2.77	0.497197	0.002802	3.90	0.499951	0.000048
2.78	0.497281	0.002718	4.00	0.499968	0.000031

UNIT 7

INTRODUCTION TO SAMPLING

CONTENTS

UNIT OBJECTIVES

After studying this unit you will be able to

- understand the meaning of the terms; sample, sampling error, census and population

- calculate estimates from sample data

- calculate confidence intervals for sample estimates

- calculate the size of sample required in order to make estimates to a specified degree of precision

- explain the meaning of both point and interval estimates

- construct simple significance tests involving means and proportions

SECTION 1

SAMPLE AND POPULATION

1. INTRODUCTION

Think about the following problems:

PROBLEM 1

A company is considering whether or not to launch a new brand of microwave precooked dinners. It would like to know how much consumers spend on such products, including competing brands.

PROBLEM 2

The Very Sensible Party is about to start campaigning in the forthcoming by-election in the UK constituency of Podville East. It would like an estimate of the amount of support presently enjoyed by each of the main political parties.

In the above two situations it is necessary to consider how such information may be obtained. As you will discover from working through this unit the kind of information required can only be found by taking samples.

That is why we are concerned with how we collect sample data, how we calculate estimates of statistics from sample data and how we interpret the estimates obtained from our sampling operations.

2. RANDOM SAMPLING

A technique called **random sampling** is at the heart of the process of estimation. We shall start with a simple example.

Case Study: The Village of Hamdon-on-the-Marsh

The village consists of 60 households, and we wish to discover the average weekly spending on groceries for every household in the village. To do this, we start by assuming that we are unable (for practical reasons) to contact every single household. We decide therefore to obtain an estimate of expenditure by just taking a sample of 12 households. How do you think we should proceed?

Firstly, we need a list of all households in the village and we find that such a list is provided by the local government registration lists.

Figure 1 below provides these data together with the average weekly grocery bill for each household. Grocery bill data would not come from local government registration lists but would have been obtained by asking the households direct.

No.	Grocery Bill	No.	Grocery Bill
1	69.60	31	87.10
2	65.20	32	78.20
3	61.50	33	55.60
4	48.00	34	72.60
5	61.20	35	76.40
6	49.80	36	72.90
7	58.40	37	61.30
8	72.80	38	55.10
9	79.10	39	81.10
10	51.30	40	68.80
11	56.30	41	86.00
12	65.30	42	72.60
13	77.00	43	64.50
14	80.80	44	68.20
15	50.40	45	85.40
16	79.80	46	75.20
17	65.10	47	72.20
18	63.20	48	92.50
19	68.20	49	80.70
20	51.60	50	91.20
21	55.80	51	77.30
22	46.00	52	80.20
23	71.90	53	73.60
24	53.10	54	91.60
25	50.40	55	75.00
26	75.40	56	78.80
27	77.00	57	67.50
28	63.50	58	69.00
29	70.00	59	83.10
30	73.90	60	82.10

FIGURE 1: **Population of Hamdon; Weekly Grocery Bills for 60 Households**

A random sample of 12 households is taken from the list. A random sample is a sample where all households in the population have the same chance of being selected.

Each household is given a number from 1 to 60 these numbers are written on slips of paper and the slips placed in a hat.

A sample of 12 households is then taken by selecting 12 slips of paper from the hat.

We could use any of two major methods of random sampling.

SAMPLING WITH REPLACEMENT

A number is selected and the household with that number is included in the sample. The number is then replaced in the hat. It is possible to pick the same number more than once using this method.

SAMPLING WITHOUT REPLACEMENT

Select a number, as before, but do not return it to the hat. This way a household can only be picked once.

Most samples used to collect business, economic and social data are taken **without replacement**. It seems reasonable to give each household only one chance of appearing in the sample. However, it must be stated that much of the theory which supports the use of sampling is based upon using the **with replacement** method. Fortunately most of the observations which will be made in this unit will apply to any simple random sample whether it is with or without replacement. Nevertheless you should be aware that certain simplifications have been made in this unit in order to make the practical applications of sampling clearer. As with many other very useful analytical techniques, the mathematical background behind sampling can be very difficult. We do not necessarily need to know all of this mathematics in order to make use of sampling techniques.

3. SELECTING A RANDOM SAMPLE

If you go back for a moment to our householders example, we have already said that a simple random sample of households is a sample where every home in the village has the same chance of being selected.

How do we actually take a simple random sample?

There is a method of random sampling available which is rather more reliable than drawing names from hats!

Since every household in the village is numbered, we can begin by taking a sample of random numbers between 1 and 60. We then include in our sample the households with corresponding numbers.

There are several ways of taking samples of random numbers. One way is to use lists of random numbers which are available in many books of statistical tables. An example is given in figure 2 below.

---

89 24 45 01 34 42 26 24 52 39 11 46 49 13 04 62 17 51 16 31 89 85 73 69 15 32 26 81 04 95 53 79 72 09 53

71 27 45 01 42 01 27 97 72 98 58 66 53 50 62 06 39 32 82 31 15 54 92 10 57 93 23 46 98 19 69 90 14 09 90

94 50 77 07 51 03 48 27 48 93 17 81 28 31 30 91 60 78 28 73 61 58 06 45 68 81 69 32 04 92 59 31 28 86 53

39 58 25 90 63 63 26 38 51 30 44 00 70 38 30 70 etc etc etc

FIGURE 2: **Extract From a Random Number Table**

Figure 2 is an extract from a much larger set of tables prepared for the use of statisticians.

Such a table consists of the digits 0-9 repeated in groups, with no apparent order in the digits, which is exactly what the term 'random' means.

Another way of generating random numbers is to use a scientific pocket calculator, many of which have random number facilities. If you have such a calculator, you may wish to use it in any sampling exercises you do here. It is also worth noting that many computer programs (statistical 'packages' and spreadsheets especially) have random number facilities.

Now back to Hamdon village. We can now tackle the problem of estimating the average grocery bill by taking a sample of 12 households.

Using the table in figure 2 to select a sample of 12 households we

(a)   number all the households in the village. (This has already been done for us in figure 1);

(b)   take 12 numbers from the table in figure 2 – I have just taken the first 12 numbers between 1 and 60, starting from the first row. (Or if you are using a calculator or computer, produce a stream of 12 random numbers);

(c)   discard any number greater than 60, or any which have already been used up, and replace it with a new number;

(d)   and finally contact the household that corresponds to each sampled number and find out how much it spends on groceries each week. This could be done by some kind of questionnaire survey.

When all of the above stages have been completed, we will have some data similar to that shown in figure 3, below.

RANDOM No.	GROCERY BILL	RANDOM No.	GROCERY BILL	RANDOM No.	GROCERY BILL
24	53.10	42	72.60	11	56.30
45	85.40	26	75.40	46	75.20
1	69.60	52	80.20	49	80.70
34	72.60	39	81.10	13	77.00

FIGURE 3: **Sample of 12 Households from Hamdon**

We can easily calculate that the mean grocery bill of the above 12 households is £73.27 and then generalise this result as

'the mean weekly grocery bill in Hamdon is £73.27 per household'.

This is obviously an estimate, since it is based upon a sample of only 12 households, rather than the whole village.

4. CAN WE TRUST SAMPLE ESTIMATES?

An immediate question arises. Suppose that we had decided to take a different set of 12 numbers. We would then have sampled a different set of 12 households and possibly obtained a different estimate for the mean weekly grocery bill in Hamdon.

ACTIVITY 1

How many different samples of 12 households is it possible to select from a village of 60 households?

There are 60 households in Hamdon, and Activity 1 requires us to calculate the number of different samples of 12 we may select from this number. Put another way, how many collections of 12 different objects could be selected from 60 different objects?

You should have recognised that this is a problem concerned with counting the number of combinations.

Here is the calculation

There are $\binom{60}{12}$ different samples of 12 households where

$$\binom{60}{12} = \frac{60!}{12!(60 - 12)!} = \frac{60 \times 59 \times 58 \times ..... \times 48}{12 \times 11 \times 10 \times ..... \times 1} =$$

$$1.399358844 \times 10^{12}$$

If you are unsure how this calculation was made, you should consult unit 5, *Probability*.

The answer, $1.399358844 \times 10^{12}$, is a very large number indeed. It implies that the sampling process could have resulted in any one of several million different possible estimates. How do we know that the particular sample estimate we may have obtained is the most accurate possible?

ACTIVITY 2

Now try taking a random sample for yourself. By using a pocket calculator (or the table of random numbers) generate 12 random numbers between 1 and 60. Use this list of numbers to take a sample (without replacement) of households in Hamdon. Use the sample to estimate the mean grocery bill. How does the estimate you made compare with the estimate obtained from the sample shown in figure 3?

Activities 1 and 2 illustrate a crucial point about estimates made from samples. Firstly, a large number of different samples of 12 households are possible, even from a village of only 60.

And secondly, it is possible by the 'luck of the draw' to select any one of these samples. Each different sample will possibly give a different estimate of the mean grocery bill. You should be able to test this theory for yourself if you are able to compare your answer to Activity 2 with other students studying this unit.

How do you know that the estimate you have obtained is an accurate one? Or do we just ignore this problem and hope for the best?

This is not a trivial matter, and we MUST be able to make some kind of statement about the level of accuracy of our results if sampling is to be at all useful.

The problem can be summarised as follows:

> we need to know the average amount spent on food per week by a household in Hamdon;

> we cannot contact every single household in the village;

> we must therefore make do with a sample of households;

> it is quite clear that the calculation of the mean grocery bill from our sample can only be an estimate of the true, unknown grocery bill. (The only way of finding the exact value would be to contact EVERY household, and this we have ruled out.)

estimates always have some degree of error in them; we must find some way of estimating how big this error is likely to be.

Here is the problem shown diagrammatically (figure 4).

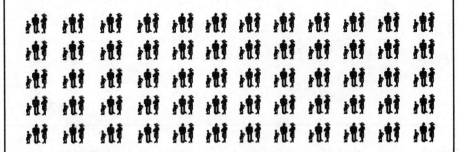

FIGURE 4: **The Sampling Problem**

Our Hamdon village example is small-scale in comparison with sampling problems normally encountered in business situations. Most analysts are usually faced with groups (or populations, to use the correct statistical term), of 60,000 or even 60,000,000 in size rather than just 60.

Having discussed our sampling problem, we can now carry on with our analysis of Hamdon village. Just how accurate is our sample estimate of grocery expenditure? We can answer this question by calculating the average grocery bill for the whole village.

ACTIVITY 3

Calculate the mean grocery bill for the whole village. You may prefer to use LOTUS 1-2-3, a statistical package, or some other appropriate computer software to help you with these figures.

Using the usual method of calculating the mean of all the data, we find that the average size of bill in Hamdon is £69.79.

I hope you produced the same figure.

ACTIVITY 4

We continue with our attempts to estimate the grocery bill of Hamdon by taking a sample of 12 households. Suppose that by sheer chance you happen to select the 12 households with the lowest bills. What estimate of the mean weekly grocery bill would you obtain from this sample?

The list of Hamdon households is given again in figure 5 but this time sorted into order, from the smallest to the largest grocery bill.

No.	Bill	No.	Bill	No.	Bill
22	46.00	2	65.20	35	76.40
4	48.00	12	65.30	13	77.00
6	49.80	57	67.50	27	77.00
15	50.40	44	68.20	51	77.30
25	50.40	19	68.20	32	78.20
10	51.30	40	68.80	56	78.80
20	51.60	58	69.00	9	79.10
24	53.10	1	69.60	16	79.80
38	55.10	29	70.00	52	80.20
33	55.60	23	71.90	49	80.70
21	55.80	47	72.20	14	80.80
11	56.30	34	72.60	39	81.10
7	58.40	42	72.60	60	82.10
5	61.20	8	72.80	59	83.10
37	61.30	36	72.90	45	85.40
3	61.50	53	73.60	41	86.00
18	63.20	30	73.90	31	87.10
28	63.50	55	75.00	50	91.20
43	64.50	46	75.20	54	91.60
17	65.10	26	75.40	48	92.50

FIGURE 5: **Hamdon Households in Order of Size of Grocery Bill**

From figure 5 we calculate the mean of the first 12 entries. The result is £51.95. This is the lowest possible estimate we would have obtained for mean expenditure using a sample of 12 households.

ACTIVITY 5

Now suppose that you happen (again by chance) to select the 12 households with the largest bills. What estimate of the mean weekly grocery bill would you obtain from this sample?

Taking the last 12 entries from the sorted table, we obtain a mean of £85.15. This is the largest possible estimate we would have obtained for mean expenditure using a sample of 12 households.

ACTIVITY 6

Consider and compare the following from the last three activities (3, 4 and 5):

(a)   the maximum and minimum grocery bills of **all households** in Hamdon (from figure 5);

(b)   the mean grocery bill for Hamdon (from your answer to Activity 4);

(c)   the maximum and minimum possible estimates of the mean grocery bill from samples of 12 households (from your answers to Activities 4 and 5).

Can you draw any conclusions from this comparison with respect to the behaviour of sample estimates of the mean?

The statistics required in Activity 6 are summarised below.

Minimum grocery bill = £46.00

Maximum grocery bill = £92.50

Minimum sample estimate of the mean grocery bill = £51.95

Maximum sample estimate of the mean grocery bill = £85.15

The maximum and minimum grocery bills have a **crude range** of 92.50 - 46.00 = 46.5.

The range between the largest and smallest sample estimates of the mean grocery bill is 85.15 - 51.95 = 33.20.

Averages differ by much less than the 'raw' figures from which they are calculated.

For example, if you took the range of heights from the smallest dwarf to the tallest giant you would see a difference of several feet. There may be a person 3 feet tall in Cardiff and a person 7 feet tall in London, giving a range of 4 ft.

However, if you compare the **average** heights of people in Cardiff and London then you would find a very much smaller difference; maybe only of fractions of inches.

All of this suggests that even if you are very unlucky and select the most unrepresentative sample possible, your estimate of the mean may still not be in such serious error as you may think. The 'averaging' process tends to even out seriously extreme values.

The above remark holds true except in the case where only a sample of one is taken. However, if you are unwise enough to base judgements on just a single sample, then you deserve the consequences!

Your answer to Activity 6 should have convinced you that although we can use samples to make estimates of quantities such as the mean, there will always be some degree of error in these estimates.

How can the analyst be sure that a particular sampling operation has given a 'good' (ie low-error) estimate of the mean?

In general, estimates from properly managed random sampling operations can be regarded as trustworthy. What is more, provided that the sample is truly random, the analyst can also quote a '**margin of error**' for any estimates made.

5. SUMMARY

In this first section we have introduced you to sampling through the case study of Hamdon-on-the-Marsh, by

- defining random **sampling**

- explaining the differences between sampling **with replacement** and **without replacement**

- showing how to select **random samples**

- examining the reliability of **sample estimates**

- comparing the mean of a **sample** with the mean of the **population** from which the sample is drawn

If you are unsure of any of the topics in this section, check back **now** before you read on.

SECTION 2

THE BEHAVIOUR OF SAMPLE ESTIMATES

1. TERMINOLOGY

So far in our discussion of sampling, we have been vague in the use of terminology. Before proceeding any further you should take note of the following definitions.

POPULATION OR 'UNIVERSE'

The totality of things which are under investigation is referred to as the **population**. Some authorities prefer to use the term '**universe**'. In the example used in section 1 of this unit, the population under investigation is the total number of households in Hamdon-on-the-Marsh. Do not make the mistake of thinking that a statistical population is necessarily human. For example, if you were a veterinary surgeon working with the Department of Agriculture, you might be concerned to find out what proportion of the dairy cattle herd is infected with bovine spongiform encephalopathy. In this case your population would be the whole dairy herd of the country. In industrial quality control the population under investigation is the total 'population' of goods produced by a business.

CENSUS

A census is a full count, or enumeration of the population. In the Hamdon village example, a census would consist of contacting every single household in the population. In Activity 3 you were asked to compute the mean grocery bill by using a census. This is feasible for a small population of 60; normally, populations are much bigger than this.

SAMPLE

For most business organisations, a census is not a feasible method of gathering data; a sample is normally used.

A sample is a proportion of the population. Normally a sample is taken, the data analysed, and the results generalised to the whole population.

For best results, random sampling is preferable to other forms of sampling.

SAMPLE ERROR

Any estimate made using a sample contains a degree of error. This is called **sampling error** and must be carefully distinguished from clerical error, or any other errors which arise from miscalculation, or mismanagement of the sampling process.

Even if all these other sources of error could be removed, sampling error would remain. There is only one way to remove sampling error, and that is to use a census.

The presence of sampling error in statistical data is not necessarily serious. As you will see later, it is possible to make some estimate of the maximum size of error incurred by random sampling, and forewarned, we can make allowances for it.

THE SAMPLE MEAN, $\bar{X}$, AND THE POPULATION MEAN μ

The Greek letter μ is commonly used to denote the **population** mean. The symbol $\bar{X}$ (the letter X with a vertical bar above it) is used to denote the **sample** mean. It is a convention in statistics to use Greek letters for population quantities and Western alphabetic characters for sample estimates.

$\overline{X}$ is an estimator of μ. We may, of course, wish to estimate other quantities as well as the mean.

For the moment however, we will just consider the problem of estimating μ.

2. THE CENTRAL LIMIT THEOREM

Much of the practice of sampling is based on something called the **central limit theorem**. This is a complex mathematical theorem, but fortunately we do not need to worry about the details. However, it is necessary to understand something of the conclusions of the theorem if you are to be able to properly interpret sample data.

In brief, this is how the theory works:

> If we wish to make an estimate of some population value – for example, the mean grocery bill in Hamdon – we know that the population mean is a constant, and the only way we can know what it is for certain is to take a census. This is usually impossible.
>
> We therefore take a sample and calculate the sample mean $\overline{X}$ as an estimate of μ. But the sample we select is subject to chance. In the case of the Hamdon example we could have picked any one of 1.399×10^{12} different samples. This means we could have had any of 1.399×10^{12} possible estimates of the mean.
>
> Therefore $\overline{X}$ is NOT a constant; it is a variable. Like any other random variable, it has a range of possible values and a probability distribution.
>
> For large random samples the distribution of $\overline{X}$ is known to be Normal and is known as the **sampling distribution of the mean.**
>
> The mean of the sampling distribution of $\overline{X}$ is μ, (the same as the mean of the population). The standard deviation of $\overline{X}$ is $\sigma/\sqrt{N}$, where N is the sample size, and s is the population standard deviation.

You can see this more clearly in figure 6 below.

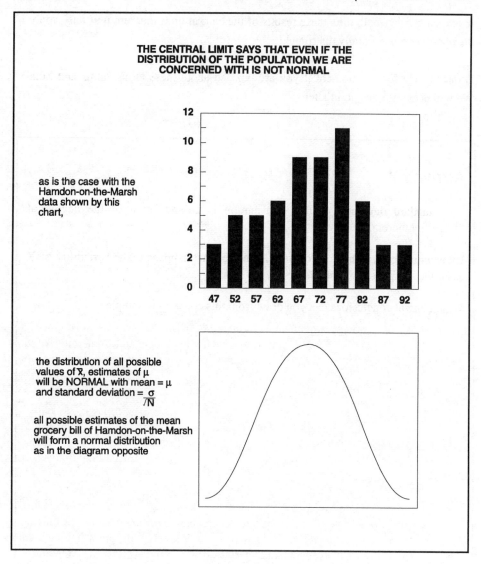

THE CENTRAL LIMIT SAYS THAT EVEN IF THE
DISTRIBUTION OF THE POPULATION WE ARE
CONCERNED WITH IS NOT NORMAL

as is the case with the
Hamdon-on-the-Marsh
data shown by this
chart,

the distribution of all possible
values of x̄, estimates of μ
will be NORMAL with mean = μ
and standard deviation = σ/√N

all possible estimates of the mean
grocery bill of Hamdon-on-the-Marsh
will form a normal distribution
as in the diagram opposite

FIGURE 6: **The Central Limit Theorem**

Be careful that you do not get X and X̄ confused. X is the population variable – in the
Hamdon example this would be size of weekly grocery bills, X̄ is the sample estimate
of μ, the **average** of the grocery bills.

X is distributed (not necessarily normally) with mean μ and standard deviation σ. X̄ is
(for large samples) distributed normally with mean μ and standard deviation σ/√N.

The result of the central limit theorem means that since we now know something about
the way sample estimates such as X̄ behave, we can make useful observations about the
accuracy of such estimates.

If our sample is small, then these results of the central limit theorem will only apply if the population is normally distributed.

Do not worry for the moment if you are puzzled about these terms 'large' and 'small'. We will deal with this point later.

ACTIVITY 7

The standard deviation of **any** distribution is an indication of the degree of variability therein.

By examining the behaviour of $\sigma/\sqrt{N}$, analyse what happens to the variability of $\bar{X}$ as N, the sample size increases.

What general conclusions can you draw from this concerning sample size?

The standard deviation of $\bar{X}$ is $\sigma/\sqrt{N}$. If you increase the size of N then you should be able to see that $\sigma/\sqrt{N}$ decreases in size. (If you increase the denominator of a fraction while holding the numerator constant, it grows smaller.)

We know that a smaller standard deviation means lower variability. This would suggest that the larger the sample size, the more accurate the sample estimate (because $\bar{X}$ is less variable).

Note
Standard Error of the Mean

The value $\sigma/\sqrt{N}$ is usually dignified with the special title of standard error of the mean. It is an important value because it tells the analyst how accurate (variable) the sample statistic is. Most sample statistics have their own standard error.

From this point, we will use the terms standard deviation when referring to the distribution of X, and standard error when referring to the distribution of $\bar{X}$.

Example

Household expenditure in Hamdon is normally distributed with mean £69.79 and standard deviation £11.82.

What is the probability that a **sample** of 12 households would have a **mean expenditure** of £73 or more?

We know that the sample mean is normally distributed with mean

$$\mu = 69.79$$

and standard error

$$\frac{\sigma}{\sqrt{N}} = \frac{11.72}{\sqrt{12}} \approx 3.3833$$

So the probability that we could find a sample of 12 households with a mean expenditure greater than £73 is

$$Pr(\bar{X} > 73) =$$

$$Pr(Z > \frac{\bar{X} - \mu}{\frac{\sigma}{\sqrt{N}}}) =$$

$$Pr(Z > \frac{73 - 69.79}{3.3833}) =$$

$$Pr(Z > 0.95)$$

You should remember from the earlier unit on probability in this series, that 'Pr' is an abbreviation for 'the probability that....'

From tables of areas under the standard normal curve the area beyond $Z = 0.95$ is 0.171056.

Approximately 17% of all possible samples of 12 will have mean expenditures greater than £73.

Notice that this does NOT mean that 17% of all Hamdon households spend more than £73 weekly. The above calculation has been concerned with average expenditures for groups (samples) of 12, and not for the population of all households.

ACTIVITY 8

A class of 25 students take an examination in accounting, for which the national result averages 50, with a standard deviation of 12. Marks are in percentages, and are normally distributed. The class can be considered as a random sample from the national population of students.

(a)   How likely is it that a **single student** selected at random would get a mark in excess of 60?

(b)   How likely is it that the mean mark for the class of 25 would exceed 60?

⇒

Activity 8 continued...

Part (a) of Activity 8 specifies that we select a single student at random from the total population. This an extreme case of a sample of 1, and is identical to the problems studied in unit 6 in this series on probability distributions.

We have a distribution of student marks which is normal, with $\mu = 50$ and $\sigma = 12$, so

Pr(Student obtains a mark in excess of 60) = Pr(X > 60)

$$Pr(Z > \frac{\overline{X} - \mu}{\sigma}) = Pr(Z > \frac{60 - 50}{12})$$

$$3 Pr(Z > 0.83)$$

$$= Pr(Z > 0.83)$$

From tables of areas under the normal curve, the area above $Z = 0.83$ is 0.203269.

There is therefore approximately a 20% chance that a student selected at random will get a mark above 60.

So part (a) of this Activity did not actually involve sampling at all unless you describe it as a sample of 1.

In part (b) of the Activity sampling is involved. We need to compute Pr(The class average exceeds 60).

Since we are dealing with samples of size $N = 25$, then

$\mu = 50$ and standard error of $\overline{X} = \sigma/\sqrt{N} = 12/\sqrt{25} = 2.4$.

So $Pr(X > 60) =$

$$Pr(Z > \frac{\overline{X} - \mu}{\frac{\sigma}{\sqrt{N}}}) = Pr(Z > \frac{60 - 50}{\frac{12}{\sqrt{25}}})$$

$$Pr(Z > \frac{10}{2.4}) \approx Pr(Z > 4.17)$$

Now the tables of areas under the normal curve do not have values as large as $Z = 4.17$.

You may therefore confidently assume that the area beyond $Z = 4.17$ is negligible.

Consequently

Pr(Class average exceeds 60) = negligible

The conclusion drawn from Activity 8 is that while it is perfectly possible for a **single individual** to get a mark above 60 (the probability is about 20%), the chances of the **class average** being above 60 is negligible. Make sure that you understand the difference between what has been calculated in questions (a) and (b) of this Activity before you read on.

ACTIVITY 9

Nine flashlight bulbs are selected at random from a large quantity of bulbs with a lifetime which is normally distributed with a mean of 20 hours, and a standard deviation of 5 hours.

(a)   What is the probability that the mean lifetime of the 9 bulbs exceeds 22 hours?

Activity 9 continued...

(b)   What is the probability that the mean lifetime of the sample of 9 bulbs is between 19 and 21 hours?

(c)   What is the probability that the mean lifetime of the sample of 9 bulbs is less than 16 hours?

(d)   What is the probability that the TOTAL combined lifetime of the sample of 9 bulbs exceeds 200 hours?

The sample mean $\overline{X}$ for samples of $N = 9$ has a normal distribution with mean $\mu = 20$ and standard error $\sigma/\sqrt{N} = 5/\sqrt{9} = 1.67$.

For question (a) we calculate

Pr(the mean life exceeds 22 hours) = $Pr(\overline{X} > 22)$ =

$$Pr(Z > \frac{\overline{X} - \mu}{\frac{\sigma}{\sqrt{N}}} = Pr(Z > \frac{22 - 20}{\frac{5}{\sqrt{9}}}) =$$

$Pr(Z > 1.2)$

The area beyond $Z = 1.2$ is 0.115069

So there is approximately an 11.5% chance that a sample of 9 bulbs will have an average life in excess of 22 hours.

For question (b) we calculate

$Pr(19 < \overline{X} < 21)$ =

$$Pr(\frac{\overline{X}_1 - m}{\frac{s}{\sqrt{N}}} < Z < \frac{\overline{X}_2 - m}{\frac{s}{\sqrt{N}}})$$

$$Pr(\frac{19 - 20}{\frac{5}{\sqrt{9}}} < Z < \frac{21 - 20}{\frac{5}{\sqrt{9}}})$$

$Pr(-0.60 < Z < 0.60) = 0.451494$

There is a 45.15% chance that the mean life of the 9 bulbs will be between 19 and 21 hours.

For question (c)

$$Pr(\bar{X} < 16) =$$

$$Pr(Z < \frac{\bar{X} - \mu}{\frac{\sigma}{\sqrt{N}}}) = Pr(Z < \frac{16 - 20}{\frac{5}{\sqrt{9}}})$$

$$Pr(Z < -2.4) = 0.008197$$

There is a 0.82% chance that the mean lifetime of the sample of 9 bulbs will be less than 16 hours.

Finally, question (d). If the total lifetime of the 9 bulbs lasts longer than 200 hours, then this must mean that the **mean lifetime** exceeds 22.2222.

Thus Pr(Total life > 200 hours) = Pr(Mean life > 22.2222 hours).

$$Pr(\bar{X} > 22.2222) > = Pr(Z > \frac{\bar{X} - \mu}{\frac{\sigma}{\sqrt{N}}}) =$$

$$Pr(Z > \frac{22.2222 - 20}{\frac{5}{\sqrt{9}}})$$

$$Pr(Z > 1.33) = 0.091759$$

There is a 9.18% chance, approximately that the total lifetime of the 9 bulbs will be greater than 200 hours. (Mean lifetime greater than 22.2222 hours.)

Here is another example for you to try.

ACTIVITY 10

In an office with a large number of employees, both male and female staff use lifts to gain access to the upper floors. The company which manufactures the lifts says that they have a tendency to break down if the total loading exceeds 1500 lbs, and suggests that no more than 10 people should use them at any one time, thus reducing the chance of breakdown to acceptable levels.

The weight of the office staff using the lifts is known to be normally distributed with an average 126 lbs, and a standard deviation of 25 lbs.

If the office staff always adhere to the 'no more than 10' rule, what are the chances of the load exceeding the recommended level if the lift is fully loaded?

The lift will exceed the recommended level when fully loaded if the 10 occupants have a combined weight of 1500 lbs or more. This is only another way of saying that the mean weight of the 10 people in the lift should not be more than 150.00 lbs.

We can consider a group of 10 getting into a lift as a random sample from the total workforce of the firm. We want

Pr(Total weight > 1500 lbs) = Pr(Mean weight > 150.00 lbs)

The mean weight of the population of workers is $\mu = 126$ lbs with a standard deviation of $\sigma = 25$ lbs.

For samples of size 10 we have a standard error of

$$\sigma/\sqrt{N} = 25/\sqrt{10} \approx 7.9057$$

$$Pr(\bar{X} > 150) = Pr\left(Z > \frac{\bar{X} - \mu}{\dfrac{\sigma}{\sqrt{N}}}\right)$$

$$Pr\left(Z > \frac{150 - 126}{\dfrac{25}{\sqrt{10}}}\right) \approx Pr(Z > 3.04) = 0.001182$$

This represents slightly more than a 1 in a 1000 chance of the lift exceeding the recommended load when it is occupied by 10 people.

ACTIVITY 11

A brand of radial tyres is manufactured to standards such that the average tread life is 30,000 miles, with a standard deviation 3,000 miles. Distribution of tread life is normal. A random sample of 4 tyres from a production run is tested. What is the probability that the mean tread life of these 4 tyres is less than 26,000 miles?

You may have wondered whether it is reasonable to assume that such a thing as tyre lifetimes is normally distributed. Actually, it quite often happens that product lifetimes are normally distributed, so it is not an unreasonable assumption.

The population of tyres has a mean life of $\mu = 30{,}000$ miles with $\sigma = 3{,}000$ miles.

For samples of 4 the standard error of $\overline{X}$ is $\sigma/\sqrt{N} = 3000/\sqrt{4} = 1500$.

Pr(A sample of 4 will average less than 26,000) =

$$Pr(\overline{X} < 26{,}000) = Pr(Z < \frac{\overline{X} - \mu}{\frac{\sigma}{\sqrt{N}}}) =$$

$$Pr(Z < \frac{26{,}000 - 30{,}000}{\frac{3{,}000}{\sqrt{4}}}) =$$

Pr(Z < -2.67) = 0.003792

There is a 0.38% chance that a sample of tyres will average less than 26,000 miles.

ACTIVITY 12

Use the tyre data from Activity 11. The company decides to test 16 tyres from each production lot. If the lot is satisfactory, what average tread life for the sample has a 0.99 chance of being exceeded?

For a sample of 16 tyres from the same population, the standard error of $\bar{X}$ is $\sigma/\sqrt{N} = 3000/\sqrt{16} = 750$.

We want the value x such that

$$Pr(\bar{X} > x) = 0.99$$

$$Pr(\bar{X} > x) = Pr(Z > \frac{\bar{X} - \mu}{\frac{\sigma}{\sqrt{N}}}) =$$

$$Pr(Z > \frac{x - 30,000}{\frac{3000}{\sqrt{16}}}) = 0.99$$

Now we can read from normal curve tables that approximately 99% of the normal distribution lies above $Z = -2.33$.

Therefore

$$Pr(-2.33 > \frac{x - 30\,000}{750}) = 0.99$$

$$So\ x = (-2.33).(750) + 30000 = 28252.5$$

There is a 99% chance that the 16 tyres will average a mean life of more than 28252.5 miles.

3. SUMMARY

In this section we have

- defined the terms **population, census, sample, sample error** and **sample mean**

- described and illustrated the results of the **central limit theorem**

- looked at several examples of **probability calculations** involving samples

If you are unsure of any of these areas, check back **now** before starting on section 3.

SECTION 3

POINT ESTIMATES AND INTERVAL ESTIMATES

1. A PROBLEM IN ESTIMATION

A town has a mean grocery bill of £50 per week with a standard deviation of £10. If we were ignorant of these facts (as we usually would be without the results of a census readily to hand), we would be forced to estimate the population mean. The only way we could do this would be to take a sample of households.

We decide to take a sample of 36 households, and from this we estimate that the mean grocery bill is £52 per week.

This figure of 52 is known as a **point estimate** because it consists of just one single figure, one single point. Point estimates can be very misleading because they give a false impression of accuracy. As you are now aware, any estimate obtained from a sample is subject to random error. Point estimates offer us no clues as to the likely magnitude of this error. It would be better if we were able to quote an **interval** rather than a single point.

So instead of making statements such as

'the mean weekly grocery bill = £52'

we could say something like

'the mean weekly grocery bill is £52 ± £2'

Such an estimate is often known as an **interval estimate** because it says that the mean weekly grocery bill is somewhere in the interval (in this case) £50 - £54.

Further, it is possible to make some statement concerning the degree of 'confidence' with which we can trust the accuracy of the interval. For instance

'we can be 95% confident that the mean weekly grocery bill is in the interval £50 ± £2'

Exactly what we mean by 'confidence' in statements such as the above is a problem we can return to after the next four Activities. Such estimates are properly known as **confidence intervals**.

Confidence interval estimates are more useful than point estimates because they not only indicate the magnitude of the statistic we are investigating, but also give the analyst some idea of the likely margin of error in the result.

2. CALCULATION OF INTERVAL ESTIMATES

Activities 13, 14, 15 and 16 demonstrate how confidence intervals may be calculated.

Activities 13 and 14 introduce you to the methods for calculating intervals for a specific sampling problem, while Activities 15 and 16 ask you to generalise these results to all large sampling problems involving the mean.

ACTIVITY 13

Consider the sampling problem in the town grocery bill example at the beginning of this section.

The population mean (the grocery bill for all households) is £50, with standard deviation £10. A sample of 36 households is taken, and the mean for this sample is calculated.

The sample mean will vary, according to the particular random sample chosen. Calculate the values a and b, such that the following three conditions are satisfied.

(i) $\Pr(a < \overline{X} < b) = 0.95$

(ii) $\Pr(\overline{X} < a) = 0.025$

(iii) $\Pr(\overline{X} > b) = 0.025$

Activity 13 requires us to find 2 values a and b which satisfy the properties summarised in figure 7, below.

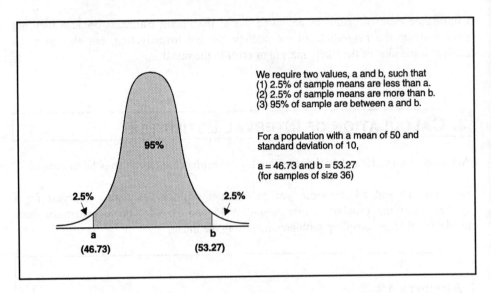

We require two values, a and b, such that
(1) 2.5% of sample means are less than a.
(2) 2.5% of sample means are more than b.
(3) 95% of sample are between a and b.

For a population with a mean of 50 and standard deviation of 10,

a = 46.73 and b = 53.27
(for samples of size 36)

FIGURE 7: **Grocery Bill Data (Activity 13)**

The problem can be tackled in a number of ways, so you may have reached the correct result with different reasoning.

First we want the value a such that

$$Pr(\bar{X} < a) = 0.025.$$

$$Pr(\bar{X} < a) = Pr(Z < \frac{a - 50}{\frac{10}{\sqrt{36}}}) = 0.025$$

Now we can read from normal curve tables that approximately 0.025 of the normal distribution area is below z = -1.96 (don't forget the minus). Therefore

Equation 1

$$\frac{a - 50}{\frac{10}{6}} = -1.96$$

$$a = -1.96 \times 10/6 + 50 = 46.73.$$

So 2.5% of all samples of 36 households will have a mean expenditure of less than £46.73.

Now consider condition (iii), ie a value b such that

$$Pr(\bar{X} > b) = 0.025$$

$$Pr(\bar{X} > b) = Pr(Z > \frac{b - 50}{\frac{10}{\sqrt{36}}}) = 0.025$$

From tables, approximately 0.025 of the normal distribution is to be found above Z = 1.96. Therefore

Equation 2

$$\frac{b - 50}{\frac{10}{6}} = 1.96$$

$$b = 1.96 \times 10/6 + 50 = 53.27$$

Therefore 2.5% of samples of 36 households will have a mean expenditure of more than £53.27.

Condition (i) is automatically fulfilled if we let a = £46.73 and b = £53.27.

ACTIVITY 14

For the same data as Activity 13, calculate the values a and b such that the following three conditions are satisfied.

(i) $Pr(a < \bar{X} < b) = 0.99$

(ii) $Pr(\bar{X} < a) = 0.005$

(iii) $Pr(\bar{X} > b) = 0.005$

➡

Activity 14 continued...

The solution to Activity 14 is tackled in the same way as that for Activity 13; see figure 8 below.

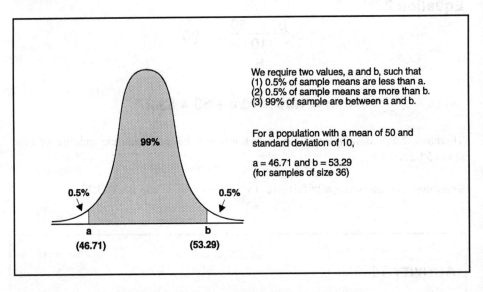

FIGURE 8: **Grocery Bill Data (Activity 14)**

We require two values a and b which satisfy all the conditions. In equation 1 of the solution to Activity 14, instead of -1.96, the value of Z becomes -2.575. In equation 2 instead of 1.96, the value of Z becomes 2.575. (I have chosen + and -2.575 rather than 2.57 or 2.58 because the appropriate area for 99% lies approximately halfway between these two latter values.)

Recalculation of these equations gives

a = £45.71

b = £54.29

ACTIVITY 15

A population has a mean of m and a standard deviation of s. A sample of size = N is taken from the population.

Calculate the values a and b such that the three conditions (i) to (iii) stated in Activity 13 are satisfied.

Activity 15 is more generalised than Activities 13 and 14. For a population with mean μ and standard deviation σ, we consider samples of size N.

First we want the value a such that

$$Pr(\bar{X} < a) = 0.025. \quad \text{Condition (ii)}$$

$$Pr(\bar{X} < a) = Pr\left(Z < \frac{a - \mu}{\frac{\sigma}{\sqrt{N}}}\right) = 0.025$$

therefore

Equation 3

$$\frac{a-\mu}{\dfrac{\sigma}{\sqrt{N}}} = -1.96$$

$$a = \mu - 1.96 \, \frac{\sigma}{\sqrt{N}}$$

Secondly we want the value b such that

$$Pr(\bar{X} > b) = 0.025. \quad \text{Condition (iii)}$$

$$Pr(\bar{X} > b) = Pr(Z > \frac{b-\mu}{\dfrac{\sigma}{\sqrt{N}}}) = 0.025$$

therefore

Equation 4

$$\frac{b-\mu}{\dfrac{\sigma}{\sqrt{N}}} = 1.96$$

$$b = \mu + 1.96 \, \frac{\sigma}{\sqrt{N}}$$

Condition (i) is now automatically met.

It seems that if we take a sample of size N, 95% of all possible sample mean estimates $(\bar{X})$ of μ which could be obtained will fall between the limits

$$\mu - 1.96\sigma/\sqrt{N} \quad \text{and} \quad \mu + 1.96\sigma/\sqrt{N}$$

ACTIVITY 16

A population has a mean of μ and a standard deviation of σ. A sample of size = N is taken from the population.

Calculate the values a and b such that the three conditions (i) to (iii) stated in Activity 14 are satisfied.

Activity 16 is solved by substituting the values Z = -2.575 and Z = 2.575 instead of ±1.96 in equations 1 and 2 of the solution to Activity 15.

By this substitution we obtain

$$a = \mu - 2.575\sigma/\sqrt{N} \qquad \text{Condition (ii)}$$
$$b = \mu + 2.575\sigma/\sqrt{N} \qquad \text{Condition (iii)}$$

Condition (i) is now automatically met.

It seems that if we take a sample of size N, 99% of all the possible sample mean estimates ($\bar{X}$) of μ will fall between the limits

$$\mu - 2.575\sigma/\sqrt{N} \quad \text{and} \quad \mu + 2.575\sigma/\sqrt{N}$$

The results of Activities 15 and 16 are generalisations of the findings of 13 and 14. These results are of great importance and are summarised below.

95% of sample means fall between the values

$$\mu - 1.96\,\frac{\sigma}{\sqrt{N}} \quad \text{and} \quad \mu + 1.96\,\frac{\sigma}{\sqrt{N}}$$

99% of all sample means fall between the values

$$\mu - 2.575\,\frac{\sigma}{\sqrt{N}} \quad \text{and} \quad \mu + 2.575\,\frac{\sigma}{\sqrt{N}}$$

Analysts wish to make observations concerning the accuracy of the sample mean, and apply the above observations to $\bar{X}$, rather than to μ. There are some dangers in taking this step, but if we substitute the sample mean $\bar{X}$ for μ, then we can (with care) use the following results:

$\bar{X}$ is a point estimate of the population mean μ

we can be 95% 'confident' that the true value of the population mean μ is in the range

$$\bar{X} \pm 1.96\,\frac{\sigma}{\sqrt{N}}$$

we can be 99% 'confident' that the true value of the population mean μ is in the range

$$\bar{X} \pm 2.575\,\frac{\sigma}{\sqrt{N}}$$

in general, a confidence interval is given by

$$\bar{X} \pm Z \frac{\sigma}{\sqrt{N}}$$

where Z depends upon the confidence level used.

EXAMPLE OF A CONFIDENCE INTERVAL

A manufacturer needs to estimate the mean lifetime of batteries they are producing. To do this they take a sample of 100 batteries and find that the mean life of this sample is 50 hours. The standard deviation of all battery lifetimes is believed to be 6 hours.

The 95% confidence interval estimate for the mean of all battery lifetimes is therefore

$$\bar{X} \pm 1.96 \frac{\sigma}{\sqrt{N}}$$

$$50 \pm 1.96 \frac{6}{\sqrt{100}}$$

$$= 50 \pm 1.176$$

The 95 % confidence interval estimate for the mean of battery lifetimes is 48.824 hours to 51.176 hours.

The 99% confidence interval for the mean of all battery lifetimes is

$$\bar{X} \pm 2.575 \frac{\sigma}{\sqrt{N}}$$

$$50 \pm 2.575 \frac{6}{\sqrt{100}}$$

$$= 50 \pm 1.545$$

We can be 99% confident that the mean is somewhere in the range 48.455 to 51.545.

3. INTERPRETATION OF CONFIDENCE INTERVALS

The narrower the confidence interval for a given level of confidence, the better. For example, consider the following two statements about the lifetime of an industrial component, estimated by testing a sample of 40 such items.

1. I am 95% confident that the average lifetime of the component is between 5 days and 80 days.

2. I am 95% confident that the average lifetime is between 37 days and 42 days.

The information contained in the first statement is practically useless, because the viable range quoted is too wide. The second statement is fairly useful, as it narrows down the actual lifetime to a much smaller range. Let us consider the meaning of this second statement a little more closely. What does it entitle us to say about the mean lifetime of the component?

We must be careful how we express ourselves when using confidence interval estimates. The following statements give both an incorrect and a correct interpretation.

INCORRECT ARGUMENT

Many people would argue the following about the above confidence interval

'the probability that the real mean lifetime of the components is between 37 and 42 days is equal to 0.95 (95%)'

This statement is incorrect.

The following is valid.

VALID ARGUMENT

I am 95% confident that the lifetime is between 37 and 42 days. If I repeatedly took samples of 40 components and computed the 95% confidence interval for each one, then 95% of these intervals would contain the mean, and 5% would not.

Does the confidence interval 37 - 42 contain μ? You cannot say with 100% certainty. All you are entitled to say is that 95% of the time, the estimation procedure called 'a 95% confidence interval' will produce an interval containing μ.

See figure 9, for a diagrammatic representation of the correct argument.

If you find the difference between the two arguments somewhat obscure, and rather philosophical, do not worry too much about it. You can think of a confidence interval as indicating something of the likely degree of error in a sample estimate.

This is, in fact, how many research scientists, biologists, economists, market analysts etc, choose to regard confidence interval estimates.

For example, I am 95% confident that my estimate of μ is within 1.96 standard errors of the real value of μ.

Or, I am 99% confident that my estimate of μ is within 2.575 standard errors of the real value of μ.

We are using a confidence interval
(5%) to estimate mean lifetime components

Suppose the population mean lifetime
of a component is 40 hours

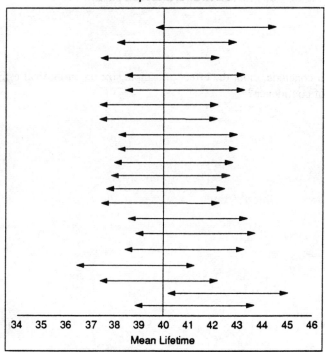

95% of possible confidence intervals
(shown by a ⟵————————⟶ above)
will contain the population mean

FIGURE 9: **Representation of Correct Argument**

4. How Precise Are Interval Estimates?

Before reading on, try the following Activity.

ACTIVITY 17

Earlier in this section, an example was given of the estimation of the life of batteries from a sample of 100.

The test result was $\bar{X} = 50$ hours and s for all batteries was 6 hours.

The 95% confidence interval was 50 ± 1.176.

Recalculate the 95% confidence interval if the sample size had been

(a)   25
(b)   1000

What do you conclude about the effect of sample size on an interval estimate for a given level of confidence?

The point estimate of μ is 50 hours, and we are told that $\sigma = 6$ hours.

In general a 95% confidence interval estimate is given by

$$\bar{X} \pm 1.96 \; \sigma/\sqrt{N}$$

We already know that for a sample size of 100 this interval estimate is 50 ± 1.176 hours.

So to answer question (a)

for a sample of size $N = 25$ we have

$$50 \pm 1.96 \times 6/\sqrt{25} \quad \text{or}$$

$$50 \pm 2.352$$

and question (b)

for a sample size $N = 1000$ we have

$$50 \pm 1.96 \times 6/\sqrt{1000} \quad \text{or}$$

$$50 \pm 0.372$$

We can summarise the results of Activity 17 as follows

If we take a sample of 25, then we can be 95% confident that the mean lifetime is in the range 50 ± 2.352, or 47.648 to 52.352 hours.

If we take a sample of 100, then we can be 95% confident that the mean lifetime is in the range 50 ± 1.176, or 48.824 to 51.176 hours.

If we take a sample of 1000, then we can be 95% confident that the mean lifetime is in the range 50 ± 0.372, or 49.628 to 50.372 hours.

We can assume that, for a given level of confidence, an increase in the sample size will reduce the size of the interval. The margin of error is reduced as N increases.

ACTIVITY 18

All of the confidence interval estimates quoted so far have been either 95% or 99%. However, there is nothing sacred about these figures; it is just as easy to calculate (say) 90% or 99.5% confidence intervals.

For the battery lifetime data of Activity 17, recalculate the interval estimate for a sample of 100 if the level of confidence required is

(a)   90%
(b)   99.5%

What do you conclude about the effect of changing the level of confidence required for a given size of sample?

If you found this Activity difficult, think back to how (for example) a 95% confidence interval was set up. See the answers to Activities 13 and 15. In those problems you had to find two values such that;

$$Pr(a < \bar{X} < b) = 0.95$$

$$Pr(\bar{X} < a) = 0.025$$

$$Pr(\bar{X} > b) = 0.025$$

where a was

$$\bar{X} - 1.96 \, \sigma/\sqrt{N}$$

and b was

$$\bar{X} + 1.96\ \sigma/\sqrt{N}$$

The crucial factor in the confidence interval is the value Z, which is 1.96 for a 95% interval.

In answer to question (a), for a 90% interval, we must find two values a and b such that

$$Pr(a < \bar{X} < b) = 0.90$$

$$Pr(\bar{X} < a) = 0.05$$

$$Pr(\bar{X} > b) = 0.05$$

These three conditions state that 90% of all sample means will have values between a and b.

These two values will be of the type

$$\bar{X} - Z\sigma/\sqrt{N}\ \text{ and }\ \bar{X} + Z\sigma/\sqrt{N}$$

where Z is determined by the size of the confidence interval.

From a study of tables, it appears that there is a value of Z; approximately -1.645 such that 5% of the normal distribution lies below. Also, by a similar argument, 5% of the normal distribution lies above Z = 1.645. (I have used 1.645 rather than 1.64 or 1.65 because the appropriate area lies almost exactly midway between these latter two Z values.)

So the 90% confidence interval for a mean is

$$\bar{X} \pm 1.645\ \sigma/\sqrt{N}$$

Therefore for the data of Activity 17, the confidence interval for a sample of 100 is given by

$$50 \pm 1.645\sigma/\sqrt{N}$$
$$50 \pm 0.987$$

We are 90% confident that the mean battery lifetime is in the interval 49.013 - 50.987.

And the second question (b), by a similar process of reasoning to that used in part (a), we can discover from tables that there are values, Z = -2.81 and Z = 2.81 such that

$$Pr(Z < -2.81) = 0.0025$$
$$Pr(Z > 2.81) = 0.0025$$
$$Pr(-2.81 < Z < 2.81) = 0.995$$

Therefore the 99.5% confidence interval for a mean is

$$\bar{X} \pm 2.81\ \sigma/\sqrt{N}$$

and for the data of Activity 17, the 99.5% confidence interval is

$$50 \pm 2.81\ \sigma/\sqrt{N}$$

$$50 \pm 1.686$$

We are 99.5% confident that the mean battery lifetime is in the range 48.314 - 51.686.

We can summarise the results of Activity 18.

The point estimate of mean battery lifetime is 50 hours, obtained from a sample of 100 batteries

- the 90% confidence interval estimate is 49.013 to 50.987;

- the 95% confidence interval estimate is 48.824 to 51.176;

- the 99.5% confidence interval estimate is 48.314 to 51.686.

It appears that for a given sample size, increasing the confidence interval gives us an interval which we can assert with increasing 'confidence' contains the true value of m. However, this is done at the expense of increasing the size of the likely margin of error.

5. How Precise Are Sample Estimates?

The results we have obtained so far can be summed up as

- it is more useful to have an interval estimate of a statistic than a point estimate;

- the size of the 'confidence' interval is a useful guide to the accuracy of our sample estimate. The accuracy of a sample estimate is sometimes referred to as its **precision**. The larger the interval, the less precise the estimate and vice versa;

- if we insist on keeping the same level of confidence, the best way of obtaining a more precise estimate is to increase the sample size (see the results of Activity 18);

- if we cannot increase the sample size, then we can obtain a smaller interval estimate by reducing the level of confidence (say from 95 to 90%). However, this means that the confidence and trust we can place in the result is materially lowered.

The business application of sampling also raises many questions.

How large a sample can we afford to take?

How much precision do we **want** in the sample results?

How much precision do we **need**?

What level of confidence do we want in the results?

6. SUMMARY

In section 3 we have discussed

- **point estimates** and **interval estimates**

- calculation of interval estimates

- examples of **confidence intervals**

- interpretation of confidence intervals

- **valid** and **non-valid** interpretations of confidence intervals

- the **accuracy** of interval estimates

- the accuracy of sample estimates

This section has covered a number of complex areas. Make sure you understand these before moving on to section 4.

SECTION 4

PROPORTIONS AND PERCENTAGES

1. INTRODUCTION

So far in this unit we have concentrated on the problems of estimating means by using samples. It is possible however, that an analyst might wish to estimate statistical quantities other than the arithmetic mean. One frequent requirement of the analyst is to estimate **proportions, fractions, or percentages**.

For example, an opinion pollster may need to have an estimate of the proportion of the electorate who are likely to vote for each of the main political parties in a forthcoming election. A market researcher may wish to estimate the percentage share of the total market for microwave foods enjoyed by each of the firms in the industry.

In both of these cases we are concerned with estimating a **proportion** not an **arithmetic mean**.

Nevertheless, we will still be able to use some of the results of sampling and the central limit theorem.

2. SAMPLING DISTRIBUTION OF PROPORTIONS

The population in which the political opinion pollster is interested consists of all adults presently on the electoral register. The proportion of people voting for each party can be estimated by taking a sample (size = N) from this population.

Suppose that we particularly wish to estimate support for the Labour Party. We will denote the real population proportion of people in favour of the Labour Party by the Greek letter Π (pronounced 'pi' – please do not confuse the use of pi here with its familiar use in the formulas for area and circumference of a circle).

We cannot, of course know the true value of Π without taking a **census** of all electors. Since it is not usually possible to do this, we take a sample and find the proportion of the sample who are in favour of the Labour Party.

We will denote this sample proportion by p.

So p is an estimate of Π.

All of the previous observations relating to $\bar{X}$ apply equally to p. Random chance could have led us into selecting any of a very large number of possible samples of size N, and consequently, we could have ended up with a correspondingly large number of possible estimates of Π. What can we say about the accuracy of the sample estimate p?

Can we calculate confidence intervals for Π as we did for μ?

Just as $\bar{X}$ was normally distributed, so also is p.

p is normally distributed with a mean of Π and a standard deviation, or as we prefer to call it, standard error equal to

$$\sqrt{\frac{\Pi(1 - \Pi)}{N}}$$

Since we do not always know the value of Π, we may have to use p as an estimate of it. In which case the standard error of a proportion becomes

$$\sqrt{\frac{p(1 - p)}{N}}$$

thereafter we proceed in the same manner as we did with sample means (but see *Notes concerning the use of sampling theory* in section 6 of this unit).

Example 1

Suppose a researcher wishes to estimate whether (or not) a particular candidate will win a forthcoming by-election. In this fictitious by-election there are only two candidates, and the analyst uses a sample of 100 voters from a large electorate. The following interpretation of the sample results has been decided upon

> conclude that the candidate will win if he/she receives 55% or more of the vote,

> otherwise assume the candidate will lose.

What is the probability that the analyst will conclude that the candidate is a winner if in fact their true share of the vote is just 49% (ie they are really losers)?

Rephrasing this question in terms of population and sample we have that

$$\Pi = 0.49$$
$$p = 0.55$$

and

$$\sqrt{\frac{\Pi(1 - \Pi)}{N}} = \sqrt{\frac{0.49(1 - 0.49)}{N}} = 0.04999$$

(Note: Π and p must always be expressed in decimal fraction form when calculating the standard error).

So if we have a population proportion of 0.49, how likely is it that we would select a sample which would lead us into wrongly concluding success. For example, how likely is it that we would take a sample where $p > 0.55$?

Firstly, we must standardise the sample proportion (obtain its Z value).
How do we accomplish this?

When working with sample means you transformed a $\bar{X}$ value into Z by taking

$$Z = \frac{\bar{X} - \mu}{\frac{\sigma}{\sqrt{N}}}$$

That is

$$Z = \frac{\text{Sample estimate} - \text{population value}}{\text{standard error}}$$

Exactly the same process works for sample proportions (allowing for the difference in standard errors). So, for the electoral data we have;

$$Pr(p > 0.55) = Pr\left(Z > \frac{p - \Pi}{\sqrt{\frac{\Pi(1 - \Pi)}{N}}}\right)$$

$$= Pr\left(Z > \frac{0.55 - 0.49}{\sqrt{\frac{0.49(1 - 0.49)}{100}}}\right) \approx Pr(Z > 1.2)$$

From tables, the area above Z = 1.2 is 0.115069.

Thus there is an 11.51% chance of wrongly concluding that a candidate will win, when in fact they only have 49% of the vote.

Example 2

Assume that 50% of live births are males. (Actually, since males have a higher perinatal mortality this is not quite true, but we will discount this.) It has been decided that in future, the size of classes in higher education will be limited to 50 students. If classes of 50 students are selected at random from among those eligible, what proportion of classes will have 35 (ie 70%) or more males?

The true (ie population) proportion of males is $\Pi = 0.5$. For samples of 50, the standard error of the population proportion is

$$\sqrt{\frac{\Pi(1 - \Pi)}{N}} = \sqrt{\frac{0.5(1 - 0.5)}{50}} \approx 0.0707$$

We need

$$\textbf{Pr}(\text{A sample of 50 will have 70\% or more males})$$

$$= \textbf{Pr}(p > 0.70)$$

$$\textbf{Pr}\left(Z > \frac{p - \Pi}{\sqrt{\dfrac{\Pi(1 - \Pi)}{N}}}\right) =$$

$$= \textbf{Pr}\left(Z > \frac{0.7 - 0.5}{\sqrt{\dfrac{0.5(1 - 0.5)}{50}}}\right) \approx \textbf{Pr}(Z > 2.83)$$

From tables, the area beyond Z = 2.83 is 0.002327.

Therefore there is a probability of 0.002327 that a sample of 50 will contain more than 70% males, and 0.23% of classes of 50 will have this proportion (or more) of male students.

ACTIVITY 19

Using the same decision making criteria as in example 1 (the electoral problem), what would be the probability that the sampling procedure used would correctly predict the winner if the candidates true share of the vote were 60%?

For Activity 19 we assume that $\Pi = 0.6$

You must also remember the analysts criteria for judging the sample results; if the sample of 100 voters has 55% or more in favour, he/she will conclude a win.

So Pr(Analyst correctly predicts a win)

$$Pr(p > 0.55) = Pr\left(Z > \frac{p - \Pi}{\sqrt{\dfrac{\Pi(1 - \Pi)}{N}}}\right)$$

$$= Pr\left(Z > \frac{0.55 - 0.60}{\sqrt{\dfrac{0.60(1 - 0.60)}{100}}}\right) = Pr(Z > -1.02)$$

$= 0.846135$ (from normal curve tables)

Therefore if the candidate really has a 60% share of the vote, there is a 84.61% chance of the analyst correctly predicting that they will win.

ACTIVITY 20

Based on past data, 30% of credit card owners use their cards for extended credit.

If a sample of 100 credit card owners is taken, what is the probability that more than 40% will be using their cards for extended credit?

In this problem $\Pi = 0.3$. We need to find

$$Pr(\text{In a sample of 100 cardholders } p > 0.4)$$

$$Pr(p > 0.4) = Pr\left(Z > \frac{p - \Pi}{\sqrt{\dfrac{\Pi(1 - \Pi)}{N}}}\right)$$

$$= Pr\left(Z > \frac{0.4 - 0.3}{\sqrt{\dfrac{0.3(1 - 0.3)}{100}}}\right) = Pr(Z > 2.18) = 0.0146$$

There is almost a 1.5% chance that among a sample of 100 cardholders, more than 40% will be using their card for extended credit (when the population proportion is 30%).

3. CONFIDENCE INTERVALS FOR PROPORTIONS

As with the mean, the most useful property of the sampling distribution of the proportion is that we can make interval estimates of the population proportion.

If you recall from the notes you read earlier, concerning interval estimates for μ, the procedure for computing (say) a 95% confidence interval was

$$\bar{X} \pm 1.96 \; \frac{\sigma}{\sqrt{N}}$$

In general, a confidence interval for a mean is given by

$$\bar{X} \pm Z \; \frac{\sigma}{\sqrt{N}}$$

where the value of Z is determined by the level of confidence we wish to use.

There is a similar procedure for calculating confidence intervals for proportions (but using the standard error of p not $\bar{X}$).

For example, for a 95% confidence interval we would have

$$p \pm 1.96 \; \sqrt{\frac{\Pi(1 - \Pi)}{N}}$$

or rather, since we do not know Π, we must use p as an estimate for it, so the formula becomes

$$p \pm 1.96 \; \sqrt{\frac{p(1 - p)}{N}}$$

The general formula for a confidence interval for p becomes

$$p \pm Z \; \sqrt{\frac{p(1 - p)}{N}}$$

where the value of Z depends upon the level of confidence used.

Example

In a survey carried out by a personnel manager, 64 out of the sample of 100 employees stated that they would purchase a private medical insurance scheme started by the company. What is the 90% confidence interval estimate for the proportion of all employees interested in the scheme?

From tables, the appropriate value of Z for a 90% interval estimate is 1.645.

The point estimate of Π (the proportion of all employees interested in the insurance scheme) is

$$p = \frac{64}{100} = 0.64$$

So a 90% confidence interval is

$$0.64 \pm 1.645 \sqrt{\frac{0.64(1 - 0.64)}{100}}$$

$$= 0.64 \pm 0.08 \text{ (to two dp)}$$

Alternatively, this interval could be written as

0.56 to 0.72   or   **56% to 72%**

This means that we are 90% confident that the true proportion of employees interested in this scheme is between 56% and 72%.

ACTIVITY 21

A random sample of 200 registered voters was selected to determine the proportion who intended to vote for a particular political party in a forthcoming election; 28 stated that they intended to vote for the party. Set up a 95% confidence interval estimate for the true proportion of the electorate who intend to vote for this party.

The sample point estimate of the proportion in favour of the party is $28/200 = 0.14$.

The 95% confidence interval estimate for the proportion in favour is

$$p \pm 1.96\sqrt{\frac{p(1 - p)}{N}}$$

$$0.14 \pm 1.96\sqrt{\frac{0.14(1 - 0.14)}{200}}$$

$$0.14 \pm 0.05 \qquad \text{(rounded to two dp)}$$

The proportion in favour is between 0.09 and 0.19 (or 9% to 19%).

ACTIVITY 22

A business has developed a new product which must obtain at least a 10% share of the market to break even. To test the market, the company contact a sample of 200 potential customers and find that 27 of them would be sufficiently interested to buy. By calculating a 99% confidence interval estimate for Π, the proportion of people likely to buy, advise the company on the likely success (or otherwise) of the product.

We have a sample proportion (point estimate) of = 0.135, or 13.5%.

The 99% confidence interval estimate is given by

$$p \pm 2.575 \sqrt{\frac{p(1-p)}{N}}$$

$$0.135 \pm 2.575 \sqrt{\frac{0.135(1-0.135)}{200}}$$

$$0.135 \pm 0.062$$

The share of the market is (with 99% confidence), likely to be in the interval 0.073 to 0.197 (or 7.3% to 19.7%).

Sadly, the margin of error in the sample estimate is too large for us to guarantee (at this level of confidence) that the product will get more than a 10% share. It could get as high a share as 19.7%, but it could also do badly and only get 7.3%.

The company would have to take a larger sample if it wished to obtain a more precise estimate.

ACTIVITY 23

A national television company in the UK regularly use an 'Exit Poll' to predict the outcome of a general election before the polls close. An exit poll consists of asking a sample of voters emerging from polling stations which party they voted for. From this sample they compute the percentage of support enjoyed by each party.

The TV company claim that with a sample of 2000 electors, the accuracy of the sample estimates is within ± 3 percentage points.

Using the example of a party predicted as having 50% of the vote, comment on the company's accuracy claim.

Try calculating a 99% confidence interval for a predicted share of 50%. This will result in

$$p \pm 2.575 \sqrt{\frac{p(1-p)}{N}}$$

$$p \pm 2.575 \sqrt{\frac{0.5(1-0.5)}{2000}}$$

$$0.5 \pm 0.03 \quad \text{(to two dp)}$$

This is where the claim of '± 3 percentage points' originates. Of course, if the level of confidence were different, then the claimed margin of error would be different too.

You will learn more about the effects of changing levels of confidence on the margin of error in section 5.

4. SUMMARY

In section 4 we concerned ourselves with proportions and percentages by looking at

- **sampling distribution** of **proportions**

- **confidence intervals** for **proportions**

Look back over this section, particularly the worked examples to make certain that you are ready to tackle the next section.

SECTION 5

SAMPLE SIZE PROBLEMS

1. INTRODUCTION

It is possible to use the theory of the distribution of the sample mean to decide on an appropriate sample size.

It often happens that analysts wish to make an estimate of some quantity or another by means of sampling. How do they decide what size sample should be taken?

In order to answer this question we should consider:

What is the maximum margin of error allowed in the estimates?

What level of confidence is required?

What is the best estimate of the population standard deviation?

The technique of determining sample size can best be explained by using an example, the result of which can then be generalised.

2. DECIDING SAMPLE SIZE: THE METHOD

Suppose that an analyst wishes to make a sample estimate the mean grocery bill of households in a certain town with a large population.

It is intended that the estimate should be accurate to within $\pm £4$ at a 95% level of confidence.

The standard deviation of household grocery bills is estimated as being in the region of £15.

What should be the minimum size of sample taken in order to achieve these aims?

We want the estimate to be within $\pm £4$ at 95% confidence. A 95% confidence interval is calculated by taking

$$\pm 1.96 \; \frac{\sigma}{\sqrt{N}}$$

Therefore in this situation, we need

$$\pm 4 = \pm 1.96 \; \frac{\sigma}{\sqrt{N}}$$

As we have an estimate of the standard deviation this becomes

Equation 5

$$\pm 4 = \pm 1.96 \; \frac{15}{\sqrt{N}} \qquad \text{(formula 5)}$$

We can solve equation 5 for the unknown N.

So from equation 5 we have

$$\sqrt{N} = \frac{1.96 \times 15}{4}$$

$$\sqrt{N} = 7.35$$

$$\therefore N = 55$$

When calculating minimum sample sizes, results are rounded up.

A sample of size 55 (or above) will mean that we will estimate the mean grocery bill to the desired level of accuracy and confidence.

ACTIVITY 24

Use the data from the above example.

Assume that the analyst is not satisfied with a maximum error of ± £4, but wishes to claim a maximum error of only ± £2 (though still at 95% confidence).

How would this affect sample size?

Assume a standard deviation of £15 as before.

For Activity 24 we want

$$\pm 2 = \pm 1.96 \times \frac{15}{\sqrt{N}}$$

$$\sqrt{N} = \frac{1.96 \times 15}{2} = 14.7$$

So

$$N = 14.7^2 = 217$$

Insisting on the maximum error being reduced to ±2 will lead to an increase in minimum sample size from N = 55 to N = 217 (if the level of confidence remains unchanged at 95%).

ACTIVITY 25

Continue using the same example. The analyst is satisfied with the original maximum error of ± £4, but now wishes to claim a confidence level of 99%.

How will this affect sample size?

If the error is to remain at ± £4 but the confidence interval changes to 99% then

$$\pm 4 = \pm 2.575 \times 15/\sqrt{N}$$

$$\div N = (2.575 \times 15)/4$$

$$N \approx 9.66^2 = 94$$

Leaving the error level unchanged, but increasing the desired level of confidence from 95% to 99% will lead to an increase in minimum sample size from $N = 55$ to $N = 94$.

We are now in a position to generalise these results:

If the level of confidence remains constant, a reduction in the desired error level of the estimate will increase the sample size (and vice versa).

If the desired error level remains the same, the effect of increasing the level of confidence will also increase the size of sample required (and vice versa).

Now try Activity 26 which asks you to obtain a general expression for sample size.

ACTIVITY 26

An analyst wishes to estimate the mean of a population by using random sampling. The maximum error which he/she is prepared to tolerate in the estimate is ±e, at a level of confidence of a%. The standard deviation of the population is estimated as σ.

Write down an expression for the size of sample required in such a case.

In this Activity you are asked to generalise the method of solution of sample size problems for any error level, ±e and any level of confidence a%.

Let σ be an estimate of the standard deviation, Z be the appropriate value for an a% interval, and N be the unknown sample size. Then we require

$$\pm e = \pm Z\, \sigma/\sqrt{N}$$

$$\sqrt{N} = (Z \times \sigma)/e \quad \text{so}$$

$$N = \{(Z \times \sigma)/e\}^2$$

You might like to check that this formula works by applying it to the data of Activities 24 and 25, and comparing the answer it gives with your responses to those Activities.

Note on Sample Size Problems

You may have noticed that in order to solve questions relating to the size of sample which should be used in order to achieve a given error and confidence level we need to have an estimate of σ, the population standard deviation. This may seem difficult to do, considering that we may know nothing of the population under investigation. In practice, this constitutes no difficulty. Commercial analysts and researchers often undertake a small 'pilot survey' prior to the full survey. The aim of the pilot survey is usually to test questionnaires and to obtain other useful information which may help in the preparation of the full survey. An estimate of the standard deviation can be obtained from the pilot study.

3. PROPORTIONS AND SAMPLE SIZE PROBLEMS

Earlier in this unit we used a procedure for determining the size of sample required to estimate a mean to within a given margin of error at a given level of confidence. In order to do this we required some estimate of σ.

A similar procedure can be used when the statistic being estimated is a proportion.

Let ε be the level of error permitted. The level of confidence chosen results in a Z value which we will symbolise, for the moment, by Z.

Therefore we have

Margin of error (confidence interval) =

$$\pm \varepsilon = \pm Z \sqrt{\frac{\Pi(1 - \Pi)}{N}}$$

Assuming ε and Z are specified, then in order to calculate N, the sample size, we need an estimate of Π.

Now this may seem to be an insoluble problem. We are carrying out a sampling exercise for the very purpose of estimating Π. How therefore can we possibly know anything about Π before the event?

This is not such an intractable problem as it seems.

The factor which determines the accuracy of a sample estimate is the standard error

$$\sqrt{\frac{\Pi(1 - \Pi)}{N}}$$

It can be shown that for any given sample size N, the standard error is at its largest if $\Pi = 0.5$.

Therefore we can proceed by assuming that $\Pi = 0.5$ and calculate the size of sample required.

If Π turns out in fact to be something other than 0.5, then no great harm has been done; our assumption will give us a 'worst case' estimate of sample size. Any other value of Π would give a smaller estimate of the required value of N.

Example

The student union at a university wish to build a swimming pool on the campus, for which they would require to charge student users. Before going ahead with the building they would like to have an estimate of the proportion of students who would be willing to pay. A questionnaire has been designed to obtain student views. What sample size will give a probability of 0.90 that the sample proportion in favour is within 0.05 of the true proportion?

For a 90% confidence interval Z would be (approximately) 1.645.

therefore

$$\pm 0.05 = \pm 1.645 \sqrt{\frac{0.5(1 - 0.5)}{N}}$$

$$0.05^2 = 1.645^2 \times \frac{0.5 \times 0.5}{N}$$

and

$$N = \frac{1.645^2 \times 0.25}{0.0562} = 270.6 \approx 271$$

Try some of these calculations for yourself in the next three Activities.

ACTIVITY 27

The director of a corporation wishes to estimate the proportion of shareholders who would favour a joint project with another company. A sample is to be used.

How large should the sample be if an estimate to within 0.04 at a 95% level of confidence is required?

We require

$$\pm\, 0.04 = \pm\, 1.96 \sqrt{\frac{\Pi(1 - \Pi)}{N}}$$

where we may assume a value of 0.5 for Π.

$$\pm\, 0.04 = \pm\, 1.96 \sqrt{\frac{0.5(1 - 0.5)}{N}}$$

$$0.04^2 = 1.96^2\, \frac{0.5 \times 0.5}{N}$$

$$N = \frac{1.96^2 \times 0.25}{0.04^2}$$

$$N = 601$$

ACTIVITY 28

The poultry and egg buyer for a supermarket chain wishes to estimate the proportion of small 'grade A' eggs contained in each shipment from a poultry farm.

How large should the sample be to make the probability 0.95 of being within 0.05 of the true proportion?

For Activity 28 we require

$$\pm 0.05 = \pm 1.96 \sqrt{\frac{0.5(1 - 0.5)}{N}}$$

$$N = \frac{1.96^2 \times 0.25}{0.05^2}$$

$$N = 385$$

ACTIVITY 29

Complete the following table

Confidence Interval	0.01	0.02	Size of Error 0.03	0.04	0.05
90%	6766				
95%					
99%					

Insert the appropriate sample size for each confidence interval/error size combination. For example, a sample size of at least 6766 is required, if an error level of ± 0.01 at a confidence level of 90% is desired. (This result has already been entered in the table.)

Some of the calculations necessary to complete this table are shown below.

For 90% confidence and a 0.01 error

$$0.01^2 = 1.645^2 \frac{0.5 \times 0.5}{N}$$

$$N = \frac{1.645^2 \times 0.25}{0.01^2} = 6766$$

For 90% confidence and a 0.02 error

$$N = \frac{1.645^2 \times 0.25}{0.02^2} = 1692$$

For 90% confidence and a 0.03 error

$$N = \frac{1.645^2 \times 0.25}{0.03^2} = 752$$

For 90% confidence and a 0.04 error

$$N = \frac{1.645^2 \times 0.25}{0.04^2} = 423$$

For 90% confidence and a 0.05 error

$$N = \frac{1.645^2 \times 0.25}{0.05^2} = 271$$

The remaining entries to the table are calculated in a similar manner. The method is always

$$N = \frac{Z^2 \times 0.25}{e^2}$$

where Z is the value required by the particular level of confidence, and e is the margin of error.

Therefore Z will be 1.96 for a 95% confidence interval, 2.575 for a 99% interval and e will take the values 0.01, 0.02, 0.03, 0.04 and 0.05 respectively. The resulting table is given in figure 10 below.

Confidence Level %	0.01 error	0.02 error	0.03 error	0.04 error	0.05 error
90	6766	1692	752	423	271
95	9604	2401	1068	601	385
99	16577	4145	1842	1037	664

FIGURE 10: **Response to Activity 31**

4. SUMMARY

In this section we have considered sample problems

- deciding on **sample size**

- methods and calculations required for specified **error** and **confidence level** requirements

- **proportions** and sample size

Look back over any of these areas if you are not sure of any of the content before you move on.

SECTION 6

SIGNIFICANCE TESTING

1. INTRODUCTION

We have already seen how sampling enables us to make estimates of important statistics and express how confident we can be in the results. In any kind of research, or investigation we often formulate **hypotheses** about things. We can also use sampling to test whether or not these hypotheses are well-founded. This area of statistical analysis is often called **significance testing**.

We will start with two examples.

Example 1

In section 1 of this unit we needed to estimate the average grocery bill for the village of Hamdon. We established that the mean bill was £69.79 (see Activity 3). Suppose also, we found that the standard deviation was £11. Sometime later, we formulate a belief that average expenditure on groceries has increased, and we decide to test this by taking another sample of 12 households and repeating the survey. After making some allowances for inflation, we **now** obtain a sample mean of $\bar{X} = £77$.

Is it likely that average expenditure in Hamdon has increased?

You may think there is no problem here. After all, £77 is plainly greater than £69.79 so therefore our hypothesis must be true.

However, we must be careful. How do we know that we have not, by chance, selected 12 of the higher spending households? This would certainly give us a mistaken impression of the average grocery bill in the village.

What we can do is answer the following question:

> What is the probability that we would have selected a sample of 12 households with a mean grocery expenditure of £77, or more, if the population mean is in fact £69.79?

We can calculate this probability as follows

$$Pr(\bar{X} > 77) = Pr\left(Z > \dfrac{\bar{X} - \mu}{\dfrac{\sigma}{\sqrt{N}}}\right) =$$

$$Pr\left(Z > \dfrac{77 - 69.79}{3.1754}\right) \approx Pr(Z > 2.27)$$

$$= 0.011603$$

The chance therefore, of getting a sample where $\bar{X}$ is £77 when the real population mean is actually £69.79 is about 1.2% or approximately 12 in 1000.

You might possibly use this result to argue that, as there is only a small probability of obtaining such a sample mean if Hamdon's average grocery is £69.79, then it implies that the real population mean for the village is probably higher than this.

The above type of reasoning is used frequently in statistics, to help us decide whether to believe, or not to believe certain statements, or hypotheses. The process can be summarised as follows:

> I assume (for the time being) that the mean (μ) grocery expenditure in Hamdon is £69.79.

However, I have just taken a sample which has given me an estimate for μ of £77;

The chance that this would have occurred randomly is (approximately) 12 in 1000.

Because this is (arguably) a low probability, I am therefore forced to reconsider my original assumption that the mean is £69.79. It is probably higher than this.

This is an example of **statistical reasoning**.

Example 2

This is a rather more trivial (though quite enlightening) example.

Suppose you believe that a coin is 'unfair', that is, it does not have even chances of showing heads and tails when tossed. You decide to test its fairness by taking a sample of 100 throws and counting the number of heads. You find that 65 heads are obtained. Now the proportion of heads you would expect to get with a fair is 0.5 (50%). You have actually obtained a proportion from your sample of 65/100 = 0.65 (65%).

Does this convince you that the coin is biased?

ACTIVITY 30

(a)   Use the coin example above. If the coin really is fair, what would be the probability of having a sample of 100 throws of the coin and finding that the proportion of heads obtained was 0.65?

(b)   Does the calculation you made in question (a) convince you that the coin is biased?

In Activity 30 we have a sample size of 100. If the coin is fair, we would expect 50% heads. Thus the population proportion should be $\Pi = 0.5$. However, we have obtained a sample proportion of $p = 0.65$.

We should not immediately jump to conclusions about the unfairness of the coin just because we have obtained more than 50% heads; perhaps such a result is not unlikely?

$$Pr(p > 0.5) = Pr(Z > \frac{p - \Pi}{\sqrt{\frac{\Pi(1 - \Pi)}{N}}})$$

$$Pr(p > 0.5) = Pr(Z > \frac{0.65 - 0.50}{0.05}) = Pr(Z > 3)$$

So we have that

$$Pr(\text{65\% plus heads with 100 throws of a fair coin}) = Pr(Z > 3)$$

This is approximately 0.001.

So we would only have a 1 in 1000 chance of such a result with a genuinely fair coin.

This is a very low probability, and we might think it reasonably safe to conclude that the coin is therefore not fair.

Here again is another example of statistical reasoning.

2. THE CONSTRUCTION OF STATISTICAL TESTS

We now need to formalise the statistical testing procedure we have rather casually used on the grocery and coin-tossing examples.

1.   First, we set up a hypothesis whose truth or falsity needs to be tested. In the grocery example, we might have stated this hypothesis as follows:

'The average grocery bill for the village of Hamdon has not increased, remaining at £69.79'.

The hypothesis is formulated in deliberately cautious terms; we deny what the new sample evidence is telling us (that there has been an increase to £77), until we have carried out tests.

Such a hypothesis is known as a **null hypothesis**, and is often abbreviated by the symbol H_0.

2. We next formulate what we can call the **alternative hypothesis**. This is the hypothesis which we might have to consider if we find that H_0 is untrue. It is usually symbolised by the abbreviation H_A. In the grocery example H_A may be written as

'The mean grocery bill for Hamdon is now greater than £69.79'

Notice we do not say that the mean has increased to £77. We are being deliberately cautious: all we are allowing ourselves to consider is that the mean has **increased**.

3. The next step is not so easy to explain. We have to formally describe the **criteria** whereby we are going to accept or reject H_0.

We have used probability as the criteria; we have reasoned that since a sample result of £77 was rather improbable in a population where the mean was £69.79, then we might reasonably start questioning whether the mean still remained at this level. However, when does something start to become too improbable to be believed? How low should the probability of an event be before we dismiss it as untrue? This probability figure is decided by the researcher at the outset of a test, and is known as the **critical value**.

Suppose, for the moment, we decide on a figure of 0.05, or 5% as our critical value. What this means is that if the probability of our sample result is 0.05 or above, then we hold that it is quite a likely result in the circumstances, and do not reject our H_0. On the other hand, if it should fall below 0.05, then we have to consider that such a sample result sheds doubt on the truth of H_0.

The probability of the sample result in the grocery example was 0.012, which is below 0.05, and would thus lead us to cast doubt on our belief that the mean bill was still £69.79. However, rather than use probability figures direct, it has become conventional to use the normal curve Z-value associated with the critical probability level.

Now if you glance down the tables of areas under the normal curve, you will find that the value $Z = 1.645$ has a probability of (approximately) 5% of being exceeded.

So $Z = 1.645$ is our **critical value**, and we reject H_0 only if the standardised value of our sample result exceeds this. The type of test here described is known as **'a significance test at level 0.05.'**

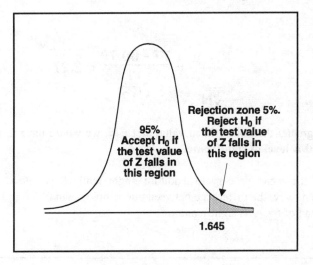

Rejection zone 5%.
Reject H_0 if
the test value
of Z falls in
this region

95%
Accept H_0 if
the test value
of Z falls in
this region

1.645

FIGURE 11: **Test of Significance**

Figure 11 illustrates the process involved in a 5% test of significance.

Now in case all of the above seems rather indigestible, we can attempt to clarify by setting up the Hamdon grocery test in a precise manner.

This is done in the following way.

The Significance Test for the Hamdon Data

H_0:   The mean grocery bill remains at £69.79.

H_A: The mean grocery bill has increased.

Significance Level: 0.05

Critical Value of Z: 1.645

Decision Rule: Standardise $\overline{X}$, if the result is
                      less than Z = 1.645, accept H_0.

In this case, when we standardise the sample mean we obtain

$$Z = \frac{\overline{X} - \mu}{\dfrac{\sigma}{\sqrt{N}}} = \frac{77 - 69.79}{\dfrac{11}{\sqrt{12}}} = 2.27$$

Since 2.27 is greater than our critical value of 1.645, we would have to reject the null hypothesis **at this level of significance**.

It looks as if the mean grocery expenditure might really have risen. To put this a slightly different way, the difference between our sample mean of 77 and the presumed population mean of 69.79 is significant.

ACTIVITY 31

Reconsider example 2, the coin-tossing example. Formally set up a hypothesis test at a significance level of 5%, and use it to decide whether the coin is fair or not.

Use the Hamdon grocery example as your model for this procedure, but remember that this problem concerns **proportions rather than means.**

If the coin is fair then the population proportion Π, should be 0.5. We have a sample of 100 giving rise to a sample proportion $p = 0.65$.

We begin by assuming that the sample evidence is misleading and that the true state of affairs is that the coin is really fair.

So we would have a formal 0.05 significance test as follows:

H_0: **The population proportion is $\Pi = 0.5$. The coin is fair.**

H_A: **The population proportion is a value $\Pi > 0.5$. The coin is biased.**

Significance level: **0.05**

Critical value: **$Z = 1.645$.**

Decision rule: **Accept H_0 if $Z < 1.645$ otherwise reject.**

Again, notice the cautious way in which H_A has been framed. We do not say that the proportion of heads is 65%; only that **it is more than 50%**.

We now conduct the test.

$$Z = \frac{p - \Pi}{\sqrt{\dfrac{\Pi(1 - \Pi)}{N}}} = \frac{0.65 - 0.5}{0.05} = 3$$

and since 3 is greater than the critical value of 1.645, we cannot accept H_0; we would have to entertain the hypothesis that the coin may not be fair.

ACTIVITY 32

There is no reason why we should necessarily have to use a level of significance of 5% (0.05). Suppose we decide to use 1% instead. What difference would this have made to the Hamdon grocery and coin-tossing problems?

Hint: look at the formal hypothesis tests for each of these problems and try to determine exactly what would change, if 5% became 1%.

If we had decided that we should use the probability level of 1% instead of 5%, then we would be conducting a 'test of significance at the 1% level'.
The part of the test which says

critical value: Z = 1.645

becomes

critical value: Z = 2.33.

We now have to compare the Z value of our test statistic $\overline{X}$ or p with 2.33. If this Z exceeds 2.33 then we conclude that there appears to be a significant difference between the hypothesised value of μ (or Π) and the sample result.

What happens to our two examples?

With the coin tossing example the result of the test remains unchanged. We obtained a Z of 3, which is clearly greater than the critical Z of 2.33. We would thus continue to question the fairness of the coin (reject H_0).

In the Hamdon grocery example however, the change in the level of significance from 5% to 1% has caused us to change our decision. The Z value for our test statistic was 2.27 in this case. Now this is NOT greater than the critical Z of 2.33, and we would therefore NOT reject H_0 **at this level of significance**.

Think about what happens when we choose a level of significance for a test. If you compare the process with what happens in a legal trial, then we can equate the level of significance with the amount of proof we need. A 1% level means we are asking for a higher level of proof (compared to 5%) before we reject H_0.

Determining the level of significance is a matter of judgement for the analyst.

We shall return to this problem before concluding this unit.

ACTIVITY 33

A machine is designed to produce screws which are declared by the manufacturer to have a nominal length of 5 mm. The machine operates to a standard deviation of 0.072 mm. It is important that the variation of lengths is kept controlled, since buyers are entitled to refunds if the screws are not as specified.

A random sample of 400 screws produced by this machine is found to have a mean length of 5.008 mm.

State, giving your reason, whether the evidence of this sample suggests that length is significantly greater than the nominal 5 mm.

Use a significance level of 5%.

We first set up the test in formal terms.

H₀: **The mean length of screws is 5 mm, as stated.**

Hₐ: **The mean length is greater than 5 mm.**

Significance Level: **0.05.**

Critical Value of Z: **1.645**

Decision Rule: **Standardise $\overline{X}$, if the result is less than Z = 1.645, accept H₀.**

Second, we obtain the Z value for the test statistic.

$$Z = \frac{\overline{X} - \mu}{\frac{\sigma}{\sqrt{N}}} = \frac{5.008 - 5}{\frac{0.072}{\sqrt{400}}} = 2.22$$

Z = 2.22 > 1.645

We would therefore have to declare the result significant at this level; it appears that average screw length is greater than that nominally declared by the manufacturer. So we therefore cannot accept H₀.

Notice that if we had used a 1% level of significance we would have accepted H₀, since Z = 2.22 < 2.33.

Whether or not the manufacturer accepts the result of the 5% test depends very much upon whether he/she accepts the 'burden of proof' implied by such a test. A 1% test is a more stringent requirement for a sample result to pass.

ACTIVITY 34

The RAMBO ll is a popular brand of micro computer and of a sample of 250 sold, 16 had to be returned for repair within the first year. It has been established that 4.5% of all micro computers have to be returned for repair within their first year.

Is there any evidence to suppose that the RAMBO ll is less reliable than the average?

We will equate the repair rate with reliability and it is generally 4.5% = 0.045. For the RAMBO it is 16/250 = 0.064. Is this significantly greater than the general rate? Or could such a difference be due to normal sampling variation?

As always, we begin by setting up the formal hypothesis test. In this case, at the outset of the test we would assume that there is no difference between the RAMBO and other machines. We begin by using a 5% significance test.

H_0:   **There is no difference between the RAMBO and other computers. $\Pi = 0.045$.**

H_A: **The population proportion for the RAMBO is a value $\Pi > 0.045$. The machine has a significantly higher repair rate.**

Significance level: 0.05

Critical Value: Z = 1.645.

Decision rule: Accept H_0 if Z < 1.645 otherwise reject.

We now conduct the test.

$$Z = \frac{p - \Pi}{\sqrt{\dfrac{\Pi(1 - \Pi)}{N}}} = \frac{0.064 - 0.045}{0.013111} = 1.45$$

$$Z = 1.45 < 1.645$$

The result is not significant, and we accept the null hypothesis that there is no difference between the RAMBO machines and others.

3. POSSIBLE MISTAKES IN STATISTICAL TESTS

Since we are making choices between conflicting hypotheses on the basis of probability rather than certainty then we will sometimes make the wrong choice. What possible mistakes could we make?

As an illustration, we will consider the data used in Activity 35 – RAMBO computers. Suppose we have carried out all the sampling and estimation, but have not yet performed a statistical test. What are the possible options?

1.   We might have decided that RAMBO computers are as reliable as other computers, and this is subsequently borne out by fact. We would have correctly accepted H_0.

2.   We might come to the conclusion that RAMBO computers are **less** reliable than others and this is later found to be true. We would have thus have correctly rejected H_0.

3.   We might conclude that RAMBO machines are as reliable as others and it later becomes apparent that they are not. In this case we would have incorrectly accepted H_0.

4.   Lastly, we might accept the hypothesis that RAMBO produce a less reliable machine than other makers, but later find that there is no difference between the products. By doing so, we would have incorrectly rejected H_0.

These decisions are shown schematically in figure 12.

	H_0 IS TRUE	H_0 IS FALSE
WE REJECT H_0	This is an error (Type 1)	Correct decision
WE ACCEPT H_0	Correct decision	This is an error (Type 2)

FIGURE 12: **Decisions Between Conflicting Hypotheses**

If the analyst accepts a null hypothesis which is true or rejects one which is false, then correct decisions have been made, and no one need worry. On the other hand, if the analyst rejects a null hypothesis which turns out to be true, then a mistaken decision has been made. This type of mistake is often called a **type 1 error**. (Some authorities use the alternative term 'type α error', where α is the Greek letter alpha.)

Also, if the researcher accepts a null hypothesis which turns out to be false, then this is also a mistake – often called a **type 2 error**. (Sometimes called a 'type β error', where β is the Greek letter beta.)

The probability of a type 1 error is easy to calculate. It is always equal to the level of significance chosen. For example, if you choose a 1% significance level, then there is a 1% chance that you might reject H_0 when it is, in fact, true. It is more difficult to calculate type 2 errors, and we will not attempt this in this unit. Suffice it to say that a great deal of a statisticians work is connected with devising tests which minimise the chances of making type 1 and 2 errors.

ACTIVITY 35

A marketing manager is considering whether or not to launch a newly designed product, and requires some evidence that it will do significantly better than break even. The product will break even if it achieves a market share in excess of 10% of sales for that product class. The business will sample potential buyers to ascertain purchase intentions.

(a)   Set up a formal hypothesis test for the survey information.

(b)   How would you explain to the manager the meaning of making a type 1 or 2 error in this case?

(c)   The sample data are now in, and for a sample size of 200 reveals a share of the market of 13%. Carry out the test you have designed in part (a) and advise the marketing manager accordingly.

Use a 5% level of significance.

⇒

Activity 35 continued...

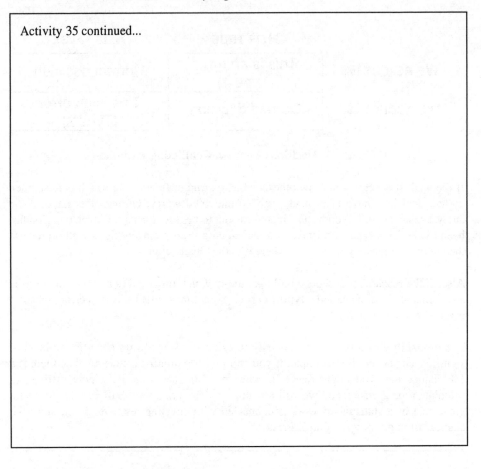

Firstly, we set out the required test in formal terms. (Using a 5% significance level.)

H$_0$:   **Π = 0.10. The share of the market is not above break even.**

H$_A$:   **Π > 0.10. The market share is significantly above break even.**

Significance level: 5%

Critical Value of Z: 1.645.

Decision Rule: Accept H$_0$ if Z < 1.645.

The test has been set out in typical cautious fashion. We adopt the initial position (in H_0) that sales will not be above break even, unless we can show otherwise. We would need to explain to the manager that we could

> make a type 1 error, which would mean concluding that the product will be successful when it is, in fact, a flop;

> make a type 2 error, which would mean concluding that the product will not achieve break even, when it would be a success.

Finally, when we have the sample information, we can actually carry out the statistical test.

We have

$$Z = \frac{p - \Pi}{\sqrt{\frac{\Pi(1 - \Pi)}{N}}} = \frac{0.13 - 0.10}{0.0212132} = 1.41$$

We obtain $Z = 1.41$, which is less than the critical 1.645. We cannot reject the null hypothesis. The sample evidence does not support the contention that the product will be a success. We would, of course, have to remind the manager of the possibility of our having made a type 2 error.

We finish looking at statistical testing by pointing out that the subject is a vast one. We have only dealt with one possible type of test; a test between a sample mean (proportion) and a hypothesised population mean (proportion). There are other possibilities.

Nevertheless, even in this limited coverage, you should have acquired a feeling for the kind of reasoning used by statisticians when they judge sample evidence.

4. NOTES CONCERNING THE USE OF SAMPLING THEORY

If you undertake any further study of the field of statistics, you will eventually find that some aspects of sampling theory have been simplified in these notes in order to make for greater clarity. You need not worry too much about this. Our aim in this unit has been to give you some idea of the kind of reasoning which is embodied in statistical analysis, rather than to give a detailed practitioners guide. No great harm has been done to the principles of sampling. The points which should be born in mind should you ever undertake further study in this subject are

(1)   The sampling theory described in these notes can only be used on non-normal populations if the sample size N is large. In practice, 'large' means a sample size of 30 or more. For smaller samples other techniques are available.

(2)   Strictly speaking, the technique for calculating confidence intervals and conducting significance tests described in these notes should only be used if σ, the population standard deviation is known. If s is unknown, and we have to use σ, the sample standard deviation as an estimate of it, then we should not use the normal distribution. Generally though, if N is large enough, this point becomes less important.

(3)   If the population size is **finite**, then the standard error should be adjusted by use of something called the 'finite population correction factor'. However, you may regard this matter as of little consequence provided that the population is very large.

5. SUMMARY

In this unit we are concerned with the problems which occur whenever samples are used to make estimates of important statistical values. The statistics estimated in these notes were the mean and the proportion, although the method could be extended to others.

Looking back through the whole of this unit we have seen that

● any sample estimate contains an error. The central limit theorem provides us with the means whereby we can not only make estimates, but also make some useful observations concerning the possible degree of sampling error. In particular, we can calculate confidence interval estimates, as well as point estimates

● given some specifications relating to level of accuracy and degree of confidence required, it is possible to compute the minimum size of sample needed in order to obtain trustworthy data

● sampling theory can help the decision maker to choose between competing hypotheses

If you are unsure of any of the topics covered in this unit, check back to the appropriate section.

REFERENCES

Students may follow up this subject by reading the following texts:

1. MORRIS, C. *Quantitative Approaches in Business Studies*. Pitman Publishing.
   Chapter 3 contains some information on sampling method – only briefly touched on in this unit. Chapters 10 and 11 give an overview of estimation and hypothesis testing.
2. CURWIN and SLATER. *Quantitative Methods for Business Decisions*. Chapman & Hall.
   Part 5 contains a good account of estimation and significance testing. In addition, this section of the book will also give you an introduction to different kinds of statistical test, which have not been dealt with in this unit.

GLOSSARY

The following is an alphabetical listing of the technical terms most often encountered in this unit.

Alternative hypothesis A hypothesis set up in competition with the null hypothesis during a significance test. If the null hypothesis is rejected, then the alternative will be considered as a possibility.

Census A full count or enumeration of the population.

Central limit theorem A complex mathematical theorem, which shows that for normal populations, the distributions of sample means and proportions drawn from an infinite population are themselves normal. The same conclusions are true of sampling from non-normal populations provided that the population standard deviation is known, and that the sample size is large (usually taken to mean size 30 or more).

Confidence interval estimate An estimate of a population value which states that this value lies between some stated maximum and minimum value, and also quotes a degree of 'confidence' or trust in this interval.

Confidence level A measure of the degree of trust with which an interval estimate can be held to contain the true population value. A 99% confidence level would be more likely to contain the population value than a 95% level.

Critical value A probability value which is used to decide between the null and alternative hypotheses. If the probability of a particular sample result is more than this, then the null hypothesis will be accepted. If less, then the null hypothesis will be rejected. In most cases, the probability value is replaced by the standard normal, or Z value associated with it.

Hypothesis test A formal test, using probability and sampling distributions to decide which of two conflicting hypotheses should be accepted. Sometimes referred to as a significance test.

Interval estimate See *confidence interval estimate.*

Large sample A sample usually held to be of size 30 or more. If the sample size is less than this, then the conclusions of the central limit theorem cannot be judged to hold for non-normal populations.

Level of significance The level of probability which is to be used to judge between acceptability, or otherwise of the null hypothesis in a significance test. See *critical value.*

Margin of error An imprecise term. Sometimes used to mean precision and sometimes sampling error.

Null hypothesis A hypothesis set up for testing during a significance test. If accepted, the sample evidence will be held to be no more than acceptable sample variation. If rejected, the sample evidence will be held to show a significant change in some population value. See alternative hypothesis.

Point estimate A single figure estimate of some population value. Does not, in itself, give any indication of the size of sampling error.

Population The totality of things under analysis by sample. The greater whole from which a sample is drawn.

Precision The precision of a sample (interval) estimate is the absolute size of the interval held to contain the population value.

Random numbers A series of numbers where the digits 0–9 have equal probabilities of occurring. Used to assist in the selection of random samples.

Random number generator A method for generating a sequence of random numbers, for example, random number tales, pocket calculators and computers.

Random sampling A method of sampling where, in its simplest form, every element of the population has equal chance of inclusion in the sample. A form of sampling generally held to produce the most reliable results.

Sample A selection of units from the population used to make inferences about that population.

Sample estimate A value calculated from sample data which is meant to be an estimate of some population value.

Sampling error The difference between a sample estimate and the population value. Sampling error is to be considered as variation inherent in the sampling process itself, and therefore to be distinguished from other kinds of error, such as miscalculations etc.

Sampling with replacement   A system of sampling where the unit is returned to the population after it has been sampled. It is therefore possible for the same unit to be included more than once in the sample. The conclusions of the central limit theorem depend upon the existence of this type of sampling.

Sampling without replacement   A sytem of sampling where the unit sampled is not returned to the population after it has been sampled. A unit may be included only once in the sample using this method. The conclusions of the central limit theorem are generalised tt such sampling methods.

Significance test   See Hypothesis test.

Standard error   The special name given to the standard deviation of a sample estimate. It is a very important statistic, since it dictates the degree of precision of a sample estimate. A larger sample size will produce a smaller standard error.

Type 1 (or α) error   This occurs where the analyst conducting a hypothesis test wrongly rejects a true null hy)thesis.

Type 2 (or β) error   This occurs where the analyst conducting a hypothesis test wrongly accepts a false null hyjthesis.

Universe   The same as population.

TABLES OF AREAS UNDER THE STANDARD NORMAL CURVE

TABLE VALUES CALCULATED USING HASTINGS BEST APPROXIMATION

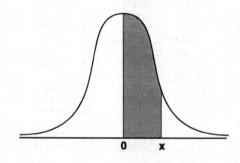

z	Area Between Mean and z	Area Beyond z	z	Area Between Mean and z	Area Beyond z
0.00	0.000000	0.500000	0.55	0.208840	0.291159
0.01	0.003988	0.496011	0.56	0.212259	0.287740
0.02	0.007977	0.492022	0.57	0.215660	0.284339
0.03	0.011965	0.488034	0.58	0.219042	0.280957
0.04	0.015952	0.484047	0.59	0.222404	0.277595
0.05	0.019938	0.480061	0.60	0.225746	0.274253
0.06	0.023921	0.476078	0.61	0.229068	0.270931
0.07	0.027902	0.472097	0.62	0.232370	0.267629
0.08	0.031880	0.468119	0.63	0.235652	0.264347
0.09	0.035855	0.464144	0.64	0.238913	0.261086
0.10	0.039827	0.460172	0.65	0.242153	0.257846
0.11	0.043794	0.456205	0.66	0.245372	0.254627
0.12	0.047757	0.452242	0.67	0.248570	0.251429
0.13	0.051716	0.448283	0.68	0.251747	0.248252
0.14	0.055669	0.444330	0.69	0.254902	0.245097
0.15	0.059617	0.440382	0.70	0.258036	0.241963
0.16	0.063558	0.436441	0.71	0.261147	0.238852
0.17	0.067494	0.432505	0.72	0.264237	0.235762
0.18	0.071423	0.428576	0.73	0.267304	0.232695
0.19	0.075344	0.424655	0.74	0.270349	0.229650
0.20	0.079259	0.420740	0.75	0.273372	0.226627
0.21	0.083165	0.416834	0.76	0.276372	0.223627
0.22	0.087063	0.412936	0.77	0.279349	0.220650
0.23	0.090953	0.409046	0.78	0.282304	0.217695
0.24	0.094834	0.405165	0.79	0.285235	0.214764
0.25	0.098705	0.401294	0.80	0.288144	0.211855
0.26	0.102567	0.397432	0.81	0.291029	0.208970
0.27	0.106419	0.393580	0.82	0.293891	0.206108
0.28	0.110260	0.389739	0.83	0.296730	0.203269
0.29	0.114091	0.385908	0.84	0.299545	0.200454
0.30	0.117910	0.382089	0.85	0.302337	0.197662
0.31	0.121719	0.378280	0.86	0.305105	0.194894
0.32	0.125515	0.374484	0.87	0.307849	0.192150
0.33	0.129299	0.370700	0.88	0.310570	0.189429
0.34	0.133071	0.366928	0.89	0.313266	0.186733
0.35	0.136830	0.363169	0.90	0.315939	0.184060
0.36	0.140575	0.359424	0.91	0.318588	0.181411
0.37	0.144308	0.355691	0.92	0.321213	0.178786
0.38	0.148026	0.351973	0.93	0.323814	0.176185
0.39	0.151731	0.348268	0.94	0.326391	0.173608
0.40	0.155421	0.344578	0.95	0.328943	0.171056
0.41	0.159096	0.340903	0.96	0.331472	0.168527
0.42	0.162756	0.337243	0.97	0.333976	0.166023
0.43	0.166401	0.333598	0.98	0.336456	0.163543
0.44	0.170031	0.329968	0.99	0.338912	0.161087
0.45	0.173644	0.326355	1.00	0.341344	0.158655
0.46	0.177241	0.322758	1.01	0.343752	0.156247
0.47	0.180822	0.319177	1.02	0.346135	0.153864
0.48	0.184385	0.315614	1.03	0.348494	0.151505
0.49	0.187932	0.312067	1.04	0.350829	0.149170
0.50	0.191462	0.308537	1.05	0.353140	0.146859
0.51	0.194973	0.305026	1.06	0.355427	0.144572
0.52	0.198467	0.301532	1.07	0.357690	0.142309
0.53	0.201943	0.298056	1.08	0.359928	0.140071
0.54	0.205401	0.294598	1.09	0.362143	0.137856

Z	Area Between Mean and Z	Area Beyond Z	Z	Area Between Mean and Z	Area Beyond Z
1.10	0.364333	0.135666	1.65	0.450528	0.049471
1.11	0.366500	0.133499	1.66	0.451542	0.048457
1.12	0.368642	0.131357	1.67	0.452540	0.047459
1.13	0.370761	0.129238	1.68	0.453521	0.046478
1.14	0.372856	0.127143	1.69	0.454486	0.045513
1.15	0.374927	0.125072	1.70	0.455434	0.044565
1.16	0.376975	0.123024	1.71	0.456367	0.043632
1.17	0.378999	0.121000	1.72	0.457283	0.042716
1.18	0.380999	0.119000	1.73	0.458184	0.041815
1.19	0.382976	0.117023	1.74	0.459070	0.040929
1.20	0.384930	0.115069	1.75	0.459940	0.040059
1.21	0.386860	0.113139	1.76	0.460796	0.039203
1.22	0.388767	0.111232	1.77	0.461636	0.038363
1.23	0.390651	0.109348	1.78	0.462462	0.037537
1.24	0.392512	0.107487	1.79	0.463273	0.036726
1.25	0.394350	0.105649	1.80	0.464069	0.035930
1.26	0.396165	0.103834	1.81	0.464852	0.035147
1.27	0.397957	0.102042	1.82	0.465620	0.034379
1.28	0.399727	0.100272	1.83	0.466375	0.033624
1.29	0.401474	0.098525	1.84	0.467115	0.032884
1.30	0.403199	0.096800	1.85	0.467843	0.032156
1.31	0.404901	0.095098	1.86	0.468557	0.031442
1.32	0.406582	0.093417	1.87	0.469258	0.030741
1.33	0.408240	0.091759	1.88	0.469945	0.030054
1.34	0.409877	0.090122	1.89	0.470621	0.029378
1.35	0.411491	0.088508	1.90	0.471283	0.028716
1.36	0.413084	0.086915	1.91	0.471933	0.028066
1.37	0.414656	0.085343	1.92	0.472571	0.027428
1.38	0.416206	0.083793	1.93	0.473196	0.026803
1.39	0.417735	0.082264	1.94	0.473810	0.026189
1.40	0.419243	0.080756	1.95	0.474411	0.025588
1.41	0.420730	0.079269	1.96	0.475002	0.024997
1.42	0.422196	0.077803	1.97	0.475580	0.024419
1.43	0.423641	0.076358	1.98	0.476148	0.023851
1.44	0.425066	0.074933	1.99	0.476704	0.023295
1.45	0.426470	0.073529	2.00	0.477249	0.022750
1.46	0.427854	0.072145	2.01	0.477784	0.022215
1.47	0.429219	0.070780	2.02	0.478308	0.021691
1.48	0.430563	0.069436	2.03	0.478821	0.021178
1.49	0.431887	0.068112	2.04	0.479324	0.020675
1.50	0.433192	0.066807	2.05	0.479817	0.020182
1.51	0.434478	0.065521	2.06	0.480300	0.019699
1.52	0.435744	0.064255	2.07	0.480773	0.019226
1.53	0.436991	0.063008	2.08	0.481237	0.018762
1.54	0.438219	0.061780	2.09	0.481691	0.018308
1.55	0.439429	0.060570	2.10	0.482135	0.017864
1.56	0.440619	0.059380	2.11	0.482570	0.017429
1.57	0.441792	0.058207	2.12	0.482997	0.017002
1.58	0.442946	0.057053	2.13	0.483414	0.016585
1.59	0.444082	0.055917	2.14	0.483822	0.016177
1.60	0.445200	0.054799	2.15	0.484222	0.015777
1.61	0.446301	0.053698	2.16	0.484613	0.015386
1.62	0.447383	0.052616	2.17	0.484996	0.015003
1.63	0.448449	0.051550	2.18	0.485371	0.014628
1.64	0.449497	0.050502	2.19	0.485737	0.014262
			2.20	0.486096	0.013903
			2.21	0.486400	0.013600

Z	Area Between Mean and Z	Area Beyond Z	Z	Area Between Mean and Z	Area Beyond Z
2.22	0.486790	0.013209	2.79	0.497364	0.002635
2.23	0.487126	0.012873	2.80	0.497444	0.002555
2.24	0.487454	0.012545	2.81	0.497522	0.002477
2.25	0.487775	0.012224	2.82	0.497598	0.002401
2.26	0.488089	0.011910	2.83	0.497672	0.002327
2.27	0.488396	0.011603	2.84	0.497744	0.002255
2.28	0.488696	0.011303	2.85	0.497813	0.002186
2.29	0.488989	0.011010	2.86	0.497881	0.002118
2.30	0.489275	0.010724	2.87	0.497947	0.002052
2.31	0.489555	0.010444	2.88	0.498011	0.001988
2.32	0.489829	0.010170	2.89	0.498073	0.001926
2.33	0.490096	0.009903	2.90	0.498134	0.001865
2.34	0.490358	0.009641	2.91	0.498192	0.001807
2.35	0.490613	0.009386	2.92	0.498249	0.001750
2.36	0.490862	0.009137	2.93	0.498305	0.001694
2.37	0.491105	0.008894	2.94	0.498358	0.001641
2.38	0.491343	0.008656	2.95	0.498411	0.001588
2.39	0.491575	0.008424	2.96	0.498461	0.001538
2.40	0.491802	0.008197	2.97	0.498510	0.001489
2.41	0.492023	0.007976	2.98	0.498558	0.001441
2.42	0.492239	0.007760	2.99	0.498605	0.001394
2.43	0.492450	0.007549	3.00	0.498650	0.001349
2.44	0.492656	0.007343	3.01	0.498693	0.001306
2.45	0.492857	0.007142	3.02	0.498736	0.001263
2.46	0.493053	0.006946	3.03	0.498777	0.001222
2.47	0.493244	0.006755	3.04	0.498817	0.001182
2.48	0.493430	0.006569	3.05	0.498855	0.001144
2.49	0.493612	0.006387	3.06	0.498893	0.001106
2.50	0.493790	0.006209	3.07	0.498929	0.001070
2.51	0.493963	0.006036	3.08	0.498964	0.001035
2.52	0.494132	0.005867	3.09	0.498999	0.001000
2.53	0.494296	0.005703	3.10	0.499032	0.000967
2.54	0.494457	0.005542	3.11	0.499064	0.000935
2.55	0.494613	0.005386	3.12	0.499095	0.000904
2.56	0.494766	0.005233	3.13	0.499125	0.000874
2.57	0.494915	0.005084	3.14	0.499155	0.000844
2.58	0.495059	0.004940	3.15	0.499183	0.000816
2.59	0.495201	0.004798	3.16	0.499211	0.000788
2.60	0.495338	0.004661	3.17	0.499237	0.000762
2.61	0.495472	0.004527	3.18	0.499263	0.000736
2.62	0.495603	0.004396	3.19	0.499288	0.000711
2.63	0.495730	0.004269	3.20	0.499312	0.000687
2.64	0.495854	0.004145	3.21	0.499336	0.000663
2.65	0.495975	0.004024	3.22	0.499358	0.000641
2.66	0.496092	0.003907	3.23	0.499380	0.000619
2.67	0.496207	0.003792	3.24	0.499402	0.000597
2.68	0.496318	0.003681	3.25	0.499422	0.000577
2.69	0.496427	0.003572	3.30	0.499516	0.000483
2.70	0.496532	0.003467	3.35	0.499595	0.000404
2.71	0.496635	0.003364	3.40	0.499663	0.000336
2.72	0.496735	0.003264	3.45	0.499719	0.000280
2.73	0.496833	0.003166	3.50	0.499767	0.000232
2.74	0.496927	0.003072	3.60	0.499840	0.000159
2.75	0.497020	0.002979	3.70	0.499892	0.000107
2.76	0.497109	0.002890	3.80	0.499927	0.000072
2.77	0.497197	0.002802	3.90	0.499951	0.000048
2.78	0.497281	0.002718	4.00	0.499968	0.000031

UNIT 8

INDEX NUMBERS

CONTENTS

UNIT OBJECTIVES

After working through this unit you will be able to

- calculate simple index numbers

- use index numbers to measure changes in value and volume

- use index numbers to remove the effect of inflation from a series

- describe the individual component movements of a time series

- use the process of 'moving averages' to deseasonalise a time series

- use the method of moving averages and regression analysis together in order to make forecasts of time series

- use the additive and multiplicative models of time series

SECTION 1

THE MEASUREMENT OF CHANGE

1. WHY MEASURE CHANGE?

In section 6 of this unit you will be introduced to some aspects of business forecasting. Most people can readily see the importance to business of forecasting change, reasoning that fairly accurate predictions of variables such as sales, volume of credit, income, etc, will help a business to anticipate change. The same people do not always see the importance of measuring **past change**. Why should we wish to measure the variations in prices, credit, income, etc over, say, the last year? Surely this is past history?

The reason why we should interest ourselves in past change is because we almost always base business forecasts on what happened in the past. If we wish to forecast what might happen in the future then it will help if we have a clear measurement of how key economic variables have changed in the past.

In this first section you will learn just how important certain quantities called **index numbers** are to the measurement of change. For example, the Retail Price Index (RPI) is an example of an index number, and is regarded as an important economic statistic.

2. SIMPLE INDEX NUMBERS

We will begin this unit covering index numbers and time series with a simple example. Figure 1 below, shows the change in volume of UK imports of a given category of goods for the years 1988 - 1992

YEAR	IMPORTS (£ billion)
1988	10.89
1989	11.41
1990	12.73
1991	14.46
1992	14.50

FIGURE 1: **Change in Volume of UK Imports**

One easy method of measuring change would be to use percentages.

ACTIVITY 1

The table below is an expanded copy of figure 1.

For each of the years 1988 to 1992 measure the change that has occurred in imports compared with 1988, as a number and as a percentage and enter your answers in the blank columns provided.

YEAR	IMPORTS	INCREASE (OVER 1988)	INCREASE AS %
1988	10.89		
1989	11.41		
1990	12.73		
1991	14.46		
1992	14.50		

Answering this Activity will mean we have to calculate each years import figure change since 1988.

The calculation for Activity 1 is shown in figure 2 below.

YEAR	IMPORTS	INCREASE (OVER 1988)	INCREASE AS %
1988	10.89	0.00	0.0
1989	11.41	0.52	4.8
1990	12.73	1.84	16.9
1991	14.46	3.57	32.8
1992	14.50	3.61	33.1

FIGURE 2: **Solution to Activity 1**

Remember that you have been asked to measure change **compared with 1988** each time, therefore you must take the difference between each import figure and the 1988 figure and express this difference as a percentage of 1988 imports. The result is the last column of figure 2. Notice that imports rose slowly from 1988 to 1989 but increased very rapidly betweem 1989 and 1991. From 1991 to 1992 the rate of increase slowed down again.

The presentation of a series of figures calculated as percentage changes on a year chosen as a **fixed base** is the key concept to understand when you are learning about index numbers. A fixed reference point – often called the base year – is chosen, and subsequent years figures are calculated as percentage changes when compared with this base year.

There is one simple but important difference between the methods of Activity 1 and the way in which index numbers are usually prepared.

In the solution to Activity 1, the current years percentage figure was calculated as follows;

$$\frac{\text{Current year imports - 1988 imports}}{\text{1988 imports}} \times 100$$

where current year means the year for which a percentage is to be calculated.

A true index number for imports would be calculated using the following formula, which we will call formula 1.

Formula 1

A Simple Index Number

An index number for a current year is calculated by

$$\frac{\text{Current year data}}{\text{Base year data}} \times 100$$

So an index number does not just measure the **difference** between base year and current year as a percentage of base year, it calculates the **whole** of the current year data as a percentage of the base year.

What effect do you think this will this have on our measure of the change for the import data of figure 1 and Activity 1?

While you are thinking about the answer look at the table in figure 3. It should answer this question, and illustrate the method of index number calculation.

YEAR	IMPORTS	CALCULATION	RESULT
1988	10.89	$\frac{10.89}{10.89} \times 100$	100.0
1989	11.41	$\frac{11.41}{10.89} \times 100$	104.8
1990	12.73	$\frac{12.73}{10.89} \times 100$	116.9
1991	14.46	$\frac{14.46}{10.89} \times 100$	132.8
1992	14.50	$\frac{14.50}{10.89} \times 100$	133.1

FIGURE 3: **Index Number Series for Import Data**

Every one of the figure 2 percentages has had 100 added to it. This is the general method for computing an index number series. The base year is always 100.

Each subsequent year will be above or below 100 depending on whether there has been an increase or decrease in the data compared with the base year.

So an index number of, say, 132.8 (the figure for 1991) will mean that imports have risen by 32.8% since 1988.

There is just one other very important thing to note when using index numbers. The statement

'the import change index for 1991 was 132.8'

is incomplete. The correct statement should be

'the import change index for 1991 was 132.8 (1988 = 100)'.

The expression '1988 = 100' is the usual way of telling the user of the statistics what the reference point, or base year is. Such an expression must be included with every quotation of index numbers, otherwise the figures will be meaningless.

Do we have to choose 1988 as the base year for the import index? Try this next Activity.

ACTIVITY 2

For this Activity, look back to the import data of figure 1. Recalculate the index number series with 1990 as the base year (ie 1990 = 100).

What will be the effect of doing this?

We must answer this question by repeating the calculations of figure 3, but this time use the 1990 figure of 12.73 as the basis for the indices. This is shown in figure 4 below.

YEAR	IMPORTS	CALCULATION	RESULT
1988	10.89	$\dfrac{10.89}{12.73} \times 100$	85.5
1989	11.41	$\dfrac{11.41}{12.73} \times 100$	89.6
1990	12.73	$\dfrac{12.73}{12.73} \times 100$	100.0
1991	14.46	$\dfrac{14.46}{12.73} \times 100$	113.6
1992	14.50	$\dfrac{14.50}{12.73} \times 100$	113.9

FIGURE 4: **Index Number Series for Import Data with 1990 = 100**

The last column shows the required index. It measures change over the same period as before but all changes are comparative to 1990 and not 1988.

Notice that the index for 1988 is now 85.5. What does this mean? The figure is below 100 which indicates that imports were below the 1990 level. In fact, they were

$$100 - 85.5 = 14.5\%$$

below their 1990 level.

It is often the case that the base year of a series is the **first year** in that series. However, as Activity 2 shows, there is no reason why this should always be so. We can vary the convention at any time provided we always make a statement such as '1988 = 100', or '1990 = 100', for the information of the user of the statistics.

3. MORE COMPLEX INDEX NUMBERS

The import index calculated earlier measured the changes in only one item. Index numbers will be of little use to us unless we can use them to measure the amount by which a collection of items has changed. We can use the example of a share price index to show how this might be done. Many world financial centres have their own share price index. You may have heard of the *Financial Times* share price index, or the Wall Street index. These are published in the financial columns of newpapers and are highly regarded as indicators of movements of stocks and share prices.

They are measures of the changes not just of one share price, but of a whole range of shares.

How do they do this?

First, the compilers of the index assemble a sample or 'basket' of shares selected so as to represent the range of financial securities normally dealt in on the world's stock exchanges. The price changes in this basket of shares are monitored day by day, and the average change is calculated.

Take a look at figure 5, which shows price movements of three shares between January and December 1991.

SHARE	PRICE JAN 1991	PRICE DEC 1991
English Products PLC	£0.10	£0.15
World Manufactures Inc	£0.40	£0.45
Anglo Euro Consolidated	£1.75	£2.55

FIGURE 5: **Share Price Movements**

ACTIVITY 3

Referring to the data in figure 5, calculate the mean share price in

(a)   January 1991
(b)   December 1991.

Use the two figures you have obtained to calculate a share price index for December 1991, given that January 1991 = 100.

Activity 3 continued...

The mean share price for January 1991 is

$$\frac{0.10 + 0.40 + 1.75}{3} = 0.75$$

and for December 1991 it is

$$\frac{0.15 + 0.45 + 2.55}{3} = 1.05$$

To create the index for December 1991 (January = 100) we can percentage the December figure on the January one. This would be

$$\frac{1.05}{0.75} \times 100 = 140$$

Therefore our share price index would be

Jan 1991 = 100
Dec 1991 = 140

which suggests that share prices have risen by 40% over the period.

Although you may think it obvious, it is necessary to stress the point that an index such as the one calculated for Activity 3 indicates the **average** movement in prices; some share prices will have risen by more and some by less. Indeed, it is quite possible that some shares not included in our sample will have fallen over the period.

4. THE 'PRICE RELATIVE' METHOD

In many cases, before the overall index number is calculated, the individual items are themselves subjected to the index number treatment. The final index number is an average of these individual components. We can use the share price data of Activity 3 to illustrate the general method. We begin by expressing each December price as a percentage of the January one.

$$\text{\textit{English Products PLC}} = \frac{0.15}{0.10} \times 100 = 150$$

$$\text{\textit{World Manufactures}} = \frac{0.45}{0.40} \times 100 = 113$$

$$\text{\textit{Anglo Euro Consolidated}} = \frac{2.55}{1.75} \times 100 = 146$$

Finally we obtain the mean of these three indices.

$$\frac{150 + 113 + 146}{3} = 136$$

We do not need to multiply by 100 at the final stage with this method since the figures being averaged are already percentages.

So now our index is

$$\text{January } 1991 = 100$$
$$\text{December } 1991 = 136$$

This method of constructing an index is often referred to as the **price relative** method. The term price relative is actually an alternative name for index number. It has become the convention to refer to individual component figures (such as the share price percentage changes) as price relatives, and reserve the term index number to describe the final average of these relatives.

The method can be summarised as

      calculate a price relative for each item comprising the index

      calculate the mean of the resulting price relatives

The resulting figure is the overall index number.

ACTIVITY 4

In Activity 3, you obtained an overall share price index of 140, suggesting a 40% average increase in prices. The price relative method has just given us a figure of 136 – a 36% increase in prices. Can you suggest a reason for the difference in these results?

In the share price data, one of the shares – Anglo Euro Consolidated – has a much higher share price than the others. Consequently it has a greater impact than the other share prices in the calculation of the arithmetic mean.

Note

you may like to look back on the section dealing with the arithmetic mean in unit 2 to remind yourself of the tendency of this measure of central tendency to be biassed towards large numbers.

Sometimes, in order to deal with this problem of the arithmetic mean, a method called the **geometric mean** is used to obtain the average of a series of numbers. The geometric mean of a series of N numbers is obtained by multiplying the N numbers and then taking the Nth root of the result. Therefore the geometric mean of the three share prices in January 1991 would be obtained as

$$\sqrt[3]{(0.10 \times 0.40 \times 1.75)} = 0.41$$

and the geometric mean of the December prices is

$$\sqrt[3]{(0.15 \times 0.45 \times 2.55)} = 0.56$$

The resulting index would then be

$$(0.56)/(0.41) \times 100 = 136.6$$

Which is less than the index of 140 given by using the arithmetic mean.

The geometric mean of a series of numbers has the effect of reducing the impact of large numbers on the averaging process. We shall not be pursuing its use any further in this unit but you should be aware that we are not restricted to the arithmetic mean when we wish to calculate an overall index number.

When we turn individual share **prices** into price **relatives** we are then working with the same common denominator of percentages and the effect of Anglo Euro's high price on the arithmetic mean calculation is removed.

This effect is one of the advantages of the price relative method.

ACTIVITY 5

In this Activity we consider whether the methods described so far can produce an index number to measure changes in retail prices.

Suppose that there are three basic products, bread, butter and milk which feature in the shopping baskets of all shoppers.

➡

Activity 5 continued...

In January 1987 the unit price of bread was 30 pence, but this had increased to 39 pence by January 1988. Milk had increased from 10 pence to 11 pence a unit over the same period, while butter had changed from 40 pence to 50 pence a unit.

Use this information to construct an all-items index for January 1988 (January 1987 = 100).

We will deal with Activity 5 by first converting each price change to a relative.

$$\textbf{\textit{Bread}} \quad \frac{39}{30} \times 100 = 130$$

$$\textbf{\textit{Milk}} \quad \frac{11}{10} \times 100 = 110$$

$$\textbf{\textit{Butter}} \quad \frac{50}{40} \times 100 = 125$$

The overall (all-items) index of retail prices would then be

$$\frac{130 + 110 + 125}{3} \approx 121.7$$

So the retail price index would be

$$\text{January 1987} = 100$$
$$\text{January 1988} = 121.7$$

suggesting an average 21.7% increase in prices over the period.

Is this the method by which index numbers, including retail price indices, are usually calculated? The honest answer to this question is 'not quite'. We have gone some way towards our goal of obtaining a measure of change but there is one additional step which we will need to take before we can describe our index number as an effective measure.

We will look at this requirement in the next section.

5. SUMMARY

In this first section we have

- examined the reasons why we should **measure change**

- calculated **simple** and **complex** index numbers

- introduced the **price relative method** for the construction of indices and practised its use

If you are unsure of any of these topics, check back **now** before you read on.

SECTION 2

WEIGHTED INDICES AND AGGREGATIVE METHODS OF CALCULATION

1. WEIGHTED INDEX NUMBERS

At the end of section 1, we asked whether the methods so far described produce an index which is a reliable measure of change. It was hinted that we needed to take one further step before we could justifiably say this. We must now describe this step.

ACTIVITY 6

In Activity 5 you were asked to calculate an all items retail price index for a fixed basket of goods.

If an index of prices is to be successful then it should try to take account of the impact of prices on the average shopper.

Do you think the index calculated in Activity 5 achieves this? Take some time to think this question through. What do you think might be the faults of the index that you calculated?

All of the indices calculated so far have implied that each item in the overall index is of equal importance. With particular respect to the retail price index in Activity 5, it would mean giving equal importance to bread, milk and butter. For most people this would not be the realistic. It may be that bread is a more important feature of the average person's expenditure than, say, milk or butter. So it could be argued that a 30% increase in bread prices will have a greater impact on a shopper than a similar sized increase in the price of the other products.

When we construct an index number it therefore seems advisable to try and reflect the varying importance of each item in the overall index.

How can we do this?

We use a **weighted average** to construct the index.

The general method for constructing any weighted average is shown in formula 2 below.

Formula 2

Constructing a Weighted Average

Consider a set of N values X_1, X_2, X_3, ... X_N
having respectively weights W_1, W_2, W_3, ... W_N

The weighted average of these numbers is calculated by taking

$$\frac{\sum WX}{\sum W} = \frac{W_1.X_1 + W_2.X_2 + W_3.X_3 + ... + W_N.X_N}{W_1 + W_2 + W_3 + ... + W_N}$$

In plain words, we multiply each number in the series by its corresponding weight, add the results and then divide by the sum of the weights.

Instead of obtaining an ordinary simple average, the result will be an average which reflects the importance of each number.

But how can we apply this concept to our index number problem?

We need some indication of the relative importance of bread, milk and butter in the budget of the shopper. Now since no two people are exactly alike in their purchasing habits, we introduce the concept of the **average shopper**. Suppose that we have carried out some research and found out that in January 1987 the average shopper distributed spending so that for every £1 spent on butter, £1 was spent on milk and £3 on bread.

It would seem reasonable to regard the numbers 3, 1 and 1 as the weights for bread, milk and butter respectively.

The calculations for the weighted index of prices is shown below (data taken from Activity 5).

ITEM	PRICE RELATIVE FOR JAN 1988 (JAN 1987 = 100)	WEIGHT	WEIGHT TIMES PRICE RELATIVE
Bread	130	3	390
Milk	110	1	110
Butter	125	1	125
		$\sum W = 5$	$\sum WX = 625$

FIGURE 6: **Weighted Price Index Calculations**

We know (from formula 2) that to calculate the weighted index we must divide the sum of price relative times weights by the sum of the weights. This will result in

$$\frac{\sum WX}{\sum W} = \frac{625}{5} = 125$$

Thus the weighted retail prices index will now be

Jan 1987 = 100
Jan 1988 = 125

There are variations in methods for different situations but this is the general method used for constructing most index numbers.

ACTIVITY 7

When calculating the (unweighted) index for prices in Activity 5, you obtained a figure of 121.7, suggesting a price rise of 21.7%.

For the weighted version we have obtained a figure of 125, suggesting a 25% price increase.

Can you suggest any reason why the weighted index should give this increased measure of price rises?

Bread has risen the most over this time period. In the unweighted index of Activity 5, it was given equal importance with butter and milk. In the weighted index, bread has a weight of 3, compared with 1 for milk and 1 for butter. Therefore a price increase for bread has three times the impact of an increase for milk and butter.

ACTIVITY 8

Now you can attempt to calculate a weighted index number using the methods developed so far in this section. However, instead of a price index, we will now consider an index of industrial production.

Suppose that the three staple products of an economy were produced in the following quantities in 1989 and 1990.

PRODUCT	PRODUCTION	
	1989	1990
A	500 tonnes	650 tonnes
B	1 million m^2	1.5 million m^2
C	1,600 barrels	1,440 barrels

Also, in 1989, the net value of output for each of these three products was recorded as £30 million for product A, £50 million for product B and £20 million for product C.

From the data provided, obtain a suitable weight to reflect the importance of each product to this economy. Hence calculate a weighted index of industrial production for 1990 (1989 = 100).

An index of production is a useful statistic to the analyst because it can indicate the degree of growth (or otherwise) in an economy. Of course, products are of varying importance to the economy; a small increase in production in one product may be regarded as many times more important than a large rise in production in another. Consequently, when we calculate an index of production we will need some measure of this importance. In other words, we need a **weight**.

What did you use for the weights in Activity 8? There is really only one figure to choose, and that is the value of net output provided for each product.

Total production (in value terms) of these products in 1989 was 30 million + 50 million + 20 million = 100 million.

Of this total net value, product A contributed 30%, product B 50% and product C 20%. For this reason, we shall use 3, 5 and 2 as weights for products A, B and C respectively.

We can now proceed with the solution. As before, we first calculate a price relative for each product. Then we multiply each relative by the appropriate weight. Finally we total up these results and divide by the sum of the weights.

The calculations are set out in figure 7 below.

PRODUCT	PRICE RELATIVE 1990 (1989 = 100)	WEIGHT	WEIGHT X RELATIVE
A	$\dfrac{650}{500} \times 100 = 130$	3	390
B	$\dfrac{1.5}{1} \times 100 = 150$	5	750
C	$\dfrac{1440}{1600} \times 100 = 90$	2	180
	TOTALS	10	1320

FIGURE 7: **Production Index Calculations**

So the final index is

$$\frac{\sum WX}{\sum W} = \frac{1320}{10} = 132$$

The completed index is therefore

$$1989 = 100$$
$$1990 = 132$$

Thus production has risen in this economy by 32%. You should also notice that product C has actually fallen by 10%.

However, the most important product (with a weight of 5) has risen by 50%, which has more than compensated for the poor performance of product C (which has a weight of only 2).

2. SELECTING SUITABLE WEIGHTS FOR INDEX NUMBERS

We have seen from the above example that it is possible to calculate an index number series which can effectively measure changes, provided we find a suitable set of weights. We must choose weights which provide an effective reflection of the importance of each item in the overall scheme. In most cases this will not constitute a problem, since economists, accountants, managers, etc, will readily agree on the figures to be chosen. For example, when calculating an index of retail prices, we have seen that it is reasonable to use consumers' proportionate expenditure on each item as weights. Also, it seems reasonably logical to use net value of commodities when compiling an index of industrial production.

However, even if we are agreed on the weights to use, we may still have a problem about what period of time the weights should be taken from.

In both the retail price and industrial production indices we use weights taken from expenditure/production in the base year.

There is no reason why we should not use other years as sources for weights if they suit our needs better.

We will look again at the retail price index to illustrate this point.

In the original index calculated earlier in the unit, we obtained the weights by examining consumer expenditure in the base year 1987. In that year for every £1 spent on milk or butter, £3 was spent on bread.

Now suppose that instead of using the base year of 1987 for our weights we had obtained data from the current year of 1988. Consumers change their expenditure patterns and there is no reason to suppose that 1988 will be identical to 1987.

ACTIVITY 9

This question refers to the retail price data of Activity 5.

Suppose that in 1988 some consumer research indicated that for every £8 spent on bread, the average shopper spent £2 on milk and £1 on butter.

Calculate the all items price index for 1988 (1987 = 100) using these weights.

Calculations for the new revised index are shown in figure 8. The only difference between the calculations required for Activity 9 and the previous version of this index is the change in weights.

ITEM	PRICE RELATIVE FOR JAN 1988 (JAN 1987 = 100)	WEIGHT	WEIGHT TIMES PRICE RELATIVE
Bread	130	8	1040
Milk	110	2	220
Butter	125	1	125
		$\Sigma W = 11$	$\Sigma WX = 1385$

FIGURE 8: **Revised Weighted Price Index Calculations**

The completed all-items index will be

$$\frac{\sum WX}{\sum W} = \frac{1385}{11} = 125.9$$

which is slightly different to our previous index of 125.

When we first calculated the price index we used weights drawn from the base year. Such indices are known as **base-weighted** indices. In Activity 9, you used weights drawn from the current year. The result is known as a **current-weighted** index.

A base-weighted price index measures the average price change in a fixed basket of goods typically purchased in the **base** year.

A current-weighted price index also measures average price changes, but in a fixed basket of goods typically purchased in the **current** year.

There is no objection in principle to your using either method provided that once you have chosen your weights you do not arbitrarily change them.

If you do change them then your index will no longer be a measure of the change in prices.

ACTIVITY 10

The following table gives the prices per unit in 1990 and 1992 of three commodities entering into average household expenditure. Also included are the amounts purchased by the household per week in each of these years.

COMMODITY	UNIT	AMOUNT PURCHASED		PRICE	
		1990	1992	1990	1992
A	Dozen	3	6	£0.60	£0.50
B	Box	1	2	£0.80	£1.00
C	500 gms	6	3	£0.10	£0.15

(a)   Devise a system of weights suitable for a base-weighted index.

(b)   Devise suitable weights for the current-weighted version of the same index.

(c)   Hence calculate both kinds of price index for 1992, taking 1990 = 100.

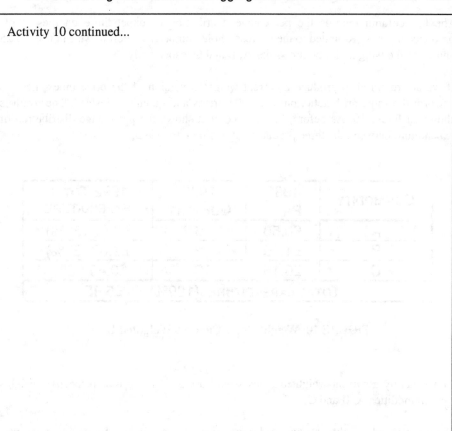

The proportionate expenditure on each of the three commodities would be suitable weights for the indices required in Activity 10. For the base-weighted index we would need to use expenditure and prices in the **base** year.

Figure 9 below, shows the calculation of weights for a base-weighted index. All prices and weights used for the calculation, must, by definition, be taken from the base year (1990).

COMMODITY	1990 PRICE	1990 QUANTITY	1990 TOTAL EXPENDITURE
A	£0.60	3	£1.80 (56%)
B	£0.80	1	£0.80 (25%)
C	£0.10	6	£0.60 (19%)
TOTAL EXPENDITURE (100%) =			£3.20

FIGURE 9: **Weights for a Base-Weighted Index**

The last column records the percentage distribution of expenditure on these three products in 1990. (Rounded to the nearest whole number.) Therefore we can use 56, 25 and 19 as the weights for commodities A, B and C respectively.

If we are required to produce a current-weighted version of the price index then we perform the same arithmetic, but use 1992 prices and quantities instead. The result is shown in figure 10. As before, the final column shows the percentage distribution of expenditure between the three products but this time for 1992.

COMMODITY	1992 PRICE	1992 QUANTITY	1992 TOTAL EXPENDITURE
A	£0.50	6	£3.00 (55%)
B	£1.00	2	£2.00 (37%)
C	£0.15	3	£0.45 (8%)
TOTAL EXPENDITURE (100%) = £5.45			

FIGURE 10: **Weights for a Current-Weighted Index**

Consequently a current-weighted index would use 55, 37 and 8 as respective weights for commodities A, B and C.

Having devised weights, all we need now are the price relatives for each commodity, and we can then do the required calculations for our retail price index.

This is shown in figure 11.

COMMODITY	PRICE RELATIVE	BASE WEIGHT × RELATIVE	CURRENT WEIGHT × RELATIVE
A	(50/60) × 100 = 83	56×83 = 4648	55×83 = 4565
B	(100/80) × 100 = 125	25×125 = 3125	37×125 = 4625
C	(15/10) × 100 = 150	19×150 = 2850	8×150 = 1200
	ΣWX =	10623	10390
	ΣW =	100	100

FIGURE 11: **Index Number Calculations**

So the index number calculations for the base-weighted index are

$$\frac{\sum WX}{\sum W} = \frac{10623}{100} \approx 106.2$$

while for the current-weighted index they are

$$\frac{\sum WX}{\sum W} = \frac{10390}{100} = 103.9$$

The final index number statement is

	Base Weighted	Current Weighted
1990 =	100	100
1992 =	106.2	103.9

The base-weighted version of the index would suggest that there has been a 6.2% average price increase while the current-weighted index would suggest a 3.9% increase.

Whatever index we use depends very much upon our intentions. For example, base weighting would be very useful if we wished to find out how much the cost of a particular basket of goods purchased in some **past** base year has gone up between then and now.

Current weighting would be the choice if we wished to discover the change in cost of **today's** typical basket of goods over past years. We would, however, have to recognise that extra costs would be involved in continually obtaining new data to construct weights for each current period.

Whichever index is chosen, it is essential that weights are kept constant throughout the index number series.

3. THE AGGREGATIVE METHOD OF CALCULATION

Finally in this section we deal with an alternative method of calculating an index number; the **aggregative method**.

So far, the method of price relatives has been used. This, as we have seen, consists in calculating a 'price relative' for each separate item in the index and then obtaining a weighted average of these relatives. If we have the right kind of information we can use a different method. For this so-called aggregative method we must have both value and volume information for the base and the current years.

We shall use the price index information of the last section as an illustration. In order to calculate a retail price index we must have:

1   The prices of the goods in a typical shopping basket bought in a reference period in both the base and current years

2   The quantities of goods bought in these periods for the base and current years.

The price data from Activity 10 will suffice as an illustration. We summarise these data in figure 12.

We will be using the following abbreviations

P_0 = Price of product in the base year.

P_1 = Price of product in the current year.

Q_0 = Quantity purchased in the base year.

Q_1 = Quantity purchased in the current year.

COMMODITY	PRODUCT UNIT PRICE		QUANTITY PURCHASED	
	1990 (P_0)	1992 (P_1)	1990 (Q_0)	1992 (Q_1)
A	£0.60	£0.50	3	6
B	£0.80	£1.00	1	2
C	£0.10	£0.15	6	3

FIGURE 12: **Price-Quantity Data**

There are two main kinds of aggregative index; the **Laspeyre** and **Paasche** indices (so-called after their originators). The Laspeyre index is a base weighted index for reasons which the following calculations will make clear. To calculate the Laspeyre index we need to carry out the following stages:

1. Calculate the expenditure incurred by these three goods in 1990 **using 1990 quantities**;

2. Similarly, calculate the expenditure incurred in 1992, **but still assuming that the consumer buys 1990 quantities**;

3. Express the 1992 expenditure as a percentage of the 1990 expenditure.

The result is the Laspeyre index for 1992 (1990 = 100).

In formal terms, the formula for a Laspeyre index calculated by this method is as shown below.

Formula 3

Aggregative Laspeyre Price Index

The Laspeyre price index for the current year is

$$\frac{\text{Current Expenditure at Base Year Quantities}}{\text{Base Expenditure at Base Year Quantities}} \times 100$$

$$= \frac{\sum (P_1 \times Q_0)}{\sum (P_0 \times Q_0)} \times 100$$

The calculations for a Laspeyre index for the data of figure 12 are shown below

Expenditure at 1990 volume is

$$1990 = (£0.60 \times 3) + (£0.80 \times 1) + (£0.10 \times 6) = £3.20$$

$$1992 = (£0.50 \times 3) + (£1.00 \times 1) + (£0.15 \times 6) = £3.40$$

Finally 1992 expenditure as a percentage of 1990 is

$$(3.40/3.20) \times 100 = 106.25$$

So the final index would be stated as

$$1990 = 100$$
$$1992 = 106.25$$

The base-weighted price relative index and the Laspeyre index will always be exactly the same; they are equivalent methods. Any small differences will be solely due to rounding.

ACTIVITY 11

By making the necessary alterations to formula 3 produce a general formula for the calculation of a Paasche index using the aggregative method.

Using the price data of Activity 10 use your formula to calculate a Paasche index for 1992 (1990 = 100).

The Paasche index is an example of a current-weighted index. The general formula for it is shown in formula 4.

Formula 4

Aggregative Paasche Price Index

The Paasche price index for the current year is

$$\frac{\underline{\text{Current Expenditure at Current Year Quantities}}}{\text{Base Expenditure at Current Year Quantities}} \times \textbf{100}$$

$$= \frac{\sum (P_1 \times Q_1)}{\sum (P_0 \times Q_1)} \times \textbf{100}$$

You will see from the above that the method is in all particulars except one the same as for the Laspeyre index. The difference is that only the **current** year quantities are used.

The required index for Activity 11 will be calculated as follows:

Expenditure at 1992 volume is

$$1990 = (£0.60 \times 6) + (£0.80 \times 2) + (£0.10 \times 3) = £5.50$$

$$1992 = (£0.50 \times 6) + (£1.00 \times 2) + (£0.15 \times 3) = £5.45$$

Finally the 1992 expenditure as a percentage of 1990 is

$$(5.45/5.50) \times 100 = 99$$

Therefore the final index would be stated as

$$1990 = 100$$
$$1992 = 99$$

Although it is a current-weighted method, do not expect the Paasche index to give the same result as the current-weighted **price relative** index described earlier. They are **not** equivalent methods.

It should not escape your notice that the Paasche index suggests that prices have fallen by 1%, whereas the Laspeyre index estimates that they have risen by 6.25%!

All of this discussion of indices should alert you to the dangers of using index numbers.

They are very useful as indicators of change but they can give different results depending upon the system of weights chosen. When using index numbers you should attempt to discover the methods used to obtain them. Only by exercising this kind of care will you be able to interpret them intelligently.

So which weights (or quantities) should you use? There is no final answer to this question. The choice will depend very much on circumstances. Base-weighted indices tend to over-emphasise the effects of price inflation because they always use fixed quantities from a past year, not taking into account the movements of demand in subsequent years.

Current-weighted indices probably err in the opposite direction. Also, since the weights used to calculate the index refer always to the current year (which is always changing) we can only compare the current indices with the base year and not with each other.

Some index numbers are constructed using neither base year **nor** current year quantities. Instead, some other year, judged to be typical is chosen. There is nothing wrong in principle with proceeding like this but it does raise unanswerable questions as to what is a 'typical' year, and who decides whether it is typical or not.

4. SUMMARY

In this second section of the unit we have

- constructed an **index number** using **price relatives**

- discussed **weighted averages** and shown how to calculate them

- seen how to select suitable **weights** for **index numbers**

- discussed the **aggregative method** of calculating indices

If you are unsure of any of these topics look back **now** before starting the next section.

SECTION 3

QUANTITY AND VALUE INDICES

1. VALUE AND VOLUME INDICES

In section 2 we discussed the calculation of a price index. In these indices the quantity consumed by the shopper was assumed to be a constant, and therefore the price could be assumed to be a measure of price changes. Such indices are typical of a wide class of measures, collectively called **value indices**. Alternatively, we may also calculate indices of **volume**, where prices are treated as a constant, and quantities allowed to change over time. Such indices can be regarded as reliable measures of change in **volume**. The production index you calculated for Activity 8 was a volume index, since the weights were based on the value of what was produced in the base year. Subsequent changes in production values were not considered. Consequently, the index obtained was a measure of changes in the **volume** of production, not its value.

It requires only a few changes in our methods to calculate a volume rather than a value index.

We will illustrate by using the retail price data first introduced in Activity 10.

A VOLUME INDEX USING THE RELATIVE METHOD

How would we proceed if we wished to compute a base-weighted index measuring the change in the volume of goods purchased between 1990 and 1992? Firstly, we require relatives for each commodity, just as before, but this time they must measure changes in **quantity** purchased, not prices. That is, we require **volume relatives** rather than **price relatives**. These relatives have been calculated and are shown below in figure 13.

	AMOUNT PURCHASED		CALCULATION OF
COMMODITY	1990	1992	VOLUME RELATIVE
A	3	6	$\frac{6}{3} \times 100 = 200$
B	1	2	$\frac{2}{1} \times 100 = 200$
C	6	3	$\frac{3}{6} \times 100 = 50$

FIGURE 13: **Volume Price Relatives**

Notice that two of the commodities have doubled in volume purchased while the third has halved. This is reflected in the relatives for 1992.

What next? As before, we need suitable weights. As we are calculating a base-weighted index we can use the proportions of expenditure from the base year. These were already obtained in the answer to Activity 10 (also see figure 9). In 1990, the average consumer spent 56% of income on commodity A, 25% on commodity B and 19% on C. These figures are our weights.

We then proceed in the usual manner by multiplying each volume relative by its appropriate weight, adding the resulting figures and dividing by the total sum of the weights.

This is shown below in figure 14.

COMMODITY	RELATIVE	WEIGHT × RELATIVE
A	200	56 × 200 = 11200
B	200	25 × 200 = 5000
C	50	19 × 50 = 950
	ΣWX =	17150
	ΣW =	100

FIGURE 14: **Base-Weighted Volume Index Calculations**

Therefore the base weighted volume index number for 1992 (1990 = 100) is

$$\frac{\sum WX}{\sum W} = \frac{17150}{100} = 171.50$$

Therefore there has been a 71.5% increase in volume consumed between 1990 and 1992 (measured at 1990 prices).

ACTIVITY 12

Now that you have seen how to construct a base weighted index of volume, see if you can produce a current weighted version of the same index.

All that changes for the index is that we use the 1992 percentage purchases; we still use the same relatives. The method and solution is shown below, in figure 15.

COMMODITY	RELATIVE	WEIGHT × RELATIVE
A	200	55 × 200 = 11000
B	200	37 × 200 = 7400
C	50	8 × 50 = 400
	ΣWX =	18800
	ΣW =	100

FIGURE 15: **Current-Weighted Volume Index Calculations**

The weights were obtained from the answer to Activity 10 (see figure 10).

The the current weighted volume index for 1992 (1990 = 100) is

$$\frac{\sum WX}{\sum W} = \frac{18800}{100} = 188.00$$

So, there has been an 88% increase in volume consumed between 1990 and 1992 (at 1992 prices).

The current-weighted index has given us a higher figure than the base-weighted index for increase in volume in this case because we are using higher weightings for the commodities (A and B) which have increased in consumption, and a lower weight for the one which has **decreased** in consumption.

VOLUME INDICES: THE AGGREGATIVE METHOD

We can now consider how we would use the aggregative method to calculate an index of volume. You may wish to revise aggregative indices in section 2 before you try the next Activity.

ACTIVITY 13

Study the method for constructing Laspeyre and Paasche value indices (see formulae 3 and 4).

How would you amend these two formulae so that they produce measures of the change in quantity purchased rather than the change in prices?

When we calculated a price index we kept the quantities constant and allowed prices to change. We must now reverse this situation for a volume index.

The formula for the Laspeyre **value** index is

$$\frac{\sum (P_1 . Q_0)}{\sum (P_0 . Q_0)} \times 100$$

Notice how Q_0 appears in both numerator and denominator of the above expression, while P_1 appears in the numerator and P_0 appears in the denominator. Quantities (the Q values) are not allowed to change, while the prices (the P values) are. We must reverse this procedure if we wish to construct a volume index. The Laspeyre index of volume would be calculated as in formula 5 below.

Formula 5

Aggregative Laspeyre Volume Index

The Laspeyre volume index for the current year is

$$\frac{\text{Current Expenditure at base Year Prices}}{\text{Base Expenditure at Base Year Prices}} \times 100$$

$$= \frac{\sum (P_0 . Q_1)}{\sum (P_0 . Q_0)} \times 100$$

Notice how in formula 5, the prices stay constant (at base year values) while the quantities are allowed to change. As a consequence, the index will now measure volume changes rather than price changes.

With the Paasche volume index, the same principle of holding prices constant is adhered to, but the prices used are those of the **current** year rather than the base year. Consequently a Paasche volume index would be calculated as in formula 6 below.

Formula 6

Aggregative Paasche Volume Index

The Paasche volume index for the current year is

$$\frac{\text{Current Expenditure at Current Year Prices}}{\text{Base Expenditure at Current Year Prices}} \times 100$$

$$= \frac{\sum P_1 \times Q_1}{\sum P_1 \times Q_0} \times 100$$

ACTIVITY 14

Now use formulae 5 and 6 and the data from Activity 10 to calculate

(a)   A Laspeyre index
(b)   A Paasche index

of volume for 1992 (1990 = 100).

To answer Activity 14 we require the following results:

1. base year expenditure at base year prices

$$\Sigma P_0.Q_0 = £0.60 \times 3 + £0.80 \times 1 + £0.10 \times 6 = £3.20$$

2. current year expenditure at base year prices

$$\Sigma P_0.Q_1 = £0.60 \times 6 + £0.80 \times 2 + £0.10 \times 3 = £5.50$$

3. base year expenditure at current year prices

$$\Sigma P_1.Q_0 = £0.50 \times 3 + £1.00 \times 1 + £0.15 \times 6 = £3.40$$

and

4. current year expenditure at current year prices.

$$\Sigma P_1.Q_1 = £0.50 \times 6 + £1.00 \times 2 + £0.15 \times 3 = £5.45$$

Therefore the Laspeyre volume index will be

$$\frac{\sum (P_0.Q_1)}{\sum (P_0.Q_0)} \times 100 = \frac{5.50}{3.20} \approx 171.9$$

ie 1992 = 171.9 (1990 = 100)

and the Paasche volume index will be

$$\frac{\sum P_1.Q_1}{\sum P_1.Q_0} \times 100 = \frac{5.45}{3.40} \approx 160.3$$

so that

1992 = 160.3 (1990 = 100)

As with the value indices, the Laspeyre and price relative volume indices give the same results (apart from a rounding difference). They are equivalent methods. The Paasche volume index does not give the same result as the current-weighted price relative index; they are **not** equivalent.

As with the value indices, whether we use the aggregative or price relative methods and the choice to be made between current and base year weighting depends upon the data we have available and the changes we wish to emphasise.

2. USING A VALUE INDEX AS A DEFLATER

Consider the following situation.

In a certain industry the average weekly wage changed as follows between 1986 and 1988:

Year	1986	1987	1988
Wage	£120	£141	£151

The trade association representing the employers of the industry claimed that wages had shown real and substantial increases during this period, but the industry trade union leaders were not so sure. In order to shed light on this situation, the union consulted the retail price index for the period which was as follows:

Year	1986	1987	1988
Price Index (1980 = 100)	157.0	182.0	197.2

Do these data tell us anything useful about wage increases over the period?

You will no doubt be only too aware that price inflation erodes wages and salaries. Is there any convenient way in which we can decide whether wages in the above industry have stayed ahead of inflation?

A convenient technique is to obtain some measure of inflation, such as a retail price index and use it to remove the effect of inflation from the wage figures.

We are, in effect, using the index as a 'deflater' to answer the question

'what would the wage changes be like if we allowed for the effect of price changes?'

This can be done by multiplying the wage figure by a factor relating to the amount of the price changes. The method is shown as in formula 7 below.

Formula 7

To Deflate a Series of Money Values

Assume that we have a series of money values V_1, V_2, V_3, ... etc, and a suitable price/value index with its base year starting from the same point as the monetary values. Then we can 'deflate' the money values as follows:

$$\text{Deflated Value} = V \times \frac{100}{\text{index number}}$$

In plain words, we divide the value we wish to deflate by a suitable index for that time period and then multiply by 100.

We shall do this with the wage data.

There is a small problem which we must deal with first before we can proceed. The price index series is based on a starting point of 1980 = 100 whereas our wage data begins in 1986.

We can easily deal with this problem by 'rebasing' the index so that 1986 = 100. How?

By simply recalculating each index afresh using the 1986 value of 157 as the base we would have results as shown in figure 16 below.

YEAR	1986	1987	1988
OLD INDEX	157.0	182	197.2
NEW INDEX	100	$\frac{182}{157} \times 100 =$ 115.9	$\frac{197.2}{157} \times 100 =$ 125.6

FIGURE 16: **Rebasing an Index**

So we now have a new index number series based on 1986 = 100 and we are now ready to deflate the wage series.

The money wage in 1986 was £120, and since this is the base year, we do not need to deflate this.

In 1987 the money wage was £141. Its 'deflated' value is

$$\frac{Value}{index} \times 100 = \frac{£141}{115.9} \times 100 = £121.66$$

In 1988, the money wage was £151. Its deflated value is

$$\frac{Value}{index} \times 100 = \frac{£151}{125.6} \times 100 = £120.22$$

We have removed from each of the wage figures a factor related to the degree of price inflation. Whilst the original values are money wages, this deflated amount is often referred to as **real wages.**

So the level of real wages in each year (measured from a base of 1986), was as follows:

Year	1986	1987	1988
Money Wage	£120.00	£141.00	£151.00
Real Wage	£120.00	£121.66	£120.22

Wages have not increased at all in real terms, any money increase has been negated by the effect of price inflation.

This technique of using an index number to convert money values into real values is a very important one. With it we can decide whether an increase in some money value series has kept pace with price inflation.

ACTIVITY 15

The following figures relate to the total and library expenditure of a local authority. Also included is the retail price index (1988=100).

Expenditure in £000s

	1988	1989	1990	1991
(a) Total	4802	5235	5805	6708
(b) Library	451	502	510	517
Price Index	100	117	125	142

A press release from the local council stated:

> '.... As you will see from the figures, expenditure by the local council has increased and library provision has shared in this increase...'.

Examine this statement, and use the figures to decide whether you think it is true or false, giving your reasons.

It is certainly true from the data that expenditure has increased in **money** terms both totally and on the libraries. You might like to note that, even in money terms, library expenditure is a falling proportion of the total; 9.4% of total expenditure in 1988 falling to 7.7% in 1991.

However, we are really concerned here with **real** expenditure. The following table (figure 17) shows the necessary calculations to deflate the series.

Notice that for this problem the index is already based on the starting year of our expenditure so that we do not have to rebase before we start.

YEAR	REAL EXPENDITURE AT 1988 PRICES	
	TOTAL	LIBRARY
1988	4802	451
1989	$\dfrac{5235}{117} \times 100 = 4474$	$\dfrac{502}{117} \times 100 = 429$
1990	$\dfrac{5805}{125} \times 100 = 4644$	$\dfrac{510}{125} \times 100 = 408$
1991	$\dfrac{6708}{142} \times 100 = 4724$	$\dfrac{517}{142} \times 100 = 364$

FIGURE 17: **Calculations for Activity 15**

You should again take notice that the first year's values do not have to be deflated. All calculations are carried out using formula 7. Note also that the second two columns in the table are entitled 'Real Expenditure at 1988 Prices'. This form of words should remind you that we are recalculating what the expenditure would be if we removed the effect of price changes since 1988.

It is quite clear that the council press release does not apply to real expenditure.

Total expenditure, in real terms has suffered a slight decline over the years, while library expenditure has declined considerably in real terms.

3. THE UK RETAIL PRICE INDEX

Before we leave the subject of index numbers it will be useful if we take a brief look at the UK Retail Price Index to which we have referred several times in this unit. The index is a key economic statistic and its monthly publication is a matter of great publicity. It is widely interpreted as a measure of inflation or cost of living. (Although to be fair, the government statisticians deny that they are trying to measure the cost of living.) Its compilation shows very clearly the kinds of problems encountered in the construction of an index.

The index is a weighted average of changes in the prices of a fixed basket of goods featuring in the expenditure of the average family. The basket of goods undergoes substantial modification from time to time to indicate changes in the pattern of buying. This is a key problem in the construction of indices. How do we decide what to include in our basket of goods? Also, of equal importance, what is the average family?

Both problems are solved by the Family Expenditure Survey (FES) which is conducted yearly by the government statistical services.

A randomly selected group of about 7,000 families keep a journal of their daily expenditure.

The FES carefully excludes households living only on a state pension and those in the top 2% income group. In this way the FES is representative of the ordinary household. It is from the records of the FES that the government is able to decide what proportions of their income the average family spend on various goods and services.

Data relating to prices is gathered nationally by investigators and the index is a base-weighted average of these movements. At the time of writing the current index is based on January 1987 = 100. The base year is changed whenever the index is thought to be out of date.

Figure 18 shows the main categories of the index and their current weighting (as at 1993).

CATEGORY	WEIGHT
Food	152
Catering	47
Alcoholic Drink	80
Tobacco	36
Housing	172
Fuel and Light	47
Household Goods	77
Household Services	48
Clothing and Footwear	59
Personal Goods and Services	40
Motoring Expenditure	143
Fares and Other Travel Costs	20
Leisure Goods	47
Leisure Services	32
ALL ITEMS	1000

FIGURE 18: **Current Categories and Weights (1993) Used in the Retail Price Index**

Remember that the weights quoted in the above table represent the proportionate expenditure by the average family on each category. Also, these categories are very broad groupings. If you wish to see a more detailed breakdown then you should consult the *Monthly Digest of Statistics* (a HMSO publication) or one of the annual FES reports. The *Employment Gazette* (Department of Employment) also carries an annual article relating to the FES, which is well worth looking at.

4. SUMMARY

In section 3 we have concentrated on

- **value** and **volume indices** using the price relative method

- volume indices using the **aggregative method**

- the use of value indices as deflaters

- the **UK Retail Price Index**

If you are unsure about any of these topics take a look back **now** before reading on.

SECTION 4

TIME SERIES

1. INTRODUCTION

There are many situations where we wish to make forecasts of sales, employment, income or some other quantity by using a **time series**.

But what is a times series?

A time series is data about the behaviour of some variable, or variables over succesive past time periods. Such data might be collected weekly, monthly, quarterly or yearly. So a firm might possibly keep monthly records of the sales of each of its products.

In this section and in section 5, we will explore how we can analyse the behaviour of a time series.

In section six we will examine a method whereby a time series can be used as the basis of a forecasting system.

2. A SALES DATA TIME SERIES

Suppose that a firm keeps a monthly record of sales stretching back over several years. What features do you think might be present in such a series?

THE SALES DATA MIGHT SHOW SOME LONG RUN TREND

If the market for the firm's products has been expanding then over a period of time its sales will probably have risen. It is also possible that the business may have been contracting over the long term, which would show up in a sales decline over time. We must bear in mind that if we are expressing sales data in value terms rather than in volume, we will often see a long run increase due to the factor of price inflation. We saw in section 3 that it is usual to deflate a value time series first by using an acceptable index. This will show the **real** behaviour of sales.

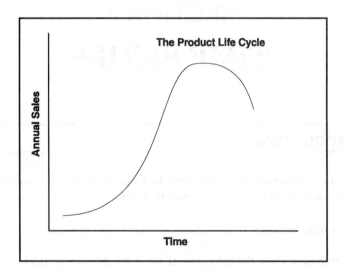

FIGURE 19: **Product Life Cycle**

In some cases, the behaviour of sales is more complex than just a rise or fall. Many products exhibit all the signs of a **product life cycle**. The behaviour of a product life cycle is shown in figure 19 above.

Initially, a new product is slow to penetrate a market, so that sales rise only slowly. If the product is successful in this early introduction stage then knowledge of it spreads more widely, subsequent penetration of the market is deeper and sales increase at a more rapid rate.

Later, as the market reaches saturation point, sales begin to level out. Finally, as happens in most cases, the product suffers from obsolescence and a decline in sales.

Sales Might Be Responsive to the Overall State of the Economy

Quite apart from the changing level of demand for goods and services of the type marketed by the company, sales might be influenced by the trade cycle. The current cycle of boom and slump particularly affects products such as package holidays.

Sales Might Show Some Seasonal Pattern

Many products have definite seasonal patterns of sales. For example, sales of ice cream and beer show a definite seasonal pattern of consumption.

Sales Might Show Random Variations

All of the above factors affecting a time series are predictable to a greater or lesser degree. But a time series such as sales will also show random, and therefore unpredictable, fluctuation. Any number of factors, such as the unpredictability of the weather or actions of competitors, will cause such variations in sales.

ACTIVITY 16

The following data relates to the quarterly sales of woodpulp (in millions of tonnes) over the period 1990 - 1992. Quarter I refers to the period Jan - March, II to April - June, and so on.

	Quarter			
	I	II	III	IV
1990	11.5	12.2	12.9	15.7
1991	18.9	20.5	21.4	23.4
1992	27.8	28.3	29.1	31.6

⟶

Activity 16 continued...

On a separate piece of graph paper draw a graph of the above data. Use the horizontal axis for time period and the vertical axis for sales. We will be using these data throughout the rest of the unit, so you will find it useful for later activities if you code the time periods so that they appear on the horizontal axis as follows:

1990 Quarter I = 1
1990 Quarter II = 2

.   .   .

.   .   .

etc   etc   etc

.   .   .

.   .   .

1992 Quarter IV = 12

What would you say are the major features of this time series?

Note It will be a considerable help to you if you use a spreadsheet program, such as LOTUS 1-2-3 for this exercise.

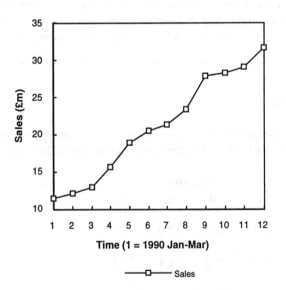

FIGURE 20: **Data from Activity 12**

Figure 20 shows the woodpulp data from Activity 16. In this instance, LOTUS 1-2-3 was used to draw the graph although any reputable spreadsheet software would do just as well. You may have chosen to sketch the graph manually. We will now deal with the various features to be found in this kind of time series data.

3. BREAKING DOWN A TIME SERIES

In general terms, you would expect to find the following features present in any time series:

> a **trend**
>
> a **cyclical** variation
>
> a **seasonal** variation
>
> a **random,** or irregular, variation.

THE TREND

The trend of a time series is the long run behaviour of the data. Do we see a broad rise or fall in the series? Is the rate of rise or fall getting more pronounced or is it generally constant?

In the case of the woodpulp data from Activity 16 there is a pronounced upward trend which is very probably linear.

You should remember what is meant by linearity. Figure 21 below shows examples of various kinds of trend.

Study each graph carefully.

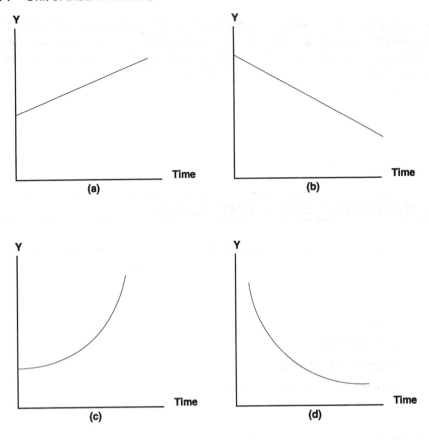

FIGURE 21: **Linear and Non-Linear Trends**

In graphs (a) and (b) the Y variable is changing linearly over time; the growth or decline is by a fixed amount per time period.

In graphs (c) and (d) the variable is growing or declining by a different amount each time period. It may be changing by a fixed **rate** rather than a fixed **amount**. If this is so, then the time series is said to be growing (or declining) **exponentially**.

CYCLICAL VARIATION

Many time series will show medium term fluctuations about the long term trend. The most obvious case of such variation is the trade cycle. Figure 22 shows how cyclical variation might show up on a graph.

These cyclical changes will be of varying length and severity and are much more difficult to predict than seasonal variation.

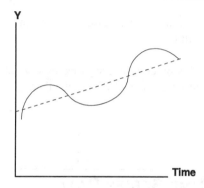

FIGURE 22: **Cyclical Variation**

SEASONAL VARIATION

A major source of variation is due to seasonal factors. Sales of many consumer goods and services show a clear seasonal pattern. The woodpulp data from Activity 10 shows clear quarterly fluctuation.

Seasonal variations are of a much shorter duration than cyclical variation as they tend to occur at weekly/quarterly/monthly intervals.

RANDOM VARIATION

Even after trying to account for the changes in a time series by referring to trend, cyclical and seasonal movements, there will still be a random, and therefore unpredictable, source of variation.

There are good reasons for breaking down a time series into trend, seasonal variation, etc. We may wish to know whether some economic indicator, such as unemployment, has risen this month. The monthly unemployment figures constitute a time series and show strong seasonal variation. We **must** know whether a rise in the unemployment figures is due to a real upward long term trend, or less seriously, to seasonal factors.

If you are a follower of the economic news, you may have noticed that UK unemployment data is published in two forms; **raw** figures, which will show all kinds of variation, and **deseasonalised** figures. In the latter, the variation due to seasonal factors has been removed so that we may be reasonably certain that much of what is left is due to trend. Therefore time series analysis will be of use to economic policy makers.

But time series analysis is also of use to business forecasters. If we wish to make a time series the basis of a forecast, then it is sensible to disaggregate the data into its component parts.

A forecast can be made for trend and seasonal variation separately and the results combined into a final overall forecast.

Before we can carry out this process of disaggregation we must first understand how the different parts of a time series interact with each other.

4. MODELS OF TIME SERIES DATA

There are two main types of interaction between the different components of a times series:

> the **additive** model and
>
> the **multiplicative** model.

We will require some mathematical shorthand to describe the differences between these two.

Let Y_t represent the value of the variable in time period t

T_t represent the trend value of Y in time period t

C_t represent the cyclical component of Y in time period t

S_t represent the seasonal component of Y in time period t

R_t represent the random component of Y in time period t.

Using the above symbols, formulae 7 and 8 below describe the interaction between the time series components in the additive and multiplicative cases.

Formula 7

The Additive Time Series Model

$$Y_t = T_t + C_t + S_t + R_t$$

Formula 8

The Multiplicative Time Series Model

$$Y_t = T_t \times C_t \times S_t \times R_t$$

Put more simply, if we use the additive model we can obtain Y_t, the overall value of the time series, by adding the various components together. If we use the multiplicative model, then we must multiply the components together to get Y_t.

In practice, it is usually a difficult exercise to identify and analyse the cyclical component of a time series. We shall therefore restrict ourselves just to trend, seasonal and random variation.

But how do we decide whether to apply a multiplicative or additive model to time series data? Usually a graph will help as Activity 17 will demonstrate.

ACTIVITY 17

Consider the following two time series both relating to quarterly sales of businesses. As before, I means Jan-March, II April-June, etc.

Time Series (a)		Time Series (b)	
Time	**Sales**	**Time**	**Sales**
1990 I	8.00	1990 I	8.00
II	17.00	II	18.20
III	15.00	III	16.20
IV	24.00	IV	26.40
1991 I	24.00	1991 I	23.40
II	33.00	II	39.00
III	31.00	III	31.60
IV	40.00	IV	45.60
1992 I	40.00	1992 I	37.80
II	49.00	II	59.80
III	47.00	III	45.00
IV	56.00	IV	64.80

Draw graphs of each time series on the same sheet of graph paper, using the same axes. Better still, use a spreadsheet to draw the graphs if you have access to one.

Now using your graph, compare the two sets of data. Do you think think the seasonal variation is roughly constant over time or is it increasing?

The graphs of the two time series are shown in figure 23, again drawn using LOTUS 1-2-3.

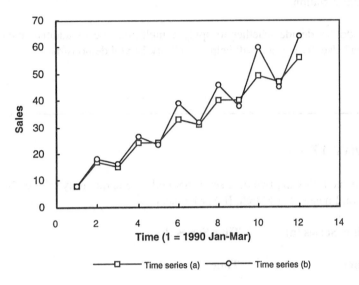

FIGURE 23: **Quarterly Sales (Activity 17)**

If you look at the graph it appears that both data sets show seasonal fluctuations. However, in data set (a) the fluctuations are generally constant over time, while the fluctuations in data set (b) seem to be increasing in intensity over time.

In the case of data set (a) the additive model is appropriate. We can just add a relatively unchanging seasonal variation factor on to our forecast for the trend. However, for data set (b), it is not appropriate to follow this course of action. Seasonal variation is increasing in size from year to year. In this case, we would have to use the multiplicative model. Multiplying the trend by a constant factor each quarter will ensure that the seasonal variation increases in intensity.

We seem then, to have a rule for deciding between additive and multiplicative models:

   if the seasonal component appears to be generally constant in absolute size over time, then the additive model is appropriate;

   if the seasonal component is increasing or decreasing in absolute size over time, then the multiplicative model is appropriate.

Of course, seasonal variation is never completely regular because of the random element. The true seasonal variation will be equal to our forecast seasonal variation but with added (and unpredictable) random variation. This situation will often make analysis of the behaviour of seasonal variation difficult, so that it will usually be a matter of judgement as to whether to use the additive or multiplicative models.

ACTIVITY 18

Now go back to the woodpulp data of Activity 16.

Which time series model do you think best describes this data?

Since you have already drawn the graph of this data for Activity 16, you will observe that the seasonal fluctuations appear to be roughly constant over time. Therefore the additive model can be used.

5. SUMMARY

In this section we covered the basics of time series. We have

- looked in detail at **sales data time series**

- broken down a time series into its **component parts**

- examined the behaviour of **the trend** and **the cyclical**, **seasonal** and **random variation components** of a time series

- looked at **two models** of time series data

Check back over all the points and exercises in this section before you read on.

SECTION 5

MOVING AVERAGES

1. INTRODUCTION

In this section we will demonstrate the general method for disaggregating a time series into trend and seasonal variation components. In particular, you will study a technique called **moving averages**.

In what follows, we will be using the woodpulp sales data which you first met in Activity 16. Although it is not essential, it is highly recommended that you use a spreadsheet to deal with the exercises in both this section and section 6.

2. MOVING AVERAGES

A moving average is a method generally used to separate a time series into trend and seasonal variation components, and is calculated by using the mean value of the series over a number of time periods. This mean value will be the trend of the data since the moving averages technique smooths out fluctuations in a time series. We will illustrate the moving averages technique by using a three period moving average.

Here is the formula for this:

Formula 9

Three-Period Moving Average

The three period moving average for time period t is calculated as follows:

$$T_t = \frac{Y_{t-1} + Y_t + Y_{t+1}}{3}$$

To use a three-period moving average we take the data, three periods at a time, and calculate the average. The average is placed at the centre of the time period it relates to. This process is shown as applied to the woodpulp data in figure 24 below.

TIME		SALES	CALCULATION OF THREE PERIOD MOVING AVERAGE
1990	I	11.5	
	II	12.2	(11.5+12.2+12.9)/3 = 12.20
	III	12.9	(12.2+12.9+15.7)/3 = 13.60
	IV	15.7	(12.9+15.7+18.9)/3 = 15.83
1991	I	18.9	(15.7+18.9+20.5)/3 = 18.37
	II	20.5	(18.9+20.5+21.4)/3 = 20.27
	III	21.4	(20.5+21.4+23.4)/3 = 21.77
	IV	23.4	(21.4+23.4+27.8)/3 = 24.20
1992	I	27.8	(23.4+27.8+28.3)/3 = 26.50
	II	28.3	(27.8+28.3+29.1)/3 = 28.40
	III	29.1	(28.3+29.1+31.6)/3 = 29.67
	IV	31.6	

FIGURE 24: **Calculation of a Three-Period Moving Average for the Sales of Woodpulp**

In figure 24, the first three sales figures have been averaged and the resulting figure, 12.20, placed at the centre of the time period. Therefore, the first average will be placed against quarter II of 1990. The first sales figure, 11.5, is dropped, and the next quarter, 15.7, is added. The mean of these sales figures forms the next moving average. This process continues until all of the sales data have been used. You will note that by the very nature of the process, there will be no moving average for the very first and last quarters.

This is where a computer spreadsheet is invaluable for calculating moving averages, since a simple formula can be entered to produce the required figures.

The resulting moving average is formally called the **three-period centred moving average** and is a **smoothed** version of the data. The moving average process tries to smooth out the fluctuations in the time series so that what remains can be taken as representative of the trend. However, before we get involved in the question of interpretation of moving averages it would be a good idea if you aquired some experience by practicing the technique.

You will need the following formula definition for the next activity.

Formula 10

Five-Period Moving Average

The five-period moving average for time period t is calculated as follows:

$$T_t = \frac{Y_{t-2} + Y_{t-1} + Y_t + Y_{t+1} + Y_{t+2}}{5}$$

ACTIVITY 19

Use formula 9 to calculate a five-period centred moving average for the woodpulp sales data.

On a separate piece of graph paper, and using the same axes, draw the following graphs

(a)   the original woodpulp sales data,
(b)   the three-period moving average data,
(c)   the five-period moving average data.

Notice the effect on the sales data of taking a moving average. What is the effect of increasing the number of periods in the moving average from 3 to 5?

The calculations for the five-period moving average are shown in figure 25.

TIME		SALES	CALCULATION OF FIVE PERIOD MOVING AVERAGE
1990	I	11.5	
	II	12.2	
	III	12.9	(11.5+12.2+12.9+15.7+18.9)/5 = 14.24
	IV	15.7	(12.2+12.9+15.7+18.9+20.5)/5 = 16.04
1991	I	18.9	(12.9+15.7+18.9+20.5+21.4)/5 = 17.88
	II	20.5	(15.7+18.9+20.5+21.4+23.4)/5 = 19.98
	III	21.4	(18.9+20.5+21.4+23.4+27.8)/5 = 22.40
	IV	23.4	(20.5+21.4+23.4+27.8+28.3)/5 = 24.28
1992	I	27.8	(21.4+23.4+27.8+28.3+29.1)/5 = 26.00
	II	28.3	(23.4+27.8+28.3+29.1+31.6)/5 = 28.04
	III	29.1	
	IV	31.6	

FIGURE 25: **Calculation of a Five-Period Moving Average for the Sales of Woodpulp**

As with the three-period moving average each figure is placed at the centre of the data, the first figure being placed at quarter III of 1990. You will notice that with a five-period moving average we obtain no data for the first and last two quarters.

The graph showing the original data, the three-period and five-period moving average is shown in figure 26. Notice that the five-period moving average has smoothed out more of the variation in the data than has been the case with the three-period moving average.

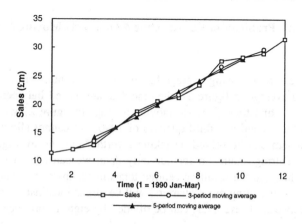

FIGURE 26: **Sales of Woodpulp**

The foregoing discussion of three and five period moving averages prompts the question, 'How do we determine the exact moving average we should employ?' Should we use a three-period, a five-period, or something quite different?

The answer is that we should use a moving average which depends on the data being analysed. In the case of the woodpulp data, since the figures are presented quarterly and seem to show a four-period regular fluctuation (see figure 20), then we should perhaps use a four-quarterly moving average. In general, if the time series shows a fluctuation which seems to repeat every n period, then we should use an n-period moving average. Usually, if data have been collected on a quarterly basis, then we can assume that this is because these show a four-quarterly pattern; if collected on a monthly basis, then these shows a 12-monthly pattern, and so on.

You will find that constructing a moving average based upon an even number of periods presents us with a problem. Take a look at figure 27 below, to see what we mean.

TIME		SALES	FOUR-PERIOD MOVING AVERAGE
1990	I	11.5	
	II	12.2	
			$(11.5+12.2+12.9+15.7)/4 = 13.1$
	III	12.9	
			$(12.2+12.9+15.7+18.9)/4 = 14.9$
	IV	15.7	
			$(12.9+15.7+18.9+20.5)/4 = 17.0$
1991	I	18.9	
	II	20.5	
etc....			

FIGURE 27: **Problems of Constructing 4-Quarterly Moving Averages**

When we try to centre a moving average based on an even number, such as the four-quarterly moving average in figure 27, then the data are placed **between** time periods. This means that the first four-quarterly moving average in figure 27 would have to be placed between the second and third quarters of 1990. We cannot allow this situation. Happily the problem can be solved by taking a further moving average, this time of **pairs** and then centring again. So for quarterly data, we can add in groups of four, centre the data, then add the resulting centred totals in groups of two and centre again. The final totals (representing eight quarters) will be aligned against exact time periods rather than in between. These totals can be divided by eight to produce four-quarterly moving averages.

This process is shown in figure 28.

TIME		SALES	4-QUARTERLY MOVING TOTAL	8-QUARTERLY MOVING TOTAL	TREND
(1)		(2)	(3)	(4)	(5)
1990	I	11.5			
	II	12.2			
			52.3		
	III	12.9		112.0	14.00
			59.7		
	IV	15.7		127.7	15.90
			68.0		
1991	I	18.9		144.5	18.00
			76.5		
	II	20.5			
	III	21.4	etc	etc	etc

Column 3, is the result of the sales figures (from column 2) being totalled in fours and centred.

These totals are further added, in pairs, and then centred (column 4).

The resulting totals now represent eight quarters, and must be divided by eight to give the trend (column 5).

FIGURE 28: **Calculation of a Four-Quarterly Moving Average**

You should notice that this process means that the first trend figure we obtain is centred on the third quarter of 1990; we lose the first two quarters.

Notice that the first moving total of the four quarters in column 3 has been obtained as follows:

$$11.5 + 12.2 + 12.9 + 15.7 = 52.3$$

and the second total

$$12.2 + 12.9 + 15.7 + 18.9 = 59.7$$

So the first total in column 4 is

$$52.3 + 59.7 = 112 = 11.5+12.2+12.9+15.7+12.2+12.9+15.7+18.9 =$$
$$11.5 + (2\times12.2) + (2\times12.9) + (2\times15.7) + 18.9 = 112$$

and the trend in column 5 will be

$$(11.5 + 2\times12.2 + 2\times12.9 + 2\times15.7 + 18.9)/8 = 112/8 = 14$$

This can be expressed as formula 11 below.

Formula 11

Centred Four Quarterly Moving Average for Time Period t

$$\frac{Y_{t-2} + 2\times Y_{t-1} + 2\times Y_t + 2\times Y_{t+1} + Y_{t+2}}{8}$$

ACTIVITY 20

Continue the process started in figure 28 and obtain a four-quarterly moving average for the woodpulp data.

As before, you will find it saves a lot of time and effort if you use spreadsheet software to do this.

The following solution (figure 29) to Activity 20 has been calculated using LOTUS 1-2-3. A single formula has been used to obtain the centred moving average.

TIME PERIOD		SALES	QUARTERLY MOVING AVERAGE
1990	I	11.50	
	II	12.20	
	III	12.90	14.00
	IV	15.70	15.96
1991	I	18.90	18.06
	II	20.50	20.09
	III	21.40	22.16
	IV	23.40	24.25
1992	I	27.80	26.19
	II	28.30	28.18
	III	29.10	
	IV	31.60	

FIGURE 29: **Solution to Activity 20**

Notice that like all moving averages we have used so far the quarterly moving average loses data at the beginning and end of the sales time period.

Also notice the way the quarterly averages are smoother than the original sales data.

The moving average is an estimate of long run trend.

3. SEASONAL VARIATION

Having obtained an estimate for trend we can now proceed to analyse the seasonal variation. We will do this by continuing to use the woodpulp sales data. We must start by examining differences between the trend and the original time series.

ACTIVITY 21

Use the solution to Activity 20 contained in figure 29. For each quarter (t) for which we have the information calculate the difference between actual sales and trend,

$Y_t - T_t$

Figure 30 shows the calculations necessary for Activity 21

TIME PERIOD (T)		SALES (Y_T)	(T_T)	QUARTERLY MOVING AVERAGE (Y_T-T_T)
1990	I	11.50		
	II	12.20		
	III	12.90	14.00	-1.10
	IV	15.70	15.96	-0.26
1991	I	18.90	18.06	0.84
	II	20.50	20.09	0.41
	III	21.40	22.16	-0.76
	IV	23.40	24.25	-0.85
1992	I	27.80	26.19	1.61
	II	28.30	28.18	0.13
	III	29.10		
	IV	31.60		

The final column shows the seasonal variation for quarter t.

FIGURE 30: **Calculation of Seasonal Variation**

Notice that we cannot obtain a seasonal variation estimate for the first two and last two quarters.

It is usual to continue the analysis by making an estimate of the **average** seasonal variation for each quarter.

We have two seasonal variations for the first quarter of the years 1991 (0.84) and 1992 (1.61). So the average quarter I seasonal variation is

$$(0.84 + 1.61)/2 = 1.22$$

for quarter II it is

$$(0.41 + 0.13)/2 = 0.27$$

for quarter III

$$(-1.10 + -0.76)/2 = -0.93$$

and finally for quarter IV

$$(-0.26 + -0.85)/2 = -0.56 \text{ (to two dp)}$$

What would you say these seasonal variation figures tell us?

Generally, it means that in the first quarter of the year sales of woodpulp will, on average, be 1.22 above the trend. In quarter II, sales will tend to run above trend by 0.27. Quarter III sales will tend to be 0.93 **below** the trend, and quarter IV 0.56 below the trend.

ACTIVITY 22

In the table below, the woodpulp sales data are shown again, along with the average seasonal variation component relevant to each quarter.

Time Period (t)	Sales (Y_t)	Seasonal Variation (S_t)
1990 I	11.50	1.22
II	12.20	0.27
III	12.90	-0.93
IV	15.70	-0.56
1991 I	18.90	1.22
II	20.50	0.27
III	21.40	-0.93
IV	23.40	-0.56
1992 I	27.80	1.22
II	28.30	0.27
III	29.10	-0.93
IV	31.60	-0.56

Deseasonalise, ie remove the seasonal component from the original data.

Remember that (ignoring cyclical and random variation) an additive model time series is $Y_t = T_t + S_t$.

Activity 22 continued...

If a time series (Y_t) is composed of the trend (T_t) plus the seasonal variation (S_t), then it follows that to deseasonalise a series we must subtract some estimate of the seasonal variation for each quarter. The result is shown in figure 31.

TIME PERIOD (T)		SALES (Y_T)	SEASONAL VARIATION (S_T)	DESEASONALISED (Y_T-S_T)
1990	I	11.50	1.22	10.28
	II	12.20	0.27	11.93
	III	12.90	-0.93	13.83
	IV	15.70	-0.56	16.26
1991	I	18.90	1.22	17.68
	II	20.50	0.27	20.23
	III	21.40	-0.93	22.33
	IV	23.40	-0.56	23.96
1992	I	27.80	1.22	26.58
	II	28.30	0.27	28.03
	III	29.10	-0.93	30.03
	IV	31.60	-0.56	32.16

FIGURE 31: **Deseasonalising an Additive Model Time Series**

The last column in figure 31 can be regarded as the trend of sales since it represents the sales minus seasonal factors.

4. SUMMARY

It has taken us sometime to reach this point, but we have derived a technique which is of great use to economists, statisticians, sales managers and policy makers generally. We can use a method called moving averages to obtain estimates of seasonal variation, which we can then use to deseasonalise a time series, leaving us with the general trend.

Even excluding other uses of this technique, it is very important for the policy maker to know when a movement in a time series is due to a fundamental long-term trend, or whether it is a mere seasonal variation.

In section 6 we will extend the method to the multiplicative model, and show how we might combine it with regression analysis to provide effective forecasts of time series.

In this section we have

- defined **moving averages**

- looked at, and calculated the three and five-period **moving averages**

- discussed, and illustrated the problems of constructing four-quarterly **moving averages**

- examined the effects of seasonal variation

If you are unsure of any of these areas, check back **now** before you start the next section.

SECTION 6

FORECASTING A TIME SERIES

1. USING REGRESSION ANALYSIS ON A TIME SERIES

In unit 4 of this series we used a technique called regression analysis to establish the mathematical form of the relationship between two variables. Having done this, we can then predict one variable, Y, or dependent variable from our knowledge of another, the independent variable.

Regression analysis can be put to good use in forecasting the progress of a time series. In such a case we make the time period, t; the independent variable and the time series (sales, employment, whatever it may be), will be the dependent variable.

We will, of course, be limited in our use of the technique, because we have only studied the linear two-variable regression model in this course and will therefore have to assume that there is a straight line relationship between time and the data.

Note

You should remember that other, more complex, regression models are available to those interested in further study.

As mentioned already in this unit, spreadsheet software will be an invaluable aid to you as you work throughout this section.

Activity 23

Use the deseasonalised woodpulp data from figure 31 for this activity.

Assume that woodpulp sales grow linearly over time. (This is quite a reasonable assumption.)

Numerically code each time period so that 1990 I becomes 1, 1990 II becomes 2 ... etc ... 1992 IV becomes 12.

Now obtain the linear regression equation of the deseasonalised time series (T_t) on the coded time period (t).

In figure 32 below, the last column which is the deseasonalised, or trend, data, will be regressed on the coded time period in the second column. It is essential to recode time period, as regression analysis can only be carried out on numerical data, and calendar time is not numerical data.

In the proper use of this technique, you must remember to make trend, T_t, the dependent variable. Do not use the original data, Y_t, for this purpose. This is because in the first instance, we wish to forecast the **trend**. We can adjust our forecast for seasonal variation afterwards.

PERIOD		CODED TIME(T)	SALES (Y_T)	VARIATION (S_T)	TREND (T_T)
1990	I	1	11.50	1.22	10.28
	II	2	12.20	0.27	11.93
	III	3	12.90	-0.93	13.83
	IV	4	15.70	-0.56	16.26
1991	I	5	18.90	1.22	17.68
	II	6	20.50	0.27	20.23
	III	7	21.40	-0.93	22.33
	IV	8	23.40	-0.56	23.96
1992	I	9	27.80	1.22	26.58
	II	10	28.30	0.27	28.03
	III	11	29.10	-0.93	30.03
	IV	12	31.60	-0.56	32.16

FIGURE 32: **The Complete Disaggregated Time Series**

The required regression equation is

$$T_t = a + bt$$

In obtaining the solution to the problem using LOTUS 1-2-3 it estimated that

$$b = 2.01$$
$$a = 8.03$$

therefore the linear regression model becomes

$$T_t = 8.03 + 2.01t. \ (t = 1, 2, 3, \ldots \text{etc})$$

ACTIVITY 24

Now use the regression equation obtained in Activity 23 to forecast the **trend** of woodpulp sales for the four quarters of 1993.

If you need some help, think about the numerical code values for 1993 I, II, III and IV.

Before you can answer Activity 24, you must obtain the numerical code values for the four quarters of 1993. Since 1992 IV was coded as 12, it follows that quarters I, II, III and IV of 1993 will be

t = 13, 14, 15 and 16

Using the regression line $T_t = 8.03 + 2.01t$ we have the forecasts as follows

$$1993 \text{ I} \quad (t = 13) \quad T_{13} = 8.03 + 2.01 \times 13 = 34.16$$
$$1993 \text{ II} \quad (t = 14) \quad T_{14} = 8.03 + 2.01 \times 14 = 36.17$$
$$1993 \text{ III} \quad (t = 15) \quad T_{15} = 8.03 + 2.01 \times 15 = 38.18$$
$$1993 \text{ IV} \quad (t = 16) \quad T_{16} = 8.03 + 2.01 \times 16 = 40.19$$

You must keep it clearly in mind that these forecasts are of the **trend** only, not of actual sales.

ACTIVITY 25

Now take the forecasts of trend made in Activity 24 and **reseasonalise** them.

Remember, you have already carried out the operation of deseasonalising data. Think how you would reverse this process.

Earlier, when you deseasonalised data, you **subtracted** the seasonal component. Therefore in order to reseasonalise, we need to **add** the seasonal factor to the trend.

We already have the quarterly seasonal factors from figure 31. The final seasonalised forecasts are as shown in figure 33 below.

Time (t)(T_t)		Trend Forecast (S_t)	Seasonal Component (Y_t)	Final Forecast
1993	I	34.16	1.22	35.38
	II	36.17	0.27	36.44
	III	38.18	-0.93	37.25
	IV	40.19	-0.56	39.63

FIGURE 33: **The Seasonalised Forecast**

These forecasts are made on the assumptions that

> the additive model remains appropriate
>
> the trend continues as it has in the past
>
> the seasonal factors remain unchanged.

2. THE MULTIPLICATIVE MODEL

So far we have used the additive model as the basis for disaggregating and forecasting a time series. Finally in this section, we turn to the multiplicative model.

We shall require some data for this, so we will use the monthly sales data for sales of the 'CONCHA', a mid-priced lounge three piece suite sold by Zarkon Furnishing Plc. The sales figures are in numbers of units sold rather than in value.

	1987	1988	1989	1990	1991	1992
Jan	154	200	223	346	518	649
Feb	96	118	104	261	404	392
Mar	73	90	107	224	300	273
Apr	49	79	85	141	210	322
May	36	78	75	148	196	189
Jun	59	91	99	145	186	257
Jul	95	167	135	223	247	324
Aug	169	169	211	272	343	404
Sep	210	289	335	445	464	677
Oct	278	347	460	560	680	858
Nov	298	375	488	612	711	895
Dec	245	203	326	467	610	664

FIGURE 34: **Sales of Furniture**

ACTIVITY 26

On a separate sheet of graph paper draw the graph of the Zarkon data and check that the multiplicative model applies.

Your graph of the Zarkon data should look like figure 35 below.

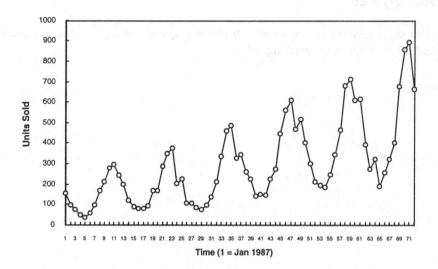

FIGURE 35: **Zarkon Furnishing – Sales of Concha Suites**

It seems fairly clear from the graph that the upswings and downswings of sales are increasing over time. It is in just such a situation that the multiplicative model applies.

To disaggregate the multiplicative time series we begin the same way as we did for the additive model, with a moving average. We now come to the problem of what time period we should use in the moving average with the Zarkon data.

The data have been collected monthly, and the graph in figure 35 clearly implies a 12-monthly cycle. Therefore we shall use a 12-monthly moving average.

Before you proceed with the next Activity, which requires you to obtain such a moving average, you should reflect on the way in which the **quarterly** moving average was obtained. A strict centred total of each four quarters has been placed **between** two time periods. We solved this problem, you might remember, by taking a second centred moving total, now representing the sum of eight quarters, and dividing by eight to obtain the quarterly trend estimate. With a centred total of 12 quarters we have a similar problem, and need to take a further moving total, this time of pairs. The resulting centred total now becomes the sum of **24** quarters, and we would divide by 24 to obtain our monthly trend estimate.

The first six months and the last six months will have no trend estimate, just as the first and last two quarters of data were lost in the four-quarterly moving average.

The general formula for a 12-month moving average is shown in formula 12, below.

Formula 12

A 12-Month Moving Average

The 12-month moving average for time period t is calculated as follows;

$$\frac{Y_{t-6} + 2 \times Y_{t-5} + 2 \times Y_{t-4} + \ldots + 2 \times Y_t + \ldots + 2 \times Y_{t+4} + 2 \times Y_{t+5} + Y_{t+6}}{24}$$

ACTIVITY 27

You can now calculate the moving average for the Zarkon data.

You will very definitely find this a tedious exercise without a spreadsheet!

Columns (1) to (6) in figure 36 below contain the solution to this problem.

Year	Month	Time Code	Sales	Moving Total	Moving Average	Sales-Trend Ratio	Seasonal Factor	De-season-alised Data
(1)	(2)	(3)	(4)	(5)	(6)	(7)	(8)	(9)
1987	Jan	1	154				1.30	118.03
	Feb	2	96				0.84	114.58
	Mar	3	73				0.66	111.07
	Apr	4	49				0.52	94.04
	May	5	36				0.44	82.75
	Jun	6	59				0.48	122.71
	Jul	7	95	3570	148.75	0.64	0.68	138.72
	Aug	8	169	3638	151.58	1.11	0.91	185.92
	Sep	9	210	3677	153.21	1.37	1.34	157.27
	Oct	10	278	3724	155.17	1.79	1.73	160.45
	Nov	11	298	3796	158.17	1.88	1.83	162.76
	Dec	12	245	3870	161.25	1.52	1.31	186.80
1988	Jan	13	200	3974	165.58	1.21	1.30	153.28
	Feb	14	118	4046	168.58	0.70	0.84	140.84
	Mar	15	90	4125	171.88	0.52	0.66	136.94
	Apr	16	79	4273	178.04	0.44	0.52	151.61
	May	17	78	4419	184.13	0.42	0.44	179.29
	Jun	18	91	4454	185.58	0.49	0.48	189.27
	Jul	19	167	4435	184.79	0.90	0.68	243.86
	Aug	20	169	4444	185.17	0.91	0.91	185.92
	Sep	21	289	4447	185.29	1.56	1.34	216.44
	Oct	22	347	4470	186.25	1.86	1.73	200.27
	Nov	23	375	4473	186.38	2.01	1.83	204.82
	Dec	24	203	4478	186.58	1.09	1.31	154.78
1989	Jan	25	223	4454	185.58	1.20	1.30	170.91
	Feb	26	104	4464	186.00	0.56	0.84	124.13
	Mar	27	107	4552	189.67	0.56	0.66	162.81
	Apr	28	85	4711	196.29	0.43	0.52	163.13
	May	29	75	4937	205.71	0.36	0.44	172.39
	Jun	30	99	5173	215.54	0.46	0.48	205.91
	Jul	31	135	5419	225.79	0.60	0.68	197.13
	Aug	32	211	5699	237.46	0.89	0.91	232.13
	Sep	33	335	5973	248.88	1.35	1.34	250.89
	Oct	34	460	6146	256.08	1.80	1.73	265.49
	Nov	35	488	6275	261.46	1.87	1.83	266.54
	Dec	36	326	6394	266.42	1.22	1.31	248.56
1990	Jan	37	346	6528	272.00	1.27	1.30	265.18
	Feb	38	261	6677	278.21	0.94	0.84	311.52
	Mar	39	224	6848	285.33	0.79	0.66	340.83
	Apr	40	141	7058	294.08	0.48	0.52	270.60
	May	41	148	7282	303.42	0.49	0.44	340.18
	Jun	42	145	7547	314.46	0.46	0.48	301.58
	Jul	43	223	7860	327.50	0.68	0.68	325.64
	Aug	44	272	8175	340.63	0.80	0.91	299.24

(Table continues overleaf).

Year	Month	Time Code	Sales	Moving Total	Moving Average	Sales-Trend Ratio	Seasonal Factor	De-season-alised Data
(1)	(2)	(3)	(4)	(5)	(6)	(7)	(8)	(9)
	Sep	45	445	8394	349.75	1.27	1.34	333.27
	Oct	46	560	8539	355.79	1.57	1.73	323.21
	Nov	47	612	8656	360.67	1.70	1.83	334.26
	Dec	48	467	8745	364.38	1.28	1.31	356.07
1991	Jan	49	518	8810	367.08	1.41	1.30	397.00
	Feb	50	404	8905	371.04	1.09	0.84	482.19
	Mar	51	300	8995	374.79	0.80	0.66	456.46
	Apr	52	210	9134	380.58	0.55	0.52	403.02
	May	53	196	9353	389.71	0.50	0.44	450.51
	Jun	54	186	9595	399.79	0.47	0.48	386.86
	Jul	55	247	9833	409.71	0.60	0.68	360.68
	Aug	56	343	9916	413.17	0.83	0.91	377.35
	Sep	57	464	9877	411.54	1.13	1.34	347.50
	Oct	58	680	9962	415.08	1.64	1.73	392.47
	Nov	59	711	10067	419.46	1.70	1.83	388.33
	Dec	60	610	10131	422.13	1.45	1.31	465.10
1992	Jan	61	613	10279	428.29	1.43	1.30	469.81
	Feb	62	392	10417	434.04	0.90	0.84	467.87
	Mar	63	273	10691	445.46	0.61	0.66	415.38
	Apr	64	322	11082	461.75	0.70	0.52	617.96
	May	65	189	11444	476.83	0.40	0.44	434.42
	Jun	66	257	11682	486.75	0.53	0.48	534.53
	Jul	67	324				0.68	473.12
	Aug	68	404				0.91	444.46
	Sep	69	677				1.34	507.02
	Oct	70	858				1.73	495.20
	Nov	71	895				1.83	488.83
	Dec	72	664				1.31	506.27

FIGURE 36: **The Zarkon Data**

Column (6) contains the 12-monthly moving average. Columns (7) - (9) contain data relevant to the next two activities (28 and 29).

You should study very carefully the way in which this moving average has been calculated, and compare it with the four-quarterly case.

So far, the moving totals and averages for this multiplicative model have been calculated in the same manner as for the additive model. However, in the next step – calculating the seasonal variation – the model uses a different procedure.

The additive model is as follows:

$$Y_t = T_t + S_t$$

That is, we **add** the trend and seasonal variation to produce the full time series. As you are now aware, we had to subtract the trend from the time series to produce a seasonal variation.

What about the multiplicative model?

This model is given by

$$Y_t = T_t \times S_t$$

So we must use a different method to obtain the seasonal variation.

ACTIVITY 28

Using the Zarkon data from your answer to Activity 27, work out the seasonal variation in each month for which there exists the relevant information.

Obtain the **average** seasonal variation for each of the months January to December.

If you require any help, remember that in the additive model, you had to **subtract** the trend from the original time series in order to do this. Think what you would need to do to obtain the seasonal data for the multiplicative model.

Figure 35 above, provides the answer to this problem. Column (7), titled Sales Trend Ratio, shows the calculations of seasonal variation for each month. Notice that the first and last six months do not have seasonal components since we have no trend data for these months.

Since $Y_t = T_t \times S_t$ for the multiplicative model, then this implies that we should **divide** Y_t (the original sales data) by T_t (the trend), to obtain S_t (the seasonal variation). So we must carry out the following calculation:

$$\text{Seasonal index} = \frac{\text{Original Data}}{\text{Moving average}}$$

For example, in July 1987 furniture sales were 95 and the moving average was 148.75.

The seasonal variation, or sales-to-trend ratio for that month is therefore

$$95/148.75 \approx 0.64$$

Put in a slightly different way, sales were 64% of trend in that particular month.

Column (8) in figure 36 shows the average seasonal variation for each month.

As an example, we have five January figures, so that to obtain the January seasonal index we simply calculate the average

$$(1.21 + 1.20 + 1.27 + 1.41 + 1.43)/5 \approx 1.30$$

which is the January seasonal index.

ACTIVITY 29

Now use the seasonal index obtained in Activity 28 to deseasonalise the Zarkon sales data.

To help you, remember that, in the additive model, data were deseasonalised by **subtracting** the seasonal factor. How would you deseasonalise data with the multiplicative model?

Column (9) of figure 36 contains the required deseasonalised data, obtained by dividing each of the original sales figures by the seasonal factor. That is, column (4) divided by column (8).

Now suppose that Zarkon wish to forecast sales for the last six quarters of 1993. How would they do this?

Firstly, if we are to use the linear regression model, we would check that the deseasonalised, or trend data, are linear. You can assume that this is the case, and if you wish, verify this for yourself by drawing a scatterplot of the trend data against time.
Next we would obtain the regression line of deseasonalised data on time period, remembering to numerically code the time period, January 1987 = 1, February = 2, and so on.

The regression equation would then be used to make the required forecasts and finally, the forecasts would be reseasonalised by using the appropriate seasonal factors.

ACTIVITY 30

Calculate the regression equation of deseasonalised data on time. (The spreadsheet will continue to be a great help here.)

Use the regression equation so obtained to forecast the sales for the months July-December of 1993.

(Remember the seasonal factor!)

Your response to this activity should have been firstly to use the equation

$$T_t = a + bt$$

where T is the trend and t is time period, and then from, say, a spreadsheet solution

$$b = 6.048 \quad \text{and} \quad a = 68.3667$$

To make the forecasts, we must remember that time period has been coded as 1, 2, 3, etc.

Consequently, the months July-December of 1993 will be represented by t = 79, 80, 81, 82, 83 and 84.

We should also remember that the regression equation only forecasts trend. Therefore, we must reseasonalise. We do this by **multiplying** the trend by the seasonal factor. Thus the forecasts will be as figure 37 below:

TIME PERIOD		NUMERIC CODE	TREND FORECAST	SEASONAL FACTOR	FINAL FORECAST
1993	Jul	79	546.16	0.68	371
	Aug	80	552.21	0.91	503
	Sept	81	558.26	1.34	748
	Oct	82	564.30	1.73	976
	Nov	83	570.35	1.83	1044
	Dec	84	576.40	1.31	755

FIGURE 37: **Reseasonalised Sales Forecasts**

Like all forecasts, we must accept that the above are only valid if the assumptions we have made (respecting linearity, additive/multiplicative nature of model, seasonality, etc) continue to be true.

Nevertheless, all reservations aside, the combination of time series analysis and regression provides us with some very powerful analytical methods.

3. SUMMARY

In the whole of this unit, we have adopted two themes concerned with the behaviour of data over time. We saw how to calculate certain measures called **index numbers**. These statistics are attempts to measure the change in the time series (prices, sales volume, productivity, etc) over a period. Change is always measured from some fixed point called the base year.

The second half of the unit showed how a time series might be broken down into separate trend and seasonal factors and how it might be possible to forecast the future behaviour of the series.

In this final section we have discussed forecasting a time series, and examined

- **deseasonalising** and **reseasonalising**

- the **multiplicative model**

- 12-monthly moving averages

- the use of **regression analysis**

If you are unsure of any of the topics, examples and activities covered in this unit then check back to the appropriate section. You should now have another look at the objectives at the very beginning of the unit and use them as a checklist for your own understanding.

REFERENCES

Students may follow up this subject by reading the following texts:

1. CURWIN and SLATER. *Quantitative Methods for Business Decisions*. Chapman & Hall. See chapters 5 and 20.
2. MORRIS. C. *Quantitative Approaches in Business Studies*. Pitman Publishing. See chapters 7 and 14.
3. *Monthly Digest of Statistics*. Published monthly HMSO. Contains many of the major indices produced by the Central Statistical Office.
4. *Employment Gazette*. Journal of the Department of Employment. In addition to producing indices of changes in wage rates, this journal carries an article each year on the results of the *Family Expenditure Survey*.

GLOSSARY

The following is an alphabetical listing of the technical terms most often encountered in this unit.

Additive time series A model of a time series where the overall series is obtained by adding the separate trend, seasonal, cyclical and random components.

Aggregative index An index number constructed by multiplying unit values by volume. Total aggregate volume for the cuurent year is then calculated as a percentage of total aggregate volume for the base year.

Base-weighted index A weighted index number series which uses data obtained from the base period to calculate the weights.

Base year, or period The base period of an index number series is the period with which all changes in the series are compared. The reference point of the series.

Current-weighted index A weighted index number series which uses data obtained from the current period to calculate the weights.

Current year, or period The current year of an index series is always the year which is being compared with the base.

Cyclical variation Cyclical variation in a time series is the long-term variation about trend.

Deflater A value index number which is being used to remove the effect of price changes from a series of money values.

Deseasonalisation The process of removing the effect of seasonal variation from a time series.

Disaggregation of a time series This is the process whereby a time series is broken down into its constituent elements of trend and seasonal, cyclical and random variations.

Index number An index number is a single value which measures change in a series.

Laspeyre index A weighted index constructed by the aggregative method which uses weights drawn from current year data.

Moving average A moving average is an average of N periods of a time series. The time series is taken N values at a time. The centred moving average is the basic method for disaggregating a time series.

Multiplicative time series A model of a time series where the overall series is obtained by multiplying the separate trend, seasonal, cyclical and random components.

Paasche index A weighted index constructed by the aggregative method which uses weights drawn from current year data.

Price relative A number expressing a current year money value of a series as a percentage of a base year money value of the same series.

Price, or volume relative method A method of constructing an index number which consists of taking the average of a series of relatives.

Random variation The unpredictable remaining variation in a time series when the trend and cyclical and seasonal variation have been removed.

Real value The value of some monetary time series expressed in terms of the prices of the base year.

Reseasonalisation of a time series The process whereby a trend figure, or forecast of the trend has the seasonal factor replaced. The resulting number will constitute the full value.

Seasonal factor A measure of the seasonal variation in a time series.

Seasonal variation The short-term variation about trend in a time series.

Simple index number An index number which measures the change in a single entity, rather than a group of entities. Usually taken to mean the same as a price or volume relative.

Time series A series of numbers expressing the changes in some variable over a period of time.

Trend The long run direction of a time series, ignoring fluctuations due to seasonal, cyclical or random factors.

Value index An index number which measures the change in some monetary series. For example, a price index.

Volume index An index number which measures the change in the physical volume of some variable, irrespective of changes in its value.

Volume relative A number expressing a current year physical volume of a series as a percentage of a base year physical volume of the same series.

Weighted average A measure of central tendency where component values are weighted with numbers before being averaged. The values are multiplied by the weights before being averaged.

Weighted index number An index number calculated by using a weighted average. The weights are chosen to reflect the degree of importance attached to each of the components of the index.